THE GREATEST LEADERS' GENERATION, OUR FOUNDING FATHERS

Copyright George McCarley ISBN:979-8-9912575-2-7

By
George McCarley

The Founders created the first modern nation-state; via the democratic principle that political sovereignty lives in the citizenry and not in a divinely sanctioned monarchy; the capitalistic principle that economic productivity depends upon release of individual energies in the marketplace rather than state policies; the moral principle that the
individual, not society or the state, is the sovereign political unit; and the judicial principle that all citizens are equal before the law.

Moreover, this formula has become the preferred political recipe for success in the modern world, vanquishing the European monarchies in the 19th century and totalitarian regimes of Germany, Japan, and the Soviet Union in the 20th century.

They defied conventional wisdom in four unprecedented achievements:

1. They won a war for colonial independence against the most powerful military and economic power in the world.
2. They established the first large-scale republic in the modern world.
3. They invented political parties that institutionalized legitimate opposition.
4. They established the principle of the legal separation of church and state.
5. We hear much about the work of Founders during warfighting and constitutional development. More than 100 risked their lives to make the USA survive until today.
6. We compiled a list of those taking the greatest risk, while contributing the greatest effort to our Revolution and Constitutional development. We follow signatories to three precious documents, followed by the States of signers of the Declaration and US Constitution. Had our revolution failed, they would be executed first.
7. Each Founding Father offered unique contributions. Samuel Adams and Franklin were world class philosophers. Washington was a great natural leader. One founder entered Harvard at age 12, others entered at 14 and 15 years. Paul Revere was our first industrialist. Franklin was equal to Thomas Edison.
8. The Founders are the most important people one can study to understand the American ideals of freedom and liberty. No ancient philosopher, nor Greco-Roman leaders reached the level of democratic republican government as our Founders.
9. While they all played important roles, they often disagreed. Debate was heated. Compromise has given us the greatest government of the past 250 years.
10. Founding Fathers were young. Washington was 43 as Commanding General. Jefferson was 33 writing the Declaration of Independence. John Adams was 40 as he argued independence. Madison was 36 at Constitutional Convention. John Jay was 43 as first Chief Justice of the Supreme Court. Alexander Hamilton was 33 as Secretary of the Treasury. Franklin was 70 at Second Continental Congress.
11. The phrase "Founding Fathers" was popularized by Warren G. Harding.
12. Many of the Founders feared new generations might not be capable of maintaining American liberty. They were acutely aware, only Greece and Rome had successful tenures as democracies and republics, Greece 800 years, Rome at 500 years.
13. The Founding Fathers were not perfect.
14. The Founding Fathers left an unparalleled legacy which grows in benefit to the entire world. More than 5 billion Christians and Catholics worship freely. Wars that characterize our world come with less frequency, at far lower death rate.
15. Many Founders took the lead establishing colleges and universities.

These achievements were won without the guillotine or firing squad, or violent revolutions such as France, Russia, and China.

TABLE OF CONTENTS

MOST PRODUCTIVE FOUNDING FATHERS

New Hampshire
William Whipple, Matthew Thorton, Josiah Bartlett
    286   287   269
Massachusetts
Robert Treat Paine, Elbridge Gerry
  288   213
Sam Adams, John Adams, John Hancock
  27   120   63
Rhode Island
Stephen Hopkins, William Ellery
  238   271
Connecticut
William Williams, Samuel Huntington, Roger Sherman, Oliver Wolcott
  289   273   147   285
New York
William Floyd, Philip Livingston, Lewis Morris, Francis Lewis
  290   291   292   275
New Jersey
Richard Stockton, John Hart, Abraham Clark, John Witherspoon, Francis Hopkinson
  293   294   295   283   248
Pennsylvania
John Morton, James Smith, George Ross, James Wilson, George Taylor
  295   296   297   237   251
Geo. Clymer, Ben Franklin, Robert Morris, Benjamin Rush
  272   37   52   204
Delaware
Caesar Rodney, George Read, Thomas McKean
  297   280   276
Maryland
Samuel Chase, William Paca, Thomas Stone, Charles Carroll
  298   300   189   162
Virginia
Benjamin Harrison, Thomas Nelson, Jr., Richard Henry Lee,
  265   301   262
Francis Lightfoot Lee, Carter Braxton, George Wythe, T. Jefferson
  265   260   227   109
North Carolina
William Hooper, Joseph Hewes, John Penn
  302   302   279
South Carolina
Thomas Heyward, Jr., Thomas Lynch, Jr., Arthur Middleton, Ed. Rutledge
  304   305   306   254
Georgia
Button Gwinnett, Lyman Hall, George Walton
  306   307   308

Signers of United States Constitution

Delaware
Gunning Bedford jun, Richard Bassett, Jaco: Broom, George Read
    309   310   310   280

Maryland
James McHenry, Dan of St Thos. Jenifer, Daniel Carroll
    256   174   176

Virginia
John Blair, James Madison
  311   135

North Carolina
Richd. Dobbs Spaight, Hu Williamson, William Blount
    312   313   314

South Carolina
J. Rutledge, Charles Cotesworth Pinckney, Charles Pinckney, Pierce Butler
  253   196   196   318

Georgia
William Few   Abraham Baldwin
  319   320

New Hampshire
Nicholas Gilman   John Langdon
  345   243

Massachusetts
Rufus King   Nathaniel Gorham
  323   246

Connecticut
Wm. Samuel Johnson   Roger Sherman
  324   147

New York
Alexander Hamilton--------- 95

New Jersey
Wil: Livingston, David Brearly, Wm. Paterson, Jona: Dayton
  325   326   327   328

Pennsylvania
Thomas Mifflin, Thos. FitzSimons, Jared Ingersoll, Gouv. Morris
    329   330   331   233
Ben Franklin, Robert Morris, Geo. Clymer, James Wilson,
  37   52   272   220

Acknowledgement: We honor the work of so many academics and publications that continue to provide this crucial information, often left out of academic curriculums.
Political Writings of the Founding Era, Britannica.com, www.battlefields.org, History.com, National Archives, American Battlefield Trust, US Army Center of Military History, Wikipedia.

THEY CAME SEEKING RELIGIOUS FREEDOM

The following paragraphs are brief descriptions of the extreme persecutions and executions our Founding Fathers families often endured. America's Founding Fathers intent was to ensure these events could never happen again. The Government product of their generation survives and protects the people of most our modern world.

Our Founding Fathers were directly descended from the millions of people worldwide who had been persecuted and executed for their religious beliefs. We see the fullest extent of persecution in the life and times of Jesus Christ. Once Jesus gave his life for all of us, a great new standard of faith in God, was established. It will be another 300 years before Roman Emperor Constantine, early 300's AD would establish Christianity as the official religion of the Roman Empire. The Roman Empire was the fourth world empire prophesied by Daniel, in his Biblical Book of Daniel. Once Constantine declared Christianity to be legal, the persecution and executions of Christians stopped immediately. It was unfortunate that there were a few Christian sects that did not understand the work of Constantine, nor did Constantine understand those other Christian sects, thus the persecutions continued against those sects. However, Christianity began to blossom through the work of the Catholic Church.

Constantine may have been the worldwide launch point for a continual wave of additional attempts to define and worship Christianity.

Most of those considered America's Founding Fathers were superbly educated at Harvard, Yale, Princeton, or other top universities in England. They had been acutely educated into these incidents detailed below, while at the same time hearing firsthand accounts from their Grandparents.

They came seeking RELIGIOUS FREEDOM. The following major points became a driving force in their zeal to find the New World more acceptable.

SPANISH INQUISITION

Beginning in 1492, the religious climate in Europe became preposterous. The very same Ferdinand and Isabella who bankrolled Christopher Columbus became heavily involved in The Spanish Inquisition which persecuted and executed all those in Spain who failed to embrace the Catholic Church. There were times when other Christians, Jews and Muslims were burned at the stake, side-by-side due to their refusal to accept the Catholic Church and continued 250 years.

Many Catholics had begun to question the worship methodology of Catholicism. Over the centuries, there had been as many as 25 Christian breakaway attempts that failed. Then by 1500's, a young Catholic Priest realizes the false direction of Catholic's due to the issue of "Indulgences."

The Catholic Church had never fully recovered from the Crusades and had begun a practice by which parishioners could be granted an "indulgence." This required payment of large tithes, or "good works" and the church then absolved the parishioner.

MARTIN LUTHER AND 95 THESES (Germany, Austria)

Luther was ordained to the Catholic priesthood in 1507. He came to reject several teachings and practices of the Roman Catholic Church; in particular, he disputed the view on indulgences. Luther attempted to resolve these differences amicably, first proposing an academic discussion of the practice and efficacy of indulgences in *Ninety-five Theses*, which he authored in 1517. In 1520, Pope Leo X demanded that Luther renounce all of his writings, and when Luther refused to do so, excommunicated him in January 1521. Later that year, Holy Roman Emperor Charles V condemned Luther as an outlaw at the Diet of Worms. When Luther died in 1546, Pope Leo X's excommunication was still in effect.

Luther taught that salvation and, consequently, eternal life are not earned by good deeds; rather, they are received only as the free gift of God's grace through the believer's faith in Jesus Christ, who is the sole redeemer from sin. Luther's theology challenged the authority and office of the pope by teaching that the Bible is the only source of divinely revealed knowledge, and opposed sacerdotalism by considering all baptized Christians to be a holy priesthood. Those who identify with Luther's wider teachings are called Lutherans, believing those who professed faith in Christ should be called "Christian" or "Evangelic." The work of Martin Luther would push along the Reformation in Europe.

NOW ENGLAND PERSECUTES AND EXECUTES CATHOLICS

On 29 April 1559, the English House of Lords by 33 votes to 12 passed a bill abolishing papal supremacy over the Christian church in England and establishing the supremacy of the English monarchs over the one and only denomination, Anglican. Also in April 1559, a bill abolishing the Mass and imposing an English language Book of Common Prayer liturgy passed in the House of Lords by a majority of three and was implemented on 24 June of that year. To refuse to take an oath of belief in royal supremacy over the church became a crime punishable by removal from public office and inability to hold any office. To defend papal authority over the church became punishable in the first offense by loss of goods; the second by imprisonment for life; the third offence was considered treason.

The 1559 bills made English Catholics guilty of high treason—a crime English law punished by hanging, drawing, and quartering offending men, and by burning offending women. The bills made a political offense out of a matter of conscience—belief in a universal church under God. As in the Roman Empire in which early Christians who refused to burn incense before statues of the emperor were condemned to death for sedition, in Elizabethan England, Catholics were killed because they did not believe an act of Parliament changed what a fifteen-century-old Christian tradition told them: that the Church was a universal institution and the Bishop of Rome was its spiritual leader. To say or attend the Catholic Mass became a criminal act punishable by fines and imprisonment. All parishioners had to attend church on Sundays and holy days under penalty of a shilling for each absence.

HUGUENOT CONTROVERSY IN FRANCE

Huguenot controversy is next in chronological order. The Huguenot rebellions were a series of rebellions of the 1620s in which French Calvinist Protestants (Huguenots), mainly located in southwestern France, revolted against royal authority. The uprising occurred a decade after the death of Henry IV who, himself originally a Huguenot before converting to Catholicism, had protected Protestants through the Edict of Nantes. His successor Louis XIII, under the regency of his Italian Catholic mother Marie de' Medici, became more intolerant of Protestantism. The Huguenots responded by establishing independent political and military structures, establishing diplomatic contacts with foreign powers, and openly revolting against central power. The Huguenot rebellions came after two decades of peace under Henry IV, following intermittent French Wars of Religion of 1562–1598.

9

The St. Bartholomew's Day Massacre of Huguenots in 1572 was a targeted group of assassinations and a wave of Catholic mob violence directed against the Huguenots (French Calvinist Protestants) during the French Wars of Religion. Traditionally believed to have been instigated by Queen Catherine de' Medici, the mother of King Charles IX,[2] the massacre started a few days after the marriage on 18 August of the king's sister Margaret to the Protestant King Henry III of Navarre. Many of the wealthiest Huguenots gathered in Catholic Paris to attend.

The massacre began in the night of 23–24 August 1572, the eve of the Feast of Saint Bartholomew the Apostle, two days after the attempted assassination of Admiral Gaspard de Coligny, the military and political leader of the Huguenots. King Charles IX ordered the killing of a group of Huguenot leaders (may be original "night of the long knives"), including Coligny, and the slaughter spread throughout Paris. Lasting several weeks, the massacre expanded to the countryside and other urban centers. Modern estimates for the number of dead across France vary widely, from 5,000 to 30,000.

Huguenot population of France was estimated at 10%. They began to leave France, drifting all over the world. North America saw them first, in a Canadian province, then they boarded ship and moved to the southerly climate of Louisiana.

The massacre marked a turning point in the French Wars of Religion. The Huguenot political movement was crippled by the loss of many of its prominent aristocratic leaders, and many rank-and-file members subsequently converted. Those who remained became increasingly radicalised. Though by no means unique, the bloodletting "was the worst of the century's religious massacres".[3] Throughout Europe, it "printed on Protestant minds the indelible conviction that Catholicism was a bloody and treacherous religion."

ROGER WILLIAMS, RHODE ISLAND, FIRST BAPTIST CHURCH

Once the Exodus to America is underway, we see cases in which many British practices that drove our revolution, accompany the 1600's migrants.

Roger Williams was such a superior student that he is apprenticed to Lord Coke, the greatest Judge in British history at the ripe old age of 13. Williams completes university and law school, with special emphasis on five languages and becomes clerk to Lord Coke. Justice Coke (often spelled Cook) took two religious freedom cases. The King loved one decision and jailed Coke for the other decision. At the jailing, Williams decided to come to America.

Williams knew that Puritan leaders planned to immigrate to the New World. He did not join the first wave of settlers, but later decided that he could not remain in England. Williams regarded the Church of England as corrupt and false, and he had arrived at the Separatist position by 1630; on December 1, he and his wife boarded the Boston-bound *Lyon* in Bristol.

The Anglican (official church of England) had become the official church of Boston. Williams commences preaching and weeks later, the General Court tried Williams in October 1635 and convicted him of sedition and heresy. They declared that he was spreading "diverse, new, and dangerous opinions" and ordered that he be banished. The execution of the order was delayed because Williams was ill and winter was approaching, so he was allowed to stay temporarily if he ceased publicly teaching his opinions. He did not comply with this demand, and the sheriff came in January 1636, only to discover that he had slipped away three days earlier during a blizzard. He traveled 55 miles on foot through the deep snow, from Salem to Raynham, Massachusetts, where the local Wampanoags offered him shelter at their winter camp. He learns their language, remains with them 3 years, and then his well-to-do friends find him. During this episode, Williams and friends arrange a purchase of large Islands for Williams. The purchase will become the State of Rhode Island, where Williams and friends built the very first Baptist Church in America.

OLIVER CROMWELL, ENGLISH MASSACRE IN IRELAND

In September 1649, Cromwell's English Commonwealth forces stormed the coastal town of Drogheda, killing more than 3,000 people. The garrison, led by Sir Arthur Aston, refused to surrender, and many civilians were also killed. The aftermath of the siege is an atrocity that continues to impact Cromwell's reputation.

In October 1649, Cromwell's forces stormed Wexford after negotiations broke down, killing around 2,000 soldiers and 1,500 civilians. Many civilians drowned while trying to escape across the River Slaney.

These massacres convinced many Irish Catholics that they would be killed even if they surrendered, prolonging resistance elsewhere. The massacres also took on the air of martyrdom for Irish Catholics fighting against English Anglicans.

Irish historians record as many as 2.5 million Irishmen in Ireland prior to Cromwell and only 500,000 remained at the end of the Cromwell catastrophe.

COLONIZATION OF AMERICA
Roanoke Colonies

Roanoke Colonies were England's first attempt to colonize The New World. The original landing date of the first Roanoke expedition was July 13, 1584, being chartered as a business and exploration enterprise. It was a colossal failure. Once the first Roanoke colony became lost, they sent another, landing on 22 July 1587. It suffered the same consequence.

The Queen of England had interest in the Roanoke colony, and along with her "confidant" Sir Walter Raliegh, they established The London Company to provide a more appropriate investment. Then wartime conditions erupted in Europe. That was the time of Great Britain destroying The Spanish Armada, August 8, 1588. Second Roanoke would not be resupplied for three years due to warfare in the Atlantic. Roanoke colonists were gone when resupply finally came.

Jamestown

Jamestown original date of landing was May 14, 1607. In June of 1606, King James I granted a charter to a group of London entrepreneurs, the Virginia Company, to establish an English settlement in the Chesapeake region of North America. In December, 104 settlers sailed from London with Company instructions to build a secure settlement, find gold, and seek a water route to the Pacific.

On May 14, 1607, the Virginia Company settlers landed on Jamestown Island to establish an English colony sixty miles from the mouth of the Chesapeake Bay. Discovery of the exact location of the first fort indicates its site was in a secure place, where Spanish ships could not fire directly into the fort. Within days of landing, Powhatan Indians attacked the colonists. The newcomers spent the next few weeks working to *"beare and plant palisadoes"* for a wooden fort.

The Virginia Company tried to intensify the focus on money-making industry with The First Supply to Jamestown. But disease, famine, and sporadic attacks from the neighboring Powhatan Indians took a tremendous toll on the population of the settlement. There were also times when trade with the Powhatan revived the colony with food in exchange for glass beads, copper, and iron implements. Captain John Smith was particularly good at this trade. But his strict leadership made enemies within and without the fort, and a mysterious gunpowder explosion severely injured him and sent him back to England in October 1609. What followed was Jamestown's darkest hour, the "starving time" winter of 1609-10.

Some years of peace and prosperity followed the 1614 wedding of John Rolfe and Pocahontas, the favored daughter of Chief Powhatan.
The first representative assembly in English North America convened in the Jamestown church on July 30, 1619. The General Assembly met in response to orders from the Virginia Company *"to establish one equal and uniform government over all Virginia"* and provide *"just laws for the happy guiding and governing of the people there inhabiting."*

Plymouth Colony

The Mayflower anchored at Plymouth Rock, near Provincetown Harbor, Cape Cod, November 11, 1620. At this time in that northern turf, the seas are becoming very cold, with ice conditions commencing soon. It took a whole month for the ship to find a suitable location to anchor. No one could leave the ship for a month, until December 10, 1620. Scouting parties went ashore and it would be December 21 by one story and December 16 by another, prior to all passengers going ashore. The First Thanksgiving would not come until the next year.

PRELUDE TO REVOLUTION
WHAT HARM DID GREAT BRITAIN INFLICT ON THE COLONIES?
WHAT CAUSED THE SPIRIT OF INDEPENDENCE?

Due to so many atrocities all over England and Europe, the early settlers were escaping England by any means possible and going into a new world to which they could not imagine what lay ahead. Spanish was having earlier success in Central and South America. The Spanish are establishing ports and cities in the 1500's, while modern writers have termed 1500's "The Lost Century in America."
Now for the next hundred years, the colonists will have to deal with a high death rate, starvation, attacks by Indians and wild animals. Suffering begins to change early in 1700's, to a time of outright war with Indians, and then French and Indians
A long series of rules and regulations from Great Britain would begin in the year 1651, a 125-year record of negative events intended to be good for Great Britain, yet considered Orwellian, restrictive, expensive, and bankrupting for the North American colonies of the day. The series of crippling laws were:

1651 - Navigation Acts	1733-	Molasses Act
1754-1763 - French and Indian War	1754-	Albany Congress
1763 - Proclamation of 1763	1764-	Sugar Act
1764 - Currency Act	1765-	Stamp Act
1765 - Quartering Act Congress	1766-	Declaratory Act
1767 - Townshend Revenue Act	1770-	Boston Massacre
1773 - Tea Act	1773-	Boston Tea Party
1774 - Intolerable or Coercive Acts	1774-	First Continental Congress
1775 – Lexington and Concord		

By the early 1620s as Britain was coming out of severe recession, colonial merchants and politicians started discussing trade policy. They concluded that to be a healthy nation their exports should exceed their imports, and the balance should be invested in military strength. Their fiercest and strongest competitor was the Dutch who dominated the navigation trade. In 1650 parliament passed an ordinance forbidding any foreign ships in British colonies.

The following year parliament, under the leadership of Oliver Cromwell, passed the first of the Navigation Acts which existed for almost two centuries to be fully repealed in 1849. The laws were designed to protect British economic interests in colonial trade and to protect its industry against the rapidly growing Dutch navigation trade. The law reinforced the 1650 ordinance under which no foreign ships were allowed in British colonies, furthermore the act added that British owned vessels be operated by a crew composed of at least fifty percent English men including colonials. Favorably for American colonies, English referred to the nationality not the place of residence thus including colonial ships and residents to conduct inter colonial trade. This law restricted trade of Asian and African goods going to British Islands and American colonies; conversely West Indies and American goods could not be shipped in foreign ships to the rest of the world. European goods could be traded in British ships or ships of the producing country. Subsequent Navigation Acts would change this last provision. A system of duties and rebates was set up to give British goods a price advantage.

Navigation Acts of Parliament gave all advantage to British shipping and businesses, while increasing the cost and difficulty of receiving import goods to the rest of the world, creating more difficulty for business and survival requirements in the North American colonies.

The system was re-enacted and broadened with the Restoration by the Navigation Act 1660, and further developed and tightened by the Navigation Acts of 1663, 1673, and 1696. Upon this basis during the 18th century, the Acts were modified by subsequent amendments, changes, and the addition of enforcement mechanisms and staff. Additionally, a major change in the very purpose of the Acts in the 1760s—that of generating a colonial revenue for Great Britain, rather than only regulating the Empire's trade—would help lead to major rebellions, and significant changes in the implementation of the Acts themselves.

1733 Molasses Act

The Molasses Act of 1733 levied a duty of six pence per gallon on foreign molasses imported into British colonies in North America. The duty was not intended to raise revenue, but to be a prohibition against the importation of molasses from foreign sugar plantations. It was at first a nullity, a dead letter, but three decades later it was enforced and amended into an act intended to produce revenue, thereby becoming part of the dispute over the authority of Parliament to tax the colonies. Molasses was important; the Molasses Act imposed other duties, but the molasses prohibition was the motivation for its enactment. John Adams, in a reflective mood long after Britain and America went separate ways, wrote to a friend, "I know not why we should blush to confess that molasses was an essential ingredient in American independence." There is a backstory to the Molasses Act, beginning in early eighteenth century.

The Molasses Trade

British sugar colonies—islands in the West Indies—were in dire competition with foreign sugar islands (French). In addition to sugar, all these islands exported the by-product of sugar production: molasses. Over time, northern colonies developed an economy dependent on molasses. The colonies distilled it into rum, an export necessary for further trade. These colonies imported molasses from all the sugar islands, most often in exchange for fish, lumber, horses, and other provisions necessary for the livelihood of the single-crop plantations. The British islands, not faring well against the competition, resented that their sister colonies supplied the French with these indispensable provisions, and complained to British officials that the trade should be prohibited.

After decades of futile argument, the British sugar planters planned to bring the matter before Parliament. This was not good news for the Americans as the sugar interests held substantial influence in the House of Commons. A blizzard of pamphlets followed, leading up to the 1731 session of Parliament.

Again, Britain ignores colonial interests. In 1773, the tax was increased again, which enriched British interests and penalized all others.

1754-1763 - French and Indian War - -This war was fought by American Colonial troops and militia. It was paid for by the colonists. Yet in the end, even after colonial troops won the war, Great Britain passed along many costs and attempted to collect even further earnings from many means. Much of the balance of these misguided acts by Great Britain are summarized herein, and lead up to our Founding Fathers declaring Independence, although they would be Hanged if we lost.

Albany Congress - - (Established by England)

Albany Congress, a conference in U.S. colonial history (June 19–July 11, 1754) at Albany, New York, which advocated a union of British colonies in North America for security and defense against the French, foreshadowing unification.

Seven colonies; Connecticut, Maryland, Massachusetts, New Hampshire, New York, Pennsylvania, and Rhode Island, sent delegates to the conference, of the British Board of Trade to work out joint defense and help cement loyalty of the Iroquois Confederacy, which wavered between the French and British, early in the French and Indian War.

After receiving presents, provisions, and promises of redress of grievances, 150 representatives of the Six Nations of the Confederacy (Indian) withdrew without committing themselve. In addition, delegates to the Congress advocated practical measures resulting in closer regulation of Indian affairs and westward migration of pioneers. Moreover, Benjamin Franklin, serving as a Pennsylvania delegate, presented the so-called Albany Plan of Union, which provided for a loose confederation presided over by a president general and having a limited authority to levy taxes to be paid to a central treasury. Although delegates approved the plan, neither the Crown (jealous of its authority) nor any of the colonial assemblies (unwilling to sacrifice sovereignty) approved it, and the war was conducted under the old system. "The different reasons of dislike to my plan made me suspect that it was really the true medium," Franklin later wrote, "and I am still of opinion it would have been happy for both sides the water if it had been adopted." Despite the fact that the issue was not independence, the Albany Plan proved to be farsighted and contained the seeds of the solution to colonial problems later adopted in the Articles of Confederation and in the Constitution.

Proclamation of 1763

Declared by the British crown at the end of the French and Indian War in North America, intended to conciliate Native Americans by checking the encroachment of settlers on their lands. In the centuries since the proclamation, it has become one of the cornerstones of Native American law in the United States and Canada.

After Native American grievances had resulted in the start of Pontiac's War (1763–64), British authorities determined to subdue intercolonial rivalries and abuses by dealing with Native American problems as a whole. To that end, the proclamation organized new British territories in America—the provinces of Quebec, East and West Florida, and Grenada (in the Windward Islands)—and a vast British-administered Native American reservation west of the Appalachians, from south of Hudson Bay to north of the Florida's. It forbade settlement on Native American territory, ordered those settlers already there to withdraw, and limited future settlement. For the first time in the colonization of North America, the proclamation formalized the concept of Native American land titles, prohibiting issuance of patents to any lands claimed by a tribe unless the Native American title had supplanted by purchase or treaty.

Although not intended to alter western boundaries, the proclamation was nevertheless offensive to the colonies as undue interference in their affairs. Treaties following Pontiac's War drew a line of settlement more acceptable to colonial settlers (*see* Fort Stanwix, Treaties of), but the continued westward movement of pioneers and the settlers' disregard of the proclamation's provisions evoked decades of continued Native American warfare throughout the area. Addition of the territory north of the Ohio River to Quebec in 1774 further exacerbated colonial conflict with Britain.

The Colonists lost again

Sugar Act, (1764),

British legislation intended to end smuggling in sugar and molasses from French and Dutch West Indies and providing increased revenues to fund enlarged British responsibilities following the French and Indian War. A reinvigoration of the ineffective Molasses Act of 1733, the Sugar Act provided strong customs enforcement of the duties on refined sugar and molasses imported into the colonies from non-British Caribbean sources.

Protests had been received from America against the enforcement of the Molasses Act, together with a plea that the duty be set at one penny per gallon. Although warnings were issued that the traffic could bear no more than that, the government of Prime Minister George Grenville refused to listen and placed a three-penny duty upon foreign molasses (the preamble bluntly declared the purpose was to raise money for military expenses). The act thus granted a virtual monopoly of the American market to British West Indies sugarcane planters. Early colonial protests at these duties ended when the tax was lowered two years later.

The protected price of British sugar actually benefited New England distillers, though they did not appreciate it. More objectionable to the colonists were the stricter bonding regulations for shipmasters, whose cargoes were subject to seizure and confiscation by British customs commissioners and who were placed under the authority of the Vice-Admiralty Court in distant Nova Scotia if they violated the trade rules or failed to pay duties. As a result of the Sugar Act, the clandestine trade in foreign sugar and, thus, much colonial maritime commerce was severely hampered.

The Currency Act of 1764

Enacted by Great Britain to ensure control of the medium of exchange in the colonial markets. Gold and Silver sources had not been discovered by English speakers at that time, although the Spanish were mining heavily to the west of Texas. Lack of precious metals made it difficult for the colonies to establish a medium of exchange. Most business was conducted by barter, not conducive to international trade.

On September 1, 1764, Parliament passed the Currency Act, effectively assuming control of the colonial currency system. The act prohibited the issue of any new bills and the reissue of existing currency. Parliament favored a "hard currency" system based on the pound sterling but was not inclined to regulate the colonial bills. Rather, they simply abolished them. The colonies protested vehemently against this. They suffered a trade deficit with Great Britain to begin with and argued that the shortage of hard capital would further exacerbate the situation. Another provision of the Currency Act established what amounted to a "superior" Vice-admiralty court, at the call of Naval commanders who wished to assure that persons suspected of smuggling or other violations of the customs laws would receive a hearing favorable to the British, and not the colonial, interests.

The Stamp Act of 1765

The first internal tax levied directly on American colonists. The act, which imposed a tax on all paper documents in the colonies, came when the British Empire was deep in debt from the Seven Years' War (1756-63) and looking to its North American colonies as a revenue source.

Arguing that only their own representative assemblies could tax them, the colonists insisted that the act was unconstitutional, and they resorted to mob violence to intimidate stamp collectors into resigning. Parliament passed the Stamp Act on March 22, 1765, and repealed it in 1766, but issued a Declaratory Act at the same time to reaffirm its authority to pass any colonial legislation it saw fit. The issues of taxation and representation raised by the Stamp Act strained relations with the colonies to the point that, 10 years later, the colonists rose in armed rebellion against the British.

British Parliament passed the Stamp Act to help replenish their finances after the costly Seven Years' War with France. Part of the revenue from the Stamp Act would be used to maintain several regiments of British soldiers in North America to maintain peace between Native Americans and the colonists. Moreover, since colonial juries had proven notoriously reluctant to find smugglers guilty, violators of the Stamp Act could be tried and convicted without juries in the vice-admiralty courts.

The Quartering Act of 1765

British parliamentary provision (actually an amendment to the annual Mutiny Act) requiring colonial authorities to provide food, drink, quarters, fuel, and transportation to British forces stationed in their towns or villages. Colonists' homes could be utilized as quarters for British troops. Resentment over this practice is reflected in the Third Amendment to the U.S. Constitution, which forbids it in peacetime.

The Quartering Act was passed primarily in response to greatly increased empire defense costs in America following the French and Indian War and Pontiac's War. Like the Stamp Act of the same year, it also was an assertion of British authority over the colonies, in disregard of the fact that troop financing had been exercised for 150 years by representative provincial assemblies rather than by the Parliament in London. The act was particularly resented in New York, where the largest number of reserves were quartered, and outward defiance led directly to the Suspending Act as part of the Townshend Acts of 1767. After considerable tumult, the Quartering Act was allowed to expire in 1770. An additional quartering stipulation was in the Intolerable Acts of 1774.

The Declaratory Act of 1766

An Act of the Parliament of Great Britain which accompanied the repeal of the Stamp Act 1765 and the amendment of the Sugar Act. Parliament repealed the Stamp Act because boycotts were hurting British trade and used the declaration to justify the repeal and avoid humiliation. The declaration stated that Parliament's authority was the same in America as in Britain and asserted Parliament's authority to pass laws that binding on the American colonies.

The Townshend revenue Act of 1767 was a series of laws that:

- Taxed goods imported to the American colonies.
- Restructured the Administration of the colonies.
- Placed duties on certain imported goods such as glass, paint, lead, tea.
- Heightened tensions between Great Britain and American colonists and were a precursor to the Revolutionary War.

The Boston Massacre of 1770

Came about due to the continuing heavy handedness of British government and troops and "tax collectors." The Sons of Liberty had formed and were agitating many means of action to convince King George to cease these Orwellian government actions.

A large crowd scene or mob gathering took place many nights. In the confusion, one of the soldiers, who were then trapped by the patriot mob near the Customs House, was jostled and, in fear, discharged his musket. Other soldiers, thinking they had heard the command to fire, followed suit. Three crowd members—including Crispus Attucks, a Black sailor, were shot and died almost immediately. Two of the eight others who were wounded died later. Hoping to prevent further violence, Lieut. Gov. Thomas Hutchinson, who had been summoned to the scene and arrived shortly after the shooting had taken place, ordered Preston and his contingent back to their barracks, where other troops had their guns trained on the crowd. Hutchinson then made his way to the balcony of the Old State House, from which he ordered the other troops back into the barracks and promised the crowd justice, calming the mob, and bringing an uneasy peace.

The soldiers stood trial, defended by future President of the United States, John Adams. The sentiment for independence and revolution is rapidly moving forward.

Tea Act of 1773

A legislative maneuver by British Lord North to make English tea marketable in America. A previous crisis had been averted in 1770 when all the Townshend Acts duties had been lifted except that on tea, which had been mainly supplied to the Colonies since then by Dutch smugglers. In an effort to help the financially troubled British East India Company sell 17,000,000 pounds of tea stored in England, the Tea Act rearranged excise regulations so that the company could pay the Townshend duty and still undersell its competitors. Also, the North administration hoped to reassert Parliament's right to levy taxes on the Colonies.

The shipments became a symbol of taxation tyranny to the colonists, reopening the door to unknown future tax abuse. Colonial resistance culminated in the Boston Tea Party (December 1773), in which tea was dumped into the ocean, and similar action in New York (April 1774).

The Boston Tea Party of 1773

An act of revolutionary defiance of heavy-handed government, in which 342 chests of tea belonging to the British East India Company were thrown into Boston Harbor by patriots disguised as Mohawks. The Americans were protesting (taxation without representation) a tea tax and monopoly of the East India Company.

The Intolerable or Coercive acts of 1774

Called Intolerable Acts by the American colonists, were passed by Parliament in 1774 in response to colonial resistance to British rule. The four acts were:
(1) Boston Port Bill, which closed Boston Harbor.
(2) Massachusetts Government Act, which replaced the elective local government with an appointive one and increased the powers of the military governor.
(3) Administration of Justice Act, which allowed British officials charged with capital offenses to be tried in another colony or in England; and
(4) The Quartering Act permitted the requisition of buildings to house troops.

Now in 1774, we see the Crown reinstating an act of 1770 to allow quartering of troops in colonial homes. Revolutionary fever is about to reach the great breaking point.

The **First Continental Congress** was a meeting of delegates of 12 of the Thirteen Colonies held from September 5 to October 26, 1774, at Carpenters' Hall in Philadelphia at the beginning of the American Revolution. The meeting was organized by the delegates after the British Navy implemented a blockade of Boston Harbor and the Parliament of Great Britain passed the punitive Intolerable Acts in response to the Boston Tea Party.

During the opening weeks of the Congress, the delegates conducted a spirited discussion about how the colonies could collectively respond to the British government's coercive actions, and they worked to make a common cause. As a prelude to its decisions, the Congress's first action was the adoption of the Suffolk Resolves, a measure drawn up by several counties in Massachusetts that included a declaration of grievances, called for a trade boycott of British goods, and urged each colony to set up and train its own militia. A less radical plan was then proposed to create a Union of Great Britain and the Colonies, but the delegates tabled the measure and later struck it from the record of their proceedings.

The First Continental Congress agreed on a Declaration and Resolves that included the Continental Association, a proposal for an embargo on British trade. They also drew up a Petition to the King pleading for redress of their grievances and repeal of the Intolerable Acts. That appeal was unsuccessful, leading colony delegates to convene the Second Continental Congress, also held in Philadelphia the following May, shortly after the Battles of Lexington and Concord, to organize defense of the colonies for the American Revolutionary War.

The **Battles of Lexington and Concord** was the first major military campaign of the American Revolutionary War, resulting in an American victory and outpouring of militia support for the anti-British cause. The battles were fought on April 19, 1775, in Middlesex County Province of Massachusetts Bay within the towns of Lexington, Concord, Lincoln, Menotomy (Arlington), and Cambridge. They marked the outbreak of armed conflict between the Kingdom of Great Britain and Patriot militias from America's thirteen colonies.

In late 1774, Colonial leaders adopted the Suffolk Resolves in resistance to the alterations made to the Massachusetts colonial government by the British parliament following the Boston Tea Party. The colonial assembly responded by forming a Patriot provisional government known as the Massachusetts Provincial Congress and calling for local militias to train for hostilities. Colonial government controlled the colony outside British-controlled Boston. In response, the British government in February 1775 declared Massachusetts to be in a state of rebellion.

About 700 British Army regulars in Boston, under Lieutenant Colonel Francis Smith, were given secret orders to capture and destroy Colonial military supplies reportedly stored by the Massachusetts militia at Concord. Through effective intelligence gathering, Patriot leaders had received word weeks before the expedition that their supplies might be at risk and had moved most of them to other locations. On the night before the battle, warning of the British expedition had been rapidly sent from Boston to militias in the area by several riders, including Paul Revere and Samuel Prescott, with information about British plans. The initial mode of the Army's arrival by water was signaled from the Old North Church in Boston to Charlestown using lanterns to communicate "one if by land, two if by sea".

The first shots were fired just as the sun was rising at Lexington. The militia was outnumbered and fell back, and the regulars proceeded on to Concord, where they broke apart into companies to search for the supplies. At the North Bridge in Concord, approximately 400 militiamen engaged 100 regulars of the King's troops at about 11:00 am, resulting in casualties on both sides. The outnumbered regulars fell back from the bridge and rejoined the main body of British forces in Concord.

British forces began their return march to Boston after completing the search for military supplies, and more militiamen continued to arrive from the neighboring towns. Gunfire erupted again between the two sides and continued throughout the day as the regulars marched back towards Boston. Upon returning to Lexington, Lt. Col. Smith's expedition was rescued by reinforcements under Brigadier General Earl Percy. The combined force of about 1,700 men marched back to Boston under heavy fire in a tactical withdrawal and eventually reached the safety of Charlestown. The accumulated militias then blockaded the narrow land accesses to Charlestown and Boston, starting the siege of Boston.

The Spanish and Georgia Indians

Once the Revolution was underway, the Spanish and Indian allies continued as an extreme problem for Georgia. Then at the very time that the British moved the war down South, at the same time as the British assault on Charleston, our Georgia delegates to Constitutional Convention were planning a Georgia militia attack on the Spanish and Indians in South Georgia. That action clearly would've starved the people of South Carolina of the greater number of troops they would need to be victorious immediately. The Southern Strategy was indeed the action that Marion Campbell, the Swamp Fox, needed to emerge at the prime time he demonstrated. You will see these details within the biographic brief for the Georgia and South Carolina delegates.

FOUNDING FATHERS BRILLIANCE
LITTLE KNOWN FACTS
WHO DID WHAT FROM FRENCH AND INDIAN WARS TO 1812

GEORGE WASHINGTON

George Washington contracted Smallpox, which killed his older brother. Many stories suggest that the British intentionally created a smallpox epidemic in the Colonies, under the guise of attempting peace with the Indians by giving them woolen blankets laced with smallpox. Washington handled some of those blankets.

Nails such as those used in wooden construction developed in Scotland, only to see business die due to the factory being too far away from the urban centers. Kegs of nails would be difficult to transport in those days by horse and buggy. A Scotsman named Adam Smith, author of "Wealth of Nations," the founder of Economics, was known to have spent a couple of weeks with leading Founding Fathers in the period following our Revolution. Smith discusses the nail issue in his classic book WEALTH OF NATIONS. Washington and Jefferson would pioneer nail factories of the day.

George Washington created the Purple Heart while he was Commanding General of our Revolutionary War. Washington kept a distillery at Mount Vernon.

Forbes Magazine found the financial records and declared Washington to have been one of the top 100 richest Americans in history, with a constant dollar adjusted net worth of some $400 million in 2024-dollar terms.

Many of the Founding Fathers engaged in Land Speculation. Washington accumulated over 20,000 acres of land during his periods between combat.

Very few World Leaders in all history would spend as many years of their life in combat as George Washington.

No other world leader in history, before or since, has won a war while being so heavily outnumbered, while facing so many stronger weapons, as did Washington. Not even the Smallpox epidemic could help the British defeat the American colonial fighters.

Washington had just a few especially important advantages over the British troops.

1. We had superior flintlock muskets with longer barrels and an early adaptation of twist, the two improving accuracy and velocity.
2. We had east coast sources of the raw materials required to produce gunpowder and thus freshness and less exposure to trans-Atlantic moisture provided a firepower advantage. We also had ironworks to produce cannon.
3. Guerilla Warfare perplexed the British military. War results in the Northern theatre were a draw. Once Cornwallis decided to move the war to the Southern Theatre, our Guerilla warfare became the deciding factor.
4. Resolve was a strong factor. All the Founding Fathers and other leaders fully expected execution if America loses. They could not allow defeat.
5. This is God's country. They came seeking Religious Freedom. God provided guidance and provenance.

6. The British treatment of prisoners was far worse than experienced by Yankee prisoners at Andersonville Prison in the American Civil War. They nearly starved some prisoners to death. They refused all medical care. Such treatment was a strong driver for all colonial fighters.
7. The captured wife of one Founding Father resulted in jail, starvation, and kept naked in northern freezing weather. She only lived a year upon release.

Bloodletting was a common and often practiced emergency medical technique in the day of the Founding Fathers. While George Washington was on his deathbed, he encouraged the doctors to "let blood," thinking it would help him recover. The doctors obliged and drained a pint of blood. When that failed to help, Washington encouraged them once again. They would drain a total of five pints of blood.

BENJAMIN FRANKLIN

Benjamin Franklin is not fully understood today. Franklin was one of the strongest performing inventors in all history. He argued against Patent and Copyright law while at constitutional convention. His reasoning was that the great inventions and written works should benefit humanity, not just the inventor. The chapter on Franklin details a huge laundry list of his known inventions.

He improved the operation of The Gutenberg Press. He not only improved mechanical components, but he also increased speed of output and improved the metal melting process that produced "typeface" letters for the press.

Franklin was a pioneer in the analysis of electricity. While he was engaged in that kite flying experiment in a lightening story, he made discoveries that became key to the development of electricity as a daily factor in modern life. Electrocution was a known danger of these experiments. Franklin would go on to invent the "lightening rod" that continues to be in use on many rooftops across America. During the kite experiment, he erected a very tall metal pole and connected one strand of cord from the kite to the pole, while another strand was connected to a glass jar. Once the lightning commenced, his glass jar was illuminated for several seconds, simply from the static electricity that the large metal rod did not trap.

Franklin and a German scientist developed a "wet cell" battery, having uncanny similarity to automotive batteries used today. It would be another 100+ years before scientists could develop electricity plants and infrastructure.

Franklin signed 4 of our most important founding documents. However, two of those were agreements with France.

The chapter on Benjamin Franklin will demonstrate two pages of bullet points of the incredible brilliance of Franklin.

THOMAS JEFFERSON

Exploration of the vast Northwestern territory was a recognized goal in early America, as it was considered a pathway to Asia. Jefferson hosted Lewis and Clark in his Whitehouse and strongly assisted planning of that massive expedition.

Jefferson invented the Jeffersonian Music Stand for no other purpose than that he and his future wife could stand closer together while playing violin duets.

Once retired to his mansion at Monticello, Jefferson engaged in "plant husbandry" as he experimented with attempts to adapt important plants for American crops. He kept a journal of these experiments. The most important of these tests was Jeffersons attempt to grow the "pulse plant" indicated in the first chapter of the Biblical book of Daniel. We know today, this plant has the name Astragalus, which Daniel tells us held immense medicinal and health benefits. Unfortunately, the experiment of Jefferson was such a failure that he ended that experiment after the very first crop. We know today, there are 3000 varieties of Astragalus. The Mesopotamian variety provided the health benefits indicated in the Book of Daniel.

ROBERT MORRIS, Financier of the American Revolution

Robert Morris was the largest financial source involved in paying the costs of The American Revolution. He developed all his wealth leadership in as little as 15 years prior to the Revolution, by continually improving his Import/Export company and the trade network he developed with colonial tradesmen and shops along with Jamaica and Great Britain. His financial performance compares favorably with the most highly performing investment houses and Hedge Funds in 2024.

Robert Morris paid our troops a bit beyond the first year of the war. He set up the gunpowder and cannon supply and paid those costs for most of the war.

Nearing midpoint of the war, he paid Benjamin Franklin to produce the first "Paper Money" in the colonies, to be funded by the fledgling colonial government. Government funding had failed before the end of our Revolution.

CARTER BRAXTON, of VIRGINIA

He built an empire of 14 ocean going ships and once the revolution commenced, all his ships engaged in privateering to help fund the Revolution.

PIERCE BUTLER of SOUTH CAROLINA, GEORGIA

Butler would become one of the richest men in early America. Once revolutionary war fighting moved into the Southern theater, he became heavily involved, in addition to engaging in combat, he paid many of the monetary costs of the southern war fighting.

Following his wife's death in 1790, Butler sold off the last of their South Carolina holdings and invested in Georgia Sea Island plantations. Butler hired Roswell King as the manager of his two plantations on St. Simon's Island and Butler Island. He pursued 1830's plans to develop cotton mills in Georgia, where he founded what became Roswell, Georgia, in 1839.

Pierce Butler recovered most of the money he paid to fund the revolution, and as the paragraph shows above, he developed what continues today as a premier island vacation resource. His work at Roswell, Georgia, did much to set the trend of major Textile companies moving into the American South.

JOHN LANGDON, NEW HAMPSHIRE

Langdon began a small business and became a shipping magnate. Once the revolution commenced, he began building ships and forming militia companies, paying all the costs. He would build the largest warship in the American navy, which contained 74 large cannon.

PAUL REVERE

Revere was not involved at Constitutional Convention but was always an important member of the founding fathers. We teach little more about Revere than the midnight ride.

Revere may have been the first modern industrialist among the Founders. In his early career he became a noted Silversmith and some of his works still exist.

He produced much of the gunpowder and cannon used in our Revolutionary War.

In late career, he revolutionized the process of copper production by coupling successful processes that had never been integrated. His REVERE COPPER AND BRASS continued production until about 2008. The Paul Revere Heritage Site in Canton, Massachusetts is maintained by the state to honor Paul Revere in Copper.

ROGER SHERMAN

Roger Sherman, the only Founding Father to sign our four most important founding documents – the Continental Association, the Declaration of Independence, the Articles of Confederation, and the Constitution, along with editing the Bill of Rights.

FOUNDING FATHER FAMILIES' ANCESTRY

While reading the individual Founding Father bio's, you will note that several of those families are descended from original pilgrims at Jamestown and The Mayflower. You will also find that an exceptionally considerable number graduated from the world's greatest Universities, such as Cambridge, Oxford, Harvard, Princeton, Yale.

STRONGEST FAMILY INVOLVEMENT IN FOUNDING PERIOD

Pinckney of South Carolina

The Pinckney family of South Carolina may have been the most prolific family in early US history. They developed an average Plantation and turned it into a most prolific producer for the entire region, by providing advance information on farm product trends. After reaching America, they mainstreamed tobacco production. Their next money crop was Indigo, which became a coveted dye source. They converted several plantations into indigo production just in time for a British chemist to invent chemical dye. They quickly shifted to Rice, which is perfect for lowland South Carolina. Then Cotton became the great monetary producer of the South.

Pinckney's had a profound influence of the Port of Charleston, South Carolina, which by the time of the American Civil War, shipped over 75% of the export volume of North America. It was not all agriculture. In fact, Fort Sumter, in the same Port, was built to protect the Port of Charleston from the Pirates of the Caribbean.

No other Founding Father family saw so many family members working on our foundational documents, with four (4) Pinckney's doing so.

Carroll of Maryland

Next comes the Carroll family of Maryland, three members and a cousin involved in the development and signing of our foundational documents. The Nephew of these Carroll's would become the very first Catholic Bishop in North America.

Adams of Massachusetts

Samuel Adams is well known as the first and most outspoken among our Founding Fathers. While Benjamin Franklin was an early key to our independence, only Samuel Adams devoted his life to America, with no other passions.

John Adams would become our second President and was heavily involved with the development of foundational documents.

Lee family of Virginia

Richard Henry Lee and Francis Lightfoot Lee are also cousins to George Washington, and forebears of Robert E. Lee, the Commander of Southern Forces in the American war of Northern Aggression, also known as the American Civil War. One of the brothers was active on Declaration of Independence, with the other in development of the United States Constitution.

Livingston family of New Jersey / New York

Philip Livingston was active in the development of the Declaration of Independence, while his brother William of New Jersey was active in the development of the US Constitution.

Morris family of New York

Lewis Morris of New York worked to develop our Declaration of Independence, and his cousin Gouverneur Morris, of New York worked on Articles of Confederation and the US Constitution. He was called The Penman of the US Constitution.

Benjamin Harrison of Virginia

This Harrison family was generous to the development of America through 3 generations. Harrison family produced two Presidents. Harrison's son, William Henry Harrison, and his great-grandson, Benjamin Harrison became President of the United States.

In the 1840 US Presidential election, William Henry defeated incumbent Martin Van Buren and died just one month into his presidency. Vice President John Tyler, a fellow Virginian and Berkeley neighbor succeeded him. William Henry's grandson, Benjamin Harrison (1833–1901), was a brigadier general in the Union Army during the American Civil War. Benjamin served in the U.S. Senate and was elected president in 1888 after defeating Grover Cleveland.

HOW DID THEY PRODUCE HUGE WEALTH?

How is it possible that any individual can work professionally 20 years, and make enough money to pay for a major war? It happened in our pre-revolution era.

Robert Morris quickly found the greatest wealth building methods of that day. Morris developed a seven-fold plan. 1) You must own the business, 2) You own ocean vessels, 3) You must engage in export and import, 4) Your company must have strong offices in favored trading destinations, 5) You must own highly productive agriculture land, 6) You must own manufacturing, 7) He owned ship builders and Iron production.

Several Founding Fathers were involved in this business outreach. Primary products were tobacco, indigo, rice, wheat, cotton, cloth, sugar, molasses, Rum; processed metal in Silver and Copper were a growing market. Oddly, the colonies produced 15% of the world's iron production. Following the revolution, Paul Revere became a major copper producer worldwide.

WHAT HAPPENED TO SLAVERY

The most contentious issue at Constitutional Convention was Slavery. All members, North and South agreed to abolish Slavery with no consensus on a method.

The great Southern Agriculture industry made heavy dependence on Slavery. The Port of Charleston shipped over 75% of our export volume, which was heavily agricultural. Cotton became most important.

Benjamin Rush of New Jersey was the most highly educated among our founders. He wrote a macroeconomics book proving that the southern planters would be far better off, with higher profits if they HIRED THE LABOR, instead of feeding, clothing, housing slaves forever.

Unspoken was a means of release and care of former slaves once freed. America had no tax base, no welfare, no food stamps, no benevolent support.

The numbers indicate that by the time of the Civil War, there were 5 million slaves in America. Even today, that is the census of our mid-population states. If today the need arose to feed and house five million people, a severe problem would ensue. Many might die before we could organize the support.

During the revolutionary era, we did not have an available labor supply as large as required to replace the slaves. On the small to medium plantations, money to pay labor might not be available until the crop was sold, which might not be quick.

The Southern states convinced the Northern states that we needed to leave it alone, agree on founding constitutional principles, establish necessary documents and agreements, such as the US Constitution, and find a solution later.

REPRESENTATION IN HOUSE OF REPRESENTATIVES AND SENATE

This was another heated issue that took a long while to achieve agreement. The Federalists wanted most responsibility in the executive and senate areas. The Democrat/Republicans wanted responsibility in the lower house.

Following years of argument more than debate, they compromised on the plan we continue with today. US Senate seat from each state would be 2 Senators. House of Representatives would be represented by population, with more representatives in the states with higher population and lesser numbers of representatives in states with lesser populations. Senate was appointed, yet soon changed to elected.

President was to be elected by popular vote, with a backup being the Electoral College. If tied in Electoral college, a House of Representatives vote broke the tie.

THE GREATEST ARGUMENT

All those chosen to participate in the foundational documents found their most unsettling decision was that of independence. All Founding Fathers argued the issue both ways, although many were strongly convinced independence would be the only solution. It was clear to all that the King and his advisors were creating far too many problems. They sent delegations to attempt to talk with the King or other political leaders, yet they were ignored. The Founders greatest fear was that if war commenced, the King would "hang them all," if the colonists lost. Throughout several years, the colonists pursued reconciliation, and while this was at least a friendly debate, they moved forward, in hopes of peace with the King.

Lexington and Concord broke the tie in favor of Independence.

LAND ISSUES?

Given the vastness of the New World, how could we have land issues? Understand that many unexpected issues arise when developing a virgin, uncharted continent. Land sales cannot occur, with any legal merit, until the establishment of mapping and survey is completed. The bio's contained herein make it clear that many of the Founders became schooled in the survey methodology, even George Washington. Neither Land deeds nor Land titles are legal, unless the corners of the property can be factually identified, marked, agreed, and allowed by a court. Nothing in North or South America had been surveyed, therefore only giant tracts of land that can be identified easily by physical features such as ridge lines or creeks and riverbeds, or shorelines, can be legally upheld by a court.

Many of our Founding Fathers sought ways to deal with this issue. Early governments attempted to identify land acreage in advance of surveys. Far too many historians and critics with incorrect understanding, have labeled Founding Fathers as "land speculators". NOT SO.

In fact, many Founders did identify these tracts of land. Early State of Georgia became involved. Many such identifiable tracts existed up and down our east coast. The bio's herein identify those founders who engaged in land issues, and all would go overboard financing our revolution, only to go bankrupt before they died.

Long Island may have been the first such plot of land. After the revolution, the area that became Washington, DC, was quickly subdivided and residential lots identified. What was called the "State of Franklin," in middle Tennessee was an example. The area around Dayton Ohio was an example. Another area continues today to have deed and title disputes, near the border of Texas and Arkansas, where the Red River becomes the state border. State of Georgia is blamed for the largest land area problem requiring Federal intervention, - the YAZOO CASE.

Many early settlers to the west of present-day Atlanta thought they had found great land deals, stretching from the west side of Atlanta across present day Alabama and Mississippi. The Yazoo is a river in Mississippi. The government made land available for prices between 50 cents and $10 dollars per acre. The government would not title less than 100 acres. It became an early and successful means of bringing people and settlers to those three states, prior to The Homestead Acts. The government realized they could have charged more for the land (consider it a tax form). After thousands of people took titles and paid, our government attempted to cancel the deals. The people took the issue to the first federal court west of the Appalachians, in Asheville, North Carolina, where a grandson of the founders denied government the right to cancel those completed contracts, as those contracts complied with the tenets of contract law that had been in effect over 1000 years. The Yazoo case should prove that our Founders were not attempting personal enrichment by means of land speculation.

- Which Founding Father was the most important Professor for six of our Founding Fathers?
- What University was the most important source of Education for the Founders?
- Learn which Founder entered University at the age of 12, and how many other Founders began University as young as 14-16.

The following pages provide a biographical history of our Founding Fathers brilliance and contributions, which created the Declaration of Independence, Articles of Confederation, United States Constitution, and the Bill of Rights. Some 90 bio's are included so that you may learn the totality of brilliance, of each of the Founders.

We have determined which Founders endured the greatest risk to life, liberty, and safety. This is a key distinction, once you understand that King George and his Generals had called for the arrest and jailing of the leaders among our Founding Fathers.

26

SAMUEL ADAMS
WAS HE LEADER OF THE "SONS OF LIBERTY"

Samuel Adams (September 27, 1727 – October 2, 1803) was the earliest leader to convince American Colonists that we should separate from Great Britain.

He was born in Boston, brought up in a religious and politically active family. A graduate of Harvard, he was an unsuccessful businessman and tax collector before politics. He was an influential official of the Massachusetts House of Representatives, and he became a part of a movement opposed to the British Parliament's efforts to tax the British American colonies without their consent. His 1768 Massachusetts Circular Letter calling for colonial non-cooperation prompted occupation of Boston by British troops, resulting in the Boston Massacre of 1770. Continuous resistance to British policy resulted in the 1773 Boston Tea Party and the coming American Revolution. Adams was involved with colonial newspapers publishing colonial sentiment over British rule, fundamental in uniting the colonies.

Biographer Mark Puls says Adams' writing tells us the "mob" was a reflective group, making Adams case with reason, not emotion.[1]

Early life (1727 – 1742)

Adams was born in Boston in the colony of Massachusetts on September 16, 1727.[2] Adams was one of twelve children born to Samuel Adams, Sr., and Mary (Fifield) Adams.[3][4][5] Adams emphasized Puritan values, especially virtue.[6]

Samuel Adams, Sr. (1689–1748) was a prosperous merchant and church deacon.[7][3] Adams became a leading figure in Boston politics through the Boston Caucus, promoting candidates who supported popular causes.[8][9][10] Members of the Caucus helped shape the agenda of the Boston Town Meeting, a form of local government with elected officials. Historian William Fowler said it was "the most democratic institution in the British empire".[11][8] Adams rose through the ranks, becoming a Justice of the Peace, a selectman, and a member of the Massachusetts House of Representatives.[12] He worked closely with the leader of the "popular party", a faction that resisted any encroachment by royal officials on the colonial rights embodied in the Massachusetts Charter of 1691.[13] In the coming years, members of the "popular party" became known as Whigs or Patriots.[15]

Young Samuel Adams attended Boston Latin School, then Harvard College in 1736. His parents hoped schooling would prepare him for the ministry, but Adams shifted to politics.[16] In his master's thesis, he argued that it was "lawful to resist the Supreme Magistrate, if the Commonwealth cannot otherwise be preserved."[18]

In 1739, Massachusetts faced a serious currency shortage, and Deacon Adams and the Boston Caucus created a "land bank" to issue paper money to borrowers who mortgaged land as security.[20] The court party used its influence to have British Parliament dissolve the land bank in 1741.[21] Directors of the land bank, including Deacon Adams, became personally liable for the currency in circulation, payable in silver and gold. For Adams, these lawsuits "served as a constant reminder that Britain's power over the colonies could be arbitrary and destructive."[22]

Early career (1743 – 1768)

After leaving Harvard in 1743, Adams considered becoming a lawyer but decided to go into business. He worked at Thomas Cushing's counting house, for a few months.[23] Adams's father then lent him £1,000 to go into business.[24]

Adams father soon made him a partner in the family's malthouse.[25] Years later, a poet poked fun at Adams by calling him "Sam the maltster".[26] Adams has often been described as a brewer, but the evidence suggests that he worked as a maltster and not a brewer.[27] Financial decisions caused the malthouse to close.[27]

In January 1748, Adams and friends were inflamed by British impressment and launched *The Independent Advertiser*, a weekly newspaper that printed many political essays written by Adams.[28] His essays drew heavily upon English political theorist John Locke's *Second Treatise of Government*, and they emphasized many of the themes that characterized his subsequent career.[29] He argued that the people must resist encroachment on their rights.[30] He cited the decline of the Roman Empire as an example of what could happen to New England if it abandoned Puritan values.[30]

When Deacon Adams died in 1748, Adams took over the family's affairs.[31] In October 1749, he married Elizabeth Checkley, his pastor's daughter.[34] Elizabeth gave birth to six children.[32] In July 1757, Elizabeth died soon after giving birth to a stillborn son.[35] Adams remarried to Elizabeth Wells,[36] but had no other children.

Elected to his first political office in 1747, he served as one of the clerks of the Boston market. In 1756, the Boston Town Meeting elected him to the post of tax collector, which provided a small income.[37] He often failed to collect taxes from his fellow citizens, which increased his popularity among those who did not pay, but left him liable for the shortage.[38] By 1765, his account was more than £8,000 in arrears. The town meeting was on the verge of bankruptcy, and Adams was compelled to file suit against delinquent taxpayers, but many taxes went uncollected.[39] In 1768, his political opponents used the situation to their advantage, obtaining a court judgment of £1,463 against him. Adams's friends paid off some of the deficit, and the town meeting wrote off the remainder.[40]

Conflict with Great Britain (Begins 1754)

Samuel Adams emerged as an important public figure in Boston soon after the British Empire's victory in the French and Indian War (1754–1763). The British Parliament found itself deep in debt, and they sought to directly tax the colonies of British America for the first time.[41] This tax dispute was part of a larger dispute between British and American interpretations of the British Constitution and the extent of Parliament's authority in the colonies.[43]

In the years leading up to and into the revolution Adams made frequent use of colonial newspapers and began openly criticizing British colonial policy and by 1775 was advocating independence from Britain.[44] Adams was foremost in actively using newspapers like the *Boston Gazette* to promote the ideals of colonial rights by publishing against the practice of taxation without representation.[46] The *Boston Gazette* had a circulation of two thousand, weekly, and its publishers, Benjamin Edes and John Gill, both founding members of the Sons of Liberty.[47]. Historian Ralph Harlow maintains the strong influence these men had in arousing public feeling.[48] In his *Boston Gazette writings*, Adams often wrote under a variety of surnames, including "Candidus", "Vindex",[49] and others, sometimes unsigned.[48]

Adams wanted to awaken his fellow citizens over the attacks on their Constitutional rights, with emphasis aimed at Massachusetts Governor Hutchinson. In each of its issues from early September through mid-October of 1771, the *Gazette* published Adams' essays, one of which criticized Parliament for using colonial taxes to pay Hutchinson's annual salary.[49] In a letter of February 1770, published by the *New York Journal* Adams asked if anyone of common sense could deny the King assumed a "personal and decisive" role against Americans.[50]

Sugar Act (1764)

The first step in the new program was the Sugar Act of 1764, which Adams saw as an infringement of colonial rights. Colonists were not represented in Parliament, he argued, therefore they could not be taxed by that body; only the colonial assemblies, and only they could levy taxes.[51] Adams highlighted the dangers of taxation without representation:

> For if our Trade may be taxed, why not our Lands? Why not the Produce of our Lands & everything we possess or make use of? This annihilates our Charter Right to govern & tax ourselves. It strikes at our British privileges, which as we have never forfeited them, we hold in common with our Fellow Subjects who are Natives of Britain. If Taxes are laid upon us in any shape without our having a legal Representation where they are laid, are we not reduced from the Character of free Subjects to the miserable State of tributary Slaves?[52]

"When the Boston Town Meeting approved Adams instructions on May 24, 1764," writes historian John K. Alexander, "it became the first body in America to go on record stating Parliament could not constitutionally tax the colonists."[54]

Adams's instructions were published in newspapers and pamphlets, and he soon became associated with James Otis, Jr., a member of the Massachusetts House[54] who boldly challenged the constitutionality of Parliament, but not go as far as Adams, who held that Parliament did not have sovereignty over the colonies.[55]

Stamp Act (1765 – 1766)

In 1765, Parliament passed the Stamp Act which required colonists to pay a new tax on most printed materials[56] and produced an uproar in the colonies.[57] In June 1765, Otis called for a Stamp Act Congress to coordinate colonial resistance.[58] The Virginia House of Burgesses passed a widely reprinted set of resolves against the Stamp,[59] calls to boycott British goods to pressure Parliament to repeal the tax.[60]

In Boston, the Loyal Nine, precursor to Sons of Liberty, organized protests of the Stamp Act. Adams was friendly with the Loyal Nine but was not a member.[61] Stamp distributor Andrew Oliver was hanged in effigy from Boston's Liberty Tree.

Governor Francis Bernard blamed the violence on Adams.[63] Scholars in the early 20th century viewed Adams as a master of propaganda,[64] with historians stating this pro and con. [62] Adams did approve of the August 14 action because he saw no other legal options to resist an unconstitutional act by Parliament, but he condemned attacks on officials.[65] Scholarly interpretation says he supported legal methods of resisting parliamentary taxation, such as petitions, boycotts, and nonviolent demonstrations, but he opposed mob.[66]

In September 1765, the Boston Town Meeting again appointed Adams to write instructions for Boston's delegation to the Massachusetts House of Representatives. He wrote his own instructions, and the town meeting selected him to replace deceased Oxenbridge Thacher as one of Boston's representatives.[67] Adams was one of the first colonial leaders to argue mans natural rights that governments could not violate.[68]

The Stamp Act was scheduled to go into effect on November 1, 1765, but it was not enforced because protestors throughout the colonies compelled stamp distributors to resign.[69] Eventually, British merchants convinced Parliament to repeal the tax.[70] By May 16, 1766, news of the repeal reached Boston. There was celebration throughout the city, and Adams made a public statement of thanks to British merchants.[71]

Adams was re-elected to the House and selected as its clerk, in which position he was responsible for official House papers. Adams used his position as clerk in promoting his message.[72] Joining Adams was John Hancock. He was initially a protégé of Adams and used his wealth to promote the Whig cause.

Townshend Acts (1767 – 1768)

After repeal of the Stamp Act, Parliament passed the Townshend Acts in 1767 establishing new duties on imported goods. These duties appear low yet untenable. The British ministry wanted[73] to enforce compliance, and created a customs agency known as the American Board of Custom Commissioners, headquartered in Boston.[74]

Adams used the Boston Town Meeting to organize a boycott. By February 1768, towns in Massachusetts, Rhode Island, and Connecticut had joined.[73] Opposition to the Townshend Acts was encouraged by *Letters from a Farmer in Pennsylvania*, essays by John Dickinson, who argued that new taxes were unconstitutional and never made to such a wide audience.[75]

In January 1768, the Massachusetts House sent a petition to King George asking for his help. [76] Adams and Otis requested the House send the petition to other colonies, along with the Massachusetts Circular Letter," a significant milestone on the road to revolution".[75] The letter written by Adams called on the colonies to join with Massachusetts in resisting the Townshend Acts.[77] The House initially voted against but politicking by Adams and Otis, approved it.[78]

British colonial secretary Lord Hillsborough, hoping to prevent a repeat of the Stamp Act, instructed the colonial governors in America to dissolve the assemblies if they responded to the Massachusetts Circular Letter. He directed Massachusetts Governor Francis Bernard to have the Massachusetts House rescind the letter.[79] On June 30, the House refused to rescind, with Adams citing their right to petition.[80] Instead, Adams sent a petition to the king asking to remove Governor Bernard. Bernard dissolved the legislature.[81]

The commissioners of the Customs Board found that they were unable to enforce trade regulations in Boston, so they requested military assistance.[82] Help came in the form of HMS *Romney*, a fifty-gun warship which arrived in Boston Harbor in May 1768.[82] Tensions escalated after the captain of *Romney* began to impress local sailors. The situation exploded on June 10, when customs officials seized *Liberty*, a sloop owned by John Hancock—a leading critic of the Customs Board—for alleged customs violations. Sailors and marines came ashore from *Romney* to tow away *Liberty*, and a riot broke out. Things calmed down in the following days, but customs officials packed up families and fled for protection to *Romney* and eventually to Castle William, in the harbor.[83]

Governor Bernard wrote to London that troops were needed to restore order.[125] Lord Hillsborough ordered four regiments to Boston.

Boston under occupation and Boston Massacre (1768 – 1770)

Learning British troops were on the way, the Boston Town Meeting met and requested Governor Bernard convene the General Court.[84] Bernard refused, so the Town Meeting called other Massachusetts towns to send representatives to Faneuil Hall.[85] The convention issued a letter insisting Boston was not lawless, and military occupation violated Bostonians' natural, constitutional, and charter rights.[86] As adjournment, British troops arrived in Boston Harbor.[87]

According to some accounts, the occupation of Boston was a turning point for Adams, after which he gave up hope of reconciliation and secretly began to work towards American independence.[88][89] Biographer Stewart Beach also questioned whether Adams sought independence before the mid-1770s, as Hutchinson, who despised Adams, never accused Adams of seeking independence, though Adams promised retaliation to troops sent to quell rebellion.[90]

Adams wrote numerous letters and essays against the occupation, which he considered a violation of the 1689 Bill of Rights.[91] The occupation was publicized throughout the colonies in the *Journal of Occurrences*, an unsigned series of newspaper articles that may have been written by Adams.[92] The *Journal* presented a factual daily account of events in Boston during the military occupation, also criticized the British impressment of colonial sailors into the Royal Navy.[93] The *Journal* ceased publication August 1, 1769, as Bernard had left Massachusetts.[94]

Adams continued to work on getting British occupational troops to withdraw. Two regiments were removed from Boston in 1769, but the other two remained.[94] Tensions between occupational troops and local colonists eventually resulted in the Boston Massacre. According to the "propagandist interpretation"[95] of historian John Miller, Adams provoked the incident to promote independence.[96] "There is no evidence that he prompted the Boston Massacre".[65]

After the Boston Massacre, Adams and other leaders met with Bernard's successor Governor Thomas Hutchinson and Colonel William Dalrymple, the army commander, to demand withdrawal of all occupational troops from Boston.[97] The situation remained explosive, so Dalrymple agreed to remove both regiments to Castle William.[98] Adams wanted the soldiers involved in the massacre to have a fair trial, to show Boston was not controlled by a mob, but was instead the victim of unjust occupation.[99] He convinced his cousins John Adams and Josiah Quincy to defend the soldiers, knowing they would not slander Boston to gain acquittal.[100] Sam Adams condemned the outcome; he thought the soldiers should be convicted of murder.[101]

"Quiet period" (1770 – 1773)

After the Boston Massacre, politics entered the "quiet period".[102] In April 1770, Parliament repealed the Townshend duties, except the tax on tea. In 1770, New York City and Philadelphia abandoned the non-importation boycott and Boston merchants faced the risk of being ruined.[103] John Adams withdrew from politics, while John Hancock and James Otis appeared more moderate.[104] Samuel Adams ran for Register of Deeds, and was beaten.[105] He was re-elected to the Massachusetts House, April 1772, but received fewer votes than ever.[106]

Boston Tea Party (1773 – 1774)

Adams took a leading role in the events that led up to the Boston Tea Party of December 16, 1773. In May 1773, the British Parliament passed the Tea Act, a tax law to help the struggling East India Company. Britons could buy smuggled Dutch tea more cheaply than the East India Company's tea, and the company amassed a huge surplus it could not sell.[106]

The Tea Act permitted the East India Company to export tea directly to the colonies for the first time, bypassing most of the merchant middlemen.[107] Merchants in New York, Philadelphia, Boston, and Charlestown received tea for resale.[108] In late 1773, seven ships were sent to the colonies carrying East India Company tea, including four bound for Boston.[109]

News of the Tea Act set off a firestorm of protest in the colonies.[110] The familiar "no taxation without representation" argument remained prominent, along with the question of the extent of Parliament's authority in the colonies.[111] Some colonists worried that, by buying the cheaper tea, they would be conceding that Parliament had the right to tax them.[110] The tea tax revenues were to be used to pay the salaries of certain royal officials, making them independent of the people.[112] Colonial smugglers played a heavy role in the protests, since the Tea Act made legally imported tea cheaper, which threatened to put smugglers of Dutch tea out of business.[112] Legitimate tea importers who had not been named as consignees by the East India Company were also threatened with financial ruin by the Tea Act.[113]

Adams and the committees promoted opposition to the Tea Act.[114] In every colony except Massachusetts, protesters were able to force the tea consignees to resign or return tea to England.[115] Governor Hutchinson convinced the tea consignees, two of whom were his sons, not to back down.[116] The Boston Caucus and Town Meeting acted to compel the consignees to resign, but they refused.[117] With the tea ships about to arrive, Adams and the Boston Committee of Correspondence contacted nearby committees to rally support.[118]

Dartmouth arrived in November, and Adams wrote a circular letter calling for a mass meeting at Faneuil Hall on November 29. Thousands arrived and the meeting was moved to the Old South Meeting House.[118] The meeting passed a resolution introduced by Adams urging the captain of the *Dartmouth* to send the ship back without paying.[119][120] Meanwhile, the meeting assigned twenty-five men to watch the ship and prevent the tea from being unloaded.[121]

Governor Hutchinson refused to grant permission for Dartmouth to leave without paying the duty. Two more tea ships, the *Eleanor* and the *Beaver*, and *William*, were stranded near Cape Cod and never arrived. December 16 was the last day of the *Dartmouth's* deadline, and about 7,000 people gathered around the Old South Meeting House.[122] Adams received a report that Governor Hutchinson had refused to let the ships leave, and he announced, "This meeting can do nothing further to save the country,"[123] some say, Adams's statement was a prearranged signal for the "tea party" to begin.[124] According to eyewitness accounts, people did not leave the meeting until fifteen minutes after Adams's alleged "signal."[125]

Adams tried to reassert control of the meeting, but people left the Old South Meeting House for Boston Harbor. That evening, 30 to 130 men boarded the vessels, some disguised as Mohawk Indians, and dumped all 342 chests of tea into the water .[126] Whether or not Adams helped plan is unknown, but Adams immediately worked to publicize and defend it.[127] He argued that the Tea Party was not the act of a lawless mob, but a principled protest and the only remaining option that the people had to defend their constitutional rights.[128]

The Chess Match Between Colonists and The King (1774)

Great Britain responded to the Boston Tea Party in 1774 with the Coercive Acts. The first was the Boston Port Act, which closed Boston's commerce until the East India Company had been repaid for the destroyed tea. The Massachusetts Government Act rewrote the Massachusetts Charter, making many officials royally appointed, and severely restricting town meetings. The Administration of Justice Act allowed colonists charged with crimes to go to another colony or Great Britain for trial. A new royal governor was appointed: General Thomas Gage, who was also commander of British military forces in North America.[129]

In May 1774, the Boston Town Meeting (Adams as moderator) organized a boycott of British goods.[130] Adams headed a committee in the Massachusetts House—with doors locked to prevent Gage from dissolving the legislature—which proposed an inter-colonial congress in Philadelphia. He was one of five delegates chosen to attend First Continental Congress.[131]

First Continental Congress (1774)

In Philadelphia, Adams promoted colonial unity while using his political skills to lobby delegates.[133] On September 16, Paul Revere brought Congress the Suffolk Resolves, one of many resolutions in Massachusetts that promised resistance to the Coercive Acts.[134] Congress endorsed the Suffolk Resolves, issued a Declaration of Rights that denied Parliament's right to legislate for the colonies, and organized a colonial boycott called the Continental Association.[135]

The Provincial Congress created the minutemen companies, who were ready for action on a moment's notice.[136] Adams served as moderator of the Boston Town Meeting, convened despite the Massachusetts Government Act.[136] He was selected to Second Continental Congress.

John Hancock had been added to the delegation, and he and Adams attended the Provincial Congress. Safety concerns caused them to stay at Hancock's childhood home in Lexington.[137] On April 14, 1775, General Gage received a letter from Lord Dartmouth advising him "to arrest the principal actors and abettors in the Provincial Congress whose proceedings appear in every light to be acts of treason and rebellion," and the night of April 18, Gage sent out a detachment of soldiers that sparked the American Revolutionary War, purpose being to seize and destroy military supplies in Concord, and Gage evidently decided against seizing Adams and Hancock, but Patriots believed otherwise, influenced by London newspapers reporting that the patriot leader would be hanged if caught.[138] From Boston, Joseph Warren dispatched Paul Revere to warn the two that British troops were on the move and might attempt to arrest them.[139] Soon after Lexington and Concord, Gage issued a proclamation granting a general pardon to all who would "lay down their arms, and return to the duties of peaceable subjects"—except Hancock and Samuel Adams, singling them out, according to Patriot historian Mercy Otis Warren, exaggerated importance of the two men.[140]

Second Continental Congress (1775 – 1776)

Continental Congress worked under a secrecy rule. Adams's worked behind the scenes as a "parliamentary whip."[141] Jefferson credits Samuel Adams with steering Congress toward independence, saying, "If there was any Palinurus to the Revolution, Adams was the man."[142] He served committees of military matters, nominated Washington as commander in chief.[143]

Adams was a cautious advocate for independence, urging Massachusetts to wait for more colonists to support separation from Great Britain, was pleased in 1775 when the colonies began to replace their old governments with republican governments.[144] He praised Thomas Paine's pamphlet *Common Sense*.[145] On June 7, Adams's ally Richard Henry Lee introduced a three-part resolution calling for Congress to declare independence, create a colonial confederation, and seek foreign aid. Congress and Adams signed the Declaration of Independence, July 4, 1776.[146]

Adams served on the Board of War in 1777.[147] He advocated bonuses to Continental Army soldiers to encourage them to reenlist.[148] He called for legislation to punish Loyalists. In Massachusetts, more than 300 Loyalists were banished and property confiscated.[148] In 1781, Adams retired, nearing age 60 with health declining.

Samuel Adams was involved in Politics for the balance of his life:

- Elected to Massachusetts State Senate
- Promoted free education for Girls and children.
- Charter member, American Academy of Arts and Sciences
- Advised the Governor on Shay's Rebellion
- Governor Bowdoin sent 4000 militiamen on Adams counsel
- Appointed to the Constitution Ratification board.
- Adams and Hancock agreed that the Bill of Rights was needed.
- Elected Lieutenant Governor of Massachusetts
- Governor of Mass upon death of Governor John Hancock
-

References
1. Puls 2006, pp. 15–16.
2. Hosmer 1885, p. 14.
3. Alexander 2002, p. 1.
4. Fowler & Fowler 1997, p. 4.
5. Puls 2006, p. 22.
6. Maier 1980, p. 41–42.
7. Miller 1936, pp. 3–4.
8. Alexander 2002, p. 2.
9. Maier 1980, p. 19.
10. Maier 1976, p. 17.
11. Fowler & Fowler 1997, p. 8.
12. Miller 1936, pp. 7–8.
13. Fowler & Fowler 1997, pp. 10–11.
14. Miller 1936, p. 9.
15. Alexander 2002, pp. 23, 74.
16. Puls 2006, p. 25.
17. Miller 1936, pp. 15–16.
18. Alexander 2002, p. 7.
19. Fowler & Fowler 1997, p. 25.
20. Alexander 2002, pp. 4–5.
21. Fowler & Fowler 1997, p. 21.
22. Alexander 2002, p. 12.
23. Miller 1936, p. 17.
24. Alexander 2002, p. 3.
25. Alexander 2002, pp. 3–4.
26. Maier, *American National Biography.*
27. Alexander 2002, p. 58.
28. Miller 1936, pp. 17–18.
29. Miller 1936, p. 21.
30. Alexander 2002, p. 8.
31. Miller 1936, p. 19.
32. Puls 2006, pp. 30–31.
33. Alexander 2002, p. 9.
34. Fowler & Fowler 1997, p. 34.
35. Puls 2006, pp. 31–32.
36. Fowler & Fowler 1997, p. 55.
37. Alexander 2002, p. 14.
38. Alexander 2002, p. 14, "The failure to collect all taxes was a Boston tradition".
39. Alexander 2002, p. 27.
40. Alexander 2002, pp. 53–54.
41. Fowler & Fowler 1997, p. 50.
42. Alexander 2002, p. 17.
43. Bailyn 1992, p. 162.
44. Alexander 2002, pp. x, 23, 65.
45. Maier 1980, pp. 13, 25.
46. Thomas 1874, p. lix.
47. Puls 2006, p. 5–6, 92.
48. Cushing 1908, pp. 250, 255.
49. Alexander 2002, pp. 100–101.
50. Alexander 2002, p. 209.

51. Fowler & Fowler 1997, p. 51.
52. Fowler & Fowler 1997, pp. 51–52.
53. Cushing 1904, pp. 1–7.
54. Alexander 2002, p. 21.
55. Alexander 2002, pp. 22–23.
56. Alexander 2002, pp. 17–18.
57. Miller 1936, pp. 50–51.
58. Fowler & Fowler 1997, p. 61.
59. Alexander 2002, p. 24.
60. Alexander 2002, pp. 24–25.
61. Alexander 2002, p. 25.
62. Miller 1936, p. 53.
63. Alexander 2002, p. 26.
64. O'Toole 1976, pp. 90–91.
65. Maier 1980, p. 27.
66. Alexander 2002, p. 29.
67. Alexander 2002, pp. 32–33.
68. Alexander 2002, p. 33.
69. Alexander 2002, p. 37; Puls 2006, p. 62.
70. Wells 1865, p. 112.
71. Alexander 2002, p. 40.
72. Alexander 2002, p. 41.
73. Alexander 2002, p. 50.
74. Alexander 2002, pp. 49–50.
75. Alexander 2002, p. 51.
76. Hosmer 1885, p. 109.
77. Alexander 2002, p. 52.
78. Fowler & Fowler 1997, pp. 78–80.
79. Alexander 2002, p. 54.
80. Fowler & Fowler 1997, p. 82.
81. Alexander 2002, p. 55.
82. Alexander 2002, p. 57.
83. Alexander 2002, pp. 57–60.
84. Alexander 2002, pp. 61–62.
85. Alexander 2002, p. 62–63.
86. Alexander 2002, p. 63.
87. Fowler & Fowler 1997, p. 88.
88. Wells 1865, p. 207.
89. Maier 1980, pp. 21–25.
90. Beach 1965, pp. 171–172.
91. Alexander 2002, p. 67.
92. Fowler & Fowler 1997, p. 90–92.
93. Alexander 2002, pp. 68–69.
94. Alexander 2002, p. 74.
95. O'Toole 1976, p. 92–95.
96. Miller 1936, p. 276.
97. Alexander 2002, p. 82.
98. Fowler & Fowler 1997, p. 105.
99. Alexander 2002, p. 82–84.
100. Alexander 2002, p. 84–85.
101. Alexander 2002, pp. 94–95.
102. Alexander 2002, p. 93.
103. Alexander 2002, p. 91.
104. Alexander 2002, pp. 97, 99.
105. Alexander 2002, p. 104.
106. Thomas 1987, pp. 248–249.
107. Labaree 1979, pp. 67, 70.
108. Labaree 1979, pp. 75–76.
109. Labaree 1979, pp. 78–79.
110. Alexander 2002, p. 120.
111. Thomas 1987, p. 246.
112. Labaree 1979, pp. 78, 106.
113. Labaree 1979, p. 102.
114. Thomas 1987, p. 256.
115. Alfred F. Young, Shoemaker and Tea Party: Memory and American Revolution (Boston: Beacon Press, 1999
116. Alexander 2002, pp. 120–122.
117. Labaree 1979, pp. 96–100.

118. Labaree 1979, pp. 109–112.
119. not official town meeting, but gathering of "body of the people" of greater Boston
120. Alexander 2002, pp. 123–124.
121. Puls 2006, p. 143.
122. Alexander 2002, p. 123.
123. Alexander 2002, p. 125.
124. Raphael 2004, p. 53.
125. Maier 1980, pp. 27, 28–32.
126. Alexander 2002, pp. 125–126.
127. Fowler & Fowler 1997, p. 124.
128. Alexander 2002, p. 129.
129. Alexander 2002, pp. 130–133.
130. Alexander 2002, pp. 131–132.
131. Alexander 2002, pp. 135–136.
132. Alexander 2002, p. 137.
133. Alexander 2002, p. 139.
134. Alexander 2002, pp. 139–140.
135. Alexander 2002, p. 140.
136. Alexander 2002, p. 143.
137. Fischer, *Paul Revere's Ride*, 94, 108.
138. Burgan 2005, p. 11.
139. Fischer, *Paul Revere's Ride*, 110.
140. Maier 1980, p. 17.
141. Nobles, "Old Republicans", 264, per Jack N. Rakove,
142. Randall, Henry Stephens, *Life of Thomas Jefferson*, J.B. Lippincott, 1871, p. 182
143. Chernow 2010, p. 186.
144. Alexander 2002, pp. 152–153.
145. Alexander 2002, p. 1
146. Maier 1980, p. 5.
147. Alexander 2002, p. 157.
148. Alexander 2002, pp. 158–159.

Bibliography

- Alexander, John K. (2002). Samuel Adams: America's Revolutionary Politician. Lanham, Maryland: Rowman & Littlefield. p. 249. ISBN 0-7425-2115-X.
- Bailyn, Bernard (1992) [1967]. The Ideological Origins of the American Revolution (enlarged ed.). Harvard University Press. ISBN 0-674-44302-0.
- Beach, Stewart (1965). Samuel Adams; the fateful years,1764-1776. New York, Dodd, Mead
- Cushing, Harry Alonzo (1904). Writings of Samuel Adams. Vol. I. New York: G.P. Putnam's Sons.
- Chernow, Ron (2010). Washington: Life. Penguin Press. ISBN 978-1-59420-266-7.
- Fowler, William M.; Fowler, Lillian M. (January 1, 1997). Handlin, Oscar (ed.). Samuel Adams: Radical Puritan. New York: Longman. p. 190. ISBN 0-673-99293-4.
- Hosmer, James K. (1885). Samuel Adams. Boston: Houghton Mifflin. p. 469.
- Labaree, Benjamin Woods (1979) [1964]. "Boston Tea Party". The New England Quarterly. **38** (2). Boston: Northeastern U Press: 255–257. ISBN 0-930350-05-7. JSTOR 363599.
- Maier, Pauline (1976). "Coming to Terms with Samuel Adams". The American Historical Review. **81** (1): 12–37. doi:10.2307/1863739. JSTOR 1863739.
- Miller, John Chester (1936). Sam Adams: Pioneer in Propaganda. Boston: Little, Brown. 437.
- O'Toole, James M. (March 1976). "The Historical Interpretations of Samuel Adams". New England Quarterly. **49** (1): 82–96. doi:10.2307/364558. JSTOR 364558.
- Puls, Mark (2006). Samuel Adams: Father of the American Revolution. New York: St. Martin's Press. p. 273. Raphael, Ray (2004). Founding Myths: Stories That Hide Our Patriotic Past. New York: The New Press. pp. 354. Thomas, Isaiah (1874). history of printing in America, bio of printers. Vol. I. New York, B. Franklin.
- Thomas, Peter David Garner (1987). The Townshend Duties Crisis: The Second Phase of the American Revolution, 1767-1773. Clarendon Press. ISBN 978-0-1982-29674.
- Wells, William V. (1865). Life and Public Services of Samuel Adams: Being a Narrative of His Acts and Opinions, and His Agency in Producing and Forwarding the American Revolution, Extracts from His Correspondence, State Papers, and Political Essays. Vol. 3. Boston: Little, Brown

BENJAMIN FRANKLIN
GENIUS OF THE ERA

Benjamin Franklin (January 17, 1706 – April 17, 1790) became a successful newspaper editor and printer in Philadelphia, the leading city in the colonies, publishing the *Pennsylvania Gazette* at age 23.[3] He became wealthy publishing this and *Poor Richard's Almanack*, using the pseudonym "Richard Saunders".[4] After 1767, he was associated with the *Pennsylvania Chronicle*, a newspaper known for its revolutionary sentiments and criticisms of the policies of the British Parliament and the Crown.[5] He was founder and first president of the Academy and College of Philadelphia, now University of Pennsylvania. He organized the American Philosophical Society. He was deputy postmaster-general for the colonies.[6]

Franklin spearheaded repeal of the Stamp Act by the British Parliament. He was the first U.S. ambassador to France and developed positive Franco–American relations. His efforts proved vital in securing French aid for the American Revolution. From 1785 to 1788, he served as President of Pennsylvania.

He charted and named the Gulf Stream. His inventions include the lightning rod, bifocals, glass harmonica and the Franklin stove.[8] He founded many civic organizations, the Library Company, Philadelphia's first fire department,[9] the University of Pennsylvania.[10] Franklin earned the title of "First American" for his campaigning for colonial unity. He was the only person to sign the Declaration of Independence, Treaty of Paris, peace with Britain and the Constitution. Franklin is called "the most accomplished American of his day."[11]

Ancestry

Benjamin Franklin's father, Josiah Franklin, was a tallow chandler, soaper, and candlemaker. Josiah Franklin was born at Ecton, Northamptonshire, England.[13]

Franklin's mother, Abiah, was born in Massachusetts Bay Colony, his grandmother was a former indentured servant, came from a Puritan family among the first Pilgrims seeking religious freedom in 1635 after King Charles I began persecuting Puritans. Her father Peter was "the sort destined to transform America."[14] As clerk of the court, he was arrested February 10, 1676, and jailed.[15]

Youthful Development

- He attended Boston Latin School but did not graduate.
- "His parents talked of the church as a career"[16]
- for Franklin, his schooling ended when he was ten.
- At 12 he became an apprentice to his brother James, a printer.[17]
- Denied a chance to write, adopted pseudonym "Silence Dogood,"
- Mrs. Dogood's letters were published and became conversation around town.
- Franklin was an advocate of free speech from an early age.
- Brother was jailed in 1722 for an article Ben wrote about the governor,
- Mrs. Dogood quoted *Cato,* "Without freedom of thought there can be no wisdom and no such thing as public liberty without freedom of speech."[18]
- He left apprenticeship without permission and was a fugitive.[19]
- Self taught translator of foreign languages, while setting type

As Young Adult

At 17, Franklin ran away to Philadelphia, seeking a new start in a new city.

When he arrived, he worked in several printing shops, but he was not satisfied.

- Pennsylvania governor Sir William Keith convinced him to go to London, to acquire equipment for establishing another newspaper in Philadelphia.
- Discovering that Keith's promises of a newspaper were empty, he worked as a typesetter in a printer's shop in Church of St Bartholomew-the-Great, London.
- He returned to Philadelphia in 1726 with the help of Thomas Denham, a merchant who employed him as a clerk, shopkeeper, and bookkeeper.[20]
- Franklin was essentially "trapped" in England for 5 years.
- In 1727, at age 21, Franklin formed the Junto, a group of "like minded aspiring artisans and tradesmen who hoped to improve themselves and the community."
- The Junto was a discussion group for issues of the day.
- Junto subsequently gave rise to organizations in Philadelphia.[21]
- The Junto was modeled after English coffeehouses, and which had become the center of the spread of Enlightenment ideas in Britain.[22][23]
- Franklin conceived a subscription library, to pool the funds to buy books.[24]
- This birthed the Library Company of Philadelphia, in 1731.[25]
- Upon Denham's death, Franklin returned to his former trade.
- In 1728, set up a printing house.
- the following year he was publisher of *The Pennsylvania Gazette*.
- The *Gazette* gave Franklin a forum for a variety of local reforms.
- As scientist and statesman, he remained 'B. Franklin, Printer.'[20]
- 1732, published first German-language newspaper in America.[26]
- Franklin printed Moravian religious books in German.[27]
- According to Ralph Frasca, Franklin promoted the printing press as a device to instruct colonial Americans in moral virtue. He saw this as a service to God.
- He saw himself uniquely qualified to instruct Americans in morality.
- He built a printing network of partnerships, Carolinas, to New England.
- He created and financed the first newspaper chain.
- He believed the press had a public-service duty.[29][30]

Franklin's Chain of Newspapers

- He began in Charleston, South Carolina, in 1731.
- He sponsored two dozen printers in Pennsylvania, South Carolina, New York, Connecticut, and even the Caribbean.
- By 1753, eight of the fifteen English language newspapers in the colonies were published by him or his partners.[31]

After his second editor died, the widow, Elizabeth Timothy, one of the first woman printers,[32] and her son Peter Timothy, took over the *South Carolina Gazette*.[33] Timothy took a patriotic stand in the crisis with Great Britain.[34][35][36]

In 1730 1731, Franklin was initiated into the Masonic lodge. He became grand master in 1734.[37][38] He edited and published the first Masonic book in the Americas, James Anderson's *Constitutions of the Free-Masons*.[39][38]

Common-law marriage to Deborah Read

At age 17, Franklin proposed to 15-year-old Deborah Read.[20]

Franklin travelled to London, and after he failed to communicate with Deborah and her family, they interpreted his silence as breaking his promises.[40][41]

Franklin returned in 1726 and resumed his courtship of Deborah.[40] They established a common-law marriage on September 1, 1730. They took in his recently acknowledged young son (William) and raised him in their household.[42]

Deborah's fear of the sea meant that she never accompanied Franklin on any of his extended trips to Europe.[43] Deborah wrote to him in November 1769, saying she was ill due to "dissatisfied distress" from his prolonged absence.[44] Deborah Read Franklin died of a stroke on December 14, 1774.[45] History records that Franklin was prevented by governmental factors from returning any sooner.

William Franklin surviving son of Benjamin Franklin was born February 22, 1730,[46] educated in Philadelphia, studied law in London. In 1763, he was appointed as the last royal governor of New Jersey.

Benjamin Franklin the Author

In 1732, Franklin began to publish *Poor Richard's Almanack*. The first issue published was for the upcoming year, 1733.[47] He developed a distinct, signature style.[48] He sold about ten thousand copies per year—it became an institution.[49]

Public Life - - Early Examples Leading to National Recognition

In 1736, Franklin created the Union Fire Company, one of the first volunteer firefighting companies.[50] In 1743, he devised a plan for the Academy, Charity School, College of Philadelphia; but his chosen leader, Rev. Richard Peters, refused. He printed, *Proposals Relating to Education of Youth in Pennsylvania*.[51]:30 He was appointed president of the Academy on November 13, 1749.[52]

In 1743, he founded the American Philosophical Society. He began electrical research that would occupy him between politics and moneymaking.[20]

During King George's War, Franklin raised a militia, the Association for General Defense as legislators took no defense action for Philadelphia. He raised money for earthworks and artillery, largest was the "Grand Battery" of 50 guns.[53][54]

In 1747, Franklin retired from printing and went into other businesses.[55] He formed a partnership with his foreman, which provided Franklin with half of the shop's profits for 18 years.

He was selected as a councilman; in June 1749, he became a Justice of the Peace for Philadelphia; and in 1751, he was elected to the Pennsylvania Assembly. August 10, 1753, he was appointed deputy postmaster-general of British North America. His most notable service in domestic politics was reform of the postal system.[20]

Franklin and Thomas Bond chartered Pennsylvania Hospital, first in the colonies.[56] He organized Philadelphia Contributionship, first homeowner's insurance company.[57][58]

Franklin the Great Educator

Between 1750 and 1753,"[59] Franklin, Samuel Johnson of Stratford, Connecticut, and schoolteacher William Smith built on Franklin's initial scheme and created what Bishop James Madison, president of the College of William & Mary, called a "new-model"[60] plan of American college. Franklin solicited, printed, and promoted an American textbook of moral philosophy by Samuel Johnson, titled *Elementa Philosophica*,[61] to be taught in colleges.

In 1753, Harvard [66] and Yale[67] awarded him honorary master of arts degrees.[68] In 1756, he was awarded an honorary Master of Arts from the College of William & Mary.[69] In 1759, the University of St Andrews awarded him an honorary doctorate.[80] He was awarded an honorary doctorate by Oxford University in 1762, often addressed as "Dr. Franklin."[1]

In June 1753, Johnson, Franklin, and Smith met in Stratford.[62] They decided the new-model college would focus on the professions, with classes taught in English instead of Latin, have subject matter experts as professors, and there would be no religious test for admission.[63] Johnson founded King's College (Columbia University) in New York City, while Franklin hired Smith as provost of the College of Philadelphia, in 1755. It later merged with University of the State of Pennsylvania, now University of Pennsylvania. Over one-third of the college-affiliated men who contributed to the Declaration of Independence studied at the college.[64]

In 1754, he headed the Pennsylvania delegation to the Albany Congress. Franklin proposed a broad Plan of Union. While the plan was not adopted, elements of it found their way into the Articles of Confederation and the Constitution.[65]

Later in 1756, Franklin organized the Pennsylvania Militia. He used Tun Tavern to recruit soldiers to go into battle against the Native Americans.[70]

Postmaster

Well known as a printer and publisher, Franklin was appointed postmaster of Philadelphia in 1737, until 1753, when he and publisher William Hunter were named deputy postmasters–general of British North America, the first to hold the office. (Joint appointments were standard at the time, for political reasons.) He was responsible for the British colonies from Pennsylvania north and east, as far as the island of Newfoundland. Franklin opened the first post office with regular, monthly mail in Halifax. He reorganized the accounting system and improved delivery between Philadelphia, New York, and Boston..[71]

When the lands of New France were ceded to the British under the Treaty of Paris in 1763, the British province of Quebec was created, and Franklin saw mail service expanded between Montreal, Trois-Rivières, Quebec City, and New York. For the greater part of his appointment, he lived in England (from 1757 to 1762, and 1764 to 1774)—about three-quarters of his term.[72] Eventually, his sympathies for the rebel cause in the Revolution led to his dismissal on January 31, 1774.[73]

On July 26, 1775, Second Continental Congress established the United States Post Office and following decades as postmaster, named Franklin the first United States postmaster general.[74]

Decades in London - - Political work while in London

In 1757, he was sent to England by the Pennsylvania Assembly as a colonial agent to protest political influence of the Penn family, the proprietors of the colony.

At this time, many members of the Pennsylvania Assembly were feuding with William Penn's heirs, who controlled the colony as proprietors. After his return to the colony, Franklin led the "anti-proprietary party" in the struggle against the Penn family and was elected Speaker of the Pennsylvania House in May 1764. The anti-proprietary party sent him to England again to seek resolution with the Penn family. During this trip, events drastically changed his mission.[75]

In London, Franklin opposed the 1765 Stamp Act. Pennsylvanians were outraged, believing that he had supported the measure all along. Franklin soon learned of the extent of colonial resistance to the Stamp Act, and he testified during the House of Commons proceedings that led to its repeal.[76] He authored popular essays on behalf of the colonies. Georgia, New Jersey, and Massachusetts appointed him as their agent to the Crown.[75]

During his missions to London between 1757 and 1775, Franklin lodged off the Strand in central London,[77] now a museum, the Benjamin Franklin House.

Scientific work

In 1756, Franklin became a member of the Society for the Encouragement of Arts, Manufactures & Commerce founded.[78]

The study of natural philosophy (today, science in general) networked him as a corresponding member of the Lunar Society of Birmingham.[79] In October 1759, he was granted Freedom of the Borough of St Andrews.[81]

In 1759, the University of St Andrews awarded him an honorary doctorate,[80] also awarded an honorary doctorate by Oxford University in 1762. Via these honors, he was often addressed as "Dr. Franklin."[1]

Franklin spoke against official recordings of patents and copyright, arguing such developments should benefit the whole of mankind instead of just the inventor.

His first notable invention - -improvements to the "Guttenberg Press," which revolutionized high speed printing 250 years earlier.

Travels around Europe

Franklin used London as a base to travel, staying at Leeds, Manchester, Lichfield.[82] In Scotland, he spent five days near Stirling and three weeks in Edinburgh. In 1759, he visited Edinburgh with his son and reported his six weeks in Scotland "six weeks of the densest happiness in any part of my life."[83]

In Dublin, Franklin was invited to sit with the members of the Irish Parliament rather than in the galley. He was the first American to receive this honor.[84] While touring Ireland, he was deeply moved by the level of poverty he witnessed. The economy of the Kingdom of Ireland was affected by the same trade regulations and laws that governed the Thirteen Colonies. He feared that the American colonies could eventually come to the same poverty if the regulations and laws apply to them.[85]

Franklin spent two months in Germany,1766. He declared his gratitude to German scientist Otto von Guericke for his early studies of electricity. Franklin co-authored the first treaty of friendship between Prussia and America in 1785.[86] News of his electrical discoveries was widespread in France. His reputation brought an introduction to influential scientists and politicians, and also to King Louis XV.[10]

Franklin Scouts French and Indian Enemy at Fort Defiance, 1755

The British had tired of the French and Indian War and sent their greatest combat General Braddock and heavy troop numbers to lead an attack on Fort Defiance, today's Pittsburgh. Franklin led a reconnaissance party that located the enemy positions and guided Braddock. The Indians were able to surveil the attacking Brit/American force. When French and Indians launched a surprise ambush, they destroyed all the British troops and only the Americans led by George Washington escaped.

Defending the American cause politically

One argument in Parliament was that Americans should share costs of the French and Indian War. Franklin said local governments had raised and paid 25,000 soldiers to fight France, America spent millions in French and Indian War alone.[88][89]

In 1773, he published his pro-American essays: "Rules by Which a Great Empire May Be Reduced to a Small One," and "An Edict by the King of Prussia."[90]

Coming of revolution

In 1763, soon after Franklin returned to Pennsylvania from England, the western frontier was engulfed in Pontiac's Rebellion. The Paxton Boys murdered a group of peaceful Susquehannock Indians and marched on Philadelphia.[91] Franklin helped to organize a local militia to defend the capital against the mob. Franklin wrote about the Paxton Boys: "If an *Indian* injures me," he asked, "does it follow that I may revenge that injury on all *Indians*?"[92][93]

He countered British surveillance by counter-surveillance and manipulation. "Waged a public relations, secured secret aid, engaged privateering, churned out effective propaganda."[94]

Declaration of Independence

By the time Franklin arrived in Philadelphia on May 5, 1775, after his second mission to Great Britain, the American Revolution had begun at the Battles of Lexington and Concord. The New England militia forced the main British army to remain inside Boston.[95] The Pennsylvania Assembly unanimously chose Franklin as their delegate to the Second Continental Congress. In June 1776, he was appointed to the Committee of Five that drafted the Declaration of Independence. Temporarily disabled by gout, he made "small but important" changes to the draft sent to him by Thomas Jefferson.[96]

At the signing, he is quoted as having replied to John Hancock, "Yes, we must, indeed, all hang together, or most assuredly we shall all hang separately."[97] (This would result if America lost Revolution!)

Ambassador to France (1776–1785)

On October 26, 1776, Franklin was dispatched to France as commissioner for the US.[106] He conducted the affairs of his country toward the French with great success, including securing a military alliance and signing Treaty of Paris.[98]

Franklin's advocacy for religious tolerance resulted in Louis XVI's signing of the Edict of Versailles in November 1787. This edict effectively nullified the Edict of Fontainebleau, which denied non-Catholics the right to practice their faith.[99]

Franklin also served as American minister to Sweden, although he never visited that country.[109] He negotiated a treaty that was signed in April 1783. On August 27, 1783, in Paris, he witnessed the world's first hydrogen balloon flight.[100] *Le Globe*, created by professor Jacques Charles and Les Frères Robert, was watched by a vast crowd as it rose from the Champ de Mars (now the site of the Eiffel Tower).[101] Franklin became so enthusiastic that he subscribed financially to the next project to build a manned hydrogen balloon.[102]

President of Pennsylvania, Delegate to Constitutional Convention

He was unanimously elected the sixth president of the Supreme Executive Council of Pennsylvania. Shortly after, he was re-elected to a full term in 1785, 1786 and 1787. He hosted the Constitutional Convention of 1787 in Philadelphia.[103]

He served as a delegate to the Convention. Mrs. Powel asked him what kind of government they had wrought. He replied: "A republic, if you can keep it."[104]

Franklin opened Constitutional Convention one morning with, "we can save much argument and debate by agreeing to implement 'The Laws of Moses' as the initial legal code of our constitution . . ."

Benjamin Franklin, in 1788, saw the difficulties that some of the newly independent American states were having in forming a government, and proposed that until a new code of laws could be agreed to, they should be governed by "the laws of Moses", as contained in the Old Testament. He justified his proposal by explaining that the laws had worked in biblical times: "The Supreme Being ... having rescued them from bondage by many miracles, performed by his servant Moses, he personally delivered to that chosen servant, in the presence of the whole nation, a constitution and code of laws for their observance."[105]

Our Founding Fathers understood these lessons as has no one before or since. They studied this vast bibliography in original languages as little more than the Bible had been translated, (see original Harvard college catalogue, "First Fruits").

Franklin on Inventions and scientific inquiries

Franklin was a prodigious inventor. A few creations were the lightning rod, Franklin stove, bifocal glasses, flexible urinary catheter. He never patented inventions; in his autobiography he wrote,"... we should be glad of an opportunity to serve others by any invention of ours; this we should do freely and generously."[106]

Franklin started exploring the phenomenon of electricity in the 1740s, after he met the itinerant lecturer Archibald Spencer, who used static electricity in his demonstrations.[107] He proposed that "vitreous" and "resinous" electricity were not different types of "electrical fluid" (as electricity was called then), but the same "fluid" under different pressures. (The same proposal was made independently that same year by William Watson.) He was the first to label them as positive and negative respectively, which replaced the then current distinction made between 'vitreous' and 'resinous' electricity,[108][109][110] and he was the first to discover the principle of conservation of charge.[111] In 1748, he constructed a capacitor, called an "electrical battery" (not a true battery like Volta's pile) by placing eleven panes of glass sandwiched between lead plates, suspended with silk cords, connected by wires.[112]

Franklin briefly investigated electrotherapy, including the use of the electric bath. This work led to the field becoming widely known.[115] The CGS unit of electric charge has been named after him: one *franklin* (Fr) is equal to one statcoulomb.

Franklin advised Harvard University in its acquisition of new electrical laboratory apparatus after a fire that destroyed the original Harvard Hall in 1764. The collection he assembled later became part of the Harvard Collection of Historical Scientific Instruments.[115]

Kite experiment and lightning rod

Franklin published a proposal for an experiment to prove that lightning is electricity by flying a kite in a storm. On May 10, 1752, Thomas-François Dalibard of France conducted Franklin's experiment using a 40-foot-tall (12 m) iron rod instead of a kite, and he extracted electrical sparks from a cloud. On June 15, 1752, Franklin may have conducted his well-known kite experiment in Philadelphia, successfully extracting sparks from a cloud. He described the experiment in his newspaper, *The Pennsylvania Gazette*, on October 19, 1752,[116][117] without mentioning that he himself had performed it.[118] This account was read to the Royal Society on December 21 and printed as such in the *Philosophical Transactions*.[119] Joseph Priestley published an account with additional details in his 1767 *History and Present Status of Electricity*. Franklin was careful to stand on an insulator, keeping dry under a roof to avoid electric shock.[120] Georg Wilhelm Richmann in Russia, were electrocuted performing lightning experiments in months following his experiment.[121]

He did not perform this experiment in the way that is often pictured, flying the kite and waiting to be struck by lightning, as it would have been dangerous.[122] Instead he used the kite to collect some electric charge from a storm cloud, showing that lightning was electrical.[123] On October 19, 1752, he sent a letter to England with directions for repeating the experiment.[124]

Franklin's electrical experiments led to his invention of the lightning rod. He said conductors with a sharp[124] rather than a smooth point could discharge silently and at far greater distance. He surmised that this could help protect buildings from lightning by attaching "upright Rods of Iron," made sharp as a Needle and gilt to prevent Rusting, and from the Foot of those Rods a Wire down the outside of the Building into the Ground. Following experiments on Franklin's house, lightning rods were installed on the Academy of Philadelphia (University of Pennsylvania) and the Pennsylvania State House (later Independence Hall) in 1752.[125]

Population studies

Franklin had a major influence on the emerging science of population studies.[126][127] He calculated America's population was doubling every 20 years and would surpass England in a century.[128] In 1751, he drafted *Observations concerning the Increase of Mankind, Peopling of Countries, etc.* Four years later, it was anonymously printed in Boston and was quickly reproduced in Britain, where it influenced economist Adam Smith and later the demographer Thomas Malthus, who credited Franklin for discovering a rule of population growth.[129][130]

Kammen (1990) and Drake (2011) say Franklin's *Observations concerning the Increase of Mankind* (1755) stands alongside Ezra Stiles' "Discourse on Christian Union" (1760) as the leading works of 18th-century Anglo-American demography; Drake credits Franklin's "wide readership and prophetic insight."[131][132] Franklin was also a pioneer in the study of slave demography.[133] In his capacity as a farmer, he wrote at least one critique about price controls, and subsidy of the poor. This is preserved in his letter to the *London Chronicle* published November 29, 1766, "On the Price of Corn, and Management of the poor."[134]

Oceanography

As deputy postmaster, Franklin became interested in North Atlantic Ocean circulation patterns.[146] Franklin worked with experienced ship captains, learning enough to chart the current and name it the Gulf Stream.[135] Phil Richardson, a Woods Hole oceanographer and Gulf Stream expert, discovered it in the Bibliothèque Nationale in Paris in 1980.[136][137][138]

Franklin's oceanographic findings, *Maritime Observations*, published 1786,[138] contained ideas for sea anchors, catamaran hulls, watertight compartments, shipboard lightning rods and a soup bowl stable in stormy weather.

Theories and experiments

Equal to Issac Newton, Franklin was among few scientists who supported Christiaan Huygens's wave theory of light, ignored by the scientific community. In the 18th century, Isaac Newton's corpuscular theory was held to be true.[140]

Franklin deduced that storms do not always travel in the direction of the prevailing wind, a concept that greatly influenced meteorology.[141] After the Icelandic volcanic eruption of Laki in 1783, and the subsequent harsh European winter of 1784, Franklin made observations on the nature of these two seemingly separate events. He wrote about them in a lecture series.[142]

Franklin used kites to pull humans and ships across waterways.[143] George Pocock in *A Treatise on The Aeropleustic Art, or Navigation in the Air, by means of Kites, or Buoyant Sails*[144] was inspired by Franklin's kite power across a waterway.

Franklin noted a principle of refrigeration by observing that on a very hot day, he stayed cooler in a wet shirt in a breeze than he did in a dry one. In 1758 on a warm day in Cambridge, England, he and fellow scientist John Hadley experimented by continually wetting a mercury thermometer with ether and using bellows to evaporate the ether.[145] With each subsequent evaporation, the thermometer read lower, reaching 7 °F (−14 °C). Another thermometer showed room temperature constant at 65 °F (18 °C). In his *Cooling by Evaporation*, he noted, "One may see the possibility of freezing a man to death on a warm summer's day."[146]

Franklin wrote to Mary Stevenson describing his experiments on the relationship between color and heat absorption.[147] He found darker color clothes got hotter when exposed to sunlight than lighter color clothes, an early demonstration of black body thermal radiation.

Franklin's experiments on non-conduction of ice are worthy, although the law of the general effect of liquefaction on electrolytes is not attributed to Franklin.[148] Franklin wrote, "... A certain quantity of heat will make some bodies good conductors, which will not otherwise conduct ..." and again, "... And water, though naturally a good conductor, will not conduct well when frozen into ice."[149]

Franklin Views on religion, morality, slavery like Great Philosophers

He felt that organized religion was necessary to keep men good to their fellow men.[149] When he met Voltaire in Paris and asked his fellow member of the Enlightenment vanguard to bless his grandson, Voltaire said in English, "God and Liberty, this is the only appropriate benediction for the grandson of Franklin."[150]

Franklin's parents were pious Puritans.[151] The family attended the Old South Church, where Benjamin was baptized in 1706.[152] Franklin's father owned a copy of a book, *Bonifacius: Essays to Do Good*, by Puritan preacher and family friend Cotton Mather, which Franklin cited as a key influence on his life. "If I have been," Franklin wrote Mather's son seventy years later, "a useful citizen, the public owes the advantage of it to that book."[153] He retained a strong faith in God as the wellspring of morality and goodness, as a Providential actor in history responsible for American independence.[159]

At a critical impasse during Constitutional Convention in June 1787, he attempted to introduce daily common prayer.[160] It was never brought to a vote.[161]

Franklin writes in his autobiography:

"... Once Preachers have been at a church about 2 years, . . . they begin to repeat sermons. I made a practice of seeking churches that had a new or visiting Preacher, saddled my horse and rode as many as 20 miles to hear a new sermon."

Franklin was an admirer of the evangelical minister George Whitefield. He admired Whitfield for preaching to worship God through good works. He published all Whitfield's sermons and journals, boosting the Great Awakening.[162]

Max Weber considered Franklin's writings a culmination of the Protestant ethic, which created the social conditions necessary for the birth of capitalism.[162]

One of his notable characteristics was his respect, tolerance, and promotion of all churches. Referring to Philadelphia, he wrote in his autobiography, "new Places of worship were continually wanted, and generally erected by voluntary Contribution, my Mite for such purpose, whatever might be the Sect, was never refused."[163] "He helped create a new type of nation that would draw strength from its religious pluralism."[163] The revivalists who were active mid-century, such as Whitefield, were the greatest advocates of religious freedom, "claiming liberty of conscience to be an 'inalienable right of every rational creature.'"[164] Franklin's rejection of dogma and doctrine and his stress on the God of ethics and morality and civic virtue made him the "prophet of tolerance."[163] He composed "A Parable Against Persecution," an apocryphal 51st chapter of Genesis in which God teaches Abraham the duty of tolerance.[165]

According to David Morgan,[16] Franklin was a proponent of "generic religion." He prayed to "Powerful Goodness" and referred to God as "the infinite." John Adams noted that he was a mirror in which people saw their own religion: "The Catholics thought him a Catholic. The Church of England claimed him. Presbyterians thought him half a Presbyterian, the Friends believed him a "wet Quaker."

On July 4, 1776, Congress appointed a three-member committee composed of Franklin, Jefferson, and Adams to design the Great Seal of the United States. Franklin's proposal (not adopted) featured the motto: "Rebellion to Tyrants is Obedience to God" and a scene from the Book of Exodus he took from the frontispiece of the Geneva Bible,[166] with Moses, the Israelites, the pillar of fire, and George III depicted as pharaoh.

The design that was produced was not acted on by Congress, and the Great Seal's design was not finalized until a third committee was appointed in 1782.[167]

Franklin strongly supported the right to freedom of speech:

In those wretched countries where a man cannot call his tongue his own, he can scarce call anything his own. Whoever would overthrow the liberty of a nation must begin by subduing the freeness of speech ... Without freedom of thought there can be no such thing as wisdom, and no such thing as public liberty without freedom of speech, which is the right of every man ...   —*Silence Dogood no. 8, 1722*[168]

In 1790, just about a month before he died, Franklin wrote to Ezra Stiles, president of Yale, who had asked him his views on religion: As to Jesus of Nazareth, my Opinion of whom you particularly desire, I think the System of Morals and his Religion, as he left them to us, the best the world ever saw or is likely to see   [23]

Musical Creation

Franklin played the violin, the harp, and the guitar. He also composed music, notably a string quartet in early classical style.[169] While in London, he improved the glass harmonica. He worked with the London glassblower Charles James to create it, and instruments based on his mechanical version soon found their way to Europe.[170] Joseph Haydn, a fan of Franklin's enlightened ideas, had a glass harmonica in his instrument collection.[171] Mozart composed for Franklin's 5glass harmonica,[172] as did Beethoven.[173] Gaetano Donizetti used the instrument in Amelia's aria "Par che mi dica ancora" in the tragic opera *Il castello di Kenilworth* (1821),[174] as did Camille Saint-Saëns in *The Carnival of the Animals*. Richard Strauss calls for the glass harmonica in *Die Frau ohne Schatten*.[174]

Anne-Robert-Jacques Turgot said: "Eripuit fulmen cœlo, mox sceptra tyrannis" ("He snatched lightning from the sky and the scepter from tyrants").[12]

References

1.   Encyclopædia Britannica, Wood, 2021
2.   Morris, Richard B. (1973). Seven Who Shaped Our Destiny: Founding Fathers as Revolutionaries. New York: Harper & Row. pp. 1, 5–30. ISBN 978-0-06-090454-8.
3.   Brands, H.W. (2010). The First American: The Life and Times of Benjamin Franklin. Knopf Doubleday Publishing. p. 390. ISBN 978-0-307-75494-3.
4.   Goodrich, Charles A. (1829). Lives of the Signers to the Declaration of Independence. W. Reed & Company. p. 267.
5.   "William Goddard and the Constitutional Post". Smithsonian National Postal Museum. Retr Oct 19, 2010.
6.   "Ben Franklin, Postmaster General"(PDF). USPS. Archived 10/ 9/22. Retr 5/29/21
7.   Nash, 2006, pp. 618–638.
8.   Franklin Institute, Essay
9.   Burt, Nathaniel (1999). The Perennial Philadelphians: Anatomy of an American Aristocracy. University of Pennsylvania Press. p. 142. ISBN 978-0-8122-1693-6.
10.   Isaacson, 2004, p.
11.   Isaacson, 2004, pp. 491–492.
12.   "To the Genius of Franklin". Philadelphia Museum of Art.
13.   Huang, Nian-Sheng (2000). "Franklin's Father Josiah: Life of a Colonial Boston Tallow Chandler, 1657–1745". Transactions American Philosophical Society. 90 (3): i–155. doi:10.2307/1586007. ISSN 0065-9746.
14.   Isaacson, 2004, p. 14.
15.   "Nantucket lands and landowners". Library of Congress, Washington, D.C. 20540 USA. Retr May 13, 2024.
16.   Franklin, Benjamin (1901) [1771]. "Introduction". Autobiography of Benjamin Franklin. Macmillan's pocket English and American classics. New York: Macmillan. p. vi. ISBN 9780758302939. Retrieved February 1, 2011.
17.   Bernhard, J. (2007). Porcupine, Picayune, & Post: How Newspapers Get Their Names. EBL-Schweitzer. Univ of Missouri Press. p. 11. ISBN 978-0-8262-6601-9. Retr June 1, 2023.
18.   Isaacson, 2004, p. 32.
19.   Seelye, J.E.; Selby, S. (2018). Shaping North America: Exploration to American Revolution [3 vols]. ABC-CLIO. p394. ISBN 978-1-4408-3669-5. Retr 6/1// 2022
20.   Carl Van Doren, Benjamin Franklin. (1938).
21.   Mumford, Michael D. (2002)."Social innovation: 10 cases Franklin". Creativity Research Journal. 14 (2): 253–266. doi:10.1207/S15326934CRJ1402_11. S2CID 143550175.
22.   David Waldstreicher, ed., A Companion to Benjamin Franklin (2011) p. 30.
23.   J. A. Leo Lemay, The Life of Benjamin Franklin, Vol 2: Printer and publisher, 1730–1747 (2005) pp.92–94, 123.
24.   Murray, Stuart A.P. (2009). The library: an illustrated history. NY: Skyhorse Pub. p. 147. ISBN 978-1-60239-706-4.
25.   Korty, Margaret Barton (1965). "Benjamin Franklin and Eighteenth-Century American Libraries". Transactions of the American Philosophical Society. 55 (9): 1–83. doi:10.2307/1006049. JSTOR 1006049.
26.   "German Newspapers in US and Canada". Arch Sept 12, 2016. Retr Oct 7, 2014.
27.   Frantz, John B. (1998). "Franklin and the Penn Germans". Penn. History: 21–34.
28.   Philip, Gleason (2000). "Trouble in the Colonial Melting Pot". Journal of American Ethnic History. 20 (1): 3–17. doi:10.2307/27502642. JSTOR 27502642. S2CID 254480258.
29.   Frasca, Ralph (1997). "Franklin's Journalism". Fides et Historia. 29 (1): 60–72.
30.   Ralph Frasca, Franklin's Printing Network: Disseminating Virtue in Early America (U Missouri Press, 2006) doi:10.1111/j.1540-6563.2007.00197_16.x online review by Robert Middlekauff.
31.   Ralph Frasca, Benjamin Franklin's Printing Network: Disseminating Virtue in Early America (2006) pp. 19, 196.
32.   Baker, Ira L. (1977)."Elizabeth Timothy: America's First Woman Editor". Journalism Quarterly. 54 (2): 280–85. doi:10.1177/107769907705400207. S2CID 143677057.

33. Ralph Frasca, "'Partnership at Carolina Having succeeded, Encourag'd to Engage in Others': Genesis of Ben Franklin's Printing Network", Southern Studies: Interdisciplinary Journal of South (2006), Vol. 13 Issue 1/2, p. 1–23

34. Smith, Jeffery A. (1993). "Impartiality and Revolutionary Ideology: Editorial Policies of the 'South-Carolina Gazette,' 1732–1735". Journal of Southern History. 49 (4): 511–26. doi:10.2307/2208674. JSTOR 2208674.

35. Frasca, Ralph (2003). "'I am now about to establish a small Printing Office ... at Newhaven': Franklin and First Newspaper in Connecticut". Connecticut History. 44 (1): 77–87. doi:10.2307/44369668. JSTOR 44369668. S2CID 254488378.

36. Frasca, Benjamin Franklin's Printing Network, pp. 161–167.

37. The History Channel, Mysteries of the Freemasons: America, video documentary, August 1, 2006, written by Noah Nicholas and Molly Bedell

38. "Freemasonry Grand Lodge of British Columbia and Yukon website". Freemasonry.bcy.ca. Retr Sept 21, 2009.

39. Anderson, James; Franklin, Benjamin; Royster, Paul (1/1/1734). "Constitutions of Free-Masons (1734). Online Electronic Edition". UNL Libraries: Faculty Publications

40. Chylinska, Bozenna (Jan 2015). Life" Polish Journal for American Studies. 9. Arch June 29, 2024. Retr 5/4/ 2024.

41. "Deborah Read". Constitutional Law Reporter. Nov 28, 2018. Retr May 4, 2024.

42. Tise, Larry E. (2000). Benjamin Franklin and women. University Park, Pa.: Pennsylvania State University Press. ISBN 0585382778. OCLC 49414692.

43. Coss, Stephen (September 2017). "What Led Benjamin Franklin to Live Estranged from His Wife for Nearly Two Decades?". Smithsonian.

44. November 1769 Letter Arch June 15, 2018, Wayback Machine from Deborah Read to Ben Franklin, franklinpapers.org

45. Coss, Stephen (Sept 2017). "What Led Benjamin Franklin to Live Estranged from His Wife for Nearly Two Decades?". Smithsonian. Retrieved Feb26, 2021.

46. Skemp SL. Wil Franklin: Son of a Patriot, Servant of a King, Oxford U Press US,1990,ISBN 0-19-505745-7, p4

47. "Poor Richard's Almanack – Ben Franklin Historical Society". Retr Dec 23, 2023.

48. "Benjamin Franklin – Biography and Literary Works of Benjamin Franklin". Literary Devices. August 20, 2014.

49. Van Doren 1938, p. 109.

50. John Kenneth Galbraith. (1975). Money: Where It Came, Whence It Went, pp. 54–54. Houghton Mifflin Co

51. Montgomery, Thomas Harrison (1900). A History of U of Pennsylvania from Its Foundation to A.D. 1770. Philadelphia: George W. Jacobs & Co. LCCN 00003240.

52. The Early Years: The Charity School, Academy and College of Philadelphia Archived Feb 5, 2012, Wayback Machine Uof Pennsylvania Archives, 1972.

53. Dorwart, Jeffery (1998). Fort Mifflin of Philadelphia: An Illustrated History. University of Pennsylvania Press. pp. 9–11. ISBN 978-0-8122-1644-8.

54. Kyriakodis, Harry (2011). "16. At Washington Avenue". Philadelphia's Lost Waterfront. The History Press. p. 114. ISBN 978-1-62584-188-9.

55. James N. Green, "English Books and Printing in Age of Franklin", Colonial Book in Atlantic World (2002), 257

56. "IN THE BEGINNING – Story of the Creation of the Nation's First Hospital". Penn Medicine. Archived Oct 15, 2002.

57. Landers, Jackson (Sept 27, 2016). "Early 19th Century, Firefighters Fought Fires ... and Each Other". Smithsonian. Smithsonian Institution. Retr Dec 10, 2017.

58. McGuire, Virginia (May 3, 2013). "What Are Those Little Shields Above Doorways of Philadelphia Homes?". Philadelphia. Metrocorp Publishing. Retr Dec10, 2017.

59. Olsen 2013, p. 174.

60. Smith, Horace Wemyss, Life and Correspondence of Rev. Wm. Smith, D.D., Philadelphia, 1880, Vol 1: pp. 566–67.

61. Samuel Johnson, Elementa philosophica: containing chiefly, Noetica, relating to the mind or understanding and Ethica, relating to moral behaviour. Philadelphia, Printed by B. Franklin and D. Hall, 1752.

62. Olsen 2013, pp. 163–274.

63. Olsen 2013, p. 163.

64. Olsen 2013, p. 308.

65. "Union: Joseph Galloway, Plan of Union". press-pubs.uchicago.edu. Retr Dec 30, 2022.

66. "History of honorary degrees". Harvard University. Retrieved December 30, 2022.

67. Honorary Degrees Arch June 10, 2010, Wayback Machine Yale U. Retr 8/20/2012

68. "Resume | Ben Franklin Exhibit". www.benfranklinexhibit.org. Retr Dec 30, 2022.

69. The History of the College of William and Mary. Richmond, VA: J.W. Randolph & English. 1874. p. 148. ISBN 978-1-4290-4333-5.

70. Thompson, Peter (1999). Rum Punch & Revolution: Taverngoing & Public Life in Eighteenth-Century Philadelphia. Philadelphia: University of Pennsylvania Press.

71. "Civilization.ca – Chronology of Canadian Postal History" www.historymuseum.ca. Retr Dec 30, 2022.

72. "Civilization.ca – Chronology Canadian Postal History– 1760–1840". www.historymuseum.ca.Retr12/30/22

73. "To Benjamin Franklin from Anthony Todd, 31 January, 1744".

74. Isaacson, 2004, pp. 206–09, 301

75. J.A. Leo Lemay, "Franklin, Benjamin". American National Biography Online, Feb 2000. https://www.anb.org/display/10.1093/anb/9780198606697.001.0001/anb-9780198606697-e-0100298?rskey=69AExU&result=10

76. "Ben Franklin's Resume – Independence National Historical Park (U.S. National Park Service)". www.nps.gov.

77. Peter Charles Hoffer, Benjamin Franklin Explains the Stamp Act Protests to Parliament, 1766 (2015)

78. "Tom Huntington". Archived from the original on October 5, 2009.

79. Nicholles, Natalie (Dec 14, 2016). "What Would Benjamin Franklin Say?". The RSA. Arch&Retr Sept 16, 2021

80. Schofield, Robert E. (Dec 1957),"Industrial Orientation of Science in Lunar Society of Birmingham", Isis, 48 (4), U Chicago Press, History of Science Society: 408–415, doi:10.1086/348607, ISSN 0021-1753, JSTOR 227513, S2CID 144950413
81. "Ben Franklin's Resume – Independence National Historical Park (U.S. National Park Service)". www.nps.gov.
82. Kate Kennedy Club". Arch March 27, 2009. Retr Sept 21, 2009.
83. "Biography of Benjamin Franklin". www.ushistory.org. Retrieved Dec 30, 2022.
84. Buchan, James (11/25/03). Crowded with Genius. Harper. p. 2. ISBN 0-06-055888-1.
85. Nathan Haskell Dole, ed. (2003). Autobiography of Benjamin Franklin. Kessinger. ISBN 978-0-7661-4375-3.
86. "Benjamin Franklin |Ken Burns| PBS | Watch Benjamin Franklin: A Ken Burns Film | Full Documentary Now Streaming| PBS". Retrieved December 30, 2022.
87. "The Avalon Project: Treaty of Amity and Commerce between His Majesty the King of Prussia, and the USA". avalon.law.yale.edu. Retrieved Dec 30, 2022.
88. James A. Henretta., ed. (2011). Documents for America's History, Vol 1: To 1877. Bedford/St. Martin's. p. 110.
89. Isaacson, 2004, pp. 229–230.
90. Franklin, Benjamin. "Reprinted on The History Carper". Archived on Jan 3, 2006.
91. Isaacson, W. (2003) Ben Franklin: An American Life. Simon&Schuster pp209–216
92. Franklin, Benjamin. "A Narrative of the Late Massacres ..." Archived April 27, 2006, at the Wayback Machine reprinted on The History Carper.
93. Calloway, C. G. (2006). "Chapter 4". The Scratch of a Pen: 1763 and the Transformation of North America. Oxford U Press. ISBN 978-0-19-530071-0.
94. Crews, Ed (Summer 2004). "Spies and Scouts, Secret Writing, and Sympathetic Citizens". Colonial Williamsburg Journal. Retrieved April 19, 2009.
95. "Princeton University Press".
96. Isaacson, 2004, pp. 311–312.
97. Sparks, Jared (1856). Life of Ben Franklin: Containing Autobiography, with Notes and Continuation. Boston: Whittemore, Niles and Hall. p. 408. Retr Dec 16, 2007
98. "Benjamin Franklin sets sail for France". history.com.
99. Miller, Hunter (ed.). "British American Diplomacy: Paris Peace Treaty of Sept 30, 1783". Avalon Project.
100. "Book338glava314dictofersailles1787html Wa365bet Vioslot". booking-help.org. Arch&Retr Dec 30, 2022.
101. "Benjamin Franklin – People – Department History – Office of the Historian". history.state.gov.
102. Piers Letcher – Jacques Charles (2003). Eccentric France: Bradt Guide to mad, magical marvelous France. Bradt Travel Guides. ISBN 978-1-84162-068-8. Retr March 17, 2010.
103. "Science and Society, Medal commemorating Charles and Robert's balloon ascent, Paris, 1783". Scienceandsociety.co.uk. Retrieved March 17, 2010.
104. "Fiddlers Green, History of Ballooning, Jacques Charles". Fiddlersgreen.net. Retrieved June 20, 2011.
105. Franklin 1834, p. 211. Franklin, Benjamin (1834), Franklin, William Temple (ed.), Memoirs (eBook), vol. 2, Philadelphia: McCarty & Davis.
106. Brands, The First American, pp. 654–55, 694.
107. Isaacson, Benjamin Franklin, An American Life, p. 459
108. Benjamin Franklin. "Part three". The Autobiography of Benjamin Franklin.
109. Cohen, I. Bernard (1990). Benjamin Franklin's Science. Harvard U Press. pp. 40–42.ISBN 0-674-06658-8
110. H. W. Brands, The First American, 2002 p.192
111. Franklin, Ben(May 25,1747) "Letter Peter Collinson". Franklin Papers. ArchOct 20, 2017. Retr May 1, 2016
112. Weisstein, Eric. "Franklin (1706–1790)". Eric Weisstein's World of Scientific Bio.
113. "Conservation of Charge". Archived on Feb 18, 2008. Retrieved Feb 15, 2006.
114. Franklin, Benjamin (April 29, 1749). "Further Experiments and Observations in Electricity". Franklin Papers.
115. Tomase, Jennifer (June 1, 2006). "'A How-To Guide' explores Ben Franklin's 'can-do' legacy". Harvard U Gazette. Archived July 25, 2010. Retrieved August 9, 2016.
116. Benjamin Franklin, "Kite Experiment" Arch Sept 22, 2010, Wayback Machine, printed in The Pennsylvania Gazette, Oct 19, 1752. In Papers of Benjamin Franklin, American Philosophical Society and Yale U; digital edition by Packard Humanities Institute, Vol. 4, p. 360a. Retr Feb 6, 2017.
117. "Pennsylvania Gazette – Ben Franklin Historical Society". Retr Dec 30, 2022.
118. Steven Johnson (2008) The Invention of Air, p. 39 ISBN 978-1-59448-401-8. Retrieved February 6, 2017.
119. "Founders Online: Kite Experiment, 19 Oct1752". founders.archives.gov. Retr Dec 30, 2022.
120. Van Doren 1938, p. 159.
121. Clarke, Ronald W. (1983). Benjamin Franklin, A Biography. Random House. p. 87. ISBN 978-1-84212-272-3.
122. "Franklin's Kite". Museum of Science (Boston). Arch 2/9/10. Retr Sept 28, 2003.
123. Wolf, Abraham (1939). History of Science, Technology, and Philosophy in the Eighteenth Century. New York: Macmillan. p. 232.
124. "Lightning Rods: Franklin Had It Wrong". NYT. June 1, 1983. Retr March 16, 2018.
125. Krider, Philip (Jan 2006). "Ben Franklin and Lightning Rods". Physics Today. 59 (1): 42. Bibcode:2006PhT......59a..42K. doi:10.1063/1 2180176. S2CID 110623159.
126. Houston, Alan (2008). Ben Franklin and Politics of Improvement. Yale U.P. pp.06–41. ISBN 978-0-300-15239-5
127. Lemay, J.A. Leo (2008). Life of Benjamin Franklin, Volume 3: Soldier, Scientist, and Politician, 1748–1757. U. Penn Press. p 245. ISBN 978-0-8122-4121-1.
128. Isaacson, 2004, p. 150.
129. Cohen, I. Bernard (2005). The Triumph of Numbers: How Counting Shaped Modern Life. W.W. Norton. p. 87.

130. Aldridge, Alfred Owen (1949). "Franklin as Demographer". Journal of Economic History. 9 (1): 25–44. doi:10.1017/S0022050700090318. JSTOR 2113719. S2CID 154647498.
131. Drake, James David (2011). The Nation's Nature: How Continental Presumptions Gave Rise to the USA. U. of Virginia Press. p. 63. ISBN 978-0-8139-3122-7.
132. Kammen, Michael G. (1990). People of Paradox: An Inquiry Concerning the Origins of American Civilization. Cornell U.P. p. 81. ISBN 978-0-8014-9755-1.
133. Van Cleve, George (2010) Slaveholders' Union: Slavery, Politics, Constitution, Early American Republic. U. Chicago Press. p.148. ISBN 978-0-226-84669-9.
134. "The Writings of Benjamin Franklin, Vol III: London, 1757 – 1775 – On the Price of Corn, and Management of the Poor". Historycarper.com. Archived from the original on December 2, 2011. Retrieved December 11, 2011.
135. Tuchman, Barbara Wertheim (1988). The First Salute. Knopf Publishing Group.pp.221–222. ISBN 0-394-55333-0
136. Anon. "1785: Benjamin Franklin's 'Sundry Maritime Observations'". Ocean Explorer: Readings for ocean explorers. NOAA Office of Ocean Exploration and Research. Archived Dec 18, 2005. Retr July 15, 2010.
137. Philip L. Richardson (February 8, 1980), "Benjamin Franklin and Timothy Folger's first printed chart of the Gulf Stream", Science, vol. 207, no. 4431, pp. 643–45.
138. John N. Wilford, "Prints of Franklin's chart of Gulf Stream found", New York Times, pp. A1, B7 (Feb 6, 1980).
139. Wood, Anthony R. (March 29, 2007). "How Franklin's chart resurfaced". www.inquirer.com. Retr Dec 30, 2022.
140. Jogn Gribbin, "In search of Schrödinger's cat", Black Swan, p. 12.
141. Heidorn, Keith C. Heidorn, PhD. Eclipsed By Storm. Weather Doctor. Oct 1, 2003.
142. "Memoirs of the literary and philosophical society of Manchester". www.dartmouth.edu. Arch June 15, 2018
143. Fisher, Sydney George (1903). The True Benjamin Franklin (5 ed.). Philadelphia: J.B. Lippincott Co. p. 19.
144. Pocock, George (1851). A Treatise on Aeropleustic Art, or Navigation in the Air, by means of Kites, or Buoyant Sails. London: Longmans, Brown, and Co. p. 9.
145. Writings of Benjamin Franklin: London, 1757–1775". Historycarper.com. ArchJan 28, 2011. Retr 9/14/10.
146. "Founders Online: Benjamin Franklin to John Lining, 17 June 1758" founders.archives.gov. Retr June 30, 2021
147. Jones, Thomas P. (1836). Journal Franklin Institute of State of Pennsylvania. Pergamon Press. pp. 182–83.
148. W. Gratzer, Eurekas and Euphorias, pp. 80–81.
149. Franklin, Autobiography, ed. Lemay, p. 65.
150. Isaacson, 2004, p. 354.
151. Isaacson, 2004, pp. 5–18.
152. "Isaacson, 2003, p. 15". Oldsouth.org. Arch May 31, 2008. Retr Sept 21, 2009.
153. Isaacson, 2004, p. 26.
154. Isaacson, 2004, p. 102.
155. Franklin, Benjamin (Nov 20, 1728). "Articles of Belief and Acts of Religion". Ben Franklin Papers. franklinpapers.org.
156. Franklin, Ben (1771). Autobiography other writings. Cambridge: Riverside. p. 52.
157. Eidenmuller, Michael E. "Online Speech Bank: Benjamin Franklin's Prayer Speech at Constitutional Convention 1787". Americanrhetoric.com. Retr Sept 21, 2009.
158. Rossiter, Clinton. 1787. The Grand Convention (1966), pp. 184–85.
159. Isaacson, 2004, pp. 107–113.
160. Isaacson, 2004, pp. 10, 102, 489.
161. Weber, Max (2002). The Protestant Ethic and "Spirit of Capitalism". Translated by Peter Baehr; Gordon C. Wells. Penguin Books. pp. 9–11. ISBN 9780486122373.
162. Franklin Benjamin "Benjamin Franklin's Autobiography". Archived Sept 5, 2008, Wayback Machine Section 2 reprinted on UShistory.org.
163. Isaacson, 2004, pp. 93 ff.
164. Bailyn, 1992, p. 249.
165. Isaacson, 2004, p. 112.
166. Coffman, Steve, ed(2012) Words of Founding Fathers: Selected Quotations of Franklin, Washington, Adams, Jefferson, Madison and Hamilton, with Sources. Jefferson, NC: McFarland. p. 97. ISBN 978-0-7864-5862-2.
167. Korn, Michael (Sep 28, 2015). "Franklin, the Composer" Institute for Music Leadership. Retrieved April 3, 2021.
168. "GFI Scientific glass blowing products and services". www.finkenbeiner.com. Retrieved December 30, 2022.
169. Watefield, Robin (August 1, 2003). Hidden Depths: The Story of Hypnosis: The Story of Hypnosis. Routledge. p. 67. ISBN 978-1-135-40367-6.
170. Apel, Willi (1969). "Glass harmonica". Harvard Dictionary of Music. Harvard. p. 347. ISBN 9780674375017.
171. Benke, Richard (Feb 25, 2001). "'Armonicists' Debate Source of Beethoven's Maladies" LA Times. Retr 8/21/18
172. Carmel, Jeffrey J. (November 22, 1983). "Franklin invented it, Mozart wrote for it: the 'armonica' returns". Christian Science Monitor. Retrieved August 21, 2018.
173. Osborne, Charles (April 1, 1994). The bel canto operas of Rossini, Donizetti, and Bellini. Amadeus Press. ISBN 978-0-931340-71-0.
174. Carnival of the Animals: Scores at International Music Score Library Project
175.

ROBERT MORRIS,

FINANCIER OF THE REVOLUTION
SIGNATORY TO AT LEAST TWO FOUNDATIONAL DOCUMENTS

Robert Morris Jr. (January 20, 1734 – May 8, 1806) Born in Liverpool, Morris was brought to North America by his father when he was 13 years old, quickly becoming a partner in a successful shipping firm based in Philadelphia. In the aftermath of the French and Indian War, Morris joined others opposing British taxation such as the 1765 Stamp Act. By 1775 he was the richest man in America.[3] After the outbreak of the Revolutionary War, he helped procure arms and ammunition for the revolution, and in late 1775 he was chosen as a delegate to the Second Continental Congress.

Morris was born in Liverpool, England, on January 20, 1734.[7] His parents were Robert Morris Sr., an agent for a shipping firm, and Elizabeth Murphet. Until he reached the age of thirteen, Morris was raised by his maternal grandmother in England. In 1747, Morris immigrated to Oxford, Maryland, where his father had prospered in the tobacco trade. Two years later, Morris's father sent him to Philadelphia, then the most populous city in British North America.[8]

Personal and family life

Personal connections established during our Revolution continue today to be some of the most important networks today, often influencing huge transactions.

In early 1769, at age 35, Morris married 20-year-old Mary White, the daughter of a wealthy and prestigious lawyer and landholder. Mary gave birth to seven children. (One son was Congressman Thomas Morris, whose wife was related to the Livingston and Van Rensselaer New York political families). Morris and his family built three manor homes, located across the Delaware River from Trenton, New Jersey. The Morrises worshiped at the Anglican Christ Church, also attended by Benjamin Franklin, Thomas Willing, and other leading citizens of Philadelphia.[21] The Morris household employed several domestic workers.[12][13]

Mary's brother, was an Episcopal priest and Senate chaplain.[14]

In 1781, Morris purchased a home on Market Street, two blocks north of Independence Hall.[15] President Washington accepted Morris's offer to make the house his primary residence.[16] Morris became close to Washington.[17] The Morris President's House, was residence of the president until Adams moved to the White House.[18]

American Revolution - - Tensions with Great Britain

In 1765, the Parliament of Great Britain imposed the Stamp Act. Morris joined with several other merchants in pressuring the British to refrain from collecting the new tax.[19] Facing colonial resistance, Parliament repealed the tax but implemented other policies to generate tax. During the decade after the Stamp Act, Morris frequently joined other merchants in protesting Parliament's taxation policies.[20] Writing to a friend, Morris stated that "I am a native of England but from principle am American in this dispute."[21][22]

In early 1774, in response to the Intolerable Acts, many colonists in British North America began calling for a boycott of British goods. In Philadelphia, Willing, Charles Thomson, and John Dickinson called for the colonies to coordinate a response to British tax policies.[21] Morris was not elected to the First Continental Congress, but frequently met with delegates and befriended Washington and John Jay. In September 1774, First Continental Congress created the Continental Association, to enforce a boycott against British goods.[23]

Continental Congress - - Pre-War issues 1775–August 1776

In April 1775, the Revolutionary War broke out following the Battles of Lexington and Concord. The Second Continental Congress met in Philadelphia, an appointed George Washington to command the Continental Army. The Pennsylvania Provincial Assembly established the twenty-five-member Committee of Safety to supervise defenses, and Morris was appointed. Morris became part of the core group that directed and served chairman when Benjamin Franklin was absent. Charged with obtaining gunpowder, Morris arranged a smuggling operation to import arms and ammunition. Morris also became the chief supplier of gunpowder to the Continental Army.[24] Later in the year, Morris was elected to Congress.[25]

In Congress, Morris was appointed to the Secret Committee of Trade, to supervise procurement of arms and ammunition.[26] As the revolutionary government lacked an executive branch, committees of Congress handled all business.[27] The dangerous and secretive nature of obtaining contraband goods made it difficult to establish competitive bidding.[28][29] Morris was also appointed to the Marine Committee, which oversaw the Continental Navy,.[30] From his position, he procured supplies and secured a formal alliance with France.[31]

Morris favored a naval strategy of attacking Britain's "defenseless places" in an effort to divide Britain's superior fleet.[32] Along with Franklin, Dickinson, and John Adams, Morris helped draft the Model Treaty, which served as a template for relations with foreign countries. Unlike Britain's mercantile trade policies, the Model Treaty emphasized the importance of free trade. In March 1776, Morris was named chairman of the Secret Committee of Trade.[33] He established agents, domestic and foreign, charged with procuring war supplies.[34]

In late February 1776, Americans learned the British Parliament passed the Prohibitory Act, making all American shipping subject to seizure by British ships.[35] In June 1776, due largely to frustration with the moderate leaders that included Morris, delegates from across Pennsylvania met to draft a new constitution and a new state government. By early July 1776, Pennsylvania was the lone congressional delegation opposed to declaring independence. With Morris absent, all congressional delegations voted to pass a resolution declaring independence on July 2, and the United States formally declared independence on July 4, 1776.[36]

Despite his opposition to independence, the Pennsylvania constitutional convention voted to keep Morris in Congress. Morris signed the Declaration of Independence.[37] In explaining his decision, he stated, "I am not one of those politicians that run testy when my own plans are not adopted - - I do not wish to see my countrymen die on the battlefield, nor do I wish to see them live in tyranny".[38]

Continued war, August 1776–1778

After the Declaration of Independence, Morris continued to supervise efforts to secure arms and ammunition and export American goods. British spies and warships captured American ships in the midst of trading operations.[39] Morris authorized American envoys in Europe to commission privateers to attack British shipping. He arranged for an agent, William Bingham, to pay for repairs on Martinique. Due to the lucrative nature of privateering, Morris also started outfitting his own privateers.[40][41] At the urging of Morris and Franklin, Congress authorized appointment of two envoys to seek a formal treaty of alliance with France; ultimately, Benjamin Franklin and Arthur Lee were appointed as those envoys.[42] Along with Silas Deane, Franklin would help expand arms shipments from France and Spain, but Lee failed to gain support from Prussia and the Habsburg monarchy.[43]

In early December 1776, Washington's army retreated across the Delaware River and into Pennsylvania, and most members of Congress temporarily left Philadelphia. Morris was one of few delegates to remain in the city, and Congress appointed Morris and two other delegates to "execute Continental business" in its absence.[44] Morris frequently corresponded with Washington, and he provided supplies that helped enable the Continental victory at the Battle of Trenton.[45] After the Continental Army was defeated in the Battle of Brandywine, Congress fled Philadelphia; Morris and his family went to live at their estate in Manheim, Pennsylvania.[46] Morris obtained a leave of absence in late 1777, but had to defend himself against attacks regarding mismanagement.[47] Morris did not play a large role in drafting the Articles of Confederation, but signed the document in March 1778. As some states objected to the Articles, it would not go into force until 1781.[48]

Morris returned to Congress in May 1778 to vote for a measure to provide pensions to Continental Army officers. He formed a relationship with Gouverneur Morris (no relation), a young New York congressman who shared many of Robert Morris's views.[48] The following month, Morris returned with Congress to Philadelphia, which had been evacuated.[49] Morris did not resume duties in Congress, seeking instead to focus on his business.[50] In late 1778, Morris won election to the state assembly as part of a slate of candidates that favored reforming the Pennsylvania constitution; he resigned from Congress to take up his seat.[51] After Morris left Congress, Henry Laurens, Thomas Paine, continued their false attacks, but in early 1779 a congressional committee cleared Morris of charges.[52]

Out of Congress, 1779–1781

With plans to call a state constitutional convention frustrated by Joseph Reed, Morris and James Wilson founded the Republican Society, a political club seeking a new state constitution, those who favored became Constitutionalists.[53]

Due to rising inflation, in mid-1779 the Constitutionalists established a committee to implement price controls; Philadelphia merchants were arrested, but Morris avoided arrest and emerged as a leading opponent of the committee.[54] The price control committee disbanded in September, but the following month a mob seized several Republican leaders. Morris and other Republicans sheltered at James Wilson's house, where the Continental Army rescued them.[55] Wilson fled the city, and popular anger resulted in Morris's defeat for re-election.[56]

Out of public office for the first time since the start of the American Revolution, Morris partnered with several out-of-state businessmen, including Jonathan Hudson of Maryland and Carter Braxton and Benjamin Harrison of Virginia, to form what biographer Charles Rappleye calls "the first national conglomerate." In these trading ventures, Morris often provided financing and oversight but left the details to his partners.[57] With national finances in tatters, Morris led a group of merchants in creating the Bank of Pennsylvania, which provided funding for the supplies of the Continental Army. The bank did not engage in the full range of modern banking activities, but it did accept deposits and provide a model for monetary reforms.[58] The success of the bank provided a boost to Morris's popularity, and he won election to the state legislature.[59]William Bingham, rumored to be the richest man in America after the Revolutionary War,[60] purchased 9.5% of the available shares of Bank of North America. The greatest share, 63.3%, was purchased on behalf of the US government by Robert Morris, using a gift in the form of a loan from France and from Netherlands.[61] This capitalized the bank with large deposits of gold and silver coin and bills of exchange. He issued new currency.[62]

Superintendent of Finance

During the American Revolution, U.S. government finances fell, as Congress lacked the power to raise revenue and states refused funding. Without revenue, Congress issued paper money, leading to rampant inflation.[63] By 1781, the U.S. faced a terrible financial crisis, underscored by the 1781 Pennsylvania Line Mutiny, when ten poorly fed, unpaid Army regiments demanded better treatment, resulting in Congress creating departments of war, marine, finance, and foreign affairs, each led by a departmental executive. Congress selected Morris Superintendent of Finance.[64] He accepted in May 1781.[65]

Morris soon emerged as the key economic official in the country and became a leader of the Nationalist faction, leaders who favored a stronger national government.[66] Robert R. Livingston was appointed as Secretary of Foreign Affairs later in the year.[67] In September 1781, Morris reluctantly agreed to serve as the Agent of Marine, giving him civilian leadership of the Continental Navy.[68] Congress filled the last of the executive positions in November, when Benjamin Lincoln accepted appointment as Secretary of War. Along with General Washington and Continental Congress secretary Charles Thomson, the three executives were the leaders of the first executive branch in U.S. history; Morris assumed an unofficial role as the leading department secretary.[69] All three executives, and Washington, aligned with the Nationalist faction, and enhanced the power of government.[70] Congress established committees to oversee executive departments; Morris supported reorganization, but foe Arthur Lee became chairman of the committee for the finance department.[71]

Morris pursued an array of reforms designed to boost the economy; inspired by the laissez-faire economic ideas of Adam Smith.[72] He quickly convinced Congress to establish the Bank of North America. Such a bank had been discussed prior to Morris's appointment. It was established as a private institution governed by its investors, subject to inspection by the Superintendent of Finance. The bank would take the national government's deposits, provide loans to Congress, and issue banknotes. Morris hoped the bank would help finance the war, stabilize currency, and bring the country together under one unified monetary policy.[73] Morris presided over issuing a new currency, referred to as "Morris notes," backed by Morris's funds.[74] Morris convinced Congress to allow him to purchase supplies for the Continental Army, Congress required states to furnish flour or meat.[75]

By 1781, the Revolutionary War had become a stalemate between Britain and the United States. The British had concentrated their military operations in the Southern theater of the war, while leaving a large force garrisoned at New York City. In August 1781, Morris met with General Washington and the comte de Rochambeau, who were planning a joint Franco-American operation against the British forces.[76] Morris redirected government funds to purchase supplies for Washington's march against British forces in Virginia, and pleaded with state and the French government for further funding,[77] with the final $20,000 needed coming from Morris's longtime collaborator, Haym Salomon.[78] At the Battle of Yorktown, Washington forced the surrender of General Cornwallis,[79] Britain abandoned its land campaign, but the naval war continued as Britain sought to cut the United States off from sources of trade.[80]

After Yorktown

Months after Yorktown, Morris issued the "Report on Public Credit," calling for full payment of the country's war debt through new revenues.[81] He pushed for a 5% federal tariff on imported goods, which required an amendment to the Articles of Confederation. This would strengthen the power of the national government, but the amendment process required consent of each state, and many were reluctant to alter the balance of power between the states and the national government.[82] The Articles gave Congress sole power to conduct foreign policy, but no power to raise funds, and lacked a mechanism to force states to provide funds owed to Congress.[83] Writing to the state governors, Morris argued that it was "high time to relieve the infamy we have sustained, and to restore the national credit. This can only be done by solid revenue."[84] By late 1782, all but Rhode Island agreed to back an amendment allowing the tariff, but that was enough to block the amendment.[85]

In January 1782, after receiving its charter from Congress, the Bank of North America commenced, and currency achieved circulation. Morris sought a national mint to provide for a single coinage and proposed the first decimal currency, but Congress was unwilling.[86] He appointed receivers, including Alexander Hamilton, to circulate banknotes, report on prices of goods, throughout the United States.[87] He reformed government procurement, saving money by delegating storage and transport of supplies to government contractors.[88]

Newburgh Conspiracy

Even after implementing financial reforms, Morris was unable to pay the soldiers.[89] The chief issue was the unwillingness of the states to supply funding; many states refused to furnish any funds at all. The Bank of North America provided loans but refused to furnish more until previous loans were paid off.[90] In December 1782, after defeat of the amendment to allow a government tariff, General McDougall led a delegation demanding payment of the Army.[91]

In March came the "Newburgh Address," in which Officers urged the Army to rise and demand payment. Washington assured the soldiers that they would be paid. Morris denied that he had played any role.[92] Nonetheless, most historians believe that Morris was one of three leaders of the "Newburgh Conspiracy."[93] Jack N. Rakove emphasizes the leadership of Robert Morris.[94] However, this conclusion overlooks several exculpatory facts: 1) Morris supplied $800,000 in his own notes to pay the soldiers, 2) The address was written by Major Armstrong, General Gate's aide-de-camp, anti-Morris partisans, 3) Armstrong went on to become a favorite of the Constitutionalists, 4) Morris's enemy, Arthur Lee, promoted articles in the Freeman's Journal, attacking Morris.[95]

National debt

Robert Morris submitted his resignation in 1783, but Hamilton and others convinced him to stay in office.[96] As of January 1, 1783, the public debt was $42 million of which 18.8% was foreign debt and 81.23% was owned at home.[97]
In a report to the President of Congress Morris wrote:
- Domestic Debt...$35,327,769
- Loan Certificates...$11,463,802 [with two years interest loan due $877,828]
- Army Debt...$635,618.00[98]
- $42,000,000 in 1790 is worth $1,779,281,739.13 today.
Morris and his colleagues were faced with yet another herculean task.
(https://www.officialdata.org/us/inflation/1790?amount=52,000,000)

The rest being unliquidated debts, and interest.[97] Morris distributed "Morris notes" to the remaining soldiers, but many soldiers departed for their homes rather than waiting for the notes.[99] After a mutiny over pay broke out in Pennsylvania, Congress voted to leave

Philadelphia. Nationalists were devastated by these events, and Hamilton resigned from Congress in mid-1783 after his proposal to revise the Articles of Confederation was ignored.[99]

In November 1784, Morris resigned. Rather than finding a successor for Morris, Congress established the three-member Board of Treasury.[100] In 1778–1779 Morris had attempted to strengthen accounts of the old Commercial Committee but had to give it up; he stated in answer to Paine "the accounts of Willing and Morris with the committee had been partially settled, but were still partially open, because the transactions could not be closed up."[101] Treasury Board was elected in 1794-1795 to settle those old accounts—a June 1796 entry in the Treasury debt against Morris for $93,312.63. Morris explained, while in debtors' prison that debt was due to John Ross and Willing.[103]

Continued Political Career - - Constitutional Convention

After leaving office, Morris once again devoted himself to business, but state and federal politics remained a factor in his life.[104] After the Pennsylvania legislature stripped the Bank of North America of its charter, Morris won election to the state legislature and helped restore the bank's charter.[105] Meanwhile, the United States suffered a sustained recession. Some members of Congress, continued to favor amendments to the Articles of Confederation, but the states refused to authorize major changes to the Articles.[106]

In 1786, Morris was one of five Pennsylvania delegates selected to attend the Annapolis Convention, Morris, James Wilson, Gouverneur Morris, George Clymer, Thomas Mifflin, Jared Ingersoll, and Ben Franklin. Except for Franklin, Pennsylvania delegates aligned with Morris's Republican faction. Many of Morris's Nationalist allies, including Hamilton, James Madison, John Dickinson, and Washington attended.[107]

With Franklin ill, Morris opened the Philadelphia Convention on May 25. His motion to nominate Washington as chair became unanimous. Morris allowed lawyers and others more experienced with the law to debate various issues.[108]

Congress simply forwarded it to each state to debate ratification. In elections held in October and November 1787, Morris's Federalist allies retained control of the state legislature elections held to select delegates to debate ratification.[110]

On September 17, Morris signed the final document produced by the convention which became the new Constitution of the United States.[109] Morris was one of just six individuals to sign both the Declaration of Independence and the United States Constitution. By the end of 1788, the Constitution was ratified. In September 1788, the Pennsylvania legislature elected Robert Morris and William Maclay, as the state's first members of the United States Senate.[111]

U.S. Senator

In the country's first presidential election, Washington became President of the United States. Washington offered Secretary of the Treasury to Morris who declined, suggesting Alexander Hamilton.[112] In the Senate, Morris pressed for many of the same policies he had sought as Superintendent of Finance: a federal tariff, a national bank, a federal mint, and the funding of the national debt.[113] Congress agreed to implement the Tariff of 1789, which created a uniform tariff on goods carried into American ports.[114] Morris defeated Maclay's proposal to establish the capital in Philadelphia.[115]

Morris's 1781 "Report On Public Credit" supplied the basis for Hamilton's *First Report on the Public Credit*, which Hamilton submitted in 1790.[116] In June 1790, Thomas Jefferson convinced Morris, Hamilton, and Madison to a compromise in which the federal government assumed state debts, while a new federal capital would be established on the Potomac River; until construction of that capital was completed, Philadelphia would serve as the nation's temporary capital. With the backing of all four leaders, the Compromise of 1790, as it became known, was approved by Congress.[117] That same year, Morris and Maclay helped secure Pennsylvania's control of the Erie Triangle, to provide access to the Great Lakes.[118]

In the early 1790s, the country became increasingly polarized between the Democratic-Republican Party, led by Jefferson and Madison, and the Federalist Party, led by Hamilton. Despite opposition of Madison and other Southern leaders, Congress approved establishment of the First Bank of the United States in 1791.[119]

(A network that rivals modern NY Venture Capital operations)

Morris now concentrates business efforts to help America pay off Revolutionary debt, as well as his own personal debt from personal money he paid into the War.

Morris refocused on his trading concerns after leaving office as Superintendent of Finance, seeking especially to expand his role in the tobacco trade.[120] He began suffering from financial problems in the late 1780s after a business partner mistakenly refused to honor bills issued by Morris, causing him to default on a loan.[121] In 1784 Morris was part of a syndicate that backed the sailing of the Empress of China (1783) for the China trade.(In 1787 Morris also sent the ex-warship Alliance to Canton China as part of the China Trade).[122] Financier James Swan on July 9, 1795, managed to do something Morris had been unable to do: the entire U.S. National debt to France of US$2,024,899 was paid in full.[123] The United States no longer owed money to foreign governments, although it continued to owe money to private investors in the United States and in Europe.[124][125][126]

From July 1778 to January 1780, Morris was an agent, normally paid on commission for John Holker. In early 1780, they became partners in William Turnbull and Co. Turnbull had worked for the secret Pennsylvania Committee of Commerce and would manage operations on their behalf. In the monumental edition of the Robert Morris Papers, the list of Holker's associates is given in a note to volume 7. It is edifying on the French side, Le Ray de Chaumont of course, Sabatier and Després, La Caze and Mallet, the bankers Le Couteulx and Ferdinand Grand; the authors have just forgotten Holker senior, Antoine Garvey and Baudard de Saint-James, associate in Sabatier's business. On the American side, three founding fathers , John Langdon , Thomas Fitzsimons and Robert Morris, Simeon and Barnabas Deane, brothers of Silas Deane, William Duer, who will be discussed again, Matthew Ridley , Mark Pringle, Jonathan Williams Sr. and Jr. 40 , Stacey Hepburn, William Smith, of Baltimore, Benjamin Harrison V , of Virginia 41.

Other land speculations that Morris was involved was the Illinois-Wabash Company and Georgia Yazoo Land Company.[127]

1796 and Panic of 1797, bankruptcy (NALC = North American Land Company)

The Washington DC Lots were not the only land problems for Morris; he began losing everything for nonpayment on interest on loans and taxes. Auctioning his properties required from 1796 to 1801, all due to his financial gifts to young America during our revolution.

The canal companies had also failed: the Schuylkill and Susquehanna was subscribed for 40,000 shares—but only 1000 were sold; the Delaware and Schuylkill company was to issue 2000 shares at $200.00 a share. Operations were suspended "Either on account of errors in plans adopted, failure to procure the necessary means, financial convulsions, or a combination, they suspended operations after an outlay of $440,000, an immense sum."[128]

Napoleonic Wars ruined the American land market and Morris's company collapsed. Financial markets of England, the United States, and Caribbean suffered deflation due to the Panic of 1797. Morris was "land rich and cash poor". He *owned* more land than any other American but did not have capital to pay creditors.[129]

Morris and his partners had failed to both pay the instalments on the Washington D.C. building lots and finished building twenty houses (they had contracted ten houses annually for seven years on said lots).[130] On July 10, 1795, Morris and Nicholson bought out Greenleaf's interest in one agreement.[131] The commissioners began legal proceedings to regain title to the 6,000 lots owned by NALC and the 1,115.25[132] owned by Greenleaf personally. The worsening financial problems of Greenleaf, Morris, and Nicholson led to increasingly poor personal relations.[133] Nicholson made public accusations against Greenleaf.[133]

When the NALC did not issue its 6 percent dividend, Greenleaf transferred one-third of the shares in the "391 trust" to the trustees.[134] The total number of shares transferred to the "381 trust" trustees was now 6,119.[135] On June 24, 1797, Morris, Greenleaf and Nicholson had conveyed their Washington D.C. Lots in trust to Henry Pratt and others in payment of their debts.[136] Poor business practices were dragging down NALC. For years, Morris and Nicholson had acted as personal guarantors for one another's notes. Now many of these notes were coming due, and neither man could pay them. Creditors began selling the notes publicly, often at heavy discounts.[137] By 1798, Morris and Nicholson's $10 million (~$234 million in 2023) in personal notes were trading at one-eighth face value.[138] NALC also discovered that some of titles to the 6,000,000 acres (24,000 km^2) of land it owned were not clear, thus the land could not be used for security. In other cases, NALC found it had been swindled, and the rich land it thought it owned turned out to be barren and worthless.[137] This proved incorrect. On October 23, 1807, all stock in the company was sold at 7 cents on the dollar to accountants managing the Aggregate Fund. In 1856, Trustees of the North American Land Company held $92,071 (~$2.44 million in 2023). After all fees and expenses, the amount available for Morris was $9,692"[139]

In 1797 Morris conveyed his household furniture to Thomas Fitzsimmons, for public auction. What was left was lent to Mrs. Morris by Fitzsimmons and Morris son-in-law Marshall; all Morris had left in his house was some bedding, clothing, part of a quarter cask of wine; part of a barrel of flour, some coffee, a little sugar and some bottled wine which was the remainder from a cask he had given to his daughter Maria.[140] Morris attempted to avoid creditors by staying outside the city at his country estate "The Hills", located on the Schuylkill River, but his creditors literally pursued him to his gate. Morris was sued by a former partner, James Greenleaf, who had been imprisoned for fraud and was serving time in debtors' prison. Unable to dodge his creditors and their lawyers, Morris was finally arrested. He was imprisoned for debt in Prune Street prison in Philadelphia from February 1798 to August 1801.[141] Of his partners Geenleaf was released;[141] Nicholson died in prison in 1800.[142] Morris wrote that the deceased Nicolson owed him $60,000 specie from all entries and transactions but "With the purest intentions."[143]

Financier of the American Revolution in Paupers Grave

Unable to pay his debts, Morris remained in debtors' prison three and a half years. Congress passed the Bankruptcy Act of 1800 partly to get Morris out of prison.[144] At the time of his release, commissioners found that he had debts of $2,948,711; the proceedings were certified October 15, 1801, after 2/3 of his creditors agreed to discharge Morris; on December 4, 1801, a certificate of bankruptcy was confirmed.[145] Morris died on May 8, 1806.[146]

References

1. Women of the Republican Court https://www.librarycompany.org/women/republicancourt/morris_mary.htm
2. "Image 1 of Robert Morris, the financier of the American revolution. A sketch". Library of Congress.
3. Kennedy, John (1894). Robert Morris and the Holland Purchase. Batavia, NY: J. F. Hall. p. 121
4. Cazorla, Frank (2019), Governor Luis de Unzaga (1717–1793) Precursor in the birth of the United States and in liberalism. Malaga Foundation/City Council. pp. 82, 90, 105, 112,
5. "APS Member History". search.amphilsoc.org. Retrieved April 6, 2021.
6. Ryan K. Smith. Robert Morris's Folly: The Architectural and Financial Failures of an American Founder. New Haven, CT: Yale University Press, 2014.
7. "Morris, Robert, (1734–1806)". Biographical Directory of the United States Congress. Retr Dec 7, 2018.
8. Rappleye 2010, pp. 7–8.
9. Raymond A. Mohl (1997), The Making of Urban America,
10. Pennsylvania Gazette, July 25, 1765
11. The Trans-Atlantic Slave Trade CD-ROM, published by the Oxford U Press
12. Rappleye 2010, pp. 26, 140, 415.
13. Rappleye 2010, pp. 11, 14, 23.
14. Rappleye 2010, pp. 22, 140.
15. Rappleye 2010, pp. 412–413.
16. Rappleye 2010, pp. 485–486.
17. Rappleye 2010, pp. 490–491.
18. "John Adams". WhiteHouse.gov.
19. Rappleye 2010, pp. 17–19.
20. Rappleye 2010, pp. 20–21.
21. Rappleye 2010, pp. 27–28.
22. Rappleye 2010, pp. 13, 22.
23. Rappleye 2010, pp. 30–32.
24. Rappleye 2010, pp. 33–38.
25. Rappleye 2010, pp. 41–42.
26. Rappleye 2010, p. 44.
27. Rappleye 2010, pp. 106–107.
28. Rappleye 2010, pp. 44–46.
29. Rappleye 2010, p. 47.
30. Rappleye 2010, pp. 47–50.
31. Rappleye 2010, pp. 56–57.
32. Rappleye 2010, pp. 49–51.
33. Rappleye 2010, pp. 51–52.
34. Rappleye 2010, pp. 55–56.
35. Rappleye 2010, pp. 59–61.
36. Rappleye 2010, pp. 70–72.
37. Rappleye 2010, p. 74.
38. Robert Morris to Horatio Gates, Philadelphia, October 27, 1776, cited in "The Founders on the Founders" ed. by John P. Kaminski, U. VA. Press 2008.
39. Rappleye 2010, pp. 78–83.
40. Rappleye 2010, pp. 104–105.
41. Rappleye 2010, pp. 121–122, 134.
42. Rappleye 2010, pp. 83–85.
43. Rappleye 2010, pp. 100–103.
44. Rappleye 2010, pp. 90–91, 114.
45. Rappleye 2010, pp. 93–94.
46. Rappleye 2010, pp. 118–120.
47. Rappleye 2010, pp. 140–143.
48. Rappleye 2010, pp. 144–145.
49. Rappleye 2010, pp. 148–150.
50. Rappleye 2010, pp. 159–161.
51. Rappleye 2010, pp. 163–164.
52. Rappleye 2010, pp. 172–177.
53. Rappleye 2010, pp. 178–180.
54. Rappleye 2010, pp. 180–186.
55. Rappleye 2010, pp. 189–193.
56. Rappleye 2010, pp. 195–196.

57.	Rappleye 2010, pp. 204–205.
58.	Rappleye 2010, pp. 215–217.
59.	Rappleye 2010, pp. 220–221.
60.	Alberts 1969, pp. 435
61.	Alberts, Robert C. (1969). The Golden Voyage: The Life and Times of William Bingham, 1752–1804. Houghton-Mifflin. OCLC 563689565. Retr March 17, 2016.
62.	Dowgin, Christopher (2016). Sub Rosa. Salem House Press. p. 83. ISBN 978-0-986-26102-2.
63.	Rappleye 2010, pp. 210–213.
64.	Rappleye 2010, pp. 225–226.
65.	Rappleye 2010, pp. 234–235, 285.
66.	Rappleye 2010, pp. 227–229.
67.	Rappleye 2010, pp. 240, 284.
68.	Rappleye 2010, pp. 263–264.
69.	Rappleye 2010, pp. 284–285.
70.	Rappleye 2010, pp. 285, 292–293.
71.	Rappleye 2010, pp. 315–316.
72.	Rappleye 2010, p. 247.
73.	Rappleye 2010, pp. 236–239.
74.	Rappleye 2010, pp. 258–259.
75.	Rappleye 2010, pp. 246–247.
76.	Rappleye 2010, pp. 253–255.
77.	Rappleye 2010, pp. 255–262.
78.	Phelps, Greg (July 4, 2016). "The Broker You Should Be Thanking This 4th Of July". Retr Sept 16, 2021.
79.	Rappleye 2010, pp. 275–277.
80.	Rappleye 2010, pp. 300–301.
81.	Rappleye 2010, pp. 303–306.
82.	Rappleye 2010, pp. 248–251.
83.	Rappleye 2010, pp. 257–258.
84.	Rappleye 2010, pp. 279–280.
85.	Rappleye 2010, pp. 325–329.
86.	Rappleye 2010, pp. 289–291.
87.	Rappleye 2010, pp. 298–299.
88.	Rappleye 2010, pp. 247, 286–288.
89.	Rappleye 2010, p. 288.
90.	Rappleye 2010, pp. 308–313.
91.	Rappleye 2010, pp. 330–333.
92.	Rappleye 2010, pp. 347–351.
93.	Kohn, "Inside History" p, 193.
94.	Jack N. Rakove, beginnings of national politics: interpretive history of Continental Congress (1979), p. 317
95.	Morris, Robert, Morris, Inside the Revolution, pp. 440–445
96.	Rappleye 2010, pp. 356–357.
97.	Financial History of the United States. p. 317
98.	Financial History of the United States. p. 316 Morris had managed to pay troops one months pay combined with personal notes payable after six months; in six days Morris signed 60,000 personal notes, $75 million
99.	Rappleye 2010, pp. 358–360, 374.
100.	Rappleye 2010, pp. 361–36.
101.	Rappleye 2010, pp. 378–381, 425.
102.	Robert Morris. p. 117
103.	Robert Morris. pp. 119–121
104.	Rappleye 2010, pp. 392–396.
105.	Rappleye 2010, pp. 397–399, 409–411.
106.	Rappleye 2010, pp. 424–426.
107.	Rappleye 2010, pp. 428–433.
108.	Rappleye 2010, pp. 432–433.
109.	Rappleye 2010, p. 437.
110.	Rappleye 2010, pp. 438–440.
111.	Rappleye 2010, pp. 449–450.
112.	Rappleye 2010, pp. 454–455.
113.	Rappleye 2010, pp. 457–458.
114.	Bordewich 2016, pp. 100–102.

115. Rappleye 2010, p. 462.
116. Rappleye 2010, pp. 460–461.
117. Ver Steeg (1954), p. 175
118. Rappleye 2010, pp. 472–473.
119. Rappleye 2010, pp. 487–488.
120. Rappleye 2010, pp. 415–420.
121. Rappleye 2010, pp. 436–437, 457.
122. Papers of Robert Morris, 9:152–156
123. Gratefull American Foundation who-paid-off-the-2024899-u-s-national-debt-today
124. When_did_the_US_pay_its_Revolutionary_War_debt_to_France History.com
125. [An example of Morris Penn Land dealings accepting land in payment of Debts owed to him can be found in the 1846 Grant vs Levan case which came up before the Penn Supreme Court Pennsylvania state Reports # 4 pp. 393–343. According to the 1881 History of Schuylkill County Penn, Judge William Donaldson, an owner of rich coal lands which were concerned regarding poll deed Schuylkill County purchases by Morris, found ten missing Poll deeds in a NY storehouse-they had been taken by Morris sons to relieve his mother the burden of keeping Morris Business papers.History of Schuylkill County. p. 303.]
126. Dec 24, 1793, Morris, and Greenleaf contracted with Washington D.C. for 6,000 lots: modified April 28, 1794. After payment of $80,000.00 the lots conveyed to Morris, Greenleaf, and Nicholson, 1,000 lots for Morris and Greenleaf; Journal... Council of City of Washington ..., Vol 64 1867 pp. 303–304
127. The Yazoo Land Companies.' 25
128. Ibid. p. 44 Two Companies in question were dissolved and reunited as "Union Canal Company, of Philadelphia" April 2, 1811,
129. Chernow 1978.
130. Journal of the ... Council of the City of Washington ..., Volume 64 1867 p. 304
131. Clark, Greenleaf and Law in the Federal City, p. 70. Accessed Nov 24, 2012.
132. "Clark71"
133. "Sakolski165"
134. Originally, there was a single trustee for the "391 trust", George Simpson. Simpson later brought in other trustees, including Henry Pratt. Pratt trustees purchased $4,725 in notes issued by Morris and Nicholson to shore up their trust—and to help keep Morris and Nicholson out of bankruptcy.
135. Livermore, p. 169.
136. Congressional Record: Proceedings and Debates of the ... Congress 1896 pp. 5075–5076
137. "Mann201"
138. "Mann202"
139. Robert Morris. p. 169
140. [William Graham Sumner The Financier and the Finances of the American Revolution p. 296]
141. [Besides speculation he defended himself in 13 lawsuits from 1797 until his death in 1843]
142. A History of the United States: Federalists and Republicans, 1789–1815 p. 112
143. William Graham Sumner "Robert Morris The Financier and Finances of the American Revolution " p. 295
144. Purvis 1997, p. 29.
145. In Jan 1830, Morris's son Henry petitioned the district Court of Philadelphia that the commission should be vacated and superseded as nothing had been done by either the assignees or the creditors; the petition was granted.The Historic Mansions and Buildings of Philadelphia: With Some Notice of ... pp. 374–375
146. Rappleye 2010, p. 515.

Primary sources
- Ferguson, E. James (editor): The Papers of Robert Morris 1781–1784 (9 volumes): U of Pittsburgh Press, 1978; (1995 reprint: ISBN 0-8229-3886-3).

Sources
- Chernow, Barbara Ann (1978). Robert Morris, land speculator, 1790–1801. New York: Arno Press. ISBN 0-405-11029-4. OCLC 3609086.
- Purvis, Thomas L. (1997). Dictionary of American History. Wiley. p. 29. ISBN 978-1-57718-099-9.
- Rappleye, Charles (2010). Robert Morris: Financier of the American Revolution. Simon&Schuster. ISBN 978-1-4165-7091-2.
- Ver Steeg, Clarence L. Robert Morris, Revolutionary Financier. Philadelphia: U of Penn Press, 1954. online
- Ver Steeg, Clarence L. "Morris, Robert" American National Biography Online 2000.
-

JOHN HANCOCK

ASSASSINATION TEAMS SENT BY KING GEORGE III

John Hancock (January 23, 1737– October 8, 1793) was an American Founding Father, merchant, statesman, and prominent Patriot of the American Revolution.[1] He was the longest-serving president of the Continental Congress, having served as the second president of the Second Continental Congress and the seventh president of the Congress of the Confederation. He was the first and third governor of the Commonwealth of Massachusetts. He is remembered for his large and stylish signature on the United States Declaration of Independence.[2] He also signed the Articles of Confederation, and used his influence to ensure that Massachusetts ratified the United States Constitution in 1788.

Before the American Revolution, Hancock was one of the wealthiest men in the Thirteen Colonies, having inherited a profitable mercantile business from his uncle. He began his political career in Boston as a protégé of Samuel Adams. Hancock used his wealth to support the colonial cause as tensions increased between colonists and Great Britain in the 1760s.

The signature of Hancock on the Declaration of Independence is the most easily recognizable. It is no surprise his part in the revolution is equally engaging.

Early life

Hancock was born on January 23, 1737,[3] in Braintree, Massachusetts, today's Quincy.[4] He was the son of Colonel John Hancock Jr. of Braintree and Mary Hawke Thaxter (widow of Samuel Thaxter Junior). As a child, Hancock became a casual acquaintance of young John Adams, whom the Reverend Hancock baptized in 1735.[5]

After Hancock's father died in 1744, he was sent to live with his uncle and aunt, Thomas Hancock, and Lydia (Henchman) Hancock. Thomas Hancock was the proprietor of a firm known as the House of Hancock, which imported manufactured goods from Britain and exported rum, whale oil, and fish.[6] Thomas Hancock's highly successful business made him one of Boston's richest and best-known residents.[7] He and Lydia, along with servants, lived in Hancock Manor on Beacon Hill. The couple, became the dominant influence on John's life.[8]

After graduating from the Boston Latin School in 1750, Hancock enrolled in Harvard College and received a bachelor's degree in 1754.[9] Upon graduation at 17, he began to work for his uncle, just as the French and Indian War had begun. Thomas Hancock had close relations with royal governors of Massachusetts and secured profitable government contracts.[10] Hancock worked hard, but he also enjoyed the role of a wealthy aristocrat and expensive clothes.[11]

From 1760 to 1761, Hancock worked in England while building relationships with customers and suppliers. Hancock gradually took over the House of Hancock as his uncle's health failed, becoming a full partner in January 1763.[12] He became a member of the Masonic Lodge of St. Andrew in October 1762, which connected him with many of Boston's most influential citizens.[13] When Thomas Hancock died in August 1764, John inherited the business, Hancock Manor, two or three household slaves, and thousands of acres of land, becoming one of the wealthiest men in the colonies.[14] The household slaves continued to work for John, but were freed through the terms of Thomas Hancock's will.[16]

Growing imperial tensions

After its victory in the Seven Years' War, the British Empire was deeply in debt. Looking for new sources of revenue, the British Parliament sought to tax the colonies, beginning with the Sugar Act of 1764.[17] The earlier Molasses Act of 1733, a tax on shipments from the West Indies, had produced hardly any revenue because it was widely bypassed by smuggling, which was seen as a victimless crime. Merchants sometimes stole impounded goods.[18]

The Sugar Act provoked outrage in Boston, where it was viewed as a violation of colonial rights. James Otis and Samuel Adams argued that because colonists were not represented in Parliament, that body could not tax them; only colonial assemblies, where colonists were represented, could levy taxes upon the colonies. Hancock criticized the tax for economic, not constitutional, reasons.[16]

Hancock emerged as a leading political figure in Boston just as tensions with Great Britain were increasing. In March 1765, he was elected as one of Boston's five selectmen.[18] Soon after, Parliament passed the 1765 Stamp Act, a tax on legal documents such as wills that had been levied in Britain for many years, but which was wildly unpopular in the colonies. Hancock initially took a moderate position: as a loyal British subject, he thought that the colonists should submit to the act even though he believed that Parliament was misguided.[19] After Bostonians learned of the impending repeal of the Stamp Act, Hancock was elected to the Massachusetts House of Representatives in May 1766.[20]

Hancock's political success benefited from support of Samuel Adams. Fifteen years older than Hancock, Adams had a somber, Puritan outlook that stood in contrast to Hancock's taste for luxury and extravagance.[21] Apocryphal stories later portrayed Adams masterminding Hancock's political rise so his wealth could further the Whig agenda.[22] William Fowler, wrote biographies of both, arguing the relationship was symbiotic, with Adams as mentor.[23]

Townshend Acts crisis

After the repeal of the Stamp Act, Parliament took a different approach passing the 1767 Townshend Acts, which established new duties on various imports and strengthened the customs agency by creating the American Customs Board. Smugglers violated the Navigation Acts by trading with ports outside of the British Empire and avoiding import taxes. Parliament hoped that the new system would reduce smuggling and generate British revenue.[24]

Hancock joined other Bostonians in calling for a boycott of British imports until the Townshend duties were repealed.[25] Hancock snubbed Governor Francis Bernard by refusing to attend functions when the customs officials were present.[26]

On April 9, 1768, two customs employees boarded Hancock's brig *Lydia* in Boston Harbor. Hancock was summoned and found that the agents lacked a writ of assistance (search warrant), he did not allow them to go below deck. When one of them later managed to get into the hold, Hancock's men forced the customs men back on deck.[27] Customs officials wanted to file charges, but the case was dropped when Massachusetts Attorney General ruled Hancock had broken no laws.[28] Hancock's most ardent admirers called this the first act of resistance to British authority and credit Hancock with initiating the Revolution.[29]

Prelude to Liberty Sloop

He apprenticed to his uncle as a clerk and proved so honest and capable that, in 1760, he was sent on a business mission to England. There he witnessed the coronation of George III and engaged some of the leading businessmen of London. In 1763, his uncle died, and John

63

Hancock inherited what was said to be the greatest body of wealth in New England. Hancock, however, soon became involved in revolutionary politics and his sentiments were, early on and clearly, for independence from Great Britain. He was in company with the Adamses and other prominent leaders in the republican movement in New England. He was elected to the Boston Assembly in 1766 and was a member of the Stamp Act Congress.

Liberty affair

The next incident proved to be a major event in the coming of the American Revolution. On the evening of May 9, 1768, Hancock's sloop *Liberty* arrived in Boston Harbor, carrying a shipment of Madeira wine. When custom officers inspected the ship the next morning, they found that it contained 25 pipes of wine, just one fourth of the ship's carrying capacity.[30] Hancock paid the duties on the 25 pipes of wine, but officials suspected that he had arranged to have more wine unloaded during the night to avoid paying the duties for the entire cargo.[31] They did not have any evidence to prove this, since the two tidesmen who had stayed on the ship overnight gave a sworn statement that nothing had been unloaded.[32]

One month later, while the British warship HMS *Romney* was in port, one of the tidesmen changed his story: he claimed that he had been forcibly held on the *Liberty* while it had been illegally unloaded.[33] On June 10, customs officials seized the.[34] A riot broke out when officials began to tow the *Liberty* out to the *Romney*, which was also arguably illegal.[35] After the riot, customs officials relocated to the *Romney* and then Castle William (an island fort in the harbor), claiming they were unsafe in town.[36] Whigs insisted customs officials were exaggerating so London would send troops.[37]

British officials filed two lawsuits stemming from the *Liberty* incident. Royal officials as well as Hancock's accuser stood to gain financially since, as was the custom, any penalties assessed by the court would be awarded to the governor, the informer, and the Crown, each getting a third.[38] Customs officials used the ship to enforce trade regulations until it was burned by angry colonists the following year.[39]

The second trial began in October 1768, when charges were filed against Hancock and five others for allegedly unloading 100 pipes of wine from the *Liberty* without paying the duties.[40] With John Adams serving as his lawyer, Hancock was prosecuted in a trial which had no jury and no cross-examination of witnesses.[68] The proceedings against Hancock were dropped without explanation.[41]

Although the charges against Hancock were dropped, many writers later described him as a smuggler.[42] Historian Oliver Dickerson argues that Hancock was the victim of an essentially criminal racketeering scheme perpetrated by Governor Bernard and the customs officials. Dickerson believes that there is no reliable evidence that Hancock was guilty in the *Liberty* case and that the purpose of the trials was to punish Hancock for political reasons and to plunder his property.[43] Lawyer and historian Bernard Knollenberg concludes the customs officials had the right to seize Hancock's ship, but towing it out to the *Romney* was illegal.[44]

Aside from the *Liberty* affair, the degree to which Hancock was engaged in smuggling has been questioned. Given the clandestine nature of smuggling, records are scarce.[45] Biographer William Fowler concludes that while Hancock was probably engaged in some smuggling, most of his business was legitimate.[26]

Boston Massacre to Tea Party

The *Liberty* affair reinforced a previously made British decision to suppress unrest in Boston with a show of military might. The decision had been prompted by Samuel Adams's 1768 Circular Letter, which was sent to other British American colonies in hopes of coordinating resistance to the Townshend Acts. Lord Hillsborough, secretary of state for the colonies, sent four regiments of the British Army to Boston to support embattled royal officials and instructed Governor Bernard to order the Massachusetts legislature to revoke the Circular Letter.[46] When Bernard returned to England in 1769, Bostonians celebrated.[47]

The British troops remained, however, and tensions between soldiers and civilians eventually resulted in the killing of civilians in the Boston Massacre of March 1770. Meeting with Bernard's successor, Governor Thomas Hutchinson, and the British officer in command, Colonel William Dalrymple, Hancock claimed that there were 10,000 armed colonists ready to march into Boston if the troops did not leave.[48] Hutchinson knew Hancock was bluffing, but soldiers were in a precarious position within the town, and so Dalrymple agreed to remove both regiments to Castle William.[49] Hancock was celebrated as a hero for his role in getting the troops withdrawn.[50] His re-election to the Massachusetts House was nearly unanimous.[51]

After Parliament partially repealed the Townshend duties in 1770, Boston's boycott of British goods ended.[52] Politics became quieter in Massachusetts, although tensions remained.[53] Hancock tried to improve his relationship with Governor Hutchinson, who in turn sought to woo Hancock away from Adams's influence.[54] In April 1772, Hutchinson approved Hancock's election as colonel of the Boston Cadets, a militia unit whose primary function was to provide a ceremonial escort for the governor and the General Court.[55]

To avoid hostile crowds in Boston, Hutchinson had been convening the legislature outside of town; now he agreed for the General Court to sit in Boston.[56]

Hutchinson had dared to hope that he could win over Hancock and discredit Adams.[57] To some, it seemed that Adams and Hancock were indeed at odds: when Adams formed the Boston Committee of Correspondence in November 1772 to advocate colonial rights, Hancock declined to join.[58] But whatever their differences, Hancock and Adams came together again in 1773 with the renewal of major political turmoil.[59] The Massachusetts House, blaming Hutchinson for the military occupation of Boston, called for his removal as governor.[60]

Even more trouble followed Parliament's passage of the 1773 Tea Act. On November 5, Hancock was elected as moderator at a Boston town meeting that resolved that anyone who supported the Tea Act was an "Enemy to America".[61] Hancock was at the fateful meeting on December 16 where he told the crowd, "Let every man do what is right in his own eyes."[62] Hancock did not take part in the Boston Tea Party that night, but he approved of the action.[63]

Over the next few months, Hancock was disabled by gout, which troubled him with increasing frequency in the coming years. By March 5, 1774, he had recovered enough to deliver the fourth annual Massacre Day oration, a commemoration of the Boston Massacre.[64] The speech, probably written by Hancock in collaboration with Adams, Joseph Warren, and others, was published and reprinted, enhancing Hancock's stature as a leading Patriot.[65]

Prelude to Revolution

The following year he delivered a public address to a large crowd in Boston, commemorating the Boston Massacre. In 1774, he was elected to the Provincial Congress of Massachusetts and simultaneously to the Continental Congress. A decree had been delivered from England in early 1776 offering a large reward for the capture of several leading figures.

Hancock was one of them. When Peyton Randolph resigned in 1776, Hancock assumed the position of President. He retired in 1777 due to problems with gout but participated in the formation of its constitution. He was then elected to the Governorship and re-elected in 1787.

Revolution begins

Parliament responded to the Tea Party with the Boston Port Act, one of the so-called Coercive Acts intended to strengthen British control of the colonies. Hutchinson was replaced as governor by General Thomas Gage, who arrived in May 1774. On June 17, the Massachusetts House elected five delegates to send to the First Continental Congress in Philadelphia, which was being organized to coordinate colonial response to the Coercive Acts. Hancock did not serve in the first Congress.[66]

Gage dismissed Hancock from his post as colonel of the Boston Cadets.[67] In October 1774, Gage canceled the scheduled meeting of the General Court. In response, the House resolved itself into the Massachusetts Provincial Congress, a body independent of British control. Hancock was elected as president of the Provincial Congress and was a key member of the Committee of safety.[68] The Provincial Congress created the first minutemen companies, consisting of militiamen who were to be ready for action on a moment's notice.[69]

On December 1, 1774, the Provincial Congress elected Hancock as a delegate to the Second Continental Congress to replace James Bowdoin, who had been unable to attend the first Congress because of illness.[70] Before Hancock reported to the Continental Congress in Philadelphia, the Provincial Congress unanimously re-elected him as president in February 1775. Hancock's multiple roles gave him enormous influence in Massachusetts, and as early as January 1774 British officials considered arresting him.[71] After attending the Provincial Congress in April 1775, Hancock and Samuel Adams decided it was not safe to return to Boston. They stayed at Hancock's childhood home in Lexington.[72]

Gage received a letter from Lord Dartmouth on April 14, 1775, advising him "to arrest the principal actors and abettors in the Provincial Congress whose proceedings appear in every light to be acts of treason and rebellion".[73] On the night of April 18, Gage sent out a detachment of soldiers on the fateful mission that sparked the American Revolutionary War. The purpose of the British expedition was to seize and destroy military supplies that the colonists had stored in Concord. According to many historical accounts, Gage also instructed his men to arrest Hancock and Adams; if so, the written orders issued by Gage made no mention of arresting the Patriot leaders.[74] Gage decided he had nothing to gain by arresting Hancock and Adams, since other leaders would take their place, and the British would be portrayed as aggressors.[75]

Although Gage had decided against seizing Hancock and Adams, Patriots initially believed otherwise. From Boston, Joseph Warren dispatched messenger Paul Revere to warn Hancock and Adams that British troops were on the move and might attempt to arrest them. Revere reached Lexington around midnight and gave the warning.[76] Hancock, still considering himself a militia colonel, wanted to take the field with the Patriot militia at Lexington, but Adams and others convinced him to avoid battle, arguing that he was more valuable as a political leader than as a soldier.[77] As Hancock and Adams made their escape, the first shots of the war were fired at Lexington and Concord. After the battle, Gage issued a proclamation granting pardon to all who would be peaceful, except Hancock and Samuel Adams. Singling out Hancock and Adams added to their renown among Patriots.[78]

President of Congress

With the war underway, Hancock made his way to the Continental Congress in Philadelphia with the other Massachusetts delegates. On May 24, 1775, he was unanimously elected President of the Continental Congress, succeeding Peyton Randolph. Hancock was a viable choice for president for several reasons.[79] He was experienced, having often presided over legislative bodies and town meetings in Massachusetts. His wealth and social standing inspired the confidence of moderate delegates, while his association with Boston radicals made him acceptable to other radicals. Like other presidents of Congress, Hancock's authority was mostly limited to that of a presiding officer.[80] He had to handle correspondence, and he found it necessary to hire clerks at his own expense.[81]

In Congress on June 15, 1775, Massachusetts delegate John Adams nominated George Washington as commander-in-chief of the army then gathered around Boston. Years later, Adams wrote that Hancock had shown great disappointment at not getting the command for himself. This brief comment from 1801 is the only source for the oft-cited claim that Hancock sought to become commander-in-chief.[82] According to historian Donald Proctor, "There is no contemporary evidence that Hancock harbored ambitions to be named commander-in-chief. Quite the contrary."[83] Hancock and Washington maintained a good relationship after the alleged incident, and in 1778 Hancock named his only son *John George Washington Hancock*.[84] Hancock admired and supported General Washington, even though he declined Hancock's request for military appointment.[85]

When Congress recessed on August 1, 1775, Hancock wed his fiancée, Dorothy "Dolly" Quincy. The couple was married on August 28 in Connecticut.[87]

While president of Congress, Hancock became involved in a long-running controversy with Harvard. As treasurer of the college since 1773, he had been entrusted with the school's financial records and about £15,000 in cash and securities.[88] In the rush of events at the onset of the Revolutionary War, Hancock had been unable to return the money and accounts to Harvard before leaving for Congress.[89] In 1777, a Harvard committee headed by James Bowdoin, Hancock's chief political and social rival in Boston, sent a messenger to Philadelphia to retrieve the money and records.[90] Hancock was offended, but he turned over more than £16,000, though not all of the records.[91] The issue dragged on after Hancock's death, as his estate paid the college more than £1,000 to resolve the matter.[92]

Hancock served in Congress through some of the darkest days of the Revolutionary War. The British drove Washington from New York and New Jersey in 1776, which prompted Congress to flee to Baltimore.[93] Hancock and Congress returned to Philadelphia in March 1777 but were compelled to flee six months later when the British occupied Philadelphia.[94] Hancock wrote innumerable letters to colonial officials, raising money, supplies, and troops for Washington's army.[95] He chaired the Marine Committee and took pride in helping to create a small fleet of American frigates, including the USS *Hancock*, named in his honor.[96]

Signing the Declaration

Hancock was president of Congress when the Declaration of Independence was adopted and signed. He is primarily remembered for his large, signature on the Declaration, so much so that "John Hancock" became, in the United States, an informal synonym for *signature*.[97] According to legend, Hancock signed his name largely and clearly so that King George could read it without his spectacles.[98]

The story, entirely unfounded, is that on signing the Declaration, Hancock commented, "The British ministry can read that name without spectacles; let them double their reward." An alternate story, has him saying, "There, I guess King George will be able to read that!".

Return to Massachusetts

In October 1777, after more than two years in Congress, Hancock requested a leave of absence.[98] He asked Washington to arrange a military escort for his return to Boston. Although Washington was short on manpower, he sent fifteen horsemen to accompany Hancock.[99] By this time Hancock had become estranged from Samuel Adams. Congress voted to thank Hancock for his service.[100]

Back in Boston, Hancock was re-elected to the House of Representatives. As in previous years, his philanthropy made him popular. Although his finances had suffered greatly because of the war, he gave to the poor, helped support widows and orphans, and loaned money to friends. According to biographer William Fowler, "Hancock was a generous man and the people loved him. He was their idol."[101] In December 1777, he was re-elected as a delegate to the Continental Congress and as moderator of the Boston town meeting.[102]

In his absence, Congress elected Henry Laurens as its new president, which was a disappointment to Hancock, who hoped to reclaim his chair. Hancock got along poorly with Samuel Adams and missed his wife and son.[103] On July 9, 1778, Hancock and the other Massachusetts delegates joined representatives from seven other states in signing the Articles of Confederation; not ratified until 1781.[104]

Hancock returned to Boston in July 1778, motivated by the opportunity to lead men in combat. Back in 1776, he had been appointed senior major general of the Massachusetts militia.[105] Now that the French fleet had come to the aid of the Americans, Washington instructed General Sullivan to lead an attack on the British garrison at Newport, Rhode Island, in August 1778. Hancock commanded 6,000 militiamen in the campaign. French Admiral d'Estaing abandoned the operation, after which Hancock's militia mostly deserted Sullivan's Continentals.[106] Hancock suffered criticism but emerged from his military career with his popularity intact.[107]

After much delay, the Massachusetts Constitution went into effect in October 1780. To no one's surprise, Hancock was elected Governor of Massachusetts in a landslide, garnering over 90% of the vote.[108] Hancock was unquestionably patriotic given his personal sacrifices and leadership of the Second Continental Congress. Bowdoin, his opponent, was cast by Hancock's supporters as unpatriotic, due to his refusal to serve in Continental Congress.[109] Bowdoin's supporters, well-off commercial interests from Massachusetts coastal communities, cast Hancock as a demagogue.[110]

Hancock governed Massachusetts through the end of the Revolutionary War and into troubled postwar, repeatedly winning re-election by wide margins. Hancock took a hands-off approach to governing, avoiding controversial issues.[111] Hancock governed until his surprise resignation on January 29, 1785. Hancock cited failing health as the reason, but he was aware of growing unrest and wanted to get out before the trouble.[112]

Hancock's critics sometimes believed that he used claims of illness to avoid difficult political situations.[113] Historian James Truslow Adams writes that Hancock's "two chief resources were his money and his gout, the first always used to gain popularity, and the second to prevent his losing it".[114] The turmoil that Hancock avoided ultimately blossomed as Shays' Rebellion, which Hancock's successor Bowdoin had to deal with. After the uprising, Hancock was re-elected in 1787, and he promptly pardoned all the rebels.[115] The next year, a controversy arose when three free blacks were kidnapped from Boston and sent to work as slaves in the French colony of Martinique, West Indies.[116] Hancock wrote to the governors of the islands on their behalf.[117] As a result, the three men were released and returned to Massachusetts.[118] Hancock was re-elected governor the remainder of his life.[119]

Final years

Hancock was again elected as a delegate to Congress, known as the Confederation Congress after the ratification of the Articles of Confederation in 1781. Congress had declined in importance after the Revolutionary War and was frequently ignored by the states. Hancock was elected to serve as its president on November 23, 1785. He sent Congress a letter of resignation in June 1786.[120]

In an effort to remedy the perceived defects of the Articles of Confederation, delegates were first sent to the Annapolis Convention in 1786 and then to the Philadelphia Convention in 1787, where they drafted the United States Constitution, which was then sent to the states for ratification or rejection. Hancock, who was not present at the Philadelphia Convention, had misgivings about the Constitution's lack of a bill of rights and its shift of power to a central government.[121] In January 1788, Hancock was elected president of the Massachusetts ratifying convention.[122] He gave a speech in favor of ratification, and Samuel Adams supported Hancock's position.[123] Even with the support of Hancock and Adams, the Massachusetts convention narrowly ratified the Constitution by a vote of 187 to 168.[124]

Hancock was put forth as a candidate in the 1789 U.S. presidential election. Like everyone else, Hancock felt Washington was going to be elected. Hancock received only four electoral votes in the election; the Massachusetts electors all voted for John Adams, who became vice president.

His health failing, Hancock spent his final years as a figurehead governor. With his wife at his side, he died in bed on October 8, 1793, at age 56. No full-length biography of Hancock appeared until the 20th century. Hancock left few writings for historians.

References
1. Bernstein, Richard B. (2009). "Appendix: The Founding Fathers, A Partial List". The Founding Fathers Reconsidered. New York: Oxford University Press. pp. 176–180. ISBN 978-0199832576.
2. Harlow G. Unger (9/21/2000).John Hancock: Merchant King, American Patriot. Wiley.ISBN 978-0-471-33209-1
3. Allan 1948, pp. 22, 372n48. The date was January 12, 1736, according to the Julian calendar then in use.
4. Allan 1948, p. 22.
5. Fowler 1980, p. 8.
6. Fowler 2000b.
7. Fowler 1980, pp. 11–14.
8. Fowler 1980, p. 18.
9. Fowler 1980, p. 31.
10. Allan 1948, p. 61.
11. Allan 1948, pp. 58–59.
12. Fowler 1980, p. 46.
13. Allan 1948, p. 85.
14. Fowler 1980, pp. 48–59.
15. Fowler 1980, p. 78.
16. Fowler 1980, p. 53.
17. Smuggler Nation, Page 15
18. Fowler 1980, p. 55.
19. Fowler 1980, p. 56.
20. Fowler 1980, pp. 63–64.
21. Fowler 1980, p. 109.
22. Fowler 1980, p. 64.

23. Fowler 1980, pp. 64–65.
24. Fowler 1980, pp. 71–72.
25. Tyler 1986, p. 111–14.
26. Fowler 1980, p. 82.
27. Dickerson 1946, p. 530.
28. Dickerson 1946, pp. 530–31.
29. Allan 1948, p. 103b; Allan does not fully endorse this view.
30. Unger 2000, p. 119.
31. Wroth & Zobel 1965, p. 174.
32. Dickerson 1946, pp. 521–22.
33. Dickerson 1946, p. 522.
34. Knollenberg 1975, p. 63.
35. Knollenberg 1975, p. 64.
36. Fowler 1980, p. 85.
37. Reid 1979, pp. 104–20.
38. Wroth & Zobel 1965, p. 186.
39. Wroth & Zobel 1965, pp. 179–80.
40. Dickerson 1946, p. 534.
41. Dickerson 1946, pp. 535–36.
42. Fowler 1980, p. 100.
43. Dickerson 1946, p. 517.
44. Dickerson 1946, pp. 518–25.
45. Knollenberg 1975, pp. 65–66, 320n41, 321n48.
46. Tyler 1986, p. 13.
47. Fowler 1980, pp. 86–87.
48. Fowler 1980, p. 112.
49. Fowler 1980, p. 124.
50. Unger 2000, p. 145.
51. Fowler 1980, p. 131.
52. Tyler 1986, p. 140.
53. Brown 1955, p. 268–69.
54. Brown 1955, pp. 289–90.
55. Fowler 1980, p. 136.
56. Fowler 1980, pp. 136–42.
57. Brown 1955, p. 285.
58. Brown 1970, pp. 57–60.
59. Fowler 1980, pp. 150–52.
60. Fowler 1980, p. 152.
61. Fowler 1980, p. 156–57.
62. Fowler 1980, p. 161.
63. Fowler 1980, pp. 159–62.
64. Fowler 1980, p. 163.
65. Fowler 1980, pp. 165–66.
66. Fowler 1980, p. 176.
67. Fowler 1980, p. 174.
68. Fowler 1980, p. 177.
69. Unger 2000, p. 185.
70. Fischer 1994, pp. 94, 108.
71. Unger 2000, p. 187.
72. Fowler 1980, p. 179.
73. Fischer 1994, p. 76.
74. Alden 1944, p. 453.
75. Alden 1944, p. 452.
76. Fischer 1994, p. 110.
77. Fischer 1994, pp. 177–78.
78. Fowler 1980, p. 193. The text of Gage's proclamation is available online from the Library of Congress
79. Fowler 1980, p. 190.
80. Fowler 2000a.
81. Fowler 1980, p. 205.
82. Proctor 1977, p. 669.
83. Proctor 1977, p. 670.
84. Proctor 1977, p. 675.
85. Unger 2000, p. 215.
86. Fowler 1980, p. 197.
87. Proctor 1977, p. 661.
88. Fowler 1980, p. 214.
89. Manuel & Manuel 2004, pp. 142–42.

90. Proctor 1977, p. 662.
91. Manuel & Manuel 2004, pp. 144–45.
92. Unger 2000, p. 248.
93. Unger 2000, p. 255.
94. Unger 2000, pp. 216–22.
95. Fowler 1980, pp. 198–99.
96. Allan 1948, p. vii. See also Merriam-Webster online and Dictionary.com
97. Fowler 1980, p. 213.
98. Fowler 1980, p. 220.
99. Fowler 1980, pp. 207, 220, 230.
100. Fowler 1980, pp. 225–26.
101. Fowler 1980, p. 225.
102. Fowler 1980, pp. 230–31.
103. Unger 2000, p. 270.
104. Fowler 1980, p. 207.
105. Fowler 1980, pp. 232–34.
106. Fowler 1980, pp. 234–35.
107. Fowler 1980, pp. 243–44.
108. Morse 1909, pp. 21–22.
109. Hall 1972, p. 134.
110. Fowler 1980, pp. 246–47, 255.
111. Fowler 1980, pp. 258–59.
112. Allan 1948, p. 222.
113. Adams 1930, p. 430.
114. Fowler 1980, pp. 265–66.
115. Slavery in the U.S.: A Social, Political, and Historical Encyclopedia, Vol 1
116. The Collected Works of Theodore Parker: Discourses of slavery
117. John Hancock: The Picturesque Patriot
118. Unger 2000, p. xvi.
119. Fowler 1980, p. 264.
120. Fowler 1980, pp. 267–69.
121. Fowler 1980, p. 268.
122. Fowler 1980, p. 270.
123. Fowler 1980, p. 271.
124. Fowler 1980, p. 274.

Sources

- Adams, James Truslow (September 1930). "Portrait of an Empty Barrel". Harpers Magazine. 161: 425–34.
- Alden, John R. (1944). "Why the March to Concord?". The American Historical Review. 49 (3): 446–54. doi:10.2307/1841029. JSTOR 1841029.
- Allan, Herbert S. (1948). John Hancock: Patriot in Purple. New York: Macmillan.
- Brown, Richard D. (1970). Revolutionary Politics in Massachusetts: The Boston Committee of Correspondence and the Towns, 1772–1774. Cambridge: Harvard University Press. ISBN 0-393-00810-X.
- Brown, Robert E. (1955). Middle-Class Democracy and Revolution in Massachusetts, 1691–1789. Ithaca, New York: Cornell University Press.
- Dickerson, O. M. (March 1946). "John Hancock: Notorious Smuggler or Near Victim of British Revenue Racketeers?". The Mississippi Valley Historical Review. 32 (4): 517–40. doi:10.2307/1895239. JSTOR 1895239.
- Fischer, David Hackett (1994). Paul Revere's Ride. New York: Oxford Uni Press. ISBN 0-19-508847-6.
- Fowler, William M. Jr. (1980). Baron of Beacon Hill: A Biography of John Hancock. Boston: Houghton Mifflin.
- Fowler, William M. Jr. (1997). Samuel Adams: Radical Puritan. New York: Longman. ISBN 0-673-99293-4.
- Fowler, William M. Jr. (2000a). "John Hancock". American National Biography Online. Oxford Uni Press.
- Fowler, William M. Jr. (2000b). "Thomas Hancock". American National Biography Online. Oxford U Press.
- Knollenberg, Bernhard (1975). Growth of American Revolution, 1766–1775. NY: Free Press. ISBN 0-02-917110-5
- Manuel, Frank Edward; Manuel, Fritzie Prigohzy (2004). James Bowdoin and the Patriot Philosophers. Philadelphia: American Philosophical Society. ISBN 978-0-87169-247-4. OCLC 231993575.
- Proctor, Donald J. (December 1977). "John Hancock: New Soundings on an Old Barrel". The Journal of American History. 64 (3): 652–77. doi:10.2307/1887235. JSTOR 1887235.
- Reid, John Phillip (1979). In a Rebellious Spirit: The Argument of Facts, the Liberty Riot, and the Coming of the American Revolution. University Park: Pennsylvania State University Press. ISBN 0-271-00202-6.
- Tyler, John W. (1986). Smugglers & Patriots: Boston Merchants and Advent of the American Revolution. Boston: Northeastern U Press. ISBN 0-930350-76-6.
- Unger, Harlow Giles (2000). John Hancock: Merchant King and American Patriot. New York: Wiley & Sons.
- Wroth, L. Kinvin; Zobel, Hiller B. (1965). Legal Papers of John Adams, Vol 2. Harvard U Press.

GEORGE WASHINGTON
FATHER OF OUR COUNTRY

George Washington (February 22, 1732 – December 14, 1799) was a Founding Father of the United States, military officer, and farmer who was the first president of the United States from 1789 to 1797. The great victory won by General Washington over the British can be compared to a flea defeating the most powerful fighting dog. Britain was the great superpower of the day, while the American colonies were at best an after-thought to the British military. In our modern military, Washington would have won Congressional Medals of Honor for his personal bravery in the face of overwhelming odds while fighting in front-line combat.

Early life (1732–1752)

George Washington was born on February 22, 1732, at Popes Creek in Westmoreland County, Virginia.[1] He was the first of six children of Augustine and Mary Ball Washington.[2] His father was a Justice of the Peace.[3] The family moved to Little Hunting Creek in 1734 before settling in Ferry Farm. When Augustine died in 1743, Washington inherited Ferry Farm. His older half-brother Lawrence inherited Little Hunting Creek and renamed it Mount Vernon.[4]

Washington did not have the formal education his elder brothers received at Appleby Grammar School in England, but he did attend the Lower Church School in Hartfield. He learned mathematics, including trigonometry, and land surveying, and became a draftsman and mapmaker. By early adulthood, he was writing with "considerable force" and "precision".[5] As a teenager, to practice his penmanship, Washington compiled over a hundred rules for social interaction styled *Rules of Civility and Decent Behaviour in Company and Conversation*, copied from an English translation of a French book of manners.[6]

Washington often visited Mount Vernon and Belvoir, the plantation of William Fairfax, Lawrence's father-in-law. Fairfax became Washington's patron and surrogate father. In 1748, Washington spent a month surveying Fairfax's Shenandoah Valley property.[9] The following year, he received a surveyor's license from the College of William & Mary. Fairfax appointed him surveyor of Culpeper County, Virginia. He familiarized himself with the frontier region, and though he resigned from the job in 1750, continued to do surveys west of the Blue Ridge Mountains.[10] By 1752, he had bought almost 1,500 acres and owned 2,315 acres.[11]

In 1751, Washington accompanied Lawrence to Barbados, hoping the climate would cure his brother's tuberculosis.[12] Washington contracted smallpox during that trip.[13] Lawrence died in 1752, and Washington leased Mount Vernon from his widow Anne; he inherited it outright after her death in 1761.[14]

Colonial military career (1752–1758)

Virginia's appointed Washington major and commander of militia districts. The British and French competed to control the Ohio Valley: the British were building forts on the Ohio, and the French between the Ohio River and Lake Erie.[15]

In October 1753, Dinwiddie appointed Washington as a special envoy. He sent Washington to demand French forces vacate land claimed by the British.[16] Washington met Iroquois chiefs, at Logstown, and gathered information about the numbers and locations of the French. Washington was nicknamed Conotocaurius by Tanacharison; meaning "devourer of villages", had been given to his great-grandfather John Washington by the Susquehannock.[17]

Washington reached the Ohio River in November and was intercepted by a French patrol. They were escorted to Fort Le Boeuf. He delivered the demand to vacate to the French commander Saint-Pierre, but he refused.[18] Washington completed the mission in 77 days, in difficult winter conditions.[19]

French and Indian War

In February 1754, Dinwiddie promoted Washington to lieutenant colonel and second-in-command of the 300-strong Virginia Regiment, with orders to confront French forces at the Forks of the Ohio,[20] and learned a French force of 1,000 had begun construction of Fort Duquesne there. In May, with a defensive position at Great Meadows, he learned that the French made camp seven miles away; he took the offensive.[21]. The French found their countrymen dead and scalped, blaming Washington, who retreated to Fort Necessity.[22]

On July 3, a French force attacked with 900 men, and the ensuing battle ended in Washington's surrender.[23] He signed a surrender document in which he unwittingly took responsibility for "assassinating" Jumonville.[24] The "Jumonville affair" ignited the French and Indian War, later the Seven Years' War.[25]

In 1755, Washington was a volunteer aide to British General Edward Braddock, who led an expedition to expel the French from Fort Duquesne and the Ohio Country.[26] Washington recommended Braddock split the army into one main column and a light "flying column".[27] Two-thirds of the British force became casualties, including mortally wounded Braddock. Washington rallied the survivors into a rear guard, allowing the force to disengage and retreat.[28]

During the engagement, he had two horses shot from under him, and his hat and coat bullet-pierced.[29] His conduct under fire redeemed his reputation following the Fort Necessity.[30]

The Virginia Regiment was reconstituted in August 1755, with Washington its commander.[31] Washington wanted a higher position but was refused.[32]

In 1758, the Virginia Regiment was assigned to the Forbes Expedition to capture Fort Duquesne.[33] Washington disagreed with Forbes' tactics and route.[34]

Under Washington, the Virginia Regiment had defended 300 miles (480 km) of frontier against twenty Indian attacks in ten months.[35] He improved the regiment as it grew from 300 to 1,000 men, and Virginia's population suffered less than other colonies. He failed to get a royal commission, but gained self-confidence, leadership skills, and knowledge of British tactics.[36]

Marriage, civilian, and political life (1755–1775)

On January 6, 1759, Washington, age 26, married Martha Dandridge Custis, 27-year-old widow of wealthy plantation owner Daniel Parke Custis. The wedding was at Martha's estate; she was intelligent, gracious, and experienced in managing a planter's estate.[37] They moved to Mount Vernon, near where he grew tobacco and wheat and was a political figure.[38]

They were unable to conceive,[39] but they raised Martha's two children John Parke Custis (Jacky) and Martha Parke Custis (Patsy), and later Jacky's two children Eleanor Parke Custis (Nelly) and George Washington Parke Custis.[40]

The marriage gave Washington control over Martha's one-third interest in the 18,000-acre Custis estate, and he managed the remaining two-thirds for Martha's children. As a result, he became one of the wealthiest men in Virginia.[41]

Governor Lord Botetourt fulfilled Dinwiddie's 1754 promise of land to all-volunteer militia during the French and Indian War.[42] In 1770, Washington inspected lands in the Ohio and Great Kanawha regions and engaged a surveyor to subdivide it. Crawford allotted 23,200 acres to Washington; the land was then subdivided among the troops.[43] He doubled Mount Vernon to 6,500 acres.[44] As a respected military hero and large landowner, Washington held local offices.[44] While serving on the Forbes Expedition, he gained election.[45]

Early in his legislative career, he became a critic of Britain's taxation policy and mercantilist policies towards the American.[46]

Washington imported luxuries and other goods from England, paying for them by exporting tobacco. Heavy spending and low tobacco prices left him £1,800 in debt by 1764, prompting him to diversify the plantation.[48] He changed his cash crop from tobacco to wheat and expanded to corn flour milling and fishing.[49]

Washington was soon counted among the political and social elite in Virginia. From 1768 to 1775, he invited some 2,000 guests to Mount Vernon, whom he considered people of rank, and was exceptionally cordial.[50] He took time for fox hunting, fishing, dances, theater, cards, backgammon, and billiards.[51]

Washington's stepdaughter suffered epilepsy from age 12, she died at Mount Vernon. The next day, he wrote to Burwell Bassett: "It is easier to conceive than to describe the distress of this Family".[52] He remained home nightly, three months.[53]

Opposition to the British Parliament and Crown

Washington played a vital role before and during the American Revolution. Opposed to taxes imposed by the British Parliament on the Colonies without proper representation,[54] he was angered by the Royal Proclamation of 1763 which banned settlement west of the Allegheny Mountains and protected the British fur trade.[55]

Washington believed the Stamp Act 1765 was an "Act of Oppression" and celebrated its repeal the following year. In March 1766, Parliament passed the Declaratory Act asserting Parliamentary law superseded colonial law.[56] In the late 1760s, the interference of the British Crown in American lucrative land speculation spurred the American Revolution.[57] Washington was a prosperous land speculator, and in 1767, he encouraged "adventures" to acquire backcountry western lands.[57] Washington helped lead widespread protests against the Townshend Acts, and urged Virginia to boycott British goods; the Acts were repealed in 1770.[58]

Parliament sought to punish Massachusetts colonists for their role in the Boston Tea Party in 1774 by passing the Coercive Acts, which Washington saw as "an invasion of our rights and privileges".[59] That July, he and George Mason drafted a list of resolutions for the Fairfax County committee, including a call to end the Atlantic slave trade, which were adopted.[60]

On August 1, Washington attended the First Virginia Convention. There, he was selected as a delegate to the First Continental Congress.[61] In 1774, he helped train militias and organized the Continental Association boycott of British goods.[62]

The Revolutionary War began April 19, 1775, at Lexington and Concord and Siege of Boston.[63] Washington was "sobered and dismayed",[64] and hastily departed Mount Vernon on May 4, 1775, to join Second Continental Congress.[65]

Commander in chief (1775–1783)

On June 14, 1775, Congress created the Continental Army and John Adams nominated Washington as its commander-in-chief, mainly because of his military experience and the belief that a Virginian would better unite the colonies. He was unanimously elected by Congress the next day.[66] Washington appeared before Congress in uniform and gave an acceptance speech on June 16, declining a salary, though he was later reimbursed expenses.[67] Washington was commissioned and appointed "General & Commander in chief of the army of the United Colonies." He took charge of the Siege of Boston on June 22, 1775.

Congress chose his primary staff officers, including Major General Artemas Ward, Adjutant General Horatio Gates, Major General Charles Lee, Major General Philip Schuyler, and Major General Nathanael Greene.[68] Henry Knox, a young bookkeeper, impressed Adams and Washington with ordnance knowledge and was promoted to colonel and chief of artillery. Washington was impressed by Alexander Hamilton's intelligence and bravery. He would later promote him to colonel and appoint him his aide-de-camp.[69]

Washington initially banned the enlistment of Black people. The British saw an opportunity to divide the colonies.[70] Washington overturned his ban.[71] By the end of the war, one-tenth of Washington's army were blacks.[72] Following British surrender, Washington enforced terms of the preliminary Treaty of Paris (1783) reclaiming freed slaves. He arranged a request to Sir Guy Carleton on May 6, 1783. Instead, Carleton issued 3,000 freedom certificates and all former slaves in New York City could leave before the British departed in 1783.[73]

Siege of Boston

Early in 1775, in response to the growing rebellious movement, London sent British troops to occupy Boston, led by General Thomas Gage.[74] Local militias surrounded the city and effectively trapped the British troops.[75]

As Washington headed for Boston, word of his march preceded him; gradually, he became a symbol of the Patriot cause.[76] Upon Washington's arrival on July 2, 1775, two weeks after the Battle of Bunker Hill, he set up headquarters in Cambridge. When he inspected the army, he found undisciplined militia.[77] After consultation, he initiated Benjamin Franklin's suggested reforms: drilling the soldiers and imposing strict discipline.[78] Washington ordered his officers to identify the skills of recruits to ensure military effectiveness, while removing incompetent officers.[98] He petitioned Gage, his former superior, to release captured Patriot officers from prison and treat them humanely.[79] In October 1775, King George III declared the colonies in open rebellion and relieved Gage of command, replacing him with General Howe.[80]

The Continental Army, reduced to only 9,600 men by January 1776 due to expiring enlistments, was backed by militia. Knox arrived with heavy artillery from Fort Ticonderoga.[81] Instead of storming Boston, he secured the Dorchester Heights, 100 feet above Boston, with Knox's artillery.[82]

On March 9, in cover of darkness, Washington's troops bombarded British ships in Boston harbor. On March 17, 9,000 British troops and Loyalists began a chaotic ten-day evacuation aboard 120 ships. Washington soon entered the city with 500 men, with orders not to plunder Boston,[83] leaving matters in local hands.[84]

New York and New Jersey - - Battle of Long Island

After victory at Boston, Washington correctly guessed the British would return to Loyalist New York City and retaliate.[85] Howe transported his army from Halifax to New York City.[86] The British forces, including more than a hundred ships and thousands of troops, began arriving on Staten Island.[84] After the Declaration of Independence was adopted, Washington informed his troops Congress declared the united colonies to be "free and independent states".[87]

Howe's troop strength totaled 32,000 regulars and Hessians, and Washington's consisted of 23,000, raw recruits and militia.[88] In August, Howe landed 20,000 troops at Gravesend, Brooklyn, and approached Washington's fortifications. Opposing his generals, Washington chose to fight, and on information Howe's army had only 8,000 troops. [89][90][91] The Royal Navy bombarded lower Manhattan Island.[92] Washington ordered his army to White Plains.[92]

Howe's pursuit forced Washington to retreat across the Hudson River to Fort Lee. Howe landed his troops on Manhattan in November and captured Fort Washington, inflicting high casualties on the Americans. Washington was delayed the retreat.[93] Now reduced to 5,400 troops, Washington's army retreated, Howe set up winter quarters in New York.[94]

Crossing the Delaware, Trenton, and Princeton

Washington crossed the Delaware River into Pennsylvania, where General John Sullivan joined him with 2,000 more troops.[95]

Howe posted Hessian troops at Trenton to hold New Jersey and the Delaware.[96] Desperate for a victory, Washington devised a surprise attack on Trenton. The army crossed the Delaware in three divisions: one led by Washington (2,400 troops), another by Ewing (700), and the third by Cadwalader (1,500).[97]

Washington ordered a 60-mile search for Durham boats to transport his army, plus the destruction of vessels that could be used by the British.[98] He risked capture while staking out the Jersey shoreline alone leading to crossing the Delaware on Christmas night, 1776.[99]. The wind churned the waters, and they were pelted with hail, but by 3:00 a.m. on December 26, they made it across with no losses.[100] Knox was delayed, managing frightened horses and about 18 field guns on flat-bottomed ferries. Once Knox arrived, Washington proceeded to Trenton.[103]

The troops spotted Hessian positions a mile from Trenton, so Washington split his force into two columns, rallying his men: "Soldiers keep by your officers. For God's sake, keep by your officers. Greene's column took the upper Ferry Road, led by Washington, and Sullivan advanced on River Road.[104] The Americans marched in sleet and snowfall, many shoeless with bloodied feet. At sunrise, Washington, aided by Colonel Knox and artillery, led a surprise attack. The Hessians had 22 killed, 83 wounded, 850 captured with supplies.[105]

Washington retreated across the Delaware to Pennsylvania and returned to New Jersey on January 3, 1777, launching an attack on British regulars at Princeton, with 40 Americans killed or wounded and 273 British killed or captured.[106] American Generals Hugh Mercer and John Cadwalader were driven back by the British when Mercer was mortally wounded.[107]

Nassau Hall, Princeton, was the target of Hamilton's cannons. Washington charged; the British surrendered quickly. 194 soldiers laid down their arms.[108]

Washington took winter quarters in Jacob Arnold's Tavern in Morristown, New Jersey,[109] while he received munitions from the Hibernia mines.[110]

He ordered smallpox inoculation of his troops.[111]

The British still controlled New York, and many Patriot soldiers did not re-enlist. Congress instituted greater rewards for re-enlisting and punishments for desertion to effect greater troop numbers.[112] Strategically, Washington's victories at Trenton and Princeton were pivotal; they revived morale and quashed the British, changing the course of the war.[113] In February 1777, word of American victories reached London, the British realized the Patriots were in position to demand unconditional independence.[114]

Philadelphia - - Brandywine, Germantown, and Saratoga

In July 1777, British General Burgoyne led the Saratoga campaign south from Quebec through Lake Champlain. General Howe blundered, taking his army to Philadelphia rather than up the Hudson River to join Burgoyne near Albany.[115]

Washington and Marquis de Lafayette rushed to Philadelphia to engage Howe. In the Battle of Brandywine, Howe outmaneuvered Washington and marched into Philadelphia. A Patriot attack failed at Germantown.[115]

In Upstate New York, General Gates led the Patriots. Concerned about Burgoyne's movements southward, Washington sent reinforcements north with Generals Benedict Arnold, his most aggressive field commander, and Benjamin Lincoln. On October 7, 1777, Burgoyne tried to take Bemis Heights but was isolated from support by Howe. He retreated to Saratoga and ultimately surrendered after the Battles of Saratoga. As Washington suspected, Gates' victory emboldened his critics.[116][117]

Valley Forge and Monmouth

Washington and his Continental Army of 11,000 men went into winter quarters at Valley Forge north of Philadelphia in December 1777, and lost between 2,000 and 3,000 men from disease, lack of food, clothing, and shelter.[118] The British were quartered in Philadelphia, paying for supplies in pounds sterling, while Washington struggled with devalued American currency. The woodlands were soon over-hunted.[119]

An internal revolt by his officers, led by Major General Thomas Conway, prompted some members of Congress to consider removing Washington from command. Washington's supporters resisted, and the matter was. [120]

He recommended that Congress expedite supplies, and Congress agreed to strengthen and fund the army's supply lines.

By late February, supplies began arriving. Meanwhile, Baron von Steuben's incessant drilling transformed Washington's recruits into a disciplined fighting force.[121] Washington promoted Von Steuben to Major General and chief of staff.[122]

In early 1778, the French noted Burgoyne's defeat and entered a Treaty of Alliance with the Americans, thus a French declaration of war against Britain. [123]

The British evacuated Philadelphia for New York that. He chose a partial attack on the retreating British at the Battle of Monmouth. Generals Charles Lee and Lafayette moved with 4,000 men and bungled their first attack on June 28. Washington relieved Lee and achieved a draw after an expansive battle. At nightfall, the British retreated to New York, and Washington moved his army outside the city.[124] Monmouth was Washington's last battle in the North.[125]

West Point espionage

Washington became America's first spymaster, designing an espionage system against the British.[127] In 1778, Major Benjamin Tallmadge formed the Culper Ring at Washington's direction to covertly collect information on the British in New York.[128] Washington disregarded incidents of disloyalty by Benedict Arnold, who distinguished himself in campaigns, including Quebec and Battle of Saratoga.[129]

In 1780, Arnold began supplying British spymaster John André with sensitive information intended to compromise Washington and capture West Point, a key American defensive position on the Hudson River.[130] Historians Philbrick and Chernow noted reasons for Arnold's defection to be anger at losing promotions, or repeated slights from Congress. He was also deeply in debt, profiteering from the war, disappointed by Washington's lack of support during his court-martial.[131]

Southern theater and Yorktown

In late 1778, General Clinton shipped 3,000 troops to Georgia and invaded Savannah, reinforced by 2,000 British and Loyalist troops. They repelled American patriots and French naval forces, which bolstered the war effort.[132]

In June 1778, Iroquois warriors joined with Loyalist rangers led by Walter Butler and killed more than 200 frontiersmen, laying waste to the Wyoming Valley in Northeastern Pennsylvania.[133] In mid-1779, in response to this and other attacks on New England towns, Washington ordered General John Sullivan to lead an expedition to force the Iroquois out of New York by effecting "the total destruction and devastation" of their villages and taking their women and children hostage.[134]

The expedition systematically destroyed Iroquois villages and food stocks and forced at least 5,036 Iroquois to flee to British Canada. The campaign killed a few hundred Iroquois, but according to historian Rhiannon Koehler, the net effect reduced the Iroquois by half. They were unable to survive the harsh winter of 1779–1780; some historians called it genocide.[135]

Washington's troops went into quarters at Morristown, New Jersey for their worst winter of the war, with temperatures well below freezing. New York Harbor was frozen, snow covered the ground and the troops lacked provisions.[136]

In January 1780, Clinton assembled 12,500 troops and attacked Charles Town, South Carolina, defeating General Benjamin Lincoln. By June, they occupied the South Carolina Piedmont.[137] Clinton returned to New York and left 8,000 troops under the command of General Charles Cornwallis.[138] Congress replaced Lincoln with Horatio Gates; after his defeat in the Battle of Camden, Gates was replaced by Nathanael Greene, Washington's initial choice, but the British had firm control of the South. Washington was reinvigorated, however, when Lafayette returned from France with more ships, men, and supplies,[139] and 5,000 veteran French troops led by Marshal Rochambeau arrived at Newport, Rhode Island in July 1780.[140] French naval forces then landed, led by Admiral de Grasse.[142]

Washington's army went into winter quarters at New Windsor, New York in December 1780; he urged Congress and state officials to expedite provisions so the army would not "continue to struggle under the same difficulties they have hitherto endured".[143] On March 1, 1781, Congress ratified the Articles of Confederation, but the government was not allowed to levy taxes, yet it held the states together.[144]

General Clinton sent Benedict Arnold, now a British General with 1,700 troops, to Virginia to capture Portsmouth and conduct raids on Patriot forces; Washington sent Lafayette south to counter Arnold's efforts.[176] Washington hoped to bring the fight to New York, drawing British forces out of Virginia, but Rochambeau advised Cornwallis in Virginia was the target. Seeing the advantage, Washington faked towards Clinton, New York, then south to Virginia.[144]

Yorktown

The siege of Yorktown was a decisive victory by the combined Continental Army commanded by Washington, the French Army commanded by General Comte de Rochambeau, and the French Navy commanded by Admiral de Grasse. On August 19, the march to Yorktown led by Washington and Rochambeau began, the "celebrated march".[145] Washington was in command of an army of 7,800 Frenchmen, 3,100 militia, and 8,000 Continentals. Inexperienced in siege warfare, he often deferred to General Rochambeau. Despite this, Rochambeau never challenged Washington's authority as the battle's commanding officer.[146]

78

By late September, Patriot-French forces surrounded Yorktown, trapped the British Army, and prevented British reinforcements from Clinton, while the French navy emerged victorious at the Battle of the Chesapeake. The final American offensive began with a shot fired by Washington.[147] The siege ended with a British surrender on October 19, 1781; over 7,000 British soldiers became prisoners.[148]

Washington negotiated the terms of surrender for two days, and the official signing ceremony took place on October 19; Cornwallis claimed illness and was absent, sending General Charles O'Hara as his proxy.[149]

Demobilization and resignation

AT THIS POINT IN THE REVOLUTION, A MAJOR STRATEGY CHANGE MOVED THE WAR INTO THE SOUTHERN THEATER, WHERE THE COMBAT BRILLIANCE OF MARION CAMPBELL, THE SWAMP FOX WOULD WIN THE DECISIVE BATTLES OF THE WAR, WITH WASHINGTON ACHIEVING THE FINAL VICTORY AT YORKTOWN. THESE HISTORIES WILL BE DELIVERED IN CHAPTERS DEALING WITH THOSE FOUNDING FATHERS.

OUR BOOK SHIFTS TO POST REVOLUTION ISSUES FOR WASHINGTON.

Demobilization and resignation

When peace negotiations began in April 1782, both the British and French began gradually evacuating their forces.[150] With the American treasury empty, unpaid and mutinous soldiers forced the adjournment of Congress. In March 1783, Washington successfully calmed the Newburgh Conspiracy, a planned munity by American officers; Congress promised each a five-year bonus.[151] Washington submitted an account of $450,000 in expenses which he had advanced to the army, equivalent to $9.53 million in 2023. The account was settled, though it was vague about large sums and included expenses his wife incurred.[152]

The following month, a Congressional committee led by Alexander Hamilton began adapting the army for peacetime. In August 1783, Washington gave the Army's perspective to the committee in his *Sentiments on a Peace Establishment*, which advised Congress to keep a standing army, create a "national militia," and establish a navy and a national military academy.[153] The Treaty of Paris was signed on September 3, 1783, and Britain officially recognized American independence. During this time, Washington oversaw the evacuation of British forces in New York and was greeted by parades and celebrations.[154] Along with Governor George Clinton, he took formal possession of the city on November 25.[155]

In early December 1783, Washington bade farewell to his officers at Fraunces Tavern and resigned as commander-in-chief.[156] In a final appearance in uniform, he gave a statement to the Congress: "I consider it an indispensable duty to close this last solemn act of my official life, by commending the interests of our dearest country to the protection of Almighty God, and those who have the superintendence of them, to his holy keeping."[157] Washington's resignation was acclaimed at home and abroad and showed a skeptical world, the new republic would not degenerate into chaos.[158]

Return to Mount Vernon

Washington longed to return home after spending just ten days at Mount Vernon out of 8+ years of war. He arrived on Christmas Eve, delighted to be "free of the bustle of a camp and busy scenes of public life".[159] He was a celebrity and was fêted during a visit to his mother at Fredericksburg, he received a constant stream of visitors to pay respects at Mount Vernon.[160]

Washington reactivated his interests in the Great Dismal Swamp and Potomac canal projects begun before the war, though neither paid him any dividends, and he undertook a 34-day, 680-mile trip to check on his land holdings in the Ohio Country.[161] He oversaw completion of the remodeling work at Mount Vernon, transforming his residence into the mansion that survives to this day—although his financial situation was not strong. His estate recorded its eleventh year of deficit in 1787, with little prospect of improvement.[162] In 1784, Washington declined an invitation from Lafayette to visit France, he could not afford the trip.[163]

To make his estate profitable again, Washington undertook a new landscaping plan and succeeded in cultivating a range of fast-growing trees and native shrubs.[164] He began breeding mules after being gifted a Spanish jack by King Charles III of Spain in 1784. Few mules in the US. He believed they would revolutionize agriculture and transportation.[163]

Constitutional Convention - -1787

Before returning to private life in June 1783, Washington called for a strong union. Though he was concerned that he might be criticized for meddling in civil matters, he sent a circular letter to the states, maintaining the Articles of Confederation were no more than "a rope of sand". He believed the nation was on the verge of "anarchy", was vulnerable to foreign intervention, and a national constitution would unify states under strong central government.[165]

When Shays' Rebellion erupted in Massachusetts over taxation, Washington was convinced that a national constitution was needed.[166] Some nationalists feared the new republic had descended into lawlessness, they met at Annapolis to ask Congress to revise the Articles of Confederation. One of their biggest efforts was getting Washington to attend.[167] A Constitutional Convention came in Spring 1787, with each state to send delegates.[168]

On December 4, 1786, Washington was chosen to lead the Virginia delegation, but he declined on December 21. He had concerns about the legality of the convention and consulted James Madison, Henry Knox, and others. They persuaded him to attend as his presence might induce reluctant states to send delegates and smooth the way for the ratification process while also giving legitimacy to the convention.[169] On March 28, Washington told Governor Edmund Randolph that he would attend the convention.[170]

Washington arrived in Philadelphia on May 9, 1787. Franklin nominated Washington to preside over the convention, and he was unanimously elected to serve as president general.[171] The convention's state-mandated purpose was to revise the Articles of Confederation, and the new government would be established when the resulting document was "duly confirmed by the several states".[172] Randolph introduced Madison's Virginia Plan on the third day of the convention. It called for a new constitution and a sovereign national government, which Washington highly recommended.[173] On July 10, Washington wrote to Alexander Hamilton: "I almost despair of seeing a favorable issue to the proceedings of our convention and do therefore repent having had any agency in the business."[174] He lent his prestige to the work of the other delegates, unsuccessfully lobbying many to support ratification of the Constitution, such as anti-federalists Edmund Randolph and George Mason.[175] The final version was voted on and signed by 39 of 55 delegates on September 17, 1787.

First presidential election

Delegates to the Convention anticipated a Washington presidency and left it to him to define the office once elected.[174] The state electors under the Constitution voted for the president on February 4, 1789, Washington suspected most Republicans had not voted for him.[176] The March 4 date passed without a Congressional quorum to count the votes, but a quorum was reached on April 5. The votes were tallied, and Washington won every state's electoral votes. He was informed of his election as president by Congressional Secretary Charles Thomson.[177] John Adams received the next highest number of votes and was elected vice president.[178] Despite feeling "anxious and painful sensations" about leaving Mount Vernon, he departed for New York City on April 16 to be inaugurated.

Presidency (1789–1797)

Washington was inaugurated April 30, 1789, at Federal Hall in New York City.[218] His coach was led by militia and a marching band followed by statesmen and foreign dignitaries, an inaugural parade with 10,000 spectators.[179] Chancellor Robert R. Livingston administered the oath, using a Bible provided by the Masons, after which the militia fired a 13-gun salute.[180] Washington read a speech in the Senate Chamber, asking "that Almighty Being ... consecrate the liberties and happiness of the people of the United States".[181] Though he wished to serve without a salary, Congress insisted, later providing Washington $25,000 per year to defray costs of the presidency, equivalent to $6.39 million today.[182] Washington wrote to James Madison: "As the first of everything in our situation will serve to establish a precedent, it is devoutly wished on my part that these precedents be fixed on true principles."[183] To that end, he preferred the title "Mr. President" over names proposed by the Senate, including "His Excellency" and "His Highness the President".[184] His executive precedents included the inaugural address, messages to Congress, and the cabinet form of the executive branch.[185]

Washington planned to resign after his first term, but political strife convinced him to remain in office.[186] He was an able administrator and a judge of talent and character, and he regularly talked with department heads to get their advice.[187] He tolerated opposing views, despite fears that a democratic system would lead to political violence, and he conducted a smooth transition of power to his successor.[189] He remained non-partisan throughout his presidency (the only United States president to do so), and opposed the divisiveness of political parties, but he favored a strong Federalist form of government.[190] Washington dealt with major problems. The old Confederation lacked the powers to handle its workload and had weak leadership, no executive, a small bureaucracy of clerks, large debt, worthless paper money, and no power to establish taxes.[191] He had the task of assembling an executive department and relied on Tobias Lear for advice selecting its officers.[192] Britain refused to relinquish its forts in the American West,[191] and Barbary pirates preyed on American merchant ships in the Mediterranean before the United States even had a navy.[193]

Cabinet and executive departments

Congress created executive departments in 1789, including the State Department in July, the War Department in August, and the Treasury Department in September. Washington appointed Edmund Randolph Attorney General, Samuel Osgood Postmaster General, Thomas

Jefferson Secretary of State, Henry Knox Secretary of War, Alexander Hamilton as Secretary of the Treasury. Washington's cabinet became an advisory body.[193]

Washington's cabinet members formed rival parties with sharply opposing views, most fiercely illustrated between Hamilton and Jefferson.[194] Washington restricted cabinet discussions to topics of his choosing, without participating in the debate. He requested cabinet opinions in writing and expected department heads to agreeably carry out his decisions.[190]

Domestic issues

Washington was apolitical and opposed the formation of parties, suspecting that conflict would undermine republicanism.[1935] He exercised great restraint in using his veto power, writing that "I give my Signature to many Bills with which my Judgment is at variance..."[196] His closest advisors formed two factions, portending the First Party System. Secretary of the Treasury Alexander Hamilton formed the Federalist Party to promote national credit and a financially powerful nation. Secretary of State Thomas Jefferson opposed Hamilton's agenda and founded the Jeffersonian Republicans. Washington favored Hamilton's agenda, however, and it ultimately went into effect—resulting in bitter controversy.[197] Washington proclaimed November 26, 1789, a day of Thanksgiving to encourage national unity. "It is the duty of all nations to acknowledge the providence of Almighty God, to obey His will, to be grateful for His benefits, and humbly to implore His protection and favor." He spent that day visiting debtors in prison to provide them food and beer.[198]

African Americans

In response to two antislavery petitions before Congress, slaveholders in Georgia and South Carolina threatened to "blow the trumpet of civil war". Washington and Congress responded with racist measures: naturalization was denied to Black immigrants; blacks were barred from serving in state militias; the Southwest Territory (later Tennessee) was permitted to maintain slavery; and two more slave states were admitted (Kentucky in 1792 and Tennessee in 1796). On February 12, 1793, Washington signed the Fugitive Slave Act, which overrode state laws, allowing agents to cross state lines to return escaped slaves.[199] Free blacks in the north decried the law believing it would allow bounty hunting and kidnapping. The Fugitive Slave Act backed the Constitution's Fugitive Slave Clause, and the Act was passed in Congress.[200]

National Bank

Washington's first term saw heavy economic concerns.[201] Establishment of public credit became a primary challenge for the federal government.[202] Hamilton submitted a report to a deadlocked Congress, and he, Madison, and Jefferson reached the Compromise of 1790 in which Jefferson agreed to Hamilton's debt proposals in exchange for moving the nation's capital temporarily to Philadelphia and then south near Georgetown on the Potomac River.[197] The terms were legislated in the Funding Act of 1790 and the Residence Act, both of which Washington signed into law. Congress authorized the assumption and payment of the nation's debts, with funding provided by customs duties and excise taxes.[203]

Hamilton caused controversy in Cabinet by advocating the establishment of the First Bank of the United States. Jefferson and Randolph insisted the federal government was going beyond its constitutional authority. Hamilton argued the government could charter the bank under implied powers granted by the constitution. Washington sided with Hamilton and signed the bank legislation on February 25, 1791. The rift between Hamilton and Jefferson became openly hostile.[204] The nation's first financial crisis occurred in March 1792. Hamilton's Federalists exploited large loans to gain control of U.S. debt securities, causing a run on the national bank,[205] markets returned to normal by mid-April.[206] Jefferson believed Hamilton was part of the scheme, despite his efforts to ameliorate.[207]

Jefferson – Hamilton Feud

Jefferson and Hamilton adopted diametrically opposed politics. Hamilton believed in a strong national government requiring a national bank and foreign loans to function, while Jefferson believed the states and the farm element should primarily direct the government; he resented the idea of banks and foreign loans. To Washington's dismay, the two men entered into disputes and infighting.[253] Hamilton demanded Jefferson resign if he could not support Washington, and Jefferson told Washington Hamilton's fiscal system would lead to the overthrow of the republic.[208] Washington urged a truce for the sake of the nation.[209]

Jefferson's political actions, support of Freneau's *National Gazette*,[210] and attempts to undermine Hamilton nearly led Washington to dismiss him from the cabinet; he resigned his position in December 1793, and Washington forsook him.[211] The feud led to the well-defined Federalist and Republican parties, party affiliation became necessary for election by 1794.[212]

Whiskey Rebellion

In March 1791, at Hamilton's urging, with support from Madison, Congress imposed an excise tax on distilled spirits to help curtail the national debt, which took effect in July.[213] Grain farmers strongly protested in Pennsylvania's frontier districts; they argued that they were unrepresented and were shouldering too much of the debt, comparing their situation to British taxation pre-Revolution. On August 2, Washington assembled his cabinet to discuss the situation. Unlike Washington, who had reservations about using force, Hamilton was eager to suppress the rebellion with federal authority.[214] Wanting to avoid involving the federal government, Washington first called on Pennsylvania state officials to take the initiative, but they declined. Washington issued his first proclamation for calling up state militias.[215]

Threats and violence against tax collectors, however, escalated into defiance against federal authority in 1794 and gave rise to the Whiskey Rebellion. Washington issued a final proclamation on September 25, threatening the use of military force to no avail.[215] The federal army was not up to the task, so Washington invoked the Militia Act of 1792 to summon state militias.[216] Governors sent troops, initially commanded by Washington, who handed over command to Henry Lee to lead them into the rebellious districts. They took 150 prisoners, and the remaining rebels dispersed. Two of the prisoners were condemned to death, but Washington exercised his Constitutional authority for the first time and pardoned them.[217] Washington's forceful action demonstrated that the new government could protect itself and its tax collectors. This represented the first use of federal military force against the states and citizens.[218]

Foreign affairs

In April 1792, the French Revolutionary Wars began between Britain and France, and Washington declared America's neutrality. The revolutionary government of France sent diplomat Edmond-Charles Genêt to America, and he was welcomed with great enthusiasm. He created a network of new Democratic-Republican Societies promoting France's interests, but

Washington denounced them and demanded that the French recall Genêt.[220] The National Assembly of France granted Washington honorary French citizenship on August 26, 1792, during the early stages of the French Revolution.[221] Hamilton formulated the Jay Treaty to normalize trade relations with Britain while removing them from western forts, and also to resolve financial debts remaining from the Revolution.[222] Chief Justice John Jay acted as Washington's negotiator and signed the treaty on November 19, 1794; critical Jeffersonians, however, supported France. Washington deliberated, then supported the treaty because it avoided war with Britain,[223] but was disappointed that its provisions favored Britain.[224] He mobilized public opinion and secured ratification in the Senate[225] but faced frequent public criticism.[226] The treaty secured peace with Britain and a decade of prosperous trade. Jefferson claimed that it angered France and "invited rather than avoided" war.[227] Relations with France deteriorated and, two days before Washington's term ended, the French Directory declared authority to seize American ships,[228] leaving president Adams with prospective war.[229]

Native American affairs

During the fall of 1789, Washington had to contend with the British refusing to evacuate their forts in the Northwest frontier and their concerted efforts to incite Indian tribes to attack American settlers.[230] The Northwest tribes under Miami chief Little Turtle allied with the British to resist American expansion, and killed 1,500 settlers between 1783 and 1790.[231]

Washington declared that "the Government of the United States are determined that their Administration of Indian Affairs shall be directed entirely by the great principles of Justice and humanity", and provided that treaties should negotiate their land interests.[232] The administration regarded powerful tribes as foreign nations, and Washington even smoked a peace pipe and drank wine with them at the President's House.[233] He attempted to conciliate;[234] he equated killing indigenous peoples with killing whites and sought to integrate them into American culture.[235] Negotiations failed between federal commissioners and Indian tribes seeking retribution. Washington invited Creek Chief Alexander McGillivray and 24 leading chiefs to New York to negotiate a treaty and treated them like foreign dignitaries. Knox and McGillivray concluded the Treaty of New York on August 7, 1790, which provided the tribes with agricultural supplies and McGillivray with the rank of Brigadier General and an annual salary of $1,200, equivalent to $29,573 in 2023.[236]

In 1790, Washington sent General Josiah Harmar to pacify the Northwest tribes, but Little Turtle routed him twice and forced him to withdraw.[237] The Northwestern Confederacy tribes used guerrilla tactics and were an effective force against the sparsely manned American Army. Washington sent Major General Arthur St. Clair from Fort Washington on an expedition to restore peace in the territory in 1791. On November 4, St. Clair's forces were ambushed and soundly defeated by tribal forces with few survivors.[238] Washington replaced the disgraced St. Clair with the Revolutionary War hero Anthony Wayne. From 1792 to 1793, Wayne instructed his troops on Native American warfare tactics and instilled discipline which was lacking under St. Clair.[239] In August 1794, Washington sent Wayne into tribal territory with authority to drive them out by burning their villages and crops in the Maumee Valley.[240] On August 24, the American army defeated the Northwestern Confederacy at the Battle of Fallen Timbers, the Treaty of Greenville opened two-thirds of the Ohio Country for settlement.[241]

Second term

Washington initially planned to retire after his first term, weary of office and in poor health. After dealing with the infighting in his own cabinet and with partisan critics, he showed little enthusiasm for a second term, while Martha also wanted him not to run.[242] Washington's nephew George Augustine Washington, managing Mount Vernon in his absence, was critically ill, further increasing Washington's desire to retire.[243] Many urged him to run for a second term. Madison told him his absence would only allow the dangerous political rift in his cabinet and the House to worsen. Jefferson also pleaded with him not to retire, agreeing to drop his attacks on Hamilton, and stating that he would also retire if Washington did.[244] Hamilton maintained Washington's absence would be "deplored as evil."[245] With the election of 1792 nearing, Washington agreed to run.[235]

On February 13, 1793, Electoral College unanimously re-elected Washington president, and John Adams as vice president by a vote of 77 to 50.[235] He was sworn into office by Associate Justice William Cushing on March 4, 1793, in the Senate Chamber of Congress Hall in Philadelphia. Afterwards, Washington gave a brief address before immediately retiring to the President's House.[246] On April 22, 1793, when the French Revolutionary Wars broke out, Washington issued a proclamation which declared American neutrality. He was resolved to pursue "a conduct friendly and impartial toward the belligerent Powers" while also warning Americans not to intervene in the conflict.[247] Although Washington recognized France's revolutionary government, he would eventually ask French minister to the United States Edmond-Charles Genêt be recalled over the Citizen Genêt affair.[248] Genêt was a diplomatic troublemaker who was openly hostile to Washington's neutrality. He procured four American ships as privateers to strike Spanish forces (British allies) in Florida while organizing militias to strike other British possessions. His efforts failed to draw the US into conflict.[249]

On July 31, 1793, Jefferson submitted his resignation.[250] Hamilton, desiring more income, resigned from office in January 1795 and was replaced by Oliver Wolcott Jr. While his relationship with Washington would remain friendly, Washington's relationship with his Secretary of War Henry Knox deteriorated after rumors that Knox profited from contracts for U.S. frigates which had been commissioned under the Naval Act of 1794 in order to combat Barbary pirates, forcing Knox to resign.[251]

Farewell Address

In 1796, Washington declined to run for a third term.[252] In May 1792, in anticipation of his retirement, Washington instructed Madison to prepare a "valedictory address", an initial draft of which was entitled "Farewell Address".[253] In May 1796, Washington sent the manuscript to Alexander Hamilton who did a rewrite, while Washington provided final edits.[254] On September 19, 1796, *American Daily Advertiser* published the final version.[255]

Washington stressed that national identity was paramount, as a united America would safeguard freedom and prosperity. He warned the nation of three eminent dangers: regionalism, partisanship, and foreign entanglements, and said the "name of AMERICAN, which belongs to you, in your national capacity, must always exalt the just pride of patriotism".[256] Washington called for men to move beyond partisanship, stressing that the United States must concentrate on its own interests. He warned against foreign alliances and their influence in domestic affairs, and bitter partisanship and the dangers of political parties.[257] He counseled friendship and commerce with all nations, but advised against involvement in European wars.[258] He stressed

the importance of religion, asserting "religion and morality are indispensable supports" in a republic.[259] Washington's address favored Hamilton's ideology and policies.[260]
He closed the address by reflecting on his legacy:

"Though in reviewing the incidents of my Administration I am unconscious of intentional error, I am nevertheless too sensible of my defects not to think it probable that I may have committed many errors. Whatever they may be, I fervently beseech the Almighty to avert or mitigate the evils to which they may tend. I shall also carry with me the hope that my country will never cease to view them with indulgence, and that, after forty-five years of my life dedicated to its service with an upright zeal, the faults of incompetent abilities will be consigned to oblivion, as myself must soon be to the mansions of rest."[262]

In 1839, Washington biographer Jared Sparks maintained Washington's "Farewell Address was printed and published with laws, by order of the legislatures, as evidence of the value, and of their affection for its author."[264] In 1972, Washington scholar James Flexner referred to the Farewell Address as receiving as much acclaim as Jefferson's Declaration of Independence and Lincoln's Gettysburg Address.[265] Ron Chernow called the *Farewell Address* one of the most influential statements on republicanism.266

Post-presidency (1797–1799) Retirement

Washington retired to Mount Vernon in March 1797 and devoted time to his plantations and business interests.[267] His plantations were minimally profitable,[32] and his lands in the west (Piedmont), had squatters refusing to pay rent. He attempted to sell these.[268] He became an even more committed Federalist. He supported the Alien and Sedition Acts and convinced Federalist John Marshall to run for Congress to weaken the Jeffersonian hold on Virginia.[269]

Washington grew restless in retirement, prompted by tensions with France; in a continuation of the French Revolutionary Wars, French privateers began seizing American ships in 1798, and relations deteriorated with France and led to the "Quasi-War". Washington wrote to Secretary of War James McHenry offering to organize President Adams' army.[270] Adams nominated him for a lieutenant general commission on July 4, 1798, and the position of commander-in-chief of the armies.[319] Washington served as the commanding general from July 13, 1798, until his death 17 months later.[271] Washington delegated the active leadership of the army to Hamilton, a major.[273]

Final days and death

On December 12, 1799, Washington inspected his farms on horseback. He returned home late and had guests for dinner, sitting down for the meal without changing his damp clothes. He had a sore throat the next day but was well enough to mark trees for cutting. That evening, Washington complained of chest congestion.[274] The next morning, he awoke to an inflamed throat and difficulty breathing. He ordered estate overseer Rawlins to remove nearly a pint of his blood; bloodletting was a common practice of the time. His family summoned doctors James Craik, Gustavus Richard Brown, and Elisha C. Dick.[275]

Brown initially believed Washington had quinsy; Dick thought the condition was a "violent inflammation of the throat."[276] They continued bloodletting to approximately five pints, but Washington's condition deteriorated. Dick proposed a tracheotomy, but the other physicians disapproved.[277] Washington instructed Brown and Dick to leave the room, while he assured Craik, "Doctor, I die hard, but I am not afraid to go."[278]

Washington's death came more swiftly than expected.[279] On his deathbed, out of fear of being entombed alive, he instructed his private secretary Tobias Lear to wait three days before his burial.[280] According to Lear, Washington died between 10 p.m. and 11 p.m. on December 14, 1799, with Martha seated at the foot of his bed. His last words were "'Tis well. He was 67.[280] Cavalry and soldiers led the procession, six colonels were pallbearers.

Washington's peak net worth was $587 million, including 300 slaves.[283] He held title to more than 65,000 acres of land in 37 different locations.[73]

On October 7, 1837, Washington's remains, still in the original lead coffin, were placed within a marble sarcophagus designed by William Strickland and constructed by John Struthers.[284] The sarcophagus was sealed and encased with planks, and an outer vault was constructed around it.[285] The outer vault has the sarcophagi of both George and Martha Washington; the inner vault has the remains of other Washington relatives.[286]

Washington was reserved in personality but was known for having a strong presence. He made speeches and announcements when required, but he was not a noted orator.[287] He was taller than most contemporaries, and accounts of his height vary from 6 ft to 6 ft 3.5 inches tall, he weighed between 210–220 pounds as an adult and was known for his great strength.[288]

He had grey-blue eyes and long reddish-brown hair. He did not wear a powdered wig; he wore his hair curled, powdered, in the fashion of the day.[289]

Jefferson describing him as "the best horseman of his age".[290] He collected thoroughbreds at Mount Vernon. He enjoyed hunting fox, deer, ducks.[291] He drank alcohol but was morally opposed to excessive drinking, smoking tobacco, gambling, and profanity.[292]

Washington grandfather was Anglican minister Lawrence Washington, whose troubles with the Church of England prompted his heirs to emigrate to America.[293] He was baptized as an infant in April 1732 and became a devoted member of the Anglican Church.[294] He served over 20 years as a vestryman and churchwarden at Fairfax Parish and Truro Parish in Virginia.[295] He prayed and read the Bible daily, and publicly encouraged the nation to pray.[296]

Washington believed in a "wise, inscrutable, and irresistible" Creator God who was active in the Universe, contrary to deistic thought.[297] He referred to God in American Enlightenment terms, including *Providence*, the *Creator*, or the *Almighty*, and the *Divine Author* or *Supreme Being*.[298] He believed in a divine power who watched over battlefields, was involved in the outcome of war, protected his life, and was involved in American politics and specifically the creation of the United States.[299] Washington frequently quoted from the Bible or paraphrased it, and often referred to the Anglican *Book of Common Prayer*.[300]

Washington emphasized religious toleration in a nation of many denominations and religions. He publicly attended services of different Christian denominations and prohibited anti-Catholic celebrations in the Army.[301] While president, he acknowledged major religious sects and gave speeches on religious toleration.[302] In 1793, speaking to members of the New Church in Baltimore, Washington said, "We have abundant reason to rejoice that in this Land the light of truth and reason has triumphed over the power of bigotry and superstition."[303]

References
1. Chernow 2010, pp. 3–6.
2. Ferling 2002, p. 3; Chernow 2010, pp. 5–7.
3. Ferling 2009, p. 9; Chernow 2010, pp. 6–8.
4. "Ten Facts About Washington & Slavery". George Washington's Mount Vernon. Mount Vernon Ladies' Association.
5. Chernow 2010, pp. 10–12; Ferling 2002, p. 14; Ferling 1988, pp. 5–6.
6. "The Rules of Civility and Decent Behaviour". George Washington's Mount Vernon. Mount Vernon Ladies' Assoc
7. Chernow 2010, pp. 10, 19; Ferling 2002, pp. 14–15; Randall 1997, p. 36.
8. "George Washington's Professional Surveys". Founders Online. U.S. National Archives.
9. Fitzpatrick 1936, v. 19, p. 510; Chernow 2010, pp. 22–23.

10. Chernow 2010, p. 24.
11. Flexner 1974, p. 8; Chernow 2010, p. 25.
12. Chernow 2010, pp. 26, 98.
13. Anderson 2007, pp. 31–32; Chernow 2010, pp. 26–27, 31.
14. Ferling 2009, pp. 15–16.
15. "Conotocarious". Washington's Mount Vernon. Mount Vernon Ladies' Association. Arch &Retr 8/9/21.
16. Ferling 2009, pp. 15–18; Lengel 2005, pp. 23–24; Randall 1997, p. 74; Chernow 2010, pp. 26–27, 31.
17. Fitzpatrick 1936, 19, pp. 510–511; Ferling 2009, pp. 15–18.
18. Chernow 2010, pp. 31–32; Ferling 2009, pp. 18–19.
19. Chernow 2010, pp. 41–42.
20. Chernow 2010, p. 42.
21. Ferling 2009, pp. 24–25.
22. Ferling 2009, pp. 23–25; Ellis 2004, pp. 15–17.
23. Ferling 2009, pp. 24–25; Chernow 2010, pp. 42–45.
24. Preston, David (Oct 2019). "When Young Washington Started a War". Smithsonian. Archived March 1, 2024.
25. Chernow 2010, p. 53.
26. Alden 1996, p. 37; Ferling 1988, pp. 35–36.
27. Alden 1996, pp. 37–46; Ferling 1988, pp. 35–36; Chernow 2010, pp. 57–58.
28. Fitzpatrick 1936, p. 511.
29. Ferling 2009, pp. 28–30.
30. Ellis 2004, p. 24; Ferling 2009, pp. 30–31.
31. Ferling 2009, pp. 31–32, 38–39.
32. Flexner 1965, pp. 206–207.
33. Flexner 1965, p. 194; Fitzpatrick 1936, p. 512.
34. Fitzpatrick 1936, p. 512; Chernow 2010, pp. 89–90; Flexner 1965, pp. 194, 206–207.
35. Fitzpatrick 1936, pp. 511–512; Flexner 1965, p. 138; Fischer 2004, pp. 15–16; Ellis 2004, p. 38.
36. Chernow 2010, pp. 92–93; Ferling 2002, pp. 32–33.
37. Ferling 2002, pp. 33–34; Wiencek 2003, p. 69.
38. Chernow 2010, pp. 97–98; Fischer 2004, p. 14.
39. Chernow 2010, p. 103.
40. Coe, Alexis (June 20, 2020). "Father of Nation, George Washington Also a Doting Dad". Smithsonian. Arch Sept 21, 2023.
41. Wiencek 2003, pp. 9–10, 67–69, 80–81.
42. Rasmussen & Tilton 1999, p. 100; Chernow 2010, p. 184.
43. Ferling 2002, pp. 44–45; Grizzard 2002, pp. 135–137.
44. Ellis 2004, pp. 41–42, 48.
45. Ferling 2009, pp. 49–54, 68.
46. Ellis 2004, pp. 49–50.
47. Chernow 2010, p. 141.
48. Chernow 2010, p. 122.
49. Ferling 2002, pp. 43–44; Ellis 2004, p. 44.
50. Chernow 2010, p. 161.
51. Higginbotham 2001, p. 154.
52. Chernow 2010, p. 136.
53. Chernow 2010, pp. 137, 148; Taylor 2016, pp. 61, 75.
54. Taylor 2016, p. 103.
55. "The Pursuit of Land". The Lehrman Institute. June 22, 2021. Arch August 12, 2021.
56. Freeman 1968, pp. 174–176; Taylor 2016, p. 75.
57. Alden 1996, p. 101.
58. Chernow 2010, p. 167.
59. Ferling 1988, p. 100; Ford, Hunt & Fitzpatrick 1904, v. 19, p. 11.
60. Ferling 1988, p. 108; Taylor 2016, pp. 126–127.
61. Taylor 2016, p. 132.
62. Chernow 2010, p. 181.
63. Chernow 2010, p. 182.
64. Taylor 2016, pp. 132–133; Ellis 2004, pp. 67–68; Chernow 2010, pp. 185–186; Fitzpatrick 1936, p. 514.
65. Rasmussen & Tilton 1999, p. 294; Fitzpatrick 1936,p. 514;Taylor 2016, pp 141–142; Ferling 2009, p. 86–87.
66. Chernow 2010, pp. 190–191; Ferling 2002, p. 108.
67. Ferling 2002, pp. 109–110; Puls 2008, p. 31.
68. Morgan 2000, pp. 290–291.
69. Collins, Elizabeth M. (March 4, 2013). "Black Soldiers in Revolutionary War".U. S Army. Arch&Retr 8/10/21.
70. Taylor 2016, p. 231.
71. Roberts, Andrew (2021). Last King of America: Misunderstood Reign of George III. Penguin Random House. 446.
72. Taylor 2016, pp. 121–123.
73. Taylor 2016, pp. 121–122, 143.
74. Chernow 2010, p. 193.
75. Taylor 2016, p. 143.
76. Isaacson 2003, p. 303; Ferling 2002, p. 112; Taylor 2016, p. 143; Fitzpatrick 1936, p. 514.

77. Ferling 2002, pp. 112–113, 116.
78. Chernow 2010, pp. 57, 160, 166, 201.
79. Chernow 2010, p. 208; Taylor 2016, pp. 133–135.
80. Lengel 2005, pp. 124–126; Ferling 2002, pp. 116–119.
81. Ferling 2009, p. 100.
82. Henderson 2009, p. 47.
83. Chernow 2010, p. 227–228; Lengel2005, p. 124–126; Ferling2002, p.116–119;Taylor2016, p.144, 153–154
84. Chernow 2010, pp. 229–230.
85. Chernow 2010, p. 235.
86. Fitzpatrick 1936, pp. 514–515; Taylor 2016, pp. 162–163.
87. Chernow 2010, p. 237.
88. Chernow 2010, pp. 244–245; Taylor 2016, pp. 162–163.
89. Taylor 2016, p. 164.
90. McCullough 2005, pp. 186–195.
91. Chernow 2010, p. 240; Davis 1975, pp. 93–94; Taylor 2016, p. 164.
92. Taylor 2016, p. 165.
93. Davis 1975, p. 136; Chernow 2010, p. 257.
94. Alden 1996, p. 137; Taylor 2016, p. 165.
95. Fischer 2004, pp. 224–226; Taylor 2016, pp. 166–169.
96. Taylor 2016, pp. 166–167, 169.
97. Ketchum 1999, p. 235; Chernow 2010, p. 264.
98. Taylor 2016, p. 169.
99. Chernow 2010, pp. 270–273.
100. Chernow 2010, pp. 270–272; Randall 1997, p. 319.
101. Willcox & Arnstein 1988, p. 164.
102. Chernow 2010, p. 273.
103. Chernow 2010, pp. 273–274; Fischer 2004, pp. 215–219; Taylor 2016, p. 171.
104. Fischer 2004, pp. 228–230.
105. Chernow 2010, pp. 270, 275–276; Ferling 2002, pp. 146–147; Fischer 2004, pp. 170, 232–234, 254, 405.
106. Fischer 2004, p. 254; Ketchum 1999, pp. 306–307; Alden 1996, p. 146.
107. Alden 1996, p. 145.
108. Ketchum 1999, pp. 361–364; Fischer 2004, p. 339; Chernow 2010, pp. 276–278.
109. Dryfoos, Delaney (July 5, 2018). 4th of July celebration: This town had reading of Declaration of Independence". NJ.com.
110. Burger, Joanna; Gochfeld, Michael (2000). 25 Nature Spectacles in New Jersey. Rutgers U Press. p. 205.
111. Lawler, Andrew (April 16, 2020). "How smallpox epidemic nearly derailed American Revolution". NationalGeo
112. Fischer 2004, p. 151.
113. Taylor 2016, p. 172; Fischer 2004, p. 367.
114. Ferling 2007, p. 188.
115. Chernow 2010, pp. 300–301.
116. Randall 1997, pp. 340–341; Chernow 2010, pp. 301–304.
117. Chernow 2010, pp. 312–313.
118. Alden 1996, p. 163.
119. Ferling 2002, p. 186; Alden 1996, pp. 165, 167; Freedman 2008, p. 30.
120. Alden 1996, p. 165.
121. Flexner 1965, p. 138; Randall 1997, pp. 354–355.
122. Randall 1997, pp. 342, 356, 359; Ferling 2009, p. 172; Alden 1996, p. 168.
123. Chernow 2010, p. 336.
124. Trickey, Erick (April 26, 2017). "Prussian Nobleman Who Helped Save the American Revolution". Smithsonian..
125. Ferling 2007, p. 296.
126. Alden 1996, pp. 176–177; Ferling 2002, pp. 195–198.
127. Chernow 2010, p. 344.
128. Nagy 2016, p. 274.
129. Rose 2006, pp. 75, 224, 258–261.
130. Chernow 2010, pp. 378–387; Philbrick 2016, p. 35.
131. Adams 1928, pp. 365–366; Philbrick 2016, pp. 250–251.
132. Chernow 2010, p. 380; Palmer 2010, p. 203; Flexner 1991, pp. 119–221; Rose 2006, p. 196.
133. Chernow 2010, pp. 378, 380–381; Lengel 2005, p. 322; Adams 1928, p. 366; Philbrick 2016, pp. 280–282.
134. Taylor 2016, p. 230.
135. Alden 1996, p. 184.
136. Koehler, Rhiannon (Fall 2018). "Hostile Nations: Quantifying Destruction of Sullivan-Clinton Genocide of 1779". American Indian Quarterly. **42** (4): 427–453. doi:10.5250/amerindiquar.42.4.0427.
137. Mann 2008, p. 108.
138. Taylor 2016, p. 234.
139. Taylor 2016, pp. 234–235.
140. Alden 1996, pp. 187–188.
141. Lancaster & Plumb 1985, p. 311.
142. Alden 1996, pp. 197–199, 206.

143. Alden 1996, p. 193.
144. Taylor 2016, p. 339.
145. Chernow 2010, p. 403.
146. Alden 1996, pp. 198–199; Chernow 2010, pp. 403–404.
147. Taylor 2016, pp. 313–315.
148. Kohn 1970, pp. 187–220.
149. Alden 1996, p. 209.
150. Chernow 2010, pp. 446, 448–449, 451; Puls 2008, pp. 184–186.
151. Randall 1997, p. 405.
152. Taylor 2016, p. 319.
153. Alden 1996, p. 210; Chernow 2010, pp. 451–452, 455.
154. Chernow 2010, p. 454; Taylor 2016, pp. 319–320.
155. Ferling 2009, p. 246.
156. Chernow 2010, p. 462; Ferling 2009, pp. 255–256.
157. Ferling 2009, pp. 247–255.
158. Ferling 2009, pp. 246–247; Chernow 2010, pp. 552–553; Ellis 2004, p. 167.
159. Nichols, Tom (October 9, 2024). "The Moment of Truth". The Atlantic. Retrieved October 21, 2024.
160. Wulf 2012, p. 52; Subak 2018, pp. 43–44.
161. "Royal Gift (Donkey)". G Washington's Mount Vernon. Mount Vernon Ladies' Association. Arch July 9, 2021.
162. Alden 1996, p. 221; Chernow 2010, p. 518; Ferling 2009, p. 266.
163. Chernow 2010, pp. 517–519.
164. Taylor 2016, pp. 373–374; Ferling 2009, p. 266.
165. Chernow 2010, p. 523; Taylor 2016, pp. 373–374.
166. Chernow 2010, pp. 520–521, 523, 526, 529; Unger 2013, p. 33.
167. Elliot, Jonathan, ed (1827). "Debates in Several State Conventions: Vols. I-V". Liberty Fund. Pub by editor.
168. Ferling 1988, pp. 359–360.
169. Alden 1996, pp. 226–227.
170. Alden 1996, p. 229.
171. Chernow 2010, pp. 559–560; Ferling 2009, p. 361.
172. Chernow 2010, p. 551.
173. Ferling 2009, p. 274.
174. Ferling 2009, pp. 274–275; Chernow 2010, pp. 559–561.
175. Irving 1857, p. 475; Alden 1996, p. 236.
176. Cooke 2002, p. 4; Chernow 2010, pp. 550–551; Fitzpatrick 1936, p. 522.
177. Chernow 2010, pp. 566–567; Randall 1997, p. 448.
178. Cooke 2002, p. 4; Chernow 2010, p. 568.
179. Randall 1997, p. 448; Alden 1996, p. 236.
180. Chernow 2010, p. 552; Fitzpatrick 1936, v. 19, p. 522.
181. Unger 2013, p. 76.
182. Bassett 1906, p. 155.
183. Unger 2013, pp. 236–237.
184. Chernow 2010, pp. 674–675.
185. Ellis 2004, pp. 197–198; Unger 2013, pp. 236–237.
186. Genovese 2009, p. 589; Unger 2013, pp. 236–237.
187. Chernow 2010, pp. 696–698; Randall 1997, p. 478.
188. Cooke 2002, p. 5.
189. Chernow 2010, p. 575.
190. Chernow 2010, p. 514.
191. Ferling 2009, pp. 281–282; Cooke 2002, pp. 4–5.
192. Cooke 2002, p. 5; Banning 1974, p. 5.
193. Elkins & McKitrick 1995, p. 290.
194. Ellis, Richard J. (1999). Founding American Presidency.Rowman&Littlefield. p.133.ISBN 978-0-8476-9499-0
195. Cooke 2002, p. 7.
196. Chernow 2010, pp. 585, 609; Henriques 2006, p. 65; Novak & Novak 2007, pp. 144–146.
197. Chernow 2010, p. 758; Taylor 2016, pp. 399–400.
198. Taylor 2016, pp. 399–400.
199. Chernow 2005, p. 345.
200. Banning 1974, pp. 5–7.
201. Cooke 2002, pp. 7–8.
202. Cooke 2002, p. 8.
203. Sobel 1968, p. 27.
204. Banning 1974, p. 9; Sobel 1968, p. 30.
205. Chernow 2010, pp. 673–674.
206. Chernow 2010, pp. 515, 627–630, 648–650; Randall 1997, pp. 452, 463, 468–471.
207. Banning 1974, p. 8; Cooke 2002, p. 9.
208. Cooke 2002, p. 9; Fitzpatrick 1936, v. 19, p. 523.
209. Elkins & McKitrick 1995, pp. 240, 285, 290, 361.

210. Cooke 2002, p. 9; Chernow 2005, p. 427.
211. Ferling 2013, pp. 222, 283–284, 301–302.
212. Chernow 2005, pp. 342–343.
213. Kohn 1972, pp. 567–568, 570.
214. Chernow 2010, pp. 719–721; Puls 2008, p. 219.
215. Coakley 1996, pp. 43–49.
216. Kohn 1972, pp. 567–584.
217. Ellis 2004, pp. 225–226.
218. Elkins & McKitrick 1995, pp. 335–354.
219. "Honorary French Citizenship". G Washington's Mount Vernon. Mount Vernon Ladies' Arch&Retr 2/2/19
220. Elkins & McKitrick 1995, ch. 9.
221. Chernow 2010, p. 730.
222. Ferling 2009, p. 340.
223. Estes 2000, pp. 393–422; Estes 2001, pp. 127–158.
224. Ferling 2009, p. 344.
225. Ferling 2009, p. 343.
226. Akers 2002, p. 27.
227. Grizzard 2005, p. 263; Lengel 2005, p. 357.
228. Fitzpatrick 1936, p. 523; Cooke 2002, pp. 9–10; Chernow 2010, p. 665.
229. Waldman & Braun 2009, p. 149.
230. Harless, Richard (2018). "Native American Policy". G Washington's Mount Vernon. Arch&Retr Oct 26, 2018.
231. Calloway 2018, p. 2.
232. Flexner 1969, p. 304; Taylor 2016, p. 406.
233. Cooke 2002, p. 10.
234. Grizzard 2002, pp. 256–257; Puls 2008, pp. 207–208.
235. Chernow 2010, pp. 667–678; Gaff 2004, p. xvii; Waldman & Braun 2009, p. 149.
236. Maulden, Kristopher (2016). "Show of Force: Northwest Indian War and Early American State". Ohio Valley History
237. Cooke 2002, p. 10; Chernow 2010, p. 668.
238. Taylor 2016, p. 406; Chernow 2010, p. 668.
239. Cooke 2002, p. 14; Taylor 2016, p. 406.
240. Chernow 2010, pp. 674–675, 678; Ferling 2009, p. 362; Randall 1997, p. 484.
241. Chernow 2010, p. 687.
242. Ferling 1988, p. 421; Randall 1997, p. 482; Chernow 2010, pp. 675, 678.
243. Chernow 2005, p. 403.
244. Chernow 2010, p. 687; Cooke 2002, pp. 10–11.
245. Ferling 2009, pp. 299, 304, 308–311; Banning 1974, p. 2; Cooke 2002, pp. 11–12.
246. Cooke 2002, pp. 12–13.
247. Chernow 2010, p. 692; Cooke 2002, p. 12.
248. Cooke 2002, p. 13.
249. Chernow 2010, p. 713.
250. Spalding & Garrity 1996, p. 58; Lurie 2018.
251. Spalding & Garrity 1996, p. 58; Lurie 2018.
252. Spalding & Garrity 1996, pp. 46–47.
253. Flexner 1972, p. 292;Chernow 2010, pp.752–753;Spalding & Garrity 1996, p. 4744;Hayes 2017,p.287–298
254. Chernow 2010, p. 754; Lurie 2018.
255. Chernow 2010, p. 755; Lurie 2018.
256. Randall 1997, p. 492; Boller 1963, p. 47.
257. Fishman, Pederson & Rozell 2001, pp. 119–120; Gregg & Spalding 1999, pp. 199–216.
258. Chernow 2010, p. 133.
259. Randall 1997, p. 492;Cooke 2002, pp. 18–19;Flexner 972, pp. 292–297;Avlon2017, p. 223;Boller 1963, p47
260. Avlon 2017, p. 280.
261. Spalding & Garrity 1996, p. 143.
262. Sparks 1839, p. 444.
263. Flexner 1972, p. 292; Spalding & Garrity 1996, p. 142.
264. Breen, Eleanor E.; White, Esther C. (2006). "A Pretty Considerable Distillery: Excavating George Washington's Whiskey Distillery" Quarterly Bulletin the Archeological Society of Virginia. **61** (4): 209–20. Arch Dec 24, 2011.
265. Ellis 2004, pp. 255–261.
266. Flexner 1974, p. 386.
267. Randall 1997, p. 497.
268. Flexner 1974, pp. 376–377; Bell 1992, p. 64.
269. Bell 1992, p. 64.
270. Fitzpatrick 1936, p. 474, vol. 36.
271. Kohn 1975, pp. 225–242; Grizzard 2005, p. 264.
272. "The Death of George Washington". George Washington's Mount Vernon. Mount Vernon Ladies' Association.
273. Chernow 2010, pp. 806–807; Lear 1799, p. 257.
274. Chernow 2010, pp. 806–810.
275. Ellis 2004, p. 269.

276. Ferling 2009, p. 365.
277. Chernow 2010, p. 808.
278. Flexner 1974, pp. 401–402; Chernow 2010, pp. 808–809.
279. Irving 1857, p. 359.
280. "The Tomb". George Washington's Mount Vernon. Mount Vernon Ladies' Assoc. Arch 4/30/18. Retr 6/13/24.
281. Strickland 1840, pp. 11–14; Carlson 2016, chapter 1.
282. Strickland 1840, pp. 11–14.
283. Ferling 2002, p. 16; Randall 1997, pp. 34, 436; Chernow 2010, pp. 29–30.
284. Ferling 2002, p. 16.
285. "Founders Online: From George Washington to Charles Lawrence, 20 June 1768" founders.archives.gov
286. Chernow 2010, pp. 123–125.
287. Chernow 2010, p. 30.
288. Fessenden, Maris (June 9, 2015)."How G Washington Did His Hair". Smithsonian. Archived April 30, 2024.
289. Chernow 2010, p. 124.
290. Chernow 2010, pp. 124, 469.
291. Chernow 2010, p. 469.
292. Chernow 2010, p. 134
293. Tsakiridis 2018.
294. Chernow 2010, p. 6; Morrison 2009, p. 136; Alden 1996, pp. 2, 26; Randall 1997, p. 17; Tsakiridis 2018.
295. Chernow 2010, p. 130; Thompson 2008, p. 40; Tsakiridis 2018.
296. Frazer 2012, pp. 198–199; Chernow 2010, pp. 119, 132; Tsakiridis 2018.
297. Randall 1997, p. 67; Tsakiridis 2018.
298. Chernow 2010, p. 131; Tsakiridis 2018.
299. Chernow 2010, pp. 131–132; Morrison 2009, p. 136; Tsakiridis 2018.
300. Boller 1963, p. 125.
301. Chernow 2010, p. 131.
302. Novak & Novak 2007, p. 117, n. 52.

Bibliography

- Akers, Charles W. (2002). "John Adams". In Graff, Henry (ed.). The Presidents: A Reference History (3rd ed.). Scribner. pp. 23–38. ISBN 978-0684312262.
- Alden, John R. (1996). George Washington: A Biography. Louisiana State U Press. ISBN 978-0807121269.
- Banning, Lance (1974). Woodward, C. Vann (ed.). Responses of the Presidents to Charges of Misconduct. Delacorte Press. ISBN 978-0440059233.
- Chernow, Ron (2005). Alexander Hamilton. Penguin Press. ISBN 978-1-101-20085-8.
- Chernow (2010). Washington: A Life. Penguin Press. ISBN 978-1594202667.
- Coe, Alexis (2020). You Never Forget Your First: A Biography of George Washington. Viking Press.
- Cooke, Jacob E. (2002). "George Washington". In Graff, Henry (ed.). The Presidents: A Reference History (3rd ed.). Scribner. pp. 1–21. ISBN 978-0684312262.
- Davis, Burke (1975). G Washington and the American Revolution. Random House. ISBN 978-0394463889.
- Elkins, Stanley M.; McKitrick, Eric (1995) [1993]. Age of Federalism. Oxford U Press. ISBN 978-0195093810.
- Ellis, Joseph J. (2004). His Excellency: George Washington. Alfred A. Knopf. ISBN 978-1400040315.
- Estes, Todd (2000). "Shaping the Politics of Public Opinion: Federalists and the Jay Treaty Debate". Journal of the Early Republic. **20** (3): 393–422. doi:10.2307/3125063. JSTOR 3125063.
- Ferling, John E. (1988). First of Men: Life of G Washington. Oxford U Press. ISBN 978-0199752751.
- Ferling, (2002). Setting the World Ablaze: Washington, Adams, Jefferson, American Revolution. Oxford U Press.
- Ferling, (2007). A Miracle: American Victory in War of Independence. OxfordU Press.
- Ferling (2009). The Ascent of George Washington: The Hidden Political Genius of an American Icon. Bloomsbury Press. ISBN 978-1608191826.
- Ferling (2013). Jefferson and Hamilton: The Rivalry That Forged a Nation. Bloomsbury Press.
- Fischer, David Hackett (2004). Washington's Crossing. Oxford U Press. ISBN 978-0195170344.
- Fitzpatrick, John C. (1936). "Washington, George". In Malone, Dumas (ed.). Dictionary American Biography. Vol. 19. Scribner. pp. 509–527.
- Flexner, James (1965). Little, Brown
- Frazer, Gregg L. (2012). The Religious Beliefs of America's Founders Reason, Revelation, and Revolution. University Press of Kansas. ISBN 978-0700618453.
- Freedman, Russell (2008). Washington at Valley Forge. Holiday House. ISBN 978-0823420698.
- Genovese, Michael A. (2009). Kazin, Michael (ed.). Princeton Encyclopedia of American Political History, Vols. I & II. Princeton U Press. ISBN 978-1400833566.
- Grizzard, Frank E. Jr. (2002). G Washington: Biographical Companion. ABC-CLIO. ISBN 978-1576070826.
- Grizzard (2005). George! A Guide to All Things Washington. Mariner Pub. ISBN 978-0976823889.
- Henderson, Donald (2009). Smallpox: Death of a Disease. Prometheus Books. ISBN 978-1591027225
- Higginbotham, Don (2001). G Washington Reconsidered. U Press of Virginia. ISBN 978-0813920054.
- Kohn, Richard H. (1970). "The Inside History of the Newburgh Conspiracy: America and the Coup d'Etat". The William and Mary Quarterly. **27** (2): 187–220. doi:10.2307/1918650. JSTOR 1918650.

- Kohn (1972). "Washington Administration's Decision to Crush Whiskey Rebellion" (PDF). The Journal of American History. **59** (3): 567–584. doi:10.2307/1900658. JSTOR 1900658. Archived Sept 24, 2015.
- Lengel, Edward (2005). General G Washington: A Military Life. Random House. ISBN 978-1-4000-6081-8.
- Mann, Barbara Alice (2008). G Washington's War on Native America. U Nevada Press. ISBN 978-0803216358
- McCullough, David (2005). 1776. Simon & Schuster. ISBN 978-0743226714.
- Nagy, John A. (2016). Geo Washington's Secret Spy War:Making of America's First Spymaster. St. Martin's Press.
- Novak, Michael; Novak, Jana (2007). Washington's God: Religion, Liberty, Father of Our Country. Basic Books
- Randall, Willard Sterne (1997). George Washington: A Life. Henry Holt & Co. ISBN 978-0805027792.
- Randall, Willard Sterne (1990). Benedict Arnold: Patriot and Traitor. NY: B&N. ISBN 978-0-7607-1272-6.
- Rasmussen, William M. S.; Tilton, Robert S. (1999). G. Washington: Man Behind the Myths. U Press of Virginia.
- Rose, Alexander (2006). Washington's Spies: Story of America's First Spy Ring. Random House Publishing Group.
- Spalding, Matthew; Garrity, Patrick(1996) Sacred Union of Citizens:Washington's Farewell Address &American Character. Lanham, Boulder, NY,: Rowman & Littlefield Publishers, ISBN 978-0847682621.
- Sparks, Jared (1839). The Life of George Washington. F. Andrews.
- Sobel, Robert (1968). Panic on Wall Street: A History of America's Financial Disasters. Beard Books.
- Strickland, William (1840).Tomb of Washington at Mount Vernon. Carey & Hart.
- Taylor, Alan (2016). American Revolutions: A Continental History, 1750–1804. W.W. Norton & Company
- Tsakiridis, George (2018). "George Washington and Religion". George Washington's Mount Vernon. Mount Vernon Ladies' Association. Archived Oct 10, 2020. Retrieved June 13, 2024.
- Unger, Harlow Giles (2013). "Mr. President": George Washington and the Making of the Nation's Highest Office. Da Capo Press, A Member of the Perseus Book Group. ISBN 978-0306822414.
- Wiencek, Henry (2003). An Imperfect God: Washington, His Slaves, Creation of America. Farrar, Straus, Giroux.
- Wood, Gordon S. (1992). Radicalism of American Revolution. Alfred A. Knopf. ISBN 978-0679404934.
- Wood (2001). Higginbotham, Don (ed.). G Washington Reconsidered. U Press

ALEXANDER HAMILTON
RIGHT HAND MAN FOR GEORGE WASHINGTON

Alexander Hamilton (January 11, 1755 or 1757[a] – July 12, 1804) was an American military officer, statesman, and Founding Father who served as the first U.S. secretary of the treasury from 1789 to 1795 during Washington's presidency.

Born out of wedlock in Charlestown, Nevis, Hamilton was orphaned as a child and taken in by a prosperous merchant. He pursued his education in New York City where, despite his young age, he was a prolific and widely read pamphleteer. He served as an artillery officer in the American Revolutionary War, saw military action against the British in the New York and New Jersey campaign, served as an aide to General George Washington, and helped secure American victory at Siege of Yorktown. After the Revolutionary War, Hamilton served as a delegate from New York to the Congress of the Confederation in Philadelphia. He resigned to practice law and founded the Bank of New York. In 1786, Hamilton led the Annapolis Convention to replace the Articles of Confederation with the Constitution of the United States, which he helped ratify by writing 51 of the 85 Federalist Papers

As a trusted member of President Washington's first cabinet, Hamilton served as the first U.S. Secretary of the Treasury. He advocated the establishment of strong manufacturing industries. He successfully argued that the implied powers of the Constitution provided the legal authority to fund the national debt, assume the states' debts, and create the First Bank of the United States, funded by a tariff on imports and a whiskey tax. Hamilton's views were the basis for the Federalist Party, opposed by Democratic-Republican Party led by Thomas Jefferson.

Jefferson and Aaron Burr tied for the presidency in the electoral college, and, despite philosophical differences, Hamilton endorsed Jefferson over Burr, whom he found unprincipled. When Burr ran for governor of New York in 1804, Hamilton again campaigned against him, arguing that he was unworthy. Burr challenged Hamilton to a duel. Burr shot Hamilton in the stomach. He was transported for medical attention but died from his wounds the following day.

Early life and education

Hamilton was born and spent the early part of his childhood in Charlestown, Nevis in the British Leeward Islands. Hamilton and his older brother[1] were born to Rachel Lavien (*née* Faucette), a married woman of half-British and half-French Huguenot descent[2] and James A. Hamilton, a Scotsman who was the fourth son of Alexander Hamilton, the laird of Grange, Ayrshire, (landowner or feudal lord).[3]

Alexander Hamilton would endure several near catastrophes in his young life. The father deserted the family, then the mother died. Alexander and his brother domiciled by a cousin who died the next year, while Alexander was a young teenager. He was able to convert these terrible situations into positive results throughout his tenure as a leading Founding Father.

Hamilton became a clerk at Beekman and Cruger, a local import-export firm that traded with the Province of New York and New England.[4] Despite being a teenager, Hamilton proved capable enough to be left in charge of the firm for five months in 1771 while the owner was at sea.[5] He remained an avid reader, and later developed an interest in writing and a life outside Saint Croix. He wrote a detailed letter to his father regarding a hurricane that devastated Christiansted on August 30, 1772.[6] The Reverend Hugh Knox, a tutor and mentor to Hamilton, submitted the letter for publication in the *Royal Danish-American Gazette.* The essay impressed the community and sent Hamilton to North American for his education.[8]

In October 1772, Hamilton arrived by ship in Boston and proceeded from there to New York City, where he took lodgings with the Irish-born Hercules Mulligan who assisted Hamilton in selling cargo that was used to pay his way through a top university.[9][10] He came under the influence of William Livingston, a leading intellectual and revolutionary for lodging.[11][12][13] Hamilton entered Mulligan's alma mater King's College, now Columbia University, in New York City, in the autumn of 1773, until officially matriculating in May 1774.[14] His college roommate and lifelong friend Robert Troup spoke glowingly of Hamilton's clarity in concisely explaining the patriots' case against the British in what is credited as Hamilton's first public appearance on July 6, 1773.[15] As King's College students, Hamilton, Troup, and four other undergraduates formed a literary society that is a precursor of the Philolexian Society.[16][17]

In 1774, Church of England clergyman Samuel Seabury published a series of pamphlets promoting the Loyalist and Hamilton responded anonymously to it, with his first published political writings, *A Full Vindication of the Measures of Congress* and *The Farmer Refuted.* Seabury tried to provoke fear in the colonies with an objective of preventing the colonies from uniting against the British.[18] Hamilton published two pieces attacking the Quebec Act,[19] and possibly authored 15 installments of "The Monitor" for Holt's *New York Journal.*[20] Hamilton was a supporter of the Revolutionary cause before the war began, although he did not approve of mob reprisals against Loyalists. On May 10, 1775, Hamilton won credit for saving his college's president, Loyalist Myles Cooper, from an angry mob by speaking to the crowd long enough to allow Cooper to escape.[21] Hamilton had to cease studies before graduating when the college closed during British occupation of New York City.[22]

Revolutionary War (1775–1782) - - Early military career

Hamilton would amass a military career in the Revolution that had him far more immersed in battle than many other leaders who became Founding Fathers.

In 1775, after the first engagement of patriot troops with the British at Lexington and Concord, Hamilton and other King's College students joined a militia company called the

Corsicans, a name reflecting the Corsican Republic suppressed six years earlier, that American patriots regarded as a model.[23]

Hamilton drilled with the company before classes in the graveyard of nearby St. Paul's Chapel. He studied military history and tactics and was soon promoted.[24] Under fire from HMS *Asia*, and with support from the Sons of Liberty, he led his unit, the "Hearts of Oak" on a raid for British cannons in the Battery. Seizure of cannons resulted in the unit being re-designated an artillery company.[25]:13

Through his connections with influential New York patriots, including Alexander McDougall and John Jay, Hamilton raised the New York Provincial Company of Artillery of 60 men in 1776, and was elected captain.[26] The company took part in the campaign of 1776 in and around New York City; as rearguard of the Continental Army's retreat up Manhattan, serving at the Battle of Harlem Heights and at the Battle of White Plains a month later. At the Battle of Trenton, the company was stationed at the high point of Trenton at present-day Warren and Broad streets to keep the Hessians pinned in their Trenton barracks.[27][28]

Hamilton participated in the Battle of Princeton on January 3, 1777. After making a brief stand, the British fell back, some leaving Princeton, and others taking refuge in Nassau Hall. Hamilton transported three cannons to the hall and had them fire upon the building as others broke down the front door. The British put a white flag out one of the windows;[28] 194 British soldiers surrendered.[29]

While being stationed in Morristown, New Jersey, from December 1779 to March 1780, Hamilton met Elizabeth Schuyler, a daughter of General Philip Schuyler and Catherine Van Rensselaer. They married on December 14, 1780, at the Schuyler Mansion in Albany, New York.[30] They had eight children.[33]

George Washington's staff - - Washington's aides-de-camp

Hamilton was invited to become an aide to Continental Army generals Nathanael Greene or Alexander McDougall.[34] He declined, believing his best chance for improving his station in life was glory on the Revolutionary War's battlefields. Hamilton received an invitation to serve as Washington's aide with the rank of lieutenant colonel.[35] Washington believed "Aides de camp are persons in whom confidence must be placed and it requires men of abilities to execute the duties with propriety and dispatch."[36]

Hamilton served four years as Washington's chief aide. He handled letters to the Continental Congress, state governors, and the leading generals of the Continental Army. He drafted many of Washington's orders under Washington's direction, and eventually issued orders on Washington's behalf over his own signature.[37] Hamilton was involved in high-level duties, intelligence, diplomacy, negotiation with senior army officers as Washington's emissary.[38][39]

Field command - - Yorktown campaign

Hamilton long sought command and a return to active combat. As the war ended, he knew opportunities for military glory were diminishing. This continued until early July 1781, when Hamilton submitted a letter to Washington with his commission enclosed, "tacitly threatening to resign if he didn't get a command."[40]

Washington assigned Hamilton as commander of a battalion of light infantry.[41] In the planning for the assault on Yorktown, Hamilton was given command of three battalions, which were to fight in conjunction with allied French troops in taking Redoubts No. 9 and No. 10 of the British fortifications at Yorktown. Hamilton and his battalions took Redoubt No. 10 with bayonets in a nighttime action. The French also suffered heavy casualties and took Redoubt No. 9. These actions forced the British surrender of at Yorktown, the *de facto* end of the war, although small battles continued two more years until the signing of the Treaty of Paris.[42][43]

Return to civilian life (1782–1789) - - Congress of the Confederation

After Yorktown, Hamilton returned to New York City. He passed the bar in July after six months of self-directed education and, in October, was licensed to argue cases before the Supreme Court of New York.[44] He also accepted an offer from Robert Morris to become receiver of continental taxes for New York state.[45] Hamilton was appointed in July 1782 to the Congress of the Confederation as a New York representative beginning in November 1782.[46]

While on Washington's staff, Hamilton had become frustrated with the wartime Continental Congress, particularly its dependence upon the states for financial support. Under the Articles of Confederation, Congress had no power to collect taxes or to demand money from the states. This lack of stable funding made it difficult for the Continental Army to obtain provisions and pay soldiers.

An amendment to the Articles had been proposed by Thomas Burke, in February 1781, to give Congress the power to collect a five percent duty on all imports, but this required ratification by all states. [47]

Congress and the army - - Newburgh Conspiracy

Most of the army was then posted at Newburgh, New York. Those in the army were funding much of their own supplies, and they had not been paid for eight months. After Valley Forge, the Continental officers had been promised in May 1778 a pension of half their pay when they were discharged.[48] By the early 1780s, due to the structure of the government under the Articles of Confederation, it had no power to either raise revenue or pay its soldiers.[49] In 1782, the officers had three demands: the army's pay, their pensions, and commutation of pensions into a lump-sum payment if Congress were unable to afford the half-salary pensions for life. Congress rejected the proposal.[49]

Several congressmen, including Hamilton, Robert Morris, and Gouverneur Morris, attempted to use the so-called Newburgh Conspiracy as leverage to secure support from the states and in Congress for funding of the national government. They encouraged MacDougall to continue his aggressive approach, implying unknown consequences if their demands were not met, that the states assume the debt, or an impost be established to pay that debt.[50]

Hamilton suggested using the Army's claims to prevail upon the states for the proposed national funding system.[51] The Morrises and Hamilton contacted General Henry Knox to suggest he and the officers defy civil authority, at least by not disbanding if the army were not satisfied. Hamilton wrote Washington to suggest that Hamilton "take direction" of the officers' efforts to secure redress.[52][53][54] After the crisis had ended, Washington warned of the dangers of using the army as leverage to gain support for the national funding plan.[52][55]

On March 15, Washington defused Newburgh by addressing the officers personally.[50] Congress ordered the Army disbanded in April 1783. In the same month, Congress approved commutation of officers' pensions to five years of full pay. Rhode Island opposed.[57]

Hamilton calls for Articles of Confederation revision.

In June 1783, disgruntled soldiers from Lancaster, Pennsylvania sent Congress a petition demanding their back pay. When they began to march toward Philadelphia, Congress charged Hamilton and two others with intercepting the mob.[58] Hamilton argued that Congress ought to adjourn to Princeton, New Jersey. Congress agreed and relocated.[59] Frustrated with weakness of the central government, Hamilton drafted a call to revise the Articles of Confederation. This resolution contained many features of the future Constitution of the US. It also included separation of powers into legislative, executive, and judicial branches.[59]

Return to New York - - Annapolis Convention (1786)

Hamilton resigned from Congress in 1783.[60] When the British left New York in 1783, he practiced Law there in partnership with Richard Harison. He specialized in defending Tories and British subjects, as in *Rutgers v. Waddington*, a claim for damages done to a brewery by the Englishmen during occupation of New York. He pleaded for the mayor's court to interpret state law consistent with the 1783 Treaty of Paris, which ended the Revolutionary War.[61][44]:64–69
In 1784, Hamilton founded the Bank of New York.[62]
Long dissatisfied with the Articles of Confederation, Hamilton became a leader at the 1786 Annapolis Convention. He drafted its resolution for a constitutional convention, which came closer to his longtime desire to have a more self-sufficient federal government.[63]
As a member of the legislature of New York, Hamilton argued forcefully and at length in favor of a bill to recognize the State of Vermont. After the Constitution of the United States went into effect, Hamilton said, "One of the first subjects of deliberation will be the independence of Kentucky. The northern will be glad to send a counterpoise in Vermont."[64] Vermont was admitted to the Union in 1791.[65]
In 1788, he was awarded a Master of Arts degree from King's College, now Columbia College.[66] It was during this period that Hamilton served on the college's board of trustees.[67]

Constitution and *The Federalist Papers*

In 1787, Hamilton was chosen as a delegate at the Constitutional Convention by his father-in-law Philip Schuyler.[68]:191[69] Governor George Clinton's faction in the New York legislature had chosen New York's other two delegates, John Lansing Jr. and Robert Yates, and both of them opposed Hamilton's goal of a strong national government.[70][71] Thus, they decided New York's vote, to ensure there were no major alterations to Articles of Confederation.[68]:195 Proposes President should serve for lifetime - -defeated by Madison.
Early in the convention, Hamilton made a speech proposing a president-for-life; it had no effect upon the deliberations of the convention. He proposed to have an elected president and elected senators who would serve for life, contingent upon "good behavior" and subject to removal for corruption or abuse; this idea contributed later to the hostile view of Hamilton as a monarchist sympathizer, held by James Madison.[72] According to Madison's notes, Hamilton said in regards to the executive, "The English model was the only good one on this subject. The hereditary interest of the king was so interwoven with that of the nation, and his personal emoluments so great that he was above the danger of being corrupted from abroad... Let one executive be appointed for life who dares execute his powers."[73]

Hamilton argued, "let me observe that an executive is less dangerous to the liberties of the people when in office during life than for seven years..."[73] In his notes, Madison saw Hamilton's proposal as claiming power for the "rich and well born."[74]

During the convention, Hamilton constructed a draft for the Constitution based on the convention debates, but he never presented it. In this draft, the Senate was to be elected in proportion to the population, being two-fifths the size of the House, and the president and senators were to be elected through complex multistage elections, in which chosen electors would elect smaller bodies of electors; they would hold office for life, but were removable for misconduct. The president would have an absolute veto. The Supreme Court was to have jurisdiction over all lawsuits involving the United States, and state governors were to be appointed by the federal government.[75]

At the end of the convention, Hamilton was still not content with the final Constitution, but signed it anyway as a vast improvement over the Articles of Confederation, and urged his fellow delegates to do so also.[76] Since the other two members of the New York delegation, Lansing and Yates, had already withdrawn, Hamilton was the only New York signer to the United States Constitution.[95]:206 He first used the popularity of the Constitution by the masses to compel George Clinton to sign, but was unsuccessful. The state convention in Poughkeepsie in June 1788 pitted Hamilton, Jay, James Duane, Robert Livingston, and Richard Morris against the Clintonian faction led by Melancton Smith, Lansing, Yates, and Livingston.[78]

Clinton's faction wanted to amend the Constitution, while maintaining the state's right to secede if their attempts failed, and members of Hamilton's faction were against any conditional ratification, under the impression that New York would not be accepted into the Union. During the state convention, New Hampshire and Virginia becoming the ninth and tenth states to ratify the Constitution, respectively, had ensured any adjournment would not happen and a compromise would be reached.[79][80] Hamilton's arguments used for the ratifications were largely iterations of work from *The Federalist Papers*, and Smith eventually went for ratification.[81] The vote in the state convention was ratified 30 to 27, on July 26, 1788.[82]

The Federalist Papers

Hamilton recruited John Jay and James Madison to write *The Federalist Papers*. He made the largest contribution to that effort, writing 51 of the 85 essays published. Hamilton supervised the entire project, enlisted the participants, wrote most of the essays, and oversaw the publication. During the project, each person was responsible for their areas of expertise. Jay covered foreign relations. Madison covered the history of republics and confederacies, along with the anatomy of the new government. Hamilton covered the branches of government most pertinent to him: the executive and judicial branches, with some aspects of the Senate, military matters and taxation.[83] TheY first appeared in *The Independent Journal* on October 27, 1787.[83]

Treasury secretaryship (1789–1795) - - Report on Public Credit

Before the adjournment of the House in September 1789, they requested Hamilton to make a report on suggestions to improve the public credit by January 1790.[84] Hamilton had written to Robert Morris as early as 1781, that fixing the public credit will win their objective of independence.[84] The sources that Hamilton used ranged from Frenchmen such as Jacques Necker and Montesquieu to British writers such as Hume, Hobbes, and Malachy Postlethwaite.[85] While writing the report he also sought out suggestions from contemporaries such as John Witherspoon and Madison. Although they agreed on additional taxes such as distilleries and duties on imported liquors and land taxes, Madison feared that the securities from the government debt would fall into foreign hands.[86][68]:244–45

In the report, Hamilton felt that the securities should be paid at full value to their legitimate owners. He argued that liberty and property security were inseparable, and that the government should honor the contracts.[83]

Hamilton divided debt into national and state, and further divided national debt into foreign and domestic debt. During the Revolution, veterans were paid promissory notes and IOUs. Veterans sold the securities to speculators for fifteen to twenty cents on the dollar.[83][85]

Hamilton felt the money from the bonds should not go to the soldiers who had shown little faith in the country's future, but the speculators that had bought the bonds from the soldiers. As for state debts, Hamilton suggested consolidating them with the national debt and label it federal debt, for efficiency on a national scale.[83]

Due to bonds being traded well below their face value, the purchases would benefit the government as securities rose in price.[86]:300 When the report was submitted to the House of Representatives, detractors spoke against it. [86]:302,86:303

The involvement of those in Hamilton's circle such as Schuyler, William Duer, James Duane, Gouverneur Morris, and Rufus King as speculators was not favorable to those against the report, though Hamilton did not own or deal a share in the debt.[86]:304[68]:250 Madison spoke against it by February 1790.[86]:305 The compromise was seen as egregious to both Hamiltonians and their dissidents such as Maclay, and Madison's vote was defeated 36 to 13.[86]:305[68]:255

The fight for the national government to assume state debt was a longer issue and lasted over four months.[68]:297–98 Duer resigned as Assistant Secretary of the Treasury, the vote of assumption was voted down 31 to 29 on April 12.[68]:258–59

Hamilton bypassed slavery in Congress, after Quakers petitioned for abolition.[87]

Report on a National Bank - - History of central banking in the United States

Hamilton's *Report on a National Bank* was a projection from the first *Report on the Public Credit*. Although Hamilton had been forming ideas of a national bank as early as 1779,[68]:268 he had gathered ideas in various ways over the past eleven years. These included theories from Adam Smith,[88] extensive studies on the Bank of England, the blunders of the Bank of North America and his experience in establishing the Bank of New York.[89] He also used American records from James Wilson, Pelatiah Webster, Gouverneur Morris, and Tench Coxe.[89] He thought a National Bank could help in any sort of financial crisis.[90]

Hamilton suggested that Congress should charter the national bank with a capitalization of $10 million, one-fifth of which would be handled by the government. Since the government did not have the money, it would borrow the money from the bank itself, and repay the loan in ten even annual installments.[24]:194 The rest was to be available to individual investors.[90] The bank was to be governed by a twenty-five-member board of directors that was to represent a large majority of the private shareholders, which Hamilton considered essential for private direction.[68]:268 Hamilton's bank model had similarities to the Bank of England, except Hamilton wanted to exclude government from being involved in public debt, but provide a large, firm, and elastic money supply for economic development, among other differences.[24]:194–95 The tax revenue to initiate the bank was the same as he had previously proposed, increases on imported spirits: rum, liquor, and whiskey.[24]:195–96

It was generally held by critics that Hamilton was serving the interests of the Northeast by means of the bank,[91] and those of the agrarian lifestyle would not benefit from it.[68]:270 Among those critics was James Jackson of Georgia, who also attempted to refute the report by quoting from *The Federalist Papers*.[68]:270 Madison and Jefferson also opposed the bank bill.[24]:199–200 *The Whiskey Rebellion* showed the distance between the classes.[93]

Madison warned the Pennsylvania congress members that he would attack the bill as unconstitutional in the House and followed up on his threat.[24]:200 The bill eventually passed in an overwhelming fashion 39 to 20, on February 8, 1791.[68]:271

Washington hesitated to sign the bill, as he received suggestions from Attorney General Edmund Randolph and Thomas Jefferson. Jefferson dismissed the Necessary and Proper Clause as reasoning for a national bank, stating that the enumerated powers "can all be carried into execution without a bank."[68]:271–72 Along with Randolph and Jefferson's objections, Washington's involvement in the movement of the capital from Philadelphia is thought to be a reason for his hesitation.[45]:202–03,"[68]:272–73 Washington eventually signed the bill.[68]:272–73

Establishing the United States Mint (Establishes the American Monetary System

Because the most circulated coins in the United States at the time were Spanish currency, Hamilton proposed that minting a United States dollar weighing almost as much as the Spanish peso would be the simplest way to introduce a national currency.[95] Hamilton differed from European monetary policymakers in his desire to overprice gold relative to silver, on the grounds that the United States would always receive an influx of silver from the West Indies.[24]:197 Despite his own preference for a gold standard,[96] he ultimately issued a bimetallic currency at a fixed 15:1 ratio of silver to gold.[45]:197[97][98]

Hamilton proposed that the U.S. dollar should have fractional coins using decimals, rather than eighths like the Spanish coinage.[99] This innovation was originally suggested by Superintendent of Finance Robert Morris, with whom Hamilton corresponded after examining one of Morris's Nova Constellatio coins in 1783.[100] He also desired minting of small value coins, such as silver ten-cent and copper cent and half-cent pieces.[45]:198,[90][24]:198

By 1792, Hamilton's principles were adopted by Congress, resulting in the Coinage Act of 1792, and creation of the mint. There was to be a ten-dollar gold Eagle coin, a silver dollar, and fractional money, from one-half to fifty cents.[96][96]

Revenue Cutter Service

Smuggling and piracy was an issue before the Revolutionary War, and after the Revolution it was more problematic.[101] In response, Hamilton proposed to Congress to enact a naval police force called revenue cutters in order to patrol the waters and assist the custom collectors with confiscating contraband.[102][103]

Hamilton wanted the first ten cutters in different areas, from New England to Georgia.[102][104] Each of those cutters was to be armed with ten muskets and bayonets, twenty pistols, two chisels, one broad-ax and two lanterns. The fabric of the sails was to be domestically manufactured;[102] and provisions were made for food supply and etiquette.[102] Congress established the Revenue Cutter Service on August 4, 1790 - birth of US Coast Guard.[101]

Whiskey as tax revenue - - Whiskey Rebellion

One of the principal sources of revenue Hamilton prevailed upon Congress to approve was an excise tax on whiskey. In his first Tariff Bill in January 1790, Hamilton proposed to raise the three million dollars needed to pay for government operating expenses and interest on

100

domestic and foreign debts by an increase on duties on imported wines, distilled spirits, tea, coffee, and domestic spirits.[105]

In response of diversifying revenues, as three-fourths of revenue gathered was from commerce with Great Britain, Hamilton attempted once again in 1790 to implement an excise tax on both imported and domestic spirits.[106][107] He realized the loathing that the tax would receive in rural areas, but thought of the taxing of spirits more reasonable than land taxes.[108]

Opposition initially came from Pennsylvania's House of Representatives. William Maclay had noted that not even the Pennsylvanian legislators had been able to enforce excise taxes in the western regions of the state.[108] Hamilton was aware of the potential difficulties and proposed inspectors to search distillers.[109] Inspectors were also tarred and feathered, blindfolded, and whipped. Hamilton had attempted to reduce tax rates, but it did not suffice.[110]

Strong opposition to the whiskey tax erupted into the *Whiskey Rebellion* in 1794; in Western Pennsylvania and western Virginia, whiskey was the basic export product fundamental to the local economy. Hamilton accompanied President Washington to the rebellion's site with General Henry "Light Horse Harry" Lee, and more federal troops than were ever assembled in one place during the Revolution. This intimidated the leaders, ending the rebellion.[110]

Manufacturing and industry

Hamilton's next report was his *Report on Manufactures*. Although he was requested by Congress on January 15, 1790, for a report for manufacturing that would expand the United States' independence, the report was not submitted until December 5, 1791.[68]:274,277 In the report, Hamilton quoted from *Wealth of Nations*[45]:233 thus calling for a far greater reliance on manufacturing for export. Hamilton refuted Smith's ideas of government noninterference.[24]:244 Hamilton also thought that the US, being a primarily agrarian country, would be at a disadvantage in dealing with Europe.[111] Hamilton stated that agriculturists' would be advanced by manufactures,[68]:276 agriculture was as productive as manufacturing.[24]:233[68]:276

In 1791, Hamilton, along with Coxe and several entrepreneurs from New York City and Philadelphia formed the *Society for the Establishment of Useful Manufactures*, a private industrial corporation. In May 1792, the directors decided to examine the Great Falls of the Passaic River in New Jersey as a location for a manufacturing center. On July 4, 1792, the directors met Philip Schuyler at Abraham Godwin's hotel on the Passaic River. The location at Great Falls of the Passaic River in New Jersey was selected due to access to raw materials, it being densely inhabited, and having access to water power from the falls of the Passaic.[24]:231

Jay Treaty

When France and Britain went to war in early 1793, all four members of the Cabinet were consulted on what to do. They and Washington unanimously agreed to remain neutral, and to have the French ambassador, recalled.[112]:336–41 However, in 1794, policy toward Britain became a major point of contention. Hamilton and the Federalists wished for more trade with Britain, the largest trading partner of the United States. The Republicans saw monarchist Britain as the main threat to republicanism and proposed instead to start a trade war.[68]:327–28

To avoid war, Washington sent Chief Justice John Jay to negotiate with the British, with Hamilton writing Jay's instructions. Republicans denounced the treaty, but Hamilton mobilized support.[113] The Jay Treaty passed the Senate in 1795.

Resignation from public office

- Hamilton's wife suffered a miscarriage[114] while he was absent during the Whiskey Rebellion.[115] In the wake of this, Hamilton tendered his resignation.[116] Before leaving his post, Hamilton submitted the *Report on a Plan for the Further Support of Public Credit* to Congress to curb the debt problem.[116]
- The two-party system began to emerge as political parties developed. A congressional caucus, led by Madison, Jefferson, and William Branch Giles, began in opposition to Hamilton's financial programs. Hamilton allies began to call themselves Federalists.[117][118]
- In 1801, Hamilton established a daily newspaper, the *New York Evening Post*, and brought in William Coleman as its editor.[119] Hamilton's and Jefferson each sought to be Washington's principal and most trusted advisor.[120][121]

Post-secretaryship (1795–1804) - - 1796 presidential election

Hamilton influenced Washington in composition of his farewell address, he consulted Madison for a draft that was used in a similar manner to Hamilton's.[122][123]

In the election of 1796, under the Constitution as it stood then, each of the presidential electors had two votes, which they were to cast for different men from different states. The Federalists planned to deal with this by having all their electors vote for John Adams, then vice president, and all but a few for Thomas Pinckney.[124]

Adams resented Hamilton's influence and considered him overambitious and scandalous in his private life. Hamilton compared Adams unfavorably with Washington and thought him too unstable to be president.[125] Hamilton urged all the northern electors to vote for Adams and Pinckney, but he cooperated with Edward Rutledge to have South Carolina's electors vote for Jefferson and Pinckney. The Federalists found out about it and northern Federalists voted for Adams but not Pinckney, Pinckney came in third and Jefferson was VP.[126] Adams resented the felt his service to the nation was much more extensive than Pinckney's.[127]

Quasi-War

During the military build-up of the Quasi-War with France, and with endorsement of Washington, Adams appointed Hamilton a major general of the army. At Washington's insistence, Hamilton was made senior major general, prompting Continental Army major general Henry Knox to decline believing it degrading to serve beneath Hamilton.[129][130]

Hamilton served as inspector general of the United States Army from July 18, 1798, to June 15, 1800. Because Washington was unwilling to leave Mount Vernon, Hamilton was the *de facto* head of the army, to Adams's displeasure. If war broke out with France, Hamilton argued that the army should conquer the North American colonies of France's ally, Spain, bordering the United States.[131] Hamilton was prepared to march through the Southern US.[132][133]

1800 presidential election

In November 1799, the Alien and Sedition Acts had left one Democratic-Republican newspaper, the *New Daily Advertiser* functioning in New York City. The last newspaper reprinted an article saying Hamilton attempted to purchase the *Philadelphia Aurora* to close it down, with "British secret service money". Hamilton urged the New York Attorney General to prosecute the publisher for seditious libel, and the prosecution compelled the owner to close.[134]

In the 1800 election, Hamilton worked to defeat the Democratic-Republicans, but also John Adams.[68]:392–99 Aaron Burr had won New York for Jefferson in May via the New York City legislative elections. Now Hamilton proposed a direct election, with carefully drawn districts where each district's voters would choose an elector—such as the Federalists would split the electoral vote of New York. Jay, who had resigned from the Supreme Court to be governor of New York, wrote on it would not become me to adopt," and declined to reply.[135]

Adams was running with Charles Cotesworth Pinckney. Hamilton toured New England, urging northern electors to support Pinckney and he intrigued South Carolina.[24]:350–51

Jefferson had beaten Adams, but both he and Aaron Burr had received 73 votes in the Electoral College. With Jefferson and Burr tied, the House of Representatives had to choose between the two men.[24]:352[68]:399 Several Federalists who opposed Jefferson supported Burr, and for the first 35 ballots, Jefferson was denied a majority. Before the 36th ballot, Hamilton threw his weight behind Jefferson, and Burr lost.[24]:350–51

Even though Hamilton did not like Jefferson and disagreed with him on many issues, he viewed Jefferson as the lesser of two evils. Hamilton spoke of Jefferson as being "not so dangerous" and of Burr as a "mischievous enemy" to the measure of the past administration.[192] The fact that Burr was a northerner and not a Virginian, that Federalist representatives voted for him.[136] Hamilton wrote many letters to friends in Congress to see otherwise.[24]:352[68]:401 Burr would become vice president after losing to Jefferson.[137][24]:353[95]:401

Duel with Burr and death!

Soon after Lewis' gubernatorial victory, the *Albany Register* published Charles D. Cooper's letters, citing Hamilton's opposition to Burr and alleging that Hamilton had expressed "a still more despicable opinion" of the vice president at an upstate New York dinner party.[140][141] Cooper claimed that the letter was intercepted after relaying the information, but stated he was "unusually cautious" in recollecting the information from the dinner.[142]

Burr, sensing an attack on his honor, and recovering from his defeat, demanded an apology in the form of a letter. Hamilton would also have been accused of recanting Cooper's letter out of cowardice.[68]:423–24 A duel was arranged on June 27, 1804.[68]:426

Before the duel, Hamilton wrote an explanation of his decision to participate intending to "throw away" his shot[143] due to his desire to be available for future political matters.[144]

The duel began at dawn on July 11, 1804, along the west bank of the Hudson River, Weehawken, New Jersey.[145] The duel took place near the location of the duel that ended the life of Hamilton's son, Philip, three years earlier.[146]

VP Burr shot Hamilton, delivering what proved to be a fatal wound. Hamilton's shot was said to have broken a tree branch directly above Burr's head.[147] Neither of the seconds, could determine who fired first.[148] After final visits from family and friends, suffering 31 hours, Hamilton died. July 12, 1804.

References
1. Ramsing, Holger Utke (1939) "Alexander Hamilton". Personalhistorisk Tidsskrift (Danish): 225–70
2. Chernow, 2005, p. 8.
3. Randall, Willard Sterne (2004). Foreword. Practical Proceedings in the Supreme Court of the State of New York. By Hamilton, Alexander. New York: New York Law Journal. p. ix.
4. "To Alexander Hamilton from Walton and Cruger, [19 Oct 1771]". Founders Online. National Archives. fn.1. Arch from Syrett, Harold C., ed. (1961) [1768–1778]. Papers Alexander Hamilton. Vol. 1. NY: Columbia U Press. p. 8 n.1.
5. "Letter on the hurricane of August 1772". Archived Jan 8, 2022. Retrieved January 8, 2022.
6. Chernow, p. 37.
7. Gordon, John Steele (April–May 2004). "Self Made Founder". American Heritage. Arch 11/19/08.

8. O'Brien, Michael J. (1916) [October 30, 1915]. "Field Day of the American Irish Historical Society Held in New York City". The Journal of the American Irish Historical Society. 1 (1): 144.
9. Newton (2015), p. 64.
10. Newton (2019), pp. 227–28. "Thus, when Alexander Hamilton arrived in Elizabethtown in October 1772 and moved in with the Livingstons, they lived in this house rented from Jacob De Hart."
11. Adair and Harvey.
12. Cornfield, Josh (July 7, 2016). "Did Martha Washington Really Name a Cat After Alex Hamilton?". Boston Globe.
13. Newton (2015), p. 69.
14. Randall, p. 78.
15. Chernow, p. 53.
16. Cardozo, Ernest Abraham (1902). A History of the Philolexian Society of Columbia University from 1802–1902. New York:.
17. Miller, p. 9.
18. Mitchell 1:65–73; Miller, p. 19.
19. Newton (2015), pp. 116, 117, 573.
20. Mitchell, I:74–75.
21. Robert Troup "Memoir of General Hamilton", March 22, 1810
22. Chernow, Ron. Alexander Hamilton. Penguin Press, (2004) (ISBN 1-59420-009-2).
23. Newton (2015), pp. 127–28.
24. McDonald, Forrest (1982). Alexander Hamilton: A Biography. W W Norton Company. ISBN 978-0-393-30048-2
25. Chernow, p. 72.
26. Stryker, William S. (1898). Battles of Trenton and Princeton Boston: Houghton, Mifflin & Co. pp. 158–59.
27. Ketchum, Richard (1999). The Winter Soldiers: The Battles for Trenton and Princeton (1st Owl Books ed.). Holt Paperbacks. p. 310. ISBN 978-0-8050-6098-0.
28. Stryker, William S. (1898). Battles of Trenton and Princeton . Boston: Houghton, Mifflin & Co. p290
29. Chernow, pp. 128–29.
30. Chernow, pp. 654–55.
31. James Alexander Hamilton obituary Arch Feb 25, 2021, Wayback Machine, NYT, Sept 26, 1878.
32. "Rundown on Alexander Hamilton's 8 Children". Mental Floss. March 7, 2022. Arch&Retr Jan 13, 2023.
33. Newton (2015), pp. 189–90
34. Newton (2015), pp. 189–90.
35. Lefkowitz, Arthur S., George Washington's Indispensable Men: The 32 Aides-de-Camp, Stackpole Books, 2003, pp. 15, 108.
36. Hendrickson, R (1976) Hamilton I (1757–1789). New York: Mason/Charter. p. 119. ISBN 978-0-88405-139-8
37. Chernow, p. 90.
38. Lodge, pp. 1:15–20
39. Miller, pp. 23–26.
40. Chernow 2004, pp. 151–52
41. Chernow 2004, pp. 153–159
42. Murray, p. 69.
43. Mitchell, pp. I:254–60.
44. Morris, Richard Brandon (1970). Peacemakers: Great Powers and American Independence. Harper & Row.
45. Murray, Joseph A. (2007). Alexander Hamilton: America's Forgotten Founder. Algora Publishing. p. 74.
46. Chernow, pp. 165–71
47. Syrett, p. III:117; for a one-year term beginning the "first Monday in November next", arrived in Philadelphia between November 18 and 25, and resigned July 1783.
48. Martin and Lender, pp. 109, 160: at first for seven years, increased to life after Arnold's treason.
49. Tucker, p. 470.
50. Kohn; Ellis 2004, pp. 141–44.
51. Kohn, p. 196.
52. Chernow, pp. 177–80.
53. Hamilton's letter of February 13, 1783; Syrett, pp. III:253–55.
54. Washington to Hamilton, March 4 and 12, 1783; Kohn; Martin and Lender, pp. 189–90.
55. "To Alexander Hamilton from George Washington, 4 April 1783". Founders Online. National Archives.
56. Rakove, pp. 322, 325.
57. Brant, p. 108.
58. Chernow, pp. 177–80
59. Chernow, pp. 182–83
60. "Timeline | Articles and Essays | Alexander Hamilton Papers | Digital Collections | Library of Congress". Library of Congress.
61. Chernow, pp. 197–99.
62. Wallack, Todd (Dec 20, 2011). "Which bank is the oldest? Accounts vary". The Boston Globe.
63. Morris, Richard B. (1988). Forging of the Union, 1781–1789. Harper & Row. p. 255. ISBN 978-0-06-015733-3.
64. "Founders Online: From Alexander Hamilton to Nathaniel Chipman, 22 July 1788". founders.archives.gov.
65. "Vermont". History.com. Oct 31, 2019. Archived & Retr Jan 25, 2023.
66. Columbia College (New York, N.Y.) (1826). Catalogue of Columbia College in the City of New-York: names of trustees, officers, graduates, together with a list of all academical honours conferred by the institution from A.D. 1758 to A.D. 1826. U.S. National Library of Medicine. New York: Printed by T. and J. Swords.
67. "Alexander Hamilton CC 1778". Columbia College Alumni Association. Dec 14, 2016. Arch & Retr Feb 13, 2023.
68. Schachner, Nathan (1946). Alexander Hamilton. New York: D. Appleton Century Co. ASIN B0006AQUG2.

69. Morton, p. 169.
70. Chernow, pp. 227–28.
71. Morton, p. 131.
72. Chernow, p. 232.
73. Madison, James (2005). Larson, Edward J.; Winship, Michael P. (eds.). Constitutional Convention: A Narrative History from Notes of James Madison. New York: Modern Library. pp. 50–51. ISBN 978-0-8129-7517-8.
74. Stewart, 2016, p. 33
75. Mitchell, pp. I:397 ff.
76. Brant, p. 195.
77. Denboer, p. 196.
78. Kaplan, p. 75.
79. Denboer, p. 197.
80. Chernow, pp. 247–48.
81. Chernow, pp. 252–57.
82. Murray, p. 121.
83. Chernow, pp. 296–99.
84. Chernow, p. 121.
85. Murray, p. 124.
86. Chernow, pp. 300–05.
87. Chernow, p. 307.
88. Kaplan, p. 21.
89. Cooke, p. 88.
90. Sylla, Richard; Wright, Robert E; Cowen, David J (2009). "Alexander Hamilton, Central Banker: Crisis Management during the U.S. Financial Panic of 1792". Business History Review. 83 (1): 61–86. doi:10.1017/s0007680500000209.
91. Cooke, p. 89.
92. Cooke, p. 90.
93. Bogin, Ruth (July 1988). "Petitioning and the New Moral Economy of Post-Revolutionary America". The William and Mary Quarterly. 45 (3): 392–425. doi:10.2307/1923642. ISSN 0043-5597. JSTOR 1923642.
94. Mitchell, p. 118.
95. Engerman; Gallman, p. 644.
96. Studentski; Krooss, p. 62.
97. Nussbaum, Arthur (Nov 1937). "Law of the Dollar". Columbia Law Review (citing 2 Annals of Cong. 2115 (1789–1791)). 37 (7): 1057–91. doi:10.2307/1116782. ISSN 0010-1958. JSTOR 1116782.
98. Cooke, p. 87.
99. Engerman; Gallman, pp. 644–45.
100. James Ferguson, John Catanzariti, Elizabeth M. Nuxoll and Mary Gallagher, eds. The Papers of Robert Morris, University of Pittsburgh Press, 1973–1999 (Volume 7, pp. 682–713)
101. Gibowicz, p. 256.
102. Chernow, p. 340.
103. Chernow, p. 32.
104. Storbridge, p. 2.
105. Stockwell, p. 357.
106. Chernow, pp. 342–43.
107. Murray, p. 141.
108. Murray, pp. 141–42.
109. Chernow, p. 468.
110. Mitchell, I:308–31.
111. Cooke, p. 100.
112. Elkins, Stanley M.; McKitrick, Eric (1994). Age of Federalism: Early American Republic, 1788–1800. Oxford U Press
113. Estes, Todd (2000). "Shaping the Politics of Public Opinion: Federalists and the Jay Treaty Debate". Journal of the Early Republic. 20 (3): 393–422. doi:10.2307/3125063. JSTOR 3125063.
114. Elkins, Stanley M.; McKitrick, Eric (1994). The Age of Federalism: The Early American Republic, 1788–1800. Oxford University Press. ISBN 978-0-19-506890-0.
115. Estes, Todd (2000). "Shaping the Politics of Public Opinion: Federalists and the Jay Treaty Debate". Journal of the Early Republic. 20 (3): 393–422. doi:10.2307/3125063. JSTOR 3125063.
116. Hamilton, Alexander. "Letter from Alexander Hamilton to Angelica Schuyler Church, 6 March 1795". Founders Online. National Archives. Arch Sept 20, 2022. Retr Dec 24, 2019.
117. "Madison to Jefferson". March 2, 1794. Arch Nov 14, 2017. Retr Oct 14, 2006.
118. See also Smith (2004), p. 832.
119. Allan Nevins, The Evening Post: A Century of Journalism (1922) ch. 1 online
120. Cooke, pp. 109–10
121. Lomask, pp. 139–40, 216–17, 220.
122. Garrity and Spalding, pp. 47, 50–55.
123. Murray, p. 207.
124. Chernow, p. 117.
125. Chernow, p. 510.
126. Elkins and McKitrick; Age of Federalism, pp. 523–28, 859.

127. Elkins and McKitrick, p. 515.
128. Brookhiser, Richard (2011).Alexander Hamilton, American. Simon & Schuster. p. 3. ISBN 978-1-4391-3545-7
129. Chernow, pp. 558–60.
130. Kaplan, pp. 147–49
131. Morison and Commager, p. 327; Mitchell II:445.
132. Ellis, Joseph J. (2004). His Excellency. Vintage Books. pp. 250–55. ISBN 978-1-4000-3253-2.
133. Hamilton, Neil A. (2010). Presidents: A Biographical Dictionary. Infobase. p. 18. ISBN 978-1-4381-2751-4.
134. James Morton Smith, Freedom's Fetters: Alien and Sedition Laws, American Civil Liberties (Ithaca,1966), p.400–17
135. Monaghan, pp. 419–21.
136. Harper, p. 259.
137. Isenberg, Nancy. Fallen Founder: Life of Aaron Burr, New York: Penguin Books, 2007, pp. 211–12.
138. T Jefferson Encyclopedia "Aaron Burr" Monticello.org.Jefferson Foundation Arch&Retr 12/3/19
139. Harper, John Lamberton (2004). American Machiavelli: Alexander Hamilton and the Origins of US Foreign Policy. Cambridge, New York: Cambridge U Press. pp. 260–61. ISBN 978-0-521-83485-8. p. 260: The result could be seen as a moral victory for Hamilton, but had he contributed to it? The answer is perhaps and to a degree.
140. Freeman, Joanne B. (April 1996). "Dueling as Politics: Reinterpreting the Burr–Hamilton Duel". William and Mary Quarterly (subscription). Third Series. 53 (2): 289–318. doi:10.2307/2947402. JSTOR 2947402.
141. Kennedy, Burr, Hamilton, and Jefferson, p. 72.
142. Chernow, pp. 680–81
143. Hamilton, Alexander. "Statement on Impending Duel with Aaron Burr, (28 June – 10 July 1804)". Founders Online. National Archives. Arch Feb 8, 2017. Retr Feb 7, 2017.
144. Freeman, Joanne B. (April 1996). "Dueling as Politics: Reinterpreting Burr–Hamilton Duel". William and Mary Quarterly Third Series. 53 (2): 289–318. doi:10.2307/2947402. JSTOR 2947402.
145. Adams, pp. 93–94.
146. Roberts, Warren (2010). A Place in History: Albany In The Age Of Revolution. Albany, NY: Excelsior Editions/State University of New York Press. p. 135. ISBN 978-1-4384-3329-5.
147. Chernow, p. 117
148. Fleming, p. 345

Sources

- Brant, Irving (1970). Fourth President: A Life of James Madison. Indianapolis: Bobbs-Merill. A 1 vol
- Chernow, Ron (2005). Alexander Hamilton. Penguin Press. ISBN 978-0-14-303475-9. OL 35261741M.
- Cooke, Jacob Ernest (1982). Alexander Hamilton. Charles Scribner's Sons. ISBN 978-0-684-17344-3.
- Denboer, Gordon R. (1987). Documentary History of First Federal Elections, 1788–1790, Vol III. Madison: U of Wisconsin Press. ISBN 978-0-299-10650-8. Arch Dec 7, 2023. Retr July 11, 2020.
- Fleming, Thomas (2000). Duel: Alexander Hamilton, Aaron Burr, and the Future of America. Basic Books.
- Gibowicz, Charles J. (2007). Mess Night Traditions. Author House. ISBN 978-1-4259-8446-5.
- Harper, John Lamberton (2004). American Machiavelli: Alexander Hamilton and the Origins of US Foreign Policy. New York: Cambridge University Press. ISBN 978-0-521-83485-8.
- Kaplan, Edward (1999). The Bank of the United States and the American Economy. Westport, CT: Praeger. ISBN 978-0-313-30866-6. Archived Dec 7, 2023. Retr July 11, 2020.
- Kaplan, Lawrence S. (2001). A Hamilton: Ambivalent Anglophile. Rowman and Littlefield. ISBN 978-0-8420-2878-3
- Kohn, Richard H. (1970). "The Inside History of the Newburgh Conspiracy: America and the Coup d'Etat". The William and Mary Quarterly. 27 (2): 188–220. doi:10.2307/1918650. JSTOR 1918650.
- Lomask, Milton (1979). Aaron Burr, Years from Princeton to Vice President, 1756–1805. New York: Farrar, Straus & Giroux. ISBN 978-0-374-10016-2. The first vol of two, contains Hamilton's lifetime.
- Miller, John Chester (1959). Alexander Hamilton: Portrait in Paradox. Harper & Row. ISBN 978-0-06-012975-0.
- Mitchell, Broadus (1957). Alexander Hamilton: Youth to Maturity (1755–1788), Vol 1. Macmillan.
- Mitchell, Broadus (1957). Alexander Hamilton: National Adventure (1788–1804), Vol 2. Macmillan.
- Monaghan, Frank (1972) [1935]. John Jay: Defender of Liberty Against Kings & Peoples, New York: AMS Press. ISBN 0404046479. LCCN 74-153339. OCLC 424884.Murray, Joseph A. (2007). Alexander Hamilton: America's Forgotten Founder. Algora. ISBN 978-0-87586-501-0.
- Rakove, Jack N. (1979). The beginnings of National Politics: an interpretive history of the Continental Congress. New York: Knopf. ISBN 978-0-394-42370-8.
- Steward, David O. (2016). America. Simon and Schuster. ISBN 978-1-4516-8859-7.
- Tucker, Spencer C. (2014). The Encyclopedia of the Wars of the Early American Republic, 1783–1812 [3 volumes]: A Political, Social, and Military History. ABC-CLIO. ISBN 978-1-59884-156-5.

THOMAS JEFFERSON

Thomas Jefferson (April 13, 1743[b] – July 4, 1826) was an American statesman, planter, diplomat, lawyer, architect, philosopher, and Founding Father who was third president of the United States.[6] He was the primary author of the Declaration of Independence. Following the American Revolutionary War and before becoming president in 1801, Jefferson was the nation's first U.S. secretary of state under George Washington and then second vice president under John Adams. Jefferson was a leading proponent of democracy, republicanism, and natural rights, and he produced formative documents and decisions at state, national, and international levels.

Early life and career of Thomas Jefferson

Jefferson was born on April 13, 1743 at the family's Shadwell Plantation in the British Colony of Virginia, third of ten children.[8] He was of English and Welsh descent, and was born a British subject.[9] His father, Peter Jefferson, was a planter and surveyor who died when Jefferson was fourteen; his mother was Jane Randolph.[c] Peter Jefferson moved his family to Tuckahoe Plantation in 1745 on the death of William Randolph III, the plantation's owner and Jefferson's friend, who in his will had named Peter guardian of Randolph's children. The Jeffersons returned to Shadwell before October 1753.[11]

Peter died in 1757, and his estate was divided between his sons Thomas and Randolph.[12] John Harvie Sr. became 13-year-old Thomas' guardian.[13]

Thomas inherited approximately 5,000 acres which included Monticello, and he assumed full legal authority over the property at age 21.[14]

Education and early family life

Jefferson began his education together with the Randolph children at Tuckahoe under tutors.[15] Thomas' father Peter, who was self-taught and regretted not having a formal education, entered Thomas into an English school at age five. In 1752, at age nine, he attended a local school run by a Scottish Presbyterian minister and began studying the natural world, which he grew to love. At this time, he began studying Latin, Greek, and French, while learning to ride horses as well. Thomas also read books from his father's modest library.[16] He was taught from 1758 to 1760 by the Reverend James Maury near Gordonsville, Virginia, where he studied history, science, and the classics while boarding with Maury's family.[16][17] Jefferson came to know various American Indians, including the Cherokee chief Ostenaco, who often stopped at Shadwell to visit on their way to Williamsburg to trade.[18][19] In Williamsburg, the young Jefferson met and came to admire Patrick Henry.[20]

Jefferson entered the College of William & Mary in Williamsburg, Virginia, in 1761, at the age of eighteen, and studied mathematics, metaphysics, and philosophy with William Small. Under Small's tutelage, Jefferson encountered ideas of British Empiricists, John Locke, Francis Bacon, and Isaac Newton. Small introduced Jefferson to George Wythe and Francis Fauquier. Small, Wythe, and Fauquier recognized Jefferson as a man of exceptional ability and included him in their inner circle, where he became a regular member of their Friday dinner parties. Jefferson later wrote that, while there, he "heard more common good sense, more rational & philosophical conversations than in all the rest of my life".[21]

Jefferson concluded his formal studies in April 1762.[24] He read the law under Wythe's tutelage while working as a law clerk in his office.[25][26] Wythe was so impressed with Jefferson that he later bequeathed his entire library to him.[27]

Jefferson treasured his books and amassed three sizable libraries. He began assembling his first library, which grew to 200 volumes, in his youth. It included books inherited from his father and left to him by Wythe.[29] His second library replenished the first. It grew to 1,250 titles by 1773, and to nearly 6,500 volumes by 1814.[30]

He organized his books into three broad categories corresponding with elements of the human mind: memory, reason, and imagination.[31] After British forces burnt the Library of Congress during the 1814 Burning of Washington, Jefferson sold his second library to the U.S. government for $23,950, hoping to help jumpstart the Library of Congress's rebuilding. He used a portion of the proceeds to pay off some of his large debt. Jefferson soon resumed collecting what amounted to his third personal library, writing to John Adams, "I cannot live without books."[32][33] By the time of his death, the library had grown to nearly 2,000 volumes.[34]

Lawyer and House of Burgesses

Jefferson was admitted to the Virginia bar in 1767, and lived with his mother at Shadwell.[35] He represented Albemarle County in the Virginia House of Burgesses from 1769 until 1775.[36] He pursued reforms to slavery, including writing and sponsoring legislation to strip power from the royal governor and courts. Jefferson persuaded his cousin to spearhead the legislation's passage, against strong opposition in a state economy largely agrarian.[37]

Jefferson took seven cases of freedom-seeking enslaved people[38] and waived his fee for one he said should be freed before the minimum statutory age for emancipation.[39] Jefferson invoked natural law, arguing "everyone comes into the world with a right to his own person and using it at his own will ... This is what is called personal liberty, and is given him by the author of nature, because it is necessary for his own sustenance." The judge stopped and ruled against his client. As consolation, Jefferson gave his client some money, which was conceivably used to aid his escape shortly thereafter.[39] Jefferson's underlying intellectual argument that all people were entitled by their creator to what he labeled a "natural right" to liberty is one he would incorporate as he set about authoring the Declaration of Independence.[40] He also took on 68 cases for the General Court of Virginia in 1767.[41]

Jefferson wrote a resolution calling for a "Day of Fasting and Prayer" and a boycott of British goods in protest of British Parliament passing the Intolerable Acts. Jefferson's resolution was expanded into *A Summary View of the Rights of British America*, in which he argued people have the right to govern themselves.[42]

Monticello, marriage, and family

In 1768, Jefferson began constructing his residence, Monticello, whose name in Italian means "Little Mountain", on a hilltop overlooking his 5,000-acre plantation. He spent most of his adult life designing Monticello as an architect and was quoted as saying, "Architecture is my delight, and putting up, and pulling down, one of my favorite amusements."[44] Construction was done mostly by local masons and carpenters, assisted by Jefferson's slaves.[45] Turning Monticello into a neoclassical masterpiece in the Palladian style was his perennial project.[46]

On January 1, 1772, Jefferson married his third cousin[47] Martha Wayles Skelton, a 23-year-old widow.[48][49] Biographer Dumas Malone described the marriage as the happiest period of Jefferson's life.[50] Jefferson often accompanied her on the violin or cello.[51] During their ten years of marriage, Martha bore six children.[52][55] Martha's father John Wayles died in 1773, and the couple inherited 11,000 acres. The debts took Jefferson years to satisfy.[48]

Shortly before her death, Martha made Jefferson promise never to marry again, telling him she could not bear to have another mother raise her children.[56] Jefferson was grief-stricken. He emerged after three weeks, taking long secluded rides with his daughter Martha.[55][57]

After serving as U.S. Secretary of State from 1790 to 1793, Jefferson returned to Monticello and initiated a remodeling based on architectural concepts he had learned in Europe. The work continued throughout his presidency, completed in 1809.[58][59]

Revolutionary War   Declaration of Independence

Jefferson was primary author of the Declaration of Independence.[61] At 33, he was one of the youngest delegates to Second Continental Congress at the outbreak of the Revolution, where a Declaration of Independence from Britain was favored.[62] Jefferson was inspired by Enlightenment ideals of sanctity of the individual, and writings of Locke and Montesquieu.[63]

Jefferson sought out John Adams, a delegate from Massachusetts and an emerging leader in the Congress.[64] They became close friends, and Adams supported Jefferson's appointment to the Committee of Five, charged by the Congress with authoring a declaration of independence. The five chosen were Adams, Jefferson, Benjamin Franklin, Robert R. Livingston, and Roger Sherman. The committee initially thought that Adams should write the document, but Adams chose Jefferson. His choice was due to Jefferson being a Virginian, popular, and considered a good writer by Adams.

Jefferson's preamble is regarded as an enduring statement on individual and human rights, and the phrase "all men are created equal" has been called "one of the best-known sentences in the English language". The Declaration of Independence, historian Joseph Ellis wrote, represents "the most potent and consequential words in American history".[69][72]

Virginia state legislator and governor

At the start of the Revolution, Colonel Jefferson was named commander of the Albemarle County Militia on September 26, 1775.[73] He was then elected to the Virginia House of Delegates for Albemarle County in September 1776, when finalizing the state constitution was a priority.[74][75] For nearly three years, he assisted with the constitution and was especially proud of his Bill for Establishing Religious Freedom, which prohibited state support of religious institutions or enforcement of religious doctrine.[76] The bill failed to pass, as did his legislation to disestablish the Anglican Church, both were revived by James Madison.[77]

In 1778, Jefferson was given the task of revising the state's laws. He proposed statutes that provided for general education, which he considered the basis of "republican government".[74] Jefferson also was concerned that Virginia's powerful landed gentry were becoming a hereditary aristocracy and took the lead in abolishing what he called "feudal and unnatural distinctions."[78] He targeted laws such as entail and primogeniture by which a deceased landowner's oldest son was vested with all land ownership and power.[78]

Member of Congress

Jefferson was appointed a Virginia delegate to the Congress of the Confederation organized following the peace treaty with Great Britain in 1783. He was a member of the committee on foreign exchange rates and recommended an American currency based on the decimal system.[99] He advised the formation of the Committee of the States to fill the power vacuum when Congress was in recess.[100] The committee met when Congress adjourned, but disagreements rendered it dysfunctional.[101]

He was the principal author of the Land Ordinance of 1784, whereby Virginia ceded to the national government the vast area that it claimed northwest of the Ohio River. He insisted that this territory should not become colonial territory by any of the thirteen states, but that it should be divided into sections that could become states. He plotted borders for nine new states in their initial stages and wrote an ordinance banning slavery in all the nation's territories. Congress made extensive revisions and rejected the ban on slavery.[102][103] The provisions banning slavery, known as the "Jefferson Proviso", were modified and implemented three years later in the Northwest Ordinance of 1787.[102]

Minister to France

On May 7, 1784, Jefferson was appointed to join Franklin and Adams in Paris as Minister Plenipotentiary for Negotiating Treaties of Amity and Commerce with Great Britain and other countries.[104] With his daughter, he departed in July 1784, arriving in Paris the next month.[106][107] Jefferson had Patsy educated at the Pentemont Abbey. Less than a year later he was assigned to succeed Franklin as Minister to France. French foreign minister Count de Vergennes commented, "You replace Monsieur Franklin, I hear." Jefferson replied, "I *succeed*. No man can replace him."[108] In five Paris years, Jefferson shaped U.S. foreign policy.[109]

During the summer of 1786, Jefferson arrived in London to meet with John Adams, the US Ambassador to Britain. Adams had official access to George III and arranged a meeting between Jefferson and the king. Jefferson later described the king's reception of the men as "ungracious." George III turned his back on both. Jefferson returned to France in August.[111]

While in France, Jefferson became a regular companion of the Marquis de Lafayette, a French hero of the American Revolution, and Jefferson used his influence to procure trade agreements with France.[114][115] As the French Revolution began, he allowed his Paris residence, the Hôtel de Langeac, to be used for meetings by Lafayette and other republicans. He was in Paris during the storming of the Bastille and consulted with Lafayette while the latter drafted the Declaration of the Rights of Man and of the Citizen.[116] Jefferson often found his mail opened by postmasters, so he invented his own enciphering device, the "Wheel Cipher"; he wrote important communications in code for the rest of his career.[117] Unable to attend the 1787 Convention, Jefferson supported the Constitution and the promised Bill of Rights.[118] Jefferson left Paris in September 1789.[119] He remained a firm supporter of the French Revolution.[120]

Secretary of State

Soon after returning from France, Jefferson accepted Washington's invitation to serve as Secretary of State.[121] He opposed a national debt, preferring that each state retire its own, in contrast to Secretary of the Treasury Alexander Hamilton, who desired consolidation of states' debts by the federal government.[122] Hamilton also had bold plans to establish national credit and a national bank, but Jefferson strenuously opposed and attempted to undermine his agenda, which nearly led Washington to dismiss him from the cabinet. He later left the cabinet.[123]

Second major issue was the capital's permanent location. Hamilton favored a capital close to the Northeast, while Washington, Jefferson, and other agrarians wanted it further south.[124] After lengthy deadlock, the Compromise of 1790 was struck, locating the capital on the Potomac River, the federal government assumed war debts of the 13 states.[124]

Jefferson and political protegé Congressman James Madison founded the *National Gazette* in 1791, along with author Phillip Freneau, to counter Hamilton's Federalist policies, which Hamilton was promoting through the influential Federalist newspaper the *Gazette of the United States*. The *National Gazette* made particular criticism of the policies promoted by Hamilton, often through anonymous essays signed by the pen name *Brutus*, which were written by Madison.[126] In Spring 1791, Jefferson and Madison took a vacation to Vermont; Jefferson had been suffering from migraines and was tiring of the in-fighting with Hamilton.[127]

Jefferson became alarmed at the political rivalries taking shape; he wrote Washington, imploring him to run for reelection that year as a unifying influence.[128] Historians see this letter as the earliest delineation of Democratic-Republican Party principles.[129] Jefferson, Madison, and other Democratic-Republican organizers favored states' rights and local control and opposed federal power, whereas Hamilton sought more power for the federal government.[130]

After the Washington administration negotiated the Jay Treaty with Britain in 1794, Jefferson saw a cause around which to rally his party and organized a national opposition from Monticello.[133] The treaty, designed by Hamilton, aimed to reduce tensions and increase trade. Jefferson warned it would increase British influence and subvert republicanism, calling it "the boldest act [Hamilton and Jay] ever ventured on to undermine the government".[134] The Treaty passed, but expired during Jefferson's presidency and was not renewed. Jefferson continued his pro-France stance; during the Reign of Terror, he declined to disavow the revolution: "To back away from France would be to undermine the cause of republicanism in America."[135]

Election of 1796 and vice presidency

In the presidential campaign of 1796, Jefferson lost the electoral college to Federalist John Adams 71–68 and was elected vice president. He allowed the Senate to freely conduct debates and confined his participation to procedural issues he called an "honorable and easy" role.[136] In 1800, he published his notes on procedure as *A Manual of Parliamentary Practice*.[137] He cast three tie-breaking votes in the Senate.

In four confidential talks with French consul Joseph Létombe in the spring of 1797, Jefferson predicted that his rival would serve only one term. He also encouraged France to invade England and advised Létombe to stall any American envoys sent to Paris.[138] This toughened the tone that the French government adopted toward the Adams administration. After Adams's initial peace envoys were rebuffed, Jefferson and his supporters lobbied for the release of papers related to the incident, called the XYZ Affair after the letters used to disguise the identities of the French officials involved.[139] However, the tactic backfired when it was revealed that French officials had demanded bribes, rallying public support against France. The U.S. began an undeclared naval war with France known as the Quasi-War.[140]

During the Adams presidency, the Federalists rebuilt the military, levied new taxes, and enacted the Alien and Sedition Acts. Jefferson believed these laws were intended to suppress Democratic-Republicans, rather than prosecute enemy aliens, and considered them unconstitutional.[141] To rally opposition, he and James Madison anonymously wrote the Kentucky and Virginia Resolutions, declaring that the federal government had no right to exercise powers not specifically delegated to it by the states.[142] The resolutions followed the "interposition" approach of Madison, that states may shield their citizens from federal laws that they deem unconstitutional. Jefferson advocated nullification, allowing states to invalidate federal laws altogether.[143] He warned that, "unless arrested at the threshold", the Alien and Sedition Acts would "drive these states into revolution and blood".[145]

Presidency (1801–1809)

Jefferson was sworn in by Chief Justice John Marshall at the Capitol in Washington, D.C., on March 4, 1801. Outgoing President Adams did not attend his inauguration. Plainly dressed, he chose to walk alongside friends to the Capitol from his nearby boardinghouse that day instead of arriving by carriage.[158] His inaugural address struck a note of reconciliation and commitment to democratic ideology, declaring, "We have been called by different names brethren of the same principle. We are all Republicans; we are all Federalists."[159][160]

He stressed "equal and exact justice to all men", minority rights, and freedom of speech, religion, and press.[161] He said that a free and republican government was "the strongest government on earth."[161] He nominated moderate Republicans to his cabinet: James Madison as secretary of state, Henry Dearborn as secretary of war, Levi Lincoln as attorney general, and Robert Smith as secretary of the navy.[160]

Widowed since 1782, he first relied on his two daughters to serve as his official hostesses.[162] In late May 1801, he asked Dolley Madison, wife of his long-time friend James Madison, to be the permanent White House hostess. She was also in charge of the completion of the White House mansion. Dolley served as White House hostess for Jefferson's two terms and another eight years as First Lady to Madison.[162]

Financial Affairs

Jefferson believed First Bank of the United States represented a "hostility" to republican government.[164] He wanted to dismantle the bank before its charter expired in 1811, but was dissuaded by Gallatin.[167] Gallatin argued the national bank was a useful financial institution and set out to expand operations.[168] Jefferson looked elsewhere to trim the growing national debt.[168] He shrank the Navy, deeming it unnecessary in peacetime, and incorporated a fleet of inexpensive gunboats intended for local defense to avoid provocation against foreign powers.[165] After two terms, he lowered national debt from $83 million to $57 million.[169]

Domestic Affairs

Jefferson pardoned many, imprisoned under Alien and Sedition Acts.[170] Congressional Republicans repealed the Judiciary Act of 1801, to remove nearly all Adams's "midnight judges". A subsequent appointment led to the Supreme Court's landmark decision in *Marbury v. Madison*, judicial review of executive branch actions.[171] Jefferson appointed three Supreme Court justices: William Johnson, Henry Brockholst Livingston, Thomas Todd.[172]

Jefferson strongly felt the need for a national military university, producing an officer engineering corps for national defense based on advancement of the sciences, rather than to rely on foreign sources.[173] He signed the Military Peace Establishment Act on March 16, 1802, founding the United States Military Academy at West Point.

Louisiana Purchase

Spain ceded ownership of the Louisiana territory in 1800 to France. Jefferson was concerned that Napoleon's interest in the vast territory would threaten the security of the continent and Mississippi River shipping. He wrote that the cession "works most sorely on the U.S. It completely reverses all the political relations of the U.S."[182] In 1802, he instructed James Monroe and Robert R. Livingston to negotiate the purchase of New

Orleans and adjacent coastal areas.[183] In early 1803, Jefferson offered Napoleon nearly $10 million for 40,000 square miles of tropical territory.[184]

Napoleon realized French military control was impractical over such a vast remote territory, he was in dire need of funds for his wars on the home front. In April 1803, he made negotiators a counter-offer to sell 827,987 square miles (2,144,480 square kilometers) of French territory for $15 million (~$371 million in 2023), doubling the size of the United States.[184]

Lewis and Clark, Dunbar and Hunter, Red River (1806), Pike Expeditions.

Jefferson anticipated further westward settlements due to the Louisiana Purchase and arranged for exploration and mapping of the uncharted territory. He sought to establish a U.S. claim ahead of competing European interests and to find the Northwest Passage.[193] Jefferson and others were influenced by exploration accounts of Le Page du Pratz in Louisiana (1763) and James Cook in the Pacific (1784),[194] and they persuaded Congress to fund an expedition to explore and map the newly acquired territory to the Pacific Ocean.[195]

Jefferson appointed Meriwether Lewis and William Clark to lead the Corps of Discovery (1803–1806).[196] In the months leading up to the expedition, Jefferson tutored Lewis in mapping, botany, natural history, mineralogy, and astronomy and navigation, giving him unlimited access to his library at Monticello, which included the largest collection of books in the world on the geography and natural history of the North American continent, along with an impressive collection of maps.[197] The expedition lasted from May 1804 to September 1806 and obtained a wealth of scientific and geographic knowledge, including many Indian tribes.[198]

Jefferson organized three other western expeditions: the William Dunbar and George Hunter Expedition on the Ouachita River (1804–1805), Thomas Freeman and Peter Custis Expedition (1806) on Red River, and the Zebulon Pike Expedition (1806–1807) into the Rocky Mountains and the Southwest. All three produced valuable information about the American frontier.[199] This interest also motivated Jefferson to meet the Prussian explorer Alexander von Humboldt several times in June 1804, inquiring into Humboldt's knowledge of New Spain's natural resources, economic prospects, and demographic development.[200]

University of Virginia Founder

Jefferson envisioned a university free of church influences where students could specialize in new areas not offered at other colleges. He believed that education engendered a stable society, which should provide publicly funded schools accessible based solely on ability.[252] He initially proposed his university in a letter to Joseph Priestley in 1800[253] and, in 1819, founded the University of Virginia. He organized the state legislative campaign for its charter and, with the assistance of Edmund Bacon, purchased the location. He was the principal designer of the buildings, planned the curriculum, and served as the first rector in 1825.[254]

When Jefferson died, James Madison replaced him as rector.[257] Jefferson bequeathed most of his library of almost 2,000 volumes to the university.[258]

During his last hours, family members and friends accompanied him. Jefferson died on July 4, 1826, at 12:50 p.m. at age 83, on the 50th anniversary of the adoption of the Declaration of Independence. In the moments prior to his death, Jefferson instructed his physician, "No, doctor, nothing more", refusing laudanum. But his final significant words were, "Is it the Fourth?" or "This is the Fourth".[280] When John Adams died later that same day, his last words were "Thomas Jefferson survives", though Adams was unaware Jefferson had died hours before.[281][282][283][284] The sitting president was Adams's son, John Quincy Adams, and he called their deaths on the nation's anniversary "visible and palpable remarks of Divine Favor".[285]

Shortly after Jefferson died, attendants found a gold locket on a chain around his neck, containing a faded blue ribbon around a lock of his wife Martha's hair.[286]

Jefferson was interred at Monticello, under an epitaph that he wrote:

HERE WAS BURIED THOMAS JEFFERSON, AUTHOR OF THE DECLARATION OF AMERICAN INDEPENDENCE, OF THE STATUTE OF VIRGINIA FOR RELIGIOUS FREEDOM, AND FATHER OF THE UNIVERSITY OF VIRGINIA.[287]

Baptized in his youth, Jefferson became a governing member of his Episcopal Church in Charlottesville, which he later attended with his daughters.[334] In 1803, Jefferson said, "I am Christian, in the only sense [Jesus] wished any one to be".[213] Jefferson defined being a Christian as one who followed the simple teachings of Jesus. Influenced by Joseph Priestley,[338] Jefferson selected New Testament passages of Jesus' teachings into a private work he called *The Life and Morals of Jesus of Nazareth*, known today as the *Jefferson Bible*.

JEFFERSON WAS INVOLVED WITH MANY OTHER ISSUES IN THE BALANCE OF HIS LIFE. IN THIS BOOK, WE CONCENTRATE ON THAT TIME LEADING UP TO OUR REVOLUTIONARY WAR, ALONG WITH THE CONSTITUTIONAL CONVENTION AND IMMEDIATE AFTERMATH.

References

6. Morris, Richard B. (1973). Seven Who Shaped Our Destiny: The Founding Fathers as Revolutionaries. Harper & Row. p. 1. ISBN 978-0060904548.

7. Cogliano, Francis (2008). "Slavery". Jefferson: Reputation and Legacy. U Virginia Press.p.217-219 ISBN 9780813927336.

8. Tucker, 1837, v. 1, p. 18.

9. Malone, 1948, pp. 5–6.

10. Brodie, 1974, pp. 33–34.

11. Kern, Susan A. (2010). Jefferson's at Shadwell. Yale U Press. ISBN 978-195169119. OCLC 51854624.

12. Malone, 1948, pp. 31–33.

13. Woods, Edgar (1901). Albemarle County in Virginia. The Michie Company, printers. p. 225.

14. Malone, 1948, pp. 437–440.

15. Tucker, 1837, v. 1, p. 19.

16. Bowers, 1945, pp. 12–13.

17. Peterson, 1970, pp. 7–9.

18. Bowers, 1945, p. 13

19. Meacham, 2012, p. 36

20. Bowers, 1945, pp. 14–15

21. Bowers, 1945, p. 25; Boles, 2017, p. 17

22. Bowers, 1945, pp. 22–23; Boles, 2017, p. 18

23. Millfeld, Becca (November 2, 2004). "Shhh! The Secret Side to the College's Lesser-Known Societies".

24. Wilson, Gaye. "Jefferson's Formal Education". Monticello. T Jefferson Foundation. Retr May 5, 2024.

25. Meacham, 2012, pp. 29, 39.

26. Chinard, 1926, book cover

27. Bowers, 1945, pp. 32–34; Boles, 2017, p. 19

28. Meacham, 2012, p. 37

29. Tucker, 1837, v. 1, p. 42.

30. Ferling, 2000, p. 43.

31. Murray, S. (2009). The library: An illustrated history. Skyhorse Publishing. p. 163.

32. Library of Congress

33. Boles, 2017, p. 458

34. Root, Daniel (October 12, 2015). "I cannot live without books". UWIRE Text.

35. Meacham, 2012, pp. 11, 49.

36. Tucker, 1837, v. 1, p. 40.
37. Meacham, 2012, pp. 47–49.
38. Gordon-Reed, 2008, p. 348.
39. Gordon-Reed, 2008, pp. 99–100.
40. Meacham, 2012, p. 49.
41. Konig, David T., Encyclopedia Virginia
42. Meacham, 2012, pp. 71–73.
43. Bear, 1967, p. 51.
44. "Building Monticello". Retrieved April 21, 2020.
45. TJF: Monticello (House) FAQ – "Who built the house?"
46. Ellis, 1996, pp. 142–144.
47. "They Did What? 15 Famous People Who Actually Married Their Cousins". Retrieved August 24, 2019.
48. Tucker, 1837, v. 1, p. 47.
49. Roberts, 1993
50. Malone, 1948, p. 53.
51. Malone, 1948, pp. 47, 158.
52. "Lucy Jefferson (1782–1784)". Thomas Jefferson's Monticello. Retrieved February 17, 2020.
53. Boyd, Julian P., ed. (1953). "To Jefferson from Francis Eppes [14Oct1784]". Papers of Jefferson, vol. 7, March 2, 1784 – Feb 25, 1785. Princeton University Press. pp. 441–442. Retrieved September 29, 2019
55. White House Archives
56. Gordon-Reed, 2008, p. 145; Meacham, 2012, p. 53.
57. Halliday, 2009, pp. 48–53.
58. TJF: Monticello Construction
59. Bernstein, 2003, p. 109.
61. Bowers, 1945, p. v
62. Tucker, 1837, v. 1, p. 77.
63. Meacham, 2012, pp. 103–104.
69. Ellis, 1996, p. 50.
70. Tucker, 1837, p. 90.
72. Ellis, 2008, pp. 55–56.
73. Brodie, 1974, p. 112.
74. Peterson, 1970, pp. 101–102, 114, 140.
75. Ferling, 2004, p. 26.
76. Tucker, 1837, v. 1, p. 102; Bernstein, 2003, p. 42.
77. Peterson, 1970, pp. 134, 142; Bernstein, 2003, pp. 68–69.
99. Tucker, 1837, v. 1, pp. 172–173.
100. Peterson, 1970, p. 275.
101. Rayner, 1834, p. 207.
102. Peterson, 1960, pp. 189–190.
104. Peterson, 1970, pp. 286.
106. Stewart, 1997, p. 39.
107. Meacham, 2012, p. 180.
108. McCullough, 2001, p. 330.
109. Bowers, 1945, pp. vii–viii
111. " Meeting of TJefferson, John Adams, and George III". engagement.virginia.edu. July 7, 2019
114. Bowers, 1945, p. 328.
115. Burstein, 2010, p. 120.
116. Meacham, 2012, pp. 222–223.
117. TJF: Coded Messages
118. Peterson (2002), pp. 40–41
119. Ellis, 1996, pp. 116–117.
120. Ellis, 1996, p. 110; Wood, 2010, pp. 179–181.
121. Tucker, 1837, v. 1, p. 334.
122. Tucker, 1837, v. 1, pp. 364–369.
123. Chernow, 2004, p. 427.
124. Cooke, 1970, pp. 523–545.
126. Bernstein, 2003, p. 96.
127. Randall (1996), p. 1.
128. Tucker, 1837, v. 1, p. 429.
129. Greider, 2010, p. 246.

130. Wood, 2010, pp. 145–149.
133. Meacham, 2012, pp. 293–294.
134. Peterson, 1970, ch.8 [e-book].
135. Yarbrough, 2006, p. xx.
136. Meacham, 2012, p. 305.
137. Bernstein, 2003, pp. 117–118.
138. Elkins, 1994, p. 566.
139. Chernow, 2004, p. 550.
140. Meacham, 2012, p. 312.
141. Tucker, 1837, v. 2, p. 54.
142. Wood, 2010, pp. 269–271.
143. Meacham, 2012, p. 318.
145. Onuf, 2000, p. 73.
158. Peterson (2002), p. 39
159. Meacham, 2012, pp. 348–350.
160. Peterson, 2002, p. 41.
161. Peterson, 2002, p. 40.
162. Hendricks 2015, pp. 21–22.
164. Peterson, 2002, pp. 43–44.
165. Wood, 2010, p. 293.
167. Wills, 2002, pp. 50–51.
168. Peterson, 2002, p. 44.
169. Meacham, 2012, p. 387.
170. Meacham, 2012, p. 357.
171. Meacham, 2012, p. 375.
172. Urofsky, 2006, p. viii.
173. Scythes, 2014, pp. 693–694.
182. Meacham, 2012, pp. 383–384.
183. Wood, 2010, p. 368.
184. Freehling, 2005, p. 69.
193. Ambrose, 1996, pp. 76, 418.
194. Ambrose, 1996, p. 154.
195. Rodriguez, 2002, pp. xxiv, 162, 185.
196. Rodriguez, 2002, pp. 112, 186.
197. Ambrose, 1996, pp. 54, 80.
198. Ambrose, 1996, pp. 154, 409, 512.
199. Berry, 2006, p. xi.
200. Daum, Andreas W. (2024). Alexander von Humboldt: A Concise Biography. Trans. Robert Savage. Princeton U Press. p. 80. ISBN 978-0-691-24736-6.
252. U Va. Library
253. Adams, 1888, p. 48.
254. Peterson, 1970, ch. 11 [e-book].
257. TJF: James Madison
258. Crawford, 2008, p. 235.
259. "Millard Fillmore". University Of Buffalo. Retrieved November 24, 2022.
280. Martin, Russell L. (June 7, 1988). "Jefferson's Last Words". Monticello.
333. Wilentz, 2005, p. 200.
338. People and Ideas: Early America's Formation". Public Broadcasting Service.

Sources

- Bear, James Adam (1967). Jefferson at Monticello. University of Virginia Press. ISBN 978-0813900223.
- Bear, James Adam (1974). "Last Few Days in Life of Jefferson". Magazine of Albemarle County History. **32**: 77.
- Bernstein, Richard B. (2003). Thomas Jefferson. Oxford University Press. ISBN 978-0195181302.
- Bear, James Adam (2004). The Revolution of Ideas. Oxford University Press. ISBN 978-0195143683.
- Boles, John B. (2017). Jefferson: Architect of American Liberty. Basic Books,626 pages. ISBN 978-0465094691.
- Brodie, Fawn (1974). Thomas Jefferson: An Intimate History. W. W. Norton & Company. ISBN 978-0393317527.
- Bowers, Claude (1945). The Young Jefferson 1743–1789. Houghton Mifflin Company.
- Isenberg, Nancy (2010). Madison and Jefferson. Random House. ISBN 978-1400067282.
- Chernow, Ron (2004). Alexander Hamilton. Penguin Press. ISBN 978-1594200090.
- Ellis, Joseph J. (1996). American Sphinx: The Character of Thomas Jefferson. Alfred A. Knopf.
- Ellis, Joseph J. (2000). Thomas Jefferson: Genius of Liberty. Viking Studio. ISBN 978-0670889334.
- Ellis, Joseph J. (2003). Founding Brothers: Revolutionary Generation. Knopf Doubleday Publishing. ISBN 978-1400077687.

- Ellis, Joseph J. (2008). American Creation: Triumphs and Tragedies in Founding of Republic. Random House LLC. ISBN 978-0307263698.
- Ferling, John (2000) Setting World Ablaze: Washington, Adams, Jefferson, American Revolution. Oxford U Press ISBN 978-0195134094.
- Ellis, Joseph (2004). Adams v. Jefferson: Tumultuous Election 1800. Oxford U Press. ISBN 978-0195167719.
- Gordon-Reed, Annette (February 20, 2020). "Thomas Jefferson's Vision of Equality Was Not All-Inclusive. But It Was Transformative". Retrieved March 11, 2022.
- Halliday, E. M. (2009). Understanding Thomas Jefferson. Harper Collins. ISBN 978-0060197933.
  - Malone, Dumas. Jefferson (6 vol. 1948–1981)
  - Malone, Dumas (1948). Jefferson, The Virginian. Jefferson and His Time. Vol. 1. Little Brown. OCLC 1823927., Ebook
  - Malone, Dumas (1951). Jefferson and the Rights of Man. Jefferson and His Time. Vol. 2. Little Brown.
  - Malone, Dumas (1962). Jefferson and the Ordeal of Liberty. Jefferson and His Time. Vol. 3. Little, Brown. ISBN 978-0316544757.
  - Malone, Dumas (1970). Jefferson the President: First Term, 1801–1805. Jefferson and His Time. Vol. 4. Little Brown.
  - Malone, Dumas (1974). Jefferson the President: Second Term, 1805–1809. Jefferson and His Time. Vol. 5. Little Brown. OCLC 1929523.
  - Malone, Dumas (1981). The Sage of Monticello. Jefferson and His Time. Vol. 6. Little Brown.
  - McCullough, David (2001). John Adams. Simon & Schuster. ISBN 978-1471104527
- Meacham, Jon (2012). Thomas Jefferson: The Art of Power. Random House LLC. ISBN 978-0679645368.
- Peterson, Merrill D. (1960). Jefferson Image in American Mind. U Virginia Press. ISBN 978-0813918518.
- Peterson, Merrill D (1970). Jefferson and New Nation; a Biography. Oxford U Press. ISBN 978-0195000542.
- Peterson, Merrill D (2002). "Thomas Jefferson". In Graff, Henry (ed.). The Presidents: A Reference History (7th ed.). Charles Scribner's Sons. pp. 39–56.
- Stewart, John J. (1997). T Jefferson: Forerunner to the Restoration. Cedar Fort. ISBN 978-0-88290-605-8.
- Tucker, George (1837). Life of Thomas Jefferson, Third President of the US; 2 vol. Carey, Lea & Blanchard.
- Tucker, George (1990). Empire of Liberty: Statecraft of Jefferson. Cogliano Press. ISBN 978-0198022763.
- Wood, Gordon S (2006). Revolutionary Characters: What Made Founders Different. Penguin Press. ISBN 978-1594200939.
- Wood, Gordon S (2010). Empire of Liberty: History of Early Republic, 1789–1815. Oxford U Press. ISBN 978-0195039146
- Wood, Gordon S (2011). The Idea of America: Reflections on the Birth of the United States. Penguin Press. ISBN 978-1594202902.Thomas Jefferson Foundation sources

JOHN ADAMS,
SECOND PRESIDENT
FIRST PRESIDENT TO RESIDE IN THE WHITE HOUSE

John Adams (October 30, 1735 – July 4, 1826) was an American statesman, attorney, diplomat, writer, and Founding Father who served as the second president of the United States from 1797 to 1801. Before his presidency, he was a leader of the American Revolution that achieved independence from Great Britain. During the latter part of the Revolutionary War and in the early years of the new nation, he served the U.S. government as a senior diplomat in Europe. Adams was the first person to hold the office of vice president of the United States.

A lawyer and political activist prior to the Revolution, Adams was devoted to the right to counsel and presumption of innocence. He defied anti-British sentiment and successfully defended British soldiers against murder charges arising from the Boston Massacre. Adams was a Massachusetts delegate to the Continental Congress and became a leader of the revolution. He assisted Jefferson in drafting the Declaration of Independence in 1776 and was its primary advocate in Congress.

Early life and education

John Adams was born on October 30, 1735, to John Adams Sr. and Susanna Boylston. He had two younger brothers, Peter and Elihu.[6] Adams was born on the family farm in Braintree, Massachusetts.[7] His mother was from a leading medical family, and his father was a deacon in the Congregational Church, a farmer, a cordwainer, and a lieutenant in the militia.[8]

Adams often praised the close relationship with his father.[9] Adams's great-great-grandfather Henry Adams immigrated to Massachusetts from Braintree, Essex, England, around 1638.[8]

Adams's formal education began at age six, centered on *The New England Primer*. He then attended Braintree Latin School under Joseph Cleverly, where studies included Latin, rhetoric, logic, and arithmetic. Adams's early education included incidents of truancy, a dislike for his master, and a desire to become a farmer, but his father commanded that he remain in school. Deacon Adams hired a new schoolmaster, and his son responded positively.[10][11]

College education and adulthood

At age sixteen, Adams entered Harvard College in 1751.[12] As an adult, Adams would study the works of Thucydides, Plato, Cicero, and Tacitus in their original languages.[13] Though his father expected him to be a minister,[14] after his 1755 graduation with an A.B. degree, he taught school temporarily in Worcester, while pondering his permanent vocation.[15]

When the French and Indian War began in 1754, Adams, aged nineteen, felt guilty he was the first in his family not to be a militia officer; he said, "I longed more ardently to be a Soldier than I ever did to be a Lawyer".[16]

Law practice and marriage

In 1756, Adams began reading law.[17] In 1758, he earned an A.M. from Harvard,[18] and in 1759 was admitted to the bar.[19] He developed a habit of diary writing; this included his impressions of James Otis Jr.'s 1761 challenge to British writs of assistance, which allowed British officials to search a home without notice or reason. Otis's argument inspired Adams to the cause of the American colonies.[20]

In 1763, Adams explored aspects of political theory in seven essays written for Boston newspapers, he ridiculed the selfish thirst for power he perceived among the Massachusetts colonial elite.[21] Adams was less well known than Samuel Adams, his influence emerged from his work as a constitutional lawyer, his analysis of history, and dedication to republicanism.[14]

In 1759, he met Abigail Smith,[22] They were married on October 25, 1764. After his father's death in 1761, Adams had inherited a 9+1/2-acre farm and a house where they lived until 1783.[24] John and Abigail had six children.[29] John Quincy launched a political career, becoming president himself.[30]

Career before the Revolution - - Opponent of Stamp Act

Adams rose to prominence in opposition to the Stamp Act. The Act was imposed by the British Parliament without consulting the American legislatures. It required payment of a direct tax by the colonies for stamped documents,[31] and was designed to pay for the costs of Britain's war with France. Power of enforcement was given to British vice admiralty courts, rather than common law courts.[33] These Admiralty courts acted without juries and were greatly disliked.[31] The Act was despised for its monetary cost and implementation without colonial consent, and encountered violent resistance.[33] Adams authored the "Braintree Instructions" in 1765, explaining to the representatives of Braintree that the Act should be opposed since it denied two fundamental rights guaranteed to all Englishmen (and which all free men deserved): to be taxed only by consent and to be tried by a jury of one's peers. The instructions were a defense of colonial rights and liberties.[34]

Adams authored articles in opposition to the Stamp Act, which were republished in *The London Chronicle* in 1768 as *True Sentiments of America*, or *A Dissertation on the Canon and Feudal Law*. He spoke in December before the governor and council, pronouncing the Stamp

Act invalid in the absence of Massachusetts representation at Parliament.[36] He noted that many protests were sparked by a popular sermon of Boston minister Jonathan Mayhew, invoking Romans 13 to justify insurrection.[37] While Adams strongly opposed the Act in writing, he rebuffed attempts by Samuel Adams, to involve him in mob actions.[38] In 1766, a town meeting of Braintree elected Adams as a selectman.[39]

With repeal of the Stamp Act in early 1766, tensions with Britain eased.[40] Putting politics aside, Adams moved his family to a Boston in April 1768 to focus on his law practice.[27] In 1768, Adams successfully defended John Hancock, who was accused of violating British acts of trade in the Liberty Affair.[41] With the death of Jeremiah Gridley and the mental collapse of Otis, Adams became Boston's most prominent lawyer.[39]

Counsel for the British: Boston Massacre

Britain's passage of the Townshend Acts in 1767 revived tensions, and an increase in mob violence led the British to dispatch more troops to the colonies.[42] On March 5, 1770, when a lone British sentry was accosted by a mob, eight of his fellow soldiers reinforced him, and the crowd around them grew to several hundred. The soldiers were struck with snowballs, ice, and stones, and in the chaos the soldiers opened fire, killing five civilians, in the Boston Massacre. The accused soldiers were arrested on charges of murder. When no other attorneys would come to their defense, Adams did. He believed no person should be denied the right to counsel and a fair trial. The trials were delayed so passions could cool.[43]

The week-long trial of the commander, Captain Thomas Preston, began on October 24 and ended in his acquittal, because it was impossible to prove that he had ordered his soldiers to fire.[44] The remaining soldiers were tried in December when Adams made his famed argument regarding jury decisions: "Facts are stubborn things; and whatever may be our wishes, our inclinations, or the dictates of our passion, they cannot alter the state of facts and evidence."[45] Adams won an acquittal for six of the soldiers. Two, who had fired directly into the crowd, were convicted of manslaughter. Adams was paid a small sum by his clients.[24]

According to biographer John E. Ferling, in jury selection Adams "expertly exercised his right to challenge individual jurors and contrived what amounted to a packed jury. Not only were several jurors tied through business arrangements to the British army, but five became Loyalist exiles." The Prosecution was weak, and Adams's "performed brilliantly."[46]

American Revolution

Adams, a conservative of the Founding Fathers, persistently held that open insurrection was unwarranted and peaceful petition with the view of remaining part of Great Britain was preferable.[50] His ideas began to change around 1772, as the British Crown assumed payment of the salaries of Governor Hutchinson and his judges instead of the Massachusetts legislature. Hutchinson delivered a speech warning that Parliament's powers over the colonies were absolute and any resistance was illegal. John Adams, Samuel, and Joseph Hawley drafted a resolution adopted by the House of Representatives threatening independence as an alternative.[51]

The Boston Tea Party, a demonstration against the Tea Act and the British East India Company's tea monopoly, took place on December 16, 1773. Protestors demolished 342 chests of tea worth about ten thousand pounds on the British schooner *Dartmouth*, anchored in Boston harbor. Adams applauded the destruction of the tea, calling it the "grandest Event" in the history of the protest movement,[52] and writing in his diary that it was an "absolutely and indispensably" necessary action.[53]

Member of Continental Congress (note official spelling of the day)

In 1774, at the instigation of Samuel Adams, the First Continental Congress was convened in response to the Intolerable Acts. Four delegates were chosen by Massachusetts, including John Adams, who agreed to attend,[54]

Shortly after he arrived in Philadelphia, Adams was placed on the 23-member Grand Committee tasked with drafting a letter of grievances to King George III. The committee soon split into conservative and radical factions.[56] Although the Massachusetts delegation was largely passive, Adams criticized many conservatives who advocated a conciliatory policy towards the British or felt that the colonies had a duty to remain loyal to Britain, although his views at the time aligned with those of conservative John Dickinson. Adams sought the repeal of objectionable policies, but at this stage he continued to see benefits in maintaining the ties with Britain.[57] He renewed his push for the right to a jury trial.[58][59] Adams ultimately helped engineer a compromise between the conservatives and the radicals.[60] Congress disbanded in October after sending the petition to the King and showing its displeasure with the Intolerable Acts by endorsing the Suffolk Resolves, and a boycott of British goods.[61]

Abigail encouraged him in his task, writing: "You cannot be, I know, nor do I wish to see you an inactive Spectator, but if the Sword be drawn, I bid adieu."[62]

News of the Battles of Lexington and Concord made Adams hope that independence would soon become a reality. Three days after the battle, he rode into a militia camp and, while reflecting positively on the high spirits of the men, was distressed by their poor condition and lack of discipline.[63] A month later, Adams returned to Philadelphia for the Second Continental Congress as the leader of the Massachusetts delegation.[64] He moved cautiously at first, noting that the Congress was divided between Loyalists, those favoring independence, and those hesitant to take any position.[65] Publicly, Adams supported "reconciliation," but privately agreed with Franklin's confidential observation that independence was inevitable.[66]

In June 1775, with a view of promoting union among the colonies against Great Britain, he nominated George Washington of Virginia as commander-in-chief of the army then assembled around Boston.[67] He praised Washington's "skill and experience" as well as his "excellent universal character."[68] Adams opposed various attempts, including the Olive Branch Petition, aimed at finding peace.[69] He wrote, "In my opinion Powder and Artillery are the most efficacious, Sure, and infallibly conciliatory Measures We can adopt."[66] In October 1775, Adams was appointed chief judge of the Massachusetts Superior Court and resigned in February 1777.[67] In response to delegate queries, Adams wrote the 1776 pamphlet *Thoughts on Government*, which laid out a framework for republican constitutions.[72]

Independence

Throughout the first half of 1776, Adams grew increasingly impatient with what he perceived to be the slow pace of declaring independence.[73] In the Second Continental Congress in Philadelphia, he pushed a plan to outfit armed ships and later in the year, he drafted the first set of regulations for the navy.[74] Adams drafted the preamble to the Lee Resolution of Richard Henry Lee.[75] He developed a rapport with Thomas Jefferson of Virginia, who agreed by early 1776 that it was necessary.[76] On June 7, 1776, Adams seconded the Lee Resolution, which stated that the colonies were "free and independent states."[77]

Prior to independence being declared, Adams organized a Committee of Five charged with drafting a Declaration of Independence. He chose himself, Jefferson, Benjamin Franklin, Robert R. Livingston, and Roger Sherman.[78] Jefferson thought Adams should write the document, but Adams persuaded the committee to choose Jefferson. Many years later, Adams recorded his reasoning to Jefferson: "Reason first, you are a Virginian, and a Virginian ought to appear at the head of this business. Reason second, I am obnoxious, suspected, and unpopular. You are very much otherwise. Reason third, you can write ten times better than I can."[79][80] Although Jefferson wrote the first draft primarily, Adams assumed a major role.[81] On July 1, the resolution was debated in Congress. It was expected to pass, but opponents such as Dickinson made a strong effort to oppose it. Jefferson, a poor debater, remained silent while Adams argued for its adoption.[82] Many years later, Jefferson hailed Adams as "the pillar of the Declaration's support on the floor of Congress, its ablest advocate and defender against the multifarious assaults it encountered."[83] On July 2, Congress officially voted for independence. Twelve colonies voted in the affirmative, New York abstained. Dickinson was absent.[84] Congress approved the Declaration of Independence on July 4.[87]

During the congress, Adams sat on ninety committees, chairing twenty-five, an unmatched workload among the congressmen. As Benjamin Rush reported, he was acknowledged "to be the first man in the House."[88] In June 1776, Adams became head of the Board of War and Ordnance, charged with recording the officers in the army, their ranks, the disposition of troops throughout the colonies, and ammunition.[89] He was a "one man war department," working up to eighteen-hour days and mastering the details of raising, equipping and fielding an army under civilian control.[90] Adams functioned as a *de facto* Secretary of War.[91] He authored the "Plan of Treaties," Congress's requirements for a treaty with France.[90]

After defeating the Continental Army at the Battle of Long Island on August 27, 1776, British Admiral Richard Howe determined that a strategic advantage was at hand and requested that Congress send representatives to negotiate peace. A delegation consisting of Adams, Franklin, and Edward Rutledge met with Howe at the Staten Island Peace Conference on September 11.[94] When Lord Howe stated he could view the American delegates only as British subjects, Adams replied, "Your lordship may consider me in what light you please, ... except that of a British subject."[95] Adams learned many years later that his name was on a list of people specifically excluded from Howe's pardon-granting authority.[96]

Diplomacy of John Adams - - Commissioner to France

Adams advocated in Congress that independence was necessary to establish trade, and conversely, trade was essential for the attainment of independence; he specifically urged negotiation of a commercial treaty with France. He was appointed, along with Franklin, Dickinson, Benjamin Harrison from Virginia, and Robert Morris from Pennsylvania, "to prepare a plan of treaties to be proposed to foreign powers." While Jefferson was writing the Declaration of Independence, Adams worked on the Model Treaty, which authorized a commercial agreement with France. By late 1777, America's finances were in tatters, in September a British army defeated General Washington and captured Philadelphia. The defeat of the British at Saratoga was expected to induce France to agree to an alliance.[99]

In November 1777, Adams learned that he was to be named commissioner to France, replacing Silas Deane and joining Franklin and Arthur Lee .[100] On February 17, 1778, Adams set sail aboard the frigate *Boston*.[101] The ship was pursued by British vessels, with Adams personally taking up arms to help capture one. On April 1, the *Boston* arrived in France, where Adams learned that France had agreed to an alliance with the United States on February 6.[102] Adams was annoyed by Lee, and Franklin, whom he found overly deferential to the French.[103] Congress increased Franklin's powers by naming him minister plenipotentiary to France. Lee was sent to Spain. Adams received no instructions.[107]

121

In late 1779, Adams was appointed as the sole minister to establish a commercial treaty with Britain and end the war.[108] Following the Massachusetts constitutional convention, he departed for France,[109] accompanied by his sons.[110] A leak forced the ship to land in Ferrol, Spain.[111] He increased his usefulness by mastering French. Lee was eventually recalled.[112]

The French, Adams wrote, meant to keep their hands "above our chin to prevent us from drowning, but not to lift our heads out of water."[113] In March 1780, Congress, trying to curb inflation, voted to devalue the dollar. Adams bluntly defended the decision. Adams wrote warships were needed to contain the British armies in the port cities and contend with the powerful British Navy. Vergennes responded he would deal only with Franklin, who sent a letter back to Congress critical of Adams.[114] Adams then left France of his own accord.[115]

Treaty of Paris

After negotiating the loan with the Dutch, Adams was re-appointed as the American commissioner to negotiate the war-ending Treaty of Paris. Vergennes and France's minister to the United States, Anne-César de La Luzerne, disapproved of Adams, so Franklin, Thomas Jefferson, John Jay, and Henry Laurens.[124]

In the final negotiations, securing fishing rights off Newfoundland and Cape Breton Island proved both especially important and very difficult. In response to very strict restrictions proposed by the British.[125] Overruling Franklin and distrustful of Vergennes, Jay and Adams decided not to consult with France, instead dealing directly with the British.[126] The independent negotiations also allowed the French to plead innocence to their Spanish allies, whose demands for Gibraltar might have caused significant problems.[127] On September 3, 1783, the treaty was signed and American independence was recognized.[128]

Ambassador to Great Britain

Adams was appointed the first American ambassador to Great Britain in 1785.[129] After arriving in London from Paris, Adams had his first audience with King George III on June 1. The pair's exchange was respectful; Adams promised to do all that he could to restore friendship and cordiality "between People who, . . . under different Governments have the Same Language, a Similar Religion and kindred Blood," and the King agreed to "receive with Pleasure, the Assurances of the friendly Dispositions of the United States. Adams replied, "That Opinion sir, is not mistaken... I have no Attachments but to my own Country." King George responded, "An honest Man will never have any other."[130]

In London, Abigail joined Adams. Suffering the hostility of the King's courtiers, they escaped when they could by seeking out Richard Price, minister of Newington Green Unitarian Church and instigator of the debate over the Revolution within Britain.[131] Adams corresponded with his sons John Quincy and Charles, both of whom were at Harvard, cautioning the former against the "smell of the midnight lamp" while admonishing the latter to devote sufficient time to study.[132] Jefferson visited Adams in 1786 while serving as Minister to France.[134]

While in London Adams wrote his three-volume *A Defense of the Constitutions of Government of the United States of America*, a response to those he met in Europe who criticized government systems of the American states.[135]

The American states had been delinquent in paying debts owed to British merchants, and in response, the British refused to vacate forts in the northwest as promised. Adams's attempts to resolve this dispute failed, and he was often frustrated by a lack of news of progress from home.[136] The news he received of tumult at home, such as Shays' Rebellion, heightened his anxiety. He asked Jay to be relieved;[137] in 1788, he took his leave of George III, who promised to uphold his end of the treaty once America did the same.[138][139]

Vice presidency (1789–1797) - - 1788–1789 United States presidential election

On June 17, 1788, Adams returned to triumphant welcome in Massachusetts.[140] Each state's presidential electors gathered on February 4, 1789, to cast their two votes for the president. The person with the most votes would be president and the second would become vice president.[141] Adams received 34 electoral college votes in the election, second behind Washington, who was a unanimous choice with 69 votes. As a result, Washington became the nation's first president, and Adams became its first vice president.[142] Alexander Hamilton convinced at least 7 of the 69 electors not to cast their vote for Adams. After finding out about the manipulation but not Hamilton's role in it, Adams wrote to Benjamin Rush that his election was "a curse rather than a blessing."[142]

1796 United States presidential election

The 1796 election was the first contested American presidential election.[168] Twice, George Washington had been elected to office unanimously but, deep philosophical differences caused a rift, leading to the founding of the parties.[169] When Washington announced he would not run again, an intense struggle for control of Congress and the presidency began.[170]

As in the previous two presidential elections, no candidates were put forward for voters to choose between in 1796. The Constitution provided for the selection of electors who would then choose a president.[171] In seven states voters chose the presidential electors. In the remaining nine states, they were chosen by the state's legislature.[172] The clear Republican favorite was Jefferson.[173] Adams was the Federalist frontrunner.[171] The Republicans held a congressional nominating caucus and named Jefferson and Aaron Burr as their presidential choices.[174] Federalist members of Congress held a nominating caucus and named Adams and Thomas Pinckney as their candidates.[173][175] The campaign was confined to newspaper attacks, pamphlets, and political rallies;[171] of the four contenders, only Burr actively campaigned. The practice of not campaigning would persist for decades.[172] Adams stated he wanted to stay out of the "silly and wicked game" of electioneering.[176]

As the campaign progressed, fears grew among Hamilton and his supporters that Adams was too vain, opinionated, unpredictable, and stubborn to follow their directions.[177]. He had remarked that Hamilton's economic program, would "swindle" the poor and unleash the "gangrene of avarice."[178] He coerced South Carolina Federalist electors, pledged to vote for "favorite son" Pinckney, to scatter their second votes among candidates other than Adams. Hamilton's scheme was undone when several New England state electors agreed not to vote for Pinckney.[179][180] Throughout his life, Adams was highly critical of Hamilton.[181]

Adams won receiving 71 electoral votes to 68 for Jefferson, who became VP; Pinckney got 59 votes, and Burr with 30.[182] This is the only election in which a president and vice president were elected from opposing tickets.[183]

For the first time in American Election History, we see a divide forming between North and South. Adams wins all the Northern States, while Jefferson wins all the Southern States. Electoral College delivers a win for Adams (The Author)

Presidency (1797–1801) - - Presidency and Diplomacy of John Adams

Adams followed Washington's lead in using the presidency to exemplify republican values and civic virtue, and his service was free of scandal.[184] He ignored the political patronage and office-seeking other officeholders utilized.[185]

The "Hamiltonians who surround him," Jefferson remarked, "are only a little less hostile to him than to me."[186] Although aware of Hamilton's influence, Adams was convinced their retention ensured a smoother succession.[187] Adams maintained the economic programs of Hamilton, who regularly consulted with key cabinet members, especially powerful Treasury Secretary, Oliver Wolcott Jr.[188] Adams was independent of his cabinet, often making decisions despite opposition.[189] Hamilton had grown accustomed to being consulted by Washington. Adams ignored Hamilton.[190]

Failed peace commission and XYZ affair.

Adams presidency was dominated by a single question of American policy to an extent seldom if ever encountered by any succeeding occupant of the office," whether to make war or peace with France.[191] Britain and France were at war as a result of the French Revolution. The French supported Jefferson for president in 1796 and were belligerent at his loss.[193] Because of the Jay Treaty, the French saw America as Britain's ally and began seizing American ships.[194]

On May 16, 1797, Adams gave a speech to the House and Senate in which he called for increasing defense capabilities in case of war with France.[195] He announced that he would send a peace commission to France but simultaneously called for a military buildup to counter any potential French threat. Republicans were outraged, for Adams not only failed to express support for the cause of the French Republic but appeared to be calling for war against it.[196]

Sentiments changed with the XYZ Affair. The peace commission that Adams appointed consisted of John Marshall, Charles Cotesworth Pinckney, and Elbridge Gerry.[197] Jefferson met four times with Joseph Letombe, the French consul in Philadelphia. According to Letombe, Jefferson called Adams "vain, suspicious, and stubborn."[198] When the envoys arrived in October, they were kept waiting for several days, and then granted only a 15-minute meeting with French Foreign Minister Talleyrand. The diplomats were then met by three of Talleyrand's agents (later code-named, X, Y, and Z), who refused to negotiations unless the US paid enormous bribes.[197][199] The Americans refused to negotiate on such terms.[200] Marshall and Pinckney returned home, Gerry remained.[201]

News of the disastrous peace mission arrived in a memorandum from Marshall on March 4. Adams, not wanting to incite violence among the populace, announced that the mission had failed without providing details.[202] Republicans voted overwhelmingly to demand Adams release the papers. Once released, the Republicans, according to Abigail, were "struck dumb."[203] Adams popularity peaked, as many called for full-scale war against the French.[204]

Alien and Sedition Acts (Note the divisive politics)

Despite the XYZ Affair, Republican opposition persisted. Federalists accused the French and their immigrants of provoking unrest. In an attempt to quell the outcry, the Federalists introduced, and the Congress passed, a series of laws collectively referred to as the Alien and Sedition Acts.[205] Passage of the Naturalization Act, the Alien Friends Act, the Alien Enemies Act and the Sedition Act all came within two weeks, in what Jefferson called an "unguarded passion." The first three acts targeted immigrants, specifically French, by giving the president greater deportation authority and increasing citizenship requirements. The Sedition Act made it a crime to publish "false, scandalous, and malicious writing" against the government.[206] Adams had not promoted these acts but signed them.[207]

The administration initiated fourteen or more indictments under the Sedition Act, as well as suits against five of the six most prominent Republican newspapers, and went to trial on the eve of the 1800 presidential election.[208] Vocal opponents of the Federalists were imprisoned or fined under the Sedition Act for criticizing the government.[209] Congressman Matthew Lyon of Vermont, who was sentenced to four months in jail for criticizing the President.[210] The alien acts were not stringently.[208] Jefferson, disgusted by the acts, wrote nothing publicly but partnered with Madison to secretly draft the Kentucky and Virginia Resolutions. Writing to Madison, he speculated that the states might have to "sever ourselves from the union we so much value."[211] Federalists reacted bitterly to the resolutions, the acts energized and unified the Republican Party, doing little to unite the Federalists.[212]

Quasi-War

In May 1798, a French privateer captured a merchant vessel off of New York Harbor. An increase in attacks on sea marked the beginning of the undeclared naval war known as the Quasi-War.[213] Adams pursued a strategy whereby America harassed French ships in an effort sufficient to stem the French assaults.[214] Despite a fear that large standing armies were subversive to liberty, in May, a provisional army of 10,000 soldiers was authorized by Congress. In July, Congress created twelve infantry regiments and provided for six cavalry companies.[215]

Federalists pressured Adams to appoint Hamilton, who had served as Washington's aide-de-camp during the Revolution.[216] Adams chose Washington without consulting him. As a condition of his acceptance, Washington demanded that he be permitted to appoint his own subordinates. He wished to have Henry Knox as second-in-command, followed by Hamilton, and then Charles Pinckney.[217] On June 2, Hamilton wrote to Washington stating that he would not serve unless he was made Inspector General and second-in-command.[218] Washington conceded that Hamilton, despite holding a rank lower than Knox and Pinckney, had, by serving on his staff, more opportunity to comprehend the whole military scene, and should therefore outrank them. Adams sent Secretary of War James McHenry to Mount Vernon to convince Washington to accept the post. McHenry put forth his opinion that Washington would not serve unless permitted to choose his own officers.[219] Washington's list consisted entirely of Federalists.[220] Adams relented and agreed to submit to the Senate the names of Hamilton, Pinckney, and Knox, in that order, although final decisions of rank would be reserved to Adams.[219] On September 21, Adams received a letter from McHenry relaying a statement from Washington threatening to resign if Hamilton were not made second-in-command.[221] Fearing Federalist backlash, Adams capitulated, despite bitter resentment.[222] The illness of Abigail, whom Adams feared was near death, exacerbated his suffering.[221]

It quickly became apparent that due to Washington's advanced age, Hamilton was the army's *de facto* commander. He exerted effective control over the War Department, taking over supplies for the army.[223] Meanwhile, Adams built up the Navy, adding six fast, powerful frigates, most notably the USS *Constitution*.[224]

The Quasi-War continued, but there was a decline in war fever once news arrived of the French defeat at the Battle of the Nile, which many Americans hoped would make them more disposed to negotiate.[225][226] Hamilton's critics, including Abigail, saw his military buildups signs of an aspiring military dictator.[227]

125

Fries' Rebellion

To pay for the military buildup of the Quasi-War, Adams and his Federalist allies enacted the Direct Tax of 1798. Though Washington had maintained a balanced budget with the help of a growing economy, increased military expenditures threatened to cause major budget deficits, and the Federalists developed taxation. The Direct Tax of 1798 instituted a progressive land value tax of up to 1% of a property's value. Taxpayers in eastern Pennsylvania resisted federal tax collectors, and in March 1799 the bloodless Fries's Rebellion broke out. Led by Revolutionary War veteran John Fries, rural German-speaking farmers protested what they saw as a threat to liberties. They intimidated tax collectors.[233]

Fries and two other leaders were arrested, found guilty of treason, and sentenced to hang, but Adams granted a pardon.[234][235]

Federalist divisions and peace

On May 5, 1800, Adams's frustrations with the Hamilton wing of the party exploded during a meeting with McHenry, a Hamilton loyalist who was universally regarded, even by Hamilton, as an inept Secretary of War. Adams named John Marshall as Secretary of State and Samuel Dexter as Secretary of War.[236] In 1799, Napoleon took over as head of the French government in the Coup of 18 Brumaire and declared the French Revolution over.[238] News of this event increased Adams's desire to disband the army, which, with Washington dead, was commanded by Hamilton. Napoleon, determining conflict was pointless, readiness for relations.[241][243] Adams proudly avoided war, but deeply split his party in the process.[244]

Establishing government institutions and moving to Washington

Adams's leadership on naval defense has sometimes led him to be called the "father of the American Navy."[245][246] In July 1798, he signed into law An Act for the relief of sick and disabled seamen, which authorized the establishment of a government-operated marine hospital service.[247] In 1800, he signed the law establishing the Library of Congress.[248]

Adams made his first official visit to the nation's new seat of government in June 1800. Amid the "raw and unfinished" cityscape, the President found the public buildings "in a much greater completion than expected."[249] He moved into the nearly completed President's Mansion (White House) on November 1.[250] The Senate of the 7th Congress met in the new Capitol building on November 17, 1800. On November 22, Adams delivered his State of the Union Address,[251] the last annual message a president would deliver to Congress for 113 years.[252]

1800 United States presidential election

With the Federalist Party deeply split over negotiations with France, and the opposition Republican Party enraged over the Alien and Sedition Acts and the expansion of the military, Adams faced a daunting reelection campaign in 1800.[172] Federalist congressmen in the spring of 1800 nominated Adams and Pinckney. Republicans nominated Jefferson and Burr.[253]

Jefferson was portrayed as an apostle of liberty and man of the people, while Adams was labelled a monarchist.[254] James T. Callender, a Republican propagandist secretly financed by Jefferson, accused Adams of attempting to make war with France. Callender was arrested and jailed under the Sedition Act, which further inflamed Republican passions.[255]

Opposition from the Federalist Party was at times equally intense. Some, including Pickering, accused Adams of colluding with Jefferson so that he would end up either president or vice president.[256] Hamilton was hard at work, attempting to sabotage the President's reelection.[257] Upon seeing a draft, several Federalists urged Hamilton not to send it. Wolcott wrote that "the poor old man" could do himself in without Hamilton's assistance[258] On October 24, he sent a pamphlet strongly attacking Adams's as "emotionally unstable, given to impulsive and irrational decisions, unable to coexist with his closest advisers, and generally unfit to be president."[235][259] Thanks to Burr, the pamphlet was distributed throughout the country by Republicans.[260] The pamphlet ended Hamilton's political career.[259]

With electoral votes counted, Adams was third with 65 votes, and Pinckney with 64 votes. Jefferson and Burr tied for first with 73 votes each. Because of the tie, the election devolved upon the House of Representatives, with each state having one vote and a majority required for victory. On February 17, 1801 – on the 36th ballot – Jefferson was elected by a vote of 10 to 4 (two states abstained).[172][182] Hamilton's divided the Federalists and helped Jefferson win yet failed in its attempt to woo Federalist electors from Adams.[261]

We now see the divide between North and South shrinking in favor of a more popular leader. Yet another factor of American History steps forward. (The Author)

Hamilton would go onto the floor of Congress and cast the Tie-breaker vote that gave Jefferson the win and Burr the loss. This became the first act by Hamilton leading to the "old-world duel" that killed Hamilton. (The Author)

Anxious to rejoin Abigail, who had already left for Massachusetts, Adams departed the White House March 4, 1801, and due to his son's death, did not attend Jefferson's inauguration.[265] Only five out-going presidents have not attended their successors' inaugurations.[266] The complications of the 1796 and 1800 elections prompted a modification to the Electoral College through the 12th Amendment.[267]

AT THIS TIME, ADAMS IS BEYOND THE PERIOD IN WHICH HE DEVELOPED AS A FOUNDING FATHER. OUR STORY CEASES THERE.

Judicial appointments (GREATEST CHIEF JUSTICE)

Adams appointed two U.S. Supreme Court associate justices during his term in office: Bushrod Washington, the nephew of George Washington, and Alfred Moore.[268] After Ellsworth's retirement in 1800, it fell to Adams to appoint the Court's fourth Chief Justice. Adams chose Secretary of State John Marshall,[269] THE GREATEST CHIEF JUSTICE.

1824 was filled with excitement in America, featuring a four-way presidential contest that included John Quincy. The Marquis de Lafayette toured the country. Adams was delighted by the election of John Quincy to the presidency.

Abigail died of typhoid on October 28, 1818, at Peacefield.

On July 4, 1826, 50th anniversary of the adoption of the Declaration of Independence, Adams died of a heart attack at Peacefield. His last words included an acknowledgement of his longtime friend and rival: "Thomas Jefferson survives," unaware Jefferson died several hours before. At 90, Adams was the longest-lived US president until Ronald Reagan surpassed him in 2001, now Jimmy Carter wins.

Adams never owned a slave and declined on principle to use slave labor.

According to biographer David McCullough, "Adams was both a devout Christian, and an independent thinker, and he saw no conflict in that." He believed that regular church service was beneficial to man's moral sense. Adams was raised in the Congregational church. In Quincy, the Unitarian faction included Adams and his father. The Calvinists opposed it. In 1825, the Unitarians split off as a separate denomination that included John Adams.

References

6. Ferling 1992, p. 11.
7. Ferling 1992, p. 317.
8. McCullough 2001, pp. 29–30.
9. Ferling 1992, pp. 11–14.
10. Ferling 1992, pp. 12–14.
11. Kirtley 1910, p. 366.
12. McCullough 2001, p. 35.
13. McCullough 2001, p. 13.
14. Ferling 1992, p. 16.
15. Ferling 1992, pp. 17–18.
16. Ferling 1992, p. 21.
17. Ferling 1992, p. 19.
19. McCullough 2001, p. 44.
20. Ferling 1992, p. 46.
21. Ferling 1992, pp. 36–39.
22. "They Did What? 15 Famous People Who Actually Married Their Cousins".
24. "Private Thoughts of a Founding Father". Life. June 30, 1961. p. 82.
29. McCullough 2001, pp. 171–172.
30. McCullough 2001, pp. 634–635.
31. "Declaration of Independence: A Transcription". United States National Arch. Nov 2015. Retr Oct 1, 2018.
33. Smith 1962a, pp. 72–76.
34. Ferling 1992, pp. 55–56.
36. McCullough 2001, pp. 59–61.
37. Mayhew, Rev. Jonathan (1750). "Discourse Concerning Unlimited Submission and Non-resistance to the Higher Powers". Ashbrook Center.
38. Ferling 1992, pp. 47–49.
39. McCullough 2001, p. 63.
40. McCullough 2001, pp. 62–63.
41. Ferling 1992, p. 59.
42. Ferling 1992, pp. 57–59.
43. McCullough 2001, pp. 65–66.
44. Morse 1884, p. 39.
45. Adams, John (Dec 1770). Argument in Defense of Soldiers in Boston Massacre. Adams Papers, Massachusetts Historical Society. Retrieved July 29, 2018.
46. Ferling 1992, p. 69.
50. Ferling 1992, pp. 72–73.
51. Ferling 1992, pp. 78–80.
52. Ferling 1992, pp. 92–94.
53. "1773. Dec. 17th. [from the Diary of John Adams]". Adams Papers, Mass Historical Society.
54. Ferling 1992, pp. 95–97.
56. Ferling 1992, pp. 107–108.
57. Ferling 1992, pp. 128–130.
59. "John Adams to Abigail Adams, 9 October 1774". Adams Papers, Mass Historical Society.
60. Ferling 1992, p. 112.
62. "Abigail Adams to John Adams, 16 Oct 1774". Adams Papers, Mass Historical Society.
63. Smith 1962a, p. 196.
64. McCullough 2001, pp. 87–88.
65. McCullough 2001, p. 90.
66. Ferling 1992, p. 136.
67. "Adams Timeline". Massachusetts Historical Society. Arch March 24, 2009. Retr August 22, 2015.
68. Ferling 1992, p. 124.
69. McCullough 2001, pp. 94–95.
72. Ferling 1992, pp. 155–157.

73. Smith 1962a, p. 263.
74. McCullough 2001, pp. 99–100.
75. Maier 1998, p. 37.
76. McCullough 2001, pp. 113–117.
77. Ferling 1992, p. 146.
78. Boyd & Gawalt 1999, p. 21.
79. McCullough 2001, p. 119.
80. Maier 1998, pp. 97–105.
81. McCullough 2001, pp. 130–135.
82. Morse 1884, pp. 127–128.
84. McCullough 2001, p. 136.
88. McCullough 2001, p. 163.
89. Smith 1962a, pp. 266–267.
90. Ellis 1993, pp. 41–42.
91. Smith 1962a, pp. 298–305.
94. Smith 1962a, p. 301.
95. McCullough 2001, p. 157.
96. McCullough 2001, p. 158.
99. Ferling 1992, pp. 189–190.
100. McCullough 2001, pp. 174–176.
101. McCullough 2001, pp. 177–179.
102. McCullough 2001, pp. 186–187.
103. McCullough 2001, pp. 198, 209.
107. McCullough 2001, p. 218.
108. Ferling 1992, p. 221.
109. Smith 1962a, p. 451.
110. Ferling 1992, p. 218.
111. Smith 1962a, pp. 452–459.
112. Ferling 1992, pp. 219–222.
113. McCullough 2001, p. 233.
114. McCullough 2001, pp. 239–241.
115. McCullough 2001, p. 242.
124. Ferling 1992, pp. 185–242.
125. Smith 1962a, pp. 545–546.
126. McCullough 2001, pp. 281–284.
127. Smith 1962a, pp. 546–547.
128. McCullough 2001, p. 285.
129. Adams & Adams 1851, p. 392.
130. "From John Adams to John Jay, 2 June 1785". Adams Papers, Mass Historical Society.
131. McCullough 2001, pp. 343–344.
132. McCullough 2001, pp. 364–365.
133. McCullough 2001, pp. 354–357.
134. McCullough 2001, pp. 348–350.
135. Chinard 1933, p. 203.
136. Smith 1962b, p. 655.
137. Smith 1962b, p. 702.
138. Smith 1962b, p. 729.
139. McCullough 2001, p. 382.
140. McCullough 2001, pp. 389–392.
141. Ferling 2009, pp. 270–274.
142. McCullough 2001, pp. 393–394.
168. Bomboy, Scott (Oct 22, 2012). "America's first dirty presidential campaign, 1796 style".
169. Constitution Daily.
170. Ferling, John (Feb 15, 2016). " Rivalry Between Jefferson and Hamilton Changed History".
171. Time Magazine.
170. Flexner 1974, pp. 360–361.
171. Smith 1962b, pp. 898–899.
173. McDonald 1974, pp. 178–181.
174. Diggins 2003, pp. 83–88.
175. Hoadley 1986, p. 54.

176. "John Adams to Abigail Adams, 10 February 1796". Adams Papers, Mass Historical Society.
177. Elkins & McKitrick 1993 pp. 513–537.
178. Chernow 2004, p. 521.
179. Smith 1962b, p. 902.
180. "John Adams to Abigail Adams, 9 January 1797". Adams Papers, Mass Historical Society.
181. Chernow 2004, p. 522.
182. "Electoral College Box Scores 1789–1996". College Park, MD: Office of Federal Register, NARA.
183. Amar, Vikram David (October 22, 2008). "Vice president: a split-ticket vote?". NYT. Retr
184. Oct 17, 2017.
184. "The 3rd Presidential Inauguration, John Adams, March 04, 1797". Washington, DC: U.S. Senate.
185. Herring 2008, p. 91.
186. Ferling 1992, p. 333.
187. McCullough 2001, p. 471.
188. Kurtz 1957, p. 272.
189. Chernow 2004, pp. 593–594.
190. Chernow 2004, p. 524.
191. Ellis 1993, p. 28.
192. Wood 2009, pp. 174–177, 240.
193. Herring 2008, p. 82.
194. Ferling 1992, pp. 342–345.
195. "John Adams – Special Message to the Senate and the House; May 16 1797".
Avalon Project, Yale Law School. September 22, 2017.
196. McCullough 2001, pp. 484–485.
197. McCullough 2001, p. 495.
198. Chernow 2004, p. 547.
200. McCullough 2001, pp. 495–496.
201. McCullough 2001, p. 502.
202. Chernow 2004, p. 550.
203. Smith 1962b, pp. 957–960.
204. McCullough 2001, p. 498.
205. Ferling 1992, pp. 365–368.
206. Ferling 1992, p. 365.
207. Ferling 1992, p. 366.
208. Ferling 1992, p. 367.
209. Chernow 2004, pp. 574–575.
210. Chernow 2004, p. 575.
211. McCullough 2001, pp. 520–521.
212. Chernow 2004, pp. 573–575.
213. Chernow 2004, p. 553.
214. Ferling 1992, pp. 356–357.
215. Chernow 2004, pp. 552–553.
216. Flexner 1974, p. 376.
217. Flexner 1974, pp. 376–377.
218. Chernow 2004, p. 555.
219. Flexner 1974, p. 378.
220. Smith 1962b, p. 978.
221. Flexner 1974, pp. 380–381.
222. Smith 1962b, pp. 982–983.
223. Kurtz 1957, p. 331.
224. McCullough 2001, p. 507.
225. McCullough 2001, pp. 516–517.
226. Chernow 2004, pp. 592–593.
227. McCullough 2001, p. 518.
233. Diggins 2003, pp. 129–130.
234. McCullough 2001, pp. 540–541.
236. McCullough 2001, pp. 538–539.
238. McCullough 2001, p. 534.
241. McCullough 2001, p. 150.
242. Ferling 1992, p. 423.
243. Chernow 2004, p. 631.

244. Chernow 2004, p. 594.
245. "John Adams I (Frigate) 1799–1867". Naval History Heritage Command.
246. Miller 1997, p. 9.
247. "Congress Passes Socialized Medicine and Mandates Health Insurance – In 1798".
248. "The John Adams Building". Library of Congress. Retrieved June 29, 2018.
249. Smith 1962b, p. 1036.
250. Smith 1962b, p. 1049.
251. Smith 1962b, p. 1050.
252. The Senate Moves to Washington. United States Senate. Retr August 15, 2017.
253. Ferling 1992, pp. 396–397.
254. McCullough 2001, pp. 543–545.
255. McCullough 2001, pp. 536–537.
256. McCullough 2001, p. 544.
257. Chernow 2004, pp. 619–620.
258. McCullough 2001, p. 549.
259. McCullough 2001, p. 550.
260. Morse 1884, pp. 320–321.
261. Chernow 2004, p. 626.
265. "The Revolutionary Inauguration of Thomas Jefferson". WHHA (en-US).
267. Levinson, Sanford V. "Election of President and Vice President". Constitution Center.
268. Perry 1986, pp. 371–410.

Sources Biographies

- Chinard, Gilbert (1933). Honest John Adams. Boston: Little, Brown, and Co. OCLC 988108386.
- Diggins, John P. (2003). Schlesinger, Arthur M. Jr. (ed.). John Adams. The American Presidents. New York: Time Books. ISBN 978-0-8050-6937-2.
- Ellis, Joseph J. (1993). Passionate Sage: The Character and Legacy of John Adams. New Yorkpublisher=W.W. Norton & Co. ISBN 978-0-393-31133-4.
- Ferling, John E. (1992). John Adams: A Life. Knoxville: U Tennessee Press. ISBN 978-0-87049-730-8.
- McCullough, David (2001). John Adams. New York: Simon & Schuster. ISBN 978-1-4165-7588-7.
- Morse, John Torey (1884). John Adams. Boston: Houghton, Mifflin, and Company. OCLC 926779205.
- Smith, Page (1962a). John Adams. Vol. I, 1735–1784. New Yorkpublisher=Doubleday & Co. ISBN 9780837123486. OCLC 852986601.
- Smith, Page (1962b). John Adams. Vol. II, 1784–1826. New York: Doubleday & Co. ISBN 978-0-8371-2348-6. OCLC 852986620.

Specialized studies

- Chernow, Ron (2004). Alexander Hamilton. London: Penguin Books. ISBN 978-1-101-20085-8.
- Elkins, Stanley M.; McKitrick, Eric (1993). Age of Federalism. Oxford, NY: Oxford U Press.
- Ellis, Joseph J. (2003). Founding Brothers: The Revolutionary Generation. New York: Knopf Doubleday Publishing Group. ISBN 978-1-4000-7768-7.
- Everett, Robert B. (1966). "Mature Religious Thought of Adams" South Carolina Historical Assoc.
- Ferling, John (2009). The Ascent of George Washington: The Hidden Political Genius of an American Icon. New York: Bloomsbury Press. ISBN 978-1-59691-465-0.
- Flexner, James Thomas (1974). Washington: The Indispensable Man. Boston: Little, Brown.
- Herring, George C. (2008). From colony to superpower: U.S. foreign relations since 1776. NY: Oxford Press.
- Hoadley, John F. (1986). Origins of American Political Parties: 1789–1803. U Press of Kentucky.
- Hutson, James H. (1968). "John Adams' Title Campaign (March 1968)". The New England Quarterly. 41 (1): 30–39. doi:10.2307/363331. JSTOR 363331.
- Kirtley, James Samuel (1910). Half Hour Talks on Character Building: By Self-made Men and Women. A. Hamming. OCLC 13927429.
- Kurtz, Stephen G. (1957). The Presidency of John Adams: The Collapse of Federalism, 1795–1800. Philadelphia: University of Pennsylvania Press. ISBN 978-0-8122-7101-0. OCLC 979781538.
- Maier, Pauline (1998). American Scripture: Making the Declaration of Independence. New York: Vintage Books. ISBN 978-0-679-77908-7.
- McDonald, Forrest (1974). The Presidency of George Washington. American Presidency. Lawrence: University Press of Kansas. ISBN 978-0-7006-0359-6.
- Miller, Nathan (1997) U.S. Navy: A History (3rd ed.). Annapolis: Naval Institute Press. ISBN 978-1-61251-892-3.
- Perry, James R. (1986). "Supreme Court Appointments, 1789–1801: Criteria, Presidential Style, and the Press of Events". Journal of the Early Republic. 6 (4): 371–410. doi:10.2307/3122645. JSTOR 3122645.
- Wood, Gordon S. (2009). Empire of Liberty: history of Early Republic, 1789–1815. Oxford U Press.
- Wood, Gordon S. (2017). Friends Divided: Adams and Jefferson. NY: Penguin. ISBN 978-0-7352-2473-5.

JAMES MADISON,
VIRGINIA
FATHER OF THE UNITED STATES CONSTITUTION

James Madison was an American statesman, diplomat, and Founding Father who served as the fourth president of the United States from 1809 to 1817. Madison was popularly acclaimed the "Father of the Constitution" for his pivotal role in drafting and promoting the Constitution of the United States and the Bill of Rights.

Early life and education

James Madison (March 16, 1751 – June 28, 1836), was born at Belle Grove Plantation near Port Conway in the Colony of Virginia, to James Madison Sr. and Eleanor Madison. His family had lived in Virginia since the mid-17th century.[1] Madison's maternal grandfather, Francis Conway, was a prominent planter and tobacco merchant.[2] His father was a tobacco planter who grew up on Mount Pleasant plantation. With a 5,000-acre plantation, Madison's father was among the largest landowners. [3] In the 1760s, the Madison family moved into a newly built house they named Montpelier.[4] Madison was the oldest of twelve children.[5]

From age 11 to 16, Madison was tutored by Donald Robertson. Madison learned mathematics, geography, and modern and classical languages, becoming exceptional in Latin.[6] At 16, Madison returned to Montpelier.[7] In 1769, he enrolled at the College of New Jersey.[8]

His college studies included Latin, Greek, theology, and the works of the Enlightenment,[9] and emphasized speech and debate.[10] During his time at Princeton, Madison's closest friend was future Attorney General William Bradford.[11] Aaron Burr and Madison completed the three-year Bachelor of Arts degree in two years, graduating in 1771.[12] Madison contemplated clergy or law but remained at Princeton in Hebrew and political philosophy.[1][13]

After returning to Montpelier, Madison tutored his younger siblings.[15] He began to study law books in 1773, asking his friend Bradford, a law apprentice, to send him a plan of study. Madison never joined the bar.[16] Following the Revolutionary War, he studied ancient democracies in preparation for the Constitutional Convention.[17]

American Revolution and Articles of Confederation

In 1765, the British Parliament passed the Stamp Act, which began a conflict that became the American Revolution.[18]

After returning to Montpelier in 1774, Madison took a seat on the local Committee of Safety, a pro-revolution group that oversaw the Patriot militia.[19] In October 1775, he was commissioned colonel of the Orange County militia, serving as his father's second-in-command until elected a delegate to the Fifth Virginia Convention, to produce Virginia's first constitution. Although Madison never battled in the Revolutionary War, he rose to prominence in Virginia politics as a wartime leader.[20] At the Virginia constitutional convention, he convinced delegates to alter the Virginia Declaration of Rights to provide "equal entitlement", rather than mere "tolerance", in the exercise of religion.[21] With the enactment of the Virginia constitution, Madison became part of the Virginia House of Delegates, subsequently elected to the Virginia governor's Council of State,[22] where he became a close ally of Governor Jefferson.[23] On July 4, 1776, the United States Declaration of Independence was formally printed.[24]

Madison participated in the debates on the Articles of Confederation,[25] and was elected to the Second Continental Congress, the governing body of the US.

During Madison's term in Congress from 1780 to 1783, the U.S. faced a difficult war against Great Britain, as well as runaway inflation, financial troubles, and a lack of cooperation between the various levels of government. Madison worked to become an expert on financial issues, becoming a legislative workhorse and a master of parliamentary coalition building.[26] Frustrated the states failed to supply troops, Madison proposed to amend the Articles of Confederation to grant Congress the power to raise revenue.[28] Though Washington, Hamilton, and others favored the tariff amendment, it failed to win ratification.[29] An advocate of westward expansion, he insisted upon navigation Rights on the Mississippi River and control of all lands east of it via Treaty of Paris, which ended the Revolutionary War.[30]

James Madison as Father of the Constitution and Constitutional Convention

As a member of the Virginia House of Delegates, Madison continued to advocate for religious freedom, and, along with Jefferson, drafted the Virginia Statute for Religious Freedom. That amendment, which guaranteed freedom of religion and disestablished the Church of England, was passed in 1786.[31] Madison also became a land speculator, purchasing land along the Mohawk River in partnership with James Monroe.[32] Throughout the 1780s, Madison became increasingly worried about the disunity of the states and the weakness of the central government.[33] He believed that direct democracy caused social decay and that a Republican government would be effective against partisanship and factionalism.[34] He was particularly troubled by laws that legalized paper money and denied diplomatic immunity to ambassadors from other countries.[35] Madison was also concerned about the inability in Congress to create foreign policy, protect American trade, and foster settlement of lands between the Appalachian Mountains and Mississippi River.[36] As Madison wrote, "a crisis had arrived which was to decide whether the American experiment was to be a blessing to the world, or to blast for ever the hopes which the republican cause had inspired."[37] Madison committed to an intense study of law and political theory, influenced by Enlightenment texts sent by Jefferson from France.[38] Madison sought out works on law and constitutions of "ancient and modern confederacies."[39] With so many competing interests, Madison hoped to minimize the abuses of majority rule.[40] He opposed John Jay that the United States concede claims to the river for 25 years.[41]

Leading up to the 1787 ratification debates for the Constitution,[42] Madison worked with Edmund Randolph and George Mason, to create the Virginia Plan, an outline for a new federal constitution.[43] It called for three branches of government (legislative, executive, and judicial), a bicameral Congress (consisting of the Senate and the House of Representatives) apportioned by population, and a federal Council of Revision that would have veto rights.[44] The Virginia Plan did not structure the executive branch, but Madison favored a single executive.[45] With the assent of prominent attendees such as Washington and Franklin, the delegates agreed in a secret session that abrogation of the Articles and creation of a new constitution was a plausible and began scheduling debate on ratification.[46] As a compromise, large states got a proportional House, small states got equal Senate representation.[47]

Madison convinced his fellow congressmen to remain neutral in the ratification debate and allow each state to vote on the Constitution.[48] Those who supported the Constitution were called Federalists; that included Madison.[49] Opponents of the Constitution, known as Anti-Federalists, began a campaign against ratification.[49] In response, starting in October 1787,[50] Hamilton and John Jay, both Federalists, began publishing pro-ratification articles in New York.[51] After Jay dropped out of the project, Hamilton approached Madison, who was in New

York on congressional business, to write some of the essays.[52] The essays were published under the pseudonym of Publius.[53] The trio produced 85 essays known as *The Federalist Papers*.[54] The 85 essays were divided into two parts: 36 letters against the Articles of Confederation, and 49 letters that favored the new Constitution.[50] The articles were also published in book form and used by the supporters of the Constitution in the ratifying conventions. Federalist No. 10, Madison's first contribution to *The Federalist Papers*, became highly regarded in the 20th century for its advocacy of representative democracy.[55] In it, Madison describes the dangers posed by the majority factions and argues that their effects can be limited through the formation of a large republic. He theorizes that in large republics the large number of factions that emerge will control their influence because no single faction becomes a majority.[56] In Federalist No. 51, he explains how separation of powers between three branches of the federal government, and between state governments and federal government, establishes checks and balances that ensures no branch becomes too powerful.[57]

As the Virginia ratification began, Madison focused on winning the support of the relatively small number of undecided delegates.[58] Randolph announced that he would support unconditional ratification of the Constitution, with amendments to be proposed after ratification.[59] Though former Virginia governor Patrick Henry gave persuasive speeches against ratification, Madison's had long responded with rational arguments to Henry's anti-Federalist appeals.[60] Madison was also a defender of federal veto rights and, according to historian Ron Chernow "pleaded at the Constitutional Convention that the federal government should possess a veto over state laws".[61] In his final speech to the ratifying convention, Madison implored his fellow delegates to ratify the Constitution, arguing failure to do so would lead to the collapse of ratification, as each state would seek favorable amendments.[62] On June 25, 1788, the convention voted 89–79 in favor of ratification. The vote came a week after New Hampshire became the ninth state to ratify, securing the Constitution's adoption and a new form of government.[63] The following January, Washington was elected our first president.[64]

Madison Election to Congress - - 1789 Virginia's 5th congressional district

After Madison was defeated in his bid for the Senate, and with concerns for both his political career and the possibility that Patrick Henry and allies would arrange for a second constitutional convention, Madison ran for the House of Representatives.[65] Henry and the Anti-Federalists were in firm control of the General Assembly in the autumn of 1788.[66] At Henry's behest, the Virginia legislature denied Madison a seat by gerrymandering congressional districts. Locked in a difficult race against Monroe, Madison promised to support constitutional amendments to protect individual liberties.[67] In an open letter, Madison wrote that, while he had opposed requiring alterations to the Constitution, he now believed that "amendments, if pursued with a proper moderation ... may serve the purpose of satisfying the minds of well-meaning opponents, and of providing additional safeguards for liberty."[68] Madison's promise paid off, as in Virginia's 5th district election, he won a seat in Congress with 57 percent.[4]

Madison became a key adviser to Washington.[67] He played a role in establishing the three Cabinet departments, his influence helped Thomas Jefferson become the first Secretary of State.[69] At start of the first Congress, he introduced a tariff bill,[70] and Congress established a federal tariff on imports by enacting the Tariff of 1789.[71] The following year, Secretary of the Treasury Hamilton introduced an ambitious economic program. After deadlock, Madison, Jefferson, and Hamilton agreed to the Compromise of 1790, which provided for enactment of Hamilton's assumption plan, in the Funding Act of 1790. In return, Congress passed the Residence Act, establishing the capital district of Washington, D.C.[73]

Bill of Rights

During the first Congress, Madison took the lead advocating constitutional amendments to the Bill of Rights.[74] His primary goals were to fulfill his 1789 campaign pledge and to prevent a second constitutional convention. He believed enumeration of specific rights would fix those rights and encourage judges to protect them.[75] After studying more than two hundred amendments proposed at the state ratifying conventions,[76] Madison introduced the Bill of Rights on June 8, 1789. His amendments contained numerous restrictions on the federal government and would protect, freedom of religion, freedom of speech, and the right to peaceful assembly.[77] While his amendments were drawn from the ratifying conventions, Madison was responsible for proposals to guarantee freedom of the press, protect property from government seizure, and ensure jury trials.[76] He also proposed an amendment to prevent states from abridging "equal rights of conscience, or freedom of the press, or the trial by jury".[78]

To prevent a permanent standing federal army, Madison proposed the Second Amendment, which gave state-regulated militia groups and private citizens the "right to bear arms." Madison and the Republicans desired a free government to be established by consent of the governed, rather than by national military force.[79]

Madison's Bill of Rights faced little opposition; he had largely co-opted the Anti-Federalist goal of amending the Constitution but had avoided proposing amendments that would alienate supporters of the Constitution.[80] His amendments were mostly adopted by the House of Representatives as proposed, but the Senate made several changes.[81] Madison's proposal to apply parts of the Bill of Rights to the states was eliminated, as was his change to the Constitution's preamble, indicating that governmental power is vested by the people.[82] He was disappointed the Bill of Rights did not include protections against actions by state governments, but the passage of the shored up his support in Virginia.[76] Ten amendments were finally ratified on December 15, 1791, becoming known as the Bill of Rights.[83]

Founding the Democratic–Republican Party

Thomas Jefferson and Madison founded the Democratic-Republican Party and broadly represented Southern interests.

After 1790, the Washington administration became polarized into two main factions. One faction, led by Jefferson and Madison, broadly represented Southern interests, and sought close relations with France. This faction became the Democratic-Republican Party opposition to Secretary of the Treasury Hamilton. The other faction, led by Hamilton and the Federalists, broadly represented Northern financial interests and relations with Britain.[84] In 1791, Hamilton introduced a plan that called for the establishment of a national bank to provide loans to emerging industries and oversee the money supply.[85] Madison and the Democratic-Republican Party fought back against Hamilton's attempt to expand the power of the Federal Government with a national bank; Madison argued that under the Constitution, Congress did not have the power to create a federally empowered national bank.[86] Despite Madison's opposition, Congress created the First Bank of the United States, which Washington signed into law.[85] As Hamilton implemented his economic program and Washington enjoyed immense prestige, Madison became concerned Hamilton would establish a monarchy.[87]

When Hamilton submitted his *Report on Manufactures*, which called for federal action to stimulate the development of a diversified economy, Madison once again challenged Hamilton's proposal.[88] Along with Jefferson, Madison helped establish the *National Gazette*, a Philadelphia newspaper that attacked Hamilton's proposals.[89] In an essay in the newspaper in

September 1792, Madison wrote that the country had divided into two factions: his faction, which believed "that mankind are capable of governing themselves", and Hamilton's faction, which allegedly sought the establishment of an aristocratic monarchy and was biased in favor of the wealthy.[90] Those opposed to Hamilton's economic policies, including many former Anti-Federalists, continued to strengthen the ranks of the Democratic–Republican Party, while those who supported the administration's policies supported Hamilton's Federalist Party.[91] In the 1792 presidential election, both major parties supported Washington for re-election, but the Democratic–Republicans sought to unseat Vice President John Adams. Because the Constitution's rules precluded Jefferson from challenging Adams, the party backed New York Governor George Clinton for the vice presidency, but Adams won nonetheless.[92]

With Jefferson out of office after 1793, Madison became the de facto leader of the Democratic–Republican Party.[93] When Britain and France went to war in 1793, the U.S. needed to determine which side to support.[94] While the differences between the Democratic–Republicans and the Federalists had previously centered on economic matters, foreign policy became an increasingly important issue.[95] Madison believed a trade war would succeed, and allow Americans to assert independence fully. The British West Indies, Madison maintained, could not live without American foodstuffs, but Americans could easily do without British manufacturers.[96] Similarly, Madison argued that British industry was highly dependent on American consumers and would suffer if this market was denied to the British.[97] Washington secured friendly trade relations with Britain through the Jay Treaty of 1794.[98] Madison and his allies were outraged; the Democratic–Republican Robert R. Livingston wrote to Madison that the treaty "sacrifices every essential interest and prostrates the honor of our country".[99] Madison's opposition ended his friendship with Washington.[98]

Marriage and family

On September 15, 1794, Madison married Dolley Payne Todd, the 26-year-old widow of John Todd.[100] Earlier that year, Madison and Dolley Todd had been formally introduced by Aaron Burr.[101] Madison and Dolly quickly became engaged and prepared for a wedding that summer.[102] Dolley became a renowned in Washington, D.C., and excelled at hosting.[12][103]

At age 50, Madison inherited the large plantation of Montpelier.[1][104] While Madison never had children with Dolley, he adopted her one surviving son.[105] Monroe and Burr, believed Madison's lack of offspring weighed on his thoughts, though he never spoke of any distress.[106]

Adams presidency

Madison remained a prominent Democratic–Republican leader in opposition to the Adams administration.[112] Madison and Jefferson believed that the Federalists were using the Quasi-War with France to justify a violation of constitutional rights by passing the Alien and Sedition Acts, and they increasingly came to view Adams as a monarchist.[113] Madison and Jefferson believed natural rights were non-negotiable even in war. Madison believed the Alien and Sedition Acts formed a dangerous precedent, allowing government to look past the natural rights of its people.[114] In response to the Alien and Sedition Acts, Jefferson argued the states had power to nullify federal law on the basis of the Constitutional compact among the states. Madison rejected this view of nullification and urged that states respond to unjust federal laws through interposition, by which a state legislature declared a law unconstitutional but did not take steps to prevent its enforcement. The incident damaged the Democratic–Republican Party as attention shifted from Alien and Sedition Acts to nullification doctrine.[115]

Secretary of State (1801–1809) Presidency of Thomas Jefferson
Louisiana Purchase and Chesapeake–Leopard affair

Jefferson appointed Madison secretary of state despite lacking foreign policy experience.[119] An introspective individual, he received assistance from his wife,[104] relying deeply on her in dealing with the social pressures of being a public.[12] The ascent of Napoleon dulled Democratic–Republican enthusiasm for the French cause, Madison sought a neutral position in the ongoing Coalition Wars between France and Britain.[120] Domestically, the Jefferson administration and the Democratic–Republican Congress rolled back many Federalist policies; Congress quickly repealed the Alien and Sedition Act, abolished internal taxes, and reduced the size of the army and navy.[121] Gallatin, however, convinced Jefferson to retain the First Bank of the United States.[122] Though Federalist political power was fading at the national level, Chief Justice John Marshall ensured that Federalist ideology was important in the judiciary. In *Marbury v. Madison*, Marshall ruled Madison unjustly refused to deliver federal commissions to individuals who had been appointed, but that the Supreme Court did not have jurisdiction. Importantly, Marshall's opinion established the principle of judicial review.[123]

Jefferson promoted western expansion and hoped to acquire the Spanish territory of Louisiana, west of the Mississippi.[124] Early in Jefferson's presidency, they learned Spain planned to retrocede the Louisiana territory to France.[125] Lacking authorization from Jefferson, Monroe, and Livingston doubled size of the US via the Louisiana Purchase, in which France sold over 827,987 square miles of land for $15 million ($271,433,333.33 in 2021).[126]

Jefferson was concerned about the constitutionality of the Louisiana Purchase and favored a constitutional amendment authorizing Congress to acquire new territories. Madison convinced Jefferson to refrain from the amendment.[127] The Senate quickly ratified the treaty, and the House passed enabling legislation.[128]

Early in his tenure, Jefferson was able to maintain cordial relations with both France and Britain, but relations with Britain deteriorated after 1805.[129] The British ended their policy of tolerance towards American shipping and began seizing American goods,[130] and impressed American sailors.[131] In response to the attacks, Congress passed the Non-importation Act, which restricted many, but not all, British imports.[130] Tensions with Britain were heightened by the *Chesapeake–Leopard* affair, a confrontation between American and British naval forces, while the French also began attacking American shipping.[132] Madison convinced Congress to pass the Embargo Act of 1807, which banned all exports to foreign nations.[133] The embargo proved ineffective.[134] Congress replaced the embargo with the Non-Intercourse Act, which allowed trade with nations other than Britain and France.[135]

1808 Presidential election JAMES MADISON ELECTED

Madison's status in the party was damaged by his association with the embargo, unpopular especially in the Northeast.[136] With the Federalists party collapsing after 1800, the chief opposition to Madison came from the Democratic–Republican Party.[137]

Randolph recruited Monroe to challenge Madison for leadership of the party.[138] Many Northerners hoped Vice President Clinton could unseat Madison as Jefferson's successor.[139] Despite opposition, Madison won his party's nomination at the January 1808 congressional nominating caucus.[140] The Federalist Party mustered little strength outside New England, and Madison defeated Federalist Charles Cotesworth Pinckney in the general election.[141]

Presidency (1809–1817) - - Presidency of James Madison

Chief Justice Marshall administered the presidential oath of office to Madison while outgoing President Jefferson watched.[142] Vice President George Clinton was sworn in for a second term, making him the first U.S. vice president to serve under two presidents. Unlike Jefferson, who enjoyed unified support, Madison faced political opposition from previous political allies. Additionally, the Federalist Party was resurgent owing to opposition to the embargo. Aside from his planned nomination of Gallatin for secretary of state, the remaining members of Madison's Cabinet were chosen merely to further political harmony.[143] Due to Monroe and Clinton, Madison faced opposition to nomination of Gallatin as secretary of state. Madison did not nominate Gallatin, keeping him in treasury department,[145] choosing Robert Smith to be the secretary of state.[144]

After bitter intra-party contention, Madison finally replaced Smith with Monroe in April 1811.[146] With a Cabinet full of those he distrusted, Madison rarely called Cabinet meetings and instead frequently consulted with Gallatin alone.[147] Early in his presidency, Madison sought to continue Jefferson's policies of low taxes and a reduction of the national debt.[147] In 1811, Congress allowed the charter of the First Bank of the United States to lapse after Madison declined to take a strong stance.[148]

War of 1812 - - Prelude to war

With sanctions and other policies having failed, Madison determined that war with Britain was the only remaining option.[153] Many Americans called for a "second war of independence," and an angry public elected a "war hawk" Congress, led by Henry Clay and John C. Calhoun.[154] With Britain already engaged in the Napoleonic Wars, many Americans including Madison believed that the United States could easily capture Canada, using it as a bargaining chip or retaining control of it.[155] On June 1, 1812, Madison asked Congress for a declaration of war. The declaration of war was passed along sectional and party lines, with opposition to the declaration coming from the Northeast.[156] In the years prior to the war, Jefferson and Madison reduced the size of the military, leaving the country with a military force consisting mostly of poorly trained militia.[157] Madison asked Congress to put the country "into an armor and attitude demanded by the crisis," recommending expansion of army and navy.[158]

Military actions

Madison initially believed the war would result in a quick American victory.[155] Madison ordered three military incursions into Canada, starting from Fort Detroit, designed to loosen British control around American-held Fort Niagara and destroy the British supply lines from Montreal. These actions would gain leverage for concessions to protect American shipping in the Atlantic.[159] Without a standing army, Madison counted on regular state militias to invade Canada: governors in the Northeast failed to cooperate.[160] The British army was more organized, used professional soldiers, and fostered an alliance with Native American tribes led by Tecumseh. Commanding General Henry Dearborn, hampered by mutinous New England infantry, retreated to winter quarters near Albany, failing to destroy Montreal's vulnerable British supply lines.[159] Lacking war funding, Madison relied on high-interest bank loans.[163]

In the 1812 presidential election, Madison was re-nominated without opposition.[164] A dissident group of New York Democratic-Republicans nominated DeWitt Clinton, to oppose

Madison in the 1812 election. This faction of Democratic-Republicans hoped to unseat the president by forging a coalition among those opposed to the war, as well as those angry with Madison for not moving more decisively toward war, northerners weary of the Virginia dynasty and southern control of the White House, and many New Englanders wanted Madison replaced. Hoping to shore up his support in the Northeast, where the War of 1812 was unpopular, Madison selected Governor Elbridge Gerry of Massachusetts as his running mate,[165] though Gerry died after two years.[166] Despite the maneuverings of the Federalists, Madison won.[167]

Madison accepted Russia's invitation to arbitrate and sent a delegation led by Gallatin and John Quincy Adams to Europe to negotiate a peace treaty.[155] While Madison worked to end the war, the United States experienced some impressive naval successes, by the USS *Constitution* and other warships.[168] Victorious in the Battle of Lake Erie, the U.S. crippled the supply of British military forces in the western theater of the war.[169] General William Henry Harrison defeated the forces of the British and of Tecumseh's confederacy at the Battle of the Thames. The death of Tecumseh in that battle marked the permanent end of armed Native American resistance in the Old Northwest.[170] In March 1814, Major General Andrew Jackson broke the resistance of the British-allied Muscogee Creek in the Old Southwest with his victory at the Battle of Horseshoe Bend (more typically known as Creek, held control of most of today's Georgia, Alabama and Mississippi).[171] The British continued to repel invasion of Canada, and a British force captured Fort Niagara and burned Buffalo in late 1813.[172]

On August 24, 1814, the British landed a large force in Chesapeake Bay and routed General William Winder's army at the Battle of Bladensburg.[173] Madison, who had earlier inspected Winder's army,[174] escaped British capture by fleeing to Virginia, though the British captured Washington and burned the White House.[175] Dolley abandoned the capital and fled to Virginia, but only after securing the portrait of George Washington.[174] The charred remains of the capital signified a humiliating defeat for Madison and America.[175] On August 27, Madison returned to Washington to view the carnage.[175] Dolley returned the next day, and the Madisons moved into the Octagon House. The British army advanced on Baltimore, but the U.S. repelled the British attack in the Battle of Baltimore.[176] That same month, U.S. forces repelled a British invasion from Canada with victory at Battle of Plattsburgh.[177] The British public turned against the war, and British leaders looked for an exit.[178]

In January 1815, Jackson's troops defeated the British at the Battle of New Orleans.[179] Just more than a month later, Madison learned that his negotiators had concluded the Treaty of Ghent on December 24, 1814, which ended the war.[180] Madison quickly sent the treaty to the Senate, which ratified it on February 16, 1815.[226] This view bolstered Madison's reputation as president.[181] Napoleon's defeat at the Battle of Waterloo brought a close to the Napoleonic Wars and ended the hostile seizure of American shipping by British and French forces.[182]

Postwar period decline of Federalist opposition - - Era of Good Feelings

There was truly a discussion of a New England secession. Madison, having become a great politician, found ways to smooth the situation. John Randolph, stated that Madison's proposals now "out-Hamiltons Alexander Hamilton".[183] Responding to Madison's proposals, the 14th Congress compiled one of the most productive legislative records at that point in history.[184] Congress granted Second Bank of the United States a twenty-five-year charter[185] and passed the Tariff of 1816, with high import duties. Madison approved spending on the Cumberland Road, with a link to western lands.

Native American policy Treaty of Fort Wayne (1809) and Tecumseh's War
(Negotiated with Indians for 23 million acres of land in Georgia-Alabama to US)
(Negotiated with Indians for 3 million acres of land in Indiana to US)

Upon becoming president, Madison said the federal government's duty was to convert Native Americans by the "participation of the improvements of which the human mind and manners are susceptible in a civilized state".[147]

On September 30, 1809, Madison agreed to the Treaty of Fort Wayne.[188] In the treaty, American Indian tribes were compensated.

Tensions continued to rise, leading to the Battle of Tippecanoe, sometimes called Tecumseh's War, and Tecumseh was defeated. In addition to the Battle of the Thames and the Battle of Horseshoe Bend, other wars with American Indians included the Peoria War, and the Creek War. Negotiated by Jackson after the Creek War, the Treaty of Fort Jackson, added 23 million acres to Georgia and Alabama.

Madison's health slowly deteriorated through the 1830s. He died of congestive heart failure at Montpelier on June 28, 1836, at the age of 85.

Madison was baptized as an Anglican and educated by Presbyterian clergymen. Madison believed in religious liberty, and he advocated Virginia's disestablishment of religious institutions sponsored by the state. The best indicator of how Madison viewed organized religion comes to us in his actions as a junior legislator.

What if your state arrested preachers who did not worship the official state religion?

Future Presidents Jefferson and Madison first worked together on this issue. At first, they took different sides. Then both realized the error of such a plan, that true religious freedom could not exist if government allowed just a single religion. Massachusetts had chosen the Anglican religion as did Virginia. This was anathema to most Americans, as the Anglican church had executed many religious leaders of other God-fearing Christian denominations.

James Madison circulated a lengthy essay; Memorial and Remonstrance against Religious Assessments, June 20, 1785. In the essay, Madison stated all the reasons against establishment of a single religion as an abject defeat for religious freedom now established in the Bill of Rights to the United States Constitution.

Madison spoke in the Virginia Assembly favoring a bill Jefferson proposed for gradual abolition of slavery, and helped defeat a bill to outlaw manumission.

Madison initially opposed the Constitution's 20-year protection of the foreign slave trade but accepted it as a compromise for the South to ratify the document.

References
1.   Ketcham 2002, p. 57.
2.   Ketcham 1990, p. 5.
3.   Montpellier Foundation.
4.   Montpellier, Life of James Madison.
5.   Ketcham 1990, p. 12.
6.   Ketcham 2003, pp. 370–371.
7.   Boyd, 2013.
8.   Gutzman 2012, p. 2.
9.   Feldman 2017, pp. 3–7.
10.   Feldman 2017, pp. 5–6.
11.   Ketcham 2003, p. 35.
12.   Ketcham 2003, p. 34.
13.   Feldman 2017, pp. 4–5.
14.   Ball 2017, pp. 45–46.
15.   Feldman 2017, pp. 7–8.
16.   Bilder 2010, pp. 390–391.
17.   McCullough 2006, p. 21.
18.   Taylor 2016, pp. 96–100.

19. Burstein & Isenberg 2010, pp. 14–15.
20. Feldman 2017, pp. 25–27.
21. Burstein & Isenberg 2010, pp. 48–49, 59–60.
22. Burstein & Isenberg 2010, pp. 65–66.
23. Library of Congress, pp. 506–507.
24. Coelho 2013, p. 61.
25. Mason 1970, pp. 274–289.
26. Stagg, 2019.
27. Burstein & Isenberg 2010, pp. 96–97.
28. Burstein & Isenberg 2010, pp. 96–98.
29. Ketcham 2003, pp. 120–123.
30. Burstein & Isenberg 2010, p. xxiv.
31. Feldman 2017, p. 70.
32. Burstein & Isenberg 2010, pp. 96–97, 128–130.
33. Allott 2003, p. 321.
34. Manweller 2005, p. 22.
35. Burstein & Isenberg 2010, pp. 129–130.
36. Rutland 1987, p. 14.
37. Burstein & Isenberg 2010, pp. 136–137.
38. Feldman 2017, pp. 56–57, 74–75.
39. Feldman 2017, pp. 98–99, 121–122.
40. Ketcham 2003, pp. 177–179.
41. Robinson 1999, p. 117.
42. Burstein & Isenberg 2010, pp. 150–151.
43. Burstein & Isenberg 2010, pp. 140–141.
44. Feldman 2017, pp. 115–117.
45. Wills 2002, pp. 25–27.
46. Feldman 2017, pp. 199–200.
47. Burstein & Isenberg 2010, pp. 164–166.
48. Cost 2021, p. 118.
49. The Federalist Papers, p. xxv.
50. Feldman 2017, pp. 177–178.
51. Feldman 2017, pp. 179–180.
52. Cost 2021, p. 130.
53. Hamilton, Madison & Jay 1992, p. xxv.
54. Wills 2002, pp. 31–35.
55. Hamilton, Madison & Jay 1992.
56. Feldman 2017, pp. 180–183.
57. Burstein & Isenberg 2010, pp. 179–180.
58. Feldman 2017, pp. 231–233.
59. Wills 2002, pp. 35–37.
60. Chernow 2004, pp. 571–574.
61. Feldman 2017, pp. 239–240.
62. Amar 2005, p. 6.
63. Mount Vernon, Essay.
64. Wills 2002, pp. 38–39.
65. Feldman 2017, pp. 247–248, 251–252.
66. Cost 2021, p. 162.
67. Feldman 2017, pp. 252–253.
68. Burstein & Isenberg 2010, pp. 189–193, 203.
69. Feldman 2017, pp. 258–259.
70. Bordewich 2016, pp. 100–102.
71. Burstein & Isenberg 2010, pp. 213–217.
72. Burstein & Isenberg 2010, pp. 217–220.
73. Burstein & Isenberg 2010, pp. 195–197.
74. Feldman 2017, pp. 264–274.
75. Ketcham 1990, p. 290.
76. Feldman 2017, pp. 267–269.
77. Feldman 2017, pp. 270–271.
78. Cost 2021, p. 331.
79. Feldman 2017, pp. 274–275.
80. Feldman 2017, pp. 275–276.
81. Labunski 2006, p. 232.
82. Labunski 2006, p. 198.
83. Thomas 2013, p. 49.
84. Burstein & Isenberg 2010, pp. 221–224.

85. Feldman 2017, pp. 199–211.
86. Feldman 2017, p. 343.
87. Feldman 2017, pp. 343–347.
88. Feldman 2017, pp. 324–326.
89. Feldman 2017, pp. 366–367.
90. Meacham 2012, pp. 405–406.
91. Feldman 2017, p. 369.
92. Burstein & Isenberg 2010, pp. 305–306.
93. Burstein & Isenberg 2010, pp. 261–262.
94. Feldman 2017, pp. 373–374.
95. Varg 1963, p. 74.
96. McCoy, Drew R. (Oct 1974). "Republicanism and American Foreign Policy: Madison and the Political Economy of Commercial Discrimination, 1789 to 1794". The William and Mary Quarterly. 31 (4): 633–646. doi:10.2307/1921607. JSTOR 1921607. Retr Sept 1, 2024 – via JSTOR.
97. Wills 2002, pp. 38–44.
98. Feldman 2017, pp. 396–398.
99. Ketcham 1990, p. 377.
100. Brant 1950, pp. 406–407.
101. Ketcham 2003, pp. 376–380.
102. Feldman 2017, pp. 479–480.
103. Feldman 2017, pp. 443–444.
104. Burstein & Isenberg 2010, pp. 321–322.
105. Ketcham 2003, p. 386.
106. Mummolo 2007.
107. Burstein & Isenberg 2010, pp. 261–262.
108. Nelson 2016, pp. 19–20.
109. Feldman 2017, pp. 408–400.
110. Feldman 2017, pp. 411–414.
111. Feldman 2017, pp. 415–417.
112. Wikisource: Virginia Resolutions of 1798
113. Time Magazine, July 5, 2004.
114. Feldman 2017, pp. 417–421.
115. Feldman 2017, pp. 424–425.
116. Feldman 2017, pp. 428–430.
117. Feldman 2017, pp. 433–436.
118. Feldman 2017, pp. 438–439.
119. McDonald 1976, pp. 36–38.
120. McDonald 1976, pp. 42–44.
121. Wood 2009, pp. 293–296.
122. Feldman 2017, pp. 465–466.
123. Wood 2009, pp. 357–359, 366–367.
124. Burstein & Isenberg 2010, pp. 374–376.
125. Burstein & Isenberg 2010, pp. 382–389.
126. Feldman 2017, pp. 463–465.
127. Ketcham 2003, p. 422.
128. Wills 2002, pp. 51–52.
129. Wood 2009, pp. 640–642.
130. Wills 2002, pp. 81–84.
131. Wood 2009, pp. 644–649.
132. Feldman 2017, pp. 493–495.
133. Feldman 2017, pp. 494–495.
134. Wood 2009, pp. 652–657.
135. Burstein & Isenberg 2010, pp. 457–458.
136. Burstein & Isenberg 2010, pp. 438–439.
137. Burstein & Isenberg 2010, pp. 434–435.
138. Burstein & Isenberg 2010, pp. 457–459.
139. Feldman 2017, p. 498.
140. Rutland 1990, p. 5.
141. Brant 1956, p. 13.
142. Rutland 1990, pp. 32–33, 51, 55.
143. Ketcham 2002, pp. 61–62.
144. Rutland 1990, pp. 32–33.
145. Ketcham 2002, p. 62.
146. Rutland 1990, p. 20.
147. Rutland 1990, pp. 68–70.
148. Rutland 1990, p. 13.

149. Feldman 2017, pp. 508–512.
150. Rutland 1990, pp. 62–64.
151. Rutland 1990, pp. 64–66, 81.
152. Feldman 2017, pp. 532–537.
153. Risjord 1961, pp. 196–210.
154. Wills 2002, pp. 97–98.
155. Feldman 2017, pp. 543–545.
156. Rutland 1990, p. 159.
157. Ketcham 1990, p. 509.
158. Ketcham 2002, p. 65.
159. Feldman 2017, pp. 551–552.
160. Cost 2021, p. 334.
161. Feldman 2017, pp. 548–550.
162. Rutland 1990, pp. 126–127.
163. Rutland 1990, pp. 92–93.
164. Wills 2002, pp. 115–116.
165. Billias 1976, p. 323.
166. 1812 Presidential Election: American Presidency Project.
167. Wood 2009, pp. 682–683.
168. Roosevelt 1999, pp. 147–152.
169. Rutland 1990, p. 133.
170. Rutland 1990, pp. 138–139, 150.
171. Feldman 2017, pp. 569–571.
172. Feldman 2017, pp. 579–585.
173. Cost 2021, p. 346.
174. Feldman 2017, pp. 586–588.
175. Ketcham 2002, p. 67.
176. Ketcham 2002, pp. 66–67.
177. Rutland 1990, pp. 165–167.
178. Wills 2002, pp. 130–131.
179. Rutland 1990, pp. 179–180.
180. Rutland 1990, p. 185.
181. American Heritage, December, 1960.
182. Rutland 1990, pp. 186–188.
183. Howe 2007, pp. 82–84.
184. Rutland 1990, pp. 198–199.
185. Rutland 1990, pp. 204–207.

Sources
1. Allott, Philip (Winter 2003). "The Emerging International Aristocracy". NYU Journal of International Law and Politics.
2. Amar, Akhil Reed (2005). America's Constitution: A Biography. New York: Random House.
3. Ball, Terence, ed (2017) James Madison. Milton Park, England: Taylor & Francis. ISBN 978-1-351-15514-4.
4. Bilder, Mary Sarah (May 2010). "James Madison, Law Student and Demi-Lawyer". Law and History Review. 28 (2): 390–391. doi:10.1017/S0738248010000052. ISSN 0738-2480. JSTOR 25701109. S2CID 143805768.
5. Billias, George (1976). Elbridge Gerry, Founding Father, Republican Statesman. NY, NY: McGraw-Hill Publishers.
6. Bordewich, Fergus M. (2016). The First Congress: How James Madison, George Washington, and a Group of Extraordinary Men Invented Government. New York, New York: Simon & Schuster.
7. Boyd-Rush, Dorothy. "Molding a Founding Father". James Madison's Montpelier. Montpelier: James Madison U
8. Brant, Irving (1950). J Madison: Father of Constitution, 1787-1800. Indianapolis: Bobbs-Merrill Co, Inc. p. 406–407.
9. Brant, Irving (1956). James Madison: President, 1809-1812. Indianapolis: Bobbs-Merrill Company, Inc. p. 13.
10. Burstein, Andrew; Isenberg, Nancy (2010). Madison and Jefferson. New York, New York: Random House.
11. Chernow, Ron (2004). Alexander Hamilton. London, England: Penguin. ISBN 978-0-14-303475-9.
12. Coelho, Chris (2013). Timothy Matlack, Scribe of the Declaration of Independence. Jefferson, North Carolina: McFarland.
13. Cost, Jay (2021). James Madison America's First Politician. N.Y.: Basic Books. ISBN 978-1-5416-9955-7.
14. Feldman, Noah (2017). Three Lives of James Madison: Genius, Partisan, President. NY, NY: Random House.
15. Gutzman, Kevin R. C. (February 14, 2012). James Madison and the Making of America. NY, NY: St. Martin's Publishing
16. Hamilton, Alexander; Madison, James; Jay, John (1992)[1787-1788]. Federalist Papers. Cutchogue, N.Y.: Buccaneer Books
17. Howe, Daniel Walker (2007). What Hath God Wrought: The Transformation of America 1815–1848. Oxford, England: Oxford University Press. ISBN 978-0-19-507894-7.
18. Ketcham, Ralph (1990). Madison: A Biography. Charlottesville: U Virginia Press. ISBN 978-0-8139-1265-3.
19. Ketcham, Ralph (2002). "James Madison". In Graff, Henry F. (ed.). The Presidents: A Reference History (Third ed.). New York, New York: Charles Scribner's Sons. pp. 57–70. ISBN 978-0-684-31226-2.
20. Ketcham, Ralph (2003). James Madison: A Biography. Newton, Connecticut: American Political Biography Press.
21. Labunski, Richard (2006). James Madison and Struggle for Bill of Rights. Oxford, England: Oxford U Press.
22. Madison, James (1817). "Detached Memoranda". University of Chicago. Retrieved February 19, 2017.
23. Madison, James (1908). Writings of James Madison: 1808–1819; Vol VIII. New York, NY:G.P. Putnam's Sons. .

24. Manweller, Mathew (2005). The People Vs. the Courts: Judicial Review and Direct Democracy in the American Legal System. Bethesda, Maryland: Academica Press, LLC. p. 22. ISBN 978-1-930901-97-1.
25. Mason, George (1970). Rutland, Robert A. (ed.). Papers of George Mason, 1725–1792. Chapel Hill: U of NC Press.
26. McCullough, Noah (2006). The Essential Book of Presidential Trivia. New York, New York: Random House Digital,
27. Nelson, Alondra (2016). The Social Life of DNA: Race, Reparations, and Reconciliation after the Genome. Boston, Massachusetts: Beacon Press. ISBN 978-0-8070-3301-2. OCLC 907702592.
28. Owens, Robert M. (2007). Mr. Jefferson's Hammer: William Henry Harrison and the Origins of American Indian Policy. Norman: University of Oklahoma Press. ISBN 978-0-8061-3842-8.
29. Risjord, Norman K. (1961). "1812: Conservatives, War Hawks and the Nation's Honor". William and Mary Quarterly.
30. Roosevelt, Theodore (1999). Naval War of 1812. London, England: Modern Library War.
31. Rutland, Robert A. (1987). Madison: Founding Father. NY, NY: Macmillan Pub Co. ISBN 978-0-02-927601-3.
32. Rutland, Robert A. (1990). Presidency of James Madison. U Press Kansas. ISBN 978-0-7006-0465-4.
33. Stagg, J.C.A. (Oct 4, 2016). "James Madison: Impact and Legacy". Miller Center. U Virginia. Retr Feb 8, 2019.
34. Taylor, Alan (2016). American Revolutions: A Continental History,1750–1804. NY,NY: W.W. Norton & Co, Inc.
35. Taylor, Alan (2002). American Colonies. New York, NY: Viking/Penguin. ISBN 978-0-14-200210-0.
36. Taylor, Elizabeth Dowling (2012). Slave in White House: Paul Jennings and Madisons. NY: Palgrave Macmillan.
37. Varg, Paul A. (1963). Fathers. Michigan State U Press. OCLC 1034677575.
38. Wills, Garry (2002). James Madison. New York: Times Books. ISBN 978-0-8050-6905-1.
39. Wood, Gordon S. (2011). The Idea of America: Reflections on Birth of United States. London,: The Penguin Press.
40. "1812 Presidential Election". The American Presidency Project. Retr Nov 11, 2022.
41. "The Charters of Freedom: The Bill of Rights". NARA. Oct31, 2015. Retrieved Feb 16, 2017.
42. The Federalist Papers. Cutchogue, New York: Buccaneer Books. 1992. ISBN 978-0-89966-695-2.
43. "James Madison". Monticello: Thomas Jefferson Foundation. Retrieved July 22, 2016.
44. "Madison's Election to the First Federal Congress,

ROGER SHERMAN

ONLY SIGNATORY FOR ALL FOUR FOUNDATIONAL DOCUMENTS

Roger Sherman was an early American statesman, lawyer, and a Founding Father of the United States. He is the only person to sign all four great state papers of the United States: The Continental Association, the Declaration of Independence, the Articles of Confederation, and the Constitution.[1][2] He also signed the 1774 Petition to the King. He represented Connecticut at the Continental Congress, and he was a member of the Committee of Five that drafted the Declaration of Independence.

Sherman is especially notable in for being the only person to sign all four great state papers of the United States, Articles of Association, United States Declaration of Independence, Articles of Confederation, and United States Constitution.[2] Robert Morris, who did not sign the Articles of Association, signed the other three. John Dickinson also signed three, the Continental Association, the Articles of Confederation, and the United States Constitution.

Sherman is one of the most influential members of the Constitutional Convention.[3][5][1] At 66 years of age, Sherman was the second eldest member at the convention following Benjamin Franklin (81 years old at the time). Sherman was one of the most active members of the convention, he made motions or seconds 160 times (compared to Madison's 177 times).[3]

Early life and family

Roger Sherman (April 19, 1721 – July 23, 1793) was born into a family of farmers in Newton, Massachusetts. His father was William and mother was Mehetabel Sherman. His education did not extend beyond his father's library and grammar school, and his early career was spent as a shoemaker.[7] He had an aptitude for learning, access to a good library owned by his father, and a Harvard-educated minister, Rev. Samuel Dunbar, who took him under his wing.

In 1743, his father's death made Sherman move with his mother and siblings to New Milford, Connecticut. There, in partnership with his brother William, he opened the town's first store,[7] and earned a position as the county surveyor in 1745. The income from this office enabled him to buy land and to earn a favorable reputation throughout the county. Sherman published a series of almanacs between 1750 and 1761. He studied law, passing the bar in 1754.

A natural ability with numbers helped Roger learn surveying. When Roger was 19, William died, and Roger assumed responsibility for the estate. He moved the family to join oldest brother William in New Milford.

Sherman's self-discipline with his surveyor training paid off two years later, when the Connecticut General Assembly appointed him surveyor of New Haven County and, later, Litchfield County, a post he held until 1758. It was during these years in New Milford that Roger began to actively participate in town affairs, motivated by his growing interest in land speculation. It was also at this time that he married his wife, Elizabeth Hartwell, on November 17, 1749, and had seven children. His three oldest sons were officers in the Continental army.

Roger soon expanded his interests into retail, opening a store that sold tables, chairs, brooms, razors, and other household items. He also began publishing almanacs. In his almanacs, Sherman included entries on astronomy, religious festivals, weather, and his views on the values of colonial currencies. These pursuits did not keep his attention for long, however. Roger began spending more time surveying and took up the study of law. Sherman passed the bar in February of 1754 and the following year became Justice of the Peace for Litchfield County, an appointment that coincided with his election to Connecticut's General Assembly. After the death of his wife in October of 1760, he resigned politics and moved his children to New Haven. [8]

At this point in his life Roger Sherman gives the appearance of a modern-day young adult, uncertain about which direction to go next, yet he is driven to perform well. At other times, he takes on the genre' of a university graduate having trouble "finding himself," he moves from one endeavor to another, always with high success. His success rate is just beginning.

Sherman married Elizabeth Hartwell, November 17, 1749. Elizabeth died October 19, 1760. He married Rebecca Prescott on May 12, 1763, and had eight children. Sherman is related to Union general William Tecumseh Sherman.

Political career

Despite the fact that Sherman had no formal legal training, he was urged to read for the bar exam by a local lawyer and was admitted to the bar of Litchfield, Connecticut in 1754, during which he wrote "A Caveat Against Injustice"[7] and was chosen to represent New Milford in the Connecticut House of Representatives from 1755 to 1758 and 1760 to 1761. Sherman was appointed Justice of the Peace in 1762 and judge of the court of common pleas in 1765. He was first elected to the Governor's Council of the Connecticut General Assembly, serving until 1785. From 1784 to 1785, he also served as a judge of the Connecticut Supreme Court of Errors.

Sherman was also appointed treasurer of Yale College and awarded an honorary Master of Arts degree. He was a professor of religion for many years and engaged in lengthy correspondence with some of the theologians of the time. During February 1776, Sherman, George Wythe, and John Adams were members of a committee to establish guidelines for U.S. Embassy officials in Canada with the committee instructions that included, "You are to declare that we hold sacred the rights of conscience, and may promise the whole people, solemnly in our name, the free and undisturbed exercise of their religion. And ... that all civil rights and the rights to hold office were to be extended to persons of any Christian denomination." In 1784, Sherman was elected mayor of New Haven, held until his death.[7]

Continental and Confederation Congress

As a member of the First Continental Congress, Sherman signed the Continental Association to impose an economic boycott on British trade. In the Second Continental Congress, Sherman was appointed to the Committee of Five that drafted the Declaration of Independence. Sherman was also a member of the committee of 13 that was responsible for preparing a draft constitution for the new nation. During debate, Sherman proposed a bicameral national legislature where states would be represented equally.[6] The committee of 13 rejected Sherman's proposal, adopting a unicameral legislature and what would become the Articles of Confederation. As a member of the Confederation Congress, Sherman was a signatory of the Treaty of Paris which ended the Revolutionary War.

Constitutional Convention

Sherman saw the convention to modify the existing government. Part of his stance was concerned with public appeal. He defended amending the articles as it was in the best interest of the people and the probable way the people would accept changes to a constitution. "The problem with the old government was, it had simply been unable to enforce decrees."[4] Sherman advanced the idea that national government needed to raise revenue and regulate commerce.[4]

The increasingly restrictive policies of the British parliament resulted in the passing of numerous acts aimed at garnering revenue from the American colonies. The announcement of the 1773 Tea Act motivated Sherman to declare his belief "that no laws bind the people but such as they consent to be Governed by." His reputation for service to the colony, along with his strong patriot sentiment, got him elected as a delegate to the first Continental Congress. [8]

His views were influenced by his personal beliefs and Puritan views.[7] He opposed slavery and used the issue for negotiation and alliance.[7] He believed that slavery was gradually being abolished and the trend was moving southward.

Sherman excelled in his new work at the national level. Throughout the Revolutionary Era, he was known as a steadfast worker and an informed, attentive legislator. He is reported to have risen every morning at 5:00 a.m., begun work at 7:00 a.m., and continued working until around 10:00 p.m. Sherman was placed on the committees that drew up the Declaration of Independence and the Articles of Confederation (the new nation's first constitution). He involved himself in issues of supply purchasing, Native American affairs, and the administration of the post office. In addition, he served on the Board of War in 1776 and on the Board of Treasury. Sherman proved a capable and efficient legislator, despite a lack of polish in his oratory skills. His good friend John Adams quipped, "is the reverse of grace; there cannot be a more striking contrast to beautiful action than the motion of his hands…it is stiffness and awkwardness itself, rigid as starched linen." [8]

In 1784, Sherman returned from Congress and was elected the first mayor of the newly incorporated city of New Haven. Three years later, while still mayor of New Haven and a judge of the Superior Court in Connecticut, he was sent to represent Connecticut at the Philadelphia Convention. At the convention, Sherman was integral in shaping the country's new constitution. In addition to being a vocal supporter of Alexander Hamilton's proposal for federal assumption of states' debts, he is credited with fathering the Connecticut Compromise.[8]

Representation in Congress   Connecticut Compromise

Two proposed options for the formation of the legislative branch emerged in the deliberations.[6] One was to form a bicameral legislature in which both chambers had representation proportional to the population of the states, which was supported by the Virginia Plan. The second was to modify the unicameral legislature that had equal representation from all of the states, which was supported by the New Jersey Plan introduced by William Paterson that Sherman helped author.[6] Sherman saw no reason for bicameralism. He defended the unicameral legislature of the Articles of Confederation by stating that the more populous states had not "suffered at the hands of less populous states on account of the rule of equal voting".[4] Sherman, Elbridge Gerry and others were of the opinion that the elected composition of the national government should be reserved for the vote of state officials and not for election by the will of the people. Sherman was wary of allowing ordinary citizen participation and stated that the people "should have as little to do as may be about the Government. They want information and are constantly liable to be misled".

While Sherman was a devout supporter of unicameral legislature, he recognized that this goal was unattainable because it would not receive the support of the more populous states. With the aide of Oliver Ellsworth, Sherman repeatedly proposed a bicameral compromise where one house had representation proportional to the population, and the other had equal representation for the states.[6] Some scholars identified Sherman as a pivotal delegate at the Convention because of his role in settling the representation debate.[3][5] At important moments in the deliberations, Sherman pushed the interests of the less populous states.

The plan that emerged from the Grand Committee, originally introduced by Sherman, and which known as became the Connecticut Compromise, was designed to be acceptable to both the more and less populous states: the people would be represented proportionally in one branch of the legislature, called the House of Representatives (the lower legislative house).[6] The states would be represented in another house called the Senate (the upper house). In the lower house, each state had a representative for every one delegate. In the upper house, each state was guaranteed two senators. In modes of election, Sherman supported allowing each state legislature to elect its own senators. In the House, Sherman proposed that membership should be according to "numbers of free inhabitants" in each state.[4]

His service only lasted until March of 1793, when he returned home to New Haven due to failing health. On July 23, 1793, Roger Sherman died of typhoid fever.

His grandson, Roger Sherman Baldwin, served as US senator and governor of Connecticut. Two grandsons, George F. Hoar and William M. Evarts, served as US Senators. Evarts was secretary of state under President Rutherford B. Hayes.

References

1.   "Roger Sherman". Architect of the Capitol. Retrieved August 13, 2019.
2.   "Roger Sherman: The Only Man Who Signed All Four Founding Documents", Journal of the American Revolution,
3.   Robertson, David B. (2005). "Madison's Opponents and Constitutional Design". American Political Science Review. 99 (2): 225–243. doi:10.1017/S0003055405051622. S2CID 145374045.
4.   Collier, Christopher, and James Lincoln Collier. Decision in Philadelphia: The Constitutional Convention of 1787. New York: Random House, 1986. Print.
5.   Phillips, Stephen C.; Smith, Alex P.; Licari, Peter R. (2022). "Philadelphia reconsidered: participant curation, the Gerry Committee, and US constitutional design". Public Choice. 190 (3): 407–426. doi:10.1007/s11127-021-00943-5. S2CID 244431495.
6.   Robertson, David B. The Original Compromise: What the Constitution's Framers Were Really Thinking. NY: Oxford U Press,
7.   Hall, Mark D. Roger Sherman, and the Creation of the American Republic. New York: Oxford U Press, 2015.
8.   (http://connecticuthistory.org/roger-sherman-revolutionary-and-dedicated-public-servant/)

JOHN DICKINSON,

DELAWARE
AUTHOR OR SIGNER OF THREE MAJOR DOCUMENTS

- "Penman of the Revolution including Letters from a Farmer in Pa
- Member of the First and Second Continental Congresses
- Fought in the Revolutionary War as a private in the Delaware Militia
- President of Pennsylvania from 1782 to 1785
- President of Delaware from 1781 to 1783
- Author of the 1774 Petition to British King George III and the 1775
- Author of the Olive Branch Petition.
- He also wrote the first draft of the Articles of Confederation.
- Along with his wife, he is the namesake of Dickinson College.

John Dickinson, a Founding Father of the United States, was an attorney and politician from Philadelphia, Pennsylvania, and Wilmington, Delaware. Dickinson was known as the **"Penman of the Revolution"** for his twelve *Letters from a Farmer in Pennsylvania*, in 1767 and 1768, and wrote "The Liberty Song" in 1768.

As a member of the First Continental Congress, where he signed the Continental Association, Dickinson drafted most of the 1774 Petition to the King, and then, as a member of the Second Continental Congress, he wrote the 1775 Olive Branch Petition. Both of these attempts to negotiate with King George III of Great Britain failed. Dickinson also reworked Thomas Jefferson's language to write the final draft of the 1775 Declaration of the Causes and Necessity of Taking Up Arms.

While in Congress, Dickinson served on the committee that wrote the Model Treaty, seeking alliances with foreign countries, but he opposed independence from Great Britain. He either abstained from the vote on the Declaration of Independence and refused to sign the document after its passage. Dickinson wrote the first draft of the 1776–1777 Articles of Confederation and Perpetual Union and served as a militia officer during the Revolution. He was elected president of the 1786 Annapolis Convention, which called for the Constitutional Convention of 1787, and as a delegate from Delaware, he signed the United States Constitution.

One of the wealthiest men in the British American colonies, Dickinson served as president of Delaware (1781–1783) and president of Pennsylvania (1782–1785). Upon Dickinson's death, President Thomas Jefferson referred to Dickinson as, "(a)among the first of the advocates for the rights of his country when assailed by Great Britain" and called him "one of the great worthies of the revolution."[1]

Together with his wife, he is the namesake of Dickinson College, Penn State Dickinson Law, and the Dickinson Complex at the University of Delaware.

Family history

John Dickinson (November 13, 1732 – February 14, 1808), was born at *Alabama*, his family's tobacco plantation near the village of Trappe in Talbot County, Province of Maryland.[2] He was the great-grandson of Walter Dickinson who came from England as an indentured servant to the Colony of Virginia in 1654 and, having joined the Society of Friends, came with several co-religionists to Talbot County on the eastern shore of the Chesapeake Bay in 1659. There, with 400 acres (1.6 km²) on the Choptank River, Walter began a plantation. Walter also bought 800 acres (3.2 km²) on St. Jones Neck in what became Kent County, Delaware.[3]

Croisadore passed through Walter's son, William, to his grandson, Samuel, the father of John Dickinson. Each generation increased the landholdings so that Samuel inherited 2,500 acres on five farms in three Maryland counties; over his lifetime he increased that to 9,000 acres. He also bought the Kent County property from his cousin and expanded it to about 3,000 acres stretching along the St. Jones River from Dover to the Delaware Bay. There he began another plantation and called it Poplar Hall. These plantations were large, profitable agricultural.[4]

Samuel married Judith Troth, April 11, 1710. They had nine children. Judith died, leaving him with two children. Samuel remarried Mary Cadwalader in 1731.

Leaving *Croisadore* to elder son Henry Dickinson, Samuel moved to Poplar Hall, where he had already taken a leading role in the community as judge of the Court of Common Pleas of Kent County. The move also placed Mary nearer her Philadelphia relations. Poplar Hall was situated on an artificially straightened section of the St. Jones River. There was plenty of activity delivering the necessities and shipping the agricultural products produced. Much of this product was wheat that along with other wheat from the region, was milled into a "superfine" flour.[5]:39

Early life and education

Dickinson was educated at home by his parents and by recent immigrants employed for that purpose. Among them was the Presbyterian minister Francis Alison, who later established New London Academy in Chester County, Pennsylvania.[6] Most important was his tutor, William Killen, who became a lifelong friend and Delaware's first chief justice and chancellor.

At age 18, Dickinson began studying law under John Moland in Philadelphia. While there, he became friends with fellow students George Read, Samuel Wharton, and others. In 1753, he went to London for three years of study at the Middle Temple. He spent those years studying the works of Edward Coke and Francis Bacon at the Inns of Court, following in the footsteps of his lifelong friend, Pennsylvania Attorney General Benjamin Chew,[7] and in 1757 was admitted to the Pennsylvania bar beginning his career as barrister and solicitor.

In protest to the Townshend Acts, Dickinson published *Letters from a Farmer in Pennsylvania*, which were first published in the *Pennsylvania Chronicle*. Dickinson's letters were reprinted by numerous other newspapers, and they emerged among the most influential American political documents prior to the American Revolution. Dickinson further warned that if the colonies acquiesced to the Townshend Acts, Parliament would lay further taxes on the colonies in the future.[8] He was elected in 1768 to the American Philosophical Society.[9]

On July 19, 1770, Dickinson married Mary Norris, known as Polly, a prominent and well educated 30-year-old woman in Philadelphia with a substantial holding of real estate and personal property, including a 1,500-volume library, one of the largest in the colonies at the time, who had been operating her family's estate, Fair Hill, for several years by herself with some support from her sister. She was the daughter of wealthy Philadelphia Quaker and Speaker of the Pennsylvania General Assembly Isaac Norris and Sarah Logan, the daughter of James Logan.[10] She was also cousin to the Quaker poet Hannah Griffitts. Dickinson and Norris had five children. Dickinson never joined the Quaker Meeting because he believed in the "lawfulness of defensive war".[11] He and Norris were married in a civil ceremony.

In Philadelphia, they lived at Fair Hill near the present-day Germantown neighborhood in Philadelphia, which they modernized through their combined wealth. On October 4, 1777, Fair Hill was burned by the British during the Battle of Germantown. While in Philadelphia as state president, Dickinson lived at the mansion of Joseph Galloway at Sixth and Market Streets.

Dickinson lived at Poplar Hall from 1776 to 1777 and from 1781 to 1782. In August 1781, Poplar Hall was sacked by Loyalists and badly burned in 1804.

Career - - Continental Congress

Dickinson was one of the delegates from the Province of Pennsylvania to the First Continental Congress in 1774 and the Second Continental Congress in 1775 and 1776. In support of the cause, he continued to contribute declarations in the name of the Congress. Dickinson wrote the Olive Branch Petition as the Second Continental Congress' last attempt for peace with King George III, who did not even read the petition. But through it all, agreeing with George Read and many others in Philadelphia and the lower counties, Dickinson's objective at first was reconciliation, not independence and revolution. Dickinson prepared the first draft of the Articles of Confederation in 1776, after others had ratified the Declaration of Independence despite his concerns that the Declaration would escalate the Revolutionary War, which began in 1775 at the Battle of Lexington and Concord. At the time, he chaired the committee charged with drafting the Articles of Confederation, Dickinson was serving in the Continental Congress as a delegate from Pennsylvania.

When the Second Continental Congress began the debate on the Declaration of Independence on July 1, 1776, Dickinson reiterated his opposition to declaring independence at that time. Dickinson believed that the Congress should complete the Articles of Confederation and secure a foreign alliance before issuing a declaration. Dickinson also objected to violence as a means for resolving the Thirteen Colonies' dispute with Britain. He abstained from the votes on July 2 that declared independence and absented himself again from voting on the wording of the formal declaration on July 4. Dickinson understood the implications of his refusal to vote saying, "My conduct this day, I expect will give the finishing blow to my once too great and, . . . now too diminished popularity."[14] Dickinson refused to sign the declaration, and since a proposal had been brought forth and carried that stated "for our mutual security and protection", no man could remain in the Continental Congress without signing it, so Dickinson voluntarily departed and joined the Pennsylvania patriot militia.[15] John Adams, a fierce advocate for independence and Dickinson's adversary on the floor of Congress, remarked, "Mr. Dickinson's alacrity and spirit certainly become his character and sets a fine example."[16]

Dickinson is one of only two members of the First Continental Congress who actively took up arms during the Revolutionary War.

In the Pennsylvania militia, known as the Associators, Dickinson was given the rank of brigadier general and led 10,000 soldiers to Elizabeth, New Jersey, to protect that area against British attack from Staten Island. Due to his abstaining from supporting independence, two junior officers were promoted above him.[15]

Return to Poplar Hall

Dickinson resigned his commission in December 1776 and went to stay at Poplar Hall in Kent County. While there, Dickinson learned that his home on Chestnut Street in Philadelphia had been confiscated and converted into a hospital. He stayed at Poplar Hall for more than two years. The Delaware General Assembly tried to appoint him as their delegate to the Second Continental Congress in 1777, but he refused. In August 1777, he served as a private with the Kent County militia at Middletown, Delaware, under General Caesar Rodney to help delay General William Howe's march to Philadelphia during the Philadelphia campaign. In October 1777, Dickinson's friend Thomas McKean appointed him brigadier general of the Delaware Militia, but Dickinson again declined the appointment. Shortly after, he learned the British had burned down his property in the Battle of Germantown.[17]

In 1777, Dickinson, then Delaware's wealthiest farmer and largest slaveholder,[18] decided to free his slaves. While Kent County was not as large a slave-holding area as southern colonies and Dickinson had only 37 slaves,[18] his action represented considerable courage. His farm had moved away from farming tobacco to less labor-intensive crops, wheat and barley.[5]:40

President of Delaware

On January 18, 1779, Dickinson was appointed a delegate for Delaware to the Second Continental Congress, which was convening at what today is Independence Hall in Philadelphia. During this term, he signed the Articles of Confederation, which he authored while serving in the First Continental Congress as a delegate from the Province of Pennsylvania. In August 1781, while still a delegate in Philadelphia, he learned that Poplar Hall had been severely damaged by a Loyalist raid. Dickinson returned to investigate damage and remained several months.

In October 1781, while at Poplar Hall, Dickinson was elected to represent Kent County in the State Senate. Shortly after, the Delaware General Assembly elected him president of Delaware. The General Assembly's vote was nearly unanimous; the only dissenting vote was cast by Dickinson himself.[20] Dickinson took office on November 13, 1781, and served until November 7, 1782. Beginning his term with a "Proclamation against Vice and Immorality," he sought ways to bring an end what he perceived to be the disorder of the American Revolution. It was a popular position and enhanced his reputation in Delaware and Pennsylvania.

Dickinson then successfully challenged the Delaware General Assembly to address lagging militia enlistments and to properly fund the state's assessment to the Confederation government. Recognizing the delicate negotiations to end the American Revolution, Dickinson secured the Assembly's endorsement of the French alliance, with no agreement on peace.

On October 10, 1782, Dickinson was elected to the Supreme Executive Council of Pennsylvania. A ballot by the Council and the Pennsylvania General Assembly elected him president of the council and thereby president of Pennsylvania. But he did not resign as president of Delaware. Even though Pennsylvania and Delaware shared the same governor until recently, many in Delaware were upset at being cast aside so readily, particularly after Philadelphia newspapers began criticizing Delaware for permitting its office holders to be non-residents. Dickinson's successor, John Cook, was considered too weak in support of the Revolution. On January 12, 1783, Cook called for a new election, leading Dickinson to resign.

President of Pennsylvania

When the Revolution began, Dickinson represented centrist views in Pennsylvania politics at a time when independence views varied. The General Assembly was dominated by Loyalists and moderates who, like Dickinson, did little to support the burgeoning Revolution or independence, except protest. The Radicals took matters into their own hands, using irregular means to write the Pennsylvania Constitution of 1776, which by law excluded from the franchise anyone who would not swear loyalty to the document or Christian Holy Trinity.

Dickinson's election to the Supreme Executive Council was the beginning of a counterrevolution against the Constitutionalists. He was elected president of Pennsylvania on November 7, 1782, garnering 41 votes to James Potter's 32. On November 6, 1784, he defeated John Neville, who also lost the election for vice president the same day. Working with small majorities in the General Assembly in his first two years and with the Constitutionalists in the majority in his last year, all issues were contentious. At first, he endured withering attacks from opponents for his alleged failure to fully support the new government in large and small ways.

United States Constitution

After his service in Pennsylvania, Dickinson returned to Wilmington, Delaware, where he was quickly appointed to represent Delaware at the Annapolis Convention, where he served as its president. In 1787, Delaware sent him as one of its delegates to the Constitutional Convention of 1787, along with Gunning Bedford Jr., Richard Bassett, George Read, and Jacob Broom. There, he supported the effort to create a strong central government but only after the Great Compromise assured that each state, regardless of size, would have an equal vote in the future United States Senate. As he had done with the Articles, he also carefully drafted it with the term "Person" rather than "Man" as was used in the Declaration of Independence. He prepared initial drafts of the First Amendment. Following the Convention, he promoted the resulting Constitution in a series of nine essays, written under the pen name *Fabius*. Dickinson did not sign the constitution, leaving early due to illness, George Read signed his name.[21]

In 1791, Delaware convened a convention to revise its existing Constitution, which had been hastily drafted in 1776. Dickinson won election as president of this convention, and although he resigned the chair after most of the work was complete, he remained highly influential in the content of the final document.

Dickinson returned to the State Senate for 1793, but served just one year, resigning with declining health. In 1801, Dickinson published two volumes of his collected works on politics.

Death and legacy

Dickinson died at Wilmington, Delaware, and was buried in Friends Burial Ground in Wilmington. Shortly before his death he unconditionally freed all his slaves. While he had been economically reliant on them, he also wanted slavery to end. By freeing all his slaves upon his death, he thought this would contribute to the United States having a future without slavery. Like many of the founders he believed slavery would die "a natural death."

In an original letter from Thomas Jefferson to Joseph Bringhurst, caretaker of Dickinson in his later years, Jefferson responds to news of Dickinson's death:

"A more estimable man, or truer patriot, could not have left us. Among the first of the advocates for the rights of his country when assailed by Great Britain, he continued to the last the orthodox advocate of the true principles of our new government and his name will be consecrated in history as one of the great worthies of the revolution."[1]

He shares with Thomas McKean the distinction of serving as chief executive of both Delaware and Pennsylvania after the Declaration of Independence.

References
1. "UD Library Discovers Thomas Jefferson letter" (Press release). U of Delaware. Dec 3, 2009. Arch & Retr Dec 5, 2009.
2. "America's Founding Fathers: Delegates to the Constitutional Convention". NARA October 30, 2015.
3. Duke of York Record 1646–1679, Printed by order of the General Assembly of the State of Delaware, 1899
4. "John Dickinson: timeline". Historyhome.co.uk. January 5, 2011. Retrieved September 12, 2012.
5. Hoffecker, Carol E. (2004). Democracy in Delaware. Wilmington, DE: Cedar Tree Books. ISBN 1-892142-23-6.
6. "History". University of Delaware. July 7, 2017.
7. Publications of the Historical Society of Pennsylvania: Life and Writings of John Dickinson [vol. 1], p. 28.
8. Middlekauff,Robert(2005)The Glorious Cause:American Revolution 1763–1789Oxford U Press. pp. 161–162
9. Bell, Whitfield J.; Greifenstein, Charles Jr. (1997). Patriot-Improvers: Biographical Sketches of Members of the American Philosophical Society. Vol. 1. Philadelphia: American Philosophical Society. pp. 383–390. ISBN 9780871692269.
10. Stillé, Charles J. (1891). Life and times of John Dickinson. Philadelphia, The Historical Society of Pennsylvania
11. Flower 1983, p. 301.
12. Ferling, John (2011). Independence: The Struggle to Set America Free. New York: Bloomsbury Press. p. 132...
13. "John Dickinson Plantation". State of Delaware, Department of State, Division of Historical and Cultural Affairs.
14. Murchison, William (Feb18, 2014). "Delaware's John Dickinson and Why You Should Care". Delaware Today.
15. Wright, Robert K.; MacGregor, Morris J. Jr. (1987), Soldier-Statesmen of the Constitution, Washington, D.C.: Center of Military History, United States Army, pp. 82–84
16. Smith 1962, p. 285.
17. Publications of Historical Society of Pennsylvania: Writings of John Dickinson [vol. 1], 315.
18. Lubert, Howard L.(2008) "John Dickinson" In Gregg; Hall,Mark David(eds.)America's Forgotten Founders. p 97
19. Calvert, Jane E. "Biography". The John Dickinson Writings Project. University of Kentucky. Retr Feb 10, 2013.
20. Bushman, Hancock & Homsey 1988, p. 17. "National Park Service – Signers of the Constitution (John Dickinson)".

JOHN JAY

FOUNDING FATHER FOR COUNTERINTELLIGENCE

John Jay (December 23 [O.S. December 12], 1745 – May 17, 1829) was an American statesman, diplomat, abolitionist, signatory of the Treaty of Paris, and a Founding Father of the United States. He served as the first chief justice of the United States Supreme Court, and from 1795 to 1801 as the second governor of New York. Jay directed U.S. foreign policy for much of the 1780s and was an important leader of the Federalist Party after the ratification of the United States Constitution in 1788.

Early life - - Family History

The Jays, a prominent merchant family in New York City, were descendants of Huguenots who escaped religious persecution in France. In 1685, the Edict of Nantes had been revoked, thereby abolishing rights of Protestants, and the French Crown confiscated their property. Among those affected was Jay's paternal grandfather, Auguste Jay. He moved from France to Charleston, South Carolina, and then New York, where he built a successful merchant empire.[1] Jay's father, Peter Jay (1704–1782), born in New York City in 1704, became a wealthy trader in commodities.[2]

Jay's mother was Mary Van Cortlandt (1705–1777), married Peter Jay in 1728.[2] They had ten children.[3] Peter Jay retired following a smallpox epidemic.[4]

Education

Jay spent his childhood in Rye. He was educated there by his mother until he was eight years old, when he was sent to New Rochelle to study under Anglican priest Pierre Stoupe.[5] In 1760, 14-year-old Jay entered King's College (now Columbia College) in New York City.[6][7] There he made many influential friends, including his closest friend, Robert Livingston.[8] Jay took the same political stand as his father, a staunch Whig.[9] Upon graduating in 1764[10] he became a law clerk.[3] Three years later, in 1767, Jay was promoted to Master of Arts.[11]

Entrance into law and politics

In 1768, after reading law and being admitted to the bar of New York, Jay opened his own law office in 1771.[3] He was a member of the New York Committee of Correspondence in 1774[12] and became its secretary, his first public role.

Jay represented the faction that was interested in protecting property rights and in preserving rule of law.[13] This faction feared the prospect of mob rule. Jay believed British tax measures were wrong and thought Americans were morally and legally justified in resisting, but as a delegate to First Continental Congress,[14] Jay became an ardent Patriot, as he decided efforts at reconciliation with Britain were fruitless.[15]

Marriage and family

On April 28, 1774, Jay married Sarah Van Brugh Livingston, eldest daughter of the New Jersey Governor William Livingston.[16] Together they had six children. She accompanied Jay to Spain and later was with him in Paris, where they and their children resided with Benjamin Franklin at Passy.[17] Jay now faced extreme family disasters. Jay's brother-in-law was lost at sea during the revolution, While Jay was in Paris, his father died. His blind brother and sister,[18] became his responsibility. His brother Fredrick was in constant financial trouble.[19]

Personal views - - Slavery

Every man of every color and description has a natural right to freedom.
—*John Jay, February 27, 1792*

The Jay family participated in the slave trade, including slave ships.[25]

A founder of New York Manumission Society, he freed all but one by 1810.[26]

In 1774, Jay drafted the "Address to the People of Great Britain,[27] and organized boycotts and provided legal counsel to free Blacks.[28] The Society helped enact the 1799 law for emancipation of slaves in New York, which Jay signed into law.[29] All slaves were emancipated by July 4, 1827.[30] In the 1792 gubernatorial election, Jay's antislavery work was expected to hurt his election in New York Dutch areas, where slavery was practiced.[30],[31]

Religion

Jay was a member of the Church of England and later of the Protestant Episcopal Church in America. Jay had been a warden of Trinity Church, New York.

Jay, who served as vice-president (1816–1821) and president (1821–1827) of the American Bible Society,[35] believed the most effective way of ensuring world peace was through propagation of the Christian gospel. In a letter addressed to Pennsylvania House of Representatives member John Murray, dated October 12, 1816, Jay wrote:

"*Real* Christians will abstain from violating the rights of others, and therefore will not provoke war. All nations have peace or war at will and pleasure of rulers whom they do not elect, and who are not always wise or virtuous. Providence has given to our people the choice of their rulers, and it is the duty, as well as the privilege and interest, of our Christian nation to select and prefer Christians for their rulers."[36] He said, "No human society has ever been able to maintain order and freedom, cohesiveness and liberty apart from the moral precepts of the Christian Religion. Should our Republic ever forget this fundamental precept of governance, we will then, be surely doomed."[37]

During the American Revolution

Jay was elected to the First and Second Continental Congresses which debated independence. He helped write the Olive Branch Petition which urged the British to reconcile with the colonies. Jay supported the revolution and Independence.

In 1774, upon the conclusion of the Continental Congress, Jay returned to New York.[38] There he served on New York City's Committee of Sixty,[39][38] Jay was elected to the third New York Provincial Congress, where he drafted the Constitution of New York, 1777;[40] his duties as a New York Congressman prevented him from voting on or signing the Declaration of Independence.[38] Jay served on the New York Committee to Detect and Defeat Conspiracies.[41] New York's Provincial Congress elected Jay the Chief Justice of the New York Supreme Court of Judicature on May 8, 1777,[38][42] which he served two years.[38]

The Continental Congress turned to Jay, only three days after Jay became a delegate and elected him President of the Continental Congress.[43]

As a diplomat - - September 27, 1779, Jay was appointed Minister to Spain.[44]

Peace Commissioner

On June 23, 1782, Jay reached Paris, where negotiations to end the American Revolutionary War would take place.[45] Benjamin Franklin was the most experienced diplomat of the group, and thus Jay wished to learn from him.[46] The United States agreed to negotiate with Britain separately, then with France.[47] In July 1782, the Earl of Shelburne offered the Americans independence, but Jay rejected the offer on the grounds that it bypassed negotiations; Jay's dissent halted negotiations until the fall.[47] The final treaty dictated that the United States would have Newfoundland fishing rights, Britain would acknowledge US independence, would withdraw its troops, United States would end the seizure of Loyalist property and honoring private debts.[47][48] The treaty granted the United States independence.[47] John Adams credited Jay with the central role negotiations."[48] Jay was summoned to receive "the Freedom" of New York City as a tribute to his successful negotiations.[49]

The Federalist Papers, 1788

Jay believed his level of authority was weak, so he joined Alexander Hamilton and James Madison in advocating for a stronger government than dictated by the Articles of Confederation.[3][51] He argued in his "Address to the People of the State of New-York, on the Subject of the Federal Constitution" that the Articles of Confederation were weak, contending:

The Congress under the Articles of Confederation may make war, but are not empowered to raise men or money to carry it on—they may make peace, but without power to see the terms of it observed—they may form alliances, but without ability to comply with the stipulations on their part—they may enter into treaties of commerce, but without power to enforce them at home or abroad ... —In short, they may consult, deliberate, recommend, make requisitions, and they who please may regard them.[52]

Jay did not attend the Constitutional Convention but joined Hamilton and Madison aggressively arguing in favor of the creation of a new and more powerful, centralized but balanced system of government. Writing under the shared pseudonym of "Publius",[53] they articulated this vision in *The Federalist Papers*, a series of eighty-five articles written to persuade New York to ratify the Constitution of the United States.[54] Jay wrote the second, third, fourth, fifth, and sixty-fourth articles. The second through fifth are on "Dangers from Foreign Force and Influence". The sixty-fourth discusses the Senate in foreign treaties.[55]

The Jay Court

Washington nominated Jay on September 24, 1789, the same day he signed the Judiciary Act of 1789 (which created the position of Chief Justice) into law.[51] Jay was unanimously confirmed by the US Senate on September 26, 1789; Washington signed and sealed Jay's commission the same day. Jay swore his oath of office on October 19, 1789.[56] Washington also nominated John Rutledge, William Cushing, Robert Harrison, James Wilson, and John Blair Jr. as Associate Judges.[57] Harrison declined the appointment, however, and Washington appointed James Iredell.[58] Jay would later serve with Thomas Johnson, who took Rutledge's seat, and William Paterson, who took Johnson's seat.[59] While Chief Justice, Jay was elected a Fellow of the American Academy of Arts and Sciences in 1790.[60] Jay served as Circuit Justice for the Eastern Circuit from the Spring of 1790, until the Spring of 1794.[61]

When Treasury Secretary Alexander Hamilton wrote to Jay requesting the Court's endorsement of legislation, Jay replied that the Court's business was restricted to ruling on the constitutionality of cases being tried and refused to take a position.[62]

For his work as chief justice, Jay was awarded an honorary Doctor of Laws degree by the University of Edinburgh on May 17, 1792.[63]

Cases That Defined our Judiciary

The Jay Court's first case *West v. Barnes* (1791), the Court had an opportunity to establish the principle of judicial review in the United States with the case, which involved a Rhode Island state statute permitting the lodging of a debt payment in paper currency. Instead of grappling with the constitutionality of the law, the Court unanimously decided the case on procedural grounds, strictly interpreting statutory requirements.[57]

Hayburn's Case (1792) concerned whether a federal statute could require the courts to decide whether petitioning veterans of the American Revolution qualified for pensions, a non-judicial function. The Jay Court wrote a letter to President Washington to say that determining whether petitioners qualified was an "act ... not of a judicial nature"[65] and that because the statute allowed the legislative branch and the executive branch to revise the court's ruling, the statute violated the separation of powes.[66]

In *Chisholm v. Georgia* (1793), the Jay Court had to decide if suits against state governments by state citizens could be heard in federal court.[67] In a 4–1 ruling (Iredell dissented, and Rutledge did not participate), the Jay Court ruled in favor of two South Carolina Loyalists whose land had been seized by Georgia. That ruling sparked debate, as it implied that old debts must be paid to Loyalists.[57] The ruling was overturned when the Eleventh Amendment was ratified, which stated that a state could not be sued by a citizen of another state or foreign country.[3][57] The case was brought again to the Supreme Court in *Georgia v. Brailsford*, and the Court reversed its decision.[68][69] Jay's original *Chisholm* decision established that states were subject to judicial review.[67][70]

In *Georgia v. Brailsford* (1794), the Court upheld jury instructions stating, "you jurors have ... a right to take upon yourselves to ... determine the law as well as the fact in controversy." Jay noted for the jury the "good old rule, that on questions of fact, it is the province of the jury, on questions of law, it is the province of the court to decide," but that amounted to no more than a presumption that judges were correct about the law. Ultimately, "both objects [law and facts] are lawfully within your power of decision."[71][72]

Jay Treaty

Relations with Britain verged on war in 1794. British exports dominated the U.S. market. Britain still occupied northern forts that they had agreed to abandon in the Treaty of Paris, as the Americans had refused to pay debts owed to British creditors or halt the confiscation of Loyalist properties. In addition, the Royal Navy impressed U.S. sailors who were alleged to be British deserters from the Navy, and seized almost 300 American merchant ships who were trading with the French West Indies between 1793 and 1794.[75] Madison proposed a trade war, "[a] direct system of commercial hostility with Great Britain," assuming that Britain was so weakened by its war with France that it would agree to American terms and not declare war.[76]

Washington rejected that policy and sent Jay as a special envoy to Great Britain to negotiate a new treaty; Jay remained Chief Justice. Washington had Alexander Hamilton write instructions for Jay that were to guide him in the negotiations.[77] In March 1795, the resulting Jay Treaty, was brought to Philadelphia.[77] When Hamilton, in an attempt to maintain good relations, informed Britain that the United States would not join the Second League of Armed Neutrality, Jay lost most of his leverage. Britain withdrew from their northwestern forts[79] and granted the U.S. "most favored nation" status.[75] U.S. merchants were also granted commercial access to the British West Indies.[75]

The treaty did not resolve American grievances about neutral shipping rights and impressment,[31] and the Democratic-Republicans denounced it, but Jay, as Chief Justice, decided not to take part in the debates.[79] The Royal Navy's continued impressment of American citizens would be a cause of the War of 1812.[80] The failure to receive compensation for American slaves freed by the British and transported away "was a major reason for the bitter Southern opposition". Washington put his prestige behind the treaty, and Hamilton mobilized public opinion. The Senate ratified by a 20–10 vote, the two-thirds majority required.[75]

The people chanted "John Jay, the arch traitor – seize him, drown him, burn him, flay him alive." Jay joked he could travel at night lighted by burning effigies.

Governor of New York

As governor, he received a proposal from Hamilton to gerrymander New; he marked the letter "Proposing a measure for party purposes which it would not become me to adopt. President Adams renominated him to the Supreme Court; the Senate quickly confirmed him, but he declined, citing poor health[72] and the court's lack of "the energy, weight and dignity which are essential to its due support to the national government." After Jay's rejection, Adams nominated John Marshall as Chief Justice.

On the night of May 14, 1829, Jay was stricken by a stroke, dying on May 17.[91]

References

1. Pellew, George: "American Statesman John Jay", p. 1. Houghton Mifflin, 1890
2. Stahr, Walter (2006). John Jay: Founding Father. Continuum Pub Group. pp.1–5. ISBN 978-0-8264-1879-1
3. "A Brief Biography of John Jay". Papers of John Jay. Columbia U. 2002. Arch Nov 27, 2015. Retr Aug20, 2008.
4. Clary, Suzanne. "From a Peppercorn to a Path Through History" Archived March 16, 2016, at the Wayback Machine. Upper East Side Magazine, Weston Magazine Publishers, Issue 53, October 2014.
5. Cushman, Clare. The Supreme Court Justices: Illustrated Biographies, 1789–2012 Wayback Machine. The Supreme Court Historical Society, SAGE Publications, 2012.
6. "Jay, John (1745–1829)". World of Criminal Justice, Gale. Farmington: Gale, 2002. Credo Ref. Web.9/24/12.
7. Stahr, p. 9
8. Stahr, p. 12 Archived September 10, 2015, at the Wayback Machine
9. Pellew p. 6
10. Barnard edu Archived February 22, 2001, Wayback Machine retr August 31, 2008
11. Columbia College (New York, N. Y.) (1826). Catalogue of Columbia College, City of New-York: names of its trustees, officers, and graduates, A.D. 1758 to A.D. 1826, inclusive. U.S. National Library of Medicine. New York: Printed by T. and J. Swords.
12. "John Jay". www.ushistory.org. Archived Jan16, 2016. Retrieved August 21, 2008.
13. Roger J. Champagne, "New York's Radicals and Coming of Independence." Journal American History 51.1 (1964): 21-40.
14. "John Jay Nomination to First Continental Congress". Arch Jan 27, 2016. Retr Dec 26, 2012.
15. Klein (2000)
16. "Urbanities: "The Education of John Jay"." City Journal. (Winter 2010): 15960 words. LexisNexis Academic. Web.
17. Jay, John (1892). "Jay, John" . In Wilson, J. G.; Fiske, J. (eds.). Appletons' Cyclopædia of American Biography.
18. Du Bois, John Jay (July 27, 2014). "Jay Family Timeline". Archived Feb 22, 2015. Retr Feb 21, 2015.
19. Morris, Richard. John Jay: The Winning of the Peace. New York: Harper & Row Publishers, 1980.
20. "Westchester Building, Rye, N.Y.". New York Evening Post. May 13, 1922.
21. Library of Congress, Local Legacies, Jay Heritage Center http://lcweb2.loc.gov/diglib/legacies/loc.afc.afc-legacies.200003400/ Archived April 2, 2015, Wayback Machine
22. Wilcox, Arthur Russell. Bar of Rye Township Arch 3/4/17, Wayback Machine. Knickerbocker Press, NY, 1918.
23. Clement, Douglas P. (March 11, 2016). "Clement, Douglas P.,"Jay Heritage Center in Rye: Young Americans," 'NYT,' New York, NY, March 10, 2016". NYT. Archi May 22, 2020. Retr March 2, 2017.
24. "Friends of John Jay Homestead". www.johnjayhomestead.org. Arch Oct 14, 2008. Retr August 24, 2008.

25. Sudderth, Jake."John Jay and Slavery" Columbia U Libraries. New York City Arch 2/7/20. Retr 5/23/20.
26. Address to the People of Great Britain. Archived Oct 4, 2015. Retr Oct 2, 2015.
27. Kennedy, Roger G. (1999). Burr, Hamilton, Jefferson: A Study in Character. Oxford U Press. p. 92.
28. McManus, Edgar J.(2001).History of Negro Slavery in New York. Syracuse U Press. ISBN 978-0815628941.
29. Sudderth, Jake (2002). "John Jay and Slavery". New York City: Columbia U. Arch 2/8/07.Retr 10/12/06
30. Herbert S. Parmet and Marie B. Hecht, Aaron Burr (1967) p. 76
31. Baird, James. "The Jay Treaty". www.columbia.edu. Archived July 9, 2008. Retr August 22, 2008.
32. Crippen II, Alan R.(2005) "John Jay: American Wilberforce?" JohnJayInstitute Arch 10/10/06 Retr 12/13/06.
33. Kaminski, John P. (March 2002). "Religion and Founding Fathers". Annotation: Newsletter of the National Historic Publications and Records commission. 30 (1). ISSN 0160-8460. 3/27/08. Retr 8/25/08.
34. Davis, Kenneth C. (July 3, 2007). "Opinion | The Founding Immigrants". The New York Times. ISSN 0362-4331.
35. "John Jay" Archived May 30, 2013, at the Wayback Machine. WallBuilders
36. Jay, William (1833). The Life of John Jay: With Selections from His Correspondence and Miscellaneous Papers. New York: J. & J. Harper. p. 376. ISBN 978-0-8369-6858-3. Retrieved August 22, 2008.
37. Loconte, Joseph (Sept 26,2005). "Why Religious Values Support American Values" Wayback Machine. The
38. "Jay and New York". The Papers of John Jay. Columbia U. 2002. Arch July 25, 2008. Retr August 23, 2008.
39. Stahr, p. 443
40. "The First Constitution, 1777". Historical Society of Courts of State of New York. NY State Unified Court System.
41. Ketchum, Richard M. (2002). Divided Loyalties: How American Revolution Came to NY. Henry Holt & Co. p. 368
42. "Portrait Gallery". Historical Society of Courts of State of New York. State Unified Court System. Arch Dec 2, 2008
43. Calvin C. Jillson; Rick K. Wilson (1994). Congressional Dynamics: Structure, Coordination, Choice in First American Congress, 1774–1789. Stanford U Press. p. 88. ISBN 9780804722933. Archi 9/15/15. Retr 6/16/15.
44. "United States Department of State: Chiefs of Mission to Spain". Archived Nov 17, 2017. Retr May 22, 2019.
45. Pellew p. 166
46. Pellew p. 170
47. "Treaty of Paris, 1783". U.S. Department of State. Office of Electronic Info, Arch 2/5/09. Retr 8/23/08.
48. "The Paris Peace Treaty of 1783". The University of Oklahoma College of Law. Archived Sept 29, 2008.
49. "American Occurrences". Warden & Russell's Massachusetts Sentinel. October 27, 1784.
50. Whitelock p. 181
51. "John Jay". Find Law. Archived August 20, 2008. Retrieved August 25, 2008.
52. "Extract from Address to people of state of New-York, on federal Constitution". Arch 1/18/09. Retr 8/23/08.
53. WSU Archived August 28, 2008, at the Wayback Machine retrieved August 31, 2008
54. "Federalist Papers".Primary Document in American History.library of Congress.Arch 8/29/08. Retr 8/21/08
55. "Federalist Papers Authored by John Jay". Foundingfathers.info. Arch August 21, 2008. Retr 8/21/08
56. "Supreme Court of US – History". US Senate Committee on Judiciary. Arch 8/5/11. Retr 10/18/11
57. "The Jay Court ... 1789–1793". Supreme Court Historical Society. Arch May 16, 2008. Retr August 21, 2008.
58. Lee Epstein, Jeffrey Segal, Harold J. Spaeth, T G. Walker, Supreme Court Compendium 352 (3d ed. 2003)
59. "Appointees Chart". The Supreme Court Historical Society. Archived 4/21/08. Retr 8/22/08.
60. "Book of Members,1780-2010: Chapter J" American Academy Arts Sciences.Arch 10/20/16. Retr 4/28/14.
61. John Jay at the Biographical Directory of Federal Judges, a publication of the Federal Judicial Center.
62. John Jay Archived April 16, 2010, at the Wayback Machine, Leftjustified.com
63. "Honorary graduate details | The U of Edinburgh". www.scripts.sasg.ed.ac.uk. Arch &Retr July 24, 2023.
64. "Hayburn's Case, 2 U. S. 409 (1792)". Justia and Oyez. Archived Oct 29, 2008. Retr August 22, 2008.
65. "Georgia v. Brailsford, Powell & Hopton, 3U.S. 3Dall. 1 1 (1794)". Oyez & Justia. Arch 12/10/08. Retr 8/21/08.
66. "Chisholm v. Georgia, 2 U.S. 419 (1793)". The Oyez Project. Retrieved Dec 6, 2022.
67. "Georgia v. Brailsford, Powell & Hopton, 3U.S. 3Dall. 1 1 (1794)". Oyez & Justia. Arch 12/10/08. Retr 8/21/08.
68. "John Jay (1745–1829)". The Free Library. Farlex. Arch May 9, 2008. Retr August 21, 2008.
69. Johnson (2000)
70. We the Jury by Jefferey B Abramson, pp. 75–76
71. Mann, Neighbors and Strangers, pp. 71, 75
72. Jenkins, John (1846). History Political Parties State of NY. Alden & Markham. Arch 4/7/14. Retr 8/25/08.
73. Sullivan, James; Williams, Melvin E.; Conklin, Edwin; Fitzpatrick, Benedict, eds. (1927), "Chapter III. Politics
74. "John Jay's Treaty,1794–95"U.S. Department State. Office Electronic Info, Arch2/5/09 Retr 8/25/08
75. Elkins and McKitrick, p. 405
76. Kafer p. 87
77. "Jay's Treaty". Archiving Early America. Arch March 3, 2009. Retr August 25, 2008.
78. Estes (2002)
79. "Wars – War of 1812". USAhistory.com. Archived Sept 15, 2008. Retr August 25, 2008.
80. Don Fehrenbacher, Slaveholding Republic (2002) p. 93; Frederick A. Ogg,

CARROLL FAMILY of MARYLAND
ONE OF THE EARLIEST FAMILIES TO SURVIVE IN AMERICA
FIRST CATHOLIC BISHOP IN AMERICA

As America is beginning to develop in the decades prior to our American Revolution, the Carroll family of Maryland becomes the most prolific presence in the fledgling colonies. There may be two or more Carroll family lineages in this story of Founding Fathers, and unfortunately the historical record missed too many details, except to record their importance.

In the Revolution and Constitution period, we have 3 different men within the Carroll family that sign the Declaration of Independence and US Constitution. One branch of the family will establish an incredible business presence. Another branch will concentrate on religion and become the very first Catholic Bishop in America.

In those early days, Catholics were ostracized due to the terrible persecutions of the Catholic Reformation practiced in Spain and France. Catholics were prohibited from taking part in our colonial political process but allowed to function fully otherwise.

The given name for many in this family is Charles, and they used other names unusual to modern readers. They became prominent and publicly known, attempting a measure of individuality, as was practiced prominently in Britain and the continent.

The great Historian Josephus, a Galilean and contemporary of Jesus Christ, writes that it often became impossible to trace historical dates due to the preponderance of the names of men repeating with such great frequency across many generations. Josephus tells us ancient historical dates are only accurate within 400 years. Within this chapter on the many men named Charles Carroll, you will see the repetition of names continue into the Revolution period.

Two of the family ancestry of Maryland signers of the Declaration of Independence and US Constitution, endured a heavy "religious freedom" clash in England prior to coming to America, and you will see how that formed their belief as to how our Constitution and laws should be written in order to protect all people.

There is an interesting anecdote revolving around Carroll's and William Penn. Pennsylvania and Maryland are neighboring states. One of William Penns' first actions upon being awarded the Pennsylvania Land Grant was to complete a grueling horseback tour of the future State of Pennsylvania. On that tour, Penn realized the incredible extent of the Land Grant. He also recognized potential American Indian problems. He became aware that neighboring Marylanders were heavily poaching the game and fish in his central state area, which became known as Gettysburg. Penn returned to Ireland and recruited a shipload of 140 men and placed them in key locations in the portion of Pennsylvania which had remained in a Wilderness Frontier category. Penns orders to the 140 men was to protect his land from the Indians and those annoying Marylanders. And this is yet another indication of the extreme religious freedom issues still pervasive among the British and Continentals. Penn was an avowed Quaker and Maryland was solidly Catholic.

CHARLES CARROLL THE SETTLER
FAMILY HISTORY IN ENGLAND AND IRELAND
RELIGIOUS PERSECUTIONS AND TENSIONS IN ENGLAND
MAJOR POINTS OF TENSION THAT FORMED COLONIAL BELIEF

Charles Carroll (1661 – 1720), sometimes called **Charles Carroll the Settler** to differentiate him from his son and grandson,[1] was an Irish-born planter and lawyer who spent most of his life in the English Province of Maryland. Carroll, a Catholic, is best known for his efforts to hold office in the Protestant-dominated colony which eventually resulted in the disfranchisement of Maryland's Catholics. The second son of Irish Catholic parents, Carroll was educated in France as a lawyer before returning to England, where he pursued the first steps in a legal career. Before that career developed, he secured a position as Attorney General of the young colony of Maryland. Its founder George Calvert, 1st Baron Baltimore and his descendants intended it as a refuge for persecuted Catholics.

Carroll supported Charles Calvert, 3rd Baron Baltimore, the colony's Catholic proprietor, in an unsuccessful effort to prevent the Protestant majority from gaining political control over Maryland. Following the overthrow of the Calvert proprietorship and the subsequent exclusion of Catholics from colonial government, Carroll turned his attention to owning slave plantations, law, business, and various offices in the proprietor's remnant organization. He was the wealthiest man in the colony by the time of his death. In the last years of his life, Carroll attempted to regain some vestige of political power for Catholics in the colony, but the Protestant colonial assembly and Governor John Hart disfranchised them. His son, Charles Carroll of Annapolis, became a wealthy planter and grandson, Charles Carroll of Carrollton, also wealthy, was the only Catholic signer of the US Declaration of Independence.

Early life

Carroll was the second of four sons born to Daniel Carroll of Aghagurty and Littermurna, an Irish Catholic whose family lost much of their land and wealth during the Wars of the Three Kingdoms. The exact place of his birth is unclear, though it likely occurred near the small town of Aghagurty that Carroll's father took as part of his name.[1] Some of the family property near Aghagurty was obtained by a friend, Richard Grace, who made Daniel Carroll the head tenant. This action gave the family a livelihood, but the family continued to have limited means compared to their former status.[2] It is likely that Charles Carroll was fostered by the wealthier Grace, who had no son; his greater resources could provide for the child's education.[3]

With Grace's support, Carroll was able to attend school in France—at Lille and at the University of Douai—where he studied the humanities, philosophy, and civil and canon law.[4] By May 1685, Carroll had moved to London, where he registered to study English common law and was accepted into the Inner Temple, one of the four Inns of Court that are able to call members to the bar and enable them to practice law.[5] According to family tradition, Carroll secured a position as clerk to William Herbert, 1st Marquess of Powis, an English nobleman who was one of two Catholic peers in the court of James II of England.[6]

According to Carroll family tradition, Powis told his new clerk that he believed King James was receiving bad advice related to the religious turmoil in England. Powis was concerned about the consequences for English Catholics. He supposedly spoke on Carroll's behalf to an associate of his, Charles Calvert, proprietor of the Maryland colony.[7] Charles Calvert's grandfather, George Calvert, 1st Baron Baltimore, was a former member of Parliament and Secretary of State to James I, whose Catholicism had effectively ended his political career. Intense lobbying by George Calvert had led to the granting of a hereditary charter to the Calvert family. The Maryland colony was established in the 1630s on land granted by this charter. It was intended as a haven for English Catholics and other religious minorities.[8] Powis may have encouraged Carroll to emigrate to Maryland with the hope that the younger man's career would come to greater fulfillment in a place with less religious conflict than England at the time.[6]

Carroll received a commission from Calvert as the colony's Attorney General on July 18, 1688, and arrived in the colony in October 1688. En route, Carroll changed his family motto from *In fide et in bello forte* (strong in faith and war) to *Ubicumque cum libertate* (anywhere so long as there be freedom).[7] Soon after, the Protestant William of Orange invaded England, James II fled, Parliament—which had been leery of James' Catholicism—recognized William and Mary as the new King and Queen two weeks after Carroll's arrival in Maryland. The event, known as the Glorious Revolution, had profound implications for the future of the Maryland colony and for Carroll.[9]

American Career Commences in Maryland

Soon after his arrival in Maryland, Carroll presented his commission to the colony's council and was recognized as the new Attorney General of the colony. He arrived in a place already riven by religious and class differences. Carroll and most of the governing structure of the colony, except for the lower house, were appointed by Calvert. Most of the appointees were Catholic and wealthy, whereas the majority of the population and the lower house of the assembly were Protestant and less wealthy.[10] Carroll arrived in Maryland just as long-standing economic, religious, and political tensions between the poorer Protestant majority and the wealthier Catholic minority were reaching a head.[11]

By the late 17th century, Maryland's economy was suffering from the effects of price fluctuations on the world market of its main cash crop, tobacco. Often in those years, the price on world markets was barely above the cost of production, leaving the colony's planter class with little to show for their efforts. This affected small Protestant planters disproportionately, as many of the larger Catholic landowners had diversified economically. This growing socioeconomic inequality exacerbated underlying religious tensions.[11] Furthermore, the new Governor, William Joseph, who arrived in the colony just before Carroll, immediately entered into an adversarial relationship with the Protestant-dominated lower house of the assembly. Into this powder keg came the news that England's Glorious Revolution had taken place; the Catholic King James II had been deposed and replaced with the Protestant William of Orange. In an attempt to maintain control in the colony, Governor Joseph quickly canceled the session of the colonial assembly scheduled for April 1689.[12]

In response to this cancellation and rumors of an anti-Protestant alliance between Catholics and Native Americans, Protestant settlers formed an association to defend themselves. In July 1689, they marched on the colonial capital, St. Mary's City. Led by John Coode, the Protestant associators were quickly able to capture St. Mary's and the other major towns of the colony. The Governor and a number of other Calvert allies fled to Virginia.[13] Charles Calvert turned for relief to the Lords of Trade and eventually to the Privy Council, but these groups sided with the Protestants and took away the power of the Calvert family to govern the colony.[14] Leaders of the colony soon barred Catholics from holding office, bearing arms, or jury duty.[15]

During the rebellion, Carroll was recovering from the "hard seasoning" often experienced by immigrants whose bodies were acclimatizing to local conditions.[16] Perhaps due to illness, he chose not to flee the colony. Instead, Carroll offered support and legal advice to

161

Calvert and became an outspoken critic of the Protestant government. He was jailed twice for insulting the new colonial leaders, including Governor Lionel Copley, who accused Carroll of "uttering several mutinous and seditious speeches".[17] Losing his position in the colonial government and the £50 (equal to £11,453 today) annual salary it entailed was a blow to Carroll. His support for Calvert earned him various positions in the private Calvert family organization, which would benefit him throughout his life.[18]

Marriage adds to Wealth.

Carroll improved his fortunes through a judicious marriage. In November 1689, he wed Martha Ridgely Underwood (née Hawks), a widow whose two former husbands had left her a small fortune. Her son by Robert Ridgely was Charles Ridgely I, father of Charles Ridgely II. Carroll inherited a portion of this fortune after Martha's death in 1690 in childbirth.[19] The child, named Anthony in honor of Carroll's brother, also died.[20] Restricted in his law practice by the new Protestant government, Carroll used the inheritance to begin importing goods to the colony.[21] He also purchased a store in the town of Annapolis.[22]

In February 1693 or 1694, Carroll remarried, this time to the 15-year-old daughter of Colonel Henry Darnall, Charles Calvert's chief agent in the colony.[23] The marriage to Mary Darnall secured Carroll a tract of land in Prince George's County, a position in the colony's land office with a £100 annual salary, and a lifelong alliance with Henry Darnall. This tract of land was the first part of what would become a vast empire of nearly 50,000 acres (20,000 ha) by the time of Carroll's death, worth approximately £20,000.[24] Some of these lands were worked by the 112 slaves he acquired during his lifetime. This was a very large number of slaves for a Maryland planter in the early colonial period.[25] After 1706, Carroll and his family resided on two properties, a town house built in the new colonial capital of Annapolis and the plantation called Dougheregan in modern-day Howard County.[26]

Children

As successful as Carroll was, he and his wife experienced many personal losses. Of the ten children born to Charles and Mary Carroll, five died within a year of their birth. Henry, their eldest son, died the year before his father in 1719, at the age of 21 or 22. Only the third child, named Charles and later known as Charles Carroll of Annapolis, and their next son Daniel would marry and have children of their own.[20]

Henry Darnall died in 1711. Carroll took over Darnall's positions as agent and receiver general for the Calvert family in the colony, both posts with significant additional salaries. Among the many uses to which he put this money was lending. After 1713, he became the largest mortgage lender in the colony, and made a number of large personal loans to other planters.[27] Carroll continued to practice law, making a small income from cases argued in the two courts where Catholics were still allowed to practice law, the chancery and prerogative courts.[28] His speculation in mercantile enterprises also continued. Together, these made Carroll the wealthiest man in the colony by 1715, and its most prominent Catholic.[29]

Final political actions and death

In 1715, political power over the Maryland colony was restored to the Calvert family after the conversion of Benedict Calvert to Protestantism. Emboldened by this turn of events, and with support from prominent Maryland Catholic families, Carroll attempted to gain government office in the state. This would have been a profound departure from the policy of excluding Catholics from government, which had existed since the Protestant takeover in 1689. Carroll's chief antagonist in this effort was the Governor, John Hart.[30] In 1716, Hart discovered Carroll was planning to travel to England to lobby Calvert's officials for restoration of office-holding rights for Catholics, something Hart vehemently opposed. Hart described Carroll as:

a professed Papist, and first fomentor of our late Disturbances, who having acquired a large estate in the Province by the offices he formerly employed, and his practice in Law...must add the Ambition of Rule to his former Felicity.[31]

Carroll travelled to England to press his case, although Hart later claimed that he was promised no such lobbying would take place. Carroll convinced the proprietor's officials to appoint him as the proprietor's chief agent in the colony.[32] He was further appointed to the positions of receiver general, escheator, and naval officer. These positions together effectively gave Carroll the power to oversee all money in the colony that was collected by the government or by Calvert's private organization.[33]

Upon Carroll's return to Maryland, Hart was incensed both at the threat to his own power and the idea of a Catholic officeholder in the colony. Hart demanded that Carroll take the oath of allegiance, which he was willing to do, and the oath of abjuration confirming the Protestant succession to the English throne, which Carroll was not willing to do. Carroll began to act in the capacity authorized by the proprietor's commission, and Hart turned to the upper house of the colonial legislature for relief.[34] Rejecting Carroll's arguments in support of his right to hold government offices, the assembly resisted his attempts to exercise the commission and, near the end of 1716, passed a series of laws confirming and restricting the oath requirements for officeholders, which were anti-Catholic by intent.[35] Carroll's case may have been undermined when he came to the defense of his nephew, who had raised a toast to the Catholic James Stuart. Stuart had tried to take the British throne during a rebellion in 1715 and was extremely unpopular with Protestants in the colony.[36] The proprietor, whose position had been so recently restored and who did not want to risk the loss of the colony, confirmed the decision of the assembly. Carroll's commission was formally revoked on 20 February 1717.[35] According to a later account Hart gave to the assembly, Carroll began a campaign to undermine the Governor. There is no evidence Hart was accurate, but the assembly passed stricter anti-Catholic laws in 1718, including stripping Catholic males of the right to vote.[37]

Carroll died only two years later, with his wealth intact but having failed to regain any political rights for Catholics in Maryland. Carroll's eldest son Henry had died a year before; the family fortune and burden of heading a Catholic family in Protestant-dominated Maryland were passed on to his sons Charles and Daniel.[38]

Carroll's descendants continued to play a prominent role. His son Charles, known as Charles Carroll of Annapolis, expanded the family fortune. His grandson, Charles Carroll of Carrollton, achieved restoration of political rights his grandfather had desired. He was the only Catholic to sign the Declaration of Independence.[39]

References
1. Hoffman, pp. 29–35
2. Hoffman, pp. 34–35
3. Hoffman, pp. 36–37
4. Hoffman, p. 37
5. Hoffman, p. 38
6. Hoffman, p. 39
7. McDermott, p. 25
8. Krugler, p. 114
9. Hoffman, pp. 40–42

10. Hoffman, pp. 41–42
11. Radoff, p. 17
12. Radoff, pp. 19–20
13. Lovejoy, pp. 266–267
14. Hoffman, pp. 43–44
15. Payne, p. 269
16. Hoffman, p. 45
17. Hoffman, pp. 45–46
18. Hoffman, p. 46
19. Hoffman, pp. 64–65
20. Hoffman, Appendix 6: Genealogical Charts
21. Hoffman, p. 65
22. McDermott, p. 29
23. Hoffman, p. 67
24. Hoffman, pp. 70–72
25. Hoffman, p. 73
26. *"Three Generations of Carroll's, "Anywhere So Long as There Be Freedom"". Charles Carroll House of Annapolis. Archived 2009-04-28. Retr 2009-05-13.*
27. Hoffman, pp. 73–75
28. Hoffman, p. 75
29. Hoffman, pp. 76–77
30. Hoffman, pp. 79–80
31. Andrews, p.226
32. The proprietor was underage at the time, colony was managed with the help of a council of family officials.
33. Hoffman, pp. 82–84
34. Hoffman, pp. 84–86
35. Hoffman, pp. 89–91
36. McDermott, p. 30
37. Hoffman, p. 94
38. Hoffman, pp. 95–97
39. Radoff, p. 28 and Hoffman, p. 309

Sources

☐ Andrews, Matthew Page (1929). A History of Maryland. Doubleday Doran & Co.
☐ Hoffman, Ronald (2000). Princes of Ireland, Planters of Maryland: A Carroll Saga, 1500–1782. Chapel Hill: University of North Carolina Press. ISBN 0-8078-5347-X.
☐ Krugler, John D. (2004). English and Catholic: The Lords Baltimore in the Seventeenth Century. Baltimore: Johns Hopkins University Press. ISBN 0-8018-7963-9.
☐ Lovejoy, David (1987). The Glorious Revolution in America. Wesleyan U Press. ISBN 978-0-8195-6177-0.
☐ McDermott, Scott (2002). Charles Carroll of Carrollton. Scepter Publishers. ISBN 978-1-889334-68-4.
☐ Payne, Roger (2003). "Maryland: Colonial to Early Republic". In Cookson, Catharine (ed.). Encyclopedia of Religious Freedom. Taylo Francis. pp. 265–269. ISBN 978-0-415-94181-5.

☐ Radoff, Morris L. (1971). The Old-Line State: A History of Maryland. Hall of Records Commission, State of Maryland. ISBN 978-0-942370-07-2.

EXTENDED CARROLL FAMILY ANCESTRY THROUGH CONSTITUTION PERIOD

The Carroll family were descendants of the Ó Cearbhaill's, who were the rulers of the Irish petty kingdom of Éile in King's County, Ireland.[6] Carroll's grandfather was Charles Carroll the Settler, an Irishman from Aghagurty who moved to London in 1685 and worked as a clerk for English nobleman Lord Powis before emigrating to Maryland in October 1688.[7] After arriving in Maryland, he settled in the colonial capital of St. Mary's City with a commission as an attorney general from Lord Baltimore.[8][9]

Carroll's mother was English and hailed from the Brooke family.[10][11] Carroll's father was Charles Carroll of Annapolis, who was born in Annapolis, Maryland, in 1702. He inherited the plantation of Doughoregan Manor from his father, but as a Roman Catholic he was forbidden from participating in the political affairs of the colony.[12][13]

The Carroll Men and their given and assumed names.
Charles Carroll the Settler, arrived in Maryland 1685
Charles Carroll of Annapolis or Charles Carroll II
Charles Carroll of Carrollton or Charles Carroll III

Declaration Signers from Maryland
Samuel Chase, William Paca, Thomas Stone, Charles Carroll of Carrollton

US Constitution signatories from Maryland
James McHenry, Dan of St Thomas Jenifer, Danl. Carroll
Thomas Stone is in the lineage of Daniel of St. Thomas Jenifer.

CHARLES CARROLL OF CARROLLTON

Charles Carroll (September 19, 1737 – November 14, 1832), known as **Charles Carroll of Carrollton** or **Charles Carroll III**,[2] was an American politician, planter, and signatory of the Declaration of Independence. He was the only Catholic signatory of the Declaration and the longest surviving, died 56 years after signing.[3]

Considered one of the Founding Fathers of the United States,[4] Carroll was known contemporaneously as the "First Citizen" of the American Colonies, a consequence of signing articles in the *Maryland Gazette* with that pen name.[5] He served as a delegate to the Continental Congress and Confederation Congress. Carroll later served as the first United States Senator for Maryland. Carroll was one of the wealthiest and most educated of the signers of the Declaration of Independence. Carroll spoke five languages fluently, a product of his Jesuit education.

Young Life

Carroll was born on September 19, 1737, in Annapolis, Maryland, the only child of Charles Carroll of Annapolis and his wife Elizabeth Brooke.[14] The young Carroll was educated at a Jesuit school on Maryland's Eastern Shore.[14] At age 11, he was sent to France, where he continued in Jesuit schools, first at the College of St. Omer in Northern France and later the Lycée Louis-le-Grand in Paris, graduating in 1755. He continued his studies in Europe and read law in London before returning to Annapolis in 1765.[14][15]

Charles Carroll of Annapolis granted Carrollton Manor to his son, Charles Carroll of Carrollton. The land name became his title "Charles Carroll of Carrollton." Like his father, Carroll was a Catholic and as a consequence was barred by Maryland statute from entering politics, practicing law and voting.[14] This did not prevent him from becoming one of the wealthiest men in Maryland (or indeed anywhere in the Colonies),[14] owning extensive agricultural estates, most notably the large manor at Doughoregan, Hockley Forge and Mill, and providing capital to finance new enterprises on the Western Shore.[16]

American Revolution - - Voice for independence

Carroll was not initially interested in politics,[14] and in any event Catholics had been barred from holding office in Maryland since the 1704 act seeking "to prevent the growth of Popery in this Province".[17] But as the dispute between Great Britain and her American colonies intensified in the early 1770s, Carroll became a powerful voice for independence. Writing in the *Maryland Gazette* under the pseudonym "First Citizen," he became a prominent spokesman against increasing legal fees to state officers and Protestant clergy. Opposing Carroll in these written debates and writing as "Antillon" was Daniel Dulany the Younger, a noted lawyer and loyalist politician.[18][19] In these debates, Carroll argued that the government of Maryland had long been the monopoly of four families, the Ogles, the Taskers, the Bladens and the Dulanys, with Dulany taking the contrary view.[19] Word spread of the true identity of the two combatants, and Carroll's fame and notoriety began to grow.[20] Dulany soon resorted to highly personal ad hominem attacks on "First Citizen", Carroll responded, in statesmanlike fashion, with considerable restraint, arguing that when "Antillon" engaged in "virulent invective and illiberal abuse, we may fairly presume, that arguments are either wanting, or that ignorance or incapacity know not how to apply them".[20] Following these debates, Carroll became an opponent of British rule and served on various committees.[21]

In the early 1770s, Carroll appears to have embraced the idea that only violence could break the impasse with Great Britain. According to legend, Carroll and Samuel Chase (who would later sign the Declaration of Independence for Maryland's) had the following exchange:

Chase: "We have the better of our opponents; we have completely written them down."
Carroll: "And do you think that writing will settle the question between us?"
Chase: "To be sure, what else can we resort to?"
Carroll: "The bayonet. Our arguments will only raise the feelings of the people to that pitch when open war will be looked to as the arbiter of the dispute."[22]

Continental Congress

Beginning with his election to Maryland's committee of correspondence in 1774, Carroll represented the colony in most of the pre-revolutionary groups. He became a member of Annapolis' first committee of safety in 1775. Carroll was a delegate to the Annapolis Convention, which functioned as Maryland's revolutionary government before the Declaration of Independence. In early 1776, the Congress sent him on a four-man diplomatic mission to the Province of Quebec, in order to seek assistance from French Canadians in the coming confrontation with Great Britain. Carroll was an excellent choice, being fluent in French and a Catholic and therefore well suited to negotiations with the French-speaking Catholics of Quebec.[22] He was joined in the commission by Benjamin Franklin, Samuel Chase, and John Carroll.[23] The commission did not accomplish its mission.

Carroll won election to the Continental Congress on July 4, 1776, and remained a delegate until 1778. He arrived too late to vote in favor of the Declaration of Independence but was present to sign the official document that survives today. After both Thomas Jefferson and John Adams died on July 4, 1826, Carroll became the last living signatory of the Declaration of Independence. His signature reads "Charles Carroll of Carrollton" to distinguish him from his father, "Charles Carroll of Annapolis," who was still living at that time, and several other Charles Carroll's in Maryland, such as Charles Carroll, Barrister, and his son Charles Carroll Jr., also known as "Charles Carroll of Homewood." He is usually referred to this way by historians. At the time, he was the richest man in America and had much to lose by identifying himself on the document. Throughout his term in the Second Continental Congress, he served on the board of war. Carroll also gave considerable financial support to the American Revolutionary War.

Post-revolution political career

Carroll returned to Maryland in 1778 to assist in the formation of a state government. Carroll was re-elected to the Continental Congress in 1780, but he declined. He was elected to the Maryland Senate in 1781 and served there until 1800. In November 1779, The Maryland

House of Delegates moved to pass a bill confiscating the property of those who had sided with the Crown during the Revolution. Carroll opposed this measure, questioning the motives of those who pressed for confiscation and arguing that the measure was unjust. Confiscation of Tory property had popular support and in 1780, the measure passed.[24]

When the United States government was created, the Maryland legislature elected him to the first United States Senate. In 1792, Maryland passed a law that prohibited any man from serving in the state and national legislatures at the same time. Since he preferred to be in the Maryland Senate, he resigned from the U.S. Senate on November 30, 1792.

Carroll did not leave a description of his expectations of the US Constitution, although he was a supporter of the document.

On Slavery

The Carroll family were slaveholders at the time of the American Revolution.[25] Carroll was opposed in principle to slavery, asking rhetorically: "Why keep alive the question of slavery? It is admitted by all to be a great evil.; let an effectual mode of getting rid of it be pointed out, or let the question sleep forever;"[26]However, although he supported its gradual abolition, he did not free his own slaves.[27] Carroll introduced a bill for the gradual abolition of slavery in the Maryland Senate, but it did not pass.[28] In 1828, aged 91, he served as president of the Auxiliary State Colonization Society of Maryland,[29] the Maryland branch of the American Colonization Society, dedicated to returning Black Americans to lives in Liberia.

Life beyond the Constitution era

Carroll retired from public life in 1801. After Thomas Jefferson became president, he had great anxiety about political activity and was not sympathetic to the War of 1812. He was elected a member of the American Antiquarian Society in 1815.[30] Carroll helped create the Baltimore and Ohio Railroad in 1827.

Carroll died on November 14, 1832, at age 95, in Baltimore. He outlived four of the first five U.S. presidents. His funeral took place at the Baltimore Cathedral (Basilica of the National Shrine of the Assumption of the Blessed Virgin Mary), and he is buried in his Doughoregan Manor Chapel at Ellicott City, Maryland.

Signature of Carroll

The story behind the unusual signature used by Carroll gives us further proof of the historical quandary of our Founding Fathers. All feared that if the Revolution should fail, the King of England would execute them.

In the 1940s, newspaper journalist John Hix's syndicated comic *Strange as It Seems* published an apocryphal explanation for Charles Carroll's distinctive signature on the Declaration of Independence. Every member of the Continental Congress who signed this document automatically became a criminal, guilty of sedition against King George III. Carroll, because of his wealth, had more to lose than most of his companions. Some of the signatories, such as Caesar Rodney and Button Gwinnett, had unusual and distinctive names which would clearly identify them to the King; other signatories, with commonplace names, might sign the Declaration without incriminating themselves.

According to Hix, when it was Carroll's turn to sign the Declaration of Independence, he rose, went to John Hancock's desk where the document rested, signed his name "Charles

Carroll", and returned to his seat. Another member of the Continental Congress, who was prejudiced against Carroll's Catholicism, commented that Carroll risked nothing in signing the document, as there must be many men named Charles Carroll. Carroll returned to Hancock's desk and added "of Carrollton.[31]

In fact, Carroll had been appending "of Carrollton" to his signature for over a decade, the earliest surviving example appearing at the end of a September 15, 1765, letter to his English friend William Gibson. Carrollton Manor was the name of a tract of more than twelve thousand acres in Frederick County, Maryland, which the Carroll family leased to tenant farmers.

References

1.   Ellis, John Tracy (1969). American Catholicism. University of Chicago. p. 72. ISBN 978-0-226-20556-4.
2.   "Signers of the Declaration: Biographical Sketches: Charles Carroll". National Park Service.Oct 26, 2012.
3.   "Charles Carroll, of Carrollton," American Catholic Quarterly Review, Vol. XXIV, 1899.
4.   Bernstein, Richard B. (2011) [2009]. "Appendix: The Founding Fathers: A Partial List". Founding Fathers Reconsidered. New York: Oxford U Press. ISBN 978-0199832576.
5.   "Charles Carroll Of Carrollton Commemorative Medal". State of Maryland. Retr March 10, 2021.
6.   "Ireland's History in Maps – Tuadmumu, Kingdom of Thomond". rootsweb.com. October 25, 2003.
7.   "Charles Carroll, Signer, Declaration of Independence". adherents.com. Arch Dec 25, 2005.
8.   "Biography of Charles Carroll of Carrollton, page 1 – Colonial Hall". colonialhall.com.
9.   "www.charlescarrollhouse.com". charlescarrollhouse.com.
10. Mary Virginia Geiger (1979). Daniel Carroll II, One Man and His Descendants, 1730-1978. U Wisconsin p. 131.
11. Charles Carroll (1902). Unpublished Letters of Charles Carroll of Carrollton. Yale U Library.
12. Hoffman, Ronald, Princes of Ireland, Planters of Maryland: A Carroll Saga, 1500–1782 Retr August 9, 2010
13. "History of Independence Hall (1859)". fairfield.edu. Archived April 12, 2006. Retrieved May 14, 2006.
14. McClanahan, Brion T., p.199, The Politically Incorrect Guide to the Founding Fathers. Retrieved Nov 2010.
15. Maier, Pauline. The Old Revolutionaries (1980), ISBN 0-394-51096-8/>
16. Andrews, Matthew Page, History of Maryland, p. 270, Doubleday Doran & Co, NY (1929)
17. Roark, Elisabeth Louise, p.78, Artists of colonial America Retrieved August 2012
18. Williamson, Claude, p.247, Great Catholics, Williamson Press (March 15, 2007). Retrieved November 2010.
19. Warfield, J. D., p. 215, The Founders of Anne Arundel and Howard Counties, Maryland. Retrieved Nov 2010.
20. McClanahan, Brion T., p.203, The Politically Incorrect Guide to the Founding Fathers. Retrieved Nov 2010.
21. "Charles Carroll". aoc.gov. Architect of the Capitol. October 10, 2014.
22. McClanahan, Brion T., p.204, The Politically Incorrect Guide to the Founding Fathers. Retr Nov 2010.
23. "Charles Carroll". aoc.gov. Architect of the Capitol. October 10, 2014.
24. Andrews, Matthew Page, History of Maryland, p. 374, Doubleday Doran & Co, NY,1929
25. "Charles Carroll of Carrollton – the Signer". March 17, 2011.
26. Quotes by Carroll Archived August 13, 2018, at the Wayback Machine. Retr Nov 2010.
27. Miller, Randall M., and Wakelyn, Jon L., p.214, Catholics in the Old South: Essays on Church and Culture Mercer University Press (1983). Retrieved January 21, 2010.
28. Leonard, Lewis A. p.218, Life of Charles Carroll of Carrollton New York, Moffat, Yard, and Company, (1918).
29. Gurley, Ralph Randolph, Ed., p.251, African Repository, Volume 3. Retr Jan 15, 2010.
30. "Member List C". American Antiquarian Society.
31. "Charles Carroll of Carrollton: The Southern Irish Catholic Planter – Abbeville Institute".

DANIEL CARROLL

Daniel Carroll (July 22, 1730 – May 7, 1796) was an American politician and plantation owner from Maryland and one of the Founding Fathers of the United States. He supported the American Revolution, served in the Confederation Congress, was a delegate to the Philadelphia Convention of 1787 which penned the Constitution of the United States, and was a U.S. Representative in the First Congress.[1] Carroll was one of five men to sign both the Articles of Confederation and the Constitution. He was a Roman Catholics among the Founders.

Early life

Carroll was born in Marlborough Town in the Province of Maryland on July 22, 1730. He was the son of wealthy planters Daniel Carroll (c.1696 - 1751) and Eleanor Darnall Carroll (1703 - 1796). His parents' home was Darnall's Chance, a plantation of 27,000 acres which his mother inherited from her grandfather.[2] Carroll was sent abroad for his education. Between

1742 and 1748 he studied at Jesuits College of St. Omer in France, established for the education of English Catholics. After a tour of Europe, he sailed home and married Eleanor Carroll.

His younger brother John was the first Roman Catholic bishop in the United States (as Bishop of Baltimore, 1790) and founder of Georgetown University; his cousin Charles Carroll of Carrollton signed the Declaration of Independence.

Career

In the 1770s, Carroll gradually joined the Patriot cause. As a slaveholder and large landholder, he was initially concerned that the Revolution might fail economically and bring about his family's financial ruin and mob rule.[1]

At the time, Maryland, though Catholic-founded, had (like the rest of the Thirteen Colonies) issued laws excluding Roman Catholics from holding public office. When Maryland declared its independence from the Crown and enacted its first constitution, these laws were nullified. Carroll was elected to the Maryland Senate, serving 1777–1781. As a state senator, he helped raise troops and money for the war. His involvement in the Revolutionary War, like that of other Patriots in his family, was inspired by the family's motto: "Strong in Faith and War".[1]

He led the effort to block the State Assembly from ratifying of the Articles of Confederation until the states that had western land claims (which Maryland did not) ceded those claims to Congress.[3] Carroll dropped his opposition only after Virginia relinquished its claims on land north of the Ohio River to Congress, and on February 2, 1781, Maryland became the thirteenth and final state to ratify the Articles.

Constitutional Convention of 1787

In 1787, Carroll was named a Maryland delegate to the Philadelphia Convention, which convened to revise the Articles, and produced the Constitution. Like his good friend James Madison of Virginia, Carroll was convinced that a strong central government was needed to regulate commerce among the states and with other nations. He also spoke repeatedly in opposition to the payment of members of the United States Congress by the states, reasoning that such compensation would sabotage the strength of the new government because "the dependence of both Houses of state Legislatures would be complete ... The new government is nothing more than a second edition of [Continental] Congress in two volumes, instead of one."[1]

When it was suggested that the president (executive branch) should be elected by the Congress (legislative branch), Carroll, seconded by James Wilson, moved that the words "by the legislature" be replaced with "by the people". He and Thomas Fitzsimons were the only Roman Catholics to sign the Constitution, but their presence was a sign of the continued advancement of religious freedom in America. Carroll played an essential role in formulating the limitation of the powers of the federal or central government. He was the author of the presumption—enshrined in the Constitution as a closing article – that powers not specifically delegated to the federal government were reserved to the states or to the people.[4] Carroll spoke about 20 times during debates at the Constitutional Convention and served on the Committee on Postponed Matters. Returning to Maryland, he campaigned for ratification of the Constitution but was not a delegate to the Maryland convention for ratification.[5]

Political career

Following the convention, Carroll continued to be involved in state and national affairs. He was a key participant in the Maryland ratification struggle of 1787–1788.[6] He defended the Constitution in the *"Maryland Journal"*, most notably in his response to the arguments advanced by the well-known Anti-Federalist and Patriot delegate Samuel Chase. After ratification was achieved in Maryland, Carroll was elected as a representative ("congressman") to the Sixth Congressional District of Maryland to the First Congress of 1789, meeting in New York City. Given his concern for economic and fiscal stability, he voted for the assumption of state debts accumulated during the war by the federal government to establish a new level of financial confidence of credible public debts as proposed by Secretary of the Treasury Alexander Hamilton as part of a "grand bargain" with Secretary of State Thomas Jefferson, for Northerners to support locating the new national capital in the upper South, along the Potomac River.

One of three commissioners was appointed to survey the newly designated District of Columbia and acquire land for the new federal capital in the District, Carroll was related to two major landowners whose land was acquired by the government, his brother-in-law Notley Young and nephew Daniel Carroll of Duddington. **The United States Capitol was built on a wooded hill owned by his nephew.**[7] As one of his first official acts, on April 15, 1791, he and fellow commissioner David Stuart of Virginia laid the cornerstone for the beginning boundary survey of the District at Jones Point, on the south bank of the Potomac near Alexandria, formerly in Virginia.[6] He served as a commissioner until 1795, when he retired because of poor health.

He was again elected to the Maryland Senate. He had many interests in his state and region, including the "Patowmack Company", which sought to build a Patowmack Canal to the West. This was a long-time project of George Washington since his western explorations and military campaigns against the French. This predated construction thirty years later of the Chesapeake and Ohio Canal.[5]

Carroll died May 7, 1796, at age 65, at his home near Rock Creek in the present neighborhood of Forest Glen, Maryland. Carroll's body was buried there in Saint John the Evangelist Catholic Church Cemetery.[8]

References

1. Robert K. Wright Jr.; Morris J. MacGregor Jr. (1987). "Daniel Carroll". Soldier-Statesmen of the Constitution. Washington D.C.: USA Center of Military History. CMH Pub 71-25. Arch 10/9/19. Retr 10/2/07.
2. Geiger, Mary Virginia. Daniel Carroll, A Framer of the Constitution, Washington, D.C.: Catholic U of America, 1943. (In 1741, Mrs. Carroll sold six acres to merchant James Wardrop, who built a house there. That house and land is now a house museum called "Darnall's Chance", listed on the National Register of Historic Places.)
3. "Maryland finally ratifies Articles of Confederation". history.com. A&E Television Networks. Retr April 28, 2019.
4. "Carter, Charles Carroll. "The Carroll Family", Catholic Ed Resource Center". Arch 10/30/18. Retr 7/5/13.
5. "Delegates to the Constitutional Convention" United States National Archives and Records Administration
6. Daniel Carroll
7. United States Congress. "Daniel Carroll (id: C000187)". Biographical Directory of the United States Congress.
8. "Signers of the Constitution" Archived April 6, 2014, Wayback Machine, National Park Service
9. "Wisconsin Historical Society". Archived April 23, 2006. Retrieved June 24, 2011.

Daniel of St. Thomas Jenifer

Daniel of St. Thomas Jenifer[a] (1723 – November 16, 1790) was an American politician and Founding Father who was one of the signers of the Constitution of the United States. He was active in the Province of Maryland's colonial government, but when conflict arose with Great Britain, Jenifer embraced the Patriot cause.

Early life and colonial career

Jenifer, born at Coates Retirement (now Ellerslie), west of Port Tobacco in Charles County, Maryland, the son of Dr. Daniel Jenifer and Elizabeth Mason. As a young man, he acted as receiver general, the local financial agent for the last two proprietors of Maryland. He was the uncle of Thomas Stone, Michael J. Stone, and John Hoskins Stone. The Jenifer family was Swedish.[1][2][3]

Jenifer served as Justice of the Peace for Charles County and the western circuit of Maryland. He sat on a commission that settled a boundary dispute between Pennsylvania and Delaware[4] (1760) and on the Governor's Council, the colony's court of appeals and as senior advisers to the governor (1773–76).

American Revolution

Despite his close ties with the colonial government, Jenifer strongly resented what he and most of the colonial gentry saw as Parliament's arbitrary interference with the colonies' affairs, especially laws concerning taxation and trade regulation. Years before the struggle for independence began, he had defended the proprietors of Maryland against those who sought to make Maryland a Royal colony. When the Revolution came, Jenifer lent his considerable support as a wealthy landowner to the Patriot cause, even though many leading Patriots had been his enemies in the proprietorship struggle. Jenifer became the president of Maryland's Council of Safety, the Patriot body established to organize Maryland's military forces for the Revolution (1775–1777). When, in 1776, a new constitution was framed for the state of Maryland, Jenifer commented on the document's neglect of popular sovereignty: "The Senate does not appear to be a Child of the people at Large, therefore will not be Supported by them longer than there Subsists a perfect Union between Legislative branches."

During and after the war, Jenifer became increasingly concerned about national affairs. He represented his state in the Continental Congress (1778–1782) while simultaneously serving as president of Maryland's first senate (1777–1780). As manager of his state's finances between 1782 and 1785, Jenifer drew on his experiences as a landholder to help the state survive the critical postwar economic depression. Along with James Madison, John Dickinson, George Mason and his good friend George Washington, Jenifer began to explore ways to solve the economic and political problems that had arisen under the weak Articles of Confederation. He attended the Mount Vernon Conference, a meeting that led to the Constitutional Convention.

Constitutional Convention

Like his old friend Benjamin Franklin, Jenifer enjoyed the status of elder statesman, which took place from May 25 to September 17, 1787, in Philadelphia, Pennsylvania. Jenifer used his prestige (as well as humor and reputation as pleasant company) to work for a strong and permanent union of the states by reconciling opposing views and formulating the compromises that made the convention a success.

Jenifer took stands on several principal issues, although his advanced age restricted his activity in the day-to-day proceedings. Business experience gained while managing a large plantation had convinced him that an active central government would ensure financial and commercial stability. Concerned with continuity in the new government, he favored a three-year term for the United States House of Representatives. Jenifer was outvoted on this point, but his reaction was to marvel at the delegates' ability to come to agreement on a plan of government:

171

"The first month we only came to grips, and the second it seemed as though we would fly apart forever, however we came as close as friends of eighty years in but days." When Maryland's other delegate, Luther Martin, said that he feared being hanged if the people of Maryland approved the Constitution, Jenifer quipped that Martin should stay in Philadelphia, so that he would not hang in his home state.

Death and Legacy

After the convention, Jenifer retired to his plantation at Stepney near Annapolis, where he died in 1790. He was buried at Ellerslie, the place of his birth, which is now on the National Register of Historic Places. In his will, Jenifer passed his roughly 16,000-acres to his nephew, Daniel Jenifer, and instructed that all his slaves be freed six years after his death.[5] The following year the younger Jenifer had a son, who was named after his great-uncle. Daniel Jenifer, like his uncle, also served as magistrate in Charles County, as well as three terms in the U.S. House of Representatives. His family home, Retreat, was located in Charles County, near one of the largest slave-trading ports of the era, Port Tobacco; it was built in the last quarter of the 18th century and is listed on the National Register of Historic Places.[6]

Jenifer Street in Madison, Wisconsin, is named in honor of Jenifer.[7] There is also a Jenifer Street in Washington, D.C. Daniel of Saint Thomas Jenifer Elementary school in Charles County was named in his honor. Jenifer Elementary School is located in the Charles County Public Schools school district.

References

1. Knorr, Lawrence; Farley, Joe; Farrell, Joe (December 5, 2018). Graves of Our Founders: Their Lives, Contributions, and Burial Sites. Sunbury Press, Inc. ISBN 978-1-62006-176-3.
2. Congress, United States (1959). Congressional Record: Proceedings and Debates of the ... Congress. U.S. Government Printing Office.
3. Shellhorn, Richard Carl (June 12, 2018). A Guide to the Formation of the Constitution. Christian Faith Publishing, Inc. ISBN 978-1-64191-703-2.
4. "The Founding Fathers: Maryland". National Archives. October 30, 2015.
5. Papenfuse, Edward C., et al., "Daniel of St. Thomas Jenifer (Jennifer)," in A Biographical Dictionary of the Maryland Legislature 1635–1789, Vol. I, I–Z (Baltimore: Johns Hopkins University Press, 1985), 485–486.
6. "Maryland Historical Trust". Retreat, Charles County. Maryland Historical Trust. June 8, 2008.
7. Odd Wisconsin Archives Archived April 23, 2006, Wayback Machine. Wisconsinhistory.org (2006-03-29).

NATIONAL PARK SERVICE DOCUMENTATION ON DAN. ST. THOS. JENIFER

As an adult, Jenifer gained a reputation for political and economic skills, which led to his serving as a Justice of the Peace in Charles County, and later as a circuit judge in Western Maryland. In 1760, Jenifer served on the Maryland commission to settle the border dispute between Maryland and Pennsylvania, which led to the Mason—Dixon Line.

While his political reputation grew, Jenifer actively purchased land, traded in mercantile goods, bought and sold enslaved African Americans, and handled contracts for indentured servants. He invested in a shipload of about 140 enslaved men and women that arrived in Annapolis, Maryland on September 29, 1767.

By 1771, Jenifer was serving on the Council of Maryland's Proprietary Governor Sir Robert Eden. Jenifer's position initially caused animosity with other Marylanders, who were beginning to question the British Parliament's authority over the colonies. Over the next four years, Jenifer cautiously renounced Great Britain's rule over the colonies, but he hoped that a reconciliation would create a semi-autonomous Maryland under the nominal authority of the British Crown.

After King George III declared the colonies in rebellion in August of 1775, Jenifer fully embraced his role as a patriot. His logistical and economic skills led him to become the President of Maryland's Council of Safety, which organized Maryland's military forces in 1775.

Soon after Jenifer's nephew, Thomas Stone, signed the Declaration of Independence, Marylanders created the state's first constitution. The subsequent elections saw Jenifer chosen as the President of the Senate, one of the most powerful positions in the new state. He noted that "The Senate does not appear to be a Child of the people at Large, and therefore will not be Supported by them...."

Once the Revolutionary War ended, an old rivalry between Maryland and Virginia reasserted itself. Both states claimed ownership over the Potomac River. While Maryland's claims were stronger, the potential for profits through trade inspired many Virginians to ignore the evidence. To settle the jurisdictional issues. James Madison of Virginia proposed a meeting between the delegates of both states. The meeting eventually took place at George Washington's home, Mount Vernon, with the Maryland delegation including Daniel of St. Thomas Jenifer and Thomas Stone. The "Mount Vernon Compact" signaled cooperation among all thirteen states must be gained. Its success led to the Annapolis Convention of 1786, which advocated improvements in interstate trade. Although the Annapolis Convention saw only five states attend, the delegates proposed a follow-up convention to take place "May next" in Philadelphia. This is now known as the Constitutional Convention.

Daniel of St. Thomas Jenifer arrived in Philadelphia on June 2, 1787, one of the oldest delegates present. William Pierce, a delegate from Georgia to the Constitutional Convention, noted that Jenifer "...is always in a good humor, never fails to make his company pleased with him." Although Jenifer rarely spoke in the convention, he used his good will behind the scenes to reconcile opposing views between delegates and to formulate the compromises that helped lead to the eventual signing of the Constitution on September 17, 1787.

Jenifer died on November 16, 1790, in Annapolis.

THOMAS STONE

Thomas Stone (1743 – October 5, 1787) was an American Founding Father, planter, politician, and lawyer who signed the United States Declaration of Independence as a delegate for Maryland. He later worked on the committee that formed the Articles of Confederation in 1777. He acted as president of Congress for a short time in 1784.[1] Stone was a member of the Maryland Senate from 1777 to 1780 and again from 1781 to 1787.[2]

Early life and education

Stone was born into a prominent family at Poynton Manor in Charles County, Maryland. He was the second son in the large family of David (1709–1773) and Elizabeth Jenifer Stone. His brothers, Michael Jenifer Stone and John Hoskins Stone, were also in politics.[3] His uncle was Daniel of St. Thomas Jenifer. Thomas read law at Thomas Johnson in Annapolis, was admitted to the bar in 1764, and opened a practice in Frederick, Maryland.[4][5] The Jenifer family was Swedish.[6][7][8]

Career

As the American Revolution neared, Stone joined the committee of correspondence for Charles County. From 1774 to 1776, he was a member of Maryland's Annapolis Convention. In 1775, the convention sent Stone as a delegate to the Continental Congress. He was re-elected and attended regularly for several years. On May 15, 1776, he voted in favor of drafting a declaration of independence, despite restrictions from the Maryland convention that prevented their delegates from supporting it. Previously, Stone had been in favor of opening diplomatic relations with Great Britain and not going to war, as he was not only a pacifist but a conservative reluctant to start a gruesome war.[4][5]

That same year Stone was assigned to the committee that drafted the Articles of Confederation, and he was struck by a personal tragedy. His wife Margaret visited him in Philadelphia, which was in the midst of a smallpox epidemic. She was inoculated for the disease, but an adverse reaction to the treatment made her ill. Her health continued to decline for the rest of her life.[4][5]

Stone accepted election to the Maryland Senate from 1779 until 1785, to promote the Articles of Confederation, which Maryland was the last state to approve. When Margaret died in 1787, he became depressed and died less than four months later in Alexandria, Virginia, reportedly of a "broken heart".[4][5]

Stone was buried at his plantation home, which still stands. After his death, the plantation remained in the family for five generations until 1936 when it sold privately. In 1977 the main structure was severely damaged by fire. The National Park Service purchased the property and restored it to its original plans. *Habredeventure* today is the centerpiece of the Thomas Stone National Historic Site and is operated as a museum by the National Park Service.

Personal life

In 1768, Stone married Margaret Brown (1751–1787), the younger sister of Gustavus R. Brown (see Rose Hill), thought to be the richest man in the county. Soon after, Stone purchased his first 400 acres and began the construction of his estate named Habre de Venture. The family made their home there, and they had three children: Margaret (1771–1809), Mildred (1773–1837) and Fredrik (1774–1793). Stone's law practice kept him away from home, so his younger brother Michael managed the plantation,[4][5] which utilized slaves for generations.[9]

References

1. "Signers of the Declaration (Thomas Stone)". National Park Service. 2004-07-04. Retr2008-04-24.
2. "Thomas Stone, MSA SC 3520-1202". msa.maryland.gov. Retrieved 2021-03-07.
3. Newman, Harry Wright (1937). The Stones of Poynton Manor: a Genealogical History of Captain William Stone, gent. and Merchant, Third Proprietary Governor of Maryland, pp. 20–30.
4. "Signers of the Declaration of Independence". US History.org.
5. "Thomas Stone". Colonial Hall.
6. Knorr, Lawrence; Farley, Joe; Farrell, Joe (2018-12-05). Graves of Our Founders: Their Lives, Contributions, and Burial Sites. Sunbury Press, Inc. ISBN 978-1-62006-176-3.
7. Congress, United States (1959). Congressional Record: Proceedings and Debates of the ... Congress. U.S. Government Printing Office.
8. Shellhorn, Richard Carl (2018-06-12). A Guide to the Formation of the Constitution. Christian Faith Publishing, Inc. ISBN 978-1-64191-703-2.
9. The quiet patriot: Thomas Stone of Haberdeventure Retrieved 15 October 2018

GEORGE MASON
FATHER OF THE BILL OF RIGHTS

George Mason (December 11, 1725 – October 7, 1792) was an American planter, politician, Founding Father, and delegate to the U.S. Constitutional Convention in Philadelphia in 1787, where he was one of three delegates who refused to sign the Constitution. His writings, including substantial portions of the Fairfax Resolves of 1774, the Virginia Declaration of Rights of 1776, and his *Objections to this Constitution of Government* (1787) opposing ratification, have exercised a significant influence on American political thought and events. The Virginia Declaration of Rights, which Mason principally authored, served as a basis for the United States Bill of Rights, of which he has been deemed a father.

YOUNG LIFE

Mason was born in present-day Fairfax County, in the Colony of Virginia, in British America, on December 11, 1725.[1][2][3] Mason's parents owned property in Mason Neck, Virginia and a second property across the Potomac in Maryland, inherited by his mother.[4][5]

Mason I settled in present-day Stafford County, Virginia,[7] where he was awarded land for bringing his family and servants to the Colony of Virginia.[8]

- His son, George Mason II (1660–1716), was the first to move to what in 1742 became Fairfax County, frontier between English and Native American controlled areas.
- George Mason III (1690–1735) served in the House of Burgesses.[7]
- George Mason IV's (1725-1792) mother, Ann Thomson Mason, daughter of a former Attorney General of Virginia who immigrated from London, Yorkshire.[9]

Colonial Virginia had few roads, and boats carried most commerce on Chesapeake Bay or its tributaries, limiting commerce. Even Williamsburg had limited economic activity. Large landowners dominated politics.[10] The Virginia economy thrived on tobacco, mostly for export to Great Britain.[11] Mason began his education with private tutors, and private libraries.[12][13]

Career - - Fairfax County

In 1747, Mason was named to the Court of Fairfax County, Virginia, 1749 and 1785.[14] He served in Fairfax County militia, rising to colonel.[15]

Mason was a justice for much of the rest of his life, though he was excluded because of nonattendance from 1752 to 1764, and resigned in 1789 when continued service meant swearing to uphold a constitution he could not support.[16] Mason resided further away than other court officers, near Tyson's Corner Alexandria.[17]

He served as a trustee of Dumfries, in Prince William County, and had business interests in Georgetown, in present-day Washington, D.C.[18]

GUNSTON HALL (The nearest plantation style home to Washington's Mount Vernon, Gunston Hall is suited even today, to host committee meetings of US Congress.)

On April 4, 1750, Mason married Ann Eilbeck, the only child of William and Sarah Eilbeck of Charles County, Maryland. At the time of his marriage, Mason lived at Dogue's Neck.[19] George and Ann Mason had nine children. Ann died in 1773.[20]

Mason began to build Gunston Hall, around 1755. William Waite or James Wren, constructed Gunston Hall.[21] Mason was proud of the layout, the four large plantations, forests, shops, and facilities that made Gunston Hall self-sufficient.[22]

Mason avoided overdependence on tobacco,[23] and diversified his crops to grow wheat for the British West Indies as Virginia's economy sank due to tobacco overproduction. Mason was a pioneer in the Virginia wine industry. Jefferson, Mason and others grew wine grapes.[24]

Mason expanded Gunston Hall, to occupy Dogue's Neck / Mason's Neck.[25]

Ohio Company Executive (200,000 acres near Pittsburgh)

One project that Mason was involved in for most of his adult life was the Ohio Company, in which he invested in 1749 and became treasurer in 1752—an office he held forty years until his death in 1792. The Ohio Company had secured a royal grant for 200,000 acres to be surveyed near the forks of the Ohio River in present-day Pittsburgh. The challenges of the French and Indian War, Revolutionary War, and competing claims from the Province of Pennsylvania eventually led to the collapse of the Ohio Company. Mason acquired considerable western lands independently. His defense against the Pennsylvania claims, *Selections from the Virginia Charters*, was widely cheered as a defense of Americans against royal decrees.

Involvement with the Ohio Company brought Mason into contact with many prominent Virginians, including George Washington, his Fairfax County neighbor.[26] Mason and Washington were friends for many years until they finally broke over their differences regarding the constitution. Washington had deep respect for Mason's intellect, and sought Mason's advice, writing in 1777, learning Mason had taken charge of issues before the General Assembly, "I know of no person better qualified ... than Colonel Mason, and shall be very happy to hear he has taken it in hand".[27] He dealt in Western lands, reasoning "little Trouble & Risqué [risk]".[28]

Virginia House of Burgesses

Little is known of Mason's political views prior to the 1760s, when he came to oppose British colonial policies.[29] In 1758, Mason was elected to House of Burgesses when George William Fairfax, chose not to seek reelection.[30] Also elected were Mason's brother Thomson for Stafford County, George Washington for Frederick County, and Richard Henry Lee, who worked closely with Mason.[31] This key network would help Mason position himself for strong involvement in the future of America:

- Mason was initially appointed to a committee concerned with raising militia.
- In 1759, appointment to the Committee on Privileges and Elections.
- Committee on Propositions and Grievances.
- Mason presented a petition of Fairfax County planters against being assessed for a tobacco wharf at Alexandria.
- Advised how to divide Prince William County as settlement expanded.
- Mason opposed the interest of the family of Thomas, Lord Fairfax, who wanted existing counties expanded instead, including Fairfax.

This difference may have brought Mason's decision not to seek re-election.[32] Broadwater did not find it surprising that Mason did not seek re-election.[33]

King George III's government felt that the North American colonies were not paying their way. The Sugar Act of 1764 had its greatest effect in New England. The Stamp Act the following year affected all 13 colonies, as it required revenue stamps to be used on papers required in trade and in the law. When word of the Stamp Act reached Williamsburg, the House of Burgesses passed the Virginia Resolves, asserting that Virginians had the same rights as if

176

they resided in Britain, and that they could only be taxed by their elected representatives. The Resolves were mostly written by a fiery-spoken new member Patrick Henry.[34]

George Washington or George William Fairfax may have asked Mason's advice in the Stamp Act crisis.[35] Mason drafted an act to allow for a most common court action, replevin, and sent it to George Washington. This action contributed to a boycott of the stamps. With the courts and trade paralyzed, the British Parliament repealed the Stamp Act in 1766.[34]

Following the repeal, a committee of London merchants issued a public letter to Americans, warning them not to declare victory. Mason published a response, to the British position, "We have, with infinite Difficulty & Fatigue got you excused this one Time; do what your Papa and Mamma bid, & hasten to return your most grateful Acknowledgements for condescending to let you keep what is your own."[36]

The Townshend Acts of 1767 were Britain's next attempt to tax the colonies, placing duties on lead and glass, which provoked calls for a boycott of British goods. In April 1769, Washington sent a copy of a resolution to Mason, asking for advice. Mason sent a corrected draft on April 23, 1769. The Burgesses passed "non-importation" from Mason's draft.[37]

In March 1773, his wife Ann died. Mason, the sole parent to nine children, and his commitments made him reluctant to accept office beyond Gunston Hall.[38]

Revolutionary War

In May 1774, Mason was in Williamsburg on real estate business. Word arrived of the passage of the Intolerable Acts, which Americans dubbed the response to the Boston Tea Party. Mason may have helped write the resolution and joined the members after dissolution at Raleigh Tavern in Williamsburg.[39][40]

New elections had to be held for burgess and for delegates to the convention which had been called by the dissolved House of Burgesses, and Fairfax County's were set for July 5, 1774. Washington met with other local leaders and selected a committee to draft resolutions Washington hoped would "define our Constitutional Rights".[41] The resulting Fairfax Resolves were drafted by Mason. The 24 propositions that made up the Resolves protested loyalty to the Crown but denied the right of Parliament to legislate for colonies. The Resolves called for a continental congress. If Americans did not receive redress by November 1, exports, including tobacco, would be cut off. According to historian Hugh Grigsby, at Alexandria, Mason "made his first great movement on the theatre of the Revolution".[42]

Washington took the Resolves to the Virginia Convention in Williamsburg. The convention elected delegates to the First Continental Congress, including Lee, Washington, and Henry, in October 1774, Congress adopted a similar embargo.[43]

Much of Mason's efforts in 1774 and 1775 were organizing a militia. Washington by January 1775 was drilling a small force, he and Mason purchased gunpowder for the company. Mason wrote in favor of the annual election of militia officers in words that would echo in the Virginia Declaration of Rights:

"We came equal into this world, and equals shall we go out of it. All men are by nature born equally free and independent."[44]

By this time, blood had been shed at the Battles of Lexington and Concord. Mason was elected and journeyed to Richmond, which, being further inland than Williamsburg, was deemed better protected from possible British attack.[45]

When the Richmond convention began in July 1775, Mason was assigned to crucial committees, to raise an army to protect the colony. According to Robert A. Rutland, "Sick or healthy, Mason was needed for his ability."[46] Despite pressure from many delegates, Mason refused to consider election as a delegate to the Second Continental Congress in place of Washington after the Congress elected Washington commanding general of the Continental Army. But Mason could not avoid election to the Committee of Safety.[47]

Declaration of Rights

With independence from Britain widely accepted as necessary among prominent Virginians,[5] the fifth convention, met in May 1776 at Williamsburg. Notables elected to the convention were Henry, George Wythe, James Madison.[48] Mason was elected for Fairfax County, with great difficulty.[49]

The May 1776 convention, unanimously instructed Congress to seek "a clear and full Declaration of Independency".[51] At the same time, the convention resolved to pass a declaration of rights.[52] On May 24, convention president Pendleton wrote to Jefferson about the committee's deliberations, "as Colonel Mason seems to have the ascendancy in the great work, I have Sanguine hopes it will be framed so as to Answer its end, Prosperity to the Community and Security to Individuals".[53]

Mason drafted a declaration of rights. Edmund Randolph recalled Mason's draft "swallowed up all the rest".[54] The Virginia Declaration of Rights and 1776 Constitution of Virginia were joint works, Mason as author, with Thomas Lee.

The draft for the Declaration of Rights drew on Magna Carta, the English Petition of Right of 1628, and that nation's 1689 Bill of Rights. Masons would be paraphrased by Jefferson in drafting the American Declaration of Independence.[55]

That all men are born equally free and independent, and have certain inherent natural Rights, of which they cannot by any Compact, deprive or divest their Posterity; among which are the Enjoyment of Life and Liberty, with the Means of acquiring and possessing Property, and pursuing Happiness and Safety.

George Mason, draft of Article 1, Virginia Declaration of Rights, 1776.[50]

From the first article, cataloging the rights of man, Mason derived the following:

- to secure and protect those rights, and if it fails to do so,
- People have a right to amend or abolish it.
- Property could not be taken for public use without the owner's consent, and
- A citizen could only be bound by a law accepted by that person.
- A citizen could only be bound by a law accepted by elected representatives.
- The accused had the right to a speedy and local trial,
- an accusation must be made known to him.
- the right to call for evidence and witnesses in his favor.[56]

Mason spoke repeatedly in the five days of debate, using oratory one hearer described as "neither flowing nor smooth, but his language was strong, his manner most impressive."[57] The Declaration of Rights was passed on June 12, 1776.[58]

Randolph credited Henry with Articles 15 and 16, but Article 16 (dealing with religious freedom), had been written by Madison.[59] Mason had imitated English law in drafting language requiring toleration of those of minority religions, but Madison insisted on full religious liberty, and Mason supported Madison's amendment.[58]

These are some of the actions that allowed George Mason to be declared a "father" of the BILL OF RIGHTS.

The committee draft (by Mason), received wide publicity and Mason's words "all men are born equally free and independent" were reproduced in constitutions from Pennsylvania to

Montana; Jefferson included the sentiments in the Declaration of Independence.[60] In 1778, Mason wrote that the Declaration of Rights "was closely imitated by the other States,"[61] as seven of the original states, and Vermont, joined Virginia in promulgating a bill of rights. Feelings were so strong in Massachusetts that voters rejected a constitution drafted by convention, insisting a bill of rights first.[62]

Virginia constitution

Even before the convention approved the Declaration of Rights, Mason was busy at work on a constitution for Virginia.[55] On June 22, 1776, William Fleming sent Jefferson a copy of the draft before the Cary Committee, telling him "the enclosed printed plan was drawn by Colo. Mason and laid before the committee".[63]

Mason submitted his plan between June 8 and 10, 1776. It named the new state the "Commonwealth of Virginia", chosen by Mason to indicate that power stemmed from the people. The constitution provided for a popularly elected House of Delegates, chosen annually by men who owned or leased property, or who fathered three or more Virginians. Most governmental power resided in the House of Delegates—the governor could not veto a bill and could only act as head of the state militia on the advice of his Council of State, whose members were elected by the legislature. The entire convention considered the document, and it was signed on June 29. Richard Henry Lee wrote prior to the passage, "I have had the pleasure to see our new plan of Government go well. 'Tis very much of the democratic kind."[64]

When the convention chose Patrick Henry as Virginia's first post-independence governor, Mason led the committee sent to inform Henry of his election.[65] Edmund Randolph later wrote that the document's faults indicated that even such a great mind as Mason's was not immune from "oversights and negligence's": it did not have an amending process and granted two delegates to each county regardless of population.[66] The 1776 constitution remained in force until 1830, when another convention replaced it.[67] According to Henry C. Riely in his journal article on Mason, "The Virginia Constitution of 1776, . . . , stands, on the authority of Jefferson, Madison, and Randolph—to mention only the highest authority—as his creation."[68]

Revolutionary War legislator

Mason devoted much effort during the American Revolutionary War to safeguarding Fairfax County and the rivers of Virginia. Tobacco export, via the West Indies, allowed imported supplies, via France and Holland, such as cloth, clothing patterns, medicines, and hardware.[69]

Mason served as a member of the House of Delegates from 1776 to 1781, which he represented in Richmond.[70] Mason's health caused him to miss meetings of the legislature or arrive days or weeks late.[71] Lee was elected in his place.[72]

Washington was frustrated at reluctance of talented men to serve in Congress, writing Benjamin Harrison that states "should compel their ablest men to attend Congress ... Where is Mason, Wythe, Jefferson, Nicholas, Pendleton, Nelson?"[73] Washington wrote Mason directly:

Where are our men of abilities? Why do they not come forth to serve their Country? Let this voice my dear Sir call upon you—Jefferson & others—do not from a mistaken opinion that we are about to set down under our own Vine and our own fig tree let our noble struggle end in ignominy.[73]

The legislation Mason introduced in the House of Delegates was war related, often aimed at raising men or money needed by Washington's Continental Army.[74] By 1777, the value of Virginia's money had dropped precipitously. Washington wrote to Custis, "It is much to be wished that a remedy could be applied to the depreciation of our Currency ... I know of no person better qualified to do this than Colonel Mason".[75]

Mason retained his interest in western affairs, hoping in vain to salvage the Ohio Company's land grant. He and Jefferson were among the few delegates to be told of George Rogers Clark's expedition to secure control of the lands north of the Ohio River. The expedition was generally successful, and Mason received a report directly from Clark.[76] Although he felt the Mason-Dixon line was unfavorable to Virginia, he voted for it enthusiastically.[77] Mason remarried Sarah Brent, from a nearby plantation. It was a marriage of convenience, with the new bride able to take some of the burden of parenting Mason's many children.[78]

Post-Revolutionary War

Following the Treaty of Paris in 1783, which established a sovereign United States and largely ended armed hostilities, life along the Potomac River returned to normal. In December 1783, Madison returned to Gunston Hall after the Second Continental Congress in Philadelphia. In 1781, the Articles of Confederation had tied the states in a loose bond, and Madison sought a more effective federal structure. He found Mason willing to consider a federal tax. The same month, Mason spent Christmas at Mount Vernon (the only larger estate than his in Fairfax County).[79][80] Mason retained political influence, writing Patrick Henry, in the House of Delegates, a letter of advice as that body's 1783 session opened.[81]

Mason scuttled efforts to elect him to the House of Delegates in 1784. His refusal disappointed Jefferson, who hoped the likelihood of land legislation would attract Mason to Richmond.[80] Mason reached agreement with Maryland delegates in March 1785 known as the Mount Vernon Conference. Mason was appointed to the Annapolis Convention of 1786, which called for a conference to consider amendments to the Articles of Confederation.[82][83]

To deter smuggling, Madison proposed a bill to make Norfolk the state's legal port of entry. The Port Act survived; additional harbors were added as entry points.[84]

Constitutional Convention (1787)

The Annapolis Convention saw only about a dozen delegates attend, it called for a meeting in Philadelphia to amend the Articles of Confederation and more durable constitutional arrangement. Accordingly in December 1786, the Virginia General Assembly elected seven men as the commonwealth's delegation: Washington, Mason, Henry, Randolph, Madison, Wythe, and John Blair. The convention opened, with at least one delegate from ten of the twelve states (Rhode Island sent none).[85]

The journey to Philadelphia was Mason's first beyond Virginia and Maryland.[86] According to Josephine T. Pacheco, "since Virginia's leaders regarded [Mason] as a wise, trustworthy man, it is not surprising that they chose him as a member of the Virginia delegation, though they must have been surprised when he accepted".[87] Broadwater suggests that Mason went to Philadelphia because he felt that body could act as a check on the powers of state legislatures.[88] As the Virginians waited for other delegates to arrive, they met each day and formulated the Virginia Plan. Within a week, Mason was bored with the social events.[89]

Going into the convention, Mason wanted a more powerful central government than under the Articles. He feared the more numerous Northern states would dominate the union and impose restrictions, so he sought a supermajority requirement for navigation acts.[90] He sought to preserve the liberty he and other free men enjoyed in Virginia, guarding against the tyranny he and others had decried under British rule. He also sought a balance of powers, thereby making a durable government. "Mason designed his home [Gunston Hall] so that no misplaced window or missing support might spoil the effect or bring down the roof; . . . , so that unprincipled men could not knock loose safeguards of liberty".[91]

He felt that the "hopes of all the Union centre in this Convention",[92] and wrote to his son George, "the revolt from Great Britain & the Formations of our new Government, were nothing compared with the great business now before us."[93]

Washington was elected the convention's president by unanimous vote, and his tremendous personal prestige as the victorious war general helped legitimize the convention but also caused him to abstain from debate. Mason had no need to remain silent, and only four or five delegates spoke as frequently. Though he ended up not signing the constitution, Broadwater says, Mason won as many debates as he lost.[95]

At the convention, Mason supported the Virginia Plan, introduced by Randolph. This plan would have a popularly elected lower house which would choose the members of the upper house from lists provided by the states.[96] Mason agreed the federal government should be more powerful than the states.[97]

The Virginia Plan would base representation in both houses of the federal legislature on population. Delaware's delegates sought an equal vote for each state, and this became the New Jersey Plan, introduced by New Jersey Governor William Paterson. The divisions in the convention became apparent in late June, when the convention voted that representation in the lower house be based on population, but the motion of Connecticut's Oliver Ellsworth for each state to have an equal vote in the upper house failed on a tie.[98] Mason had not taken as strong a position on the legislature as had Madison, and he was appointed to the committee. The committee met over July 4 recess and proposed what became known as the Great Compromise: a House of Representatives based on population, in which money bills must originate, and a Senate with equal representation for each state. The clause requiring money bills to start in the House most likely came from him or was the price of his support, as he had inserted such a clause in the Virginia Constitution, and he defended that clause once convention debate resumed.[99] Mason called to adopt the compromise:

However liable the Report of Committee might be to objections, he thought it preferable to an appeal to the world, as had been talked of by some Gentlemen. It could not be more inconvenient to a gentleman to remain absent from his private affairs, than it was for him: but he would bury his bones in this city rather than expose his Country to Consequences of dissolution of the Convention without anything being done.[100]

Road to dispute

North Carolina's William Blount was unhappy that those from his state "were in Sentiment with Virginia. Madison at their Head though Randolph and Mason also great".[101] Mason successfully argued that the minimum age for service in Congress should be 25, telling the convention younger men were too immature.[102] Mason proposed the national seat of government not be in a state capital. He voted against representation on a state's wealth or taxes and supported regular reapportionment of the House of Representatives.[103]

On August 6, 1787, the convention received a tentative draft written by a Committee of Detail chaired by South Carolina's John Rutledge; Randolph had represented Virginia. The draft was acceptable to Mason as a basis for discussion, containing such points important to him as the requirement that money bills originate in the House and not be amendable in the Senate. Mason felt the upper house was too powerful, as it had the power to make treaties, appoint

Supreme Court justices, and adjudicate territorial disputes. The draft lacked a council of revision, something Mason and others considered serious.[104]

Mason continued to work constructively to build a constitution, serving on another grand committee that considered customs duties and ports.[105]

On August 31, 1787, Massachusetts's Elbridge Gerry spoke against the document as a whole, as did Luther Martin of Maryland. When Gerry moved to postpone consideration of the final document, Mason seconded him, stating, according to Madison, that "he would sooner chop off his right hand than put it to the Constitution as it now stands".[106] As the final touches were made to the constitution, Mason and Gerry held meetings to discuss strategy.[107]

Mason's misgivings about the constitution increased on September 12, when Gerry proposed and Mason seconded that there be a committee to write a bill of rights, as text of the constitution. Connecticut's Roger Sherman noted the state bills of rights would remain in force, to which Mason responded, "the Laws of the United States are to be paramount [supreme] to State Bills of Rights." Although Massachusetts abstained in deference to Gerry, the Virginians showed no desire to conciliate Mason, as the motion failed with no states in favor and ten opposed.[109] As the convention continued clause-by-clause consideration of the draft, Mason, Randolph, and Gerry stated they would not sign the constitution.[110]

Mason's objections:

"There is no declaration of rights, and the laws of the general government being paramount, the declarations in the separate states are no security ... The president has no constitutional council. From this defect spring the improper powers of the Senate and the unnecessary office of the vice-president, who, as president of the Senate, dangerously blends executive and legislative powers ... There is no section preserving liberty of the press or trial by jury in civil cases, nor is there one concerning the danger of standing armies". *George Mason, Objections to this Constitution of Government.[108]* The document was sent to the Articles of Confederation's Congress, and to Richard Henry Lee, a member of Congress.[111]

Ratification battle

Broadwater notes, "given the difficulty of the task he had set for himself, his stubborn independence, and his lack, by 1787, of any concern for his own political future, it is not surprising that he left Philadelphia at odds with the great majority of his fellow delegates".[112] Madison recorded that Mason, believing that the convention had given his proposals short shrift in a hurry to complete its work, began his journey back to Virginia "in an exceeding ill humor".[113] Mason biographer Helen Hill Miller notes that before Mason returned to Gunston Hall, he was injured in body and spirit after an accident on the road.[114] Mason sent Washington a copy of his objections,[115] but Washington believed the choice was ratification or disaster.[116]

The constitution was to be ratified by state conventions, with nine approvals necessary for it to come into force. In practice, opposition by large states such as New York or Virginia would make it hard for the new government to function.[117] Mason remained a member of the House of Delegates, and in late October 1787, the legislature called a convention for June 1788; in language crafted by John Marshall, it decreed that the Virginia Ratifying Convention would be allowed "free and ample discussion".[118] Mason was less influential in his final session in the House of Delegates because of his opposition to ratification, and his age (61) may have caused him to be less effective.[119]

As smaller states ratified the constitution, most prominent in support were the pamphlets later collected as *The Federalist*, written by Madison and two New Yorkers, Alexander Hamilton and John Jay; Mason's objections were widely cited by opponents.[120] Lee and Mason believed that if proper amendments were made, the constitution would be a fine instrument of governance.[121] The *Objections* were widely cited in opposition to ratification,[120] and Mason was criticized for placing his own name on it, at a time when political tracts were signed, if at all, with pen names such as Junius, so that the author's reputation would not influence the debate. Mason's *Objections* were among the most influential Anti-Federalist works, and its opening line, "There is no Declaration of Rights", the most effective slogan.[122]

Virginians were reluctant to believe that greatly respected figures such as Washington and Franklin would be complicit in setting up a tyrannical system.[123] There were broad attacks on Mason; New Haven *Gazette* suggested he had not done much for his country during the war, in marked contrast to Washington.[120] Oliver Ellsworth blamed the Virginia opposition on the Lee family, who had tensions with the Washington family, and on "the madness of Mason".[124]

George Nicholas, a Federalist friend of Mason, believed that Mason felt he could lead Virginia to gain concessions from the other states.[125] On March 10, 1788, Mason finished first in the polls in Stafford County, and veteran delegate Andrew Buchanan won the other seat[126] over Colonel Carter and William Fitzhugh. Two days later, a Richmond essayist criticized Mason and Richard Henry Lee for the "barefaced impudence and folly" of public protests.[127] The Federalists were believed to have a slight advantage in elected delegates; Mason thought the convention would be unlikely to ratify, without demanding amendments.[125]

Mason moved that the convention consider the document clause by clause, which played into the hands of the Federalists, who feared an immediate vote.[128]

John Marshall, a future Chief Justice of the United States, downplayed the concern regarding the judiciary, but Mason would be proved correct in the case of *Chisholm v. Georgia* (1793), which led to passage of the Eleventh Amendment.[129]

Mason led a group of Anti-Federalists which drafted amendments: even the Federalists were open to supporting them, though the constitution's supporters wanted the document drafted in Philadelphia ratified first.[130]

After Kentuckians declared for ratification, the convention considered a resolution to withhold ratification pending the approval of a declaration of rights.[130][131] Supported by Mason but opposed by Madison, Light-Horse Harry Lee, Marshall, Nicholas, Randolph and Bushrod Washington, the resolution failed, 88–80.[131] Mason voted in the minority as Virginia ratified the constitution on June 25, 1788.[131] Unreconciled to the result, Mason prepared a fiery written argument, but some felt the tone too harsh, and Mason agreed not to publish it.[130]

Conclusion

He enjoyed a seriously strong career through the "Constitution" phase. His status as creator and refiner of the US Constitution is second to none.

Mason was a staunch anti-slavery leader. Mason routinely spoke out against slavery, even before independence. In 1773, he wrote that slavery was "that slow Poison, which is daily contaminating the Minds & Morals of our People. Every Gentlemen here is born a petty Tyrant." In 1774, he advocated ending the international slave trade.

The concluding element of George Masons life may be considered as the launching of GEORGE MASON UNIVERSITY.

A Former US Supreme Court Justice wrote that: "Mason lost his battle against ratification ... [but] his ideals and political activities have significantly influenced our constitutional jurisprudence." (O'Connor, p. 119)

References

1. "George Mason (1725-1792)" at Encyclopedia Virginia]
2. "George Mason" at Encyclopædia Britannica
3. "George Mason" at Battlefields.org
4. Copeland & MacMaster, p. 65.
5. Tarter, Brent (February 2000). "Mason, George". American National Biography. Retrieved Sept 26, 2015.
6. Miller, p. 3.
7. Pikcunas, p. 20.
8. Miller, p. 4.
9. Copeland & MacMaster, pp. 54–55.
10. Miller, pp. 3–7.
11. Miller, pp. 11–12.
12. Copeland & MacMaster, pp. 65–67.
13. Copeland & MacMaster, pp. 84–85.
14. Encyclopedia Virginia, "G Mason 1725–1792", Mason was required to be member in good standing, Anglican communion.
15. Horrell, pp. 33–34.
16. Horrell, pp. 35, 52–53.
17. Horrell, pp. 33–35.
18. Miller, pp. 33–34.
19. Copeland & MacMaster, p. 93.
20. Broadwater, pp. 4–5.
21. Copeland & MacMaster, pp. 97–98.
22. Tompkins, pp. 181–183.
23. Copeland & MacMaster, pp. 106–107.
24. Copeland & MacMaster, pp. 103–104.
25. Riely, p. 8.
26. Bailey, pp. 409–413, 417.
27. Henriques, pp. 185–189.
28. Copeland & MacMaster, pp. 162–163.
29. Broadwater, pp. 36–37.
30. Cynthia Miller Leonard, The Virginia General Assembly 1619–1978 (Richmond: Virginia State Library 1978) pp. 88, 114, 117, 119, 122, 125, 129, 133, 137, 160, 164, 174
31. Miller, pp. 68–69.
32. Copeland & MacMaster, pp. 108–109.
33. Broadwater, p. 18.
34. Miller, pp. 88–94.
35. Broadwater, pp. 29–31.
36. Broadwater, p. 39.
37. Broadwater, pp. 48–51.
38. Miller, pp. 99–100.
39. Broadwater, p. 58.
40. Miller, pp. 101–102.
41. Broadwater, p. 65.
42. Broadwater, pp. 65–67.
43. Broadwater, pp. 65–69.
44. Broadwater, p. 68.
45. Miller, pp. 116–118.
46. Rutland 1980, pp. 45–46.
47. Miller, pp. 117–119.
48. Broadwater, p. 153.
49. Miller, p. 137.
50. Broadwater, pp. 81–82.
51. Miller, p. 138.
52. Miller, pp. 138–139.
53. Miller, p. 142.
54. Broadwater, pp. 80–81.
55. Broadwater, pp. 80–83.
56. Miller, p. 148.
57. Rutland 1980, pp. 68–70.
58. Broadwater, pp. 85–87.
59. Broadwater, pp. 84–86.
60. Broadwater, pp. 89–91.
61. Miller, p. 153.
62. Miller, p. 154.
63. Miller, pp. 157–158.
64. Miller, pp. 159–160.

65. Copeland & MacMaster, p. 191.
66. Broadwater, pp. 96–99.
67. Broadwater, p. 99.
68. Riely, 16 p.
69. Copeland & MacMaster, pp. 191–194.
70. Miller, p. 163.
71. Broadwater, pp. 102–104.
72. Miller, pp. 165–166.
73. Broadwater, p. 108.
74. Broadwater, pp. 102–104, 112.
75. Broadwater, pp. 111.
76. Miller, pp. 182–186.
77. Copeland & MacMaster, pp. 210–211.
78. Copeland & MacMaster, pp. 208–209.
79. Copeland & MacMaster, p. 217.
80. Rutland 1980, p. 78.
81. Broadwater, pp. 133–137.
82. Rutland 1980, pp. 78–79.
83. Broadwater, pp. 153–156.
84. Broadwater, pp. 143–144.
85. Miller, pp. 231–234.
86. Miller, p. 243.
87. Pacheco, pp. 61–62.
88. Broadwater, pp. 175–177.
89. Miller, pp. 233–235.
90. Broadwater, pp. 160–162.
91. Tarter, pp. 286–288.
92. Rutland 1980, pp. 82–84.
93. Pacheco, p. 63.
94. Broadwater, p. 162.
95. Broadwater, pp. 162–165.
96. Broadwater, pp. 166–168.
97. Pacheco, p. 64.
98. Miller, pp. 245–247.
99. Broadwater, pp. 173–176.
100. Miller, p. 247.
101. Miller, p. 248.
102. Broadwater, pp. 169–170.
103. Broadwater, pp. 179–190.
104. Broadwater, pp. 181–184.
105. Broadwater, pp. 187–194.
106. Miller, p. 261.
107. Miller, pp. 161–162.
108. Miller, pp. 262–263.
109. Miller, p. 162.
110. Miller, pp. 163–164.
111. Miller, pp. 165–66.
112. Broadwater, p. 158.
113. Broadwater, pp. 208–210.
114. Miller, p. 269.
115. Miller, pp. 269–270.
116. Henriques, p. 196.
117. Broadwater, pp. 208–112.
118. Broadwater, pp. 217–218.
119. Rutland 1980, pp. 93–94.
120. Miller, pp. 270–272.
121. Broadwater, pp. 208–12.
122. Broadwater, pp. 211–12.
123. Kukla, p. 57.
124. Broadwater, p. 212.
125. Broadwater, pp. 224–227.
126. Leonard p. 174
127. Rutland 1970, p. 1047.
128. Rutland 1980, pp. 95–98.
129. Broadwater, pp. 229–232.
130. Broadwater, pp. 202–205.

131. Grigsby, Hugh Blair (1890). Brock, R.A. (ed.). The History of the Virginia Federal Convention of 1788 with Some Account of the Eminent Virginians of that Era who were Members of the Body. Collections of the Virginia Historical Society. New Series. Volume IX. Vol. 1. Richmond, Virginia: Virginia Historical Society. pp. 344–346.

Sources:

- Broadwater, Jeff (2006). George Mason, Forgotten Founder. Chapel Hill, North Carolina: University of North Carolina Press. ISBN 978-0-8078-3053-6. OCLC 67239589.
- Copeland, Pamela C.; MacMaster, Richard K. (1975). The Five George Masons: Patriots and Planters of Virginia and Maryland. University Press of Virginia. ISBN 0-8139-0550-8.
- Miller, Helen Hill(1975).George Mason, Gentleman Revolutionary. U NorthCarolina Press. ISBN 0-8078-1250-1
- Pacheco, Josephine T. (1989). "George Mason and Constitution". In Senese, Donald J. (ed.). George Mason and Legacy of Constitutional Liberty. Fairfax County History Commission. pp. 61–74. ISBN 0-9623905-1-8.
- Riely, Henry C. (Jan 1934)."George Mason". Virginia Magazine of History and Bio. 42 (1): 1–17.
- Rutland, Robert Allen (1980) [1961]. George Mason, Reluctant Statesman (Louisiana paperback ed.). The Louisiana State University Press. ISBN 978-0-8071-0696-9.
- Rutland, Robert Allen (1989). "George Mason's Objections and Bill of Rights". In Senese, Donald J.(ed.). George Mason Legacy of Constitutional Liberty. Fairfax County History Commission. pp. 75–81.
- Rutland, Robert (1970). Papers of George Mason. Vol.3. U North Carolina Press. ISBN 978-0-8078-1134-4.
- Tarter, Brent (July 1991). "George Mason and the Conservation of Liberty". The Virginia Magazine of History and Biography. 99 (3): 279–304. JSTOR 4249228.

BENJAMIN RUSH

NEW JERSEY
LEADER OF MEDICAL AND CONSTITUTION ACTIVITY

Dr. Rush is one of the most productive and greatest Academicians of the past 500 years, as the following brief biography of his accomplished life indicates.

Dr. Benjamin Rush (January 4, 1746 – April 19, 1813) was an American revolutionary, a Founding Father of the United States and signatory to the U.S. Declaration of Independence, and a civic leader in Philadelphia, where he was a physician, politician, social reformer, humanitarian, educator, and the founder of Dickinson College. Rush was a Pennsylvania delegate to the Continental Congress.[1] He described his efforts in support of the American Revolution, saying: "He aimed right."[2][3] He was surgeon general of the Continental Army and professor of chemistry, medical theory, and clinical practice at University of Pennsylvania.[4]

Revolutionary period

Rush was active in the Sons of Liberty and was elected to attend the provincial conference to send delegates to the Continental Congress. Thomas Paine consulted Rush when writing the pro-independence pamphlet *Common Sense*. Starting in 1776, Rush represented Pennsylvania and signed the Declaration of Independence.[1] He also represented Philadelphia at Pennsylvania's own Constitutional Convention.[1]

In an 1811 letter to John Adams, Rush recounted in stark fashion the signing of the Declaration of Independence. He described it as a scene of "pensive and awful silence". Rush said the delegates were called up, one after another, and then filed forward somberly to subscribe to what each thought was their ensuing death warrant.[17] He related that the "gloom of the morning" was briefly interrupted when the rotund Benjamin Harrison of Virginia said to a diminutive Elbridge Gerry of Massachusetts, at the signing table, "I shall have a great advantage over you, Mr. Gerry, when we are all hung for what we are now doing. From the size and weight of my body I shall die in a few minutes and be with the Angels, but from the lightness of your body you will dance in the air an hour or two before you are dead."[17]

Rush accompanied the Philadelphia militia during the battles after which the British occupied Philadelphia and most of New Jersey. He was depicted serving in the Battle of

Princeton in the painting *The Death of General Mercer at the Battle of Princeton, January 3, 1777,* by the American artist John Trumbull.[18]

The Army Medical Service was in disarray, between military casualties, high losses from typhoid, yellow fever and camp illnesses, political conflicts between Dr. John Morgan and Dr. William Shippen Jr., inadequate supplies and guidance from the medical committee.[19]:29–43,65–92 Rush's order "Directions for preserving the health of soldiers" became one of the foundations of preventive military medicine and was republished as late as 1908.[20][21]:36–41

Rush criticized General George Washington in two handwritten but unsigned letters while still serving under the surgeon general. At the time, the supposed Conway Cabal was reportedly trying to replace Washington with Horatio Gates as commander-in-chief.[14]:133–34 Rush's letter relayed General Sullivan's criticism that forces directly under Washington were undisciplined and mob-like, and contrasted Gates' army as "a well-regulated family".[22]:212–215 Ten days later, Rush wrote John Adams relaying complaints inside Washington's army, including "bad bread, no order, universal disgust," praising Conway, as inspector general.[14]:136–37

Post-Revolution

Rush believed that, while America was free from British rule, the "American Revolution" had yet to finish. As expressed in his 1787 'Address to the People of the United States', "The American war is over: but this is far from being the case with the revolution. On the contrary, nothing but the first act of the great drama is closed."[24]

In 1783, he was appointed to the staff of Pennsylvania Hospital, and he remained a member until his death. He was elected to the Pennsylvania convention which adopted the Federal constitution and was appointed treasurer of the United States Mint, serving from 1797 to 1813.[1] He was elected a fellow of the American Academy of Arts and Sciences in 1788.[25]

He became a professor of medical theory and clinical practice at the University of Pennsylvania in 1791, he advocated bloodletting for almost any illness, long after its practice had declined. While teaching at the University of Pennsylvania, one of his students was future president Harrison, who took a chemistry class from Rush.[26]

He was also founder of Dickinson College in Carlisle, Pennsylvania. In 1794, he was elected a foreign member of the Royal Swedish Academy of Sciences.[27]
He supported Thomas Jefferson for president in 1796 over John Adams.[30]

Corps of Discovery

In 1803, Jefferson sent Meriwether Lewis to Philadelphia to prepare for the Lewis and Clark Expedition under the tutelage of Rush, who taught Lewis about frontier illnesses and bloodletting. Rush provided the corps with a medical kit that included:
- Turkish opium for nervousness
- emetics to induce vomiting.
- medicinal wine
- fifty dozen of *Dr. Rush's Bilious Pills,* laxatives containing more than 50% mercury, which have since colloquially been referred to as "thunderclappers". Their meat-rich diet and lack of clean water during the expedition gave the men cause to use them frequently. Although their efficacy is questionable, their high mercury content provided a tracer by which archaeologists have been able to verify one of the Corps' campsites on their route to the Pacific. As of 2024, Travelers' Rest State Park, near Lolo, Montana, is the only location to be confirmed via the analysis of the Corps' latrines.[31][32][33][34]

REFORMS - Anti-Slavery

In 1766, when Rush set out for his studies in Edinburgh, he provided a bold and respected voice against the slave trade.[35] He warmly praised the ministry of "Black Harry" Hosier, the freedman circuit rider who accompanied Bishop Francis Asbury during the establishment of the Methodist Church in America,[36] but the highlight of his involvement was the pamphlet he wrote in 1773, "An Address to the Inhabitants of the British Settlements in America, upon Slave-Keeping." Rush argued that slavery, "is so foreign to the human mind, that the moral faculties, as well as those of the understanding are debased, and rendered torpid."[37]

Anti-capital punishment

Rush proposed private confinement, labor, solitude, and religious instruction for criminals, and he opposed the death penalty.[38] His outspoken opposition to capital punishment pushed the Pennsylvania legislature to abolish the death penalty for all crimes other than first-degree murder.[4] He authored a 1792 treatise on punishing murder by death in which he made three principal arguments:[39]

I. Every man possesses an absolute power over his own liberty and property, but not over his own life...

II. The punishment of murder by death, is contrary to reason, and to the order and happiness of society...

III. The punishment of murder by death, is contrary to divine revelation.

Rush led the state of Pennsylvania to establish the first state penitentiary, the Walnut Street Prison, in 1790. Rush campaigned for long-term imprisonment, the denial of liberty, as both the most humane but severe punishment.[40] This 1792 treatise was preceded by comments on the efficacy of the death penalty that he self-references and which appeared in the second volume of the *American Museum*.[39]

Status of women

After the Revolution, Rush proposed a new model of education for elite women that included English language, vocal music, dancing, sciences, bookkeeping, history, and moral philosophy. He was instrumental founding the Young Ladies' Academy of Philadelphia, a chartered women's institution of higher education in Philadelphia.[41]

And so, the ideal of Republican motherhood emerged, lauding women's responsibility of instructing the young in the obligations of patriotism, the blessings of liberty and the true meaning of Republicanism. He insisted on the need to instruct all youth in Christian religion.[42]

Medical contributions - - Physical Medicine

Rush was a leading proponent of heroic medicine. He firmly believed in such practices as bloodletting [43] (a practice now known to be generally harmful,[44] but at the time common practice), as well as purges using calomel and other substances. He wrote many other references to the Pro's and Con's of medical "bleeding."[45][46]

Rush also wrote the first case report on dengue fever (published in 1789 on a case from 1780).[47] Perhaps his greatest contributions to physical medicine were his establishment of a public dispensary for low-income patients (Philadelphia Dispensary), and public works associated with draining and rerouting Dock Creek (eliminating mosquito breeding grounds,). Rush's medical views drew criticism as in his analysis of race differences in medicine.[48]

Rush was interested in Native American health, seeking why Native Americans were susceptible to certain illnesses and whether they had higher mortality.[49]

Mental health

Rush published one of the first descriptions and treatments for psychiatric disorders in American medicine, *Medical Inquiries and Observations, Upon the Diseases of the Mind* (1812).[50][51] He undertook to classify different forms of mental illness and to theorize as to their causes and possible cures. Rush believed (incorrectly) that many mental illnesses were caused by disruptions of blood circulation or by sensory overload and treated them with devices meant to improve circulation to the brain such as a centrifugal spinning board, and inactivity/sensory deprivation via a restraining chair with a sensory-deprivation head enclosure ("tranquilizer chair").[52] After seeing mental patients in appalling conditions in Pennsylvania Hospital, Rush led a successful campaign in 1792 for the state to build a separate mental ward where the patients could be kept in more humane conditions.[53]

Some aspects of his approach were similar to *Moral Therapy,* which would rise to prominence in the wealthier institutions of Europe and the United States.[54][55]

Furthermore, Rush was one of the first people to describe Savant Syndrome. In 1789, he described the abilities of Thomas Fuller, an enslaved African who was a lightning calculator. His observation would later be described by notable scientists like John Langdon Down.[56]

Rush pioneered the therapeutic approach to addiction.[57][58] Rush believed that the alcoholic loses control over himself and identified the properties of alcohol, rather than the alcoholic's choice, as the agent. He developed the concept of alcoholism as a medical disease and proposed alcoholics should be weaned from their addiction via less potent substances.[59]

He is quoted to have said, "Terror acts powerfully upon the body, through the medium of the mind, and should be employed in the cure of madness."[60] He also championed the idea of "partial madness," or that people could have varying degrees of mental illness.[61]

The American Psychiatric Association's seal bears an image of Rush's profile at its center.[62][63][64] The outer ring of the seal contains the words "American Psychiatric Association 1844".[64] The Association's history of the seal states:

The choice of Rush (1746–1813) for the seal reflects his place in history   Rush's practice of psychiatry was based on bleeding, purging, and the use of the tranquilizer chair and gyrator. By 1844 these practices were considered erroneous and abandoned. Rush, however, was the first American to study mental disorder in a systematic manner, and he is considered the father of American Psychiatry.[64]

Educational legacy

During his career, he educated over 3,000 medical students, who established Rush Medical College in Chicago in his honor after his death. His students included Valentine Seaman, who mapped yellow fever mortality patterns in New York and introduced the smallpox vaccine to the United States in 1799.[65] One of his last apprentices was Samuel A. Cartwright, later a Confederate States of America surgeon charged with improving sanitary conditions in the camps around Vicksburg, Mississippi, and Port Hudson, Louisiana.[66]

Religious views

Rush advocated Christianity in public life and in education and sometimes compared himself to the prophet Jeremiah.[67] Rush regularly attended Christ Church in Philadelphia and counted William White among his closest friends (and neighbors). Ever the controversialist, Rush became involved in internal disputes over the revised Book of Common Prayer and splitting the Episcopal Church from Church of England.

In a letter to John Adams, Rush describes his religious views as "a compound of the orthodoxy and heterodoxy of most of our Christian churches."[68] Christian Universalists consider him one of their founders, although Rush stopped attending that church after the death of his friend, Baptist pastor Elhanan Winchester, in 1797.[69]

Rush fought for temperance[13]:379–380 and both public and Sunday schools. He helped found the Bible Society at Philadelphia (now known as the Pennsylvania Bible Society)[70][71] and promoted the American Sunday School Union.[72] When many public schools stopped using the Bible as a textbook, Rush proposed that the U.S. government require such use, as well as furnish an American Bible to every family at public expense. In 1806, Rush proposed inscribing "The Son of Man Came into the World, Not To Destroy Men's Lives, But To Save Them."[73] above the doors of courthouses and other public buildings. Earlier, on July 16, 1776, Rush complained to Patrick Henry about a provision in Virginia's constitution which forbade clergymen from serving in the legislature.[74]

Rush felt that the United States was the work of God: "I do not believe that the Constitution was the offspring of inspiration, but I am as perfectly satisfied that the Union of the United States in its form and adoption is as much the work of a Divine Providence as any of the miracles recorded in the Old and New Testament".[75] In 1798, after the Constitution's adoption, Rush declared: "The only foundation for a useful education in a republic is to be laid in Religion. Without this there can be no virtue, and without virtue there can be no liberty, and liberty is the object and life of all republican governments."[72]

The Constitution of this republic should make special privilege for medical freedom as well as religious freedom," is a misattribution. No primary source for it has been found, and the words "un-American" and "undercover" are anachronisms, as their usage as such did not appear until after Rush's death.[76]

Writings

- Rush, Benjamin (1773). "An Address to the Inhabitants of the British Settlements in America, Upon Slave-keeping". Philadelphia: J. Dunlap. Retrieved January 1, 2017.
- Rush, Benjamin (1819) [1791]. An inquiry into the effects of ardent spirits upon the human body and mind: with an account of the means of preventing, and of the remedies for curing them. Josiah Richardson.
- Rush, Benjamin (1794). An account of the bilious remitting yellow fever, as it appeared in the city of Philadelphia, in the year 1793. Philadelphia: Thomas Dobson.
- Rush, Benjamin (1798). Essays: Literary, Moral, and Philosophical. Philadelphia: Thomas & Samuel F. Bradford. 1989 reprint: Syracuse University Press, ISBN 0-912756-22-5
- Rush, Benjamin (1799). "Observations Intended to Favour a Supposition That Black Color (As It Is Called) of Negroes Is Derived from Leprosy". Transactions American Philosophical Society. 4: 289–297. doi:10.2307/1005108. JSTOR 1005108.
- Rush, Benjamin (1806). "A plan of a Peace-Office for the United States". Essays, Literary, Moral and Philosophical (2nd ed.). Philadelphia: Thomas and William Bradford. pp. 183–88. Retrieved June 3, 2010
- Rush, Benjamin (1808) [1778]. Directions for preserving the health of soldiers: addressed to the officers of the Army of the United States. Philadelphia: Thomas Dobson.
- Rush, Benjamin (1812) Medical Inquiries And Observations Upon The Diseases Of The Mind, 2006 reprint: Kessinger Publishing, ISBN 1-4286-2669-7. Free digital copies of original published in 1812 at http://deila.dickinson.edu/theirownwords/title/0034. or https://web.archive.org/web/20121024024628/http://collections.nlm.nih.gov/muradora/objectView.action?pid=nlm%3Anlm uid-2569036R-bk

- Rush, Benjamin (2003). "Medical Inquiries and Observations, Upon the Diseases of the Mind: Philadelphia: Published by Kimber & Richardson, no. 237, Market Street; Merritt, printer, no. 9, Watkins Alley, 1812". Their Own Words. Carlisle, Pennsylvania: Dickinson College. OCLC 53177922. Arch Jan 7, 2004. Retr Oct 20, 2017.
- Rush, Benjamin (1815). "A Defence of Bloodletting, as a Remedy for Certain Diseases". Medical Inquiries and Observations. 4. Retrieved October 24, 2012.
- Rush, Benjamin (1830). Medical Inquiries and Observations upon Diseases of the Mind (4 ed.). Philadelphia: John Grigg. pp. 98, 197.
- Rush, Benjamin (1835). Medical Inquiries and Observations Upon the Diseases of the Mind (Fifth ed.). Philadelphia: Grigg and Elliott, No. 9 North Fourth Street. OCLC 2812179. Retrieved October 20, 2017 – via Internet Archive.
- Rush, Benjamin (1947). selected writings Benjamin Rush. NY: Philosophical Library. p.448. ISBN 978-0-8065-2955-4
- Butterfield, Lyman H., ed. (1951). Letters of Benjamin Rush. Memoirs of the American Philosophical Society. Princeton University Press. OCLC 877738348.
- The Spur of Fame: Dialogues of John Adams and Benjamin Rush, 1805–1813 (2001), Liberty Fund, ISBN 0-86597-287-7
- Rush, Benjamin (1970) [1948]. George Washington Corner (ed.). The autobiography of Benjamin Rush; his Travels through life together with his Commonplace book for 1789–1813. Westport, CT: Greenwood Press.
- Fox, Claire G.; Miller, Gordon L.; Miller, Jacquelyn C. (1996). Benjamin Rush, M.D: A Bibliographic Guide. Greenwood Press. ISBN 978-0-313-29823-3.

References

1. "Benjamin Rush: 1745–1813: Representing Pennsylvania at the Continental Congress". Signers of the Decl of Independence. ushistory.org. Archived Feb 7, 2018. Ret Feb 7, 2018.
2. Renker, Elizabeth M. (1989). "'Declaration-Men' and the Rhetoric of Self-Presentation". Early American Literature. 24 (2): 123 and n. 10 there. JSTOR 25056766.
3. Rush, Benjamin (1970) [1948]. George Washington Corner (ed.). The autobiography of Benjamin Rush; his Travels through life together with his Commonplace book for 1789–1813. Westport, CT: Greenwood Press.
4. "Benjamin Rush (1746–1813)". University of Penn. Arch June 10, 2011. Retr Aug 20, 2011.
5. Fraser, James (2019). The school in the United States: a documentary history (Fourth ed.). New York, NY: Routledge. p. 25. ISBN 978-1-138-47887-9.
6. Muccigrosso, Robert, ed. (1988). Research Guide to American Historical Biography. Vol. 4. pp. 1139–42.
7. Shorter, Edward (1997). A History of Psychiatry: From the Era of the Asylum to the Age of Prozac. Wiley.
8. Irvine, James (1893). "Descendants of John Rush". Pennsylvania Magazine History Biography. 17 (3): 334. JSTOR 20083549.
9. "About the Author: Benjamin Rush (1745–1813)". Their Own Words. deila.dickinson.edu. July 9, 2004. Archived from the original on January 26, 2004. Retrieved October 20, 2017.
10. The identity of Rush's siblings is confused: there are web pages saying Rush and one brother were responsible for the entire family, and also giving Rush's brothers names as William (a lawyer) and Samuel "Descendants of Thomas Rush". Arch Oct 9, 2012. Retr 2012-12-30. lists Rush's siblings as Jacob, James, John, Rebecca, Rachel, and Stephenson..
11. "Benjamin Rush". Signers of the Declaration of Independence. Archived June 29, 2015. Retr Dec 7, 2014.
12. Goodrich, Rev. Charles A. (1856). "Benjamin Rush, 1745–1813". Archived Jan 8, 2010. Retr Dec 16, 2017.
13. Hawke, David Freeman (1971). Benjamin Rush: Revolutionary Gadfly. Indianapolis: Bobbs-Merrill.
14. Binger, Carl (1966). Revolutionary Doctor / Benjamin Rush (1746–1813). New York: Norton & Co.
15. North RL (2000). "Benjamin Rush, MD: assassin or beloved healer?". Proc Bayl Univ Med Cent. 13 (1): 45–9. doi:10.1080/08998280.2000.11927641. PMC 1312212. PMID 16389324.
16. Bell, Whitfield J., and Charles Greifenstein, Jr. Patriot-Improvers: Biographical Sketches of Members of the American Philosophical Society. 3 vols. Philadelphia: American Philosophical Society, 1997, I:26, 33, 61–62, 184, 193, 250, 452–64, 453,466, 504, II: 136,257, 369, 386, 393, III:49, 54, 135, 204, 254, 272, 408, 524, 573.
17. "Benjamin Rush to John Adams, July 20, 1811".National Park Service. Arch July 26, 2024. Retr Nov 22, 2019
18. "Death of General Mercer at Battle of Princeton, January 3, 1777". Yale U Art Gallery. Arch Jan 5, 2016. Retr Feb 26, 2019.
19. Gillette, Mary (1981). The Army Medical Department 1775–1818. Army Medical Department Office of Medical History. Archived Jan 14, 2013. Retr Oct 24, 2012.
20. Rush, Benjamin (1808). Directions for preserving the health of soldiers: addressed to the officers of the Army of the United States. Philadelphia: Thomas Dobson.
21. Bayne-Jones, Stanhope (1968). Evolution of Preventative Medicine in the United States Army 1607–1939 (PDF). Office of the Surgeon General, Department of the Army. Archived August 1, 2013. Retr Oct. 24, 2012.
22. Brodsky, Alyn (2004). Benjamin Rush: Patriot and Physician. NY: Truman Talley Books/St. Martin's Press.
23. McCullough, David G (2006). 1776: America and Britain at war. London: Penguin.
24. "Rush 1787". kdhist.sitehost.iu.edu. Archived Feb 27, 2023. Retr February 27, 2023.
25. "Book of Members, 1780–2010: Chapter R". American Academy Arts and Sciences. ArchMarch 13, 2016. Retr July 28, 2014.
26. Rabin, Alex (January 25, 2017). "With a Penn graduate in the Oval Office for the first time, here's a look at former President William Henry Harrison's time at University". The Daily Pennsylvanian. ArchAugust 7, 2020. Retrieved April 3, 2019.
27. Johnson, Charles R.; Smith, Patricia; Blight, David; Else, Jon H.; Fields, Barbara; Frey, Sylvia; Gates Jr., Henry Louis; Gill, Gerald; Harding, Vincent (1998). Africans in America: America's Journey Through Slavery (1st ed.). United States: Harcourt Brace. p. 237. ISBN 978-0-15-100339-6.
28. "The Prison Society – About Us". The Pennsylvania Prison Society. Arch Nov 5, 2008. Retr Nov 16, 2008.
29. "The Philadelphia Society for Alleviating the Miseries of Public Prisons". Library Company of Philadelphia. World Digital Library. Archived January 2, 2014. Retr Jan 1, 2014.
30. McCullough, David (2008)[2001]. John Adams.New York:Simon and Schuster. p.470. ISBN 978-1-4165-7588-7
31. "Travelers' Rest State Park". Montana Fish, Wildlife & Parks. Archived March 30, 2024. Retr July 4, 2024.
32. Woodger, Elin; Toropov, Brandon (2009). Encyclopedia of the Lewis and Clark Expedition. Infobase Publishing. pp. 304–06.

33. Duncan, Dayton; Burns, Ken (1997). Lewis & Clark: The Journey of the Corps of Discovery. New York: Alfred A. Knopf, Inc. pp. 9–10. ISBN 978-0-679-45450-2.

34. Ambrose, Stephen (1996). Undaunted Courage: Meriwether Lewis, Thomas Jefferson, and the Opening of the American West. New York: Simon & Schuster. pp. 81, 87–91. ISBN 978-0-684-82697-4.

35. D'Elia, Donald J (1969). "Dr. Benjamin Rush and the Negro". Journal of the History of Ideas. 30 (3): 413–22. doi:10.2307/2708566. JSTOR 2708566.

36. Webb, Stephen H. (March 2002). "Introducing Black Harry Hoosier: The History Behind Indiana's Namesake". Indiana Magazine of History. 98 (1). Trustees of Indiana U: 30–42. Arch Sept 5, 2014. Retr Feb 20, 2017.

37. Dolbeare, Kenneth M.; Cummings, Michael S. (2010). American political thought (6 ed.). p. 44.

38. "Amendment VIII: Benjamin Rush, Punishing Murder by Death". press-pubs.uchicago.edu. Arch July 26, 2024. Retr Sept 4, 2018.

39. "The Founders' Constitution, Vol 5, Amendment VIII, Document 16". University of Chicago Press. Arch July 26, 2024. Retrieved October 8, 2013.

40. Manion, Jen (2015). Liberty's Prisoners: Carceral Culture in Early America. University of Pennsylvania Press.

41. Savin, Marion B.; Abrahams, Harold J. (1957). "Young Ladies' Academy of Philadelphia" History Education Journal. 8 (2): 58–67.

42. Straub, Jean S (1987). "Benjamin Rush's View on Women's Education". Pennsylvania History. 34 (2): 147–57.

43. Rush, Benjamin (1815). "A Defence of Bloodletting, as a Remedy for Certain Diseases". Medical Inquiries and Observations. 4. Archived Oct 22, 2012. Retrieved Oct 24, 2012.

44. "Why fair tests are needed". jameslindlibrary.org. 2009. Arch Jan 2, 2007. Retr Jan 8, 2017.

45. "Introduction: Thomas Jefferson to Meriwether Lewis: "bring back your party safe"". U of Virginia: Historical Collections at the Claude Moore Health Sciences Library: Medicine and Health on the Lewis and Clark Expedition. Rector and Visitors of the U of Virginia. 2007. Archived on Oct 20, 2017. Retr Oct 20, 2017.

46. "Benjamin Rush and the State of Medicine in 1803". Jefferson National Expansion Memorial. National Park Service: United States Department of the Interior. April 10, 2015. Archived Oct 17, 2015. Retr Oct 20, 2017.

47. Rush, Benjamin (1794). Account of bilious remitting fever, as appeared in Philadelphia in 1793. Philadelphia, Pa.: Thomas Dobson.

48. Rush, Benjamin (1799). "Observations Intended to Favour a Supposition That the Black Color (As It Is Called) of the Negroes Is Derived from Leprosy". Transactions American Philosophical Society. 4: 289–297. doi:10.2307/1005108. JSTOR 1005108.

49. J. Kunitz; Benjamin Rush (1970). "Benjamin Rush on Savagism and Progress Stephen". Ethnohistory. 17 (1/2). Duke University Press: 31–42. JSTOR 481523.

50. "Rush, Benjamin. Medical Inquiries and Observations, Upon the Diseases of the Mind: Philadelphia: Published by Kimber & Richardson, no. 237, Market Street; Merritt, printer, no. 9, Watkins Alley, 1812". Their Own Words. Carlisle, Pennsylvania: Dickinson College. July 17, 2003. OCLC 53177922. Arch 1/7/04. Retr Oct 20, 2017.

51. Rush, Benjamin (1835). Medical Inquiries and Observations Upon the Diseases of the Mind (Fifth ed.). Philadelphia: Grigg and Elliott, No. 9 North Fourth Street. OCLC 2812179. Retr Oct 20, 2017 – via

52. Beam, Alex (2001). Gracefully Insane: Life and Death Inside America's Premier Mental Hospital.

53. Deutsch, Albert (2007). The Mentally Ill in America: Their Care and Treatment From Colonial Times.

54. Rush, Benjamin (1830). Medical Inquiries and Observations upon Diseases of the Mind (4 ed.). Philadelphia: John Grigg. pp. 98, 197.

55. Gamwell, Lynn; Tomes, Nancy (1995). Madness in America: Cultural and Medical Perceptions of Mental Illness before 1914. State University of New York at Binghamton.

56. Treffert, Darold A. (2009). "Savant Syndrome: An Extraordinary Condition: A Synopsis: Past, Present, Future". Philosophical Transactions of the Royal Society B: Biological Sciences. 364 (1522). The Royal Society Publishing: 1351–1357. doi:10.1098/rstb.2008.0326. PMC 2677584. PMID 19528017.

57. Elster, Jon (1999). Strong Feelings: Emotion, Addiction, and Human Behavior. MIT Press. p. 131. ISBN 978-0-262-55036-9. Archived on July 26, 2024. Retr Nov 17, 2020.

58. Durrant, Russil; Thakker, Jo (2003). Substance Use & Abuse: Cultural Historical Perspectives. Thousand Oaks, CA: Sage Publications.

59. Rush, Benjamin (1805). Inquiry into Effects of Ardent Spirits upon Human Body and Mind. Phil: Bartam.

60. "Medical Inquiries and Observations Upon the Diseases of the Mind" Author Benjamin Rush. Ca 1835. P. 209.

61. Madden, Etta (2006). "PhD". Early American Literature. 41 (2): 241–272, 396. doi:10.1353/eal.2006.0022. S2CID 161899076. ProQuest 215394022.

62. "American Psychiatric Association Logo". U of California, San Francisco. Arch&Retri(JPEG) on October 20, 2017.

63. Moran, Mike (May 28, 2015). "New APA Logo Unifies Image of Psychiatry". Psychiatric News. 50 (11). American Psychiatric Association: 1. doi:10.1176/appi.pn.2015.6a14.

64. Ozarin, Lucy D. (April 17, 1998). Ramchandam, Dilip (ed.). "History Notes: The Official Seal of the APA". Psychiatric News. American Psychiatric Association. Archived August 29, 2008. Retrieved Oct 20, 2017.

65. Wilson, James Grant (1893). Memorial History of City of New-York: From First Settlement to 1892. NY History Co.

66. "History". Rush University. Archived on April 16, 2019. Retrieved Sept 30, 2015.

67. Hawke, p.5, citing Jeremiah's lament, "Woe is me, my mother, that thou has borne me, a man of strife, and a man of contention to the whole earth. I have neither lent on usury, nor have men lent to me on usury, yet every one of them doth curse me," in Letter to John Adams, December 26, 1811.

68. Letter to John Adams, April 5, 1808, in Butterfield, Letters of Benjamin Rush, pp. 2:962–963

69. "Benjamin Rush". Unitarian Universalist Association. July 8, 2010. Archived July 27, 2010. Retr July 8, 2010.

70. "Dr. Benjamin Rush Diary". Archived from the original on Oct 6, 2017. Retr July 23, 2013.

71. "Benjamin Rush, Signer of Declaration of Independence". adherents.com. Nov 28, 2005. Arch Feb 15, 2006.

72. America's God and Country Encyclopedia Quotations, by William Federer, 1999, ISBN 1-880563-09-6, p. 543
73. (1) Rush, Benjamin (1806). "Plan of a Peace-Office for United States". Essays, Literary, Moral Philosophical (2 ed.). Philadelphia: Thomas and William Bradford. pp. 183–88. Archived July 26, 2024. Retr June 3, 2010. (2) Runes, Dagobert D., ed. (1947). "A Plan of a Peace-Office for the United States". The Selected Writings of Benjamin Rush. New York: Philosophical Library. pp. 19–24. ISBN 978-0-8022-1448-5. Retr Dec 15, 2011.
74. Rush, Benjamin (July 16, 1776). "To: Patrick Henry". Delegates to Congress: Letters of Delegates to Congress, 1774–1789, Vol 4, May 16, 1776 – August 15, 1776. Electronic Text Center, U of Virginia Library. Arch Dec 15, 2012. Retr Oct 20, 2017.
75. To Elias Boudinot July 9, 1788. Letters of Benjamin Rush L. H. Butterfield, ed., (American Philosophical; Society, 1951), Vol. I, p. 475.
76. Szasz, Thomas (March 1, 2005). "A bogus Benjamin Rush quote: contribution to the history of pharmacracy". History of Psychiatry. 16 (1): 89–98. doi:10.1177/0957154X05044554. ISSN 0957-154X. PMID 15981368.

PINCKNEY FAMILY

SOUTH CAROLINA
SIGNATORIES TO DECLARATION OF INDEPENDENCE AND US CONSTITUTION

The Pinckney's held a huge position in the earliest business development of colonial America. They were expert farmers and developed huge wealth for many Plantations prior to Cotton becoming King.

Four Pinckney men would participate in the Declaration of Independence and US Constitutional Convention on behalf of South Carolina. It was the mother of those men who vastly expanded family mega income while allowing many other farm communities to profit from her developments.

In this story, most readers will be surprised to learn that cotton was the fourth major commodity crop grown in America, with first being tobacco, then rice, indigo, and then cotton would replace indigo with rice giving way more slowly to cotton. Indigo is grown in the fields, not unlike soybeans. The plant is processed and converted into "indigo ink, and indigo dyes," with the greatest application being in clothing, mostly known as "blue jeans." The color was not originally blue, but indigo purple.

Impact of the Pinckney's was so huge that their Seaport at Charleston, SC would handle more than 75% of the total export volume of all of America until the Civil War. Fort Sumter, the very first reinforced military base built in America, would ensure the Pirates of the Caribbean could not interfere with the important export volume.

Elizabeth "Eliza" Pinckney (Lucas; December 28, 1722 – May 27, 1793)[1] transformed agriculture in colonial South Carolina, where she developed indigo as its most important cash crop. Its cultivation and processing as dye produced one-third the total value of the colony's exports before the Revolutionary War. The manager of three plantations,[2] Eliza Pinckney, had a major influence on the colonial economy. Eliza Pinckney was the first woman inducted into South Carolina's Business Hall of Fame.

Elizabeth (known as Eliza) Lucas was born on December 28, 1722, on the island of Antigua, in the colony of the British Leeward Islands in the Caribbean. Lucas grew up on Poorest, one of her family's three sugarcane plantations on the island. She was the eldest child of Lieutenant Colonel George Lucas, of Dalzell's Regiment of Foot in the British Army, and Ann (probably Meldrum) Lucas.[3]

Colonel and Mrs. Lucas sent all their children to London for schooling. It was customary for elite colonists to send boys to England for their education when they might be as young as 8 or 9. Girls would not be sent until their mid-teens when nearing marriageable age. During this period, many parents believed that girls' futures of being wives and mothers made education in more than "the three Rs" and social accomplishments less necessary. Eliza's ability was recognized and she treasured her education at boarding school, where studies included French and music, but she said her favorite subject was botany.[4] She wrote to her father that she felt her "education, which [she] esteems a more valuable fortune than any [he] could have given [her], ... Will make me happy in my future life."[5]

Move to South Carolina

In 1738, the year Eliza would turn 16, Colonel Lucas moved his family from Antigua to South Carolina, where he had inherited three plantations from his father.[6] With tensions increasing between Spain and England, he believed his family would be safer in Carolina than on the tiny, exposed island in the West Indies. Eliza's grandfather, John Lucas, had acquired three tracts of land: Garden Hill on the Combahee River (1,500 acres), another 3,000 acres on the Waccamaw River, and Wappoo Plantation (600 acres) on Wappoo Creek—a tidal creek that connected the Ashley and Stono Rivers.[7] They chose to reside at Wappoo, which was 17 miles by land to Charleston (then known as Charles Town) and six miles by river.[8]

In 1739, Colonel Lucas had to return to his post in Antigua to deal with the political conflict between England and Spain. He was appointed lieutenant governor of the island. England's involvement in the War of the Austrian Succession thwarted his attempts to move back to South Carolina with his family. Eliza's letters to him show that she regarded her father with profound respect and deep affection and demonstrated that she acted as head of the family in terms of managing the plantations. Her mother died shortly after they moved.[5]

Eliza was 16 years old when she became responsible for managing Wappoo Plantation and its twenty slaves, plus supervising overseers at two other Lucas plantations, one inland producing tar and timber, and a 3,000 acres (12 km^2) rice plantation on the Waccamaw River.[6] In addition, she supervised care for her young sister, as their two brothers were still in school in London. As was customary, she recorded her decisions and experiments by copying her letters.

From Antigua, Colonel Lucas sent Eliza several types of seeds for trial on the plantations. They and other planters were eager to find crops for the uplands that could supplement their cultivation of rice. First, she experimented with ginger, cotton, alfalfa, and hemp. Starting in 1739, she began experimenting with cultivating and improving strains of the indigo plant, for which the expanding textile market created demand for its dye. When Colonel Lucas sent Eliza *indigofera* seeds in 1740, she expressed "greater hopes" for them, as she intended to plant them earlier.[5]

After three years of persistence and many failed attempts, Eliza proved that indigo could be successfully grown and processed in South Carolina. While she had first worked with an indigo processing expert from Montserrat, she was most successful in processing dye with the expertise of an indigo-maker of African descent hired from the French West Indies.[9]

Eliza used her 1744 crop to make seed and shared them with other planters, leading to an expansion in indigo production.[9] She proved that colonial planters could make a profit in an extremely competitive market. Due to her successes, the volume of indigo dye exported increased dramatically from 5,000 pounds in 1745–46, to 130,000 pounds by 1748.[4] Indigo became second only to rice as the South Carolina colony's commodity cash crop and contributed greatly to the wealth of its planters. Before the Revolutionary War, indigo accounted for more than one-third of the value of exports from the American colonies.[10]

These accomplishments are among the most well documented in early America, as Eliza became a persistent and dedicated writer.

Indigo plantation fortunes had a chance to continue until about 1856, when a young British Chemist accidently discovered how to synthesize many colors of dye. Then cotton takes over most plantations and farms.

From the time that she began her life in South Carolina on Wappoo Plantation to the time that she died in Philadelphia in 1793, Eliza carefully copied all her conversations and letters into a "letter-book."[11] She organized her writings into multiple volumes, each depicting with great detail a different period during her life. The volumes recount most of her life, with the bulk of her writings referring to the time between 1739 and 1762.[12]

The first few volumes range from the years 1739 to 1746. They begin with her description of her family's move to the plantation in South Carolina when she was about 17 years old. Throughout these years, she began to experiment with the indigo seeds along with others that her father had sent to her. Her letters describe the many years of experiments that she did on the crop to make it successful. They also detail her marriage to longtime friend and neighbor Charles Pinckney, 1744.[12]

The second set of volumes begins around 1753 and ends around 1757. By this time, Eliza and Charles had begun their new life together and had children. These sets reference the time she and her family moved to London for her husband's job. They lived there for about five years while Charles worked as the commissioner of the South Carolina colony.[12]

The third set of volumes covers 1758 through 1762. It corresponds with the family's return to South Carolina and soon after, the death of her husband. She managed her family's plantations along with her late husband's as well. She lived as a widow for more than thirty years until her death in 1793 while she was searching for a cure for breast cancer. Though she kept copies of her letters, very few of them remain today.[12]

This letter-book is one of the most complete collections of writing from 18th century America and provides a valuable glimpse into the life of an elite colonial woman living during this age. Her writings detail goings on at the plantations, her pastimes, social visits, and even her experiments with indigo over several years. Many scholars consider this letter-book extremely precious because it describes everyday life over an extended period rather than a singular event in history. Eliza passed her letter-book on to her daughter Harriott. It was passed down from mother to daughter well into the 20th century, at which point the Lucas-Pinckney family donated it to the South Carolina Historical Society.[11]

George Lucas, Eliza's father, presented two potential suitors—both wealthy, connected, South Carolina socialites—to Eliza years before she fell in love with and married Charles Pinckney. Eliza rejected both. This was strange and unheard of in 18th-century America.[12]

Eliza and Charles Pinckney, a planter on a neighboring plantation, became attached after the death of his first wife. Eliza had been close to the couple before his wife's death. They were married on May 25, 1744. She was 21.

Mr. Pinckney was South Carolina's first native-born attorney and served as advocate general of the Court of Vice-Admiralty, Justice of the Peace for Berkeley County, and attorney general. He was elected as a member of the Commons House of Assembly and Speaker of that body intermittently from 1736 to 1740, and he was a member of the Royal Provincial Council. Eliza was unlike many women of her time, as she was "educated, independent, and accomplished." When the Pinckney's lived in Charleston, Eliza was soon planting oaks and magnolias at their mansion overlooking the bay and corresponding with major British botanists.

Eliza soon gave birth to three sons and a daughter: Charles Cotesworth (1746–1825), George Lucas, Harriott Pinckney (1749–1830), and Thomas (1750–1828). George Lucas Pinckney, her father's namesake, died soon after birth in June 1747. In 1753, the family moved to London for five years.[13] Shortly after their return in 1758 to South Carolina, Charles

Pinckney died.[14] Widowed, Eliza continued to manage their extensive plantations, in addition to Lucas holdings.[15] Most of her agricultural experiments took place before this time.[13]

The surviving Pinckney sons became influential leaders. Charles was a signatory of the United States Constitution and was the Federalist vice-presidential candidate in 1800. In 1804 and 1808, he was the Federalist candidate for president. Thomas was appointed Minister to Spain, where he negotiated Pinckney's Treaty in 1795, guaranteeing American navigation rights on the Mississippi River to New Orleans. He was the Federalist vice presidential candidate in 1796. Harriott married Daniel Huger Horry, Jr. and lived at Hampton Plantation, now a South Carolina State Historic Site.

Eliza Lucas Pinckney died of cancer, in Philadelphia, in 1793.[16]

At the end of the 17th century, Antiguan political opponents of Eliza's grandfather, John Lucas, believed that the Lucas family had powerful influence in London through Henry Grey (1664–1740), later Duke of Kent, a senior member of Queen Anne's government; and Robert Lucas, 3rd Lord Lucas (1649–1705), then governor of the Tower of London. There is documentary evidence that the family used this influence for their own purposes.[17] The West India merchant Thomas Lucas (c. 1720–1784) and his business partner were prominent.

Honors and legacy

- 2008 - Inducted into the South Carolina Hall of Fame[18]
- 1989 - For her contributions to South Carolina's agriculture, Eliza Lucas Pinckney was the first woman to be inducted into the South Carolina Business Hall of Fame.[19]
- 1793 - President George Washington served as a pallbearer at her funeral at St. Peter's Church, in Philadelphia where she had traveled for treatment.
- 1753 - At an audience with Augusta, the Dowager Princess of Wales, in London, Eliza presented the princess a dress made of silk produced on the Pinckney plantations.[5]

References:

1. "Pinckney, Eliza Lucas (1722–1779)", encyclopedia.com. Accessed February 7, 2024.
2. Pearson, Ellen Holmes. Colonial Teenagers, teachinghistory.org. Accessed July 13, 2011.
3. "Eliza Lucas Pinckney's Family in Antigua, 1668–1747," Carol Walter Ramagosa, The South Carolina Historical Magazine, July 1998, vol. 99, no. 3
4. "Eliza Lucas Pinckney", Distinguished Women of Past & Present, accessed December 7, 2008.
5. Elise Pinckney and Marvin R. Zahniser, eds., The Letterbook of Eliza Lucas Pinckney: Intriguing Letters by One of Colonial America's Most Accomplished Women, Eliza Lucas Pinckney, Columbia, South Carolina: University of South Carolina Press, 1972, Google Books, accessed December 7, 2008.
6. Norman K. Risjord, "Eliza Lucas Pinckney", Representative Americans, the Colonists, Lanham, Maryland: Rowman & Littlefield, 2001, p. 240.
7. The South Carolina Genealogical Magazine; vol. 16.
8. Louise S. Grinstein, Carol A. Biermann, Rose K. Rose, "Eliza Lucas Pinckney," Women in the Biological Sciences, Westport, Connecticut: Greenwood Publishing, 1997, p. 401.
9. "Eliza Lucas Pinckney", The Devil's Blue Dye: Indigo and Slavery, archived from the original on 2012-03-22
10. "Eliza Lucas Pinckney" Arch Nov 21, 2008, Wayback Machine, Biographies, National Women's History Museum, 2007, accessed Dec 7, 2008.
11. Williams, Harriet Simons. "Eliza Lucas and Her Family: Before the Letterbook". South Carolina Historical Magazine. 99 (3): 259–279.
12. Bellows, Barbara L. "Eliza Lucas Pinckney: Evolution of an Icon". South Carolina Historical Magazine. 106 (April–July 2005): 148–155.
13. Grinstein et al. (1997), Women in the Biological Sciences, p. 405.
14. Norman K. Risjord, "Eliza Lucas Pinckney", Representative Americans, the Colonists, Lanham, MD: Rowman & Littlefield, 2001, p.249
15. "Eliza Lucas Pinckney", Infoplease, accessed December 7, 2008.
16. The Gentry, by Adam Nicolson, chapter 'Courage', London, 2011.
17. Calendar of State Papers Colonial, America and West Indies, Volume 16: 1697-1698, p. 605
18. South Carolina Hall of Fame: Eliza Lucas Pinckney, theofficialschalloffame.com. Accessed February 8, 2024.
19. Bellows, Barbara L. (2005). "Eliza Lucas Pinckney: The Evolution of an Icon". The South Carolina Historical Magazine. 106 (2/3): 147–165. ISSN 0038-3082. JSTOR 27570748.

To continue this reading, you must understand the duplication of names:

- Colonel Charles Pinckney is the elder of the family.
- Charles Cotesworth Pinckney is the eldest son of the Colonel.
- Thomas Pinckney is the second son of the Colonel.
- Charles Pinckney is related through another branch of Pinckney's.

Colonel **Charles Pinckney** (March 7, 1732 - September 22, 1782), was a South Carolina lawyer and planter residing in Charleston, South Carolina. Commissioned as a colonel for the Charles Towne Militia in the colonial era, he was widely known as "Colonel Pinckney". He had a rice and indigo plantation known as Snee Farm along the Wando River, about nine miles from Charleston, and a townhouse on Queen Street in the city.

Captured by the British in 1780 in the fall of Charleston, Pinckney was among more than 160 men who signed loyalty oaths to protect their properties, which the British would otherwise have confiscated or destroyed. After the war, to penalize his Loyalist oath, the state legislature assessed a fine against Pinckney based on property.

His son and namesake Charles Pinckney inherited the plantation and became a prominent politician after the American Revolution. After participating in the constitutional convention, he was elected to three non-consecutive terms as governor of the state, and as a US Senator and US Representative.

Pinckney was born to William Pinckney and Ruth Brewton in 1732 in Charleston. He was educated and grew up in a planter family. His grandfather, Thomas Pinckney immigrated at the age of 17 to Yorktown in 1698 from Shropshire and worked as a baker's assistant. His father served as Master of Chancery. William had joined his older brother, Charles Pinckney, in setting up "the first fire insurance company in America, the Friendly Society."[1] Then an extensive fire in 1740 in Charleston resulted in high damages, and William suffered financially. He sent his son to be educated by his wealthier brother Charles.

The younger Charles Pinckney studied law, passing the bar in 1752.[1] Pinckney became a leading attorney in the city of Charleston. He bought his first plantation, now known as Snee Farm, in 1754, as a mark of his early success. The 715-acre plantation was used to produce the commodity crops of rice and indigo.[2]

References:

1. Pinckney Family: "Colonel Charles Pinckney", Snee Farm - History & Culture, National Park Service. Accessed February 8, 2024.
2. "Charles Pinckney", Snee Farm, History&Culture, National Park Service
3. Susan Hart Vincent, of Historic Land Design, *Charles Pinckney National Historic Site: Cultural Landscape Report*, pp. 16-18, Department of Interior, 1998, full text at Internet Archive. Accessed February 8, 2024.

Charles Cotesworth Pinckney (February 25, 1746 – August 16, 1825) was an American statesman, military officer and Founding Father who served as United States Minister to France from 1796 to 1797. A delegate to the Constitutional Convention where he signed the Constitution of the United States, Pinckney was twice nominated by the Federalist Party as its presidential candidate in 1804 and 1808, losing both elections.

Charles Cotesworth Pinckney was born in Charlestown in the Province of South Carolina on February 25, 1746. He was the son of Charles Pinckney, who would later serve as the chief justice of the Province of South Carolina, and Eliza Lucas, a celebrated planter and agriculturalist, who is credited with developing indigo cultivation in this area.[2] His younger brother, Thomas Pinckney, later served as governor of South Carolina, as did his first cousin, Charles Pinckney.[3]

Pinckney enrolled in Christ Church, Oxford, in 1763 and began studying law at Middle Temple in 1764. After a short stint at a military academy in France, Pinckney completed his studies in 1769 and was admitted to the English bar. He briefly practiced law in England before establishing a legal practice in Charleston.[4]

After returning to the American colonies in 1773, Pinckney married Sarah Middleton. Her father Henry Middleton later served as the second president of the Continental Congress, and her brother Arthur Middleton signed the Declaration of Independence. Sarah died in 1784. In 1786, Pinckney married again, to Mary Stead, who came from a wealthy family of planters in Georgia. They had three daughters.

Pinckney studied botany in France in 1769 . For his assistance to French botanist André Michaux, he was honored by a species named for him: Pinckneya pubens.[5][6]

After returning to South Carolina from Europe, Pinckney began to practice law in Charleston. He was first elected to a seat in the colonial legislature in 1770. In 1773 he served as a regional attorney general. When war erupted between the thirteen American colonies and Great Britain in 1775, Pinckney stood with the American Patriots; in that year he was a member of the first South Carolina provincial congress, which helped South Carolina transition from being a British colony to being an independent state.[2] During the American Revolution, he served in the lower house of the state legislature and as a member of the South Carolina Senate, in addition to his military service.

After this, the British Army shifted its focus to the northern and mid-Atlantic states. Pinckney led his regiment north to join General Washington's troops near Philadelphia. Pinckney and his regiment participated in the Battle of Brandywine and the Battle of Germantown. Around this time, he first met fellow officers Alexander Hamilton and James McHenry, who became future Federalist statesmen.

With the conclusion of the Revolutionary War, Pinckney returned to his legal practice, becoming one of the most acclaimed attorneys in South Carolina. He also returned to the lower house of the South Carolina legislature, and he and his brother Thomas became major political powers. He became an advocate of the landed elite of the South Carolina Lowcountry, who dominated the state's government during this period. Pinckney also took the lead in negotiating the end to a border dispute with the state of Georgia, and he signed the Convention of Beaufort, which temporarily solved some of the disputes.[8]

The Revolutionary War had convinced many in South Carolina, including Pinckney, that the defense of the state required the cooperation of the other colonies. As such, Pinckney advocated a stronger national government than that provided by the Articles of Confederation, and he represented South Carolina at the Constitutional Convention of 1787,[9] where his younger cousin Charles Pinckney also served as a delegate.[10] Pinckney advocated that African American slaves be counted as a basis of representation. According to a book review in *The New York Times* in January 2015:

Pinckney advocated for a strong national government (albeit one with a system of checks and balances) to replace the weak one of the times. He opposed as impractical the election of representatives by popular vote. He also opposed paying senators, who, he thought, should be men of independent wealth. He also opposed placing a limitation on the size of a federal standing army.[12]

Pinckney played a prominent role in securing the ratification of the Federal Constitution in the South Carolina convention of 1788, and in framing the South Carolina Constitution in the convention of 1790. At the ratification convention, Pinckney distinguished three types of government and said republics were where "the people at large, either collectively or by representation, form the legislature". After this, he announced his retirement from politics.

Presidential candidate

With the support of Hamilton, Pinckney became the Federalist vice presidential nominee in the 1800 presidential election. [a] Pinckney's military and political service had won him national stature, Federalists hoped Pinckney could win southern votes against Democratic-Republican nominee Thomas Jefferson. Hamilton had even greater hopes, as he wished to displace Adams as president and viewed Pinckney as more amenable to his policies. In-fighting between Adams and Hamilton plagued the Federalists, and the Democratic-Republicans won the election. Pinckney refused Hamilton's plans to make him president and promised not to accept the votes of any elector who was not also pledged to Adams.[15]

Federalists saw little hope of defeating the popular Jefferson in the 1804 election; though the party remained strong in New England, Jefferson was widely expected to win the southern and mid-Atlantic states. With little hope of winning the presidency, the Federalists nominated Pinckney as their presidential candidate, but neither Pinckney nor the Federalists pursued an active presidential campaign. The Federalists hoped Pinckney's military reputation and status as a southerner would show that the Federalist Party remained a national party, but they knew Pinckney had little chance of winning even his own home state. Jefferson won, taking 162 electoral votes compared to Pinckney's 14. Pinckney's defeat in South Carolina made him the first major party presidential nominee to lose his own home state.[16]

Memorials

- Castle Pinckney in Charleston Harbor, completed 1810, and an earlier fort Pinckney.
- Pinckney Island National Wildlife Refuge, a national wildlife refuge Pinckney plantation.
- In 1942, a 422-foot liberty ship built in Wilmington, North Carolina, SS *Charles C. Pinckney*
- Pinckney Street on Beacon Hill in Boston and Madison, Wisconsin.
- Pinckneyville, Illinois, and Pinckney, Michigan, were named after him.
- Pinckney Highway (SC 9) in Chester, South Carolina, was named in his honor.

References

This article incorporates public domain material from websites or documents of the United States Army Center of Military History.

1. *Carrillo, Richard (1972). ""Archeological Excavations at Pinckneyville, Site of Pinckney District, 1791-1800"". University of South Carolina Scholar Commons.*
2. *DeConde, Alexander (1976). "Pinckney, Charles Cotesworth". In William D. Halsey (ed.). Collier's Encyclopedia. Vol. 19. New York: Macmillan Educational Corporation. pp. 51–52.*
3. Southwick (1998), pp. 27–29
4. Southwick (1998), p. 29
5. *"CHARLES COTESWORTH PINCKNEY". www.history.army.mil. Retrieved November 26, 2023.*
6. *Grimm, William Carey (1966). The Book of Trees. Harrisburg Pennsylvania: The Stackpole Company. p. 414.*
7. *"CHARLES COTESWORTH PINCKNEY". history.army.mil. Archived May 12, 2013. Retrieved June 21, 2009.*
8. *Zahniser, Marvin(1967) Charles Cotesworth Pinckney: Founding Father. U North Carolina Press.pp.78–83, 101*
9. Zahniser, pp. 86-87
10. Collier and Collier, p. 111
11. Quote taken from book review by Kevin Baker, January 28, 2015, of *Gateway to Freedom* by Eric Foner"
12. Fields, William and Hardy, David. "The Third Amendment and the Issue of the Maintenance of Standing Armies: A Legal History," American Journal of Legal History (1991), volume 35, p. 393: Elbridge Gerry ... proposed that the Constitution limit the size of the standing army. Charles Cotesworth Pinckney, at the investigation of Washington, responded that such a proposal was satisfactory so long as any invading force also agreed to limit its army.
13. Zahniser, pp. 191-197
14. Southwick (1998), p. 32
15. Zahniser, pp. 208-214, 231-233
16. Zahniser, pp. 243-246

Bibliography

- Buchanan, John (1997). The Road to Guilford Courthouse. John Wiley & Sons. ISBN 9780471327165.

- Chisholm, Hugh, ed. (1911). "Pinckney, Charles Cotesworth" . Encyclopædia Britannica. Vol. 21 (11th ed.). Cambridge University Press. pp. 616–617.
- Lander, Ernest M. Jr. (1956). "The South Carolinians at the Philadelphia Convention, 1787". The South Carolina Historical Magazine. **57** (3): 134–155. JSTOR 27566067.
- Morison, Samuel E. (1912). "The First National Nominating Convention, 1808". The American Historical Review. **17** (4): 744–763. doi:10.2307/1832458. JSTOR 1832458.
- Sharp, James Roger (2010). Deadlocked Election of 1800. U Press of Kansas. ISBN 978-0-7006-1742-5.
- Southwick, Leslie (1998). Presidential Also-Rans and Running Mates, 1788 through 1996 (Second ed.). McFarland. ISBN 0-7864-0310-1.
- Williams, Francis Leigh (1978). A Founding Family: The Pinckneys of South Carolina. Harcourt Brace Jovanovich. ISBN 978-0151315031.
- Zahniser, Marvin R. (1967). Charles Cotesworth Pinckney: Founding Father. UNC Press.
- Collier, Christopher, and James Lincoln (1986). Decision in Philadelphia: The Constitutional Convention of 1787. Ballantine. ISBN 0-345-34652-1.

Readers must note that several members of the Pinckney family were active in the Constitutional Convention and many other States matters that had a yeoman's effect on our modern-day government. Three of these men held the name Charles Pinckney. Each contributed thoughts and Clauses of the eventual US Constitution.

Charles Pinckney (October 26, 1757 – October 29, 1824) was an American Founding Father, planter, politician who was a signer of the United States Constitution. He served as the 37th governor of South Carolina, later serving two more non-consecutive terms. He also served as a U.S. Senator and a member of the House of Representatives. He was first cousin once removed from fellow signer Charles Cotesworth Pinckney.

Pinckney's descendants included seven future South Carolina governors, including men related to the Maybank and Rhett families.

Pinckney was born and educated in Charles Town in the Province of South Carolina. His father, Colonel Charles Pinckney, was a rich lawyer and planter. His mother was Frances Brewton (b. 1733), daughter of a goldsmith and sister of Miles Brewton and Rebecca Brewton Motte, who were prominent in Charleston history.

Busy with the war and politics, Pinckney did not marry until 1788. He married Mary Eleanor Laurens on April 27, 1788. Mary was the daughter of Henry Laurens, a wealthy and politically powerful South Carolina family. They had at least three children.

Among his in-laws were father-in-law Henry Laurens, Colonel John Laurens, and U.S. Representative David Ramsay. A brother-in-law married the daughter of South Carolina Governor John Rutledge.

Please note that these names are integral to the key places and maps of the modern state of South Carolina.

Pinckney would become a huge landowner in and around Charleston, South Carolina -- with a position in life allowing him to develop the Port of Charleston as the most important in American export up until the American Civil War.

Constitutional Convention

Although one of the youngest delegates, he later claimed to have been the most influential one and contended he had submitted a draft, known as the Pinckney Plan, that was the basis of the final Constitution. This was strongly disputed by James Madison and some of the other framers.[2] Pinckney submitted an elaborate form of the Virginia Plan, proposed first by Edmund Randolph, but it was disregarded by the other delegates. Historians assess him as an important contributing delegate.[3] Pinckney boasted that he was 24, allowing him to claim distinction as the youngest delegate, but he was 29 years old at the time of the convention.[4] He attended full-time, spoke often and effectively, and contributed to the final draft and to resolution of problems during the debates. He also worked for the ratification of the Constitution in South Carolina (1788)

Author of Significant Constitutional Clauses

NO RELIGIOUS TESTS. Pinckney introduced a clause into the Constitution in opposition to an established state religion. His No Religious Test Clause read as follows:

no religious test shall ever be required as a qualification to any office or public trust under the United States

The phrase was voted upon and passed with little opposition. For the first time, an official of a national government was not required to have a religion.[7][8]

HABEAS CORPUS Pinckney is also responsible for the inclusion of the writ of habeas corpus into the Constitution.[9][10] Initially introduced as "Nor shall the privilege of the Writ of Habeas Corpus ever be suspended, except in case of rebellion or invasion",[11] it is now a part of Article 1 of the United States Constitution.

LOUISIANA PURCHASE He facilitated Spanish acquiescence in the transfer of Louisiana from France to the US in 1803 by the Louisiana Purchase. (Spain had already returned rule of this territory to France under Napoleon.)

References

1. Susan Hart Vincent, of Historic Land Design, Charles Pinckney National Historic Site: Cultural Landscape Report, pp. 16-18, Department of Interior, 1998, full text at Internet Archive
2. James Madison on the Pinckney Plan, Farrand's Records of the Federal Convention, http://oll.libertyfund.org/titles/farrand-the-records-of-the-federal-convention-of-1787-vol-3#lf0544-03_head_424.
3. MacDonald Forrest, E Pluribus Anum: The Formation of the American Republic 1776–1790(Houghton Mifflin Company: Library of Congress Catalog Card: 65-111322) 1965 pp. 166–167.
4. Yates Publishing. U.S. and International Marriage Records, 1560–1900 [database on-line]. Provo, UT, US: The Generations Network, Inc., 2004.
5. Paul Finkelman, Slavery, and the Founders: Race and Liberty in the Age of Jefferson, p. 82, 2nd Edition, 2001.
6. The vote in the House was 69 for repeal and 38 against, which was short of the two-to-one vote required to amend the Constitution. See the Congressional Globe, 38th Cong., 1st Sess., 1325 (1864)
7. Drawn from original source: Charles C. Haynes (1991). "Overview: history of religious liberty in America". A Framework for Civic Education. Council for the Advancement of Citizenship and the Center for Civic Education.
8. Drawn from original source: "The Individual Liberties within the Body of the Constitution: A Symposium: The No Religious Test Clause and the Constitution of Religious Liberty: A Machine That Has Gone of Itself." Case Western Reserve Law Review 37: 674–747. Dreisbach, Daniel L. 1999. "The Bill of Rights: Almost an Afterthought
9. A Constitutional History of Habeas Corpus, p. 127; William Duker, University of Michigan, 1980
10. The Contribution of Charles Pinckney to the Formation of the American Union, p. 74; Andrew J. Bethea, 1937
11. The Privilege of the Writ of Habeas Corpus Under the Constitution

The Pinckney family continued to hold many important positions in the new American government. For purposes of this book which identifies those characteristics that propelled these individuals to become Founding Fathers of the United States, we need move no further from this point, although they all continued to contribute to the early development of America. These biographies indicate that our Founding Father Hero's often had to overcome a poor upbringing along with serious setbacks yet persevered to establish success and reputations that resonate.

PAUL REVERE

METALSMITH AND MASTER INDUSTRIALIST

Paul Revere: December 21, 1734 – May 10, 1818) was an American silversmith, military officer and industrialist who played a major role in the American Revolutionary War, engaging in a midnight ride in 1775 to alert nearby minutemen of the approach of British troops prior to the battles of Lexington and Concord. Paul Revere is not considered a Founding Father, but was a prominent figure in the American Revolution

Born in Boston, Revere became a prosperous and prominent Bostonian, deriving his income from silversmithing and engraving. During the American Revolution, he was a strong supporter of the Patriot cause and joined the Sons of Liberty. His midnight ride transformed him into an American folk hero, being dramatized in Henry Wadsworth Longfellow's 1861 poem, "Paul Revere's Ride". He helped to organize an intelligence alarm system to keep watch on the movements of British forces. Revere was later an officer in the Massachusetts Militia.

During the Revolution, Revere developed strong Industrialist acumen as he started up and operated many war supply industries for our military.

In 1800, he became the first American to successfully roll copper into sheets for use as sheathing on naval vessels.

Early life and education

Born in Boston,[3] his father, Apollos Rivoire, a French Huguenot who came to Boston at the age of 13, was a silversmith.[4] By the time he married Deborah Hitchborn, a member of a long-standing Boston family that owned a small shipping wharf, in 1729, Rivoire had anglicized his name to Paul Revere. The Hitchborn family was of English origin; Deborah's maternal great grandparents, David and Catherine Hitchborn, arrived in Boston, Massachusetts, in 1641 from Boston, England.[5][6] Their son, Paul Revere, was the third of 12 children.[2] Revere grew up in the extended Hitchborn family, and never learned his father's native language.[7]

At age thirteen, Paul Revere left school and became an apprentice for his father. Silversmithing afforded young Paul connections that would serve him well in the American Revolution.[8] Though his father attended Puritan services, Revere was drawn to the Church of England.[9] In 1750, aged 15, Revere was part of the first group of change ringers to ring the new bells (cast in 1744) at Christ Church, in the north of Boston (the Old North Church).[10][11] Revere eventually began attending services of the political Jonathan Mayhew at West Church.[9]

Revere's father died in 1754, when Paul was legally too young to take over the family silver shop.[13] In February 1756, during the French and Indian War (the North American theater of the Seven Years' War), he enlisted in the provincial army, as army service promised consistent pay.[14] Commissioned a second lieutenant in a provincial artillery regiment, he spent the summer at Fort William Henry at the southern end of Lake George in New York as part of an abortive plan for the capture of Fort St. Frédéric. Following a short stay in the army, he returned to Boston and assumed control of the silver shop in his own name. On August 4, 1757, he married Sarah Orne (1736–1773).[15] He and Sarah had eight children.[16]

During the economic depression that followed the French and Indian War, Revere began working as a copperplate engraver, later revolutionizing the copper production process. He produced illustrations for books and magazines, business cards, political cartoons, bookplates, a song book, and bills of fare for taverns. He also practiced as a dentist from 1768 to 1775, to the extent that his time and skills allowed. He cleaned teeth, mounted false teeth, and sold toothpaste. Contrary to popular myth, he did not make George Washington's false teeth. There is no evidence he made full sets of dentures.

1765–1774: the developing revolution

Revere's business began to suffer when the British economy entered a recession in the years following the Seven Years' War, and declined further when the Stamp Act of 1765 resulted in a further downturn in the Massachusetts economy.[17] Business was so poor that an attempt was made to seize his property in late 1765.[18] To help make ends meet he even took up dentistry, a skill set he was taught by a practicing surgeon who lodged at a friend's house.[19] One client was Joseph Warren, a local physician and political opposition leader with whom Revere formed a close friendship.[20][21] Revere and Warren, in addition to having common political views, were also both active in the same local Masonic lodges.[22]

Although Revere was not one of the "Loyal Nine"—organizers of the earliest protests against the Stamp Act—he was well connected with its members, who were laborers and artisans.[23] Revere did not participate in some of the more raucous protests, such as the attack on the home of Lieutenant Governor Thomas Hutchinson.[24] In 1765, militants who would become known as the Sons of Liberty formed, of which Revere was a member.[25][26] From 1765 on, in support of the dissident cause, he produced engravings with political themes. Among these engravings are a depiction of the arrival of British troops in 1768 (which he termed "an insolent parade") and a famous depiction of the March 1770 Boston Massacre. Although the latter was engraved by Revere and he included the inscription, "Engraved, Printed, & Sold by Paul Revere Boston", it was modeled on a drawing by Henry Pelham.[27] Revere also produced a bowl commemorating the Massachusetts assembly's refusal to retract the Massachusetts Circular Letter. (This letter, adopted in response to the 1767 Townshend Acts, called for united action against the acts. King George III issued a demand for retraction.)[27]

In 1770 Revere purchased a house, now a museum on North Square in Boston's North End. The house provided space for his growing family while he continued to maintain his shop at nearby Clark's Wharf.[29] Sarah died in 1773, and on October 10 of that year, Revere married Rachel Walker (1745–1813).[30]

In November 1773 the merchant ship *Dartmouth* arrived in Boston harbor carrying the first shipment of tea made under the terms of the Tea Act.[31] This act authorized the British East India Company to ship tea (of which it had huge surpluses due to colonial boycotts organized in response to the Townshend Acts) directly to the colonies, bypassing colonial merchants.[32] Revere and Warren, as members of the informal North End Caucus, organized a watch over the *Dartmouth* to prevent unloading of tea. Revere took turns on guard duty,[33] and was one of the ringleaders in the Boston Tea Party of December 16, when colonists dumped tea from the *Dartmouth* and two other ships into the harbor.[34]

From December 1773 to November 1775, Revere served as a courier for the Boston Committee of Public Safety, traveling to New York and Philadelphia to report on the political unrest in Boston. Research has documented 18 such rides. Notice of some of them was published in Massachusetts newspapers, and British authorities received further intelligence of them from Loyalist Americans.[35] In 1774, his cousin John on the island of Guernsey wrote to Paul that John had seen reports of Paul's role as an (courier) in London newspapers.[36]

In 1774, the military governor of Massachusetts, General Thomas Gage, dissolved the provincial assembly. Governor Gage closed the port of Boston and forced private citizens to quarter (provide lodging for) soldiers in their homes.[2]

During this time, Revere and a group of 30 "mechanics" began meeting in secret at his favorite haunt, the *Green Dragon*, to coordinate the gathering and dissemination of intelligence by "watching the Movements of British Soldiers".[37] Around this time Revere contributed political engravings to Patriot monthly, *Royal American Magazine*.[38]

He rode to Portsmouth, New Hampshire, in December 1774 upon rumors of an impending landing of British troops, a journey known as the Portsmouth Alarm.[39] Although the rumors were false, his ride sparked a rebel success by provoking locals to raid Fort William and Mary, defended by just six soldiers, for its gunpowder supply.[40]

Midnight Ride

Paul Revere's Midnight Ride was an alert given to minutemen in the Province of Massachusetts by local Patriots on the night of April 18, 1775, warning them of the approach of British troops prior to the battles of Lexington and Concord. In prior weeks, Patriots learned of a planned crackdown on the Massachusetts Congress.

Sons of Liberty members Paul Revere and William Dawes prepared the alert, which began when Robert Newman, the sexton of Boston's Old North Church, used a lantern signal to warn colonists in Charlestown of the British Army's advance by way of the Charles River. Revere and Dawes then rode to meet John Hancock and Samuel Adams in Lexington, ten miles away, alerting other Patriot riders, then onward to Concord with Samuel Prescott.[41]

The trio were intercepted by a British Army patrol in Lincoln. Prescott and Dawes escaped but Revere was returned to Lexington by the patrol and freed after questioning. The ride played a crucial role in the Patriot victory in the subsequent battles at Lexington and Concord. The ride has been commemorated, most notably Henry Wadsworth Longfellow's 1861 poem, "Paul Revere's Ride."

War years

Because Boston was besieged, he boarded in Watertown, where he was eventually joined by Rachel and most of his children (Paul Jr., then 15, remained in Boston to mind the family properties).[42] After he was denied a commission in the Continental Army, he was retained by the provincial congress as a courier, and he printed local currency which the congress used to pay the troops around Boston.[43]

Since there was a desperate shortage of gunpowder, the provincial congress decided in November 1775 to send him to Philadelphia to study the working of the only powder mill in the colonies, in the hopes that he might be able to build a second one in Massachusetts. Revere called on the mill's owner, Oswald Eve, armed with a letter from Continental Congressmen Robert Morris and John Dickinson asking Eve to "Cheerfully & from Public Spirited Motives give Mr. Revere such information as will enable him to Conduct the business on his return home."[46][47] He also acquired, through the work of Samuel Adams, plans for another powder mill. This information enabled Revere to set up a powder mill at Stoughton (present-day Canton).[46][48] The mill produced tons of gunpowder for the Patriot cause.[49]

With the outbreak of hostilities, Revere turned industrialist and constructed a much-needed powder mill to supply colonial arms. In 1776 he was put in command of Boston Harbor's principal defense at Castle William. He resumed his stride as a successful industrialist after the war, however, and set up a rolling mill for the manufacture of sheet copper at Canton, Massachusetts. From this factory came sheathing for many U.S. ships, including the

Constitution, and for the dome of the Massachusetts State House. The foundry survived into the 21st century as Revere Copper Products, Inc. (Britanica.com)

Revere's friend and compatriot Joseph Warren was killed in the Battle of Bunker Hill on June 17, 1775.[50] On March 21, 1776, after the British army left Boston, Revere and Warren's brothers, went to the battlefield and found a grave.[51] Revere identified Warren's body by a false tooth he placed in Warren's mouth.[52]

Militia service

Upon returning to Boston in 1776, Revere was commissioned a major of infantry in the Massachusetts militia that April and transferred to the artillery a month later.[53] In November he was promoted to lieutenant colonel, and was stationed at Castle William, defending Boston harbor. He was generally second or third in the chain of command, and on several occasions he was given command of the fort.[53] He applied his engineering skills to maintaining the fort's armaments, even designing and building a caliper to accurately measure cannonballs and cannon bore holes, improving cannon trajectory and velocity.[53] The service at Castle William was relatively isolated, and personality friction prompted some men to file complaints against Revere.[54] In late August 1777, Revere and his military unit escorted prisoners from the Battle of Bennington to Boston, to prison ships,[55][56] and again in September when he was briefly deployed to Rhode Island.[57]

In August 1778 Revere's regiment served in a combined Franco-American expedition to capture the British base at Newport, Rhode Island.[58] His regiment was responsible for erecting and maintaining artillery batteries on Aquidneck Island.[59] The attempt was abandoned by the French when their fleet was scattered in a storm, Revere's regiment returned to Boston before the British sortied from Newport to force the Battle of Rhode Island.[60]

Business and social connections

A factor preventing Revere's success as a merchant was the economic climate of the time period after the war, known as the Confederation Period. While the colonies had seen economic growth before the war, the colonies experienced a severe post-war depression, constraining the overall success of his business.[61]

Rolling mills greatly improved the productivity of his silver shop and enabled his business to move further away from manufacturing high-end customized products in order to focus instead on the production of a more standardized set of goods.[62] In the 18th century, the standard of living improved in America, as genteel goods became increasingly available to the masses.[63] Revere responded well to this trend because his business was not solely manufacturing custom, purchases. Smaller products accounted for the majority of his work, allowing him to build a broad customer base.[64]

Revere's increased efficiency left financial and human resources available for the exploration of other products, which was essential to overcoming the fluctuating post-war economic climate.[65] In addition to increasing production, the flatting mill enabled Revere to move towards a more managerial position.[66]

Later years: entrepreneurship, manufacturing, and politics

By 1788 he had invested some of the profits from his growing silverworking trade to construct a large furnace, which would allow him to work with larger quantities of metals at higher temperatures. He soon opened an iron foundry in Boston that produced utilitarian cast iron items.[67] Many of Revere's business practices changed when he expanded his practice into ironworking, because he transitioned from just being an artisan to also being an entrepreneur and a manager. In order to make this transition successfully, Revere invested substantial capital and time in his foundry.[68]

Technological practices

The quasi-industrialization of his practice set Revere apart from his competition. "Revere's rapid foundry success resulted from fortuitous timing, innate technical aptitude, thorough research, and the casting experience he gained from silverworking."[69] Revere was entering the field of iron casting in a time when New England cities were becoming centers of industry. The nature of technological advancement was such that many skilled entrepreneurs worked together, in what is known by Nathan Rosenberg as technological convergence, by which a number of companies work together on challenges in order to spur advances.[70]

Labor practices

An artisan, Revere managed to avoid many of these labor conflicts by adopting a system of employment that still held trappings of the craft system in the form of worker freedoms such as work hour flexibility, wages in line with skill levels, and liquor on the job.[71]

Manufacturing: church bells, cannon, and copper products

Revere identified a burgeoning market for church bells in the religious revival known as the Second Great Awakening that followed the war. Beginning in 1792 he became one of America's best-known bell casters, working with sons Paul Jr. and Joseph Warren Revere in the firm Paul Revere & Sons. This firm cast the first bell made in Boston and produced hundreds of bells, a number remain in operation.[72]

In 1794, Revere expanded his bronze casting work by learning to cast cannon for the federal government, state governments, and private clients.[73]

By 1795, a growing percentage of his foundry's business came from a new product, copper bolts, spikes, and other fittings that he sold to merchants and the Boston naval yard for ship construction. In 1801, Revere became a pioneer in the production of rolled copper, opening North America's first copper mill south of Boston in Canton. He revolutionized much of the copper production processes. Copper from the Revere Copper Company was used to cover the original wooden dome of the Massachusetts State House in 1802. His copper and brass works grew, through sale and merger, into a large corporation, Revere Copper and Brass, Inc.[74]

Revere expanded his business interests in the years following the Revolution. His plan was to turn the day-to-day operations of his silver shop over to his oldest son, Paul, Jr. and use the profits to invest in new businesses. From 1783 to 1789 he operated a hardware store in downtown Boston where he sold locally made and imported English goods, including hammers, chisels, ink stands, looking glasses, and rolls of wallpaper. At times he operated his silver shop and hardware store at the same location. By 1788 he had opened a foundry which supplied bolts, spikes, and nails for shipyards in Boston and elsewhere (including brass fittings for USS *Constitution*), produced cannons of many sizes and, after 1792, cast bells. One of his largest bells still rings in Boston's Kings Chapel. https://www.paulreverehouse.org/biography/

Revere opened the first successful copper rolling mill in North America. He provided copper sheeting for the dome of the Massachusetts State House in 1802, and the hull of USS *Constitution* in 1803. Revere Copper and Brass, Inc., the descendent of Revere's rolling mill, is best known for "Revere Ware" copper-bottomed pots and pans. Revere Ware is now manufactured by a different company. https://www.paulreverehouse.org/biography/

Steps towards standardized production

As he shifted to ironworking, he produced more standardized products, thus reducing costs.[75] Standardization was achieved via identical molds, especially for mass-produced items.[76] His bells and cannons were all unique products: these large objects required extensive fine-tuning and customization, and the small number of bells and cannon minimized the potential benefits of standardizing them.[77] "He came to realize that the foundry oven melded the characteristics of tools and machines: it required skilled labor and could be used in a flexible manner to produce different products, but an expert could produce consistent output by following a standard set of production practices."[79]

Politics and final years

Alexander Hamilton's national policies regarding banks and industrialization exactly matched his dreams, and he became an ardent Federalist committed to building a powerful nation. Of particular interest to Revere was the question of protective tariffs; he and his son sent a petition to Congress in 1808 asking for protection for his sheet copper business.[83] In 1814 he circulated a petition offering the government the services of Boston's artisans in protecting Boston during the War of 1812.[84] Revere died on May 10, 1818, at the age of 83.[85] He is buried in the Granary Burying Ground on Tremont Street.[86][87]

His son[88] took over the copper works which continues as Revere Copper Company, with divisions in Rome, New York, and New Bedford, Massachusetts.[89]

Revere's silverware, engravings, and other works are highly regarded, and can be found in the Museum of Fine Arts, Boston[90] and Metropolitan Museum of Art.

References

1.   Gill 1891, pp. 10–11.
2.   Fischer 1994, p. 297.
3.   Triber 1998, p. 7.
4.   Triber 1998, pp. 7–9.
5.   Paul Revere Memorial Association (1988). Paul Revere: Artisan, Businessman, and Patriot--the Man Behind the Myth. Paul Revere Memorial Association. p. 21. ISBN 978-0-9619999-1-9.
6.   "Paul Revere's Ancestry". Paul Revere House.
7.   Fischer 1994, p. 9.
8.   Triber 1998, pp. 14–16.
9.   Miller 2010, p. 21.
10. "Our Change Ringing Bells | The Old North Church". November 26, 2019. Retrieved January 31, 2020.
11. "Bell Ringer's Agreement" (PDF). The Old North Church. Retrieved January 31, 2020.
12. Miller 2010, pp. 25, 103.
13. Triber 1998, p. 21.
14. Triber 1998, pp. 21–22.
15. Miller 2010, p. 33.
16. Fischer 1994, pp. 15, 297.
17. Triber 1998, pp. 38–43.
18. Fischer 1994, p. 20.
19. Miller 2010, p. 104.
20. Martello 2010, p. 55.
21. Triber 1998, p. 117.
22. Triber 1998, p. 67.
23. Triber 1998, p. 43.
24. Triber 1998, pp. 46–47.

25. Goss 1891, pp. 1:112–115.
26. Triber 1998, pp. 36, 42.
27. Fischer 1994, p. 22.
28. Fischer 1994, p. 24 and note 53.
29. Triber 1998, pp. 71–72.
30. Forbes 1999, pp. 485–487.
31. Goss 1891, p. 1:119.
32. Alexander 2002, p. 120.
33. Miller 2010, p. 163.
34. Miller 2010, p. 165.
35. Fischer 1994, pp. 27, 54, Appendix C.
36. Triber 1998, p. 101.
37. Miller 2010, p. 181.
38. Goss 1891, pp. 1:83–100.
39. New Hampshire's role in the Revolutionary War, WMUR-TV
40. Fischer 1994, pp. 52–57.
41. "10 Things You May Not Know About Paul Revere". history.com. April 16, 2013.
42. Triber 1998, p. 115.
43. Miller 2010, pp. 201–208.
44. "Early Paper Money of America, Massachusetts, 1776 October 18". Newman Numismatic Portal at Washington University in St. Louis. Retrieved June 8, 2021.
45. Jordan, Louis, Massachusetts Currency, October 18, 1776-Codfish, Colonial Currency, U Notre Dame, Dept of Special Collections, retrieved June 8, 2021
46. Martello 2010, p. 62.
47. Gettemy 1905, p. 169.
48. Triber 1998, p. 148.
49. Miller 2010, p. 214.
50. Miller 2010, p. 208.
51. Ketchum 1999, p. 195.
52. Miller 2010, p. 215.
53. Martello 2010, p. 80.
54. Miller 2010, p. 217.
55. Gettemy 1905, pp. 148–151.
56. Drake 1899, p. 128.
57. Gettemy 1905, pp. 152–153.
58. Forbes 1999, p. 343.
59. Triber 1998, p. 132.
60. Triber 1998, p. 133.
61. Martello 2010, p. 94.
62. Martello 2010, pp. 107–110.
63. Federhen 2010, p. 153.
64. Federhen 2010, p. 154.
65. Falino 2001, p. 77.
66. Martello 2010, pp. 111–114.
67. Martello 2010, pp. 151–155.
68. Martello 2010, p. 137.
69. Martello 2010, p. 154.
70. Martello 2010, p. 252.
71. Martello 2010, pp. 276, 146.
72. Martello 2010, pp. 168–171.
73. Martello 2010, pp. 179–184.
74. Martello 2010, pp. 331–332.
75. Martello 2010, p. 155.
76. Martello 2010, p. 141.
77. Martello 2010, p. 301.
78. Registration Book No.1 (1736–1797), Grand Lodge of Scotland. Pp. 127 and 188.
79. Cracking the Freemasons Code. Robert L. D. Cooper. 2006. ISBN 978-1-84604-049-8.
80. "Paul Revere Grand Master". www.mwsite.org. Retrieved October 2, 2023.
81. So, What Was in That Boston Time Capsule?, Rebecca Onion, Slate.com, Jan 6, 2015, accessed Jan 8, 2015
82. Stanwood, Edward. American Tariff Controversies in the Nineteenth Century. pg. 117
83. Miller 2010, p. 257.
84. Miller 2010, p. 258.
85. "Five Historic Cemeteries to Visit in Boston". October 21, 2016.
86. PRMA 1988, p. 33.
87. Miller 2010, pp. 255, 260.
88. "About the Revere Copper Company". Revere Copper Company. Arch March 1, 2017. Retr May 26, 2016.
89. "Boston Museum of Fine Arts Search for Paul Revere". Arch August 4, 2012. Retr April 24, 2009.

90.   "Metropolitan Museum of Art Search for Paul Revere". Metropolitan Museum of Art. Retr Jan 24, 2013.

Sources

- Drake, Samuel Adams (1899). Historic Mansions and Highways Around Boston. Boston: Little, Brown. p. 128.
- Falino, Jeannine (2001). "Pride Which Pervades thro every Class": Customers of Paul Revere. Boston, Massachusetts: University Press of Virginia.
- Martello, Robert (2010). Midnight Ride, Industrial Dawn: Paul Revere and the Growth of American Enterprise. Johns Hopkins Studies in the History of Technology. Baltimore: The Johns Hopkins University Press.
- Miller, Joel J. (2010). Revolutionary Paul Revere. Nashville: Thomas Nelson. ISBN 978-1-59555-074-3.
- Paul Revere, Artisan, Businessman Patriot: Man Behind the Myth. Boston: Paul Revere Memorial Association (PRMA). 1988.
- Revere, Paul (1961). Paul Revere's Three Accounts of His Famous Ride. Introduction by Edmund Morgan. Boston: Massachusetts Historical Society. ISBN 978-0-9619999-0-2.
- Triber, Jayne (1998). A True Republican: Life of Paul Revere. Amherst, Mass: U of Mass Press. ISBN 978-1-55849-139-7.
- United States, National Archives and Records Service. Papers of the Continental Congress, 1774–1789. National Archives and Records Administration, General Services Administration.

ELBRIDGE GERRY

SIGNATORY OF TWO FOUNDATIONAL DOCUMENTS

Elbridge Gerry (July 17, 1744 – November 23, 1814) was an American Founding Father, merchant, politician, and diplomat who served as the fifth vice president of the United States under President James Madison from 1813 until his death in 1814.[1] He is known to be the father of the political practice of gerrymandering.[2]

Gerry was born on July 17, 1744, in the North Shore town of Marblehead, Massachusetts. His father, Thomas Gerry (1702–1774), was a merchant who operated ships out of Marblehead, and his mother, Elizabeth (Greenleaf) Gerry (1716–1771), was the daughter of a successful Boston merchant.[4] Gerry's first name came from John Elbridge, one of his mother's ancestors.[5] Gerry's parents had 11, Elbridge was the third.[6] He entered Harvard College shortly before turning 14. After receiving a Bachelor of Arts degree in 1762 and a Master of Arts in 1765, he entered his father's merchant business. By the 1770s, the Gerrys numbered among the wealthiest Massachusetts merchants, with trading connections in Spain, the West Indies, and the North American coast.[4][7] Gerry's father, emigrated from England in 1730, was active in local politics and had a leading militia role.[8]

Colonial business and politics

Gerry was from an early time a vocal opponent of Parliamentary efforts to tax the colonies after the French and Indian War ended in 1763. In 1770, he sat on a Marblehead committee to enforce importation bans on taxed British goods. He communicated with other opponents of British policy, including Samuel Adams, John Adams, Otis Warren, and others.[4]

In May 1772, he won election to the Great and General Court of the Province of Massachusetts Bay, which served as the state's legislative assembly. He worked closely with Samuel Adams to advance colonial opposition to Parliamentary colonial policies. He established Marblehead's committee of correspondence, one of the first to be set up after that of Boston.[9] An incident of mob action prompted him to resign the next year. Gerry and other Marbleheaders had established a hospital for smallpox inoculations on Cat Island. Because transmission of the disease was not known, fears amongst the local population led to protests and violence that wrecked the hospital and other properties.[10]

Gerry reentered politics after the Boston Port Act closed that city's port in 1774, and Marblehead became an alternative port to which relief supplies from other colonies could be delivered. As one of the town's leading merchants and Patriots, Gerry played a major role in ensuring the storage and delivery of supplies from Marblehead to Boston, interrupting those activities only to care for his dying father. He was elected as a representative to the First Continental Congress in September 1774, but declined, still grieving the loss of his father.[11]

American Revolution

Gerry was elected to the provincial assembly, which reconstituted itself as the Massachusetts Provincial Congress after Governor Thomas Gage dissolved the body in October 1774.[12] He was assigned to its committee of safety, responsible for ensuring that the province's limited supplies of weapons and gunpowder did not fall into British hands. His actions were partly responsible for the storage of weapons and ammunition in Concord; these stores were the target of the British expedition that sparked the start of the American Revolutionary War with the battles of Lexington and Concord in April 1775.[13] (Gerry was staying at an inn at Menotomy, now Arlington, when the British Army marched through on the night of April 18.)[14] During the Siege of Boston that followed, Gerry continued to take a leading role in supplying the nascent Continental Army, something he would continue to do as the war progressed.[15] He leveraged business contacts in France and Spain to acquire munitions, and supplies of all types, and was involved in the transfer of financial subsidies from Spain to Congress. He sent ships to ports all along the American coast and dabbled financing privateers against British shipping.[16]

He spoke out against price gouging and in favor of price controls, although his war-related merchant activities increased the family's wealth.[17]

Gerry served in the Second Continental Congress in Philadelphia from February 1776 to 1780, when matters of the ongoing war occupied the body's attention. He was influential in convincing several delegates to support passage of the Declaration of Independence. John Adams wrote of him, "If every Man here was a Gerry, the Liberties of America would be safe against the Gates of Earth and Hell."[19] He was implicated as a member of the so-called "Conway Cabal", a group of Congressmen and military officers who were dissatisfied with the performance of General George Washington during the 1777 military campaign. However, Gerry took Pennsylvania leader Thomas Mifflin, one of Washington's critics, to task early in the episode and specifically denied knowledge of any sort of conspiracy against.[20]

Gerry's political philosophy was one of limited central government, and he regularly advocated for the maintenance of civilian control of the military. He held these positions fairly consistently throughout his political career (wavering principally on the need for stronger central government in the wake of the 1786–87 Shays' Rebellion) and was well known for his personal integrity.[21] He opposed the idea of political parties.[22]

Gerry was convinced to rejoin the Confederation Congress in 1783, when the state legislature agreed to support his call for needed reforms.[26] He served in that body, which met in New York City, until September 1785. The following year, he married Ann Thompson, the daughter of a wealthy New York City merchant who was 20 years his junior; his best man was his good friend James Monroe.[19][27] They had ten children between, straining Ann's health.[19]

The war made Gerry sufficiently wealthy so that when it ended, he sold off his merchant interests and began investing in land. In 1787, he purchased the Cambridge, Massachusetts, estate of the last royal lieutenant governor of Massachusetts, Thomas Oliver, which had been confiscated by the state. This 100-acre property, known as Elmwood, became the family home for the rest of Gerry's life.[28] He owned shares in the Ohio Company, prompting opponents to characterize him as owner of vast lands.[29]

Constitutional Convention

Gerry played a major role in the Constitutional Convention held in Philadelphia during the summer of 1787.[30] Gerry's opposition to popular election of representatives was rooted in part by the events of Shays' Rebellion in western Massachusetts in the year preceding the convention. He sought to maintain individual liberties by providing checks on government power.[31]

He supported the idea that the Senate composition should not be determined by population; the view that it should instead be composed of equal numbers of members for each state prevailed in the Connecticut Compromise. The compromise was adopted on a narrow vote in which the Massachusetts delegation was divided, Gerry and Caleb Strong voting in favor.[32] Gerry further proposed that senators of a state, rather than casting a single vote on behalf of the state, vote instead as individuals.[33] Gerry was also vocal in opposing the Three-fifths Compromise, which counted slaves as three-fifths of a person for the purposes of determining the number of each states' votes in the House of Representatives and the Electoral College. The Southern states wanted each slave to count as a full person, whereas the Northern states did not want them to count at all. Gerry asked, why should "blacks, in the South", count toward representation "any more than the Cattle & horses of the North"?[34][35] Gerry opposed slavery and said the constitution should have "nothing to do" with slavery so as "not to sanction it."[36]

Because of his fear of demagoguery and belief the people of the United States could be easily misled, Gerry also advocated indirect elections. Although he was unsuccessful in obtaining them for the lower house of Congress, Gerry did obtain such indirect elections for the Senate, whose members were to be selected by the state legislatures. Gerry also advanced proposals for indirect elections of the President, most of them involving limiting the right to vote to the state governors and electors.[38]

Gerry was unhappy about the lack of enumeration of any individual liberties in the proposed constitution and opposed proposals that strengthened government. He was one of three delegates who voted against the constitution, the others being George Mason and Edmund Randolph."[39] Gerry refused to sign because of concerns over the rights of private citizens and the power of the legislature to raise armies and revenue.[40]

State ratification and Bill of Rights

During the ratification debates that took place in the states following the convention, Gerry continued his opposition, publishing a widely circulated letter documenting his objections to the proposed constitution.[41] In the document, he cites the lack of a Bill of Rights as his primary objection but also expresses qualified approval of the Constitution, indicating that he would accept it with some amendment.[42] Strong pro-Constitution forces attacked him in the press, comparing him unfavorably to the Shaysites. Henry Jackson was particularly vicious: "[Gerry has] done more injury to this country by that infamous Letter than he will be able to make atonement in his whole life",[41] and Oliver Ellsworth, a convention delegate from Connecticut, charged him with deliberately courting the Shays faction.[43]

One consequence of the furor over his letter was that he was not selected as a delegate to the Massachusetts ratifying convention[44] although he was later invited by the convention's leadership. Dominated by Federalists, Gerry was not given any formal opportunity to speak. He left the convention after a shouting match with chair Dana.[45] Massachusetts ratified the constitution 187 to 168.[46] The debate cost Gerry allies, including Dana and Rufus King.[47]

211

U.S. House of Representatives

Anti-Federalist forces nominated Gerry for governor in 1788, but he was predictably defeated by the popular incumbent John Hancock.[48] Following its ratification, Gerry recanted his opposition to the Constitution, noting that other state ratifying conventions had called for amendments that he supported.[49] He was nominated by friends (over his own opposition to the idea) for a seat in the inaugural House of Representatives, where he served two terms.[50]

In June 1789, Gerry proposed that Congress consider all of the proposed constitutional amendments that various state ratifying conventions had called for (notably those of Rhode Island and North Carolina, which had at the time still not ratified the Constitution).[51] In the debate that followed, he led opposition to some of the proposals, arguing that they did not go far enough in ensuring individual liberties. He successfully lobbied for inclusion of freedom of assembly in the First Amendment and was a leading architect of the Fourth Amendment protections against search and seizure.[52] He sought to insert the word "expressly" into the Tenth Amendment, which might have more significantly limited federal power.[53]

He was successful in efforts to severely limit the federal government's ability to control state militias.[54] In tandem with this protection, he had once argued against federal government controlling a large standing army, saying, "A standing army is like a standing member. It is an excellent assurance of domestic tranquility, but a dangerous temptation to foreign adventure."[55]

Gerry vigorously supported Hamilton's reports on public credit, including the assumption at full value of state debts, and supported Hamilton's Bank of the United States, positions consistent with earlier calls he had made for economic centralization.[56] Although he had speculated in depreciated Continental bills of credit (the IOUs at issue), there is no evidence he participated in large-scale speculation that attended the debate when it took place in 1790, and he became a major investor in the new bank.[57] He used the floor of the House to speak out against aristocratic and monarchical tendencies he saw as threats to republican ideals, and opposed laws and provisions he thought limited individual and state liberties. He opposed giving officers of the executive significant powers, opposing Treasury Department because its head might gain more power than the president.[58] He opposed measures to strengthen the presidency, such as the ability to fire Cabinet officers, and sought more legislative appointment power.[59]

Gerry did not stand for re-election in 1792, returning home to raise his children and care for his sickly wife.[60] He agreed to serve as a presidential elector for John Adams in the 1796 election.[61] During Adams' term in office, Gerry maintained good relations with both Adams and VP Thomas Jefferson, hoping that the divided executive might lead to less friction. The split between Federalists (Adams) and Democratic-Republicans (Jefferson) widened.[62]

XYZ Affair

President Adams appointed Gerry to be a member of a special diplomatic commission sent to Republican France in 1797.[63] Tensions had risen between the two nations after the 1796 ratification of the Jay Treaty, made between the United States and Great Britain. It was seen by French leaders as signs of an Anglo-American alliance, and France had consequently stepped up seizures of American ships.[64] Adams chose Gerry over his cabinet's opposition (on political grounds that Gerry was insufficiently Federalist), Adams described Gerry as one of the "two most impartial men in America" (Adams himself being the other).[63]

Gerry joined co-commissioners Charles Cotesworth Pinckney and John Marshall in France in October 1797 and met briefly with Foreign Minister Talleyrand. Some days after that meeting, the delegation was approached by three French agents (at first identified as "X", "Y", and "Z" in published papers, leading the controversy to be called the "XYZ Affair") who demanded substantial bribes from the commissioners before negotiations could continue.[66] The commissioners refused and sought unsuccessfully to engage Talleyrand in negotiations.[67] Believing Gerry to be most approachable of the commissioners, Talleyrand successively froze first Pinckney and then Marshall out of the informal negotiations, and they left France in April 1798.[68] Gerry, who sought to leave with them, stayed behind because Talleyrand threatened war if he left.[69] Gerry refused to make significant negotiations and left Paris in August.[70]

By then, dispatches describing the commission's reception had been published in the United States, raising calls for war.[71] The undeclared naval Quasi-War (1798–1800) followed.[72] Federalists, notably Secretary of State Timothy Pickering, accused Gerry of supporting the French and abetting breakdown of the talks, while Adams and Republicans such as Jefferson supported him.[73] Negative press damaged Gerry's reputation, and he was burned in effigy by protestors in front of his home. He was later vindicated, when his correspondence with Talleyrand was published in 1799.[62] In response to the Federalist attacks, and because of his perception that the Federalist-led military threatened republican values, Gerry joined the Democratic-Republican Party, standing for election as Governor of Massachusetts.[74]

Governor of Massachusetts

For years (in the 1800, 1801, 1802, and 1803 elections) Gerry unsuccessfully sought the governorship of Massachusetts.[76] His opponent in these races, Caleb Strong, was a popular moderate Federalist, whose party dominated the state's politics despite a national shift toward the Republicans.[77] In 1803, Republicans in the state were divided, and Gerry only had regional support of the party. He decided not to run in the 1804 election, returning to semi-retirement[78] and to deal with a personal financial crisis. His brother Samuel Russell had mismanaged his own business affairs, and Gerry had propped him up by guaranteeing a loan that was due. The matter ultimately ruined Gerry's finances for his remaining years.[79]

Gerry's first year as governor was less controversial than his second, because the Federalists controlled the state senate. He preached moderation in the political discourse, noting that it was important that the nation present a unified front in its dealings with foreign powers.[85] In his second term, with full Republican control of the legislature, he became notably more partisan, purging much of the state government of Federalist appointees. The legislature also enacted "reforms" of the court system that resulted in an increase in the number of judicial appointments, which Gerry filled with Republican partisans. However, infighting within the party and a shortage of qualified candidates played against Gerry, and the Federalists scored points by complaining vocally about the partisan nature of the reforms.[86]

Other legislation passed during Gerry's second year included a bill broadening the membership of Harvard's Board of Overseers to diversify its religious membership, and another that liberalized religious taxes. The Harvard bill had significant political slant because the recent split between orthodox Congregationalists and Unitarians also divided the state along party lines, and Federalist Unitarians had recently gained control over the Harvard board.[87]

Gerry also engaged in partisan investigations of potential libel against him by elements of the Federalist press, further damaging his popularity with moderates. The redistricting controversy, along with the libel investigation and the impending War of 1812, contributed to Gerry's defeat in 1812 (once again at the hands of Caleb Strong, whom the Federalists had brought out of retirement).[93][94] The gerrymandering of the state Senate was a notable success in the 1812 election: the body was thoroughly dominated by Republicans, even though the house and the governor's seat went to Federalists by substantial margins.[75]

Vice presidency and death

Gerry's financial difficulties prompted him to ask President Madison for a federal position after his loss in the 1812 election (which was held early in the year).[94] He was chosen by the Congressional nominating caucus to be Madison's vice-presidential running mate in the 1812 presidential election. Madison narrowly won re-election.[95] Gerry's duties included advancing the administration's agenda in Congress and dispensing patronage positions in New England.[96] Gerry's actions in support of the War of 1812 had a partisan edge: he expressed concerns over Federalist seizure of Fort Adams (Boston's Fort Independence) as a prelude to Anglo-Federalist cooperation and sought the arrest of printers of Federalist newspapers.[97]

On November 23, 1814, Gerry suffered a heart attack,[98] died at 70.[99]

He is buried in the Congressional Cemetery in Washington, D.C.[100] He is the only signer of the Declaration of Independence buried in the nation's capital. The estate he left his wife and children was rich in land and poor in cash, he managed to repay his brother's debts.[99]

Gerry is generally remembered for the use of his name in the word *gerrymander*, for his refusal to sign the United States Constitution without a Bill of Rights, and for his role in the XYZ Affair and for his time as Vice President. Biographer Billias posits that Gerry was a consistent advocate of republicanism and his role in the Constitutional Convention had a significant impact on the document.

References

1. Bernstein, Richard B. (2011) [2009]. "Appendix: The Founding Fathers: A Partial List". The Founding Fathers Reconsidered. New York: Oxford University Press. ISBN 978-0199832576.
2. Bischoff, Manon. "Geometry Reveals Tricks behind Gerrymandering". Scientific American. Retr 3/26/23.
3. "The Signers". harvard.edu. Declaration Resources Project, Harvard U. Retr Feb 9, 2023.
4. Purcell, p. 46
5. Greenleaf, p. 77
6. Billias, p. 5
7. Billias, p. 4
8. Billias, p. 3
9. Austin, pp. 6–27
10. Gilje, pp. 44–45
11. Billias, pp. 42–44
12. Billias, p. 46
13. Billias, p. 49
14. Billias, p. 52
15. Billias, pp. 55–56
16. Billias, pp. 124–30
17. Billias, pp. 56, 123
18. Billias, pp. 134–35
19. Hatfield, Mark. "Vice Presidents of United States: Elbridge Gerry (1813–1814)" Senate Historical Office.
20. Billias, pp. 76–77
21. Billias, pp. 140, 152, 192
22. Billias, p. 105
23. Billias, p. 101
24. Billias, p. 102
25. "Book of Members, 1780–2010: Chapter G" (PDF). American Academy of Arts and Sciences.
26. Billias, p. 103
27. Ammon, p. 61
28. "National Register Nomination for Elmwood". National Park Service. Retrieved October 24, 2012.
29. Billias, p. 137
30. Billias, p. 158
31. Billias, pp. 153–54
32. Billias, p. 178
33. Billias, p. 182
34. Black Perspectives: A Compact for the Good of America? Slavery and the Three-Fifths Compromise
35. Billias, p. 168
36. Thomas III, William G., A Question of Freedom: The Families Who Challenged Slavery from the Nation's Founding to the Civil War. New Haven, Connecticut: Yale University Press. 2020, p. 35.
37. Billias, p. 203

38. https://www.archives.gov/publications/prologue/2006/spring/gerry.html Archived July 19, 2017, Wayback Machine "A Founding Father in Dissent, Elbridge Gerry Helped Inspire Bill of Rights in His Opposition to the Constitution".
39. Billias, p. 159, 200
40. Billias, pp. 199-201
41. Billias, p. 209
42. Billias, pp. 207–08
43. Billias, p. 212
44. Billias, p. 211
45. Billias, p. 213
46. Billias, p. 214
47. Billias, pp. 207–08, 213
48. Billias, p. 215
49. Billias, p. 207
50. Billias, pp. 216, 243
51. Billias, p. 229
52. Billias, p. 231
53. Billias, pp. 233–34
54. Billias, p. 232
55. Isaacson, Walter (2003). Benjamin Franklin: An American Life. New York, NY: Simon & Schuster. p. 456.
56. Billias, pp. 223, 237
57. Billias, pp. 240, 242
58. Billias, p. 225
59. Billias, p. 226
60. Billias, p. 243
61. Billias, p. 245
62. Purcell, pp. 51–52
63. Ferling, p. 345
64. Elkins and McKitrick, pp. 537–38
65. Stinchcombe, pp. 596–97
66. Billias, pp. 268–69
67. Billias, pp. 272–75
68. Stinchcombe, pp. 598–613
69. Billias, p. 280
70. Billias, p. 283
71. Ferling, pp. 354–57
72. Smith, p. 130
73. Billias, pp. 289–93
74. Billias, pp. 289, 301
75. Griffith, pp. 72–73
76. "Biography of Elbridge Gerry 1744–1814; American History –Revolution to Reconstruction and Beyond".
77. Buel, pp. 39–44
78. Billias, pp. 304–305
79. Billias, pp. 305–06
80. Buel, pp. 73–82, 103–04
81. Billias, p. 313
82. Buel, pp. 104–07
83. Buel, pp. 116–17
84. Formisano, p. 74
85. Buel, pp. 107–08
86. Buel, pp. 144–47
87. Formisano, p. 76
88. Hart, p. 3:458
89. Chisholm, p. 904
90. Billias, p. 317
91. Elster, p. 224
92. "Gerrymandering: You're Saying It Wrong!" Arch May 6, 2021, Wall Street Journal 5/24/18
93. Buel, pp. 148–49
94. Billias, p. 323
95. Billias, p. 324
96. Billias, p. 327
97. Morison, p. 2:57
98. "To John Adams from Rufus King, 23 Nov 1814". archive.gov. Arch on May 18, 2015. Retr May 12, 2015.
99. Billias, p. 329
100. Purcell, p. 53

Sources

- Ammon, Harry (1990) [1971]. James Monroe: The Quest for National Identity. Charlottesville: University of Virginia Press. ISBN 9780813912660. OCLC 20294950.

215

- Austin, James (1828–1829). Life of Elbridge Gerry. Boston: Wells and Lily. OCLC 3672336. Volume 2
- Billias, George (1976). Elbridge Gerry, Founding Father, and Republican Statesman. McGraw-Hill Publishers.
- Buel, Richard (2005). America on the Brink. New York: Palgrave Macmillan.
- Elster, Charles (2005). The Big Book of Beastly Mispronunciations. Boston: Houghton Mifflin.
- Ferling, John (1992). John Adams: A Life. Knoxville: University of Tennessee Press. ISBN 0870497308.
- Formisano, Ronald (1983). The Transformation of Political Culture: Massachusetts Parties, 1790s–1840s. New York: Oxford University Press. ISBN 9780195035094. OCLC 18429354.
- Gilje, Paul (1999). Rioting in America. Bloomington, IN: Indiana U Press. ISBN 9780253212627. OCLC 185656124.
- Greenleaf, James (1910). Genealogy of the Greenleaf Family. Boston: F. Wood. p. 77. OCLC 4652345.
- Morison, Samuel Eliot (2006) [1913]. The Life and Letters of Harrison Gray Otis. Kessinger Publishing. hdl:10111/UIUCOCA:lifelettersofhar02moris. ISBN 9781428606494. OCLC 706649803.
- Purcell, L. Edward (2010). Vice Presidents: A Biographical Dictionary. New York: Facts on File. .
- Roberts, Rebecca Boggs; Schmidt, Sandra K (2012). Historic Congressional Cemetery. Charleston, SC: Arcadia Publishing.

JAMES WILSON
PENNSYLVANIA
PRINCIPAL ARCHITECT OF THE EXECUTIVE BRANCH

James Wilson was a Scottish-born American Founding Father, legal scholar, jurist, and statesman who served as an associate justice of the United States Supreme Court from 1789 to 1798. Wilson was elected twice to the Continental Congress, was a signatory of the Declaration of Independence, and was a participant in drafting the U.S. Constitution, one of only six people to sign both documents.[2] A leading legal theorist, he was one of the first four Associate Justices appointed to the Supreme Court by George Washington. In his capacity as the first professor of law at the College of Philadelphia (University of Pennsylvania), he taught the first course on the new Constitution to President Washington and his Cabinet.

Early life and education

James Wilson (September 14, 1742 – August 21, 1798) was born at Carskerdo, near Ceres, Fife, Scotland, on September 14, 1742. He was the fourth of the seven children of Alison Landall and William Wilson, a Presbyterian farming family.[4] He studied at the universities of St Andrews, Glasgow and Edinburgh.[5] While he was a student, he studied Scottish Enlightenment thinkers, including Francis Hutcheson, David Hume and Adam Smith.[6] He also played golf.[7] Imbued with the ideas of the Scottish Enlightenment, he moved to Philadelphia, in British America in 1765, carrying letters of introduction that enabled him to begin tutoring and then teaching at The academy and College of Philadelphia (University of Pennsylvania). He was awarded an honorary Master of Arts.[8] In 1790, he was awarded the honorary LL.D.[8]

While tutoring and teaching, Wilson began to study law in the office of John Dickinson. Admitted to the bar in Philadelphia in 1767, he established a practice in Reading, Pennsylvania. By then he had a small farm near Carlisle, Pennsylvania, was handling cases in eight local counties, became a founding trustee of Dickinson College, and was lecturing at the academy and College of Philadelphia. In 1768 he was elected to membership of the American Philosophical Society, and from 1781 to 1783 he was the vice president of the society.[9] Wilson's religious beliefs are disputed, as there are writings from which it can be argued that he leaned towards Presbyterianism, Anglicanism, Thomism, or Deism, favoring Christianity.[10]

On November 5, 1771, he married Rachel Bird, daughter of William Bird and Bridget Hulings; they had six children together.[11]

American Revolution

In 1774, Wilson published "Considerations on the Nature and Extent of the Legislative Authority of the British Parliament."[11] In this pamphlet, Wilson argued that the Parliament had no authority to pass laws for the American colonies because the colonies had no representation in Parliament. It presented his views that all power derived from the people. Scholars considered his work on par with the works of Thomas Jefferson and John Adams. However, it was actually penned in 1768, perhaps the first cogent argument to be formulated against the authority of the Crown. Some scholars see Wilson as a leading revolutionary while others see him as a reluctant, elite revolutionary reacting to events of radicals on the ground.[12]

In 1775, he was commissioned colonel of the 4th Cumberland County Battalion[5] and became brigadier general of the Pennsylvania State Militia.[13]

As a member of the Continental Congress in 1776, Wilson was a firm advocate for independence. Believing it was his duty to follow the wishes of his constituents, Wilson refused to vote until he caucused his district. Only after he received more feedback did he vote for independence. While serving in the Congress, Wilson was clearly among the leaders in the formation of French policy. "If the positions he held and the frequency with which he appeared on committees concerned with Indian affairs are an index, he was until his departure from Congress in 1777 the most active and influential single delegate in laying down the general outline that governed the relations of Congress with the border tribes."[14]

Wilson also served from June 1776 on the Committee on Spies, along with Adams, Jefferson, John Rutledge, and Robert R. Livingston.[15]

On October 4, 1779, the Fort Wilson riot began. After the British had abandoned Philadelphia, Wilson successfully defended at trial 23 people from property seizure and exile by the radical government of Pennsylvania. A mob whipped up by liquor and the writings and speeches of Joseph Reed, president of Pennsylvania's Supreme Executive Council, marched on Congressman Wilson's home at Third and Walnut Streets. Wilson and 35 of his colleagues barricaded themselves in his home, later nicknamed Fort Wilson. In the fighting that ensued, six died, and 17 to 19 were wounded. The city's soldiers, the First Troop Philadelphia City Cavalry[16] and Baylor's 3rd Continental Light Dragoons, eventually rescued Wilson and his colleagues.[17] The rioters were pardoned and released by Reed.[18]

Wilson closely identified with the aristocratic and conservative republican groups, multiplied his business interests, and accelerated his land speculation. He became involved with the Illinois-Wabash Company during the War for Independence and was made its president in 1780.[11] He became the company's largest single investor, owning one and a half shares outright and two shares by proxy, totaling over 1,000,000 acres of land. Additionally, Wilson individually bought huge quantities of land in Pennsylvania in 1784 and 56,000 acres of land in Virginia during the 1780s. To round out his holdings, Wilson, in conjunction with 5 other men, purchased 321,000 acres of land south of the Ohio River.

During the war, Wilson took a position as advocate general for France in America (1779–1783), dealing with commercial and maritime matters, and legally defended Loyalists and their sympathizers. He held this post until his death 1798.[11]

Constitutional Convention

One of the most prominent lawyers of his time, Wilson was the most learned of the Framers of the Constitution.[20] He was one of the most prolific speakers at the Constitutional Convention, with James Madison's notes indicating that Wilson spoke 168 times, second only in number to Gouverneur Morris.[21][22] Wilson argued in support of greater popular control of governance, a strong national government, and for legislative representation to be proportional to population. To this end, he championed the popularly elected House of Representatives, opposed the Senate (and, unable to prevent its inclusion, advocated for the direct election of senators), supported a national popular vote for the selection of the president, and argued that the Constitution should be ratified directly by citizens in state conventions rather than by state legislatures.[23][24] Wilson also advocated for broader suffrage (he was, one of the few delegates who believed the vote should not be restricted only to property owners[25]) and was one of the few major Founders to articulate a belief in the principle of one man, one vote (that is, the belief that districts should each contain approximately the same number of people so that each person's vote has equal weight), which would not become a feature of American constitutional law until *Baker v. Carr* (1962).[26] As historian Nicholas Pederson puts it:[27]

"Wilson, more than any other delegate, consistently advocated placing as much power as feasible with the people—giving them as direct control as was possible over operation of the federal government's machinery...Wilson alone, who wielded formidable intellect on behalf of democracy throughout the Convention, is a major part of the reason why the Constitution ended up as democratic a document as it did."

When Wilson joined the Philadelphia Convention in May 1787, he was viewed among the legal leaders in the country. Besides Gouverneur Morris, no delegate spoke more throughout the Convention than Wilson. In the first days of the Convention, Wilson remained silent, but once he arose on May 31, he spoke every day going forward. His remarks, according to Madison's notes, established Wilson's vision for the Constitution:

"He contended strenuously for drawing the most numerous branches of the Legislature immediately from the people. He was for raising the federal pyramid to a considerable altitude, and for that reason wished to give it as broad a basis as possible. No government could long subsist without the confidence of the people. In a republican Government this confidence was essential. He also thought it wrong to increase the weight of the State Legislatures by making them the electors of the national Legislature. All interference between the general and local Governments should be obviated." https://constitutioncenter.org/blog/forgotten-founders-james-wilson-craftsman-of-the-constitution

Despite owning a household slave himself, he argued against slavery. While he remained quiet on the issue throughout the convention out of fear of alienating the pro-slavery delegates, whose support was needed to ratify the new constitution, he believed that the thrust of the constitution laid the foundation for "banishing slavery out of this country" and made certain technical objections to clauses like the Fugitive Slave Clause.[28] Ultimately, his most substantial contribution on this issue was his proposal of the Three-fifths Compromise, which would count three-fifths of each state's slave population toward that state's total population for the purposes of representation in the House of Representatives. As the Convention proceeded, he disavowed the compromise; yet it was accepted into the new constitution.[24][21]

Wilson has been credited with adding the word "We" as first word of the constitution leading to the now famous phrase "We the people. "[29]

On economics, Wilson wished to make clear that the federal government had no power to make anything but gold or silver a tender payment of debts.

Developing our Presidency and Executive Branch

Wilson has been variously called by scholars the "principal architect of the executive branch",[3] "probably the single most important author of Article II",[30] and the man whose "conception of the presidency...was in the final analysis the presidency we got".[31] Using his understanding of civic virtue as defined by the Scottish Enlightenment, Wilson was active in the construction of the presidency's structure, its power, and its manner of selection. He spoke 56 times,[31] calling for a chief executive who would be energetic, independent, and accountable.[32] Wilson, however, maintained that a single chief executive would provide for greater public accountability than a group and thereby protect against tyranny by making it plain who was responsible for executive actions. He also submitted that a singular chief executive was necessary to ensure promptness and guard against deadlock, essential in times of national emergency.[33] Wilson's unitary executive was adopted.

The executive as well as the legislative power ought to be restrained. The restraints on the legislative authority must from its nature, be chiefly internal; that is, they must proceed from some part or division of itself. This is best done, when one object only, distinguished, and responsible, is conspicuously held up to the view and examination of the public. In planning, forming, and arranging laws, deliberation is always becoming, and always useful. But in the active scenes of government, there are emergencies, in which the man, as, in other cases, the women *[sic]*, who deliberates is lost. Secrecy may be equally necessary as dispatch. But can either secrecy or dispatch be expected, when, to every enterprise, mutual communication, mutual consultation, and mutual agreement among men, perhaps of discordant views, of discordant tempers, and of discordant interests, are indispensably necessary? How much time will be consumed! And when it is consumed, how little business will be done! When the time is elapsed; when the business is finished; when the state is in distress, perhaps on the verge of destruction; on whom shall we fix the blame? Whom shall we select as the object of punishment? *James Wilson[34]*

One of the issues that most divided the convention was the method of selecting the president, with Wilson observing that the issue had "greatly divided" the Convention and was "in truth the most difficult".[35] For his part, Wilson forthrightly supported the direct election of the president through a national popular vote. He believed that a popular election would make the presidency accountable to the people,[25] and he believed more broadly that direct elections would make each branch of government "as independent as possible of each other, as well as of the states".[36] In an attempt to accommodate these objections, Wilson proposed selection by an electoral college, which would divide the states into districts in number proportional to their population, from which voters would choose electors who would in turn cast ballots for the president on their behalf.[39]

The proposal that at first received the greatest traction was one that Wilson disliked: selection by the legislature (Wilson tried to accommodate the desires of these "congressionalists" in his electoral college proposal by including a contingent election, which would hand the selection of the president to Congress if no candidate received a majority of electoral votes).[39] Yet further discussion uncovered consequences of legislative selection that many delegates considered objectionable; they worried that if the president was allowed to seek a second term (a widely supported notion), then legislative selection would make the president dependent on the legislature for re-eligibility, imperiling separation of powers.[40]

Deadlocked on the method for selecting the president, the issue was ultimately left to the Committee of Unfinished Parts (also referred to as the Committee of Postponed Parts or the Committee of Eleven[41]), which near the end of the months-long Constitutional Convention was tasked with resolving the remaining unfinished portions of the constitution. It was in this committee that an "eleventh-hour compromise", as Supreme Court Justice Elena Kagan has described it,[42] was struck, which settled on the use of an electoral college very similar to the one Wilson had earlier proposed. The committee constructed a complex structure that, with few alterations, would become the Electoral College. In this system, each state would be awarded electors equal to its number of House Representatives and Senators (this encoded within it the Three-fifths Compromise, boosting the slave states' representation in the Electoral College above their voting populations). Each state's legislature would decide the way that state's electors would be chosen, and the electors would cast votes for the presidency. In the event that no presidential candidate received a majority of electoral votes, a contingent election would be triggered, handing the selection of the president to the Senate.   After the Committee released their proposal, at Wilson's urging, the election was shifted from the Senate to the House of Representatives.[43] With this alteration, the Electoral College—embodying a "web of compromises" that functioned as a "consensus second choice, acceptable in part, by complexity of the electoral process"—was accepted.[44]

Wilson did not consider the possibility of bitterly polarized political parties. He saw popular sovereignty as the cement that held America together linking the interests of the people and of the presidential administration. The president should be a man of the people who embodied the national responsibility for the public good and provided accountability by being a highly visible national leader.[45][46][47]

Committee of Detail

Wilson's most lasting impact on the country came as a member of the Committee of Detail, which wrote out the first draft of the United States Constitution. He wanted senators and the president to be popularly elected. Along with Madison, he was perhaps the best versed of the framers in the study of political economy. He understood clearly the central problem of dual sovereignty (nation and state) and held a vision of an almost limitless future for the United States. A witness to Wilson's performance during the convention, Dr. Benjamin Rush, called Wilson's mind "one blaze of light."[48] Madison and Wilson far outdistanced the others as political theorists, and were two of the closest allies in debates and ratification effort.[49]

Though not in agreement with all of the final Constitution, Wilson stumped for adoption, and Pennsylvania became the second state to accept the document.[11]

Statehouse Yard speech

His October 6, 1787, "speech in the statehouse yard" (delivered in the courtyard behind Independence Hall) has been seen as particularly important in setting the terms of the ratification debate, both locally and nationally. During the debates, it was more influential than *The Federalist Papers*. It was printed in newspapers, and copies of the speech were distributed by George Washington to generate support for the ratification of the Constitution.[50][51] It focused on the fact that there would be a popularly elected national government for the first time. He distinguished "three simple species of government": monarchy, aristocracy, and "a republic or democracy, where the people at large retain the supreme power, and act either collectively or by representation."[52] During the speech, Wilson criticised the proposed Bill of Rights. Powers over assembly, the press, search and seizure, and others covered in the Bill of Rights were, according to Wilson, not granted in the Enumerated powers so therefore were unnecessary.[53]

Supreme Court (1789–1798)

After the ratification of the Constitution, Wilson, a learned legal mind, desired to be the first chief justice of the Supreme Court of the United States.[57] President Washington selected

220

John Jay for that position. Instead, on September 24, 1789, Washington nominated Wilson to be an associate justice of the United States Supreme Court. He was confirmed by the United States Senate on September 26, 1789,[54] and was sworn into office on October 5, 1789.[1]

American Founder, lawyer, professor, and U. S. Supreme Court Justice James Wilson supported natural and unalienable rights in his 1790-1791 *Lectures on Law* and in his 1793 court decision *Chisholm vs. Georgia*. In his *Lectures*, he observed that all human beings possess natural rights which are upheld by the universal moral law of God and Nature. He writes, …

In US Supreme Court Case *Chisholm vs. Georgia*, Wilson, like Locke, referenced ideas from Genesis 1, Ephesians 2:10, and Psalm 139:14 (in which the individual is described as "fearfully and wonderfully made"). He thus defended from the Bible a person's God-given rights that should be protected by civil government. Likewise expressing the idea of man as God's workmanship found in Ephesians 2:10, Wilson expounds, "MAN, fearfully and wonderfully made, is the **workmanship** of his all-perfect CREATOR. A State, as useful and valuable as the contrivance is, is the inferior contrivance of man and from man's native dignity derives all its acquired importance." Because the state consists of the people, Wilson asserted, if the state diminishes rights and dignity of the individual citizen, it diminishes rights of the state itself. thefounding.net/the-american-bible-based-defense-of-unalienable-rights-life-liberty-

Wilson and the other early judges spent most of their time circuit riding, overseeing cases on the circuit courts rather than on the Supreme Court bench.[19] Only nine cases were heard by the court from his appointment in 1789 until his death in 1798. Important among these was *Chisholm v. Georgia* (1793), which granted federal courts the affirmative power to hear disputes between private citizens and states. This ruling was superseded by the Eleventh Amendment, which conflicted with Wilson's view that states did not enjoy sovereign immunity from suits made by citizens of other states in federal court. Two other important cases were *Hylton v. United States* (1796), which clarified the power of Congress to levy taxes, and *Ware v. Hylton* (1796), which held that treaties take precedence over state law under the U.S. Constitution. Wilson concurred on both rulings.[55] During Wilson's last two years, on the Supreme Court bench he rode circuit in the South.[21] He served on Supreme Court until his death on August 21, 1798.[1]

Wilson became the first professor of law at the College of Philadelphia in 1790—only the second at any academic institution in the United States.[56] Wilson mostly ignored the practical matters of legal training; he viewed the study of law as a branch of a general cultured education, rather than a prelude to a profession.[56]

He assumed heavy debts investing in land that became liabilities in the Panic of 1796–1797. In debt, Wilson was briefly in a debtors' prison in Burlington, New Jersey. In 1798, he suffered malaria and then died of a stroke at age 55. He was buried in the Johnston cemetery on Hayes Plantation near Edenton but was reinterred in 1906 at Christ Churchyard, Philadelphia.

References
1. "Justices 1789 to Present". Washington, D.C.: Supreme Court of the United States. Retrieved Feb 15, 2022.
2. "Top myths about the Constitution on Constitution Day | Constitution Center". National Constitution Center – constitutioncenter.org. Retrieved December 3, 2023.
3. McConnell 2019, p. 23
4. "Wilson, James (1742–1798), revolutionary politician in America and jurist in the United States". Oxford Dictionary of National Biography (online ed.). Oxford U Press. 2004. doi:10.1093/ref:odnb/68676. Retr Jan 30, 2019. (Subscription or UK public library membership required.)
5. "Signers of the Declaration of Independence". ushistory.org. Independence Hall assoc. Arch July 10, 2015. Retr Feb 24, 2014.
6. "James Wilson". University of St. Andrews. Archived April 21, 2016. Retr Nov 30, 2012. (this source claims Wilson graduated from St. Andrews, but that is contradicted by the previous source)
7. Davies, Ross E. (2010). "The Ancient and Judicial Game: James Wilson, John Marshall Harlan, and the Beginnings of Golf at the Supreme Court". Journal of Supreme Court History. 35 (2): 122–123. doi:10.1111/j.1540-5818.2010.01237.x. S2CID 144483764. SSRN 1573857..

8. Archives and Records Center. "Penn Biographies: James Wilson (1742–1798)". archives.upenn.edu/. Philadelphia, PA: U of Pennsylvania. Arch May 23, 2016. Retr Feb 8, 2018.
9. Bell, Whitfield J., and Charles Greifenstein, Jr. Patriot-Improvers: Biographical Sketches of Members of the American Philosophical Society. 3 vols. Philadelphia: American Philosophical Society, 1997, 2:270–280.
10. Mark D. Hall, "James Wilson: Presbyterian, Anglican, Thomist, or Deist? Does it Matter?" Archived November 9, 2021, at the Wayback Machine, in Daniel L. Dreisbach, Mark David Hall, Jeffrey Morrison, Jeffry H. Morrison, eds., The Founders on God and Government (2004). p. 181, 184–195.
11. Smith 1956
12. Mark Alcorn, "James Wilson's Considerations on Nature and Extent of Legislative Authority of the British Parliament." W Political Science Assoc 2010 Annual Meeting Paper Arch 3/25/20, Wayback Machine
13. Alexander, Lucien Hugh (1906). James Wilson, Patriot, and Wilson Doctrine. Philadelphia: The North American Review. p. 1
14. Smith 1956, p. 72
15. See "The Founders' Constitution" Vol 4, Article 3, Section 3, Clauses 1 and 2, Doc 9 online Wayback Machine
16. Pennsylvania National Guard (1875). History of First Troop Philadelphia City Cavalry. Princeton U p. 17.
17. An Historical Catalogue of The St. Andrew's Society of Philadelphia. Press of Loughead & Co. Philadelphia. 1907. p. 66. Archived Nov 9, 2021. Retr Sept 5, 2018.
18. Alexander, John K. (1976). "The Fort Wilson Incident of 1779: A Case Study of the Revolutionary Crowd". The William and Mary Quarterly. 3. 31 (4): 589–612. doi:10.2307/1921605. JSTOR 1921605.
19. Marcus 2019, p. 151
20. Aaron T. Knapp, "Law's Revolutionary: James Wilson and the Birth of American Jurisprudence." Journal of Law & Politics 29 (2013): 189+.
21. Mosvick, Nicholas (July 13, 2020). "Forgotten Founders: James Wilson, craftsman of the Constitution". National Constitution Center. Archived Dec 15, 2020.
22. Wegman 2020, p. 48
23. Pederson 2010, p. 259
24. Wegman 2020, pp. 35–56
25. DiClerico 1987, p. 305
26. Marcus 2019, p. 277
27. Pederson 2010, p. 269
28. Pederson 2010, pp. 273–275
29. see https://scholarship.law.upenn.edu/faculty_scholarship Repository Citation Ewald, William, "The Committee of Detail" (2012). Faculty Scholarship at Penn Carey Law. 3228. https://scholarship.law.upenn.edu/faculty_scholarship/3228 page 247
30. McCarthy 1987, p. 689
31. DiClerico 1987, p. 303
32. Yoo 2019, p. 52
33. Yoo 2019, pp. 55–57
34. DiClerico 1987, p. 304-305
35. Keyssar 2020, p. 17
36. Keyssar 2020, p. 19
37. Amar, Akhil Reed (Nov 8, 2016). "Troubling Reason the Electoral College Exists". Time. Arch Jan 16, 2021.
38. Codrington III, Wilfred (Nov 17, 2019). "Electoral College's Racist Origins". The Atlantic. Arch Jan 29, 2021.
39. DiClerico 1987, p. 306
40. Yoo 2019, pp. 66–69
41. Keyssar 2020, p. 23
42. Kagan, Elena (July 6, 2020). "CHIAFALO ET AL. v. WASHINGTON" (PDF). supremecourt.gov. Supreme Court of the United States. p. 2. Archived Jan 18, 2021.
43. Wegman 2020, pp. 71–74
44. Keyssar 2020, p. 24
45. Taylor, Michael H.; Hardwick, Kevin (2010). "Presidency of James Wilson Arch Nov 9, 2021, Wayback Machine". White House Studies. 9 (4): 331–346
46. McCarthy 1987, pp. 689–696
47. DiClerico 1987, pp. 301–317
48. "James Wilson: A Forgotten Father," St. John, Gerald J., in The Philadelphia Lawyer, www.philadelphiabar.org.
49. Ketcham 1971, p. 191
50. Read 2000, p. 93
51. Konkle, Burton Alva. "James Wilson and the Constitution," an address to the Law Academy of Philadelphia, Nov14, 1906, published by the academy in 1907 Archive.org. Retr July 25, 2014.
52. Natelson, Robert G. (2002). "A Republic, not a Democracy? Initiative, Referendum, and the Constitution's Guarantee Clause". Texas Law Review. 80: 807 [p. 836]. SSRN 1979002. from Elliot, Jonathan,
53. Allison 2011, p.97
54. Marcus 2019, p. 147
55. McMillion, Barry J. (Jan 28, 2022). Supreme Court Nominations, 1789 to 2020: Actions by Senate, Judiciary Committee, and President (Report). Washington, D.C.: Congressional Research Service. Retr Feb 15, 2022.
56. Marcus 2019, pp. 159–166
57. "James Wilson". Biographical Directory of the United States Congress.
58. "Remembering Founding Father James Wilson, Law School Founder, on Constitution Day". Penn Carey Law School, University of Pennsylvania. September 17, 2021. Retrieved October 5, 2022.

Sources
- Allison, Robert (2011). American Revolution: A Concise History. NY: Oxford U Press. ISBN 978-0195312959.
- DiClerico, Robert E. (Spring 1987). "James Wilson's Presidency". Presidential Studies Quarterly. 17 (2): 301–317. JSTOR 40574453 – via JSTOR.
- Ketcham, Ralph (1971). James Madison: A Biography. U Press of Virginia. ISBN 9780945707332.
- Keyssar, Alexander (2020). Why Do We Still Have Electoral College? Harvard U Press.
- Marcus, Maeva (2019). "Wilson as a Justice". In Barnett, Randy E. (ed.). The Life and Career of Justice James Wilson (PDF). Washington, D.C.: Georgetown Center for Constitution. pp. 180–204. ISBN 978-1-7341939-2-3.
- Pederson, Nicholas (January 2010). "The Lost Founder: James Wilson in American Memory". Yale Journal of Law & the Humanities. 22 (2) – via Yale Law School Legal Scholarship Repository.
- Read, James H. (2000). Power Versus Liberty: Madison, Hamilton, Wilson, and Jefferson. Charlottesville: University Press of Virginia. ISBN 978-0-8139-1911-9.
- Smith, Charles Page (1956). James Wilson, Founding Father, 1742–1798. Chapel Hill: North Carolina Press.
- Wegman, Jesse (2020). Let People Pick the President: Case for Abolishing the Electoral College. New York: St. Martin's Press.
- Yoo, Christopher S. (2019). "James Wilson as the Architect of the American Presidency". In Barnett, Randy E. (ed.). The Life and Career of Justice James Wilson (PDF). Washington, D.C.: Georgetown Center for the Constitution. pp. 51–77.

GEORGE WYTHE

Mentored Thomas Jefferson, John Marshall, and Henry Clay

- He taught at the College of William and Mary
- Wythe was a delegate to the Second Continental Congress
- He was the first Virginian to sign the Declaration of Independence.
- Wythe was a delegate to the 1787 Constitutional Convention
- Wythe helped ensure that Virginia ratified the Constitution.
- Wythe was a judge on Virginia's high court from 1789 until his death in 1806.
- In Commonwealth v. Caton, Wythe introduced judicial review in Virginia.
- Wythe became first law professor in the United States
- Wythe was an early advocate for the abolition of slavery. He freed his slaves and provided for their support until they could earn a living.

George Wythe was an American academic, scholar, and judge who was one of the Founding Fathers of the United States. The first of the seven signatories of the United States Declaration of Independence from Virginia, Wythe served as one of Virginia's representatives to Continental Congress and the Philadelphia Convention and served on a committee that established the convention's rules and procedures.

Early life and education

George Wythe (1726 – June 8, 1806)[1][2] was born in 1726 at Chesterville, the plantation operated by three generations of the Wythe family in what was then Elizabeth City County but is now Hampton, Virginia.

Career

Wythe was admitted to the bar in Elizabeth City County in 1746, the same year his mother died.[9] He then moved to Spotsylvania County to begin legal practice in several Piedmont counties. In 1747, he married Ann Lewis, the daughter of his mentor Zachary Lewis. However, his wife died on August 10, 1748."[10]

Colonial politician and mentor

Although known for his modesty and quiet dignity, Wythe eventually gained a radical reputation for his opposition to the Stamp Act of 1765 and later attempts by the British government to regulate the overseas colony. Meanwhile, Wythe maintained close friendships with successive Governors Francis Fauquier and Norborne Berkeley, 4th Baron Botetourt. In 1762, college professor William Small suggested Wythe supervise the legal training of a star student, Thomas Jefferson, which had a profound impact beyond their lives.[21]

Law practice

In the summer of 1766, three events occurred that profoundly influenced Wythe, Jefferson, and several other Virginians who became Founding Fathers and insisted upon the separation of powers between three branches of the new government. When John Robinson, the powerful speaker of the House of Burgesses, died, his estate was nearly insolvent (with many debts, as well as outstanding loans), and the accounts Robinson kept as treasurer were irregular. Instead of destroying redeemed paper currency after the French and Indian War, Robinson lent it to his political supporters (fellow southern Virginia planters). Robinson's executors kept the names of the politically powerful loan beneficiaries secret for decades but did not manage to end the John Robinson estate scandal.[22]

On June 20, 1766, Colonel John Chiswell (father of Robinson's widow and business partner of Robinson), Governor Fauquier, and William Byrd III killed merchant Robert Routledge (to whom he owed money) at the Cumberland Court House. Indicted for murder, Chiswell was brought under armed guard to Williamsburg for trial in the next session of the General Court (which included many men from distant counties who also served as Burgesses and was thus usually held at the same time). Before the group reached the Williamsburg jail, three judges (John Blair, Presley Thornton, and Byrd) stopped them on the street and allowed Chiswell to post bail until September, since the next court session began in October.

Wythe continued his thriving legal practice with Jefferson's assistance. In 1767, Wythe introduced Jefferson to the bar of the General Court, and Jefferson was appointed clerk to the House of Burgesses. The following year, Wythe wrote the colony's London agent to secure copies of the burgesses' complete journals from the colony's founding until 1752, which were supposed to be transmitted annually to the king, secretary of state, and Lords of Trade, stressing "it be not made public nor attended with great expense."[29] The secrecy may have related to continuing unrest in Massachusetts against the Townshend Acts or the administrative interregnum between Fauquier's death in March and Botetourt's arrival in October.[30]

Botetourt arrived on October 26, 1768, as Virginia's first governor to rule the colony in person in sixty years. Although Botetourt dissolved the House of Burgesses the following spring, following a royal order to all colonial governors after protests in Massachusetts against the Townshend Acts, Wythe managed to stave off the governor's clerk so the delegates could publish a resolution of protest before receiving the dissolution order.[31] The burgesses then repaired to the Raleigh Tavern, where they passed the Virginia Nonimportation Resolutions on May 18, 1769. Some speculate that Wythe's status as clerk kept his name off that document. In any event, the burgesses held a spectacular party for Botetourt that Christmas and his funeral ceremonies were the most elaborate in Virginia's history. They also voted for a marble statue of the governor to be erected at public expense.[32]

Revolution

The next royal governor, John Murray, 4th Earl of Dunmore, brought Wythe and Virginia to the brink of revolution. Dunmore arrived in Williamsburg from New York on September 26, 1771.[33] Although some cheered his military offensive against the Indians (later known as Lord Dunmore's War) as strengthening Virginia's land claims, Wythe, Jefferson, and many others took offense at Dunmore's haughty personality.[34] Dunmore attempted to govern without the burgesses, but counterfeiting and other money troubles forced him to convene the assembly in early 1773. Delegates began by voicing concerns that suspects who burned the revenue vessel *Gaspee* in Rhode Island could be tried in England. When on March 1773, they established a Committee of Correspondence, Dunmore prorogued (postponed) the assembly.[35] Moreover, Parliament passed the Tea Act in May 1773, and on December 16, the Sons of Liberty instigated the Boston Tea Party. Dunmore tried to reconvene the delegates the following May. On May 24, 1774, the House of Burgesses passed a resolution declaring June 1 as a day of fasting and prayer, which Wythe signed and posted. Enraged, Dunmore dissolved the assembly. The delegates conducted business at Raleigh Tavern and met again in mid-March in Richmond.

Wythe attended the Second Virginia Convention as Williamsburg's representative. The meeting was held in St. John's Episcopal Church. Patrick Henry stirred the delegates with his "Give me liberty or give me death!" speech. The delegates agreed to convene militia, and the prospect of armed resistance caused Dunmore to try to remove gunpowder stores from Williamsburg to Royal Navy ships stationed offshore. Wythe enlisted in the militia immediately upon returning home.[35] In the Gunpowder Incident of April 20, 1775, Peyton Randolph, Robert Carter Nicholas, and Carter Braxton helped defuse Henry's attempt to force the return of the gunpowder by negotiating payment from Dunmore.

On May 10, 1775, the Second Continental Congress convened in Philadelphia. When war seemed inevitable, Wythe was elected as Virginia's delegate to replace George Washington, who took command of the Continental Army. George and Elizabeth Wythe moved to Philadelphia by September and were inoculated against smallpox, as were fellow delegate Francis Lightfoot Lee and his lady and others. By October, Jefferson rejoined the Congress to work with his former teacher and delegates, although personal tragedy forced him to leave for five months in the winter and spring. Wythe accepted many assignments relating to the military, currency, and other matters. He, John Dickinson, and John Jay went to New Jersey and convinced that colony's assembly to show a united front.[37]

When petitions and other attempts failed to resolve the crisis by the following summer while Dunmore's raiders harassed Virginia settlements from its waterways, Wythe moved and then voted in favor of the resolution for independence that Jefferson had drafted upon his return. His fellow Virginia delegates in Philadelphia held Wythe in such esteem that they left the first space open for him when they signed the Declaration of Independence.[38] Moreover, John Adams, who did not like many Virginians, thought so highly of Wythe that he wrote "Thoughts on Government" concerning the establishment of postwar constitutions for state governments.[39][40] Earlier in the session, Wythe had also exchanged humorous verses with his friend and delegate William Ellery of Rhode Island despite their political differences.[41] Wythe signed the Declaration of Independence upon return to Philadelphia. The signers' names were not made public until the following January, for all knew the declaration was an act of treason, punishable by death, should they fail.[42]

During the war, Virginia became a battleground between Patriot and Loyalist forces. The farmer to whom he had leased Chesterville, Hamilton Usher St. George, was secretly a Loyalist, though he was acquitted of charges of being a British spy on April 23, 1776.[43][44] St. George supported British raiding parties based in Portsmouth, which targeted local plantations as well as Williamsburg and other colonial settlements along the James River in raids such as the skirmish at Waters Creek. In January 1781, Benedict Arnold led 1,600 American Legion troops, which forced Jefferson to flee Richmond and burned the fledgling state capital, destroying many colonial records. Just weeks earlier, on New Year's Eve, Wythe had reportedly helped scare another British raiding party back to their ship.[45] Finally, four boatloads of neighbors attacked St. George at his house on Hog Island on September 21, 1781, forcing him to flee to Chesterville, then to New York, and ultimately to England. Chesterville sustained damage before Wythe evicted Mrs. St. George to move into the house with Elizabeth while French troops occupied their Williamsburg home.[46] During Yorktown leading to General Cornwallis' surrender, American and French troops camped at Williamsburg, and Count Rochambeau, and occupied the George Wythe house. On December 21, 1781, a fire burned down the Governor's Palace and destroyed the college wing, which included Wythe's beloved library and physics instruments.[47][48]

Founding Father

Hurrying back to Virginia from Philadelphia, on June 23, 1776, Wythe began helping Virginia establish its new state government. Virginia's constitutional convention had begun months earlier (and had voted on May 15 to instruct its federal delegates to move toward a declaration of independence).[49][50] Despite late arrival, Wythe served on a committee with George Mason, which jointly designed the Seal of Virginia, inscribed with the motto *Sic Semper Tyrannis*, which remains today. The reverse shows three Roman goddesses, Libertas surrounded by Ceres and Aeternitas.[51][52][53]

Wythe's most noteworthy contributions in establishing the new state government began when he again returned from Philadelphia that winter. Wythe served on a committee with Jefferson and Edmund Pendleton to revise and codify its laws and helped establish the new state court system. Although few of their more than 100 proposed bills were passed, some concepts, such as religious freedom, public records access, and public education, became important in the new republic, as did the idea of intermediate appellate courts.[54][55] When a fall incapacitated Pendleton, Jefferson and Wythe redrafted his portion (much to Pendleton's dismay). Wythe also replaced Pendleton as speaker of the Virginia House of Delegates, (1777–1778).

Wythe continued working to establish the nation. In 1787, Wythe became a Virginia delegate to Constitutional Convention. Fellow delegate William Pierce considered Wythe "one of the most learned legal Characters of the present age" and known for his "exemplary life," but "no great politician" because he had "too favorable opinion of Men."[56][57] Wythe, Hamilton, and Charles Pinckney served on the committee of the convention's rules and procedures.

Teacher

Wythe's teaching career began with his appointment in 1761 to the Board of Visitors of the College of William & Mary. It often overlapped and drew upon his legal and judicial careers. For more than twenty years, Wythe taught many legal apprentices, as well as students at the college. Among the most famous were future presidents Jefferson and James Monroe; future senators Henry Clay, Littleton Waller Tazewell, and John Breckinridge; future Virginia judges St. George Tucker and Spencer Roane; future Chief Justice of the Supreme Court John Marshall; and future Associate Justice of the Supreme Court Bushrod Washington.

In 1779, Governor Jefferson appointed Wythe to the newly created Chair of Law and Police, making Wythe the first law professor in the United States.[59] As a law professor, Wythe introduced a lecture system based on the Commentaries published by William Blackstone, as well as Matthew Bacon's New Abridgement of the Law, and Acts of Virginia's Assembly. Wythe also developed experiential tools, including moot courts and mock legislative sessions, which are still used today.[60] However, apprenticeship remained the main mode of learning law in that era, followed by examination before several practicing lawyers.[61]

Virginia judge

Although Wythe served as what would now be called a Justice of the Peace during colonial times, his reputation as the "American Aristides"[65] derived from Wythe's judicial service after Virginia became a state and his scholarship. The oath Wythe drafted for its admiralty judges indicates his judicial philosophy, "You shall swear that ... you will do equal right to all manner of people, great and small, high and low, rich and poor, according to equity and good conscience, and the laws and usages of Virginia, without respect to persons   And, finally, in all things belonging to your said office, during your continuance therein you shall faithfully, justly and truly, according to the best of your skill and judgment, do equal and impartial justice, without fraud, favor or affection, or partiality."[66] Wythe designed the chancery court seal to illustrate punishment of Persian judge Sisamnes, killed and skinned for taking a bribe.[67]

In 1777, Wythe became one of three judges on the newly formed High Court of Chancery. Administering equity and developing that branch of law became his mission for the rest of his life.[68] Wythe was elected to serve as a federal judge on the Court of Appeals in Cases of Capture in 1780, but he declined to serve.[69][70] Wythe particularly despised lawyers who protracted litigation at great cost to the parties, though to their benefit, and in his last days, he regretted the delays placed upon those seeking justice from his court.[71] In the judicial reorganization of 1788, Wythe became sole judge of the Chancery Court of Virginia, refusing to be promoted with Edmund Pendleton to the Supreme Court of Appeals. Both men refused offers from President Washington of judgeships on new federal courts. Their colleague John Blair accepted appointment to the United States Supreme Court.[72] The legislature created two more territorial Chancery Courts, but Wythe remained in Richmond.[73]

In the 1782 *Commonwealth v. Caton*[74] opinion, Wythe upheld judicial review of legislative actions, in what became a predecessor to Justice Marshall's decision in Marbury v. Madison. After Virginia courts had convicted Caton and two other men of treason, they appealed to the legislature for pardons. The House of Delegates approved their pardon request, but the state Senate refused. Wythe decided the court had the right to review that pardon and that the judiciary was obliged to "say to them, here is the limit of your authority; and hither, shall you go, but no further."[75] Pendleton and Blair agreed with judicial review, although on different grounds. After the decision, both legislative houses pardoned the men.[76]

However, Chancellor Wythe's decisions were often modified or overruled, particularly by the appeals court that his former student Spencer Roane joined in 1794. In 1795, Wythe published analyses of some of his cases and subsequent appellate decisions and added more pamphlets later.[77] Although this publication offended Pendleton, he decided against replying in kind.[78] One of Wythe's most famous decisions (unpopular at the time), *Page v. Pendleton,* upheld the authority of the 1783 federal peace treaty with Great Britain, which required debts to British merchants be paid under the contract terms. However, Virginia passed a law allowing payment in depreciated paper currency.

In *Roane v. Innes,* Wythe upheld Revolutionary War soldiers' pension claims but was reversed. Pendleton died in 1803, just before he could deliver an opinion attempting to reverse Wythe in *Turpin v. Lockett,* which dealt with selling the disestablished church's glebe lands, nominally at least to support the poor.[79]

In 1790, he received the LL.D. from the College of William & Mary.
In his will, Wythe left his large book collection to Thomas Jefferson. This was part of the collection that Jefferson later sold to create the Library of Congress.

Places associated with Wythe remain preserved today, and over the centuries, other places have been named in his honor:

- The Marshall-Wythe School of Law at the College of William & Mary.
- George Wythe University in Salt Lake City, Utah.

References

1. Wythe's exact date of birth is not known. Hemphill, William Edwin, "George Wythe the Colonial Briton: A Biographical Study of the Pre-Revolutionary Era in Virginia," PhD diss., University of Virginia, 1937, 31.
2. Tyler, Lyon G., "Ancestry of George Wythe, LL. D.," William and Mary College Quarterly 2, no. 1 (July 1893), 69. Wythepedia. Retrieved January 20, 2022.
3. usconstitution.net Notes on the Constitution, U.S. Constitution
4. Virginia's Attitude Toward Slavery and Secession by Beverley Bland Munford pg. 102
5. Munford, Beverley Bland (1914). Virginia's Attitude Toward Slavery and Secession - Beverley Bland Munford - Google Books. L.H. Jenkins, Edition Book Manufactures. ISBN 9780722298015. Retrieved 2022-09-14.
6. Dill, p. 5.
7. Dill, p. 12, indirectly citing George Wythe Mumford.
8. "George Wythe". Colonial Williamsburg. Retrieved April 9, 2017.
9. Dill, p. 10.
10. Dill, p. 3.
11. Dill, pp. 12–15.
12. Brown, pp. 38–39.
13. Stanard, p. 133.
14. Stanard, pp. 135, 137, 139, 140–146.
15. Brown, pp. 47–48 argues that Wythe served as a burgess from Elizabeth City Country during 1756 and the College of William & Mary in 1758, but Chiswell defeated Wythe for the Williamsburg seat, and he also lost the Elizabeth City County election.
16. Kirtland, p. 89.
17. Stanard, pp. 146–154.
18. Dill, p. 15.
19. Stanard, pp. 154–179.
20. Brown, p. 36, citing William Meade, Old Churches, Ministers and Families of Virginia (Vol. 1)(Philadelphia 1856) p. 238 and a eulogy by Parson Weems reprinted in R.D. Anderson, "Chancellor Wythe and Parson Weems," William and Mary Quarterly series 1, vol. 25 (July 1916) pp. 13–19.
21. Brown, pp. 75–79.
22. Kirtland, p. 63.
23. Kirtland, pp. 66-71.
24. Kirtland, p. 73.
25. Kirtland, p. 82.
26. Kirtland, pp. 82–83.
27. Kirtland, p. 84. Since Routledge died intestate without heirs, his estate ultimately became a substantial endowment for Hampden–Sydney College.
28. Kirtland, p. 86, quoting Marcus Fabius and Marcus Curtius, "To Metriotes," Virginia Gazette (P&D), 12 September 1766.
29. Brown, pp. 85–86.
30. Brown, pp. 97–100. Wythe was Fauquier's executor with Robert Carter III.
31. Kirtland, pp. 95–96.
32. Brown, pp. 100–101.
33. Brown, p. 101 citing Griffith, Virginia House of Burgesses, p. 51.
34. Brown, p. 101.
35. Brown, pp. 102–103.
36. "Key to Trumbull's picture", AmericanRevolution.org
37. Brown, p. 121.
38. Dill, p. 1.
39. Brown, pp. 114–116.
40. Kirtland, p. 104.
41. Brown, pp. 149–157.
42. Brown, p. 144.
43. Brown, pp. 93–94, 103–104, 143.
44. Kirtland, p. 9.
45. Brown, p. 228.
46. Brown, p. 210.
47. Brown, pp. 210–212.
48. Kirtland, pp. 128–129.
49. Kirtland, p. 106.
50. Brown, pp. 140–141.
51. Kirtland, pp. 107-108.
52. Brown, p. 142.
53. Dunn, Susan, Dominion of Memories: Jefferson, Madison & Decline of Virginia (NY: Basic Books, 2007) p. 31.

54. Kirtland, pp. 110–118.
55. Brown, pp. 174–196.
56. Kirtland, p. 5.
57. Ferrand, Max, The Records of the Federal Convention of 1787, Vol. III p. 94
58. Brown, p. 220.
59. Courthouse History, U.S. District Court, Washington, DC Archived 2009-08-26 at the Wayback Machine
60. Brown, p. 203.
61. Kirtland, pp. 155–158.
62. Brown, p. 88.
63. Brown, p. 227.
64. William & Mary Quarterly, series I, Vol. 6, pp. 182–183.
65. Brown, p. 225.
66. Strahan, Thomas W., Retainer from the Lord (Iowa, 1976) p. 34.
67. Noonan, p. 31.
68. Kirtland, pp. 172–188.
69. Library of Congress, Journals, Vol. 16, 79.
70. Library of Congress, Journals, Vol. 16, 254.
71. Kirtland, pp. 183, 187.
72. Brown, pp. 254–257.
73. Kirtland, pp. 180–181.
74. "Commonwealth v. Caton 1782". Virginia1774.org. Retrieved 2013-09-11.
75. Stanard, p. 39.
76. Brown, p. 249.
77. Kirtland, pp. 179–180.
78. Mays, p. 296.

Sources
- Brown, Imogene, American Aristides (New Jersey: Fairleigh Dickinson University Press 1981)
- Dabney, Virginius, Richmond: The Story of a City, (Charlottesville: U Press of Virginia, rev. ed. 1990).
- Dill, Alonzo Thomas, George Wythe, Teacher of Liberty (Williamsburg, 1979)
- Kirtland. Robert Bevier, George Wythe: Lawyer, Revolutionary Judge, University of Michigan thesis, 1983 (University microfilms available through ProQuest)
- Kolchin, Peter, American Slavery, 1619–1977, New York: Hill and Wang, 1993.
- Mays, David J., Edmund Pendleton (Harvard University Press, 1953) vol. II
- Noonan Jr., John T., Persons, and Masks of Law (New York: Farrar Straus, 1976)
- Stanard, William G. and Mary Newton Stanard, The Virginia Colonial Register (Albany, NY: Joel Munsell's Sons Publishers, 1902). OCLC 253261475, Retrieved July 15, 2011.

GOUVERNEUR MORRIS

PENNSYLVANIA
PENMAN OF THE US CONSTITUTION
WROTE PREAMBLE TO UNITED STATES CONSTITUTION

Gouverneur Morris was an American statesman, a Founding Father of the United States, and a signatory to the Articles of Confederation and the United States Constitution. He wrote the Preamble to the United States Constitution and has been called the "Penman of the Constitution".[2] While most Americans still thought of themselves as citizens of their respective states, Morris advanced the idea of being a citizen of a single union of states.[3] He was also one of the most outspoken opponents of slavery among those at the Constitutional Congress. He represented New York in the United States Senate from 1800 to 1803.

Early life

Gouverneur Morris (January 31, 1752 – November 6, 1816) was born on January 31, 1752, the son of Lewis Morris Jr. (1698–1762) and his wife, Sarah Gouverneur (1714–1786). Morris's mother was from a Huguenot family that moved to Holland, then New Amsterdam.[4] In Dutch and French, *Gouverneur* means Governor.

Morris's half-brother Lewis Morris was a signer of the Declaration of Independence. Another half-brother, Staats Long Morris, was a Loyalist major-general in the British Army

229

during the American Revolution, and Morris's grandfather, Lewis Morris, was the chief justice of New York and British governor of New Jersey.

Gouverneur Morris was born on the family estate, Morrisania, on the north side of the Harlem River. Morris, a gifted scholar, enrolled at King's College (now Columbia University) at age 12. He graduated in 1768 and received a master's degree in 1771. He studied law with Judge William Smith and attained admission to the bar in 1775.

Career

On May 8, 1775,[5] Morris was elected to represent his family household in southern Westchester County (now Bronx County), in the New York Provincial Congress. As a member of the congress, he, along with most of his fellow delegates, concentrated on turning the colony into an independent state. His advocacy of independence brought him into conflict with his family, as well as with his mentor, William Smith, who abandoned the Patriot cause when it pressed independence. Morris was a member of the New York State Assembly,1777–78. After the Battle of Long Island, the British seized New York City.

Continental Congress

Morris was appointed as a delegate to the Continental Congress and took his seat in Congress on 28 January 1778. He was selected to a committee coordinating reforms of the military with George Washington. After witnessing the army encamped at Valley Forge, he was so appalled by the conditions of the troops that he became the spokesman for the Continental Army in Congress and subsequently helped enact substantial reforms in its training, methods, and financing. He signed the Articles of Confederation in 1778 and was its youngest signatory.

In 1778, when the Conway Cabal was at its peak, some members of the Continental Congress attempted a no-confidence vote against George Washington. If it had succeeded, Washington would have been court-martialed and dismissed. Gouv Morris cast the decisive tie-breaking vote in favor of keeping Washington.[6]

Lawyer and merchant

In 1779, he was defeated for re-election to Congress, largely because his advocacy of a strong central government was at odds with the decentralist views prevalent in New York. Defeated in his home state, he moved to Philadelphia, to work as a lawyer and merchant.

Despite an exemption from military duty because of his handicap, he joined a special club for the protection of New York City, a forerunner of the New York Guard.

Public office and Constitutional Convention

Morris wrote the Preamble to the United States Constitution.

In Philadelphia, he was appointed assistant superintendent of finance of the United States and served under Robert Morris.[7] He was selected as a Pennsylvania delegate to the Constitutional Convention in 1787. During the Convention, he was a friend and ally of Washington and others who favored a strong central government. Morris was elected to serve on the Committee of Style and Arrangement, a committee of five (chaired by William Samuel Johnson), which drafted the final language of the proposed constitution. Morris has been credited by most historians with authorship of the final version of the preamble, including changing the opening line "We, the People of the States" to "We, the People of the United States."[8][9] Catherine Drinker Bowen, in her 1966 book *Miracle at Philadelphia*, called Morris the committee's "amanuensis," meaning that it was his pen that was responsible for most of the draft and its final polished form.[10][11]

It is said by some that Morris was "an aristocrat to the core," who believed that "there never was, nor ever will be a civilized Society without an Aristocracy."[12][13]

Morris opposed admitting new western states on an equal basis with the existing eastern states for fear that the interior "wilderness" could not furnish "enlightened" national statesmen.[14] Madison's summary of Morris's speech at the Convention on 11 July 1787 stated that his view "relative to the Western Country had not changed his opinion on that head. Among other objections it must be apparent they would not be able to furnish men equally enlightened, to share in the administration of our common interests." His reason given: "The Busy haunts of men not the remote wilderness, was the proper School of political Talents. If the Western people get power into their hands, they will ruin Atlantic interests."[15][16]

At the Convention, he gave more speeches than other delegates, 173. As a matter of principle, he often vigorously defended the right of anyone to practice his chosen religion without interference, and he argued to include such language in the Constitution.[17] During the Convention Morris boarded at Miss Dally's boarding house, along with Hamilton and Elbridge Gerry.[18][19] Researchers believe the five-member Committee on Style and Arrangement, which included Gouv Morris, Hamilton and Madison, may have met at Miss Dally's boarding house.[20]

Opposition to slavery

Gouverneur Morris was one of the few delegates at the Philadelphia Convention who spoke openly against domestic slavery. According to James Madison, Morris spoke openly against slavery on 8 August 1787 and stated that it was incongruous to say that a slave was both a man and property at the same time.

Upon what principle is it that slaves shall be computed in the representation? Are they men? Then make them citizens and let them vote. Are they property? Why, then, is no other property included? The Houses in this city [Philadelphia] are worth more than all the wretched slaves which cover the rice swamps of South Carolina.
According to Madison, Morris felt:

The admission of slaves into the Representation when fairly explained comes to this: that the inhabitant of Georgia and S. C. who goes to the Coast of Africa, and in defiance of the most sacred laws of humanity tears away his fellow creatures from their dearest connections & damns them to the most cruel bondages, shall have more votes in a Govt. instituted for protection of the rights of mankind, than the Citizen of Pa. or N. Jersey who views with a laudable horror, so nefarious a practice.[22]

Minister Plenipotentiary to France

Morris witnessed two of history's greatest revolutions, and both had a profound influence on his idea of government. His service as a soldier and as a key member of the Continental Congress during the American Revolution convinced him that a strong central government was needed to preserve and enhance the liberties and boundless opportunities won in the war. As ambassador to Paris during the cataclysmic French Revolution, he came to fear the excesses of power that could be perpetrated in the name of liberty. Influenced by these events, he would reject what he saw as unjustified assertions of authority by his government.[51]

231

Morris went to France on business in 1789 and served as Minister Plenipotentiary to France from 1792 to 1794. His diaries during that time have become a valuable chronicle of the French Revolution and capture much of that era's turbulence and violence and document his affairs with women there. Compared to Thomas Jefferson, Morris was far more critical of the French Revolution and considerably more sympathetic to the deposed queen consort, Marie Antoinette.[23] Commenting on her grandfather's sometimes Tory-minded outlook of the world, Anne Cary Morris stated, "His creed was to form the government to suit the condition, character, manners, and habits of the people. In France, this led him to take the monarchical view, firmly believing a republican form of government would not suit the French character."[24]

Morris was "the only foreign representative who remained in his post throughout the worst days of the Terror."[25] On one occasion, when Morris "found himself the center of a hostile mob in favor of hanging him on the nearest lamppost, he unfastened his wooden leg, brandished it above his head, and proclaimed himself an American who had lost a limb fighting for liberty," upon which "[t]he mob's suspicions melted into enthusiastic cheers" (even though, as noted above, Morris had in fact lost his leg as a result of a carriage accident).[26]

While Morris was minister, the Marquis de Lafayette, who had been an important participant in the American Revolution, was exiled from France and his family imprisoned, and Thomas Paine, was arrested and imprisoned in France. Morris's efforts on their behalf have been criticized as desultory and insufficient.[27][28] After a change of the French government and after Morris was replaced as minister, his successor, James Monroe, secured Paine's release.

U.S. Senate

He returned to the United States in 1798 and was elected in April 1800, as a Federalist, to the U.S. Senate, filling the vacancy caused by the resignation of James Watson. Morris served from May 3, 1800, to March 3, 1803, and was defeated for re-election in February 1803.

Later career

He was elected an honorary member of Society of the Cincinnati.

After leaving the Senate, he served as Chairman of the Erie Canal Commission from 1810 to 1813. The Erie Canal helped to transform New York City into a financial capital, the possibilities of which were apparent to Morris when he said "the proudest empire in Europe is but a bubble compared to what America will be, in the course of two centuries, perhaps one."[29]

He was one of the three men who drew up the Commissioners' Plan of 1811, which laid out the Manhattan Street grid.[30]

Morris's final public act was to support the Hartford Convention during the War of 1812. He pushed for secession to create a separate New York-New England Confederation because he saw the war as slaveholders, who wanted to expand their territory. In the words of biographer Richard Brookhiser "The man who wrote the Constitution judged it to be a failure and was willing to scrap it."[31] Morris was elected to the American Antiquarian Society in 1814.[32]

Personal life

In 1809, at age 57, he married 35-year-old Ann Cary Randolph (1774–1837), nicknamed "Nancy," who was the daughter of Ann Cary and Thomas Mann Randolph Sr. and the sister of Thomas Mann Randolph Jr,[34] who was the husband of Thomas Jefferson's daughter, Martha Jefferson Randolph.

Death

Morris died on November 6, 1816, due to an infection.[44][45] He died at the family estate, Morrisania, and was buried at St. Ann's Church in The Bronx.[46]

References

1. Brookhiser, Richard (Spring 2002). "The Forgotten Founding Father". City Journal. New York, NY: Manhattan Institute for Policy Research. Arch 2016-03-04. Retr 2015-01-15.
2. "Documents from the Constitutional Convention and the Continental Congress". Library of Congress.
3. Wright, Robert K. Jr. (1987). "Gouverneur Morris". Soldier-Statesmen of the Constitution. United States Army Center of Military History. CMH Pub 71-25. Arch 2019-10-09. Retrieved 2009-06-02.
4. "Gouverneur Morris [1752–1816]". New Netherlands Institute. Retrieved 17 June 2014.
5. ANB "Gouverneur Morris"
6. "The True George Washington," written by Paul Leicester Ford, published by J. Lippincott, the printing of the year 1900.
7. Raphael, Ray (2009). Founders: The People Who Brought You a Nation. New York, NY: The New Press. p. 404. ISBN 978-1-59558-327-7.
8. "Historical Background on the Preamble". Constitution Annotated. Washington, DC: Library of Congress. Retr March 19, 2023.
9. Mosvick, Nicholas (June 8, 2020). "Forgotten Founders: Gouverneur Morris". Constitution Center.org. Philadelphia, PA: National Constitution Center. Retrieved March 19, 2023.
10. Bowen, Catherine Drinker. Miracle at Philadelphia. 1986 edition. p. 236.
11. Chernow, Ron. Alexander Hamilton. Penguin, 2004. p. 239.
12. "Toward An American Revolution". Cyberjournal.org. Arch 2010-06-07. Retr 2010-03-19.
13. Duff Cooper, Alfred (2001) [1932]. Talleyrand. New York: Grove Press. p. 43. ISBN 0802137679.
14. Bowen. p. 178.
15. Quoted in Amar, Akhil Reed, America's Constitution: A Biography, New York: Random House, 2005, p. 87.
16. Jon Elster, Securities Against Misrule, (2013), pp. 79–80
17. Gregg Frazer. "Gouverneur Morris, Theistic Rationalist". Allacademic.com. p. 26. Retrieved 2010-03-19.
18. "Breaking News: Long-sought receipt from the Constitutional Convention has been located – Statutes and Stories".
19. "Miss Dally's boarding house: Historic Marker Application – Statutes and Stories".
20. "Committee on Style Venue Hypothesis: Miss Dally Part IV – Statutes and Stories".
21. Robinson, Raymond H. (1999). "The Marketing of an Icon". George Washington: American Symbol. Hudson Hills. p. 117. ISBN 9781555951481. Figure 56 John Henry Hintermeister (American 1869-1945) Signing of the Constitution, 1925...Alternatively labeled Title to Freedom and the Foundation of American Government...".
22. James Madison (1787). "James Madison, The Debates in the Several State Conventions of the Adoption of the Federal Constitution vol. 5 [1827]". Retrieved 2009-07-29.
23. Antonia Fraser, Marie Antoinette:The Journey, 2002, p.476; Vincent Cronin,Louis and Antoinette, (1974), p 295
24. Anne Cary Morris, ed.,"The Diary and Letters of Gouverneur Morris; Minister of the United States to France; Member of the Constitutional Convention, etc.," (1888), Vol. I, p. 15.
25. Duff Cooper, Alfred (2001) [1932]. Talleyrand. New York: Grove Press. pp. 43–44. ISBN 0802137679.
26. Duff Cooper, Alfred (2001) [1932]. Talleyrand. New York: Grove Press. p. 44. ISBN 0802137679.
27. Whitridge, Arnold (July 1976). "A Representative of America". American Heritage. 27 (4). Retr 12 June 2019.
28. Conway, Moncure D. (1893). The Life of Thomas Paine. G.P. Putnam's Sons.
29. Will Wilkinson from the July 2004 issue (July 2004). "The Fun-Loving Founding Father: Gouverneur Morris, the First Modern American". Reason. Retrieved 2010-03-19.
30. Morris, Gouverneur, De Witt, Simeon, and Rutherford, John (March 1811) "Remarks Of The Commissioners For Laying Out Streets And Roads In The City Of New York, Under The Act Of April 3, 1807". May 7, 2008.
31. Brookhiser, Richard (2003). Gentlemen Revolutionaries: Gouverneur Morris, the Rake who wrote the Constitution. Free Press.
32. American Antiquarian Society Members Directory
33. Brookhiser, Richard (Spring 2002). "The Forgotten Founding Father". City Journal. Retr Dec 4, 2018.
34. Roosevelt, Theodore (1888). Gouverneur Morris. Boston, MA: Houghton, Mifflin, and Company. p. 340.

STEPHEN HOPKINS

SIGNER OF DECLARATION OF INDEPENDENCE
FIRST CHANCELLOR OF BROWN UNIVERSITY
FAMILY TREE TO PROVIDENCE AND PLYMOUTH
CANNON PRODUCER FOR REVOLUTIONARY WAR
PAMPHLETEER, RIGHTS OF THE COLONIES EXAMINED

Stephen Hopkins (March 7, 1707 – July 13, 1785) was a Founding Father of the United States,[2] governor of the Colony of Rhode Island and Providence Plantations, chief justice of the Rhode Island Supreme Court, and signer of the Continental Association and Declaration of Independence. He was from a prominent Rhode Island family, the grandson of William Hopkins who was a prominent colonial politician. His great-grandfather Thomas Hopkins was an original settler of Providence Plantations, sailing from England in 1635 with his cousin Benedict Arnold, who became first governor of Rhode Island colony under the Royal Charter of 1663.

Ancestry and early life

Hopkins was born in Providence in the Colony of Rhode Island and Providence Plantations, the second of nine children of William and Ruth (Wilkinson) Hopkins.[5] His grandfather William Hopkins was very prominent in colonial affairs, having served for more than 40 years as a deputy from Providence, speaker of the House of Deputies, and major.[6] His grandmother Abigail Whipple Hopkins was a daughter of Providence settler John Whipple, sister of wealthy Providence merchant Joseph Whipple, and aunt to Deputy Governor Joseph Whipple Jr.[6] His great-grandfather was Thomas Hopkins, one of the earliest settlers of Providence Plantations.[7] Thomas Hopkins was orphaned and raised by his uncle William Arnold, and he sailed to New England in 1635 with his Arnold relatives, including his cousin Benedict Arnold, who became first governor of the colony under the Royal Charter of 1663.[6][7]

The early part of Hopkins's life was spent in the wooded northern part of Providence known as Chopmist Hill, an area that became Scituate, Rhode Island.[8]. Hopkins gained skills in surveying from his grandfather Samuel Wilkinson.[8] He used his surveying skills to revise streets and create a map of Scituate, and later did the same for Providence.[10] His father gave him 70 acres when he was 19 because of his responsibility as a youth, and grandfather Hopkins gave him an additional 90 acres.[11]

Hopkins was interested in astronomy and other scientific endeavors and was involved in observation of the transit of Venus across the face of the Sun on June 3, 1769. Joseph Brown had obtained a complete set of necessary instruments, including a reflecting telescope, a micrometer, and a sextant, and an observatory was erected on a hill in Providence (later named "Transit Street" in honor of the event). The observation enabled them to very accurately determine the latitude of Providence to the nearest second of arc, after which the longitude was determined by comparing observations of the Moons of Jupiter with similar observations made in Cambridge, England.[12] He was elected to the American Philosophical Society,1768.[13]

Hopkins married Sarah Scott in 1726, the daughter of Sylvanus Scott and Joanna Jenckes, a descendant of Providence Plantations settlers Richard Scott and Katharine Marbury; youngest sister of Anne Hutchinson.[20] Richard Scott was the first Quaker in Providence.[56]

Political and mercantile pursuits

Hopkins began his public service in 1730 at age 23 when he became a Justice of the Peace in the newly formed town of Scituate, a position that he held until 1735.[14] He also became the clerk of Scituate in 1731 which he held for 11 years until moving to Providence in 1742.[15] Following his tenure as Justice of the Peace, he became a justice of the Inferior Court of Common Pleas and General Sessions from 1736 to 1746, serving as the clerk of the court for the last five of those years.[16] Other positions held during this period included president of the Town Council, deputy, and speaker of the House of Deputies.[15] In 1744, he was elected deputy from Providence, for seven years, and was speaker of the House of Deputies two years.[17]

In 1742, Hopkins sold his farm in Scituate and moved to the settled part of Providence.[10] Here he devoted much energy to commercial interests which helped Providence grow.[17] He became a merchant who built, owned, and outfitted ships, and he was part owner of the privateering vessel *Reprisal* in 1745, in partnership with John Mawney, sheriff of Providence and son of Colonel Peter Mawney.[18]

One of Hopkins's enterprises was as a manufacturer, and he became a partner with brothers Moses, Nicholas, Joseph, and John Brown in establishing the Hope Furnace.[18] This enterprise produced iron works which made pig iron and cannons for the Revolutionary War.[20] Hopkins's son Rufus managed the business four decades.[18]

Governorships

In 1755, Hopkins was elected to his first term as governor, defeating his predecessor William Greene by a small margin.[17] The year was mostly occupied with legislation and work related to the pending war with France. Braddock's defeat and the occupation of Crown Point led the colony to send forces to Albany. Late in the previous year, Hopkins and his Attorney-General Daniel Updike were delegates from Rhode Island to the Albany Congress, which convened to discuss the common defense of the collective colonies and to hold a conference with the five Indian tribes to secure their assistance in thwarting French encroachment.[17][21] He and others considered Benjamin Franklin's early plan for uniting the colonies, but the principles of the plan were rejected in both the colonies and Great Britain.[22] As the war with France developed in February 1756, the General Assembly ordered the raising of 500 Rhode Island men for the expedition to Lake George in New York.[17]

After two years in office, Hopkins was defeated by William Greene for the governorship, but Greene died in office in February 1758, and Hopkins once again became governor.[23] The most divisive political issue of the day was the use of hard money, or specie, versus the use of paper money, and Hopkins sided with paper.[24] Another issue was Newport interests versus Providence interests.[17] For several years, Hopkins was locked in a bitter rivalry with Samuel Ward of Westerly, a strong supporter of hard currency and champion of Newport, and Hopkins sued Ward for slander, putting damages at £40,000. The case was moved to Massachusetts for fair trial; the judgment went against Hopkins in 1759, and he paid the costs.[24]

In 1763, Hopkins won back the governorship, and signs of reason between the two men appeared the following year when Ward wrote to Hopkins proposing that both resign their "pretensions to the chief seat of government."[23] On the same day, without the knowledge of this letter, Hopkins wrote to Ward inviting him to accept the position of deputy governor, which had just been vacated by the death of John Gardner.[26] Neither accepted the proposal of the other, but the stage was set for cooperation.[26]

In early 1765, the Stamp Act was passed by both houses of Parliament in England. This act was a scheme for taxing the colonies, directing that all commercial and legal documents must be written on stamped paper sold at fixed prices by governmental officers, also directing that a duty be applied to newspapers. Parliament assumed the right to tax the colonies and put additional duties on sugar, coffee, and other articles, required lumber and iron from the colonies only be exported to England.[25]

The news of the act infuriated Americans, and Samuel Adams of Massachusetts invited all the colonies to a congress of delegates to meet in New York to discuss relief from the unjust taxes. The Rhode Island General Assembly passed resolutions in August 1765 following the lead of Patrick Henry of Virginia. Rhode Island's appointed stamp distributor was Attorney General Augustus Johnson, who refused to execute his office "against the will of our Sovereign Lord the People."[25] The Rhode Island General Assembly met again at East Greenwich, choosing delegates to the New York congress and appointing a committee to consider the Stamp Act.[27] The committee reported six resolutions that pointed to absolving all allegiance to the British Crown unless the grievances were removed. The Stamp Act was repealed in 1766.[28]

The Rights of Colonies Examined

In November 1764, the Rhode Island General Assembly published Hopkins's pamphlet *The Rights of Colonies Examined*.[26] This pamphlet was directed primarily at the Stamp Act and helped build Hopkins's reputation as a revolutionary leader, with its broad distribution and criticism of taxation and Parliament.[30] The text begins, "Liberty is the greatest blessing that men enjoy, and slavery the heaviest curse that human nature is capable of;" it goes on to present logical review of the relationship of the American colonies with England. Historian Thomas Bicknell called it "the most remarkable document issued during the period preceding the War of the Revolution." Massachusetts Governor Thomas Hutchinson wrote of the paper, "it was conceived in a higher strain than any that were sent out by others." It was printed widely, and Hopkins became recognized as one of the leaders of public opinion in the colonies.[29]

Chief Justice

In May 1747, Hopkins was first appointed as a justice of the Rhode Island Superior Court, whose long title was the "Superior Court of Judicature, Court Of Assize, and General Gaol Delivery."[31] In 1751, he became the third Chief Justice of this court, which he held until 1755 when he became governor.[32] Hopkins was once again appointed as Chief Justice of the court in 1770 after a total of nine years as governor; he served until October 1775 while simultaneously serving as a delegate to the Continental Congress.[33]

One of the most important events with which Hopkins dealt in final tenure as Chief Justice was the Gaspee Affair. In March 1772, Deputy Governor Darius Sessions in Providence sent a letter of concern to Governor Joseph Wanton in Newport, having consulted with Chief Justice Hopkins. Sessions expressed alarm that the British schooner *Gaspee* had been cruising the Narragansett Bay, disrupting the traffic by stopping and searching commercial ships.[34] Sessions wrote:

I have consulted with the Chief Justice thereon, who is of the opinion that no commander of any vessel has any right to use any authority in the Body of the Colony without previously applying to the Governor and showing his warrant for so doing and also being sworn to a due exercise of his office – and this he informs me has been the common custom in this Colony.[34]

Sessions went on to request that the governor take measures to bring the ship's commander into account. A chain of threatening correspondence ensued between the governor and *Gaspee*'s commander Lieutenant William Dudingston, and Dudingston's superior Admiral John Montagu. On the night of June 9–10, a party of incensed colonists attacked the vessel and burned it to the waterline.[18] Officially, Sessions was outraged at the incident and offered the colony's assistance in bringing the perpetrators to justice. To ameliorate retribution by the British, Rhode Island officials took steps to find the culprits who burned the ship.[18]

This egregious threat to local liberty prompted the colonists to form the Committees of Correspondence.[18] Loyalist Massachusetts Governor Hutchinson further aggravated colonists' by urging Britain to rescind the Rhode Island Royal Charter.[18]

Adams replied by urging Rhode Island to remain defiant, or to stall matters by appealing the creation of the royal commission.[18] The vast majority of Rhode Island's citizens were supportive of the attackers and kept quiet. A year after the incident, the royal commission was terminated without a single indictment.[18]

Continental Congress

In 1774, the First Continental Congress convened, and both Ward and Hopkins were chosen as the delegates from Rhode Island. Hopkins, at age 68, was senior to every delegate there, and only he and Benjamin Franklin had attended the Albany Congress 20 years earlier.[35] Over the previous several years, Hopkins had developed palsy in his hands, greatly affecting his ability to write. At the seating of this congress, Henry Arniett Brown wrote, "yonder sits the oldest of them all. His form is bent, his thin locks, fringing a forehead bowed with age and honorable service, and his hands shake as he folds them in his lap. It is Stephen Hopkins."[35]

Congress assembled to protest the actions of Great Britain and to secure the rights and privileges of the 13 colonies. Both Hopkins and Ward had predicted independence would only come with war. Hopkins told his associates in Congress, "Powder and ball will decide this. The gun and bayonet alone will finish the contest in which we are engaged, and any of you who cannot bring your minds to this mode of adjusting the quarrel, had better retire in time."[35]

Hopkins was again elected as a delegate to the Second Continental Congress which met on May 10, 1775, following the April attacks on Concord and Lexington.[35] This congress convened to manage the war effort, and eventually declared independence from Great Britain. In July 1775, they adopted a national postal system that was devised by William Goddard, with Benjamin Franklin appointed as the first Postmaster General. This was an idea that had already been implemented in Rhode Island a month earlier.[36] Hopkins used his influence to secure the position of commander in chief of the new navy for his brother Esek Hopkins, an appointment that proved to be unfortunate.[37]

The Colony of Rhode Island and Providence Plantations declared its absolute independence from Great Britain by a nearly unanimous vote on May 4, 1776; the Continental Congress adopted the United States Declaration of Independence two months later on July 2. Hopkins had to support his palsied right hand with his left to sign, remarking, "my hand trembles, my heart does not."[36]

John Adams appreciated Hopkins's contributions at congressional sessions:

Governor Hopkins of Rhode Island, above seventy Years of Age kept us all alive, and the flow of his Soul made all his reading our own and seemed to bring to recollection in all of Us all We had ever read. I could neither eat nor drink in those days. The other Gentlemen were very temperate. Hopkins never drank to excess, but all he drank was immediately not only converted into Wit, Sense, Knowledge and good humour, but inspired Us all.[41]

Hopkins and slavery

Stephen Hopkins was a slave owner, like the majority of the signers of the Declaration of Independence, and he mentioned five slaves in his 1760 will.[43]

Hopkins felt that bondage of self-sufficient "rational creatures" was against God's will; he also thought that unconditional freedom for some slaves would be irresponsible on his part. To this end, he refused to free his woman slave Fibbo, even though it cost him his membership in the Quaker meeting.[44] His rationale was that "she had Children that needed the Immediate Care of a Mother."[45][46]

Hopkins introduced a bill in 1774 while serving in the Rhode Island Assembly which prohibited the importation of slaves.[47] This became one of the first anti-slave trade laws in the United States,[48] pushed along by the high Quaker population.[49]

In September 1776, poor health forced Hopkins to resign from Continental Congress and return home to Rhode Island, though he remained a member of Rhode Island's general assembly from 1777 to 1779. He died at his home in Providence on July 13, 1785, at age 78.[50]

Hopkins established the College in the English Colony of Rhode Island and Providence Plantations (now Brown University) and was first Chancellor.

References

1. Romig, Walter (1973). Michigan Place Names. 081431838X: Wayne State University Press. p. 272. ISBN 9780814318386. Retrieved February 16, 2016.
2. Bernstein, Richard B. (2009). "Appendix: The Founding Fathers, A Partial List". The Founding Fathers Reconsidered. New York: Oxford University Press. pp. 176–180. ISBN 978-0199832576.
3. Manual - the State of Rhode Island and Providence Plantations (1891), p. 208-13.
4. Hopkins, Donald R. (2011). "A Slave Called Saint Jago" (PDF). Rhode Island History Journal. **69** (1). Archived from the original (PDF) on October 22, 2022. Retrieved December 17, 2020.
5. Austin 1887, p. 325.
6. Austin 1887, p. 324.
7. Moriarity 1944, pp. 224–25.
8. Bicknell 1920, p. 1078.
9. Sanderson & Conrad 1846, p. 143.
10. Sanderson & Conrad 1846, p. 136.
11. Sanderson & Conrad 1846, p. 135.
12. Arnold 1894, p. 294.
13. Bell, Whitfield J., and Charles Greifenstein, Jr. Patriot-Improvers: Biographical Sketches of Members of the American Philosophical Society. 3 vols. Philadelphia: American Philosophical Society, 1997, I:481-87.
14. Smith 1900, pp. 52–68.
15. Bicknell 1920, p. 1079.
16. Smith 1900, pp. 74–115.
17. Bicknell 1920, p. 1080.
18. Gaspee Virtual Archives 2009.
19. Merchants Satirized in Art 2009.
20. Sanderson & Conrad 1846, p. 145.
21. Sanderson & Conrad 1846, pp. 136–37.
22. Sanderson & Conrad 1846, p. 137.
23. Bicknell 1920, p. 1081.
24. Bicknell 1920, p. 1074.
25. Bicknell 1920, p. 1075.
26. Bicknell 1920, p. 1082.
27. Bicknell 1920, p. 1076.
28. Bicknell 1920, p. 1077.
29. Bicknell 1920, p. 1083.
30. Sanderson & Conrad 1846, p. 140.
31. Smith 1900, p. 129.
32. Smith 1900, pp. 149–77.
33. Smith 1900, pp. 290–325.
34. Staples 1845, p. 3.
35. Bicknell 1920, p. 1084.

36. Bicknell 1920, p. 1085.
37. Richman 1905, pp. 215–18.
38. Interactive Declaration of Independence.
39. Key to Declaration of Independence (Am Rev).
40. Key to the Declaration of Independence.
41. John Adams autobiography.
42. Bamberg & Hopkins 2012, p. 12.
43. Bamberg & Hopkins 2012, p. 13.
44. Bamberg & Hopkins 2012, p. 14.
45. Bamberg & Hopkins 2012, p. 15.
46. Bamberg & Hopkins 2012, p. 16.
47. Sanderson & Conrad 1846, p. 141.
48. Richman 1905, p. 170.
49. Richman 1905, p. 171.
50. Rogak, Lisa (2004). Stones and Bones of New England: A Guide to Unusual, Historic, and Otherwise Notable Cemeteries. Globe Pequot. p. 159. ISBN 9780762730001.

Bibliography

☐ Arnold, Samuel Greene (1894). History of the State of Rhode Island and Providence Plantations. Vol. 2. Providence: Preston and Rounds. ISBN 9781429022767.

☐ Austin, John Osborne (1887). Genealogical Dictionary of Rhode Island. Albany, NY: J. Munsell's Sons.

☐ Bamberg, Cherry Fletcher; Hopkins, Donald R. (January 2012). "The Slaves of Gov. Stephen Hopkins". New England Historical and Genealogical Register. **33**: 11–27. ISBN 978-0-7884-0293-7.

☐ Bicknell, Thomas Williams (1920). History of State of Rhode Island and Providence Plantations. Vol. 3. New York:

☐ Moriarity, G. Andrews (April 1944). "Additions and Corrections to Austin's Genealogical Dictionary of Rhode Island". The American Genealogist. **20**: 224–25.

☐ Richman, Irving Berdine (1905). Rhode Island: Study in Separatism. Boston and NY: Houghton Mifflin p.191

☐ Sanderson, John; Conrad, Robert Taylor (1846). Biography of the Signers to the Declaration of Independence. Philadelphia: Thomas, Cowperthwait & Company. Stephen Hopkins.

☐ Smith, Joseph Jencks (1900). Civil and Military List of Rhode Island,1647–1800 Providence, RI:

JOHN LANGDON
NEW HAMPSHIRE
BUILT GUNSHIPS AND PAID TROOPS

- Langdon was a member of the Continental Congress in 1775 and 1776.
- Built ships, 74 gun battleship, personally paid troops in his unit.
- Langdon was a delegate to the 1787 Constitutional Convention.
- Langdon was a member of the U.S. Senate from 1789 to 1801,
- President of New Hampshire in 1785, re-elected in 1788, 1805, and 1810.
- Langdon was also a privateer owner, and citizen-soldier.
- Personally paid the militia he organized.
- Presided the electoral college count that elected George Washington.

John Langdon (June 26, 1741 – September 18, 1819) was an American politician and Founding Father from New Hampshire. He served as a delegate to the Constitutional Convention, signed the United States Constitution, and was one of the first two United States senators from New Hampshire.

Pre-Revolution

British control of the shipping industries limited Langdon's business. He served on the New Hampshire committee of correspondence and a nonimportation committee and also attended various Patriot assemblies. In 1774, he participated in the seizure and confiscation of British munitions from Fort William and Mary.

Revolution Activity

Langdon served as a member of the Second Continental Congress from 1775 to 1776, as a member of the Marine Committee. He was one of the signatories of the U.S. Constitution. He resigned Congress in June 1776 to become an agent for Continental forces against the British and superintended construction of warships including the *Raleigh*, the *America*, and the *Ranger*. In 1777, he equipped an expedition against the British, fought in the Battle of Bennington and commanded Langdon's Company of Light Horse Volunteers at Saratoga and Rhode Island.

Langdon grew impatient with the political process. He joined militiamen who removed the gunpowder stored at the local fort before the Royal governor could seize it. In 1775 New Hampshire selected him and another leader of the gunpowder raid, John Sullivan, to attend Second Continental Congress. Langdon immediately cast his lot for independence. [11]

Langdon made an important contribution to the war effort during his year in the Continental Congress. In November 1775 he traveled to the northern front as part of a three-man committee to confer with Major General Philip Schuyler on preparations for the coming campaign. He stopped en route to investigate the situation along the Hudson River and approved the organization of the first regiment of Canadian volunteers in the Continental Army. More significantly, Congress, recognizing Langdon's maritime experiences, appointed him to the committee that oversaw the establishment of the Continental Navy. [11]

In early 1776 Langdon resigned to accept appointment as the Marine Agent for New Hampshire, the national government's primary official within the state. Employing his local contacts, he established a shipyard in Portsmouth and began work on one of the first Continental frigates, the Raleigh. While he operated his own fleet of privateers, he also supervised the construction of the Navy's first major warship, the 74-gun *America*. The most ambitious shipbuilding project in the country to that time, America, was launched near the end of the war. Another of Langdon's major responsibilities as marine agent involved supervising the importation and distribution of arms. Shipped from France to ports in New England, these vital weapons were disguised in a complicated trade deal to maintain the appearance of French neutrality. Thanks in part to Langdon's efforts they reached the regiments of the Continental Army in time for the crucial campaigns of 1777. [11]

Langdon's efforts as marine agent made it clear to him that the lack of efficient central administration was an impediment to the success of the war effort. To equip his warships, he had to spend much time persuading the various states to contribute precious resources to projects that did not promise immediate return. Even the distribution of weapons taxed his diplomatic skills to the utmost, for he had to weigh and assign priorities to the competing claims of New England governments, at the risk of losing their vital support for other projects. [11]

In 1777 Langdon assumed a more direct role in the defense of the country. Serving as speaker of the lower house of New Hampshire's legislature—a position he would hold for the rest of the war—he devoted much energy to reorganizing the state militia. Under Washington's strategic concept, the citizen-soldiers were expected to provide local security against sudden raids and to reinforce the Continental Army during specific campaigns. Langdon and his colleagues now formed the New Hampshire militiamen into two brigades. One was based in the east to protect the coast from attack by the Royal Navy and to support the other New England states. A second brigade was organized in the west to guard the frontier against attack from Canada. Langdon took command of elite infantry in General Whipple's east brigade. [11]

By September, Burgoyne's army had been halted near Saratoga, New York, by the combined efforts of continentals and various militias from New York and New England. To help break the stalemate, additional militia units were called up, including Langdon's company. They arrived in time to surround the British, cutting off retreat to Canada. On 17 October 1777 "Gentleman Johnny" Burgoyne and his entire army surrendered. Langdon witnessed this "grand scene' " as he called it, the result of the cooperative efforts of the regulars and the militia of four separate states. He also took considerable satisfaction with the fact that he had paid out of his own pocket for much of the equipment used by his militia company, saying:

"If we defend our homes and our firesides, I may get my pay; if we do not defend them, the property will be of no value to me." [11]

Political

In 1784, he built at Portsmouth the mansion now known as the Governor John Langdon House. Langdon was elected to two terms as president of New Hampshire, once between 1785 and 1786 and again between 1788 and 1789. He was a member of the Congress of the Confederation in 1787 and became president of the Constitutional Convention in 1787, serving as a member of the New Hampshire delegation. Langdon was elected to the U.S. Senate. He was elected the first president pro tempore of the Senate on April 6, 1789, and served as president pro tempore in Second Congress.

The Rhode Island campaign marked the end of Langdon's active duty. At the conclusion of the war, he declined further service in the Continental Congress but retained his seat in the state legislature. In 1785 he became president of the state, a title for New Hampshire governors. Defeated for reelection, he returned to the legislature. [11]

Langdon joined this effort when in 1787 New Hampshire appointed him to represent the state in the Constitutional Convention. In fact, he was so anxious to participate that when the legislature failed to provide funds, Langdon personally paid his own way and that of fellow delegate Nicholas Gilman. As expected from his wartime experiences, Langdon was particularly forceful in advocating centralized authority for regulation of commerce, taxation, and military matters. [11]

Following the Convention, Langdon served briefly in the Continental Congress, returning to New Hampshire later in the year to participate in the state's ratification convention. Although many feared the new government would be rejected nationally, New Hampshire's ratification, as the ninth state to do so, put the Constitution into effect. [11]

Langdon went on to serve another term as governor before resigning in 1789 to become one of the first United States senators. He presided over the Senates first session in which the electoral votes that elected George Washington our President were counted. He became one of New England's earliest supporters of the political party forming around Jefferson. Langdon had espoused a simple philosophy:

The people must grant the government sufficient authority to promote their interests but must impose sufficient controls to protect their liberties. He lived to see these ideas perpetuated in a living Constitution. [11]

During the 1787 debates in Philadelphia, Langdon spoke out against James Madison's proposed "negative" on state laws simply because he felt that should the Senate be granted this power and not the House of Representatives, it would "hurt the feelings" of House members.[1] Langdon was an ardent supporter of the drive to ratify the Constitution of the United States in New Hampshire. On June 21, 1788, it was ratified by New Hampshire by a vote of 57-47. He immediately wrote to George Washington to inform him that New Hampshire had become the ninth state, described as the "Key Stone in the Great Arch. Joshua Atherton, who campaigned against ratification, accepted the result and stated, 'It is adopted. Let us try it.'"[2]
Langdon died in Portsmouth in.[7]

References

241

1. "Avalon Project – Madison Debates – July 10". Retrieved July 30, 2016.

2. "A New Constitution for a New Nation, June 6". Nashua Telegraph. 1988.

3. Eva Gerson, "Ona Judge Staines: Escape from Washington" Arch 5/14/11, Wayback Machine, Black History,

4. "TO PASS H.R. 119, (APP. 7/9/1798, 1 STAT 578), Senate Vote #141, Jul 6, 1798". GovTrack.us. Retr 9/7/23

5. "Calvin Howard Bell Family". extract from Bell Family History. Access Genealogy. April 23, 2012. Arch Nov 4, 2011. Retr April 19, 2012. Judge Woodbury Langdon, of Portsmouth, N. H.; Delegate to the Continental Congress, 1779; President of N. H. Senate, 1784; Judge of the Superior Court of N. H., 1782–91

6. "John Langdon". The Weekly Register. June 27, 1812. p. 4. Retrieved June 8, 2024 – via Newspapers.com.

7. "North Cemetery - Portsmouth, NH". waymarking.com. Retrieved August 24, 2019.

8. Gannett, Henry (1905). The Origin of Certain Place Names in United States. U.S. Gov Printing Office. p. 181.

9. "Wisconsin Historical Society". Archived from the original on April 23, 2006. Retrieved July 30, 2016.

10. "Juan Agustin Langdon Eustis n. 20 May 1805 Baltimore, Maryland, Estados Unidos f. 18 Ago 1876 Buenos Aires, Argentina: Genealogía Familiar". www.genealogiafamiliar.net. Retrieved March 24, 2023.

11. US Army Center of Military History, https://www.history.army.mil/books/revwar/ss/langdon.htm pp100-102

NATHANIEL GORHAM
MASSACHUSETTS
SIGNER OF UNITED STATES CONSTITUTION

Nathaniel Gorham (May 27, 1738 – June 11, 1796) Starting at 15, Gorham served an apprenticeship with a merchant in New London, Connecticut, after which he opened a merchant house in Charlestown, Massachusetts, in 1759.[2] He took part in public affairs at the beginning of the American Revolution: he was a member of the Massachusetts General Court (legislature) from 1771 until 1775, a delegate to the Provincial congress from 1774 until 1775, and a member of the Board of War from 1778 until its dissolution in 1781. In 1779, he served in the state constitutional convention. He was a delegate to the Congress of the Confederation from 1782 until 1783, and also from 1785 until 1787, serving as its president for five months from June 6 to November 5, 1786, after the resignation of John Hancock. Gorham also served a term as judge of the Middlesex County Court of Common Pleas.[3]

Gorham married Rebecca Call (May 14, 1744 – November 18, 1812), who was descended from Anglicans.[4] They were the parents of nine children.[5]

Nathaniel Gorham was a self-made businessman who contributed significantly to the success of the Revolution by assuming a key role as a civilian in the management of his state's military affairs. Gorham's practical experiences in commercial matters led him to realize that a strong central government would benefit the nation economically.[15]

CAREER BEFORE THE CONSTITUTIONAL CONVENTION. Gorham was the son of a packet-boat operator and member of an Old Bay Colony family of modest means. He received little formal education, but was apprenticed at age fifteen to Nathaniel Coffin, a merchant in New London, Connecticut. Gorham succeeded in business because of personal ability rather than family prominence. Already well known in Charlestown by 1770, he began his public career as a notary, soon winning election to the colonial legislature (1771-75) where he emerged an ardent Patriot. He served on the Board of War, which organized Massachusetts' military logistics and manpower (1778-81). [15]

In recognition of Gorham's work during the war, Massachusetts appointed him a delegate to Continental Congress (1782-83,1785-87) he served as president.[15]

CONTRIBUTIONS TO THE CONSTITUTIONAL CONVENTION. Gorham played an influential part in the Constitutional Convention, speaking frequently, sitting on the Committee of Detail, and serving as chairperson of the Committee of the Whole. Representing the commercial-cosmopolitan interests in Massachusetts, he pushed for central government strong enough to protect interstate commerce, promote international trade, regulate the use of paper money. He believed, in the aftermath of Shays' Rebellion, Massachusetts would divide between east and west "on the question [of the Constitution] as it has on all questions for years past;" and the country, because of its great size, would divide into independent nations within 150 years.[15]

Political

For several months in 1787, Gorham served as one of the Massachusetts delegates to the United States Constitutional Convention.[3] Gorham frequently served as chairman of the Convention's Committee of the whole, meaning that he (rather than the president of the Convention, George Washington) presided over convention sessions during the delegates' first deliberations on the structure of the new government in late May and June 1787. After the convention, he worked hard to see that the Constitution was approved in his home state.

Huge Land Deal

In connection with Oliver Phelps, he purchased from the state of Massachusetts in 1788 pre-emption rights to an immense tract of land in western New York State which straddled the Genesee River, all for the sum of $1,000,000 (about $18 million today).[8][9] The land in question had been previously ceded to Massachusetts from the state of New York under the 1786 Treaty of Hartford. The pre-emption right gave them the first or preemptive right to obtain clear title to this land from the Native Americans. They soon extinguished the Native American title to the portion of the land east of the Genesee River, as well as a 185,000 acres tract west of the Genesee, the Mill Yard Tract, surveyed all of it, laid out townships, and sold large parts to speculators and settlers. His son Nathaniel Gorham Jr. was a pioneer settler of this tract, having been placed in charge of his father's interests there.[10] In 1790, after Gorham and Phelps defaulted in payment, they sold nearly all of their remaining lands east of the Genesee to Robert Morris, who eventually resold those lands to The Pulteney Association. It also was eventually acquired by Robert Morris, who resold most of it to the Holland Land Company.

Gorham died in Charlestown in 1796.[8][11]

References

1. Editors. "GORHAM, Nathaniel, (1738–1796)". Bio Dictionary of United States Congress: 1774–present. US Congress. Retr April 18, 2018. Member Continental Congress in 1782, 1783, 1786, 1787, and 1789, President June 6, 1786, to Feb 2, 1787
2. Lettieri, Ronald J. (1999). "Gorham, Nathaniel". American National Biography (online ed.). New York: Oxford University Press. doi:10.1093/anb/9780198606697.article.0100334. (subscription required)
3. Morton, p. 118.
4. Waters, p. 366.
5. Morton, p. 117.
6. Krauel, Richard (1911). "Prince Henry of Prussia and the Regency of the United States, 1786". The American Historical Review. 17 (1): 44–51. doi:10.2307/1832837. JSTOR 1832837.
7. Fradin, Dennis Brindell (2005). The Founders: The 39 Stories Behind the U.S. Constitution. Bloomsbury Publishing USA.
8. Morton, p. 120.
9. McKeveley, Blake (January 1939). "Historic Aspects of the Phelps and Gorham Treaty of July 4–8, 1788" Rochester History. 1 (1). Rochester Public Library. ISSN 0035-7413. Arch Dec 3, 2007. Retr April 29, 2010.
10. Wilson, J. G.; Fiske, J., eds. (1900). "Gorham, Nathaniel" Appletons' Cyclopædia American Biography. NY: D. Appleton.
11. US Army Center of Military History
12. "Odd Wisconsin Archives". www.wisconsinhistory.org. Archived from the original on April 23, 2006.
13. Gannett, Henry (1905). Origin of Certain Place Names in United States. U.S. Gov Printing Office. p. 140.
14. Roberts, Gary Boyd (2001). "#54 Royal Descents, Notable Kin, and Printed Sources: Harvard, Its Presidents, and Kings". New England Ancestors.org. New England Historic Genealogical Society. Retrieved July 5, 2012.
15. https://www.history.army.mil/books/revwar/ss/gorham.htm pp 155-156

FRANCIS HOPKINSON

NEW JERSEY
SIGNER OF THE DECLARATION OF INDEPENDENCE
WORKS INCLUDE PROFESSIONAL MUSICIAN
Asked for quarter cask of Wine as reward for designing US Flag

Francis Hopkinson (October 2, 1737 – May 9, 1791) was an American Founding Father, lawyer, jurist, author, and composer.[1] He designed Continental paper money and two early versions of flags, one for the United States and one for the United States Navy.[2][3] He was a signer of the Declaration of Independence in July 1776 as a delegate from New Jersey.[1] Hopkinson served in various roles in the early United States government including as a member of the Second Continental Congress and as a member of the Navy Board. He became the first federal judge of the Eastern District Court of Pennsylvania on September 30, 1789.[4]

He was a professional musician and composer.

In 1776, Hopkinson served as a delegate to the Second Continental Congress (Continental Congress) from June 21 through November 18.[7]:212[7]:218 He was a signer of the United States Declaration of Independence, representing New Jersey.[6] He was the Chairman of the Navy Board in Philadelphia from November 18, 1776, to mid-August 1778.[7]:218[7]:234 He was treasurer for the Continental Loan Office in Philadelphia from 1778 to 1781. He was judge of the Admiralty Court of Pennsylvania from 1779 to 1789.[5]   .[10][11] He was a member of the Pennsylvania Convention which ratified the US Constitution.[7]:chapter VI:325[6]

Hopkinson was nominated by President George Washington on September 24, 1789, to the United States District Court for the District of Pennsylvania, to a new seat authorized by 1 Stat. 73. He was confirmed by the US Senate, September 26, 1789.[5]

Cultural contributions

Hopkinson wrote popular airs and political satires, widely circulated and assisted in fostering the spirit of political independence that led to the American Revolution. His principal writings are *A Pretty Story . . .* (1774), a satire about King George; *The Prophecy* (1776); and *The Political Catechism* (1777).[12] Other notable essays are "Typographical Method of conducting a Quarrel", "Essay on White Washing", and "Modern Learning". Hopkinson began to play the harpsichord at age seventeen and, during the 1750s, hand-copied arias, songs, and instrumental pieces by many European composers. He is credited as being the first American-born composer with his 1759 composition "My Days Have Been So Wondrous Free". By the 1760s, he was playing with professional musicians in concerts.

Some of his more notable songs include "The Treaty", "The Battle of the Kegs", and "The New Roof, a song for Federal Mechanics". He also played organ at Philadelphia's Christ Church and composed or edited a number of hymns and psalms including: "A Collection of Psalm Tunes with a few Anthems and Hymns Some of them Entirely New, for the Use of the United Churches of Christ Church and St. Peter's Church in Philadelphia" (1763), "A psalm of thanksgiving, Adapted to the Solemnity of Easter: To be performed on Sunday, the 30th of March, 1766, at Christ Church, Philadelphia" (1766), and "The Psalms of David, with the Ten Commandments, Creed, Lord's Prayer, &c. in Metre" (1767). In the 1780s, Hopkinson modified a glass harmonica with keyboard inventing the **Bellarmonic**, that utilized tone of metal balls.[13]

Books by Francis Hopkinson

- *The Miscellaneous Essays and Occasional Writings of Francis Hopkinson, Esq* Printed by T. Dobson, 1792. Available via Google Books: Volume I, Volume II, Volume III
- *Judgments in the Admiralty of Pennsylvania in four suits* Printed at T. Dobson and T. Lang, 1789. Available via Internet Archive
-

Essays by Francis Hopkinson

- *A Pretty Story Written in the Year of Our Lord 1774.* Printed by John Dunlap, 1774.
- "Dissertation IV," in *Four Dissertations, on the Reciprocal Advantages of a Perpetual Union between Great-Britain and Her American Colonies.* Printed by William & Thomas Bradford, 1766. Available via the U.S. National Library of Medicine, Digital Collections
-

Musical compositions by Francis Hopkinson

- *Collection of Plain Tunes with a Few Anthems and Hymns.* Benjamin Carr, 1763.
- *Temple of Minerva.* (The First American Opera)[15] Printed by Benjamin Carr, 1781.
- *Seven Songs for the Harpsichord or Forte Piano.* Printed by T. Dobson, 1788.[16]
- No. 3: "Beneath a weeping willow's shade"

Great Seal of the United States

In 1776. Hopkinson designed the Great Seal of New Jersey with assistance from Pierre Eugene du Simitiere in 1776.[17] He was chosen as a consultant to design the Great Seal of the United States,[18][19][20][21] finalized on June 20, 1782.[22]

In the current rendition of the Great Seal of the United States, the 13 stars (constellation) representing the 13 original states have five points. They are arranged in the shape of a larger star with six points. The constellation comprising 13 smaller stars symbolizes the national motto, "E pluribus unum." Originally, the design had individual stars with six points, but this was changed in 1841 when a new die was cast. This seal is impressed upon the reverse of the United States one-dollar bill. Reverse of the seal, contains an unfinished pyramid below a radiant eye. The unfinished pyramid image was used to design the $50 bill.[23][24][25]

United States Flag

On June 14, 1777, the Second Continental Congress adopted the Stars and Stripes as the first official national flag of the United States (later celebrated as Flag Day). At the time of the flag's adoption, he was the chair of the Navy Board, which was under the Marine Committee. Today, the United States Secretary of the Navy.[28]

Hopkinson is recognized as a designer of the Flag of the United States, and the journals of the Continental Congress support this.[29] On May 25, 1780, Hopkinson wrote a letter to the Continental Board of Admiralty mentioning several patriotic designs he had completed during the previous three years.[30] One was his Board of Admiralty seal, which contained a shield of seven red and six white stripes on a blue field. Others included the Treasury Board seal, "7 devices for the Continental Currency," and "the Flag of the United States of America."[31]

Hopkinson noted he had not asked for compensation but was seeking a reward: "a Quarter Cask of public Wine." The board sent that letter to Congress.

Hopkinson submitted another bill on June 24 for his "drawings and devices." In this second letter, Hopkinson did not mention designing the flag of the United States. Instead, the first item listed was "the great Naval Flag of the United States" along with the other contributions.[32] This flag with its red outer stripes was designed to show up well on ships at sea.[32] A parallel flag for the national flag was most likely intended by Hopkinson with white outer stripes[32] as on the Great Seal of the United States and on the Bennington flag, which commemorated 50th anniversary of the founding of the US in 1826. The Navy flag was preferred as the national flag.

Hopkinson was the son of Thomas Hopkinson[7]:30 and Mary Johnson Hopkinson.[7]:16 448 He married Ann Borden on September 1, 1768.[7]:164 They had five children.[7]:449 and 450 Hopkinson died[5] of a sudden apoplectic seizure.[7]:449

References

1. Bernstein, Richard B. (2009). "Appendix: The Founding Fathers, A Partial List". The Founding Fathers Reconsidered. New York: Oxford University Press. pp. 176–180. ISBN 978-0199832576.
2. Leepson, Marc; DeMille, Nelson (May 30, 2006). Flag: An American Biography. St. Martin's Griffin. p. 33.
3. Williams, Earl P. Jr. (Oct 2012). "Did Francis Hopkinson Design Two Flags?" NAVA News (216): 7–9.
4. Hastings, George E. (1926). The Life and Works of Francis Hopkinson. Chicago: U of Chicago Press. p. 325.
5. Francis Hopkinson at Biographical Directory of Federal Judges, a publication of the Federal Judicial Center.
6. United States Congress. "Francis Hopkinson (id: H000783)". Biographical Directory of US Congress.
7. Hastings, George (1926). Life and Works of Francis Hopkinson. U of Chicago Press.
8. Hastings, pp. 157 and 158.
9. Bell, Whitfield J., and Charles Greifenstein, Jr. Patriot-Improvers: Biographical Sketches of Members of the American Philosophical Society. 3 vols. Philadelphia: American Philosophical Society, 1997, I: 27—28, 30, 335, 415, II: 9, 24–32, 26, 193, 195, 277, 308, 406, III: 58, 78, 79, 160, 190, 308, 464.
10. "Minnesota State Law Library: Trial Collection Bibliography, part 4". www.lawlibrary.state.mn.us.
11. The Pennsylvania State Trials: Containing the Impeachment, Trial, and Acquittal of Francis Hopkinson, and John Nicholson, Esquires. The Former Being Judge of the Court of Admiralty, and the Latter, the Comptroller-general of the Commonwealth of Pennsylvania. Francis Bailey. 1794. Retrieved June 16, 2023. |p22-24; 56-62
12. Charles Wells Moulton, ed. (1902). The Library of Literary Criticism of English and American Authors: 1785–1824. Buffalo, NY: The Moulton Publishing Company. pp. 131.
13. Francis Hopkinson biography Library of Congress Performing Arts Digital Library; accessed Sept 30, 2015.
14. "Hopkinson | Fisher College House". fh.house.upenn.edu. Retrieved June 2, 2016.
15. "Pennsylvania Center for the Book on Hopkinson and his writings".
16. "Seven Songs for Harpsichord or Forte Piano". Early American Secular Music, European Sources, 1589–1839.
17. Hastings, p. 217.
18. Patterson, Richard Sharpe; Dougall, Richardson (1978) [1976 i.e., 1978]. The Eagle and the Shield: A History of the Great Seal of the United States. Department and Foreign Service series; 161 Department of State publication; 8900. Washington: Office of the Historian, Bureau of Public Affairs, Dept. of State: for sale by the Supt. of Docs., U.S. Govt. Print. Off. p. 32.
19. "Journals of the Continental Congress --FRIDAY, OCTOBER 27, 1780". memory.loc.gov.
20. Buescher, John. "All Wrapped up in the Flag" Arch Sept 23, 2011, Wayback Machine, Teachinghistory.org Arch
21. Williams, Earl P. Jr. (June 14, 1996). "A Civil Servant Designed Our National Banner: The Unsung Legacy of Francis Hopkinson". New Constellation (Newsletter of the National Flag Foundation). Special Edition #7: 8.
22. "The eagle and the shield: a history of the great seal of the United States". archive.org. 1978.
23. "wikimedia.org/wikipedia/commons/c/c9/Continental_$50_note_1778".
24. "Continental Currency: September 26, 1778". coins.nd.edu.
25. Patterson and Dougall, p. 68
26. Williams, Earl P. Jr. (October 2012). "Did F Hopkinson Design Two Flags?" (PDF). NAVA News (216): 7–9.
27. Williams (2012), p.7.
28. Zall, Paul M. (1976). Comical Spirit of Seventy-Six: Humor of Francis Hopkinson. San Marino, Cal: Huntington Library. p.10
29. Furlong, William; McCandless, Byron (1981).So Proudly We Hail. Washington,D.C. Smithsonian Press. p. 101
30. Hastings, p. 240.
31. Leepson, p. 33
32. Williams (2012), pp. 7–9.

GEORGE TAYLOR

PENNSYLVANIA

Indentured Servant, Cannon Producer, Signed Declaration

- Arrived in America, 1736, as an Indentured Servant
- Ironmaster, politician, Member of the Pennsylvania Militia
- Colonel in the Bucks County Militia
- Only Indentured Servant to sign Declaration of Independence
- Negotiated a peace treaty with the Six Indian Nations

George Taylor (c. 1716 – February 23, 1781) was born in the North of Ireland (now Northern Ireland), possibly Ulster, in 1716. He emigrated to the American colonies at age 20, landing in Philadelphia in 1736.[3] According to early 18th century biographies of the signers of the Declaration of Independence.[4] To pay for his passage, Taylor was indentured to Samuel Savage Jr., ironmaster at the French Creek Iron Works northwest of Philadelphia.

Career- - Iron worker

In 1738, his brother-in-law Samuel Nutt Jr., and his mother Anna Savage Nutt built Warwick Furnace, a cold blast, charcoal furnace they named Warwick. Savage died in 1742, and the following year, Taylor married Savage's widow, Ann.[6] In 1745, Taylor was made manager of the furnace and Coventry Forge.[7]

The Taylors lived at Warwick Furnace until 1755, when Taylor formed a partnership to lease Durham Furnace.[3] The ironworks, built in 1727, was started by investors who were among Pennsylvania's wealthiest, including James Logan, proprietor of the Pennsylvania colony for the Penn family, and William Allen.[8]

Political career

Shortly after becoming ironmaster at Durham, Taylor entered public life for the first time, serving as a Justice of the Peace in Bucks County, Pennsylvania from 1757 to 1763.[9] When the lease for the Durham mill expired, the Taylors relocated to Easton, the county seat of Northampton County. Taylor was commissioned as a Justice of the Peace in and elected to the Pennsylvania Provincial Assembly.[6]

In 1767, Taylor purchased 331 acres near Allentown at Biery's Port. The house was completed in 1768, but Taylor's wife Ann died shortly after.[2]

While still at Biery's Port, Taylor arranged another lease to operate the Durham ironworks in 1774. The ironworks had just been acquired by Joseph Galloway, a Philadelphia attorney and speaker of the Pennsylvania General Assembly (1766–1774).[6] After failing to gain support in the First Continental Congress for his, Galloway resigned as speaker and refused to attend the Second Continental Congress in 1775. In July, as colonial forces prepared for war, he was commissioned as a colonel in the third battalion of the Pennsylvania militia.[9]

Taylor secured a contract with Pennsylvania's Committee of Safety for cannon shot.[3] On August 25, with a shipment of 258 round balls weighing from 18 to 32 pounds each, Durham Furnace became the first in Pennsylvania to supply munitions to the Continental Army.[7]

Founding father and signer of the Declaration of Independence

In 1776, the Continental Congress voted for independence on July 2 and adopted the Declaration of Independence two days later, on July 4.[10] Before the vote for independence, five of Pennsylvania's delegates were forced to resign. On July 20, Taylor was among the replacements.[2] One of his first duties as a member of Congress was to affix his signature to the Declaration of Independence, which he did on August 2, along with most delegates. Of the 56 signers, he was one of eight foreign-born, the only one to be indentured, and only ironmaster.[11]

Durham Furnace

Taylor continued overseeing cannon shot and shells production at Durham Furnace for the Continental Army and Navy. Not long after independence was achieved, however, Joseph Galloway fled Philadelphia, seeking refuge with British General William Howe and escaping to England.[15] Galloway was convicted by the Assembly as a traitor, and his properties, including Durham mill, were seized.[6]

Taylor appealed to the Supreme Executive Council and enabled him to finish his lease, but in 1779, the Commissioner of Forfeited Estates sold Durham.[8] Forming a new partnership, Taylor leased Greenwich Forge in Warren County, NJ.[2]

In failing health, Taylor moved back to Easton in April 1780 and died there on February 23, 1781, at 65.[3] Taylor had been experiencing financial difficulties in the last few years of his life, and legal entanglements over the Durham and Greenwich forges dragged on until 1799, at which point his estate was judged insolvent.[7]

References

1. Thompson, Kirk. "George Taylor". University Park, Pennsylvania: Pennsylvania Center for the Book, Penn State University Libraries. Arch June 11, 2010. Retrieved August 22, 2008.

2. "Delaware and Lehigh National Heritage Corridor: George Taylor House". nps.gov. Washington, DC:

3. Ely, Warren S. (1926). "George Taylor, Signer of the Declaration of Independence". A Collection of Papers Read Before the Bucks County Historical Society. V. Easton, Pennsylvania: Bucks County Historical Society:

4. Goodrich, Rev. Charles H. (1829). Lives of Signers to Declaration of Independence. Philadelphia, W Reed & Co. pp. 296–99

5. Judson, L. Carroll (1839). A Biography of the Signers of the Declaration of Independence. Philadelphia, Pennsylvania: J. Dobson and Thomas, Coperthwait & Co. pp. 174–76.

6. Kurtz, Kathleen (2011). "George Taylor". dsdi1776.com. Descendants of Signers, Declaration of Independence.

7. Fackenthal, Ben Franklin (1926). "Homes of George Taylor". A Collection of Papers Read Before Bucks County Historical Society. V. Meadville, Pennsylvania: Bucks County Historical Society: 112–33. Retr Jan 8, 2022

8. The Committee on Historical Research, Pennsylvania Society of the Colonial Dames of America (1914). "Forges and Furnaces in the Province of Pennsylvania". Lancaster, Pa: New Era Printing Company. pp. 43–57.

9. "George Taylor". Biographical Directory of the United States Congress. Retr August 22, 2008.

10. "Signers of the Declaration: Historical Background". Washington, DC: Retr Feb 27, 2024.

11. "Signers of the Declaration: Biographical Sketches". Washington, DC: Retr Aug 22, 2008.

12. Whelan, Frank (June 15, 1984). "George Taylor: A Historical Perspective Founding Father's Patriotic Beliefs Cost Him Everything". The Morning Call. Retrieved August 21, 2021.

RUTLEDGE BROTHERS JOHN, EDWARD

SOUTH CAROLINA
SIGNERS OF CONTINENTAL ASSOCIATION,
DECLARATION OF INDEPENDENCE
UNITED STATES CONSTITUTION

Another great family of Founding Fathers emerges. Between the two brothers, they strategized in committee and signed two founding documents of the United States. Both hailed from South Carolina. The eldest was John Rutledge who was of age to attend Law School in England. He signed the CONTINENTAL ASSOCIATION. John Rutledge was elected Governor of South Carolina and went home. His younger brother Edward, then at the age of 26, moved onto committee just in time to sign the DECLARATION OF INDEPENDENCE. Following our Revolution, John Rutledge returned to Continental Convention and worked on our new Constitution and ratification, signing the new CONSTITUTION OF THE UNITED STATES.

JOHN RUTLEDGE then became one of the first group of US Supreme Court Justices. EDWARD RUTLEDGE earned a George Washington appointment for a SCOTUS Justiceship only to decline. Please read their biographical briefs.

JOHN RUTLEDGE OF SOUTH CAROLINA
SIGNER OF UNITED STATES CONSTITUTION
FIRST ASSOCIATE JUSTICE OF SUPREME COURT OF THE UNITED STATES
SECOND CHIEF JUSTICE OF SUPREME COURT OF THE UNITED STATES

John Rutledge Jr. (September 17, 1739 – June 21, 1800) was an American Founding Father, politician, and jurist who served as one of the original associate justices of the Supreme Court and the second chief justice of the United States. Additionally, he served as the first president of South Carolina and later as its first governor after the Declaration of Independence was signed.

Born in Charleston, South Carolina, Rutledge established a legal career after studying at Middle Temple in the City of London. He was the elder brother of Edward Rutledge, a signatory of the Declaration of Independence. Rutledge served as a delegate to the Stamp Act Congress, which protested taxes imposed on the Thirteen Colonies by the Parliament of Great Britain. He also served as a delegate to the Continental Congress, where he signed the Continental Association, before being elected as governor of South Carolina. He served as governor during much of the American Revolutionary War.

Returning to Congress, Rutledge was appointed to the South Carolina Court of Chancery. He was a delegate to the 1787 Philadelphia Convention, which wrote the United States Constitution. During the convention, he served as chairman of the Committee of Detail, which produced the first full draft of the Constitution. The following year he participated in the South Carolina convention to ratify the Constitution.

In 1789, President George Washington appointed Rutledge as one of the inaugural associate justices of the Supreme Court of the United States. Rutledge left the Supreme Court in 1791 to become chief justice of the South Carolina Court of Common Pleas and Sessions. He returned to the Supreme Court, this time as chief justice, following the resignation of John Jay in June 1795. As the vacancy came during a long Senate recess, Washington named Rutledge as the new chief justice by a recess appointment. When the Senate reconvened in December 1795, it rejected Rutledge's nomination by a 10–14 vote. Rutledge resigned his commission shortly thereafter and withdrew from public life until his death in 1800. He holds the record for the shortest tenure of any chief justice. He was the first Supreme Court nominee to be rejected, and remains the only "recess appointed" justice not to be confirmed by the Senate.

Associate Justice OF SCOTUS

On September 24, 1789, George Washington nominated Rutledge for one of the five associate justice positions on the newly established Supreme Court. His appointment (along with those of: John Blair Jr., William Cushing, Robert H. Harrison, and James Wilson; plus that of John Jay for Chief Justice) was confirmed by the Senate two days later.[35] His service on the Court began February 15, 1790, when he took the judicial oath, and continued until March 5, 1791.[1] Rutledge resigned from the Supreme Court, without having ever heard a case, in order to become chief justice of the South Carolina Court of Common Pleas and General Sessions.[36]

Chief Justice

On June 28, 1795, Chief Justice John Jay resigned, having been elected governor of New York. Washington selected John Rutledge to succeed Jay as chief justice, and, as the Senate would not be meeting again until December, gave Rutledge a recess appointment so that he could serve as chief justice during the upcoming August session. He was commissioned as chief justice on June 30, 1795,[37] and took the judicial oath on August 12.[1]
John Rutledge would resign by December 1795.

He would remain private, outside of serving a single term in the South Carolina House of Representatives. He died on June 21, 1800, at age 60.

EDWARD RUTLEDGE, SOUTH CAROLINA
SIGNED CONTINENTAL ASSOCIATION and DECLARATION OF INDEPENDENCE

- At 26, Rutledge was the youngest to sign the Declaration of Independence.
- He was a captain in the Charleston Battalion of Artillery.
- 1774-1776 Delegate to Continental Congress.
- 1775-1776 delegate to first and second provincial congress.
- 1798-1800 SC governor. (https://www.tompsc.com/291/Edward-Rutledge)
- Was taken prisoner when the British captured Charleston in 1780.
- Rutledge served as the 39th governor of South Carolina from 1798–1800.
- 1796-1798 State Senator.
- 1788, 1792, 1796 College of Electors.
- He was author of the act abolishing the law of primogeniture in 1791.
- In 1794, President Washington offered Rutledge the appointment of Associate Justice of the United States Supreme Court, but did not accept.

Edward Rutledge (November 23, 1749 – January 23, 1800) was an American Founding Father and politician who signed the Continental Association and was the youngest signatory of the Declaration of Independence. He later served as the 39th governor of South Carolina.

Rutledge was born in Charleston, South Carolina. He was the youngest of seven children (5 sons and 2 daughters) born to Dr. John Rutledge and Sarah Hext. His father was a physician and colonist of Scots-Irish descent; his mother was born in South Carolina and was of English descent. Following his elder brothers, John and Hugh, he studied law in London at the Inns of Court. In 1772 he was admitted to the English bar (Middle Temple) [1] and returned to Charleston to practice.

American Founding Father Edward Rutledge, the youngest brother of John Rutledge, was born to Dr. John Rutledge and Sarah Hext Rutledge in Christ Church Parish on November 23, 1749. His father was an Irish immigrant and one of the first to practice medicine in the parish. His mother was a member of the prestigious Boone family. Thus, Edward Rutledge was a great grandson of Major John Boone and Elizabeth Patey Boone who founded Boone Hall Plantation. His parents lived on a plantation in the vicinity of today's Laurel Hill Plantation on Route 41 in Mount Pleasant. (https://www.tompsc.com/291/Edward-Rutledge)

He was married on March 1, 1774, to Henrietta Middleton (17 November 1750 – 22 April 1792), daughter of Henry Middleton. The couple had three children:

Rutledge had a successful law practice Charles Cotesworth Pinckney, from an iconic South Carolina family detailed within these Founding Fathers.

Career - - American Revolution

During the American Revolution, Rutledge along with his brother John represented South Carolina in the Continental Congress (1774–1776). He worked to have African Americans expelled from the Continental Army.[2] A firm supporter of colonial rights, he (as a delegate) was instructed initially to oppose Richard Henry Lee's Resolution of independence; South Carolina's leaders were unsure the time was "ripe".[3] At age 26 he was the youngest delegate to sign the Declaration of Independence.

He returned home in November 1776 to take a seat in the General Assembly. He served as a captain of artillery in the South Carolina militia and fought at the Battle of Beaufort in 1779. In May 1780, Rutledge was captured along with his co-signers of the Declaration of Independence, Arthur Middleton and Thomas Heyward during the siege of Charleston and were taken to St. Augustine, Florida. They were released during a prisoner exchange in July 1781.[4]

Professional Life

Most notably, at 26 years of age he was the youngest delegate to sign the Declaration of Independence. He proved himself to be a persuasive force within the South Carolina delegation. Rutledge rose to prominence just as political elders such as Henry Middleton, Christopher Gadsden, and Thomas Lynch Sr. were retiring. Prior to the revolution, he was invited along with John Adams and Benjamin Franklin to discuss peace with British Admiral Lord Richard Howe on Staten Island. (https://www.tompsc.com/291/Edward-Rutledge)

Later life and death

In 1779, fought in Battle of Beaufort (captured in Charleston in May 1780, and imprisoned until July 1781); After his release he returned to the General Assembly, where he served until 1796. He was known as an active legislator and an advocate for the confiscation of Loyalist property. Like John Rutledge, Edward Rutledge opposed the Jay Treaty and the

Anglophilic stance he perceived in the Federalist Party.[5] As an elector in the 1796 presidential election, Rutledge voted for Southern candidates, Thomas Jefferson and Thomas Pinckney.[6]

Rutledge approved of Adams's defense policies towards France during the Quasi-War.[7] The opposition afforded Adams's measures by Vice President Jefferson, and the Congressional Republicans angered Rutledge because he now saw the Republicans as more partial to France than to American interests.[8] Rutledge ceased communication with Jefferson.[8]

Governor Rutledge, while attending an important meeting in Columbia, had to be sent home because of his gout. He died in Charleston before the end of his term. Some said at the time that he died from apoplexy resulting from hearing the news of George Washington's death.[2] Since 1971, his home in Charleston is now a National Historic Landmark.

JAMES MCHENRY (Fort McHenry)
Home of United States National Anthem, Star Spangled Banner

James McHenry (November 16, 1753 – May 3, 1816) was a Scotch-Irish American military surgeon, statesman, and a Founding Father of the United States. McHenry was a signer of the United States Constitution from Maryland, initiated the recommendation for Congress to form the Navy, and was the eponym of Fort McHenry. He represented Maryland in the Continental Congress. He was a delegate to the Maryland State Convention of 1788, to vote whether Maryland should ratify the Constitution of the United States.[1] He served as United States Secretary of War from 1796 to 1800, bridging the administrations of George Washington and John Adams.

Early life and education

Born into a Presbyterian Scots Irish family in Ballymena, County Antrim, Ireland, in 1753. Alarmed that he was becoming sick from excessive studying, his family in 1771 sent him to North America to recuperate. Upon arrival, McHenry lived with a family friend in Philadelphia before finishing his preparatory education in Delaware. He apprenticed under Benjamin Rush and became a physician.[5][6]

Medical career

McHenry served as a skilled and dedicated surgeon during the American Revolutionary War. On August 10, 1776, he was appointed surgeon of the Fifth Pennsylvania Battalion, stationed at Fort Washington (New York). He was taken prisoner the following November when the fort was taken by Sir William Howe. While in British custody, he observed that prisoners were given very poor medical attention and initiated reports to that effect, to no avail.[7]

He was paroled in January 1777, then released from parole in March 1778. Having sufficiently impressed George Washington, he was appointed aide as secretary to the commander-in-chief in May 1779. McHenry was present at the Battle of Monmouth. In August 1780, he was transferred to Lafayette's staff, where he remained until he retired.[7][8]

Although eligible, McHenry did not join The Society of the Cincinnati as an original member when it was established in 1783. His son John was admitted as a member in the state of Maryland in 1816, representing his father.[9]

Political career

He was elected by the legislature to the Maryland Senate on September 17, 1781, and as delegate to Congress on December 2, 1784. In 1787, he was a Maryland delegate to the Constitutional Convention, which drafted the United States Constitution.[10] After a controversial campaign, he was elected to the Maryland House of Delegates on October 10, 1788. Two years later he retired from public life and spent a year actively engaged in mercantile business. On November 15, 1791, he accepted a second term in the Maryland Senate.[7]

After several other candidates had declined, Washington appointed McHenry secretary of war in 1796 and immediately assigned him the task of facilitating the transition of Western military posts from Great Britain's control to that of the US under terms of the Jay Treaty.

McHenry advised the Senate committee against reducing military forces. He was instrumental in reorganizing the United States Army into four regiments of infantry, a troop of dragoons, and a battery of artillery.[7] He established the United States Department of the Navy, based on his recommendation that the "War Department should be assisted by a commissioner of marine" on March 8, 1798.[7]

During President John Adams's administration (1797–1801), McHenry continued as Secretary of War, as Adams had decided to keep the newly established institution of the presidential cabinet intact. Adams gradually found that three members of the cabinet repeatedly opposed him: McHenry, Secretary of State Timothy Pickering, and Treasury Secretary Oliver Wolcott Jr. They appeared to listen more to Alexander Hamilton than to the president and publicly disagreed with Adam, particularly with regard to France. Although many liked McHenry personally, Washington, Hamilton, and Wolcott were said to have complained.[8]

McHenry attributed Adams's troubles as chief executive to his long and frequent absences from the capital, leaving business in the hands of secretaries who bore responsibility without the power to properly conduct it.[7] After a stormy meeting, Adams requested McHenry's resignation, which he submitted on May 13. During the election of 1800, McHenry goaded Hamilton into releasing his indictment against the president, which questioned Adams's loyalty and patriotism, sparking public quarrels over the major candidates and eventually paving the way for Thomas Jefferson to be elected as the next president.[11]

Later life

In 1792, McHenry had purchased a 95-acre tract from Ridgely's Delight and named it Fayetteville in honor of the Marquis de Lafayette.

An attack of paralysis in 1814 left him in severe pain and complete loss of the use of his legs. He died two years later.[7] Upon the death of her beloved husband, Mrs. McHenry wrote:

Here we come to the end of a life of a courteous, high-minded, keen-spirited, Christian gentleman. He was not a great man, but participated in major events and great men loved him, while all men appreciated his goodness and purity of soul. His highest titles to remembrance are that he was faithful to every duty and that he was the intimate and trusted friend of Lafayette, of Hamilton, and of Washington.[7]

Legacy and honors

- Elected member of the American Philosophical Society in January 1786.[7]
- Elected president of the Bible Society of Baltimore in 1813[7] (later known as the Maryland Bible Society).
- Elected a member of the American Antiquarian Society in July 1815.[12]
- McHenry is memorialized at Independence Hall and National Constitution Center in Philadelphia.

- Fort McHenry in Baltimore was named after him. A battle there during the War of 1812 inspired Francis Scott Key to write what became the national anthem, "The Star-Spangled Banner".
- The Fort McHenry Tunnel is named for Fort McHenry which in turn is named for him.
- Henry Street in Madison, Wisconsin, is named in his honor.[13]
- McHenry, Maryland, is named after him.[14]

References

1. Secretary of State of Maryland (1915). Maryland Manual 1914–1915: A Compendium of Legal, Historical and Statistical Information relating to the State of Maryland. Annapolis, Maryland, USA: The Advertiser-Republican.
2. Robbins, Karen (2003). "Power Among the Powerless: Domestic Resistance by Free and Slave Women in the McHenry Family of the New Republic". Journal of the Early Republic. **23** (1): 48–50. doi:10.2307/3124985. JSTOR 3124985. Retrieved 7 March 2023.
3. "James McHenry—Fort McHenry's Namesake" nps.gov.Washington,DC: National Park Service. 3/7/23
4. "Biographical Series: James McHenry". msa.maryland.gov. Maryland State Archives. Retr 7 March 2023.
5. Steiner, Bernard Christian (1907). "Chapter I: Early Years Medical Study: 1753—1775". Correspondence of James McHenry: Secretary of War under Washington and Adams. Cleveland: Burrows Brothers Company. pp. 1–4. LCCN 07024607. OCLC 563557689. Retrieved 5 Dec 2020 – via Internet Archive.
6. Robbins, Karen (2013) James McHenry, Forgotten Federalist. Athens and London: U Ga Press pp.9, 12–16
7. Steiner, Bernard Christian (1907). Life and Correspondence James McHenry: Secretary of War Washington and Adams. Cleveland: Burrows Brothers Company. LCCN 07024607. OCLC 563557689. Retr 5 Dec 2020 –.
8. Lengel, Edward G. (2007). General George Washington: A Military Life. New York: Random House.
9. Metcalf, Bryce (1938). Original Members and Other Officers Eligible to the Society of the Cincinnati, 1783-1938: With the Institution, Rules of Admission, Lists of Officers of General and State Societies. Strasburg, VA: Shenandoah Publishing House, Inc., p. 216.
10. United States Army Center of Military History, 1985, pp. 1—2, 6.
11. Diggins, John Patrick (2003). John Adams. New York: Times Books.
12. American Antiquarian Society Members Directory
13. "Origins of Madison Street Names". Wisconsin Historical Society. Archived 3 March 2016. Retr 24 June 2011.
14. "Historical Markers". Archived from the original on 2 July 2015.

Sources

- United States Army Center of Military History (1985). James McHenry. CMH Pub 71-4. Washington, D.C.: United States Army Center of Military History. OCLC 1047471045. Retr 6 Dec 2020 – via Internet Archive.

FORT MCHENRY AND NATIONAL ANTHEM OF THE USA
By Lawyer Francis Scott Key

Fort McHenry is a historical American coastal pentagonal bastion fort on Locust Point, now a neighborhood of Baltimore, Maryland. It is best known for its role in the War of 1812, when it successfully defended Baltimore Harbor from an attack by the British navy from Chesapeake Bay on September 13–14, 1814.

The fort was built in 1798 and was used continuously by U.S. armed forces through World War I and by the United States Coast Guard in World War II. It was designated a national park in 1925, and, in 1939, a U.S. National Monument.

During the War of 1812, an American flag, 17 by 25 feet flew over Fort McHenry during British bombardment of the fort. The flag was replaced early on the morning of September 14, 1814, with a larger American garrison flag, 30 by 42 feet. The larger flag signaled American victory over the British in the Battle of Baltimore.

The sight of the ensign inspired Francis Scott Key to write "Defence of Fort M'Henry," later set to music in the song "To Anacreon in Heaven", later designated as "The Star-Spangled Banner", national anthem of the United States.

War of 1812 Battle of Baltimore

Beginning at 6:00 a.m. on September 13, 1814, British warships under the command of Vice Admiral Alexander Cochrane continuously bombarded Fort McHenry for 25 hours.[15] The

American defenders had 18-, 24- and 32-pounder cannons. The British ships were unable to pass Fort McHenry and penetrate Baltimore Harbor because of its defenses, including a chain of 22 sunken ships, and the American cannons. The British vessels were able to fire their rockets and mortars at the fort only at the weapons' maximum range. Only one British warship, a bomb vessel, received a direct hit from the fort's return fire.

The Americans, under the command of Major George Armistead, lost four killed—one woman was cut in half by a bomb as she carried supplies to the troops—and 24 wounded, including one black soldier, Private William Williams. At one point during the bombardment, a bomb crashed through the fort's powder magazine. However, either the rain extinguished the fuse, or the bomb was a dud.[17]

Star-Spangled Banner

Flag that flew over Fort McHenry during its bombardment in 1814, which was witnessed by Francis Scott Key. The family of Major George Armistead, the commander of the fort, donated the flag to the Smithsonian Institution in 1912.[18]

Washington lawyer Francis Scott Key went to Baltimore to negotiate the release of Dr. William Beans, a civilian prisoner of war, and there he witnessed the bombardment from a nearby truce ship. An oversized American flag had been sewn by Mary Pickersgill for $405.90[19] in anticipation of the British attack on the fort. Key saw the flag emerge intact in the dawn of September 14,[16] and he was so moved that he began to compose "Defence of Fort M'Henry" set to the tune "To Anacreon in Heaven". It was renamed "The Star-Spangled Banner" and became the United States' national anthem, and has even been translated into various languages, targeted mostly for US immigrants who later acquired American citizenship.

References

15. "A Moment of Triumph". Retrieved 12 January 2009.

16. "Fort McHenry". Retrieved 24 January 2016.

17. "The Star-Spangled Banner, 1814". 4 August 2015.

18. "The Star-Spangled Banner: Making the Flag". National Museum of American History. Smithsonian Institution. Retrieved 2009-10-05.

19. Steve Whissen (Oct 1996). "National Register of Historic Places Registration: Fort McHenry National Monument & Historic Shrine" Maryland Historical Trust. Retr 2016-04-01.

CARTER BRAXTON, VIRGINIA
SIGNER OF DECLARATION OF INDEPENDENCE
REVOLUTION FINANCIER

Carter Braxton (September 10, 1736 – October 10, 1797)[1] was a Founding Father of the United States, signer of the Declaration of Independence, merchant, and Virginia planter.[2] A grandson of Robert "King" Carter, one of the wealthiest and powerful landowners in Virginia, Braxton was active in Virginia's legislature for more than 25 years, generally allied with Landon Carter, Benjamin Harrison V, Edmund Pendleton and other conservative planters.[3][4]

Early life

Braxton was born on Newington Plantation in King and Queen County, Virginia, on September 10, 1736, but wrongly reported as dead along with his mother, Mary Carter Braxton, who "unhappily catching a Common Cold," died shortly after his birth.[5]

Educated at the College of William & Mary like his father and brother, Braxton followed family tradition at age 19 by marrying Judith Robinson, a wealthy heiress and the Speaker's niece. However, she died giving birth to their daughter, leaving Braxton two daughters, Mary, and Judith. Returning to the colonies in 1760, following a stay in England, Braxton bought Chericoke plantation, moved, married again and built a manor house in 1767.[9]

Braxton's elder brother died in October 1761, so Braxton inherited the rest of his grandfather's estate, which was by then burdened with significant debts so that creditors persuaded some land to be sold, but even after doing so Braxton owned more than 12,000 acres in the 1770s.[10] Braxton purchased a small schooner after his second marriage and like his father turned his energies to trade. Braxton traded between the West Indies and American colonies, building relationships with Bayard & Son of New York and Willing & Morris of Philadelphia.

Early political career

Braxton began his long career representing King William County in the Virginia House of Burgesses, taking his seat in 1761. His brother George died on October 3, 1761, leaving an insolvent estate, so the family lost Newington. Although both high-living Braxton's had been considered wealthy, as well as political allies of Speaker John Robinson, when the John Robinson estate scandal broke in 1766, they turned out to be among the largest beneficiaries of the late speaker's interest-free loans of redeemed paper money supposedly burned.[15][16]

In addition to his duties as a Burgess, Braxton served as sheriff of King William County (a lucrative position for which he briefly resigned his position as Burgess), colonel of its militia, and vestryman of the troubled St. John's Church about ten miles east of his Chericoke plantation. Factional disputes within the parish (which assessed members to support not only the rector but the parish poor) grew so severe that the House of Burgesses held hearings and passed a special bill dissolving the vestry, as Braxton had wished.

Although always considered a moderate or conservative politician, Braxton signed the First Virginia Association intended to protest the Townshend duties on tea and other products. However, in 1774 Braxton returned to Williamsburg as King William County's delegate, and joined 108 others in the Fourth Virginia Association, which authorized volunteer militia. When Lord Dunmore seized the colony's gunpowder and rifles, Braxton negotiated a compromise.

Reluctant revolutionary and Virginia moderate

Braxton was "a moderate politician during the Revolution—often viewed as sympathetic to the British (but not a Loyalist)." Although absent at some sessions, he had represented his county sixteen times between 1761 and Lord Dunmore's dissolution of the House of Burgesses; Braxton also served as the county delegate to all five sessions of the Virginia Convention. In 1774, Braxton joined the patriots' Committee of Safety in Virginia, as well as chaired the legislative committee considering legal penalties for Tories.

In the spring of 1775, Braxton was instrumental in preventing the outbreak of war in Virginia. On April 20, the day after the clashes at Lexington and Concord, Royal Governor Lord John M. Dunmore seized the gunpowder in the Williamsburg magazine. Several colonial militia units prepared to retaliate, but moderate leaders such as George Washington and Peyton Randolph restrained them. Patrick Henry, however, refusing to be pacified, led a group of the Hanover County militia into Williamsburg and demanded the return of the gunpowder or payment for it. Before any hostilities occurred, Braxton, as spokesman for Henry, met with crown official Richard Corbin, his father-in-law, and convinced him to pay for the powder. [a]

When Peyton Randolph died unexpectedly in Philadelphia in October 1775, fellow Virginia legislators elected Braxton to take his place in the Continental Congress. He served in the Congress from February 1776 until August, when Virginia reduced its delegation to five members. In that capacity Braxton signed the Declaration of Independence, although he had previously opposed it as premature in Committee of the Whole and explained his stance in several letters to his uncle Landon Carter. Braxton also drew revolutionaries' criticism for his pamphlet, *Address to the Convention*, which he had printed in reply to the proposals of John Adams's *Thoughts on Government*.

Financial speculation and troubles

Braxton invested a great deal of his wealth in the American Revolution. Like Robert Morris, Braxton loaned money to the cause, as well as funded shipping and privateering (and lost about half of the 14 ships in which he held interests). Braxton (with fellow businessmen including Morris and Benjamin Harrison) sold Virginia and Carolina tobacco and corned meat abroad, and secured arms and ammunition (unsuccessfully, most colonies preferring arms supplied by foreign governments on favorable terms), as well as wheat and salt, and cloth and other trade goods.[17] In 1780, the Continental Congress censured Braxton for his role in the *Phoenix* affair of 1777, in which his privateer seized a Portuguese vessel from Brazil, prompting diplomatic protests. The British also destroyed some of Braxton's plantations.

In 1787, Braxton sued Robert Morris in Henrico County court for £28,257, but the lawsuit continued for eight years before commissioners were appointed, then Morris appealed. Finally, Virginia's Court of Appeals led by Edmund Pendleton decided mostly in favor of Braxton before Morris was forced into bankruptcy by his own continued land speculations (although Morris as late as 1800 believed he should have won £20,000). In 1791, Braxton also purchased Strawberry Hill outside Richmond for his wife (who had received nothing upon her father's death, all his property being given to his sons), and conveyed it to his sons Carter Jr. and Corbin to hold for their mother's benefit. Braxton's biographer does not believe that Braxton hid assets from his creditors by placing them in relatives' names, although his widow later attempted to recover rights in land that her husband sold in his last years. His sons-in-law, Robert Page and John White (husbands of Molly and Judith, his daughters by his first wife) paid creditors more than £2,000 on Braxton's behalf.[17]

Death and legacy

The War of Independence brought financial hardships to Braxton. At its beginning, he had invested heavily in shipping, but the British captured most of his vessels and ravaged some of his plantations and extensive landholdings. Commercial setbacks in later years ruined him. In 1786, though he retained Chericoke, he moved to Richmond, where he died in 1797 at the age of 61. He is buried in the family cemetery adjacent to Chericoke. [a]

Note

a. https://www.nps.gov/parkhistory/online_books/declaration/bio4.htm

References

1. "Biography of Carter Braxton, page 1 - Colonial Hall". colonialhall.com. Retrieved 2 July 2018.
2. Bernstein, Richard B. (2011) [2009]. "Appendix: The Founding Fathers: A Partial List". The Founding Fathers Reconsidered. New York: Oxford University Press. ISBN 978-0199832576.
3. Lyon Gardiner (1915). Encyclopedia of Virginia Biography. Vol. 2. pp. 5–6.
4. Dill, Alonzo Thomas. "Carter Braxton (1736–1797)". Encyclopedia Virginia. Retr 9 Dec 2022.
5. Dill, Alonzo (1976). Carter Braxton: Last Virginia Signer. Virginia Independence Bicentennial Commission. p. 2.
6. Dill, p. 4.

7.   Dill, p. 3
8.   Dill p. 3.
9.   Dill, Alonzo Thomas. "Carter Braxton (1736–1797)". Encyclopedia Virginia. Retrieved 9 Dec 2022.
10. encyclopediavirginia
11. "providencejournal.com: Local & World News, Sports & Entertainment in Providence, RI". providencejournal.com. Retrieved 2 July 2018.
12. "Brown University Library, Center for Digital Scholarship". dl.lib.brown.edu. Retrieved 2 July 2018.
13. Dill, Carter Braxton, Virginia Signer: Conservative in Revolt at p. 183 citing levies against Carter Braxton in King William, York, Halifax, Hanover and Henrico counties, 1782-83, 1787-88 and 1794-95 in Land and Personal Property Tax Records, Virginia State Library.
14. Dill, p.9
15. Dill at pp. 14-15 (jointly third from the top of the list of largest debtors)
16. David J. Mayes, Edmund Pendleton, Vol. I, pp. 181-184.
17. Dill at pp. 56-57.

RICHARD HENRY LEE

FATHER OF RICHARD LIGHTFOOT LEE

A cousin of George Washington, Richard Henry Lee, was a leading voice in objection to federal taxes. He put forth the Lee Resolution to declare our country independent from Britain. He also insisted we should utilize the extensive lands in America to pay national debts and to create income to pay for our government. [a]

An active participant in many key events in the Revolutionary War, Lee protested the Stamp Act in Virginia (1765), sat on the committee that named George Washington Commander-in-Chief of the Continental army (1775), and introduced the motion that led to the Declaration of Independence (1776).

Richard Henry Lee (January 20, 1732 – June 19, 1794) was an American statesman and Founding Father from Virginia,[1] best known for the June 1776 Lee Resolution, the motion in the Second Continental Congress calling for the colonies' independence from Great Britain leading to the United States Declaration of Independence, which he signed. Lee also served as the president of the Continental Congress, proposed and was a signatory to the Continental Association, signed the Articles of Confederation, and was a United States Senator from Virginia from 1789 to 1792, serving part of that time as the second president *pro tempore*.

He was a member of the Lee family, of Virginia politics.

Early life and education

Richard Henry Lee (January 20, 1732 – June 19, 1794) was born in Westmoreland County, Virginia, to Colonel Thomas Lee and Hannah Harrison Ludwell Lee on January 20, 1732. Lee spent most of his early life in Stratford, Virginia, at Stratford Hall. Here he developed a variety of skills. In 1748, at 16, Lee left Virginia for Yorkshire, England, to complete his formal education at Queen Elizabeth Grammar School, Wakefield. Both parents died in 1750. In 1753, he returned to Virginia to help settle the estate his parents had left behind.[2]

Career

In 1757, Lee was appointed Justice of the Peace of Westmoreland County. In 1758, he was elected to the Virginia House of Burgesses, where he met Patrick Henry. Lee remained a "valuable ally of...Henry and Samuel Adams" throughout the American Revolutionary War.[3] An early advocate of independence, Lee became one of the first to create Committees of Correspondence among the many independence-minded Americans in the various colonies. In

1766, almost ten years before the American Revolutionary War, Lee is credited with having authored the Westmoreland Resolution[4] against the British Stamp Act 1765, which was publicly signed by three brothers and one close cousin of George Washington.

American Revolution

In August 1774, Lee was chosen as a delegate to the First Continental Congress in Philadelphia. In Lee's Resolution on June 7, 1776, during the Second Continental Congress, Lee put forth the motion to the Continental Congress to declare Independence from Great Britain, which read (in part):

Resolved: That these united colonies are, and of right ought to be, free and independent States, that they are absolved from all allegiance to the British crown, and that all political connection between them and the state of Great Britain is, and ought to be, totally dissolved.

Lee returned to Virginia by the time Congress voted on and adopted the Declaration of Independence, but he signed the document when he returned to Congress.

President of Congress

Lee was elected the sixth president of Congress under the Articles of Confederation on November 30, 1784. Congress convened on January 11, 1785, in the old New York City Hall, with Lee presiding until November 23, 1785.

Throughout Lee's term, he maintained that the states should relinquish their claims in the Northwest Territory, enabling the federal government to fund its obligations through land sales. He wrote to friend and colleague Samuel Adams:

"I hope we shall shortly finish our plan for disposing of the western Lands to discharge the oppressive public debt created by the war & I think that if this source of revenue be rightly managed, that these republics may soon be discharged from that state of oppression and distress that an indebted people must invariably feel."[6]

Debate began on the expansion of the Land Ordinance of 1784 and Thomas Jefferson's survey method; namely, "hundreds of ten geographical miles square, each mile containing 6086 and 4-10ths of a foot" and "sub-divided into lots of one mile square each, or 850 and 4-10ths of an acre" on April 14.[7]

The Land Ordinance of 1785 passed on May 20, 1785,[8] yet the federal government lacked the resources to manage the newly surveyed lands. Not only did Native Americans refuse to relinquish their hold on the platted territory, but much of the remaining land was occupied by squatters. With Congress unable to muster magistrates or troops to enforce the dollar-per-acre title fee, Lee's plan failed.[9]

Lee served in the US Senate in the First and Second Congresses from 1789 to 1792. In 1792 he became the second president *pro tempore*, but later that year he was obliged to resign due to his failing health, and he retired from public life.[10]

Political offices
- Member of the Continental Congress (1774–1779, 1784–1785, 1787)
- Virginia House of Delegates (1777, 1780, 1785)
- President of the Confederation Congress (Nov 30, 1784 – Nov 4, 1785)
- United States Senator from Virginia (March 4, 1789 – October 8, 1792)
- President pro tempore during Second Congress (April 18 – October 8, 1792)

Personal life and family

On December 5, 1757, he married Anne Aylett, Anne died on December 12, 1768. The couple had six children. Lee remarried in June or July 1769 Anne (Gaskins) Pinckard, with seven children, five of whom survived infancy.

Lee honored his brother, Francis Lightfoot Lee (signer of the Articles of Confederation and Declaration of Independence), by naming his son after him.

Lee died on June 19, 1794, at the age of 62.

Note   a.   https://www.loc.gov/collections/continental-congress-and-constitutional-convention-from-1774-to-1789/articles-and-essays/to-form-a-more-perfect-union/richard-henry-lee/

References

1. Bernstein, Richard B. (2009). "Appendix: The Founding Fathers, A Partial List". The Founding Fathers Reconsidered. New York: Oxford University Press. pp. 176–180. ISBN 978-0199832576.
2. McGaughy, J. K. Richard Henry Lee (1732–1794). (March 18, 2014). In Encyclopedia Virginia. Retrieved from http://www.EncyclopediaVirginia.org/ Lee Richard Henry 1732–1794
3. Davis, Kenneth C. (2003). Don't Know Much About History: Everything You Need to Know About American History but Never Learned (1st ed.). New York: HarperCollins. p. 82. ISBN 978-0-06-008381-6.
4. Washington, Lawrence; McKim, Randolph Harrison; Beale, George William (Jan 1, 1912). Westmoreland County, Virginia: Parts I and II: a Short Chapter and Bright Day in Its History. Whittet & Shepperson, printers. p. 42.
5. Estimate of Annual Expenditure Civil Departments of United States, on present Establishment President Richard Henry Lee
6. "President Richard Henry Lee to Samuel Adams, NY May 20. 1785". Arch Oct 28, 2014. Retr Sept 22, 2016.
7. Plat of Township 2, Range 7 in the Ohio Seven Ranges ca. 1786 Richard Henry Lee, President United States in Congress
8. Olsen, J.S., & Mendoza, A.O. (2015). Land Ordinance 1785. American economic history: dictionary and chronology, (p. 367)
9. Staff (May 29, 2012). "The Public Land Survey System (PLSS)". National Atlas of the United States. U.S. Department of the Interior. Archived June 7, 2012. Retrieved June 20, 2012.
10. richardhenrylee.org (retrieved March 9, 2024)

RICHARD LIGHTFOOT LEE

SIGNATORY OF TWO FOUNDATIONAL DOCUMENTS

Francis Lightfoot was a Founding Father of the United States and a member of the House of Burgesses in the Colony of Virginia.[1] As an active protester regarding issues such as the Stamp Act of 1765, Lee helped move the colony in the direction of independence. Lee was a delegate to the Virginia Conventions and the Continental Congress. He was a signer of the Declaration of Independence and Articles of Confederation for Virginia. In addition to his career in politics, Lee owned a tobacco plantation. He was a member of the Lee family, a prominent Virginia dynasty.

Richard Lightfoot Lee (October 14, 1734 – January 11, 1797) was born on October 14, 1734, at Stratford Hall Plantation, in Westmoreland County, Virginia. Lee was the fourth son of Thomas Lee and Hannah Harrison Ludwell. He was of English descent and born into one of the First Families of Virginia. He grew up at Stratford Hall, a large tobacco plantation, his father completed in 1738. He was educated at home, and studied classics under Dr. Craig.

In 1772, Lee married Rebecca Plater Tayloe. Lee lived his entire life between the Rappahannock River and Chesapeake Bay (known as the Northern Neck).

In 1774, Lee called for a general congress and the first of the Virginia Conventions. He served in the Virginia State Senate from 1778 to 1782 and was a delegate to the First Continental Congress until 1779. As a congressional representative of Virginia, signed both Declaration of Independence and Articles of Confederation. He was elected to the American Philosophical Society in 1768.

Lee died of pleurisy at his residence (named "Menokin") in Richmond County, Virginia, on January 11, 1797, following his wife's death four days prior.

BENJAMIN HARRISON of Virginia
FATHER/GRANDFATHER OF TWO UNITED STATES PRESIDENTS

- Chaired debates on Articles of Association, signed on October 20, 1774.
- Read draft Declaration of Independence to delegates, July 1, 1776
- Signed Declaration of Independence on August 2.

Benjamin Harrison V was a politician who served as a legislator in colonial Virginia, following his namesakes' tradition of public service. He was a signer of the Continental Association, and the United States Declaration of Independence, and one of the nation's Founding Fathers. He was Virginia's governor, 1781 to 1784.

As a delegate to the Continental Congress and chair of its committee of the whole, Harrison presided over the final debate of the Declaration of Independence. He was one of its signers in 1776. The Declaration included a foundational philosophy of the US: "We hold these truths to be self-evident, that all men are created equal, that they are endowed by their Creator with certain unalienable Rights, that among these are Life, Liberty and the pursuit of Happiness."

Harrison was elected as Virginia's fifth governor; his administration was marked by its futile struggle with a state treasury decimated by the Revolutionary War. He later returned to the Virginia House for two final terms. In disagreement with his traditional ally George Washington, Harrison, in 1788, cast one of his last votes in opposition to the nation's Constitution for its lack of a bill of rights. Two descendants became United States presidents— son William Henry Harrison and great-grandson Benjamin Harrison.

Family - - Parents and siblings

Benjamin Harrison V (April 5, 1726 – April 24, 1791) was born April 5, 1726, in Charles City County, Virginia; he was the eldest son and 3rd oldest of ten children of Benjamin Harrison IV (1693–1745) and Anne Carter (1702–1743); Anne was a daughter of Robert Carter I. The first Benjamin Harrison arrived in the colonies around 1630 and by 1633 began a family tradition of public service when he was recorded as clerk of the Virginia Governor's Council.[1]

Marriage and children - -Son and great-grandson presidents

In 1748, Harrison married Elizabeth Bassett (1730–1792) of New Kent County; she was the daughter of Colonel William Bassett (1709–1744) and Elizabeth Churchill (1709–1779). Harrison and his wife had eight children.[2]

The youngest child was General William Henry Harrison (1773–1841), who became a congressional delegate for the Northwest Territory and also was governor of the Indiana Territory. In the 1840 United States presidential election, William Henry defeated incumbent Martin Van Buren but fell ill and died just one month into his presidency. Vice President John Tyler, a fellow Virginian and Berkeley neighbor succeeded him.[3] William Henry's grandson, Benjamin Harrison (1833–1901), was a brigadier general in the Union Army during the American Civil War. Benjamin served in the U.S. Senate and was elected president in 1888.[4]

Virginia delegate

In his first year in the House of Burgesses in 1752, Harrison was appointed to the Committee of Propositions and Grievances and participated in a confrontation with King George, Parliament, and Governor of Virginia, Robert Dinwiddie. A dispute began with the governor over his levy of a pistole (a Spanish gold coin) upon all land patents, which presaged the core issue of the American Revolution two decades later—taxation without representation.[6]

Harrison again joined the fray with Britain after it adopted the Townshend Acts, formally asserting Parliament's right to tax the colonies. He was appointed in 1768 to a special committee to draft a response for the colony. A resolution asserted the right of British subjects to be taxed only by their elected representatives.[7] The American colonies achieved their objective with a repeal of the Townshend Acts, although Lord North, continued the tax on tea.[8]

Harrison was a 1770 signer of the Virginia Association, an association of Virginia lawmakers and merchants boycotting British imports until the British Parliament repealed its tea tax.[10] Early in 1772, Harrison and Thomas Jefferson were among a group of six Virginia house delegates assigned to prepare and deliver an address to the king which called for an end to the importation of enslaved people from Africa. Biographer Howard Smith indicates that the request was delivered and was unambiguous to close the slave trade; the king rejected it.[9]

Congressional delegate in Philadelphia

In 1773, colonists protested the British tax on tea. The British Parliament responded to the protest by enacting more punitive measures, which colonists called the Intolerable Acts.[10] Despite his qualms, Harrison was among 89 members of the Virginia Burgesses who signed a new association on May 24, 1774, condemning Parliament's action. The group also invited other colonies to convene a Continental Congress and called for a convention to select its Virginia delegates.[11] At the First Virginia Convention, Harrison was selected on August 5, 1774, as one of seven delegates to represent Virginia at the Congress, in Philadelphia.[12]

Harrison set out that month, leaving his home state for the first time. He had a positive reputation, which Edmund Randolph articulated to the Congress."[5]

Harrison arrived in Philadelphia on September 2, 1774, for the First Continental Congress. According to biographer Smith, he gravitated to the older and more conservative delegates in Philadelphia; he was more distant from the New Englanders and the more radical, particularly John and Samuel Adams.[13] Harrison aligned with John Hancock and Adams with Richard Henry Lee, whom Harrison had adamantly opposed in the House of Burgesses.[14]

In October 1774, Harrison signed the Continental Association, dictating a boycott of exports and imports with Britain. The First Congress concluded that month with a Petition to the King, signed by all delegates, requesting the king's attention to the colonies' grievances and restoration of harmony with the crown.[16]

In March 1775, Harrison attended a convention at St. John's Parish in Richmond, made famous by Patrick Henry's "Give me liberty, or give me death!" speech. A defense resolution passed by a vote of 65–60 for raising a military force.

Second Continental Congress and Declaration of Independence

When the Second Continental Congress convened in May 1775, Harrison took up residence in north Philadelphia with two roommates—his brother-in-law Peyton Randolph and George Washington.[17] The two men left him to reside alone when Randolph suddenly died, and Washington assumed command of the Continental Army.[18] Harrison was kept busy with the issues of funding and supplying Washington's army and corresponded with him at length.[18]
In spring of 1775, Congress attempted reconciliation with the King of Britain through the Olive Branch Petition, of John Dickinson. A heated debate ensued with Dickinson's disapproval of only one word in the petition, Congress.[19]

In November 1775, Harrison was appointed to a select committee to review the army's needs. He went to Cambridge, Massachusetts with Washington, Benjamin Franklin, and Thomas Lynch to assess the needs, as well as the morale, of the forces. After a 10-day inspection, the committee concluded that the pay for the troops should be improved and that the ranks should be increased to over 20,000 men.[20] Harrison then returned to Philadelphia to work with delegates for the defense of his state as well as South Carolina, Georgia, and New York.[21]

Harrison attended until the session's end, serving as chair of the Committee of the Whole.[22] He presided over final debates of the Lee Resolution of Richard Henry Lee. This was Congress' first expression of its objective of freedom from the Crown. Harrison oversaw the final debates and amendments of the Declaration of Independence.[13] The Committee of Five presented Jefferson's draft of the Declaration on June 28, 1776, and Congress resolved on that the Committee of the Whole should debate content.[23] The Committee amended it on July 2 and 3, adopted final form on Thursday, July 4. Harrison gave a final reading of the Declaration.[24] Congress unanimously resolved to have the Declaration engrossed and signed.[25]

Revolutionary War

From December 1775 until March 1777, the Congress was on two occasions threatened by British forces and forced to remove itself—first to Baltimore and later to York, Pennsylvania. In 1777, Harrison became a member of the new Committee of Secret Correspondence. The committee's objective was to establish secure communication with American agents in Britain concerning the colonies' interests.[21] Harrison was named as Chairman of the Board of War, whose purpose was to review movements of the army in the north and exchange of prisoners.[26]

Harrison found himself at odds with Washington over Marquis de Lafayette's commission, that Harrison insisted was honorary.[27] He stirred controversy by endorsing the rights of Quakers not to bear arms.[28] He unsuccessfully argued throughout the Articles of Confederation that Virginia should be given greater representation based on its population. Biographer John Sanderson indicates that when Harrison retired, "his estates had been ravaged" and "his fortune had been impaired."[28]

He was elected Speaker in 1777, defeating Jefferson by a vote of 51–23.[29]

In January 1781, a British force of 1,600 was positioned at the mouth of the James River, led by Benedict Arnold; Harrison returned to Philadelphia to request military support.[30] Berkeley was one of Arnold's primary targets, so he relocated his family before setting out.[30] In Philadelphia, he obtained increased gunpowder, supplies, and troops. Meanwhile, Arnold advanced up the James, wreaking havoc.

Governor of Virginia

The new nation secured its Revolutionary War victory in October 1781 at Yorktown, Virginia–this provided only brief respite for Harrison, who began to serve a month later as the fifth Governor of Virginia.[31] He was also the fourth governor to assume the office in that year–wartime events in Virginia occasioned multiple successions.[32] Money was the primary problem he confronted, as the war had drained the coffers of the Virginia treasury, and creditors, both domestic and foreign, plagued the government.[32] Hence, there was no capacity for military action outside of the immediate area.[32] He instead pursued a policy of treating with the Cherokee, Chickasaw, and Creek Indian tribes, which allowed peace to last for the remainder of his term. The situation resulted in some contentious exchanges with General George Rogers Clark who urged aggressive operations in the west.[32]

He joined Patrick Henry to provide funds for teachers of the Christian religion. The proposal failed, and the assembly enacted Jefferson's famous Virginia Statute for Religious Freedom, establishing a separation of church and state.[33]

Harrison participated as a member of the Virginia Ratifying Convention for the United States Constitution in 1788. However, along with Patrick Henry, George Mason, and others, he was skeptical of a large central government and opposed the Constitution because of the absence of a bill of rights.[33] Washington promoted the Constitution, yet praised Harrison, saying, "Your individual endeavors to prevent inflammatory measures redound greatly to your credit."[33]

He died on April 24, 1791, at his home after celebrating re-election.

References

1	Harrison 1975, p. 46.
2	Smith 1978, pp. 4–5.
3	Dowdey 1957, pp. 301–308.
4	Dowdey 1957, pp. 308–315.
5	Smith 1978, p. 10.
6	Smith 1978, p. 12.
7	Smith 1978, p. 19.
8	Smith 1978, p. 21.
9	Smith 1978, p. 22.
10	Smith 1978, p. 23.
11	Dowdey 1957, p. 173
12	Smith 1978, pp. 24–25
13	Smith 1978, pp. 37–39
14	Smith 1978, pp. 26–28
15	
16	Smith 1978, p. 28.
17	Dowdey 1957, p. 188.
18	"To Geo. Washington from Benj. Harrison, July 22–24, 1775". National Archives. R
19	Smith 1978, p. 32.
20	Smith 1978, pp. 33–34
21	Smith 1978, p. 35.
	"Continental Congress: Monday, July 1–Thursday, July 4, 1776".
22	Journals of the Continental Congress,1774–1789. 5. Library of Congress: 504–16. 1904–1937.
23	Smith 1978, p. 37
24	Smith 1978, p. 38
25	Smith 1978, p. 39
26	Smith 1978, p. 42
27	Smith 1978, p. 45
28	Smith 1978, p. 46
29	"Final Meeting of the Burgesses". Encyclopedia of Virginia. Va. Foundation for Humanities.
30	Dowdey 1957, p. 262.
31	Smith 1978, p. 59
32	Smith 1978, pp. 57–59
33	Smith 1978, p. 62.

Sources

- Dowdey, Clifford (1957). The Great Plantation (1st ed.). New York: Rinehart & Co. OCLC 279919.
- Harrison, J. Houston (1975). Settlers by the Long Grey Trail. Genealogical Publ. Co. ISBN 0806306645.
- Smith, Howard W. (1978). Edward M. Riley (ed.). Benjamin Harrison and the American Revolution. Williamsburg: Virginia Independence Bicentennial Commission. OCLC

JOSIAH BARTLETT

NEW HAMPSHIRE
SIGNED TWO OF OUR FOUNDATIONAL DOCUMENTS
Quinine Developer

Josiah Bartlett (December 2, 1729– May 19, 1795), born in Amesbury, in the Province of Massachusetts Bay, was the seventh and last child of Hannah (Webster) and Stephen Bartlett, a shoemaker. Bartlett had some education from the town schoolmaster and circuit schools. He learned Latin and Greek, from a relative, Reverend Doctor John Webster. In 1745, Bartlett studied medicine under Dr. Nehemiah Ordway, a relative. After a five-year apprenticeship, he moved to Kingston, New Hampshire, where he lived with Rev. Joseph Secombe.

On January 15, 1754, he married Mary Bartlett of Newton, New Hampshire. The Bartletts had twelve children, eight who lived to adulthood. All three of his sons and seven of his grandsons would become physicians.

Bartlett was a freemason and encouraged his son Josiah to join. Bartlett and Mary remained married until her death on July 14, 1789.

Career In Medicine

In 1750, he moved to Kingston, New Hampshire, in Rockingham County, and opened his medical practice. Kingston at that time was a frontier settlement.

Bartlett actively practiced medicine for 40 years. During that time, he tested both traditional and new treatments for optimal efficacy. A virulent form of throat distemper or diphtheria, with a fever and canker, spread throughout Kingston in 1754. Bartlett experimented with therapy using several available drugs and empirically discovered that Peruvian bark, also known as quinine, relieved symptoms long enough to allow recovery. He realized the benefits of curing fevers with cool liquids, like apple cider, taken at intervals. He tried this when ill, against physician's orders, with success. Beginning June 25, 1765, Bartlett and Dr. Amos Gale were partners in a medical practice.

Bartlett believed in fostering wellness, including exercise, diet, fresh air, and following cues of one's body, like drinking when thirsty and covering up when sick with the chills. He also believed "to keep the mind as Easy and Contented as possible" were "of much more Service than a multiplicity of Medicines".

In 1790, Bartlett secured legislation recognizing the New Hampshire Medical Society. He was elected chief executive of New Hampshire, serving as president in 1791 and 1792. In 1790, he delivered the commencement address at Dartmouth College when his son Ezra graduated. Bartlett was awarded an honorary Doctor of Medicine the same day his son was awarded the same degree.

Politics

Bartlett became active in the political affairs of Kingston, and in 1765, he was elected to the Provincial Assembly. Bartlett conducted discussions with Colonial Governor Benning Wentworth (1741–1766) and the Provincial Assembly to mediate dissension caused by the Stamp Act of 1765 (enacted by the Parliament of Great Britain). He opposed the Townshend Acts of 1767 and 1768 and aligned with the patriots, or Whigs. Bartlett was a member of the colonial legislature until 1775.

While a legislator, Bartlett was at odds with Governor Wentworth who endorsed the Kingdom of Great Britain's agenda over the people of New Hampshire. In an unsuccessful attempt to influence Bartlett, Governor Wentworth appointed him as Justice of the Peace in 1765. Two years later, Colonial Governor John Wentworth (1767–1775) did the same. Bartlett organized the 7th Regiment of New Hampshire Militia and in 1770, he was a colonel of militia.

Wanting independence from the Kingdom of Great Britain, Bartlett participated in revolutionary causes beginning in 1774. He joined the Provincial Assembly's Committee of Correspondence and the Committee of Safety in May. In response, the governor immediately dissolved the Provincial Assembly, which resulted in the termination of the royal government in New Hampshire. A temporary government was organized, when that assembly was not in session, the Committee of Safety took the lead. Bartlett retained his seat in the Assembly. The Committee of Correspondence reassembled the representatives and selected delegates to the Continental Congress.

Also in May, his house was burned down by Tories. He was chosen to represent New Hampshire at the First Continental Congress but declined because his house was razed.[6] He moved his family to the farmhouse and rebuilt. Josiah Bartlett House was declared a National Historic Landmark in 1971.

He was named an "accessory after the fact" for the Capture of Fort William and Mary (December 14, 1774) in New Hampshire.

Bartlett was a member of the Continental Congress in 1775, 1776 and 1778. He attended the Second Session of the Continental Congress where he sat on the civil government, secrecy, safety, marine, and munitions Committees.

When the question of independence from Great Britain was brought up in 1776, as a representative of the northernmost colony Bartlett was the first to be asked, and he answered in the affirmative. He was the second signer of the Declaration of Independence (July 4, 1776). He signed on August 2, 1776.

Bartlett in 1777, organized regiments to respond to an anticipated threat from Montreal. He led the troops with supplies to Bennington, New Hampshire to join up with Gen. John Stark's forces. He brought medical supplies that were needed for the Battle of Bennington (August 16, 1777). In 1779, Bartlett was made a colonel in the militia. He lent his medical skills to Gen. John Stark's force of New Hampshire militia and Continental troops. They defeated a German element of Gen. John Burgoyne's command in the Battle of Bennington, N.Y.—one of the reverses that helped force him to surrender 2 months later at Saratoga, N.Y. Bartlett's last tour in Congress was in 1778-79, after which he refused reelection because of fatigue·

Bartlett was reelected to the Continental Congress on March 14, 1778, and returned to Pennsylvania by May 21, 1778. He served on the committee that drafted the Articles of Confederation and he signed the instrument. Bartlett withdrew on October 31, 1778, to return to New Hampshire for personal business.

Later career
- He became chief justice of the Court of Common Pleas in 1778.
- 1782 associate justice for the New Hampshire Supreme Court.
- delegate at convention that framed the Constitution of the United States
- In 1788, Bartlett was made the chief justice of the state supreme court.
- Governor of New Hampshire from 1790, initially called chief executive.
- Bartlett retired to his home in Kingston and died there on May 19, 1795.

WILLIAM ELLERY
SIGNATORY OF TWO FOUNDATIONAL DOCUMENTS

William Ellery (December 22, 1727 – February 15, 1820) was a Founding Father of the United States, one of the 56 signers of the United States Declaration of Independence, and signed the Articles of Confederation for Rhode Island.

In 1764, the Baptists consulted with Ellery and Congregationalist Reverend Ezra Stiles on writing a charter for the college that became Brown University. Ellery and Stiles attempted to give control of the college to the Congregationalists, but the Baptists withdrew until changes assured Baptist control. Neither Ellery nor Stiles accepted appointments to the Congregationalist seats on the board of trustees. Ellery was not engaged in any warfighting.

Ellery was born in Rhode Island on December 22, 1727, the second son of William Ellery Sr. and Elizabeth Almy, a descendant of Thomas Cornell. He received his early education from his father, a merchant and Harvard College graduate. He graduated from Harvard College in 1747, where he excelled in Greek and Latin. He returned to Newport where he worked first as a merchant, next a customs collector, then as clerk of the Rhode Island General Assembly. He began practicing law in 1770 at age 43 and became active in Rhode Island Sons of Liberty.

Statesman Samuel Ward died in 1776, and Ellery replaced him in the Continental Congress. He was a signer of the Articles of Confederation and one of the 56 signers of the Declaration of Independence in 1776. The size of his signature on the Declaration is second only to John Hancock's famous signature.

Ellery served as an associate justice of the Supreme Court of Rhode Island from May 1780 to May 1781, and chief justice from June 1785 to May 1786. He had become an abolitionist by 1785. He was the first customs collector of the port of Newport under the Constitution, serving until his death, he worshipped at Second Congregational Church of Newport.

Ellery died on February 15, 1820, at age 92 and was buried in Common Burial Ground in Newport.[9] The Rhode Island Society of the Sons of the Revolution and the William Ellery Chapter of the Daughters of the American Revolution make an annual commemoration at his grave on Independence Day.

GEORGE CLYMER
SIGNATORY OF MULTIPLE FOUNDATIONAL DOCUMENTS

George Clymer (March 16, 1739 – January 23, 1813) Clymer was born in Philadelphia. Orphaned when only a year old, he was apprenticed to his maternal aunt and uncle, Hannah and William Coleman, a wealthy Quaker merchant and one of Penn's founders and first trustees to prepare to become a merchant. He married Elizabeth Meredith on March 22, 1765.

Several other Founding Fathers had the same experience, such as Alexander Hamilton, losing both parents. President Hoover was also orphaned at an early age.

Motivated at least partly by the impact of British economic restrictions on his business, Clymer adopted the Revolutionary cause and was one of the first to recommend independence. He attended patriotic meetings, served on the Pennsylvania council of safety, and in 1773 headed a committee that forced the resignation of Philadelphia tea consignees appointed by Britain under the Tea Act. Given his economic background, he channeled his energies into financial matters. In 1775-76 he acted as one of the first Continental treasurers, personally underwriting the war by exchanging all his own specie for Continental currency.

Clymer was a patriot and leader in the demonstrations in Philadelphia resulting from the Tea Act and the Stamp Act. Clymer accepted the command as a leader of a volunteer corps belonging to General John Cadwalader's brigade. As an elected member of Continental Congresses, Clymer signed the Declaration of Independence.

In 1759, he was inducted to the original American Philosophical Society. He became a member of the Philadelphia Committee of Safety in 1773 and was elected to the Continental Congress 1776–1780. He served on several committees during his first congressional term and was sent to inspect the northern army at Fort Ticonderoga in the fall of 1776. When Congress fled Philadelphia in the face of Sir Henry Clinton's threatened occupation, Clymer stayed behind with George Walton and Robert Morris. Clymer's business ventures during and after war served to increase his wealth. In 1779 and 1780, Clymer and his son Meredith engaged in a lucrative trade with Saint Eustatius. Although not partial to the merchant business, Clymer continued with his father-in-law and brother-in-law until 1782.

In Continental Congress (1776-77-1780-82) the quiet and unassuming Clymer rarely debated but influenced committee efforts, especially those pertaining to commerce, finance, and military affairs. During the War for Independence, he also served on a series of commissions that conducted important field investigations. In December 1776, when Congress fled from Philadelphia to Baltimore, he, George Walton, and Robert Morris remained behind to carry on congressional business. Within a year of victory at the Battle of Brandywine, (September 11, 1777), British troops advancing on Philadelphia detoured to vandalize Clymer's home in Chester County about 25 miles outside the city. His wife and children hid in the woods.

As a state legislator, he advocated a bicameral legislature and reform of the penal code and opposed capital punishment. At Constitutional Convention, he rarely missed a meeting, spoke seldom but played a role in shaping the document.

He resigned Congress in 1777 and in 1780 was elected to the Pennsylvania Legislature. In 1782, he toured southern states in an attempt to get the legislatures to pay up to the central government. He signed the United States Constitution on behalf of Pennsylvania. He was re-elected to Constitutional Convention in 1787. He was elected to the first U.S. Congress in 1789.

He was the first president of The Philadelphia Bank and the Pennsylvania Academy of the Fine Arts and vice-president of the Philadelphia Agricultural Society. He was also one of the commissioners to negotiate a treaty with the Creek Indian confederacy at Colerain, Georgia on June 29, 1796. He is benefactor of Indiana Borough, as he donated property for a county seat in Indiana County, Pennsylvania.

Clymer, as a member of the Pennsylvania delegation during the framing of the Constitution, unsuccessfully opposed the slave trade. The question of the slave trade, i.e., the import of new slaves into the United States, was one of the most contentious issues for the framers. Clymer was on the committee to draft a Slave Trade Compromise to postpone the slave trade decision until 1808. Clymer supported an "export tax" (tariff), which was a way to indirectly tax slavery, and like the slave trade question was opposed by southern states. The tariff became part of the compromise.

After the Revolution Clymer served as a member of the Pennsylvania Assembly, and later as a member of the Constitutional Convention. Under the new government, he served as a Pennsylvania representative to the first U.S. Congress. During the 1790s he was appointed a negotiator of a treaty with the Creek and Cherokee Indians. After retiring from public life, he served as president of Pennsylvania Academy of Fine Arts and president of Pennsylvania Bank.

Clymer was elected trustee of the Academy and College of Philadelphia in 1779. He did not serve as a trustee of the University of the State of Pennsylvania during its existence from

1779 to 1791, but at the union of this institution with the College he was elected trustee of the resulting University of Pennsylvania. He served until his death in 1813.

In 1795-96 he sat on a Presidential commission that negotiated a treaty with the Cherokee and Creek Indians in Georgia and served as the first president of the Philadelphia Bank. At the age of 73, in 1813, he died at Summerseat, an estate a few miles outside Philadelphia at Morrisville that he had purchased and moved to in 1806. His grave is in the Friends Meeting House Cemetery at Trenton, NJ. Clymer died January 23, 1813, buried at Friends Burying Ground NJ.

Samuel Huntington
SIGNATORY OF TWO FOUNDATIONAL DOCUMENTS

Samuel Huntington (July 16, 1731 – January 5, 1796) was born to Nathaniel and Mehetabel Huntington on July 16, 1731, in Windham, Connecticut Colony /Scotland, Connecticut. He was the fourth of ten children and the oldest son. He had a limited education in the common schools, then was self-educated. When he was 16, he was apprenticed to a cooper but also continued to help his father on the family farm. His education was a product of books he read from the library of Rev. Ebenezer Devotion and books from local lawyers. In 1754, Huntington was admitted to the bar, and moved to Norwich, Connecticut, to practice law.

Connecticut Assembly

After service as a selectman, Huntington began his political career in earnest in 1764 when Norwich sent him as a representative to the lower house of the Connecticut Assembly and in 1773 was appointed to the colony's supreme court, known as Supreme Court of Errors. He was chief justice of the Supreme Court from 1784 to 1787.

American Revolution

Huntington was an outspoken critic of the Coercive Acts of the British Parliament. In October 1775, the assembly elected him to be one of their delegates to the Second Continental Congress in Philadelphia.

In January 1776, he joined Roger Sherman and Oliver Wolcott, who represented the Connecticut delegation in the Second Continental Congress. He voted for and signed the Declaration of Independence and the Articles of Confederation. He served in the Congress in 1776, 1778–1781, and 1783. He suffered smallpox while in Congress.

President of the Continental Congress

When John Jay left to become minister to the Spain, Huntington succeeded him as President of the Continental Congress, which is one reason he is sometimes considered the first president. President of Congress was a mostly ceremonial position with no real authority, but the office required Huntington to handle a good deal of correspondence and official documents. The Articles of Confederation were ratified during his term.

Huntington remained as President of Congress until July 9, 1781, when ill health forced him to resign. He returned to the Congress as a delegate for the 1783 session to see the success of the revolution embodied in the Treaty of Paris. In that same year, he was elected a member of the American Philosophical Society.

Governor of Connecticut

In 1785, Huntington built his mansion house just off the green in Norwichtown, Connecticut. In 1785, he was elected as lieutenant governor of Connecticut, to Governor Matthew Griswold. In 1786, he became governor.

In his first year as governor, in a reprise of his efforts in Congress, he brokered the Treaty of Hartford that resolved western land claims between New York and Massachusetts. In 1787, he lent his support to the Northwest Ordinance that completed the national resolution of these issues. In 1788, he presided over the Connecticut Convention that was called to ratify the United States Constitution. In later years he saw the transition of Connecticut into a U.S. state. He developed a permanent state capital at Hartford and oversaw the construction.
He received electoral votes in the first U.S. presidential election.

Huntington married Martha Devotion (Rev. Devotion's daughter) in 1761. They remained together until her death in 1794. The couple did not birth any children, but when his brother (Rev. Joseph Huntington) died they adopted their nephew and niece. They raised Samuel Huntington "Jr." and Frances as their own. Huntington died while in office at his home in Norwich on January 5, 1796.

Because Huntington was the president of the Second Continental Congress when the Articles of Confederation were ratified, some unconventional biographers and civic groups consider Huntington the first President of the United States.

FRANCIS LEWIS
SIGNER OF TWO OF OUR FOUNDATIONAL DOCUMENTS
Fifth Wealthiest Founding Father

Francis Lewis (March 21, 1713 – December 31, 1802) was an American merchant and a Founding Father of the United States. He was signatory of the United States Declaration of Independence and Articles of Confederation for New York in Continental Congress.

It is unlikely that many Americans today, even many New Yorkers, have heard of Francis Lewis. Even though he is one of only sixteen to have signed both the Declaration of Independence and the Articles of Confederation, he seems not to have had much impact on the political direction or the constitutional development.

Francis Lewis (March 21, 1713 – December 31, 1802) was born in Llandaff, Wales, on March 21, 1713. He was the only child of Morgan Lewis and Anne Lewis (Pettingale) of Newport. Lewis was educated at Westminster School in London.

Lewis entered a mercantile house in London until he turned 21 and inherited some properties left by his father. Lewis sold the properties and used the proceeds to acquire merchandise, set sail for New York City, arriving there in 1734 or 1735. He left some goods in New York to be sold by his business partner and brought the rest to Philadelphia. After two years in Philadelphia, he returned to New York.

Lewis made several trans-Atlantic trips, visiting several northern European ports, Saint Petersburg, northern Scotland, and Africa. He was taken prisoner while he served as a British mercantile agent in 1756 and sent to France for imprisonment. On his release and his return home, he became active in politics.

Having become a successful businessman with contacts in several countries, he was entrusted by the British military with a contract to supply uniforms during the French and Indian

War. In 1756, the first official year of war, Lewis was at Fort Oswego in upstate New York. During his stay, the French and their Indian allies attacked in August. Lewis was standing next to the English commander when the latter was killed in the battle. The British surrendered the fort to the French, and Lewis was captured and taken to France, confined in a box or crate during that voyage. His harrowing captivity ended through a prisoner exchange when peace was achieved in 1763. The British awarded him 5,000 acres in New York as compensation for his lost years.

Lewis was a member of the Committee of Sixty, a member of the New York Provincial Congress, and a delegate to the Continental Congress from 1775 to 1779, (his age 66-69). In 1776 he signed the United States Declaration of Independence, and in 1778 he signed the United States Articles of Confederation.

Lewis once more turned his attention to business, and he quickly prospered. With his large fortune firmly established, he retired from running his businesses and became active in politics. When Parliament passed the Stamp Act in 1765, he joined the Stamp Act Congress organized to protest the tax.

Thereafter, his political activism deepened. That same year, he was a founding member of the local chapter of the Sons of Liberty, one of a loosely-connected collection around the colonies of silk-stockinged rabble-rousers with their lower-class auxiliaries as enforcers. When the crisis between Britain and her colonies began to worsen, Lewis joined the Committee of Fifty-one, organized in New York in 1774 to protest the closing of the port of Boston to commerce. Lewis advanced to the Committee of Sixty in 1775 to enforce the colonies' trade embargo against British goods, which had been adopted by the First Continental Congress. The Assembly soon elected Lewis a delegate to the Second Continental Congress, where he served between 1775 and 1779.

In the Congress, he signed the Olive Branch Petition on July 5, 1775. Written by John Dickinson of Pennsylvania, this was a last attempt by the moderates in Congress to avert war. The petition failed to achieve its purpose, as the King refused to read it. Instead, on August 23, 1775, he declared the American colonies to be in rebellion. The message of peace and compromise of the Olive Branch Petition was undermined by Congress' adoption the following day of the Declaration of the Causes and Necessity of Taking Up Arms. Drafted in parts by Thomas Jefferson and John Dickinson, that document castigated Parliament's policies and its punitive acts. It did so in an incendiary language, in sharp contrast to the tone of the Olive Branch Petition. John Adams' letter, intercepted by the British and forwarded to London, belittled the petition, and complained that the Americans should have built up a navy and taken British officials' prisoner, could not have helped to persuade the British of Americans' sincerity.

As the final break with Britain loomed, the Second Continental Congress adopted the Declaration of Independence. The vote on Richard Henry Lee's resolution to declare independence, on July 2, 1776, won by 12 delegations. After his delegation received the proper authorization from New York, Lewis and other members signed the Declaration on August 2.

Lewis used his wealth and business acumen to assist the country. He is estimated as the fifth-wealthiest signer of the Declaration. Before and during the war, he was instrumental in procuring uniforms, arms, and supplies for the Continental Army, on his own account and through his administrative talents. Lewis' service in Congress also included approving the Articles of Confederation in 1777 and being Chairman of the Continental Board of Admiralty.

In 1745, Lewis married Elizabeth Annesley (died 1779), a sister of his business partner, Thomas Annesley. They were the parents of seven children.

In 1775, Lewis acquired and relocated his family to an estate located in Whitestone, in present-day Queens. The home was later destroyed after the Battle of Long Island by British forces, who also arrested his wife Elizabeth. Sources say conditions of her captivity were inhumane in that the British denied her a bed, a change of clothing, or adequate food over several weeks. She was eventually released in a prisoner exchange for the wives of two wealthy Loyalists from Philadelphia, though the hardships Elizabeth endured in captivity ruined her health and led to her death in 1779.

Lewis died on December 31, 1802, although his memorial in Trinity Church Cemetery gives his year of death as 1803, ancient at the age of 90.

THOMAS MCKEAN
DELEGATE TO FIRST AND SECOND CONTINENTAL CONGRESS

Thomas McKean was an American lawyer, politician, and Founding Father. He was a Delaware delegate to the Continental Congress in Philadelphia, where he signed the Continental Association, the Declaration of Independence, and the Articles of Confederation. McKean served as a President of Congress.

Thomas McKean (March 19, 1734 – June 24, 1817) was born in New London Township in the Province of Pennsylvania to William McKean and Letitia Finney. His father, William, immigrated to Pennsylvania in 1720.

During his education, McKean took on a boyhood attitude. Though the school was simply for boys, McKean did interact with some females, which included Reverend Alison's wife, and her toddler half-sister, Sarah Armitage.

In 1750, McKean finished his studies with Dr. Alison, and moved in with his uncle, John Finney, who was a wealthy lawyer. McKean studied with David Finney, and after four years, in 1754, he was admitted to the Bar (law).

McKean married Mary Borden, the daughter of Colonel Joseph Borden of New Jersey. The wedding was July 21, 1763, in Mary's hometown of Bordentown. They had six children, and Mary died on March 12, 1773, of an unknown cause.

Shortly after, McKean married Sarah Armitage, on September 16, 1774.

Career

In 1755, he was admitted to the bar of the Lower Counties, as Delaware was then known, and likewise in the Province of Pennsylvania the following year. In 1756, he was appointed deputy attorney general for Sussex County. From the 1762–1763 session to the 1775–1776 session, he was a member of the General Assembly of the Lower Counties, serving as its speaker in 1772–1773. In November 1765, his Court of Common Pleas became the first such court in the colonies to establish a rule for all the proceedings of the court to be recorded on unstamped paper. In 1768, McKean was elected to the revived American Philosophical Society.

Eighteenth-century Delaware was politically divided into loose political factions known as the "Court Party" and the "Country Party". The majority Court Party was Anglican, was strongest in Kent and Sussex counties, worked well with the colonial Proprietary government, and supported reconciliation with the British government. The minority Country Party was Irish Presbyterian (also referred to as "Scotch-Irish" in America), was centered in New Castle County, and quickly advocated independence from the British. The revolutionary slogan "no taxation without representation" had originated in the north of Ireland under the British Penal Laws, which denied Presbyterians and Catholics the right to vote for members of the parliament.

McKean was the epitome of the Country Party politician and was, as much as anyone else, its leader.[4] He worked with Caesar Rodney and in opposition to, George Read.

At the Stamp Act Congress of 1765, McKean and Caesar Rodney represented Delaware. McKean proposed the voting procedure that the Continental Congress later adopted: each colony, regardless of size or population, would have one vote. That decision set the precedent, Congress of the Articles of Confederation adopted the practice, and the principle of state equality has continued in the United States Senate.

McKean quickly became one of the most influential members of the Stamp Act Congress. He was on the committee that drew the memorial to parliament and, with John Rutledge and Philip Livingston, revised its proceedings. When the business session ended, Timothy Ruggles, president of the body, and others refused to sign. McKean then disputed his use of the word "conscience" so loudly and so long that Ruggles issued a duel challenge, accepted in the presence of Congress. Ruggles left the next morning the duel did not take place.

American Revolution

Despite his residence in Philadelphia, McKean remained the leader for independence in Delaware. Along with Read and Caesar Rodney, he was one of Delaware's delegates to the First Continental Congress in 1774 and Second Continental Congress in 1775 and 1776.

Being an outspoken advocate of independence, McKean was a key voice in persuading others to vote for a split with Great Britain. When Congress began debating a resolution of independence in June 1776, Rodney was absent. Read was against independence, which meant that the Delaware delegation divided between McKean and Read and therefore could not vote in favor of independence. McKean requested that the absent Rodney ride all night from Dover to break the tie. After the vote in favor of independence, McKean participated in the debate over wording of the official Declaration of Independence, approved on July 4.

A few days after McKean cast his vote, he left Congress to serve as colonel of the Fourth Battalion of the Pennsylvania Associators, a militia unit created by Benjamin Franklin in 1747. They joined Washington's defense of New York City at Perth Amboy, New Jersey.

In a reaction against the advocates of American independence, the 1776-1777 Delaware General Assembly did not reelect either McKean or Rodney to the Continental Congress in October 1776. However, the British occupation after the Battle of Brandywine swung opinions enough that McKean was returned to Congress in October 1777 by the 1777–1778 Delaware General Assembly. During that time, he avoided pursuit by British forces. Over the following years, he relocated his family five times.

He served continuously in the Congress until February 1, 1783. McKean helped draft the Articles of Confederation and voted for their adoption on March 1, 1781. When poor health caused Samuel Huntington to resign as president of Congress in July 1781, McKean was elected as his successor. He served from July 10 to November 4, 1781. The position was mostly ceremonial, but the office required McKean to handle a good deal of correspondence and sign official documents.[9] During his time in office, Lord Cornwallis surrendered at Yorktown.

Government of Delaware

Meanwhile, McKean led the effort in the General Assembly of Delaware to declare its separation from the British government, which it did on June 15, 1776. In August, he joined the special convention to draft a new state constitution. Upon hearing it, McKean made the long ride to Dover, Delaware, from Philadelphia in a single day, went to a room in an inn, and that night, by himself, drafted the document; adopted September 20, 1776. Delaware Constitution of 1776 became the first state constitution produced after the Declaration of Independence.

McKean was elected to Delaware's first House of Assembly for both the 1776–1777 and the 1778–1779 sessions, succeeding John McKinly as speaker on February 12, 1777, when McKinly became president of Delaware. Shortly after President McKinly's capture and imprisonment, McKean served as the president of Delaware for a month, from September 22 to October 20, 1777. That was the time needed for George Read to return from the Continental Congress in Philadelphia and to assume the duties.

Immediately after the Battle of Brandywine, the British Army occupied Wilmington and much of northern New Castle County. Its navy also controlled the lower Delaware River and Delaware Bay. As a result, the state capital, New Castle, was unsafe as a meeting place, and the Sussex County seat, Lewes, was sufficiently disrupted by Loyalists that it was unable to hold a valid general election that autumn. As president, McKean was occupied with recruitment of the militia and keeping civic order in the portions of the state still under his control.

Government of Pennsylvania

McKean started his long tenure as chief justice of Pennsylvania on July 28, 1777, and served in that capacity until 1799. There, he set the rules of justice for revolutionary Pennsylvania. According to the biographer John Coleman, "only the historiographical difficulty of reviewing court records and other scattered documents prevents recognition that McKean, rather than John Marshall, did more than anyone else to establish an independent judiciary in the United States. As chief justice under a Pennsylvania constitution he considered flawed, he assumed it the right of the court to strike down legislative acts it deemed unconstitutional, preceding by ten years the U.S. Supreme Court's establishment of the doctrine of judicial review. He augmented the rights of defendants and sought penal reform."

He was a member from Pennsylvania that ratified the Constitution of the United States. In the Pennsylvania State Constitutional Convention of 1789/90, he argued for a strong executive and was himself a Federalist. In 1796, dissatisfied with the Federalists' he became a Jeffersonian Republican, or Democratic-Republican.

Chief justice of Pennsylvania, McKean played a role in the Whiskey Rebellion. On August 2, 1794, he took part in a conference on the rebellion. In attendance were Washington, his Cabinet, the governor of Pennsylvania, and other officials. Washington interpreted the rebellion as a grave threat which could mean "an end to our Constitution and laws." Washington advocated "the most spirited and firm measure" but held back on what that meant. McKean argued that the matter should be left up to the courts, not the military. Alexander Hamilton insisted upon the "propriety of an immediate resort to Military force." Some weeks later, McKean and General William Irvine wrote to Pennsylvania Governor Thomas Mifflin and discussed the mission of federal committees to negotiate with the Rebels, describing them as "well disposed."

McKean was elected governor of Pennsylvania and served three terms from December 17, 1799, to December 20, 1808. In the 1799 election, he defeated the Federalist Party nominee James Ross and again more easily in the 1802 election. At first, McKean ousted Federalists from state government positions and so he has been called the father of the spoils system.

Some of McKean's accomplishments included expanding free education for all and, at age eighty, leading a Philadelphia citizens group to organize defense during the War of 1812.

McKean was a member of the Pennsylvania Society of the Cincinnati in 1785. McKean was bestowed LL.D. degrees (a) in 1781 by the College of New Jersey (Princeton), (b) in 1782 by Dartmouth College, and (c) in 1785 by his alma mater, University of Pennsylvania. With James Wilson (Founding Father), McKean published "Commentaries on the Constitution of the United States" in 1790.

JOHN PENN

SIGNER OF DECLARATION OF INDEPENDENCE and CONSTITUTION

John Penn (May 17, 1741 – September 14, 1788) was an American Founding Father who served multiple terms in the Continental Congress and signed both the Declaration of Independence and Articles of Confederation for North Carolina.

Penn was born near Port Royal in Caroline County, Virginia, the only son of Moses Penn and Catherine (Taylor) Penn. He attended a common school for two years as his father did not consider education to be important. At age 18, after his father's death, Penn privately read law with his uncle, Edmund Pendleton. He became a lawyer in Virginia in 1762.

On July 28, 1763, Penn married Susannah Lyne. They had three children. Daughter, Lucy, married John Taylor of Caroline, a political leader from Virginia.

In 1774, Penn moved to Stovall, North Carolina. There, he was a representative at the colony's Third Provincial Congress in August 1775. In 1775 Penn was elected to the Continental Congress. He was re-elected in 1777, 1778 and 1779 and served with distinction. During his tenure, he signed the Declaration of Independence and the Articles of Confederation.

In 1780 Penn was appointed to the North Carolina board of war. Following his appointment to the Congress, he practiced law until his death in 1788.

The naval ship USS *John Penn* was named in his honor. A historical highway marker honoring Penn was erected near his home in Stovall in 1936.

GEORGE READ

LEADER FOR STATES RIGHTS OF SMALLER POPULATIONS

George Read (September 18, 1733 – September 21, 1798) was the son of John and Mary Read. John Read was born in Dublin, Ireland, the son of an Englishman of large fortune. The death of his beloved left him bereft, John Read came to the colonies and entered into extensive enterprises in Maryland and Delaware.

Soon after his arrival in America, John Read purchased a large estate in Cecil County, Maryland, and founded with six associates the city of Charlestown on Chesapeake Bay, with the intention of creating a new market. They developed northern Maryland and built-up iron works, in which the Washington family, and General Washington, were largely interested.

George Read was born in Cecil County, Maryland, on September 18, 1733. When he was an infant, the family moved to New Castle County, Delaware, settling near the village of Christiana. As he grew up, Read joined Thomas McKean at the Rev. Francis Allison's Academy at New London, Pennsylvania, and then studied law in Philadelphia with John Moland. He gained admission to the Pennsylvania Bar in 1753, and a year later he returned home to establish a practice at New Castle.

In 1763 he married Gertrude Ross Till, daughter of the Rev. George Ross, the Anglican rector of Immanuel Church in New Castle and widowed sister of George Ross, also a future signer of the Declaration of Independence. They lived on The Strand in New Castle, and their house was in what is now the garden of the present Read House and Gardens, owned by the Delaware Historical Society. They were members of Immanuel Episcopal Church.

In 1763 John Penn, the proprietary governor, appointed Read crown attorney general for the three Delaware counties, and he served in that position until leaving for the Continental

Congress in 1774. He also served in the Colonial Assembly of the lower Delaware counties for twelve sessions, from 1764/65 through 1775/76.

American Revolution

Eighteenth-century Delaware was politically divided into loose factions known as the "Court Party" and the "Country Party." The majority Court Party was generally Anglican, strongest in Kent and Sussex Counties, worked well with the colonial proprietary government and was in favor of reconciliation with the British government. The minority Country Party was largely Ulster-Scot, centered in New Castle County, and quickly advocated independence from the British. Read was often the leader of the Court party faction, and as such he generally worked in opposition to Caesar Rodney and his friend and neighbor Thomas McKean.

Read, like most other people in Delaware, was in favor of trying to reconcile differences with Great Britain. He opposed the Stamp Act and similar measures of Parliament but supported anti-importation measures and dignified protests. Nevertheless, from 1764 he led the Delaware Committee of Correspondence and was elected to serve along with the more radical McKean and Rodney in the First and Second Continental Congress from 1774 to 1777. He was frequently absent, and when Congress voted on American Independence on July 2, 1776, Read voted against it. That meant Rodney had to ride overnight to Philadelphia to break the deadlock in Delaware's delegation for independence. When the Declaration of Independence was finally adopted, Read signed it despite caution.

Iron and Cannon - - This section from: https://www.nps.gov/hofu/learn/historyculture/hopewellintheamericanrevolution.htm

In 1771 Hopewell Furnace went into blast for the first time, enhanced through such partners and in-laws as James Wilson, George Ross (ironmaster) and George Read, all future signers of the Declaration of Independence. By that same year America was well on the way to revolution. America's iron industry was then producing some 15% of the world's supply of iron, more than Great Britain.

From 1775 to early 1778 the Americans had to look primarily to furnaces like Hopewell for iron cannon, shot and shell. Yet none of these sites had ever before cast ordnance. Despite the difficulties of "learning by doing," the iron industry met the challenge. Hopewell alone produced 115 cannon for the Continental Navy. Even more importantly, Hopewell provided shot and shell to the Army and Navy throughout the war, including 10-inch mortar shells to help win at Yorktown, Virginia.

Government of Delaware

Anticipating the Declaration of Independence, the General Assembly of the lower counties declared its separation from the British government on June 15, 1776, in the New Castle Court House. Once the Declaration of Independence was actually adopted, the General Assembly called for elections to a constitutional convention and Read was elected to this convention, became its president, and guided the passage of the Delaware Constitution of 1776.

Read was elected to the first Legislative Council of the Delaware General Assembly and was selected as the speaker in both the 1776/77 and 1777/78 sessions. At the time of the capture of President John McKinly, Read was in Philadelphia attending Congress; after narrowly escaping capture himself while he was returning home, he became president on October 20, 1777, serving until March 31, 1778. The British occupied Philadelphia and were in control of the Delaware River. Read tried, mostly in vain, to recruit additional soldiers and to protect the state from raiders from Philadelphia and off ships in the Delaware River. The

Delaware General Assembly session of 1777/78 had to be moved to Dover, Delaware, for safety, because disruptions at the polls had negated the election results.

On the Constitution - - quoted from US Army Center for Military History. https://www.history.army.mil/books/revwar/ss/read.htm pp. 167-168

In reference to the Stamp Act, a tax which Parliament sought to use to recoup the cost of the French and Indian War, he said that if enforced, "the colonists will entertain an opinion that they are to become the slaves" of Great Britain and will endeavor "to live as independently of the mother country as possible."

Read represented Delaware in the Continental Congress (1774-76). An irregular attendee, he moved into conservative Patriot circles with delegates such as his friend John Dickinson. They were willing to fight for colonial rights but were wary of extremism. Although he voted against independence on 2 July 1776 because he thought reconciliation was possible, fully supported the Declaration.

Read presided over Delaware's constitutional convention (1776), where he exercised more influence than any other member. He chaired the drafting committee, serving as a voice for moderation by balancing the revolutionary impulses of the people with the legitimate rights of property owners. His service as speaker of the Legislative Council (the upper house of the Delaware legislature) made him, in effect, the assistant governor of the state. In November 1777, after narrowly escaping capture by British troops while en route from Philadelphia to Dover, he assumed the presidency (governorship) of Delaware, a post he held until March 1778. Back in the Legislative Council in 1779, he drafted the act authorizing Delaware's ratification of the Articles of Confederation. Reflecting the views of the smaller states, Read argued taxes levied by Congress should be based on the population, rather than on the value of lands and improvements, and that the title to western lands should be held with specific limits on claims of states to them.

Following a brief retirement necessitated by ill health, he resumed his seat in the Legislative Council (1782-88) and served as judge on the state's court of appeals and on a commission to settle land claims in disputes with Massachusetts and New York. He was primarily active in promoting measures to improve the state's commerce and finances. Ignoring popular pressure, he opposed inflationary measures that he feared would impair Delaware's long-term financial credit.

CONTRIBUTIONS TO THE CONSTITUTIONAL CONVENTION. At the Convention, Read immediately pushed for a new national government based on a new Constitution. As he put it: "to amend the Articles was simply putting old cloth on a new garment." He was a leader in the fight for a strong central government, advocating, at one time, the abolition of the states altogether and the consolidation of the country under one powerful national government. "Let no one fear the states, the people are with us;" he declared to a Convention shocked by this radical proposal. With no one to support his motion, he settled for protecting the rights of the small states against the infringements of their larger, more populous neighbors who, he feared, would "probably combine to swallow up the smaller ones by addition, division or impoverishment." He favored giving Congress the right to veto state laws, making the federal legislature immune to popular whims by having senators hold office for nine years or during good behavior, and granting the President broad appointive powers. Outspoken, he threatened to lead Delaware out of the Convention unless the rights of small states were guaranteed in the new Constitution.

Federalist

Read was again called to service in 1786 when he represented Delaware at the Annapolis Convention. Few states were represented, and this meeting produced only a report calling for a broader convention next year. At what became the Constitutional Convention, Read again represented Delaware.

Once the rights were assured, he led the ratification in Delaware, which, because of his efforts, became the first state to ratify, and unanimously.

Senator

Following the adoption of the U.S. Constitution, the Delaware General Assembly elected Read as one of its two U.S. Senators. His term began on March 4, 1789, and he was reelected in 1791 but resigned on September 18, 1793. Read served with the Pro-Administration Party majority in the First and Second Congress, under President Washington. He supported the assumption of state debts, establishment of a national bank, and the imposition of excise taxes.

He died September 21, 1798, from a non-reported condition.

JOHN WITHERSPOON

PROFESSOR FOR JAMES MADISON, RECOGNIZED PHILOSOPHER

John Witherspoon (February 5, 1723 – November 15, 1794) was a Scottish American Presbyterian minister, educator, farmer, slaveholder, and a Founding Father of the United States. Witherspoon embraced the concepts of Scottish common-sense realism, and while president of the College of New Jersey (1768–1794; now Princeton) became an influential figure in the development of the United States. Politically active, Witherspoon was a delegate from New Jersey to the Second Continental Congress and a signatory to the July 4, 1776, Declaration of Independence. He was the only college president to sign the Declaration. Later, he signed the Articles of Confederation and supported ratification of the Constitution of the United States.

In 1789 he was convening moderator of the First General Assembly of the Presbyterian Church in the United States of America.

Early life and ministry in Scotland

John Witherspoon was born in Yester, Scotland, documented in the Old Parish Register as the eldest child of the Reverend James Alexander Witherspoon and Anne Walker, a descendant John Knox. He attended Haddington Grammar School and obtained a Master of Arts from the University of Edinburgh in 1739. He remained at the university to study divinity. In 1764, he was awarded an honorary doctoral degree in divinity by the University of St Andrews.

Witherspoon was a staunch Protestant, nationalist, and supporter of republicanism. Consequently, he was opposed to the Roman Catholic Legitimist Jacobite rising of 1745–46. Following the Jacobite victory at the Battle of Falkirk, he was imprisoned at Doune Castle, which had a long-term effect on his health.

He became a Church of Scotland (Presbyterian) minister at Beith, Ayrshire (1745–1758), where he married Elizabeth Montgomery of Craighouse. They had ten children, with five surviving to adulthood.

278

Princeton

At the urging of Benjamin Rush and Richard Stockton, whom he met in Paisley, Witherspoon finally accepted their renewed invitation to become president and head professor of the Presbyterian College of New Jersey in Princeton.

At the age of 45, he became the sixth president of the college, later known as Princeton University. Upon his arrival, Witherspoon found the school in debt, with weak instruction, and a library collection which clearly failed to meet student needs.

An advocate of natural law within a Christian and republican cosmology, Witherspoon considered moral philosophy vital for ministers, lawyers, and those holding positions in government (magistrates).

Nonetheless, Witherspoon transformed a college designed to train clergymen into a school that would equip the leaders of a new country. Students who later played prominent roles in the new nation's development included James Madison, Aaron Burr, Philip Freneau, William Bradford, and Hugh Henry Brackenridge. From among his students came 37 judges (three of whom became justices of the U.S. Supreme Court); 10 Cabinet officers; 12 members of the Continental Congress, 28 U.S. Senators, and 49 U.S. Congressmen.

Revolutionary War

Long wary of the power of the British Crown, Witherspoon saw the growing centralization of government, progressive ideology of colonial authorities, and establishment of episcopacy authority as a threat to the liberties of the colonies. Of particular interest to Witherspoon was the Crown's growing interference in the local and colonial affairs which previously had been the prerogatives and rights of the American authorities. When the Crown began to give additional authority to its appointed episcopacy over church affairs, British authorities hit a nerve in the Presbyterian Scot, who saw such events in the same lens as his Scottish Covenanters. Soon, Witherspoon came to support the American Revolution, joining the New Jersey Committee of Correspondence and Safety in early 1774. His 1776 sermon "The Dominion of Providence over the Passions of Men" was published in many editions, and he was elected to the Continental Congress as part of the New Jersey delegation. In Congress, he was appointed congressional chaplain, and in July 1776, he voted to adopt the Virginia Resolution for Independence (or Lee Resolution). In answer to an objection that the country was not yet ready for independence, according to tradition he replied that it "was not only ripe for the measure, but in danger of rotting for the want of it."

He spoke often in concurrence; helped draft the Articles of Confederation; helped organize the executive departments; played a major role in shaping public policy; and drew up instructions for peace commissioners. He fought against the flood of paper money and opposed the issuance of bonds without provision for their amortization. "No business can be done, some say, because money is scarce", he wrote. He also served twice in the New Jersey Legislature and supported adoption of the United States Constitution during the New Jersey debates.

In November 1777, as British forces neared, Witherspoon closed and evacuated the College of New Jersey. The main building, Nassau Hall, was badly damaged, and his papers and personal notes were lost. Witherspoon was responsible for its reconstruction after the war, which caused him great personal and financial difficulty. In 1780 he was elected to a one-year term in the New Jersey Legislative Council representing Somerset County. At age 68, he married a 24-year-old widow, with whom he had two more children.

Witherspoon suffered eye injuries and was blind by 1792. He died in 1794 on his farm Tusculum, just outside Princeton.

Witherspoon married Elizabeth Montgomery on 14 August 1748 documented in the old parish register in Beith, North Ayrshire. They were both from the parish.[4] His brother James, the eldest, graduated from Princeton in 1770 and joined the Continental Army as an aide to General Francis Nash, with the rank of major and was killed at the Battle of Germantown on October 4, 1777.

Philosophy

According to Herbert Hovenkamp, Witherspoon's most lasting contribution was the initiation of the Scottish common-sense realism, which he had learned by reading Thomas Reid and his expounders Dugald Stewart and James Beattie.

At the College of New Jersey, Witherspoon revised the moral philosophy curriculum, strengthened the college's commitment to natural philosophy, and positioned Princeton in the larger transatlantic world of the republic of letters. Witherspoon was a proponent of Christian values, his common sense approach to public morality of civil magistrates was influenced by the ethics of Scottish philosophers Francis Hutcheson and Reid rather than Jonathan Edwards. Regarding civil magistrates, Witherspoon thus believed moral judgment should be pursued as a science. He held to old concepts from the Roman Republic of virtuous leadership by civil magistrates, but he regularly recommended his students read such philosophers as Machiavelli, Montesquieu, and David Hume, though he disapproved of Hume's "infidel" stance on religion.

In his lectures on moral philosophy at Princeton, required of all juniors and seniors, Witherspoon argued for the revolutionary right of resistance and recommended checks and balances within government. He made a profound impression on his student James Madison, whose suggestions for the United States Constitution followed Witherspoon's and Hume's ideas.

Witherspoon owned slaves and lectured against the abolition of slavery. However, in his "Lectures on Moral Philosophy", Dr. Witherspoon advocated for the humane treatment of laborers and servants (including slaves), stating:

The settled opinion among the American founding fathers, including Dr. Witherspoon, was that slavery would eventually disappear naturally within a generation. For this reason, Rev. Witherspoon advocated for "gradual emancipation" of slaves:

In this connection it may be noted that in 1790 President Witherspoon, while a member of the New Jersey Legislature, was chairman of a committee on the abolition of slavery in the state, and brought in a report advising no action, on the ground that the law already forbade the importation of slaves and encouraged voluntary manumission.
— *Witherspoon, John (1912). Lectures on Moral Philosophy. Princeton, N.J.: Princeton University Press. p. 74.*

OLIVER WOLCOTT

Yes, Oliver Wolcott (1726-1797) was a Founding Father of the United States:

- He was major general in Connecticut militia under Washington. Commanded 14 regiments.
- Member of Continental Congress, signed Declaration of Independence.
- Wolcott helped negotiate a settlement with the Iroquois in 1784.

Oliver Wolcott Sr. (November 20, 1726 – December 1, 1797) was born in Windsor, Connecticut, the youngest of 10 children born to colonial Governor Roger Wolcott and Sarah Drake Wolcott. He attended Yale College, graduating in 1747 as first in his class. Upon graduation, New York Governor George Clinton granted Wolcott a captain's commission to raise a militia company to fight in the French and Indian Wars (King George's War (1744–1748)). Captain Wolcott served on the northern frontier defending the Canadian border against the French until the Treaty of Aix-la-Chapelle of 1748. He moved to Goshen in northwestern Connecticut to practice and study medicine with his brother Alexander. He married Lorraine Collins of Guilford, Connecticut.

American Revolutionary War

Wolcott had two careers during the war years as one of Connecticut's principal delegates to the Continental Congress and also a militia officer. He participated in the American Revolutionary War as brigadier general and then as major general in the Connecticut militia. As a representative in the Continental Congress, he was a strong advocate for independence.

Wolcott saw extensive militia service during the American Revolution. On August 11, 1776, Connecticut officials ordered him to march the Seventeenth Regiment of militia to New York and join George Washington's army. Upon arriving at Washington's camp, Connecticut Governor Jonathan Trumbull appointed Wolcott brigadier general in command of all the state's militia regiments in New York. He led 300 to 400 volunteers from his brigade to help General Horatio Gates and Benedict Arnold defeat General John Burgoyne at the Battles of Saratoga.

In May 1779, Wolcott earned promotion to major general in command of all Connecticut militia. He was largely unsuccessful in his combat with Major General William Tryon. Over the course of the war, he showed great disdain towards his opposition, describing the British in his memoirs as "a foe who have not only insulted every principle which governs civilized nations but by their barbarities offered the grossest indignities to human nature."

Continental Congress

At the beginning of the Revolution, Congress made Wolcott a commissioner of Indian affairs to persuade the northern Indian nations to remain neutral. He was asked, along to negotiate a peace treaty with the Six Nations.
He was elected to the Continental Congress in 1775.

Beyond his postwar diplomatic role, Wolcott aspired to higher office. He was elected Lieutenant Governor of Connecticut as a Federalist in 1786 and served in that position for ten years. Wolcott became governor when Samuel Huntington died on January 5, 1796, holding the office until his own death at age 71.

Wolcott died on December 1, 1797, in Litchfield. Historian Ellsworth Grant remembers Wolcott stating: "It is doubtful if any other official during this period carried so many public duties."

WILLIAM WHIPPLE

NEW HAMPSHIRE

William Whipple Jr. was an American Founding Father and signatory of the United States Declaration of Independence. He represented New Hampshire as a member of the Continental Congress from 1776 through 1779. He was engaged in heavy combat throughout the War for Independence.

William Whipple Jr. (January 25, 1731– November 28, 1785) was born in Kittery in the Province of Massachusetts Bay (now Maine. Whipple was a descendant of Samuel Appleton, an early settler in Ipswich, Massachusetts. Whipple left his business in 1775 to devote himself to the Revolution. He served in the Continental Congress from 1776 to 1779, alongside future presidents Jefferson and John Adams. He commanded militia including the Battle of Saratoga.

By the outbreak of the Revolution, Whipple had become one of the leading citizens of Portsmouth. In 1775, his fortune well established, he left business to devote his time to public affairs. His congressional tour, interrupted intermittently by militia duty, lasted until 1779. He concerned himself with military, marine, and financial matters. A tough-minded, independent individual, he recommended military aggressiveness in the war instead of diplomacy.

In 1775, New Hampshire dissolved the British Royal government and organized a House of Representatives and an Executive Council known as a Provincial Congress. Whipple was elected to represent Portsmouth. He became a member of the Committee of Safety. He was then elected to the Continental Congress and signed the United States Declaration of Independence. He was the second cousin of fellow signatory Stephen Hopkins. In January 1776, Whipple wrote Josiah Bartlett of the approaching convention:

This year, my Friend, is big with mighty events. Nothing less than the fate of America depends on the virtue of her sons, if they do not have virtue enough to support the most Glorious Cause ever human beings were engaged in, they do not deserve the blessings of freedom.

The New Hampshire Provincial Congress gave Whipple his first commission in 1777. His enslaved servant Prince Whipple joined him. William offered Prince his freedom if he continued military service. Prince agreed and by end of the war, William granted his freedom.

At Saratoga, Whipple commanded a brigade of four militia regiments. As a result of their meritorious conduct at the Battle of Saratoga, Whipple and Colonel James Wilkinson were chosen by Major General Horatio Gates to determine terms of capitulation with two representatives of General John Burgoyne. Whipple then signed the Convention of Saratoga, the surrender of General Burgoyne.

Whipple was ordered to escort Burgoyne and his army back to Winter Hill, Massachusetts. Whipple passed the news of the victory at Saratoga to John Paul Jones, who informed Franklin, who was in Paris at the time. News of the victory proved valuable to Franklin throughout alliance negotiations with the French. In 1778, Whipple followed his commanding officer, General John Sullivan to the Battle of Rhode Island.

During his last years, Whipple was a state legislator (1780-84), associate justice of the New Hampshire Superior Court (1782-85), receiver of finances for Congress in New Hampshire (1782-84), and in 1782 president of a commission that arbitrated the Wyoming Valley land dispute between Connecticut and Pennsylvania.

On November 28, 1785, he suffered from a heart ailment and died after fainting from atop his horse while traveling his court circuit.

MATTHEW THORNTON
NEW HAMPSHIRE

Matthew Thornton was a Founding Father of the United States and a signer of the Declaration of Independence. He played a key role in New Hampshire's founding. He was President of the committee that drafted the first state constitution, adopted **January 5, 1776**, the first of thirteen states to establish a constitution.

Matthew Thornton (March 3, 1714 – June 24, 1803) was born in Ireland in 1714 to James and Elizabeth (*née* Jenkins) Thornton, James Thornton lived on a farm within a mile of Derry, and this is where Matthew was probably born.

In 1716, Thornton's family immigrated to North America when he was three years old, settling first in Wiscasset, Maine. On July 11, 1722, the community was attacked by Native Americans. James and Elizabeth Thornton fled from their burning home with Matthew, moving shortly thereafter to Worcester, Massachusetts. Thornton completed studies in medicine at Leicester. He became a physician and established a medical practice in Londonderry, New Hampshire. He was appointed as a surgeon for the New Hampshire Militia troops in an expedition against Fortress Louisbourg in 1745. He served in the New Hampshire Provincial Assembly from 1758-1762, had royal commissions as Justice of the Peace, and served as colonel in the militia from 1775 until his resignation in 1779. In 1760, Thornton married Hannah Jack, and had five children.

Thornton served as president of the New Hampshire Provincial Congress in 1775, and from January to September 1776, speaker of the New Hampshire House of Representatives. He was elected to the Continental Congress after debates on independence had occurred. He did not arrive in Philadelphia until November 1776, he was granted permission to sign the Declaration of Independence.

He became a political essayist. He retired from his medical practice, and in 1780, moved to Merrimack, New Hampshire, where he farmed and operated Thornton's ferry. He served as a judge on the New Hampshire Superior Court.

In 1783, Thornton represented the towns of Merrimack and Bedford in the New Hampshire House of Representatives, and then Hillsborough County in the New Hampshire Senate from 1784 to 1787, while simultaneously serving as a state counselor from 1785 to 1786 and as a state representative again for Merrimack in 1786. His wife Hannah died in 1786.

Thornton died in Newburyport, Massachusetts. He was 89 years old.

ROBERT TREAT PAINE
MASSACHUSETTS

Robert Treat Paine was a lawyer, politician and Founding Father of the United States who signed the Continental Association and Declaration of Independence as a representative of Massachusetts. He was the state's first attorney general and associate justice of the Massachusetts Supreme Judicial Court.

Robert Treat Paine (March 11, 1731 – May 11, 1814) was born in Boston, Province of Massachusetts Bay, in British America, on March 11, 1731. He was one of five children of the Rev. Thomas Paine and Eunice (Treat) Paine. His father was pastor of Franklin Road Baptist Church in Weymouth. His mother was the daughter of Rev. Samuel Treat, whose father Maj. Robert Treat was one of the principal founders of Newark, New Jersey, and later a governor of Connecticut. Robert Treat Paine's Treat family can trace a lineage back to the *Mayflower*.

Paine attended Boston Latin School, then entered Harvard College at age 14; he graduated at age 18. He taught school and began the study of law in 1755.

Paine served as a chaplain in the Crown Point Expedition during the French and Indian War. Returning to civilian life, he did some occasional preaching and returned to legal studies and was admitted to the bar in 1757. He moved his law practice from Portland, to Taunton, Massachusetts, then back to Boston in 1780.

In 1768, he was a delegate to a provincial convention in Boston. Paine, and Samuel Quincy, prosecuted Captain Thomas Preston and eight soldiers under following the Boston Massacre of March 5, 1770. John Adams was opposing counsel, Adams' arguments won and most of the troops were let off.

Paine served in the Massachusetts General Court from 1773 to 1774, in Provincial Congress, represented Massachusetts at Continental Congress, signing the final appeal to the king (the Olive Branch Petition of 1775) and helped frame the rules of debate and acquire gunpowder, in 1776, signed the Declaration of Independence.

He returned to Massachusetts at the end of December 1776 and was speaker of the Massachusetts House of Representatives in 1777, a member of the executive council in 1779, and a member of the committee that drafted the state constitution in 1780. He was Massachusetts Attorney General from 1777 to 1790 and prosecuted the treason trials following Shays' Rebellion. In 1780, he was a charter member of the American Academy of Arts and Sciences. He last served as a justice of the State Supreme Court from 1790 to 1804 when he retired.

Paine died at age 83 in 1814 and was buried in Boston's Granary Burying Ground. Many of his papers, including correspondence and legal notes, are now held by the Massachusetts Historical Society.

WILLIAM WILLIAMS

- Signer of the Declaration of Independence.
- Helped draft Articles of Confederation
- Williams fought in the French and Indian War
- Fought in the Revolutionary War.
- Delegate to the 1788 convention that ratified the Constitution.
- Involved in the construction of the United States Capitol.
- He graduated from Harvard in 1751 and studied theology.

William Williams (April 8, 1731 – August 2, 1811) was an American Founding Father, born in Lebanon, Connecticut, the son of minister Solomon Williams and Mary Porter. He studied theology and law at Harvard in 1751. He studied for the ministry but then joined the militia to fight in the French and Indian War.

On February 14, 1771, he married Mary Trumbull, age 25. She was the daughter of Connecticut Governor Jonathan Trumbull, who served as the second speaker of the United States House of Representatives. They had three children.

Williams spent many years in the Connecticut House of Representatives, serving from 1757 to 1762, 1763 to 1776, and 1780 to 1784, while serving as Speaker of that body in 1775 and from 1781 to 1783.

He was a member of the Sons of Liberty and later served on Connecticut's Committee of Correspondence and Council of Safety. He was a staunch supporter of the non-importation agreements implemented in 1769 to oppose the Townshend Acts and the occupation of Boston by British Regulars.

On July 1, 1774, one month after the enactment of the Coercive Acts to punish Boston, Williams pseudonymously published an address "To the King" from "America" in the *Connecticut Gazette*. The document, an angry satire, read in part:

"We don't complain that your father made our yoke heavy and afflicted us with grievous service. We only ask that you govern us upon the same constitutional plan, and with the same justice and moderation that he did, and we will serve you forever. And what is the language of your answer...? Ye Rebels and Traitors...if ye don't yield implicit obedience to all my commands, just and unjust, ye shall be drag'd in chains across the wide ocean, to answer your insolence, and if a mob arises among you to impede my officers in the execution of my orders, I will punish and involve in common ruin whole cities and colonies, with their ten thousand innocents, and ye shan't be heard in your own defense, but shall be murdered and butchered by my dragoons into silence and submission. Ye reptiles! ye are scarce intitled [*sic*] to existence any longer Your lives, liberties and property are all at the absolute disposal of my parliament."

Upon the outbreak of the Revolution, Williams threw his weight behind the cause. Besides writing tracts for the press expressing the colonial viewpoint, he prepared state papers for Governor Trumbull. Williams also raised money and personally contributed to the war effort. Between 1773 and 1776 he was a colonel in the Connecticut militia. In Congress (1776-78 and 1783-84), he sat on the Board of War and helped frame the Articles of Confederation. During the winter of 1780-81, with a French regiment stationed in Lebanon, he moved out of his home and turned it over to the officers.

Williams was pastor of First Congregational Church in Lebanon, Connecticut. He died August 2, 1811, he was buried in Lebanon's Old Cemetery.

WILLIAM FLOYD of New York

- Signed the Declaration of Independence.
- Floyd served multiple terms in the Continental Congress from 1774 to 1783.
- Major General in the Revolutionary War, New York State militia.
- Floyd was elected to the first U.S. Congress in 1789.

William Floyd (December 17, 1734 – August 4, 1821) was an American Founding Father, wealthy farmer, and political leader from New York. Floyd served as a delegate to the Continental Congress and was a signer of the Continental Association and Declaration of Independence. In August 1776, a few weeks after the Declaration was signed, British forces defeated an American army at the battle of Long Island and confiscated Floyd's house and estate, using the property as a base for their cavalry units over the next seven years. Floyd remained active in politics throughout the Revolutionary Era, served as a major general in the New York State militia, and was elected to the first U.S. Congress in 1789.

Floyd was born December 17, 1734, in Brookhaven, Province of New York, on Long Island. He was the son of Tabitha Floyd and Nicoll Floyd (1705–1755).

William's great-grandfather was Richard Floyd, who was born in Brecknockshire, Wales, in about 1620 and was the last of his brothers to leave England, first visiting Jamestown, Virginia, before settling in the Province of New York around 1640. Around 1688, his grandfather purchased 4,400 acres from in the Mastic Neck of the Town of Brookhaven.

After his father's death in 1755, William took over the family farm. He became a member of the Suffolk County Militia in the early stages of the American Revolution, becoming Major General. He was a delegate from New York to Continental Congress from 1774 to 1776.

Respected by his community, he was appointed Colonel in the militia just as the Revolutionary War exploded across the Colonies. He would eventually achieve the rank of Major General. He was selected to serve as a New York representative to the First Continental Congress in September of 1774, and attended in Philadelphia, when he risked everything, and signed the Declaration of Independence. It was a risk he took freely, and one he paid for.

History records the Battle of Setauket as a major event in the war. Floyd was in Philadelphia as a Delegate during this time, and when he returned to Long Island after the British left in 1777, he found his estate ransacked, his property stolen, and his lands plundered. His family evacuated during the occupation, strain of the ordeal sickened his wife, who died in 1781.

PHILIP LIVINGSTON

NEW YORK

Our Founding Fathers interfaced the leading figures in America and sometimes in Great Britain. Philip Livingston and his family were among that gentry. He remained a formidable force during constitutional development, the economic actions, as well as early war fighting, only to die just before the revolution heated up.

Philip Livingston (January 15, 1716 – June 12, 1778) was an American Founding Father, merchant, politician, from New York City. He represented New York at the October 1774 First Continental Congress, where he favored imposing economic sanctions upon Great Britain as a way of pressuring Parliament to repeal the Intolerable Acts. Livingston was a delegate to the Second Continental Congress and signed the Declaration of Independence.

Livingston was born in Albany, New York, on January 15, 1716, the fourth surviving son of Philip Livingston (1686–1749), 2nd Lord of the Manor, and Catherine Van Gogh Livingston, the daughter of New York Mayor Pieter Van Brugh. Along with his brother, William Livingston (1723–1790), he grew up in Albany, dividing time between his father's townhouse and the manor in Linlithgo, at the junction of the Roeliff Jansen Kill and Hudson River.

Philip the Founding Father learned the importance of extreme business earnings from his father who built a large fortune from many sources, including shipping, grist mills, iron foundries and farming. The estate was 160,000 acres.

Livingston graduated from Yale in 1737. Livingston moved to New York City and worked in the import business, trading with the British West Indies. During King George's War, he made a fortune provisioning British forces and in privateering.

Livingston also became involved in the establishment of King's College and helped to organize the New York Society Library in 1754. In 1756 he was president and founding member of the St. Andrew's Society, a benevolent organization.

In 1754, Livingston went as a delegate to the Albany Congress. There, he joined delegates from several other colonies to negotiate with Indigenous nations and discuss plans for dealing with the French and Indian War. Livingston became an active promoter to raise and fund troops for the war. According to Cynthia A. Kiemer, he owned shares in six privateers, making him one of the colony's leading investors.

The second lord of Livingston Manor (an estate encompassing approximately 160,000 acres on the Hudson River, a home in Manhattan, and a forty-acre estate in Brooklyn Heights), a graduate of Yale University and a prosperous merchant of considerable wealth, Philip Livingston initially opposed American independence. Livingston opined that "[…] the thought of establishing a republic in America, breaking off our connection with Great Britain, and becoming independent: [was] the most vain, empty, shallow, and ridiculous project that could possibly enter into the heart of man." Over time, and upon repeated transgressions against the colonies, Great Britain would erode Livingston's fealty to the Crown—beginning in 1765.

He served as a member of the provincial house of representatives from 1763 to 1769 and in 1768 served as speaker. In October 1765, he attended the Stamp Act Congress, which produced the first formal protest to the Crown as a prelude to the American Revolution. He joined New York City's Committee of Correspondence to continue communication with leaders in the other colonies, and New York City's Committee of Sixty. When New York established the New York Provincial Congress in 1775, he was named its president.

He was selected as one of the delegates to the Continental Congress. His brother William, a prominent lawyer in New Jersey, was also a delegate to the Continental Congress from 1774 to June 1776. In July 1775, Philip signed the Olive Branch Petition, a final attempt to achieve an understanding with the Crown.

When the British occupied New York City, Philip and his family fled to Kingston, New York, where he maintained another residence. After the Battle of Long Island, General George Washington and his officers met at Philip's residence in Brooklyn Heights and evacuated. The British used Philip's Duke Street home as a barracks and his Brooklyn Heights residence as a Royal Navy hospital.

After adoption of the New York State Constitution, he was appointed to the New York State Senate southern district in 1777, while in the Continental Congress.

On April 14, 1740, he married Christina Ten Broeck (1718–1801), daughter of Dirck Ten Broeck (1686–1751) and Margarita Cuyler. They had nine children.

In August 1776, true to his oath, Livingston would flee New York after the Continental Army's defeat at the Battle of Long Island. Two years later, Livingston traveled to York, Pennsylvania, for a secret session of Congress. Without knowing whether the fledgling nation would survive, Philip Livingston died of congestive heart failure, July 2, 1778, shortly after arriving in York. He was sixty-two years old.

LEWIS MORRIS of New York

This Morris family is one of the most solidly networked and family-connected we may see among all the famous families of the period of our Revolution – from the atrocities of Oliver Cromwell in Great Britain, to the many leading families of our Revolution. You will see Lewis Morris initially arguing AGAINST independence. Then, during the 10-year period of King George atrocities, Morris fully calls for Revolution.

Lewis Morris (April 8, 1726 – January 22, 1798) Morris born on April 8, 1726, at his family's estate, Morrisania, presently in Bronx County, Province of New York. He was the son of Lewis Morris (1698–1762) and Katrintje "Catherine" Staats (1697–1731). He graduated from Yale in 1746, and in 1762, he inherited the estate.

Morris' father had seven children, including his siblings, Staats Long Morris and Richard Morris and his half-siblings, Mary Lawrence, Gouverneur Morris, Isabella, and Catherine. His uncle was Robert Hunter Morris, the governor of Pennsylvania. His cousin was William Paterson, the governor of New Jersey and father-in-law of Stephen Van Rensselaer, the lieutenant governor of New York, who was the brother of Philip Schuyler Van Rensselaer, mayor of Albany, New York.

His great-grandfather, Richard Morris (died 1672), immigrated to New York after being part of Oliver Cromwell's army in the English Civil War of 1648. He purchased the first tract of land in the Bronx that became Morrisania manor. Richard and his young wife died, leaving behind an infant son, Lewis Morris (1671–1746). Col. Morris and his wife were childless.

When he came of age, Lewis Morris expanded and patented the estate. He married Isabella and went on to serve as the 8th colonial governor of New Jersey.

When active revolution began, he was a member of the New York Provincial Congress, and government, from 1775 until 1777. That body, in turn, sent Morris to the Continental Congress for those same years. While in Congress, he supported independence and signed the Declaration of Independence in 1776. Warned by his brother, a British army General, of the consequences that would follow signing the document, Morris stated, "Damn the consequences. Give me the pen." His sons served in the Revolutionary War with distinguished military careers.

July 1, 1783, he returned to the New York State Senate and served from the 7th Legislature through 13th Legislature, ending on June 30, 1790. Morris was a presidential elector in the 1796 election casting votes for Adams and Pinckney.

In 1784, Morris was elected to the New York Society of the Cincinnati. On May 1 of the same year, he was appointed to the first Board of Regents of the University of the State of New York and served until his death.

After the war, he offered the land, now part of the South Bronx neighborhood of Morrisania, as the site of the U.S. capital. He died on the estate and is buried in the family vault beneath St. Ann's Church in the Bronx.

RICHARD STOCKTON of New Jersey

- Stockton graduated College of New Jersey/Princeton University in 1748.
- Member Continental Congress, signed Declaration of Independence.
- Imprisoned by the British, subjected to starvation and freezing weather.
- Stockton was a trustee of Princeton University.

Richard Stockton (October 1, 1730 – February 28, 1781) was the son of John Stockton (1701–1758), a wealthy landowner helped bring what is now Princeton University (then College of New Jersey) to Princeton, New Jersey. Stockton and his wife had six children, four daughters and two sons: Julia Stockton (married to Benjamin Rush, also a signer of the Declaration), His son, Commodore Robert Field Stockton, was a hero of the War of 1812.

Stockton was admitted to the bar in 1754 and soon rose to great distinction.

Stockton served the college, known as Princeton, as a trustee for 26 years. In 1766 and 1767, he gave up his law practice to visit England, Scotland, and Ireland. In 1768 he was elected to the American Philosophical Society.

In 1776, Stockton was elected to the Second Continental Congress, where he took a very active role. That August, when elections were held for the state governments of the new nation, Stockton and William Livingston each received the same number of votes to be the governor of New Jersey on the first ballot. Although Livingston later won the election by one vote, Stockton was unanimously elected to serve as the chief justice of the New Jersey Supreme Court, but he turned it down to remain in Congress. Stockton was the first from New Jersey to sign the Declaration of Independence.

Stockton was sent by Congress, along with fellow signer George Clymer, on an exhausting two-month journey to Fort Ticonderoga in New York to assist the Continental Army in the American Revolutionary War. On his return to Princeton, he traveled 30 miles to the home of a friend, John Covenhoven, to evacuate his family. While there, on November 30, 1776, he and Covenhoven were captured in the middle of the night, dragged from their beds by Loyalists, stripped of their property, marched to Perth Amboy, and turned over to the British. The day Stockton was captured, General William Howe wrote a proclamation of protection and a full pardon to those willing to remain in peaceable obedience to the king. As many took the pardon, Stockton did but was placed in irons and treated as a criminal. They moved him to Provost Prison in New York, denied him food and subjected him to freezing weather. Washington inquired into the circumstances; not long afterward. After five weeks, Stockton was released with his health impaired. His estate in Princeton was occupied by Cornwallis during Stockton's imprisonment. The home of Richard Stockton was denuded of its library and furniture.

On March 25, 1777, General Howe wrote to Lord George Germain, secretary of state for the Colonies, "My Lord, We have the honor to enclose to your Lordship a state of the Declarations subscribed in consequence of our Proclamation of the 30th of November. 'Although none of the Leaders, nor principal Instigators and Abettors of the Rebellion, thought fit to avail themselves of the opportunity to return to their Duty', we have some satisfaction in observing that so considerable a number of His Majesty's deluded Subjects, of inferior Rank, in those Provinces where the Proclamation could be expected to have Effect, were disposed to relinquish the unjust Cause they had been once induced to support." 4,836 declarations were subscribed but Stockton, a signer of the Declaration of Independence, never did, according to General Howe.

In 1777, all members of Congress and Washington's Continental Army were required to take the oath of allegiance to the United States. Stockton, as a prisoner of war and taken behind enemy lines, was also required to take the oath.

Two years after his parole from prison, he developed cancer of the lip and throat. He was never free of pain until he died on February 28, 1781, at Morven.

After Stockton's death, his wife Annis, one of America's first published female poets, became a favorite correspondent of Washington.

JOHN HART of New Jersey

John Hart (1713 – May 11, 1779) was an American Founding Father and politician in colonial New Jersey. As a delegate to the Continental Congress, Hart signed the Declaration of Independence. He died before the end of the Revolutionary War.

Sources disagree on the year and place of Hart's birth. His U.S. Congress biography cites 1713 as a likely birth year and Stonington, Connecticut. He was the son of Captain Edward Hart, Justice of Peace, and leader of a local militia unit.

In 1741, Hart married Deborah Scudder (1721–1776). The couple had thirteen children. His wife, died on October 28, 1776.

When New Jersey formed a revolutionary assembly (or provincial congress) in 1776, he served as its vice president. Prior to June 1776, New Jersey opposed independence. As a result, Hart was one of those selected for the Second Continental Congress. He joined in time to vote for and sign the Declaration of Independence. He served until August of that year, then became speaker of the newly formed New Jersey General Assembly.

Historical marker for John Hart's cave in East Amwell Township, New Jersey.

In December 1776, reached his home, a marked man because of his status as speaker of the Assembly, Hart escaped and hide in the nearby Sourland Mountains. His farm was raided by British and Hessian troops, who damaged but did not destroy the property. The Continentals' capture of Trenton on December 26 allowed Hart to return home. Prior to the Battle of Monmouth, Hart invited Washington and the Continental Army to make camp on his farm, 12,000 men occupied his fields, Washington dined with Hart, before winning the Battle of Monmouth.

On November 7, 1778, Hart returned to Hopewell from the Assembly in Trenton. Two days later, he indicated he was too ill with "gravel" (kidney stones) to return. He continued to suffer for six months until his death on May 11, 1779, at age 65. Hart is a forefather of Congressman John Hart Brewer and House majority leader Steny Hoyer.

ABRAHAM CLARK of New Jersey
NEW JERSEY

Abraham Clark (February 15, 1726 – September 15, 1794) was born in Elizabethtown in the Province of New Jersey. His father, Thomas Clark, realized that he had a natural grasp on math, so he hired a tutor to teach Abraham surveying. While working as a surveyor, he taught himself law and went into practice.

Clark married Sarah Hatfield circa 1749 and had 10 children. While she raised the children on their farm, Clark was able to enter politics as a clerk of the Provincial Assembly. Later he became high sheriff of Essex County and in 1775 was elected to the Provincial Congress. He was a member of the Committee of Public Safety.

Early in 1776, the New Jersey delegation to Continental Congress was opposed to independence. Clark was highly vocal that the colonies should have their independence, they appointed him, and John Hart, Francis Hopkinson, Richard Stockton, and John Witherspoon new delegates. They arrived in Philadelphia on June 28, 1776, and voted for the Declaration of Independence in early July.

Clark remained in the Continental Congress through 1778, when he was elected as Essex County's Member of the New Jersey Legislative Council. New Jersey returned him twice more, from 1780 to 1783 and from 1786 to 1788. Clark was one of New Jersey's three representatives at the aborted Annapolis Convention of 1786, along with William C. Houston and James Schureman. In an October 12, 1804 letter to Noah Webster, James Madison recalled that Clark was the delegate who formally motioned for the Constitutional Convention, because New Jersey's instructions allowed for consideration of non-commercial matters.

Clark, more than many of his contemporaries, was a proponent of democracy and the common man, supporting the societal roles of farmers and mechanics. Unlike many Founding Fathers who demanded deference to elected officials, Clark encouraged constituents to petition representatives when necessary.

In May 1786, Clark, aided by thousands of petitions in the preceding months, pushed a pro-debtor paper money bill through the New Jersey legislature.

Clark retired before the state's Constitutional Convention in 1794. He died from sunstroke at his home. Statements attributed to Abraham Clark:

- I was a signer of the Declaration of Independence.
- I was born into a farm family in Elizabeth in 1726, but unable to do heavy labor.
- I learned law and offered free advice; they called me "the poor man's counselor."
- I was among the first to argue against Parliament as they reduced our rights.
- I was appointed to the Continental Congress and voted for independence.
- I signed the Declaration of Independence, two of my sons were captured and imprisoned on the *Jersey*, the enemy's deadliest prison ship.

JOHN MORTON of Pennsylvania

- Decisive vote for Pennsylvania's independence in Continental Congress
- Signed the Declaration of Independence,
- Chaired the committee that authored the Articles of Confederation
- John Morton died in 1777 thus he had fewer years to contribute to the cause.

John Morton (1725 – April 1, 1777) was an American farmer, surveyor, and jurist from the Province of Pennsylvania and a Founding Father of the United States. As a delegate to the Continental Congress during the American Revolution, he was a signatory to the Continental Association and Declaration of Independence. Morton was the vote that allowed Pennsylvania to vote for the Declaration. Morton chaired the committee that wrote the Articles of Confederation yet died before signing.

Morton was born in Ridley, in Chester County, present-day Delaware County, Pennsylvania, in 1725, the exact month is unknown.

He was a delegate to the Stamp Act Congress in 1765. His judicial career peaked as associate justice of the Supreme Court of Pennsylvania in 1774.

Morton was elected to the First Continental Congress in 1774 and the Second Continental Congress in 1775. He cautiously helped move Pennsylvania towards independence, though he opposed the radical Pennsylvania Constitution of 1776. When in June 1776 Congress began the debate on a resolution of independence, the Pennsylvania delegation was split, with Benjamin Franklin and James Wilson in favor, and John Dickinson and Robert Morris opposed. Morton was uncommitted until July 1 when he sided with Franklin and Wilson.

Morton was chairman of the committee that wrote the Articles of Confederation, and he died before the Articles were ratified. He was the first signer of the Declaration of Independence to die, nine months after the Declaration's signing on July 4, 1776.

JAMES SMITH of Pennsylvania

- He was also a Brigadier General in the Pennsylvania Militia
- Smith was a delegate to the Continental Congress
- Signed the Declaration of Independence

James Smith (September 17, 1719 – July 11, 1806, was born in Ireland; his family immigrated to Chester County, Pennsylvania, in 1729. Smith attended the Philadelphia Academy. He studied law with his brother George. He gained bar admittance in 1745 and relocated to York, where he began Iron manufacturing.

Smith emerged as an early Whig leader. In 1774, at a provincial convention in Philadelphia, he supported nonimportation measures and advocated an intercolonial congress. That same year, at York he raised a militia company, in which he served as captain and later an honorary colonel. At two provincial meetings in 1775-76, he championed the interests of the western counties and helped formulate resolutions calling for independence, the strengthening of defenses, and establishment of a new provincial government. During the latter year, he sat on the drafting committee in the State constitutional convention. Elected to Congress on July 20, 1776, after the vote on independence, he arrived in Philadelphia in time to sign the Declaration.

He became captain of the militia. He was appointed to the provincial convention in Philadelphia in 1775, to the state constitutional convention in 1776, and was elected to Continental Congress, and signed the Declaration of Independence.

Smith died on July 11, 1806, and is buried in York, Pennsylvania.

GEORGE ROSS of Pennsylvania

- Continental Congressman (1774–1777), signer Declaration of Independence
- Militia colonel negotiated a peace treaty with the Indians.
- His uncle married Betsy Ross

George Ross Jr (May 10, 1730 – July 14, 1779) was born May 10, 1730, in New Castle, Delaware. He was educated at home and studied law, admitted to the bar in Philadelphia, family line of Farquhar Ó Beólláin (1173–1251) whom King Alexander II of Scotland named 1st Earl of Ross 1226 after great victories in battle.

George's sister married George Read, a signer of the Declaration of Independence.

Ross was a member of the committee of safety and was elected to the Continental Congress. He was a colonel in the Pennsylvania militia and vice-president of the first constitutional convention for Pennsylvania. Ross was the last of the Pennsylvania delegation to sign the Declaration of Independence.

In 1750, he was admitted to the Pennsylvania Bar when he was 20 years old, and he established his own practice in Lancaster, where he married Ann Lawler in 1751. Together they had two sons and a daughter.

Initially a Tory, he served as Crown prosecutor for 12 years from 1768 to 1776. His sympathies changed and he became a strong supporter of the colonial assemblies in their disputes with Parliament. In 1768 he was elected to the provincial legislature of Pennsylvania. He was elected to the Continental Congress in 1774, 1776, and 1777. He was a colonel in the Continental Army in 1776. In 1776, he undertook negotiations with the northwestern Indians on behalf of his colony and acted as vice president of the state constitutional convention, leading to helping draft a declaration of rights. He was re-elected to Continental Congress in January 1777 but resigned because of poor health. He was vice president of the Pennsylvania constitutional convention and Judge of the Admiralty Court of Pennsylvania in 1779. He resigned from Continental Congress in 1777 from poor health and was appointed to the Pennsylvania Court of Admiralty where he died in 1779 at age 49.

CAESAR RODNEY of Delaware

- Delaware militia, French and Indian War, American Revolutionary War.
- He also fought under General George Washington at Trenton.
- Continental Congress from 1774–76 and 1777–78.
- Signed the Declaration of Independence in 1776.
- Served as president of Delaware from 1778–1782.
- Associate justice of the Delaware Supreme Court from 1769 to 1777.
- College of Philadelphia (University of Pennsylvania)

Caesar Rodney (October 7, 1728 – June 26, 1784) was born on October 7, 1728, on St. Jones Neck Delaware. Caesar was the eldest son of William Rodney, who emigrated in 1681–1682, with William Penn. Caesar was educated when 13 or 14 years old at The Latin School, and College of Philadelphia until his father's death.

Professional and political career

At age twenty-seven in 1755, he became sheriff of Kent County. This was a powerful and financially rewarding position. During the French and Indian War, he was commissioned captain of the Dover Hundred company in Col. John Vining's regiment of the Delaware militia. From 1769 through 1777, he was associate justice of the Supreme Court of the Lower Counties.

Rodney joined McKean as a delegate to the Stamp Act Congress in 1765 and was a leader of the Delaware Committee of Correspondence.[12] He began his service in the Assembly of Delaware in the 1761/1762 session and continued in office through the 1775/1776 session. Several times he served as speaker, including the momentous day of June 15, 1776, when "with Rodney in the chair and Thomas McKean leading the debate," the Assembly of voted to sever all ties with the British Parliament and King.

Rodney served in the Continental Congress with McKean and Read from 1774 through 1776. Rodney was in Dover when he received word that he and Read were deadlocked on the vote for independence. To break the deadlock, Rodney rode 70 miles through a thunderstorm on the night of July 1, 1776, arriving in Philadelphia "in his boots and spurs" on July 2, just as the voting had begun. Wording of the Declaration of Independence was approved two days later; Rodney signed it on August 2. Backlash in Delaware led to Rodney's defeat in Kent County in the Delaware Constitutional Convention and new Delaware General Assembly.

Upon learning of the death of his friend John Haslet at Battle of Princeton, Rodney rushed to the Continental Army to fill his place. General Washington returned Rodney home to be governor and major-general of Delaware militia.

Amidst the catastrophic events following the Battle of Brandywine and the British occupation of Wilmington and Philadelphia, a new General Assembly was elected in October 1777. First, it promptly put Rodney and McKean back into the Continental Congress. Then, with state President John McKinly they elected Rodney President of Delaware, March 31, 1778.

Meanwhile, Rodney scoured the state for money, supplies, and soldiers to support the national war effort. Delaware Continentals had fought well in many battles from the Battle of Long Island to the Battle of Monmouth, Rodney resigned his office on November 6, 1781, just after the conclusive Battle of Yorktown.

Rodney was elected to the United States Congress under the Articles of Confederation in 1782 and 1783 but was unable to attend because of ill health.

Rodney was tormented throughout his life by asthma, and his adult years were plagued by facial cancer. Caesar wore a green scarf to hide his disfigured face. He died from the disease after eight years.

SAMUEL CHASE of Maryland

Samuel Chase was a Founding Father of the United States, signer of the Continental Association and United States Declaration of Independence as a representative of Maryland, and Associate Justice of the United States Supreme Court. In 1804, Chase was impeached by the House of Representatives on grounds of letting his partisan leanings affect his court decisions but was acquitted by the Senate and remained in office. He is the only United States Supreme Court Justice to be impeached.

Born near Princess Anne, Maryland, Chase established a legal practice in Annapolis, Maryland. He served in the Maryland General Assembly for several years and favored independence during the American Revolution. In 1796, President Washington appointed Chase to the United States Supreme Court.

After the 1800 elections, President Thomas Jefferson and the Democratic-Republicans sought to weaken Federalist influence on the federal courts. Chase's actions on the court demonstrated bias, and Jefferson believed Chase should be removed from office, a process that required a vote in both the Senate and the House of Representatives. The House passed eight articles of impeachment, all centering on Chase's alleged political bias. The Senate voted to acquit Chase on all counts, and Chase served on Supreme Court until his death in 1811. Some historians argue Chase's acquittal set an important precedent for independence of the judiciary.

Samuel Chase (April 17, 1741 – June 19, 1811) was the only child of the Reverend Thomas Chase (c. 1703–1779) and his wife, Matilda Walker (1705–1741), born near Princess Anne, Maryland.

In May 1762, Chase married Anne Baldwin and had three sons and four daughters. Anne died in 1776. In 1784, Chase traveled to England to deal with Maryland's Bank of England stock, and married Hannah Kilty.

In 1764, Chase was elected to the Maryland General Assembly for 20 years.

In 1766, he became embroiled in a war of words with a number of loyalist members of the Maryland political establishment. He co-founded Anne Arundel County's Sons of Liberty chapter with his close friend William Paca, as well as leading opposition to the 1765 Stamp Act.

In early 1775, the quarrel with Parliament worsened. Chase was determined to resist British violations of Colonial Rights. He believed that the British: "must either give up the Right of Taxation, or force obedience by the Sword."
Chase's apprehensions came true in April 1775 at Lexington and Concord.

During this period, American military forces began military operations in Canada that failed due to Congress' lack of funding and to poor generalship. Even before leaving Canada, Chase's position on rebellion had changed. He now believed open resurrection was inevitable. On April 28, he wrote John Adams to press for Congress' full attention to the war effort.

Immediately, Chase returned to Annapolis from Philadelphia. Between the middle of June to the end of the month, Chase and Charles Carroll visited the counties throughout the province, inflaming and rousing the "middling sort" and other supporters to action. On June 28, faced with a horde of citizens clamoring for independence from British rule, the provincial convention in Annapolis unanimously authorized its delegates to vote for independence.

From 1774 to 1776, Chase was a member of the Annapolis Convention. He represented Maryland at the Continental Congress, was re-elected in 1776 and signed the United States Declaration of Independence. He remained in the Continental Congress until 1778. Chase was elected to the Maryland Ratifying Convention to ratify the 1787 Constitution. In Convention, Chase was a prominent Antifederalist, Maryland became the seventh state to ratify.

On January 26, 1796, President Washington nominated Chase and Senate confirmed him associate justice of the SCOTUS. Chase was sworn in on February 4, 1796, and served until his death June 19, 1811.

Impeachment and Acquittal of Samuel Chase
President Jefferson, alarmed at the seizure of power by the judiciary through the claim of exclusive judicial review, led his party's efforts to remove the Federalists from the bench. His allies in Congress had, shortly after his inauguration, repealed the Judiciary Act of 1801, abolishing the lower courts created by the legislation and terminating their Federalist judges despite lifetime appointments; Chase, two years after the repeal in May 1803, had denounced it in his charge to a Baltimore grand jury, saying that it would "take away all security for property and personal liberty, and our Republican constitution will sink into a mobocracy.

On March 12, 1804, the House voted 73 to 32 to impeach Chase. The US Senate—controlled by the Jeffersonian Democratic-Republicans—began the impeachment trial of Chase on February 9, 1805, with Vice President Aaron Burr presiding and Virginia Representative John Randolph leading the prosecution.

Chase argued his actions were justified by precedent, judicial duty to restrain advocates from improper statements of law, and considerations of judicial efficiency.

The Senate voted to acquit Chase of all charges on March 1, 1805. There were 34 senators present (25 Democratic-Republicans and 9 Federalists), and 23 votes would reach the two-thirds majority for conviction/removal from office. Of the eight votes taken, the closest vote was 18 for conviction/removal from office and 16 for acquittal in regard to the Baltimore grand jury charge. He is the only U.S. Supreme Court justice to have been impeached. Judge Alexander Humphrey recorded in the *Virginia Law Register,* the impeachment trial and acquittal.

The acquittal of Chase—by lopsided margins on several counts—set an unofficial precedent that many historians say helped ensure the so-called independence of the judiciary. As Chief Justice William Rehnquist noted in his book *Grand Inquests*, some senators declined to convict Chase despite their partisan hostility to him, apparently because they doubted that the mere "quality" of his judging was grounds for removal. All impeachments of federal judges since Chase have been based on allegations of legal or ethical misconduct, not on judicial performance. For their part, federal judges were much more cautious than Chase in trying to avoid the appearance of political partisanship. Samuel Chase died of a heart attack in 1811.

WILLIAM PACA of Maryland

William Paca (October 31, 1740 – October 13, 1799), Born on October 31, 1740, in Abingdon, Province of Maryland, British America, He attended the Inner Temple in London and read law in 1761 and was admitted to the bar that year. Paca entered private practice in Annapolis starting in 1763. He married Mary Chew. They had three children.

Paca was a delegate to the First Continental Congress and the Second Continental Congress from Maryland from 1774 to 1779. He was a signer of the United States Declaration of Independence in 1776. He was a member of the Maryland Senate from 1776 to 1777, and from 1778 to 1780. He was a judge of the Maryland General Court in 1778. He was a judge of the Court of Appeals in Cases of Capture from 1780 to 1782. He was governor of Maryland from 1782 to 1785. He was a member of the Maryland House of Delegates in 1786. He was influential in establishing Washington College in Chestertown, Maryland, in 1786. He was a delegate to the Maryland State Convention of 1788, to vote whether Maryland should ratify the proposed Constitution of the United States.

Another young lawyer in Annapolis was Samuel Chase, who became a close friend and colleague of Paca. Paca and Chase led opposition to the Stamp Act of 1765 and established the Anne Arundel County chapter of the Sons of Liberty.

Paca received a recess appointment from President George Washington on December 22, 1789, to the United States District Court for the District of Maryland. He was nominated to the same position by President Washington on February 8, 1790. He was confirmed by the United States Senate on February 10, 1790.

Paca's career on the federal bench had a significant impact on the admiralty jurisdiction of the Federal courts and what was to become the principal business of the Supreme Court over four decades. Paca argued on solid precedents of law that the District Court did not have jurisdiction over the awarding of prizes brought into ports by foreign privateers. The Supreme Court asserted otherwise in seriatim opinions and established an exclusive jurisdiction over prize cases vested in the Federal District Courts that had been the responsibility of foreign consulates. Paca's opinion provides insight into the extensive legal training of a signer of the Declaration of Independence and an author/compiler of the Bill of Rights.

Paca's judicial service terminated on October 13, 1799, due to his death at his estate of Wye River, in Queen Anne's County. Paca was admitted as an honorary member of The Society of the Cincinnati in the state of Maryland in 1783.

THOMAS NELSON, JR. of Virginia

- Second Continental Congress, signer of Declaration of Independence.
- Nelson was a Brigadier General in the Continental Army
- He fought in the siege of Yorktown, the decisive battle of the war.
- Nelson was elected governor of Virginia in 1781, succeeding Thomas Jefferson.
- Coordinated Virginia's defense against Cornwallis.
- Helped organize Yorktown Tea Party, sacrificed his home, livelihood, life.

Thomas Nelson Jr. (December 26, 1738 – January 4, 1789) was the grandson of Thomas "Scotch Tom" Nelson, Cumberland, England, an early pioneer at Yorktown. Nelson was third cousin of U.S. President George Washington. He graduated Christ's College, Cambridge in 1760, returned to Virginia the following year.

York County voters elected Nelson to the Virginia House of Burgesses as a young man in 1761; he succeeded Robert Carter Nicholas in this part-time position.

Digges and Nelson were elected to represent York County during the five Virginia conventions that preceded statehood. At the Fifth Virginia Convention, in the summer of 1776, Nelson left to attend the Continental Congress.

Nelson's first term in Congress continued until 1776 when illness forced his resignation for the 1778–1779 term. After his recovery, he was again elected and served another year. During his first stint in Congress, Nelson returned to Virginia to play a key role in its Constitutional Convention in the spring of 1776. He returned to Congress to sign the Declaration of Independence that summer.

Thomas Nelson was one of thirteen committee members to "prepare and digest the form of confederation," they drafted the Articles of Confederation.

He was a brigadier general of the Lower Virginia Militia and succeeded Thomas Jefferson as governor of Virginia. Nelson was engaged in the final siege of Yorktown. According to legend, he urged General Washington to fire on his own home, the Nelson House, where Cornwallis was headquartered. Nelson died at his son's home in Hanover County, Virginia, nine days after his fiftieth birthday.

WILLIAM HOOPER of North Carolina

William Hooper (June 28, 1742 – October 14, 1790) was a Founding Father, lawyer, and politician. As a member of the Continental Congress of North Carolina, Hooper signed the Continental Association and the Declaration of Independence.

Hooper was the first child of five, born in Boston, Massachusetts on June 28, 1742. Hooper's father had hoped that William would follow in his footsteps as an Episcopal priest and placed his son at the age of seven in Boston Latin School. In 1757, at age 16, Hooper entered

Harvard University where he was highly regarded. In 1760, Hooper graduated from Harvard with honors, obtaining a Bachelor of Arts. He decided on a career in law, studying under James Otis. In 1767, Hooper married Anne Clark. They had three children.

Initially, Hooper supported the British colonial government of North Carolina. As deputy attorney general, in 1768 Hooper worked with Colonial Governor William Tryon to suppress a rebellious group known as the. The Regulators dragged Hooper through the streets and his home was destroyed. By 1774 Hooper was appointed one of North Carolina's three delegates to first Continental Congress. With Jefferson, Hooper served on a committee to draft and sign the Declaration of Independence. Hooper advised Governor Tryon to use as much force as necessary to stamp out the rebels and accompanied troops at the Battle of Alamance in 1771.

Hooper missed the initial vote approving the Declaration of Independence on the Fourth of July 1776 but was able to sign it on August 2, 1776.

Hooper's support of the colonial governments began to erode, causing problems for him because of his past support of Governor Tryon. He recognized independence was likely, mentioning this in a letter to his friend James Iredell."

During his time in the assembly Hooper slowly became a supporter of the American Revolution and independence. Hooper was also appointed to the Committee of Correspondence and Inquiry. In 1774, Hooper was appointed a delegate to the First Continental Congress, where he served on numerous committees. Hooper elected to the Second Continental Congress, but his time was split between congress and work in North Carolina, forming a new government.

In 1777, because of continued financial concerns, Hooper resigned from Congress and returned to North Carolina to resume his law career. Throughout the Revolution the British attempted to capture Hooper. In 1781, the British captured Wilmington, where Cornwallis and his forces fell back after the Battle of Guilford Court House.[11] The British burned his estates in Finian and Wilmington.

After the Revolution Hooper was called to public service in 1786, when he was appointed a federal judge in a border dispute between New York and Massachusetts, though the case was settled out of court. In 1787 and 1788, Hooper campaigned heavily for North Carolina to ratify the new United States Constitution, but Hooper had become quite ill, and he died on October 14, 1790, at the age of 48.

JOSEPH HEWES of North Carolina

Joseph Hewes (July 9, 1730– November 10, 1779) was an American Founding Father, signer of the Continental Association and U.S. Declaration of Independence. Hewes was a native of Princeton, New Jersey, born in 1730. His parents were members of the Society of Friends, commonly known as Quakers.

In 1763, he formed "Hewes and Smith." The firm had "offices, three warehouses, a wharf and five ships, three sloops and two brigs." Hewes was the owner of a ship repair and ship building yard. In 1777 Hewes created a rope factory for braiding ropes, twine, hawsers and cables used in rigging of ships. It became one of the main suppliers to the shipping industry.

First Continental Congress (September 5, 1774 – October 22, 1774)
The British Parliament responded to the Boston Tea Party by passing the Coercive Acts (Intolerable Acts In the American colonies) closing the Boston harbor and restricting town meetings in Massachusetts, applied only to Massachusetts. A proposal circulated for an inter-

colonial congress to meet in Philadelphia. The North Carolina Committee selected delegates to the Philadelphia congress.

The Provincial Congress gave the delegates two instructions: (1) to contend for their rights as Englishmen, and (2) to prohibit all imports and exports to Great Britain.

On September 18 Congress passed the Suffolk Resolves calling for the end of trade with Great Britain. On October 15 the Congress adopted a Declaration of Rights and Grievances and the Continental Association- - the end of all imports and exports to England, Ireland, and the West Indies effective September 1, 1775.

Second Continental Congress first session (May 10, 1775 – August 1, 1775)

The 2nd North Carolina Provincial Congress convened in New Bern on April 3, 1775. Hewes, Hooper, and Caswell were reappointed to serve as delegates to the 2nd Continental Congress. Hewes and Caswell left for Philadelphia. He met the Virginia delegation and Washington the Potomac. From then to Philadelphia, at each county line, troops marched with them to the next county line.

Congress convened on the 10th. Hewes was appointed to three committees: the finance committee, the army and a committee to inquire into the ore and lead resources. For the first three months of Congress, attention was on reconciliation and organizing a defensive military.

Hooper, Hewes, and Caswell were again selected to represent North Carolina in the Continental Congress. The Provincial Congress rejected the Draft of Articles of Confederation. The creation of a confederation was considered one step too far.[16] Caswell resigned, and John Penn was named in his place.

Second Continental Congress, second session (August 13, 1775)

Congress was reconvened August 13, 1775. In November, the king officially declared the colonists' rebels. Late in 1775 Hewes was appointed to the Naval Board and to the Marine Committee. These committees drafted regulations that would govern the navy and began acquiring ships, officers and men who would operate them. These acts laid the foundations for the American Navy. Hewes was responsible for getting John Paul Jones his Navy commission.

During the winter of 1776, Congress turned towards independence. In February, a resolution rejected independence. Writing to Samuel Johnston he said "I see no prospect of reconciliation. Nothing, but to fight it out."

April 12, North Carolina authorized its delegation to "declare Independence. " Richard Henry Lee of Virginia offered a resolution on June 7 for independence "that these United Colonies are, and of right ought to be, free and independent States."

The Continental Congress voted to politically separate from Britain on July 2, 1776. On July 4, the wording of the Declaration of Independence was ratified.

At the end of October 1775, the Continental Congress created a committee to fit out two vessels, one with no more than 20 guns and the other with no more than 26 guns. Hewes was appointed along with two others that became the Naval Committee, soon to be, the Marine Committee. Hewes was selected due to his marine experience. Stephen Hopkins chaired the committee and Hewes kept accounts.

On February 14, 1776, Hewes leased one of the firm's brigantines to the Secret Marine Committee of the Continental Congress for the sum of 400 Spanish dollars per month. Hewes agreed that the "said Brigt shall be Tight, stiff, Strong & Staunch, well & sufficiently fitted, found, Victualed & Manned for this Voyage. " The committee agreed to pay all port charges. For insurance purposes, value of the brigantine became 4 thousand 600 Spanish milled dollars. He died November 10, 1779.

THOMAS HEYWARD JR. of South Carolina

- Signed the Declaration of Independence and the Articles of Confederation.
- Heyward served as a captain in the Charles Town Battalion of Artillery.
- Captured during the Siege of Charleston in 1780, held prisoner two years.

Thomas Heyward Jr. (July 28, 1746 – March 6, 1809) was an American Founding Father, lawyer, jurist, and politician. As a member of the Continental Congress, he signed the Declaration of Independence and Articles of Confederation. Heyward's British imprisonment led to being proclaimed a martyr of the revolution.

Heyward was born in St. Luke's Parish (Jasper County), South Carolina. He was educated at home, then the Middle Temple. He was elected to the Continental Congress and was the last delegate to sign the Declaration of Independence.

Revolution Military Duty

Heyward was deeply involved in the revolutionary movement in South Carolina, both politically and militarily. He was elected to the South Carolina Provincial Congress, which became the ruling body of government at the outset of the Revolution. With this experience under his belt, South Carolina sent him as one of five delegates to Continental Congress in 1776.

Heyward returned to South Carolina in 1778 to serve as a judge. In 1778, he presided over a trial in which several persons were tried for treason; they were convicted and executed within view of the British lines.

When not involved with civic duties, Heyward served as an officer with an elite militia unit, the Charles Town Ancient Battalion of Artillery. Artillerymen, particularly officers, needed to have a mastery of science, mathematics, and engineering to professionally manage cannon.

Originally a single company, the Charles Town Battalion of Artillery was organized into three companies. Heyward commanded one of the companies while a fellow signer of the Declaration, Edward Rutledge, commanded another company.

After returning from the Continental Congress in 1778, he devoted more time to military duties. He fought close to his home, near Beaufort. The British planned to reclaim southern colonies with the capture of Savannah in December 1778.

Looking to establish a base of operations for naval forces, Major James Gardiner landed a British detachment of 300 men on Port Royal Island in early February 1779. An American force countered them. Among the troops were the Charles Town Battalion of Artillery, led by Heyward and Rutledge.

At the Battle of Port Royal on February 3, 1779, the British had the advantage of tree cover, but the Americans had two six-pound field pieces while the British had only one cannon. Haywards shots rendered British cannon inoperable.

Heyward's next major action occurred in April and May 1780 when British forces besieged Charleston, the longest siege of the Revolutionary War. In recognition of his ability as an artilleryman, Heyward was given charge of the cannon in the hornwork fortification. He and his twenty-six men were under fire regularly as the British directed many shells against the hornwork. On August 27, 1780, British troops took him from his Charleston home and detained him in the Old Exchange Building. It was this loss that resulted in his being proclaimed a martyr of the revolution. Hours after arrest, he and 28 other "ringleaders of the rebellion" rowed out to guardship confinement in the harbor. On September 4, they were transported to St. Augustine, Florida, for 11 months until freed in a prisoner exchange. While in prison, Heyward transposed a popular English song, "God Save the King" into "God Save the States". In 1784, he was elected a member of the American Philosophical Society.

Heyward was married twice; each wife was named Elizabeth. His first wife, died in childbirth in 1782 in Philadelphia, where she had gone to be with Heyward upon his release as a POW. He had three children with his second wife.

THOMAS LYNCH JR. of South Carolina

Thomas Lynch Jr. (August 5, 1749 – December 17, 1779) was a signer of the United States Declaration of Independence as a representative of South Carolina and a Founding Father of the United States. His father Thomas Lynch was a member of the Continental Congress and had signed the 1774 Continental Association. When he resigned with illness, Thomas Lynch Jr. filled his post.

Lynch Jr. was born at Hopsewee Plantation, Georgetown, South Carolina, and schooled at the Indigo Society School in Georgetown, South Carolina. He received honors at Eton College and Cambridge. Lynch Jr. studied law and political philosophy at the Middle Temple in London.

Lynch Jr. married Paige Shubrick on May 14, 1772. Following their marriage, they lived at Peach Tree Plantation, located near his homeland plantation.

His father died from a stroke in December 1776. His widowed mother later married South Carolina Governor William Moultrie.

Lynch was elected to the Provincial Congress on February 11, 1775, formed to prepare a plan of government and represent the people of South Carolina. Lynch served alongside Charles Cotesworth Pinckney, John Rutledge, Charles Pinckney, Henry Laurens, Christopher Gadsden, Rawlins Lowndes, Arthur Middleton, Henry Middleton, Thomas Bee, and Thomas Heyward Jr.

Lynch became a company commander in the First South Carolina regiment on June 12, 1775. He gathered men and led a march into Charlestown, South Carolina.

On March 23, 1776, the General Assembly of South Carolina named Lynch Jr. to the Continental Congress. Lynch Jr. traveled to Philadelphia to sign the Declaration of Independence. Thomas Lynch Sr. and Thomas Lynch Jr. were the only father and son to serve successively in the Continental Congress. Lynch Jr. was the second youngest delegate in the Continental Congress. South Carolinian Edward Rutledge was younger.

Less than a month after signing the Declaration of Independence, Lynch Jr. threatened that South Carolina would secede from the United States; his threat expressed the interests of his constituents, the elite planter class.

After signing the Declaration of Independence, Thomas Lynch Jr. set out for home with his ailing father. Enroute to South Carolina, his father had a second stroke. He died in December 1776. Thomas Lynch Jr. retired in early 1777.

Lynch suffered for two more years of where he resided with his wife at Peachtree Plantation on the South Santee River. He and his wife sailed for respite on the brigantine *Polly* to St. Eustatius in the West Indies on December 17, 1779. The ship disappeared. He and his wife were lost at sea.

ARTHUR MIDDLETON of South Carolina

- Delegate to the Continental Congress
- Middleton signed the Declaration of Independence on August 2, 1776
- He organized raids on royal armories, raised money for the patriot cause.
- Middleton was captured during the Siege of Charleston and held captive.
- Educated at Westminster School and St. John's College, Cambridge University.
- He studied law at the Middle Temple.
- 1787 Death at age 44 were a premature end to his contribution to America.

Arthur Middleton (June 26, 1742 – January 1, 1787) was a Founding Father of the United States, signer of the United States Declaration of Independence, and a representative from South Carolina in the Second Continental Congress.

Middleton was born in Charleston, Province of South Carolina, in 1742. He was educated in Britain at Harrow School, Westminster School, and Trinity Hall, Cambridge. He studied law at the Middle Temple and traveled extensively in Europe. In 1764, Arthur and his bride Mary Izard settled at Middleton Place.

Keenly interested in Carolina, he was a leader of the American Party in Carolina and one of the boldest members of the Council of Safety and its Secret Committee. In 1776, Middleton was elected to succeed his father in the Continental Congress and was a signer of the United States Declaration of Independence. Also in 1776, he and William Henry Drayton designed the Great Seal of South Carolina. His attitude toward Loyalists was ruthless, this stood in contrast to South Carolina patriots such as Francis Marion who led the effort to reconcile.

During the Revolutionary War, Middleton served in the defense of Charleston. After the city's fall to the British in 1780, he was sent as a prisoner of war to St. Augustine, Florida (along with Edward Rutledge and Thomas Heyward Jr.), until exchanged in July the following year.

Middleton died on January 1, 1787, at age 44 and was buried in the family tomb in the Gardens at Middleton Place.

BUTTON GWINNETT of Georgia

Button Gwinnett story is a great assist to explain how ready for war most men were in England and the continent in 16th, 17th, 18th centuries. Royalty had persecuted everyone of all stripes and all measures of wealth. They had persecuted and executed the leaders of all religious groups and all other groups that royalty believed to be a threat. Gwinnett arrives in America just 11 years prior to the American Revolution, yet quickly becomes a leader. He will only survive for the next 20 years, therefore his contributions to the independence movement and Constitutional government that emerged is brief.

Button Gwinnett (March 3, 1735 – May 19, 1777) was a British-born American Founding Father who, as a representative of Georgia to the Continental Congress, was one of the signers of the United States Declaration of Independence. Gwinnett was also, briefly, the provisional president of Georgia in 1777, and Gwinnett County (a major suburb of metro Atlanta) was named for him. Gwinnett was killed in a duel by rival Lachlan McIntosh after a failed invasion of East Florida.

Gwinnett was born in 1735 in the parish of Down Hatherley in the county of Gloucestershire, England. On 19 April 1757 he married Ann Bourne. In 1762, the couple, who parented three daughters, emigrated to America.

Gwinnett's business activities took him from Newfoundland to Jamaica. He bought St. Catherine's Island to attempt to become a planter.

Gwinnett did not become a strong advocate of colonial rights until 1775, when St. John's Parish, which encompassed his lands, threatened to secede from Georgia. During his tenure in Assembly, Gwinnett's chief rival was Lachlan McIntosh, and Lyman Hall was his closest ally.[8]

Gwinnett was appointed to represent Georgia at Continental Congress, where he voted for the Declaration of Independence, adopted by Congress on July 2, 1776. He signed the famous parchment copy on August 2, 1776. Gwinnett became a candidate for brigadier general to lead 1st Regiment in the Continental Army but lost to McIntosh, which embittered Gwinnett.

Gwinnett served in the Georgia state legislature and wrote the original draft of Georgia's first state constitution. He became Speaker of the Georgia Assembly, until the death of the President (Governor) of Georgia Archibald Bulloch.

The Revolutionary crisis brought him back into politics. He united coastal and rural dissidents into a loose coalition and was elected commander of Georgia's Continental battalion. When his election proved controversial, Gwinnett accepted an appointment to the Continental Congress, then meeting in Philadelphia.

He voted for independence and signed the Declaration of Independence in August (along with George Walton and Lyman Hall) and returned to Georgia. Gwinnett continued to lead opposition and Georgia's Provincial Congress elected him, Speaker. He played a key role in passage of the Constitution of 1777.

Gwinnett proposed a military foray into British East Florida, a defensive measure that he argued would secure Georgia's southern border.

McIntosh challenged him to a duel. Though each man shot the other, only Gwinnett's wound proved fatal. He died on May 19, 1777.

LYMAN HALL of Georgia

- He was a member of the Second Continental Congress from 1775 to 1780.
- Chartered University of Georgia while Governor

Lyman Hall (April 12, 1724 – October 19, 1790) was born in Wallingford, Connecticut. He studied with his uncle Samuel Hall and graduated from Yale College in 1747, a tradition in his family. He was a grandnephew of Capt. Theophilus Yale of the Yale family. In 1752, he married Abigail Burr, she died the following year. In 1757, he married Mary Osborne.

He migrated to South Carolina, established himself as a physician at Dorchester, South Carolina, near Charleston, then moved to Liberty County – in Georgia

On the eve of the American Revolution, St. John's Parish, was a hotbed of radical sentiment in a Loyalist colony. Though Georgia was not initially represented in the First Continental Congress, through Hall's influence the parish was persuaded to send a delegate to Philadelphia to the Second Continental Congress. Hall was admitted to a seat in the Congress in 1775. He was one of three Georgians and four doctors to sign Declaration of Independence.

In January 1779, Sunbury was burned by the British. Hall's family fled to the North, where they remained awhile, then returned to Savannah.

After the Revolution (1775-83), Hall resumed his medical practice in Savannah. In January 1783 he was elected governor. During his administration he had to deal with difficult issues, including confiscated estates, frontier problems, and a bankrupt and depleted treasury. In January 1783, he was elected governor of Georgia. While governor, Hall advocated and led the chartering of the University of Georgia. In 1790, he died on October 19 at the age of 66.

GEORGE WALTON of Georgia

- One of 3 Georgians to sign Declaration of Independence, July 4, 1776.
- At the age of 26, he was one of the youngest signers of the document.
- Walton was a colonel in the Georgia militia during the Revolutionary War.
- He fought in the First Battle of Savannah
- Captured by the British and held prisoner for ten months.

George Walton (c. 1749 – February 2, 1804) was born in Cumberland County, Virginia. His parents died when he was an infant. Walton moved to Savannah, Georgia to study law, admitted to the bar in 1774. By the end of the American Revolution, he had become one of the most successful lawyers in Georgia.

He became an advocate of the Patriot cause, was elected secretary of the Georgia Provincial Congress, and president of the Council of Safety. In 1776, he was in the Second Continental Congress. On July 2, 1776, he voted in favor of the Declaration of Independence, along with Button Gwinnett and Lyman Hall.

On January 9, 1778, Walton received a commission as colonel of the First Georgia Regiment of Militia. During the Battle of Savannah in 1778, Walton was injured and taken prisoner - released in a prisoner exchange in October 1779.

In October 1779, Walton was elected governor of Georgia.

In November 1795, he was appointed to the US Senate. He was an ally of Scottish General Lachlan McIntosh and a foe of Button Gwinnett.

Walton liked the Yazoo land sales, the massive land settlement plan in the mid-1790s by Governor George Mathews and the Georgia General Assembly.

In 1788, Alexander McGillivray and other Creek Indian leaders met with Georgia leaders at Rock Landing but failed to result in a peace treaty. The Treaty of New York (1790) ceded Creek Indian lands to the state of Georgia.

During the 1780s, Walton was devoted to Georgia politics. He was a delegate to the Constitutional Convention in 1787. In 1789, he was a presidential elector. Walton was elected to a second term as governor in 1789. During this term, Georgians adopted the new Georgia Constitution, moved the capital to Augusta, and settled the western frontier. He was a founder and trustee of Franklin College (University of Georgia). During his second term, he built Meadow Garden, where he died in 1804.

GUNNING BEDFORD, Jr. of Delaware

- A delegate from Delaware to the Constitutional Convention in 1787.
- Bedford also served in the Continental Congress, was the attorney general of Delaware, and a presidential elector on the Federalist ticket in 1789 and 1793.
- He graduated from Princeton in 1771.
- James Madison was his college roommate.
- Fought in the War for Independence and read law in Philadelphia.

Gunning Bedford Jr. (1747 – March 30, 1812) was born in 1747, in Philadelphia, Province of Pennsylvania, British America. He graduated from the College of New Jersey (Princeton University) on September 25, 1771, with honors, as a classmate of James Madison, admitted to the Delaware bar 1779 to 1783.

On July 17, 1775, the Second Continental Congress resolved to elect Bedford to deputy-muster-general for New York in the Continental Army. On February 28, 1776, he was assigned to the northern army in Canada to muster troops there monthly. On June 18, 1776, he was promoted to muster-master-general in New York. He served as an aide to General Washington.

He was a delegate to the Congress of the Confederation from 1783 to 1785. He was Attorney General of Delaware, a delegate to the Constitutional Convention in 1787, which drafted the United States Constitution and signed the Constitution. During the convention, Bedford's threat, "the small ones would find some foreign ally of more honor and good faith, who will take them by the hand and do them justice" was shouted down as treasonous.

CONTRIBUTIONS TO THE CONSTITUTIONAL CONVENTION. At first, he joined with those who sought to amend the Articles of Confederation. But when the idea of drafting a new Constitution was accepted, he supported the New Jersey Plan, that provided equal representation for the states in the national legislature, a point on which the Delaware legislature had instructed its delegates not to compromise. He called for limitations on powers of the executive branch and recommended measures by which the states could maintain control over the national legislature and judiciary, including the appointment of federal judges by state legislatures. Bedford's speeches in support, led Georgia delegate William Few to describe him as a "bold" speaker, with "a very commanding and striking manner;" "warm and impetuous in his temper and precipitate in his judgement." He agreed to the Great Compromise, which settled representation and the Convention's acceptance of the new plan of government.

He was a member of the Delaware convention which ratified the Constitution in 1787. He was a member of the Delaware Legislative Council (now Delaware Senate). Bedford was nominated by President Washington on September 24, 1789, to the US District Court for the District of Delaware, to a new seat authorized by 1 Stat. 73. He was confirmed by the US Senate on September 26, 1789, and received his commission the same day. Bedford was a leading advocate for the abolition of slavery.

Bedford was a cousin of Gunning Bedford Sr., a Governor of Delaware. In late 1772 or early 1773, Bedford married Jane Ballareau Parker, the daughter of James Parker, a printer who learned his trade from Benjamin Franklin. He died in office as a federal judge, March 30, 1812.

RICHARD BASSETT of Delaware

Richard Bassett (April 2, 1745 – September 15, 1815) Born on April 2, 1745, in Cecil County, Province of Maryland, British America, Bassett pursued preparatory studies, then read law. He was admitted to the bar in Delaware. He was a member of the Delaware constitutional conventions of 1776 and 1792. He was a member of the Council of Safety in Dover, Delaware from 1776 to 1786.

He served in the Delaware State Militia as a company captain of the Dover Light Horse Regiment from 1777 to 1781. He coordinated the all-important task of selecting officers, measuring nominees against the military criteria of the day: patriotism, sufficient popularity to attract recruits, and military competence. Bassett's selections were clearly a success; Haslet's regiment became the best in Washington's command.

Bassett was instrumental in raising a militia unit to serve as Delaware's contribution to the Flying Camp, a mobile reserve that provided Washington with some 10,000 men to join the continentals holding New York City. He helped organize Captain Thomas Rodney's Dover Light Infantry, volunteer militia which served in the Trenton-Princeton campaign in 1776.

During the summer of 1777, the British entered upper Chesapeake Bay with to capture Philadelphia. Under Washington's plan, Delaware mobilized its militia under General Caesar Rodney. Rodney's units were expected to delay any British drive south toward Baltimore until Washington's continentals could reach the scene.

Bassett raised troops and supplied them so well, his state repeatedly called on him to manage mobilization. As events propelled him from local leadership to a key role in state affairs, Bassett came to appreciate the more general point that cooperation between states was vital.

He was a member of the Delaware Legislative Council in 1782.[2] He was a member of the Delaware House of Representatives in 1786. Although he rarely addressed the Constitutional Convention, Bassett strongly supported the Great Compromise. Designed to protect the rights of small states, the compromise gave an equal voice to all thirteen states in a Senate composed of two senators from each, but House of Representation was based on population.

He was a delegate to the Constitutional Convention in 1787, and a signer of the United States Constitution. He was a member of the Delaware convention which ratified the US Constitution in 1787, and in private practice in Delaware, 1787 to 1789.

Bassett was nominated by President Adams on February 18, 1801, to the US Circuit Court for the Third Circuit. After leaving the federal bench, Bassett became a planter. He died September 15, 1815, on his estate *Bohemia Manor* in Cecil County.

JACOB BROOME of Delaware

- Operated a Cotton Mill and Operated a Machine Shop
- His Cotton Mill became headquarters for DUPONT.

Jacob Broom (October 17, 1752 – April 25, 1810) was an American Founding Father, businessman, and politician from Wilmington, Delaware. As a delegate to the U.S. Constitutional Convention of 1787, he was a signer of the United States Constitution. He was also appointed as a delegate to the Annapolis Convention in 1786 but did not attend, and he served in the Delaware General Assembly.

His father was James Broom, and his mother was Esther Willis, a Quaker. In 1773 he married Rachel Pierce, and they raised eight children.

Broom was a resolute supporter of a strong central government who had been appointed as a commissioner to the Annapolis Convention in 1786, although he failed to attend. When George Washington visited Wilmington in 1783, Broom urged him to "contribute your advice and influence to promote that harmony and union of our infant governments which are so essential to the permanent establishment of our freedom, happiness, and prosperity."

Broom carried these opinions with him to Philadelphia, where he consistently voted for measures that would assure a powerful government responsive to the needs of the states. He favored a nine-year term limit for members of the Senate, where the states would be equally represented. He wanted the state legislatures to pay their representatives in Congress, which in turn, would have the power to veto state laws. He sought to vest state legislatures with the power to select presidential electors, and he wanted the president to hold office for life. Broom faithfully attended the Convention in Philadelphia and spoke out on issues that he considered crucial, but he left most of the speech-making to more influential and experienced delegates.

For many years, he chaired the board of directors of Wilmington's Delaware Bank. He also operated a cotton mill, as well as a machine shop that produced and repaired mill machinery. In 1802 He sold his mill property, which became the center of the DuPont manufacturing empire. Broom was also involved in bog iron ore.

He died at age 57 in 1810 while in Philadelphia on business and was buried there at Christ Church Burial Ground.[2] A cenotaph was placed in his honor at the Christ Episcopal Church by the Delaware State Society in 1987. His home near Brandywine, the Jacob Broom House, was declared a National Historic Landmark in 1974. Broom Street in Madison, Wisconsin, is named in his honor.

JOHN BLAIR of Virginia

- Blair was a delegate to the Constitutional Convention of 1787 and
- Signed the Constitution as one of three Virginia delegates.
- Delegate to the Virginia Ratification Convention of 1788.
- President Washington nominated Blair to the Supreme Court in 1789
- He helped establish principles of judicial review, separation of powers, and constitutional interpretation.

John Blair Jr. (April 17, 1732 – August 31, 1800) was a Virginia lawyer since 1757, Blair represented the College of William and Mary in the House of Burgesses. A widely respected legal scholar, he avoided the tumult of state politics, preferring to work behind the scenes. He was devoted to the idea of a permanent union of the newly independent states and was a loyal supporter of fellow Virginians James Madison and at the Constitutional Convention.

Contemporaries praised Blair for his ability to penetrate to the heart of legal questions, as well as his gentleness and benevolence.

John Blair was born in Williamsburg, Colony of Virginia, in 1732, to Mary (Monro) (1726–1768) John Blair. As had his father, Blair attended William & Mary, receiving a Bachelor of Arts in 1754. In 1755, he went to London to study law at the Middle Temple. He married Jean Balfour Blair.

Returning home to practice law, Blair was admitted to the Virginia bar in 1757 and quickly thrust into public life. He began his public career shortly after the close of the French and Indian War with his election to the seat reserved for the College of William and Mary in the House of Burgesses (1766–1799).

John Blair was one of the best trained jurists of his day. But he was devoted to the idea of a permanent union of the newly independent states and loyally supported fellow Virginians James Madison and George Washington at the Constitutional Convention. His greatest contribution came as a judge on the Virginia court of appeals and on the US. Supreme Court, where he influenced interpretation of the Constitution in important decisions.

Blair originally joined the moderate wing of the Patriot cause. He opposed Patrick Henry's extremist resolutions in protest of the Stamp Act, but the dissolution of the House of Burgesses by Parliament profoundly altered his views. In response to a series of taxes on the colonies passed by Parliament, Blair joined George Washington and others in 1770 and again in 1774 to draft nonimportation agreements which pledged their supporters to cease importing British goods until the taxes were repealed. In 1775, he reacted to the British Parliament's passage of the Intolerable Acts by joining those calling for a Continental Congress and pledging support for the people of Boston suffering hardship due to Parliament's actions.

When the American Revolution began, Blair became deeply involved in the government of his state. He served as a member of the convention that drew up Virginia's constitution (1776). He served on the Privy Council, Governor Patrick Henry's major advisory group (1776–1778). The decision was a precursor to the United States Supreme Court decision *Marbury v. Madison.*

306

In 1786, the legislature, recognizing Blair's prestige as a jurist, appointed him Thomas Jefferson's successor on a committee revising the laws of Virginia. The following year, he was appointed as a delegate to the Constitutional Convention.

On September 24, 1789, President George Washington nominated Blair for one of the five associate justice positions on the new U.S. Supreme Court. He was confirmed by the US Senate two days later, serving from February 2, 1790, until October 25, 1795. Blair participated in the court's landmark case of Chisholm v. Georgia, considered the first United States Supreme Court case of significance and impact. Blair died in Williamsburg on August 31, 1800.

RICHARD DOBBS SPAIGHT of North Carolina

Richard Dobbs Spaight (March 25, 1758 – September 6, 1802) was an American Founding Father, politician, planter, and signer of the United States Constitution. Spaight was the eighth governor of North Carolina from 1792 to 1795. He ran for the North Carolina Senate in 1802, and U.S. Congressman John Stanly called him unworthy. Stanly challenged him to a duel and mortally wounded Spaight.

Spaight was the father of North Carolina Governor Richard Dobbs Spaight Jr. and the grandfather of U.S. Representative Richard Spaight Donnell.

Spaight was born in New Bern, North Carolina, grand nephew of North Carolina Governor Arthur Dobbs. Orphaned at eight, he was sent to Dobbs relatives at Carrickfergus Northern Ireland and University of Glasgow.[1]

During the American Revolutionary War Spaight returned to North Carolina, serving as aide-de-camp to Major General Richard Caswell at the Battle of Camden. Although a member of the North Carolina legislature, Spaight remained active in the militia, eventually rising to the rank of lieutenant colonel in command of an artillery regiment. Under General Washington's strategy for the War, militia forces had an exact and vital role. Washington planned for a main force of regulars to serve as a Continental Army in opposition to major British forces while the militia protected isolated areas, conducted security missions against Loyalist units.

The fall of Charleston, South Carolina, to the British in 1780 was a crushing blow to American fortunes. In hastily devising a defense strategy, the Continental Congress called on Governor Caswell to recruit 4,000 militiamen to take to the field under his command. Spaight wrestled with the mechanics of mobilization and helped train the recruits who began trickling into central camps. These units were to be combined with a similar militia force raised in Virginia by Governor Jefferson and a division of continentals sent to the region by Washington. This force, under the command of Major General Horatio Gates, the hero of Saratoga, was expected to counter the British army of General Cornwallis. In early July Spaight marched with the militia units. to attack the British at Camden. US Patriots were heavily defeated.

Spaight remained on active duty during the aftermath of the defeat. Once more he was involved with his state's efforts to raise forces to cope with an invasion. Hhe also witnessed Major General Nathanael Greene's successful effort to restore American control over the south.

The North Carolina General Assembly elected Spaight a delegate to the Congress of the Confederation between 1782 and 1785; he then served in the North Carolina House of Commons from and was named Speaker of the House. In 1787, he was a delegate to the Philadelphia Convention drafting the U.S. Constitution, and signed the document when he was 29 years old.

He married Mary Leach, who had the distinction of being the first lady to dance with George Washington in the Governor's Palace, New Bern, in 1791.

Spaight died on September 6, 1802, following injuries sustained in a duel.

HUGH WILLIAMSON of North Carolina

- Williamson was a delegate to the 1787 Constitutional Convention
- Williamson was elected to the U.S. Congress in 1789,
- Scientist, publishing works on reptiles, lightening rods, climate and disease.

Hugh Williamson (December 5, 1735 – May 22, 1819) was a scholar of international renown. During the American Revolution, He volunteered his talents as physician and natural scientist to the war effort.

Williamson was born in West Nottingham Township, in what was then the frontier region of the Province of Pennsylvania. His parents sent him to New London Academy and the College of Philadelphia (University of Pennsylvania). Williamson graduated in the school's first class, on May 17, 1757, five days before his father died. Williamson studied theology with his neighbor, the Rev. Samuel Finley (later president of College of New Jersey, today's Princeton

In career shift four years later, Williamson turned to the study of medicine. After a year at University of Edinburgh, he matriculated in 1760s at University of Utrecht in the Netherlands, wrote a thesis, and received his Medical Degree. He witnessed the Boston Tea Party.

Williamson came of age politically during this encounter. In response to questions by Council members, who were in the process of formulating punitive measures against Massachusetts, he went on to express the argument that was becoming the core of the Patriot position: Americans were entitled to the full rights of Englishmen, including representation in the decisions of the English government. A mutual interest in scientific matters cemented a solid working relationship with Benjamin Franklin. While there he learned that the colonies had declared their independence. He rushed back to Philadelphia in early 1777 and volunteered for service in the Medical Department of the Continental Army. The department had no opening, so Williamson imported medicines through the British blockade.

Facing the threat of a British invasion of the region from the sea and bases in Florida, the state legislature voted to raise a force of 4,000 men to assist South Carolina. When Governor Richard Caswell, with the rank of major general, took to the field at the head of these citizen-soldiers, he named Williamson to serve as the Physician and Surgeon General, a post Williamson held until the end of the war.

Gates attempted to attack the British advance base near Camden, South Carolina, but his tired militia units were routed. Williamson volunteered to pass behind enemy lines to care for the American wounded.

In the fall of 1780 Williamson returned to the field. Major General Nathanael Greene began his brilliant campaign to recover the south. Francis Marion nicknamed "Swamp Fox", and others in South Carolina are most remembered for this type of guerrilla warfare. Williamson was attached to a force under Brigadier General Isaac Gregory whose mission was to limit British activity in eastern North Carolina. Gregory established his base in the vast reaches of the Dismal Swamp where he could pin the British down in Wilmington without jeopardizing his small force. Williamson's bold innovations in preventive medicine, especially his strenuous efforts to indoctrinate raw troops in the importance of sanitation and diet, kept the command free of disease, a rare feat in 18th-century warfare.

He was chosen to serve in the Continental Congress in 1782. His appointment represented a natural political progression for Williamson, who was evolving into a champion of federalism. At Convention sessions, he lodged with Alexander Hamilton and James Madison. His intellectual stature and international background propelled him into a leadership role in the North Carolina delegation. On 11 July 1787, James Wilson of Pennsylvania proposed the three fifths compromise, and a similar motion was passed two days later. Williamson was opposed to the institution of slavery.

Shortly before the Convention adjourned, Williamson wrote a series of public letters in defense of a strong federal system. Williamson explained to both groups the dual dangers of finances and taxes that would stunt the growth of manufacture. Here he participated in a successful effort to support the Constitution. Williamson married Maria Apthorpe in January 1789. They had two sons. On May 22, 1819, Williamson died in New York City, at age of 83.

WILLIAM BLOUNT of North Carolina
DONATED PROVISIONS TO REVOLUTIONARY MILITARY
ESTABLISHED "STATE OF FRANKLIN"
FOUNDER OF TENNESSEE

William Blount (April 6, 1749 – March 21, 1800)[1] was an American politician, landowner and Founding Father who was one of the signers of the Constitution of the United States. He was a member of the North Carolina delegation at the Constitutional Convention of 1787 and led the efforts for North Carolina to ratify the Constitution in 1789 at the Fayetteville Convention. He played a leading role helping gain admission as the state of Tennessee.

He was elected to the North Carolina legislature in 1781, where he remained for most of the decade, except for two terms in the Continental Congress in 1782 and 1786. Blount pushed the legislature to open the lands west of the Appalachians to settlement. As governor of the Southwest Territory, he negotiated the Treaty of Holston in 1791, bringing thousands of acres of Indian lands under U.S. control.

An aggressive land speculator, Blount gradually acquired millions of acres in Tennessee and the Trans-Appalachian West. He owned slaves as well. His risky land investments left him in debt, and in the 1790s, he conspired of his to have Great Britain take over Spanish-controlled Louisiana and Florida in the hope of boosting land prices. When the conspiracy was uncovered in 1797, he was expelled from the Senate and became the first federal official to face impeachment. Blount remained popular and served in the state senate in his last years.

Blount was born on Easter Sunday at Rosefield, the home of his maternal grandfather, John Gray, in Windsor, Province of North Carolina.[6]:5[7] He was the eldest child of Jacob Blount (1726–1789) and Barbara Gray Blount. Following his birth, Jacob Blount built a plantation, Blount Hall, in Pitt County, North Carolina.[2]:7

Outside of tutors, William and his brothers had little formal education but were involved in their father's business ventures at a young age. Jacob Blount raised livestock, cotton, and tobacco, produced turpentine, and operated a mill and horse racing track.[2]:7 His land acquisitions - several thousand acres by end of the 1760s, taught profits of land speculation.[2]:11

During the Regulator Movement of the late 1760s and early 1770s, the Blount's remained loyal to the North Carolina government. Jacob Blount, a Justice of the Peace, furnished Governor William Tryon's army with supplies as it marched to defeat the Regulators at the Battle of Alamance in 1771. William Blount, along with his brother, were among Tryon's soldiers, though they saw little action.[2]:17

American Revolution

As tensions heightened between Great Britain and the Thirteen Colonies in the 1770's, the Blount family gradually aligned themselves with the Patriot cause. In April 1776, Jacob Blount was appointed paymaster of the 2nd North Carolina Regiment, and William Blount was appointed paymaster for the New Bern District Brigade of the North Carolina militia.[2]:32 William's brothers, Reading and Thomas, accepted commissions in the Continental Army. The Blount's provided provisions for the Continental Army and militias, and they profited financially and politically from the war.[6]:43 They looked westward, with John Gray Blount acquiring a portion of Richard Henderson's Transylvania Purchase in mid-1776.[2]:32

In December 1776, William Blount was appointed paymaster of the 3rd North Carolina Regiment and spent the first few months of 1777 with the unit as it marched north to join Washingtons in defense of Philadelphia.[2]:36 In November 1777, political rivals in the North Carolina removed Blount as paymaster, though he was restored to office in April 1778.[2]:38 He helped organize defense of Charleston, which fell to the British in the 1780 siege of Charleston. William's brother, Thomas, was captured.[2]:38

In early 1780, Blount was appointed commissary to General Horatio Gates, who had arrived in North Carolina to command Patriot forces.[2]:42 Blount was present at Gates's defeat at Battle of Camden, in confusion of battle lost $300,000 intended to pay Patriot soldiers.[2]:43

North Carolina politics and the Continental Congress

In late 1779, Blount ran for the vacant New Bern state House of Commons seat against Richard Dobbs Spaight in a campaign described as "violent in an age of fierce elections."[2]:40 Spaight won narrowly, but Blount convinced election officials that voter fraud had occurred, and the election was voided.[2]:41 Following the Battle of Camden, Blount won and took his seat in the House of Commons in January 1781.

In May 1782, Blount was elected one of North Carolina's four delegates to the Continental Congress. At the Congress's 1782 session, Blount helped defeat a poll tax and a liquor tax and opposed a reduction of the army. He also agreed to consider a land cession act to satisfy North Carolina's massive tax debt owed to the Confederation.[2]:57–59 Blount left Philadelphia in January 1783 and accepted appointment to the North Carolina House of Commons steering committee.[2]:66

During the House's 1783 and 1784 sessions, Blount introduced bills that would prove critical in early history of Tennessee. One bill, known as the "Land Grab Act," opened the state's lands west of the Appalachians (not under Indian domain) to settlement. Another bill rendered soldiers with at least two years of military service eligible for land grants.[2]:69 In 1784, Blount sponsored a bill establishing Nashville in what was then the Cumberland settlements.[2]:88

State of Franklin

In June 1784, Blount sponsored another bill critical to early Tennessee history—a bill calling for North Carolina lands west of the Appalachians (i.e., modern Tennessee) to be ceded to the Continental Congress. The bill was hotly contested but passed by a 52-43 margin.[2]:89 Opponents of the cession gained control of the House and repealed the act in October,[2]:94 but not before a movement by the Tennessee Valley residents to establish a separate state, known as the State of Franklin, had gained momentum. A friend of both North Carolina Governor Richard Caswell and John Sevier, Blount waffled on the Franklin issue four years.[2]:99

Despite the cession debacle, Blount was elected to the Continental Congress for the 1785 session.[2]:94 As he prepared to depart, however, word came that the Congress had appointed a commission to negotiate a new treaty, eventually known as the Treaty of Hopewell, with the southern tribes. Fearing the new treaty would be unfavorable to North Carolina, Blount, with Governor Caswell's blessing, headed south in hopes of negotiating a separate treaty for the state. He arrived too late, however, and the Hopewell Treaty negotiated by the commissioners returned a sizeable portion of western lands claimed by North Carolina speculators to the Indians. Fearing a backlash back home, Blount signed the treaty as a witness.[2]:103–6

In March 1786, Blount hurried to New York to take his seat in the Continental Congress, hoping to prevent ratification of the Hopewell Treaty, but once again he arrived too late, and the treaty was ratified.[2]:114 Disappointed, he went home, but with anger rising over his handling of the Hopewell Treaty, he returned to the Continental Congress in November 1786.[2]:118 In March 1787, Blount was chosen as one of five delegates to represent North Carolina at the Constitutional Convention in Philadelphia. Blount arrived at the convention on June 20, after debates had already begun. He sent a copy of the Virginia Plan (in violation of Convention rules), and, expressing pessimism in the Convention's outcome, he stayed for just a few days before heading to New York to rejoin the Continental Congress in early July.[2]:126 He was present for the Congress's debate and passage of the Northwest Ordinance and heard Henry Knox's report recommending a North Carolina land cession.[2]:128 By August 7, he had returned to the Convention in Philadelphia. Still reeling from the Hopewell Treaty, he was wary of signing but was convinced by Gouverneur Morris to do so.[2]:133

Confident that North Carolina would gain more than it would lose with the new Constitution, Blount returned home to campaign for its ratification. Elected to the North Carolina Senate from Pitt County in 1788 and 1789, Blount and his allies successfully countered attempts by anti-federalists to thwart adoption of the Constitution, and North Carolina voted for its ratification in November 1789.[2]:147–165 Blount sought one of North Carolina's first U.S. Senate seats but was defeated by Benjamin Hawkins.[2]:166–7

Southwest Territory (Earliest Tennessee)

Congress accepted North Carolina's western cession, which consisted of what is now Tennessee, on April 2, 1790. In May, the Southwest Territory was created and was to be governed under the Northwest Ordinance. On June 8, President George Washington appointed Blount governor of the new territory. Blount visited Washington at Mount Vernon on September 18 and was sworn in by Supreme Court Justice James Iredell two days later.[6]:182–3 In October 1790, he set up a temporary capital in Piney Flats, Tennessee, and organized government.

The western frontiersmen were initially skeptical of Blount, but he gained their trust, by recommending John Sevier and James Robertson as brigadier generals of the territorial militia, and appointing Landon Carter, Stockley Donelson and Gilbert Christian as colonels. Former Franklinites appointed to lower government offices included Joseph Hardin, William Cage, James White, Dr. James White and Francis Alexander Ramsey. Others receiving appointments included future president Jackson, future governor Roane and naval officer George Farragut.[6]:189–90 Blount hired his half-brother as a secretary,[2]:212 and recruited Fayetteville, North Carolina, publisher Roulstone to establish a newspaper, the Gazette.[2]:181

In December 1790, following his trip to the Cumberland territories, Blount's family joined him at Rocky Mount. The next year, he chose James White's Fort, near the confluence of the Holston and French Broad rivers, as the new capital, and named it "Knoxville" after his superior, the US Secretary of War Henry Knox.[2]:208

Throughout his term as governor, Blount was torn between angry western frontiersmen, who demanded war against hostile Indians, and a War Department that consistently pushed for peaceful negotiations with the Indians.[2]:233 In June 1791, he negotiated the Treaty of Holston with Cherokee leader John Watts.

Following attacks by the Chickamauga's against Ziegler's Station and against Cavet's Station in 1793, Blount called up the militia. Sevier led the militia into Georgia and destroyed several Chickamauga villages. Knox blasted Blount for the invasion and refused to pay for the militiamen.[2]:236 Blount negotiated a truce with the Chickamauga at Tellico Blockhouse in 1794.

Toward the middle of his term, Blount began implementing the steps in the Northwest Ordinance for statehood. On September 15, 1795, he directed county sheriffs to conduct a census which found the population at 77,000, with 60,000 required for statehood. Blount ordered a state constitutional convention to be held at Knoxville in January 1796.[2]:284–7 The government of the new state convened in March 1796, before it had been officially admitted to the Union.[2]:292

Blount realized he had little chance of defeating Sevier in a race for governor of the new state, so he sought one of the state's two US Senate seats. He received this appointment (with William Cocke) on March 30, 1796, and headed to Philadelphia to campaign for Tennessee's statehood. Blount's brother, Thomas (Congressman from North Carolina), and James Madison, convinced the house to vote for Tennessee's admission to the Union on May 6. Tennessee became a new state on May 31.[2]:292–5

Returning to Knoxville, he was paraded in triumph. Tennessee allies, Andrew Jackson, Joseph Anderson, James White, Charles McClung and William C. C. Claiborne, helped repair his image. He died March 21, 1800.[2]:346

References

1. Chisholm, Hugh, ed. (1911)."Blount, William" Encyclopædia Britannica(11th ed.).Cambridge U Press.
2. Masterson, William Henry (1954). William Blount. Baton Rouge: LSUPress. ISBN 978-0-8371-2308-0

PIERCE BUTLER of South Carolina

- Butler was a British military officer who fought in the American Revolutionary War.
- Butler was a delegate to the 1787 Constitutional Convention
- He proposed the Fugitive Slave Clause, which protected slavery.
- Butler was one of only 40 people to sign the Constitution.
- Paid Southern Troops and purchased war material.

Pierce Butler (July 11, 1744 – February 15, 1822) was an Irish-born American politician who was one of the Founding Fathers of the United States. Born in the Ireland, Butler emigrated to the North America and fought in the Revolutionary War. He served as a delegate to the 1787 Constitutional Convention, where Butler signed the US Constitution: also a US Senator.

He had private misgivings about the Atlantic slave trade. He introduced the Fugitive Slave Clause, and the Three-fifths Compromise that counted only three-fifths of the enslaved population in state totals.

Butler was an Anglican until after the American Revolution when he became a member of the Episcopal Church. He resigned a commission in the British Army in 1773 and settled with his wife, Mary, in South Carolina.

Marriage led him to seek new directions, for when his British unit received orders to return to Great Britain in 1773, he decided to leave the army. He sold his commission and used the proceeds to purchase a plantation in the coastal region of South Carolina. Management skills proved useful as he increased his land holdings to over 10,000 acres. He also began to accumulate a small fleet of coastal vessels.

When war broke out between Great Britain and the colonies in 1775, Butler joined other former British officers (including the future generals Horatio Gates, Charles Lee, and Richard Montgomery) in casting his lot with the American cause. In Butler's case the success of his business interests as well as the significant role played by the Middleton family in the Patriot movement in South Carolina clearly influenced his decision. He began public service in 1776 when his neighbors elected him to the South Carolina legislature, a post that he held until 1789.

In early 1779, Governor John Rutledge asked Butler to help reorganize South Carolina's defenses. Butler assumed the post of state adjutant general, a brigadier general rank.

By 1778, King George III faced a new military situation in the Colonies. Their forces in the northern and middle colonies had reached a stalemate with Washington's Continentals, more adequately supplied and better trained after the hard winter at Valley Forge. There was a risk France would enter the war as ally of the Americans. They believed that the many Loyalists in the southern states (British had an active trade through cotton, rice and tobacco) would rally to the Crown. They planned a reconquest of the rebellious colonies one at a time, moving north from Georgia. They launched their new strategy by capturing Savannah in December 1778.

Butler served as a volunteer aide to General Lachlan McIntosh during the operation, which climaxed with an attempted attack on Savannah.

In 1780, the British captured Charleston, South Carolina, and with it most of the colony's civil government and military forces. Butler escaped as part of a command group deliberately located outside the city. Over the next two years, he developed a counterstrategy to defeat the southern operations of the Brits. Refusing to surrender, allies in South Carolina and the occupied portions of Georgia and North Carolina organized guerrilla operations against the British. As adjutant general, Butler worked with former members of the militia and Continental Army veterans such as Francis Marion and Thomas Sumter to integrate the partisan efforts into a unified campaign, under the command of Horatio Gates and later Nathanael Greene.

Throughout the closing phases of the southern campaign, he donated cash and supplies to help sustain the American forces.

Military operations in the final months of the Revolutionary War left Butler poor. Many of his plantations and ships were destroyed, the international trade for his business was in shambles. To secure loans and new markets, he traveled to Europe when the war ended.

In late 1785, Butler returned to the US. Attesting to his growing political influence, the South Carolina legislature asked Butler to represent the state at the Constitutional Convention in Philadelphia in 1787. At convention, he urged the president be given the power to initiate war, all delegates rejected his proposal.

Butler's experiences as a soldier and planter-legislator led to his forceful support for a strong union of the states. He introduced the Fugitive Slave Clause (Article 4, Section 2), which established protection for slavery in the Constitution. In addition, while criticizing the international trade in enslaved Africans, he supported the passage in the Constitution that prohibited regulation of the trade for 20 years. He advocated counting the entire slave population in the states' totals for Congressional apportionment but compromised to count three-fifths of the enslaved people.

Vice President Aaron Burr was Butler's guest at his St. Simons plantations in September 1804. Burr was lying low after shooting Hamilton in the July 1804 duel.

Following his wife's death in 1790, Butler sold off their South Carolina holdings and invested in Georgia Sea Island plantations. He also pursued plans in the 1830s to develop cotton mills in the Piedmont of Georgia, where he founded what became Roswell, Georgia, in 1839. Through his business ventures, he became one of the wealthiest men in the nation, with substantial land holdings in several states.

WILLIAM FEW of Georgia

- Leading organizer of Georgia Militia before and during Revolution
- Few was elected to represent Georgia at 1787 Constitutional Convention
- Signed the U.S. Constitution
- Few was a founding trustee of the University of Georgia
- President of the City Bank of New York, predecessor to Citigroup,

The Colony of Georgia was the last to be established during the colonial period. They were on the border of two hostile forces, the Spanish in Florida and a heavy force of Indians supported by the British. The men of Georgia colony were more involved in battles with these forces than with Independence and Constitutional development.

William Few Jr. (June 8, 1748 – July 16, 1828) was born into a poor yeoman farming family, Few achieved both social prominence and political power later in life. Comparing William Few to stories of Davy Crockett is largely accurate.

Descendant of Quaker shoe polisher Richard Few from the county of Wiltshire, England, he emigrated to Maryland.

In time the Few family achieved a measure of prosperity, emerging as political leaders in rural Orange County. Like many other western settlers, the family became involved with the Regulators. Few's brother James was hanged for his part in the uprising, and the Few family farm was ransacked by William Tryon's militia troops. This led to Few's ambivalence towards capital punishment. The family fled to Wrightsboro, Georgia, leaving Few to settle affairs.

Few was called to active duty in 1778, when Georgia faced the threat of invasion by a force of Loyalist militia. The Georgians' first military campaign ended in disaster. A force of state and Continental units successfully combined to repulse an enemy raid on Sunbury near the states southeastern border, but a counterattack orchestrated by Major General Robert Howe of the Continental Army and Governor John Houston bogged down before the Patriots could reach St. Augustine. Few, in command of a company of Georgia Militia, watched the collapse of the campaign's logistical support and then the disintegration of the force. At the end of the year a sudden amphibious invasion by British forces resulted in the capture of Savannah, Georgia. Throughout 1779 the regiment, with Few as second in command, skirmished with probing British units, forcing the enemy to abandon Augusta.

Enemy operations in Georgia in 1779 were part of a new "southern strategy" by which the British planned to use the state as a base. Few's military service in the later years of the war proved critical both in frustrating this strategy and in enhancing his credentials as a state leader. The western forces, in which Few's regiment played a prominent role, kept the British from consolidating their position. Few emerged as a gifted administrator and logistics expert in maintaining a viable military force in Georgia. He also turned into a bold commander. Most importantly, he displayed the raw physical stamina required of guerrilla warfare.

Few returned to Congress in 1782, where he remained to serve throughout most of the decade. While a member of that body, Few was asked by his state to serve concurrently in the Constitutional Convention in 1787. This dual responsibility caused him to split his time between the two bodies and therefore to miss portions of the constitutional proceedings. He also participated in the Georgia ratification.

Georgia selected Few as one of its original United States senators. In the Senate, Few opposed the creation of the First Bank of the United States. He was a founding trustee of the University of Georgia (UGA) in Athens in 1785.

At the urging of his wife, a native New Yorker, Few left Georgia in 1799 and moved to Manhattan. He served as president of the City Bank of New York, the predecessor of present-day Citigroup, and remained in this position until 1817. Few retired in 1815 to his home in Fishkill, New York, where he died on July 16, 1828.

ABRAHAM BALDWIN of Georgia

Abraham Baldwin (November 22, 1754 – March 4, 1807) minister, patriot, politician, and Founding Father who signed the United States Constitution. Born and raised in Connecticut, he was a 1772 graduate of Yale. After the Revolutionary War, he became a lawyer. He moved to Georgia in the mid-1780s and founded the University of Georgia. Baldwin was a member of Society of the Cincinnati. Baldwin served as a United States Senator from Georgia from 1799 to 1807.

Abraham Baldwin was born in 1754 in Guildford in the Connecticut Colony, the son of Lucy (Dudley) and Michael Baldwin, a blacksmith, and descended from Elder John Strong. His half-brother, Henry Baldwin, was an Associate Justice of the Supreme Court of the United States. After attending Guildford Grammar School, he attended Yale College in nearby New Haven, where he was a member of the Linonian Society. He graduated in 1772.

After theological study, he was licensed as a Congregationalist minister. He served as a tutor at the college. He held that position until 1779. During the American Revolution, he served as a chaplain in the Connecticut Continental Army. He did not see combat while with the Continental troops. Two years later at the conclusion of the war, Baldwin declined an offer from Yale's president, Ezra Stiles, to become Professor of Divinity. He turned to law and in 1783 was admitted to the Connecticut bar.

Move to Georgia

Encouraged by his former commanding officer General Nathanael Greene, who had acquired the plantation at Mulberry Grove where Eli Whitney would later invent the cotton gin, Baldwin moved to Georgia. He was recruited by fellow Yale alumnus Governor Lyman Hall, another transplanted New Englander, to develop a state education plan. Baldwin was named the first president of the University of Georgia and became active in politics to build support for the university, which had not yet enrolled its first student. He was appointed as delegate to the Congress of the Confederation and then to the Constitutional Convention; in September 1786 he was one of the state's two signatories to the U.S. Constitution.

Baldwin remained president of the University of Georgia during its initial development phase until 1800. During this period, he also worked with the legislature on the college charter. In 1801, Franklin College, the University of Georgia's initial college, opened to students. Josiah Meigs was hired to succeed Baldwin as first acting president and oversee the inaugural class of students. The first buildings of the college were architecturally modeled on Baldwin's and Meigs's alma mater Yale where they both taught. (The university sports adopted as its mascot the bulldog, also mascot of Yale, a tribute to Baldwin and Meigs)

Politics

Baldwin was elected to the Georgia Assembly, where he became highly active, working to develop support for the college. He was able to mediate between the rougher frontiersmen, perhaps because of his childhood as the son of a blacksmith, and the aristocratic planter elite who dominated the coastal Lowcountry. He became one of the most prominent legislators, pushing significant measures such as the education bill through the Georgia Assembly.

He was elected as representative to the U.S. Congress in 1788. The Georgia legislature elected him as U.S. Senator in 1799 (the practice until popular election in 1913.) He served as President pro tempore of the United States Senate from December 1801 to December 1802, re-elected and served in office until his death.

On March 4, 1807, at age 52, Baldwin died while a U.S. senator from Georgia. Later that month the Savannah Republican and Savannah Evening Ledger reprinted an obituary that had first been published in a Washington, D.C., newspaper: "He originated the plan of The University of Georgia, drew up the charter, and with infinite labor and patience, in vanquishing all sorts of prejudices and removing every obstruction, he persuaded the assembly to adopt it." His remains are interred at Rock Creek Cemetery in Washington, DC.

NICHOLAS GILMAN of New Hampshire

- Gilman fought in the Continental Army during the Revolutionary War.
- Gilman was a delegate to the Constitutional Convention in Philadelphia
- Signed the U.S. Constitution as a representative of New Hampshire.

Nicholas Gilman Jr. (August 3, 1755 – May 2, 1814) was born in Exeter, Province of New Hampshire, to Ann (Taylor) and Nicholas Gilman Born during the French and Indian War, he was soon aware of the military responsibilities that went with citizenship in a New England colony. Gilman's father, along with Nathaniel Folsom and Enoch Poor, emerged as a leader of the Patriot cause in Exeter.

In November 1776, a committee of the state legislature appointed Gilman to serve as adjutant officer, of the 3rd New Hampshire Regiment. A superb combat officer, Scammell made effective use of Gilman's administrative talents in the task of creating a potent fighting force out of the limited manpower resources at hand. In time the 3rd New Hampshire would become one of the mainstays of the Continental Army.

In the spring of 1777 Gilman and the rest of the officers and men of the 3rd New Hampshire marched to Fort Ticonderoga on Lake Champlain to participate in an attempt by American forces to halt the advance of a powerful army of British and German regulars and Indian auxiliaries under General John Burgoyne. Difficulties in coordinating the efforts of several different states turned Gilman's first military experience into one of defeat. The veteran British troops outflanked the fort, and only at the last minute, escape by night retreat. This delay allowed time for a mass mobilization of New England militia, including a New Hampshire Regiment of volunteers led by John Langdon and Gilman's father. It also provided Major General Horatio Gates time to establish new positions near Saratoga, New York, to block Burgoyne's advance, and then, to cut off the British line of withdrawal to Canada. During this campaign, Gilman was busily employed in supervising the training and readiness of Scammell's men. He participated in two important battles at Freeman's Farm, where Burgoyne surrendered.

Neither Gilman nor Scammell was granted a respite after this great victory. Less than a week after the British surrender, the 3rd New Hampshire set out to reinforce Washington's main army near Philadelphia. The American capital had recently fallen to a larger British force, and the New Englanders had to spend a harsh winter in the snows of Valley Forge. When Washington selected Colonel Scammell to serve as the Continental Army's Adjutant General, Scammell made Gilman his assistant. Promotion to the rank of captain followed in June 1778.

For the remainder of the war, Gilman found himself near the military leaders of the Continental Army. His duties in carrying out the myriad tasks necessary to keep a force in the field placed him in daily contact with Washington, Baron von Steuben, Henry Knox, Nathanael Greene, and others. He personally saw action at Monmouth and Yorktown.

Gilman was elected one of the 31 original members of the Society of the Cincinnati. In 1786, New Hampshire appointed Gilman to the Continental Congress.

The outbreak of unrest and insurrection in western Massachusetts in late 1786 further strengthened Gilman's commitment to changing the Articles of Confederation. That same year, he helped to suppress the Paper Money Riot. He was pleased to serve his state as a representative at the Constitutional Convention that met in July 1787. Although he and fellow New Hampshire delegate John Langdon, reached Philadelphia after the proceedings were well under way, they both joined in the debates and helped hammer out the compromises needed to produce a document that might win approval in every state and region.

During this time, Gilman's political loyalty began to change. Ever a staunch nationalist, he had supported the Federalists while that party led the fight for a more binding union of the states. Once that concept developed, Gilman became increasingly concerned with the need to protect all people from abuse of power by the government. He supported the Democratic-Republican Party forming around Thomas Jefferson. He remained an influential member of the Senate until his death in 1814.

RUFUS KING

MASSACHUSETTS PRESIDENTIAL CANDIDATE

Rufus King (March 24, 1755 – April 29, 1827) was an American Founding Father, lawyer, politician, and diplomat. He was a delegate from Massachusetts to the Continental Congress and the Philadelphia Convention and was one of the signers of the United States Constitution in 1787. After formation of Congress, he represented New York in the United States Senate. Federalist Party last presidential nominee during the 1816 presidential election.

The son of a prosperous Massachusetts merchant, King studied law before he volunteered for the militia during the American Revolutionary War. He won election to the Massachusetts General Court in 1783 and to the Congress of the Confederation the following year. At the 1787 Philadelphia Convention, he emerged as a leading nationalist and called for increased powers for the federal government. King returned to Massachusetts, where he used his influence to help ratify the Constitution. At the urging of Alexander Hamilton, he abandoned his law practice and moved to New York City.

He won election to represent New York in the US Senate in 1789 and remained in office until 1796. That year, he accepted President George Washington's appointment to the position of Minister to Great Britain. Though King aligned with Hamilton's Federalists, the Democratic-Republican President Jefferson retained King after Jefferson's victory in the 1800 presidential election. King served as the Federalist vice-presidential candidate in the 1804 and 1808 elections and ran unsuccessfully with Charles Cotesworth Pinckney of South Carolina.

King was born on March 24, 1755, in Scarborough, which was then part of Massachusetts but is now in Maine. He was a son of Isabella (Bragdon) and Richard King, a prosperous farmer, merchant, lumberman, and sea captain who had made a modest fortune. His financial success angered his neighbors, and when the Stamp Act 1765 was imposed, a mob ransacked his house and destroyed the furniture. Nobody was punished, and the next year, they burned down his barn.

King attended Dummer Academy (now The Governor's Academy) at the age of twelve. He attended Harvard College, where he graduated first in his class in 1777. He read law but volunteered during the Revolution. Appointed a major, he served as an aide to General John Sullivan during the Battle of Rhode Island.

His wife, Mary Alsop, was born in New York on October 17, 1769, and died in Jamaica, New York, June 5, 1819. They married in New York City, March 30, 1786.

When the chance arose in 1778 to drive the last of the enemy from New England, King quickly volunteered. American victory at Saratoga in the fall of 1777 had freed New England from the threat of attack from Canada. Frances's entry into the war led the British to withdraw from Philadelphia, allowing Washington to concentrate near New York. Three of his brigades were available to reinforce New England, and the appearance of a French naval squadron off the American coast provided the occasion to attack the British at Newport.

King was first elected to the Massachusetts General Court in 1783 and returned there yearly until 1785. Massachusetts sent him to the Confederation Congress from 1784 to 1787. He was one of the youngest men at the conference.

In 1787, King was sent to the Constitutional Convention, which was held in Philadelphia. Despite his youthful stature, King held a significant position at the convention since "he numbered among the most capable orators." Along with James Madison, "he became a leading figure in the nationalist causes."

Although when he came to the convention, he was still unconvinced that major changes should be made in the Articles of Confederation, his views underwent a startling transformation over the debates. He worked with Chairman William Samuel Johnson, James Madison, Gouverneur Morris, and Alexander Hamilton on the Committee of Style and Arrangement to prepare a final draft of the U.S. Constitution. King was one of the most prominent delegates, namely because of playing "a major role in the laborious crafting of the fundamental governing character." The Constitution was signed on September 17 but needed to be ratified by the states. After signing the Constitution, he returned home. He went to work to get the Constitution ratified. Ratification passed by the narrow margin of 187–168.

After his early political experiences during the Constitutional Convention, King decided to switch his vocational calling by "abandoning the law and moving from the Bay State to Gotham and entering the New York political forum." Shortly afterwards, he was elected as Senator from New York and was re-elected in 1795. King declined an appointment as Secretary of State to succeed Edmund Randolph. In 1795, King helped Hamilton defend the controversial Jay Treaty by writing pieces for New York newspapers under the pseudonym "Camillus." King wrote nine numbers 23–30, 34, and 35, in which he discussed the treaty's maritime and commercial aspects. He was re-elected in 1795 but resigned on May 23, 1796, after he had been appointed U.S. Minister to Great Britain. Even though King was an outspoken Federalist, President Jefferson, refused to recall him. In 1803, King voluntarily relinquished his position.

King and signer of the Constitution, Charles Cotesworth Pinckney, were candidates for vice president and president, only to lose by wide margins to Jefferson and Madison.

Rufus King died on April 29, 1827, and his funeral was held at his New York home in Jamaica, Queens.

WILLIAM SAMUEL JOHNSON of Connecticut

- Johnson was educated at home and graduated from Yale College in 1744,
- He received an honorary degree from Harvard in 1747.
- Johnson attended all four founding American Congresses.
- Drafted the definitive version of the Constitution.
- Johnson was first president of Columbia College, 1787 to 1800.

William Samuel Johnson was born in Stratford, Connecticut, on October 7, 1727, to Samuel Johnson, a well-known Anglican clergyman, educator, and later president of King's College, and first wife, Charity Floyd Nicoll. He graduated from Yale College in 1744, winning the George Berkely Scholarship. He received a master's degree from Yale in 1747 and an honorary degree from Harvard. He received an honorary master's degree from King's College in 1761 and Doctor of Law from Oxford in 1766.

Self-educated in the law, he quickly developed an important clientele and network and was frequently consulted on inter-colony legal issues. He also held a commission in the Connecticut militia over 20 years, rising from ensign to colonel.

Johnson was attracted to the Patriot cause by what he and his associates considered Parliament's unwarranted interference in the colonies. At this time, he was somewhat of a radical, writing about "chains and shackles," "stamps and slavery," and the "late fatal acts" that would reduce America to "Roman provinces in the time of the Caesar." He started forming alliances with the Son's of Liberty.

He was elected one to the Stamp Act Congress. He authored the *Report of Committee at Congress on Colonial Rights,* which evolved into the *Stamp Act Declaration of Rights and Grievances,* the final version of which is in his handwriting.

The declaration, petitions, and pressure from London merchants forced Parliament to repeal the Stamp Act in 1766. But that year, Connecticut faced a new problem with a seventy-year-old unsettled legal case involving Mohegan Indians lands. The British wanted to use the case as a pretext to cancel Connecticut's Royal Charter of 1662. Johnson left his family, his political career, and his legal practice to argue in London for Connecticut's charter, where he lived from 1767 to 1771.

While a Colonial Agent he sharply criticized British policy toward the colonies. His experience in Britain convinced him that Britain's policy developed more by ignorance of American conditions, not through the sinister designs of a wicked government, as Patriots alleged. As the Patriots became more radical in their demands, Johnson found it difficult to commit himself wholeheartedly to the cause. Although he believed British policy unwise, he found it difficult to break his own connections with the native country. A scholar of international renown, he had many friends in Britain and among the British and American Loyalists.

He was elected as a delegate in 1774 to the Continental Congress but turned down the honor in favor of his protégée Roger Sherman. The Connecticut assembly, after the Battles of Lexington and Concord, over his strong personal objections, sent him on a dangerous visit through both Patriot Massachusetts militia and British army lines in Boston to the British commander General Thomas Gage to negotiate an end to the fighting by making a separate peace with the British. He succeeded, but on returning across the lines again to Connecticut, he found the Assembly had changed their mind, voted for war, then adjourned.

WILLIAM LIVINGSTON of New Jersey

- **Committee of Five**: that drafted the Declaration of Independence
- Negotiated Louisiana Purchase in 1803, doubled size of the United States
- Sponsored development of first successful steamboat with Robert Fulton
- Administered Presidential oath of office to George Washington in 1789
- Represented New York in the Continental Congress from 1776-1783
- A member of the second, third, and fourth Provincial Congresses of New York

Livingston was born in Albany in the Province of New York on November 30, 1723. He was the son of Philip Livingston (1686–1749), the 2nd Lord of Livingston Manor, and Catherine Van Brugh, the only child of Albany mayor Pieter Van Brugh.

Livingston received his early education from local schools and tutors. At age 13, he was sent to live for a year and prepare for college with the Anglican missionary and Yale College graduate Henry Barclay. Livingston enrolled at Yale in 1737 and graduated in 1741. He went on to New York City, where he studied law and became a law clerk with lawyer James Alexander.

By raising divisive issues, he managed to divert half the funds raised by a state lottery for the college to fund the construction of a new jail and a detention house for sailors from diseased ships. In July 1754, King's College was defiantly opened under its first president, Samuel Johnson, and on October 31, 1754, King George III granted a charter to the institution.

In 1772, he moved to Elizabethtown in the colonial-era Province of New Jersey, where he rented a house in town. A young Alexander Hamilton lived with Livingston while he attended Francis Barber's grammar school.

Livingston started construction of a large country home to house his growing family, Liberty Hall, still stands. After attaining considerable influence among the patriots, Livingston was elected to serve as delegate to the Continental Congress in Philadelphia. New Jersey's Provincial Congress declined to reappoint him to the Second Continental Congress, however, since he did not favor immediate independence. William Livingston's older brother, Philip Livingston, a strong member of the New York delegation, became one of the signers.

On the eve of independence, Livingston left his seat in the Congress to assume full-time military duties. When a massive buildup of British ships and troops in New York harbor indicated that a major invasion was imminent, Congress called on the states to reinforce Washington. Livingston took to the field with New Jersey's militia to secure the northern shoreline against enemy landing, break communication between the British and Loyalists. With militia headquarters nearby, Livingston used Liberty Hall as barracks for his men.

Livingston joined the New Jersey Delegation to the 1787 Constitutional Convention in Philadelphia and was one of the signers of the U.S. Constitution.

Livingston married Susannah French. They had 13 children, including:

- Susannah became the stepmother-in-law of President William Henry Harrison.
- Sarah Van Brugh Livingston (1756–1802), who married John Jay (1745–1829).

Livingston died on July 25, 1790, in Elizabeth, New Jersey.

DAVID BREARLEY of New Jersey

Born on June 11, 1745, to Mary and David Brearley Sr. (1703–1785) in Lawrence Township, New Jersey, Province of New Jersey, Brearley attended the College of New Jersey (Princeton) and read law.

Prior to the start of the American Revolution, Brearley was on one occasion arrested for his opposition to the rule of the British Parliament but was freed by a mob. With the outbreak of the Revolutionary War, Brearley was at first a captain in the Monmouth County militia after speaking out against Parliamentary absolutism.

While New Jersey was taking its final steps toward independence, a massive British armada appeared. These forces clearly outnumbered Washington's continentals, and Congress called on nearby states to mobilize their citizen-soldiers to resist the coming assault. Included in New Jersey's 3,300-man quota was Colonel Philip Van Cortlandt's regiment, in which Brearley was second in command.

Despite the efforts of Washington's regulars and the massed militia, New York and its strategic harbor fell to the enemy in September 1776. This defeat provided an important lesson that Washington and his senior officers pressed on the Continental Congress: it would take full-time soldiers to engage British and Hessian regiments successfully in open battle. Congress accepted this argument, authorizing a significant increase in the Army and directing that it retained for the duration of the war.

General Sir William Howe's Redcoats eventually boarded ships and, sailing by way of Chesapeake Bay, attacked Philadelphia from the rear. Washington hastily redeployed his units to face the new danger, eventually establishing a defensive line along Brandywine Creek. On the morning of 11 September Hessians and some British light troops appeared before Chad's Ford and immediately engaged the New Jersey Brigade. Hard skirmishing lasted all morning as the outnumbered continentals appeared to be holding their own; in the afternoon Howe's main force, which had crossed far upstream at an unguarded ford, appeared on Washington's flank and eventually forced the Americans to retreat. Brearly and the rest of Maxwell's men helped cover the withdrawal as Philadelphia fell. When the Americans counterattacked at Germantown three weeks later, the New Jersey Brigade formed the reserve.

During the following winter, the men's confidence increased during training of Frederick von Steuben at Valley Forge. In June 1778, the regiment joined in a pursuit of British forces across New Jersey, forming part of the American advance guard and acquitting itself with honor at the battle of Monmouth.

Unable to mass the strength required to take on Washington's full force, the British adopted a new strategy in 1778, concentrating their military effort on the southern states. With operations drawing down in the north, New Jersey sought retirement. Brearley retired in August 1779 to resume his legal career.

He eventually rose to the rank of colonel in Nathaniel Heard's New Jersey militia brigade. From 1776 to 1779 he served in the New Jersey Line of the Continental Army, seeing action at Brandywine, Germantown, and Monmouth.

While at Constitutional Convention in 1787, Brearley was Chair of the Committee on Postponed Parts, which played a substantial role in the final document. The committee addressed questions related to the taxes, war-making, patents and copyrights, relations with Native American tribes, and Franklin's compromise to require money bills to originate in the House of Representatives. The biggest issue was the presidency, and the final compromise was written by James Madison with the committee's input. They adopted the earlier plan for choosing the president by the Electoral College and settled on the method of choosing the president if no candidate had an Electoral College majority, which many such as Madison thought would be "nineteen times out of twenty". The committee also shortened the president's term from seven years to four years, freed him to seek re-election, and moved impeachment trials to the Senate. They created the vice president, whose only role was to succeed the president and preside over the Senate. This transferred important powers from the Senate to the president to make treaties and appoint ambassadors.

Death   He is interred in the churchyard of Saint Michael's Episcopal Church

WILLIAM PATTERSON of New Jersey

William Paterson was born December 24, 1745, in County Antrim, Ireland, to Richard Paterson, an Ulster Protestant. At 14, he began college at Princeton. After graduating, he was admitted to the bar in 1768.

Paterson was selected as the Somerset County delegate for the first three provincial congresses of New Jersey, where he recorded the 1776 New Jersey State Constitution. Paterson was appointed as the first attorney general of New Jersey, serving from 1776 to 1783, establishing himself as one of the state's most prominent lawyers.[6] He was sent to the 1787 Philadelphia Convention, where he proposed the New Jersey Plan for a unicameral legislative body with equal representation from each state. The Constitution of the United States was signed with the Connecticut Compromise with a bicameral Congress and Senate that equally represented each state and House of Representatives with population-based representation.

As attorney general, William Paterson prosecuted Loyalists and helped to maintain order during a turbulent period. In 1783, he continued his law practice.

In 1787, William Paterson was sent to the Constitutional Convention as an advocate for New Jersey. At convention, Paterson devised the "New Jersey Plan" with Roger Sherman and representatives from small states. This plan promoted the idea of equal representation for all states. The "Virginia Plan" held that representation should be proportional. The skills Paterson honed as an attorney led to a compromise. In this "Great Compromise", a bicameral government with a House of Representatives based on population and a Senate chamber with each state represented by two legislators was agreed. Paterson was called "Father of the US Senate".

When New Jersey's first governor William Livingston died in 1790, William Paterson was a natural choice for the office. William Paterson was a member of the Federalist Party, the same political party as George Washington. He was instrumental in passage of S.U.M. (Society for Establishing Useful Manufacture).

Washington re-nominated Paterson to the court on March 4, 1793, after his term as Senator expired; Paterson was immediately confirmed by the Senate.

He resigned from the governorship to become an associate justice of the U.S. Supreme Court. On the circuit, he presided over the trials of individuals indicted for treason in the Whiskey Rebellion, a revolt by farmers in western Pennsylvania over the federal excise tax on whiskey, the principal product of their cash crop.

In 1779, Paterson married Cornelia Bell (1755–1783), daughter of John Bell, a wealthy Somerset County landowner. Together, they had three children.

On September 9, 1806, Paterson, aged sixty, died from the lingering effects of a coach accident suffered in 1803 while on circuit court duty in New Jersey.

JONATHAN DAYTON of New Jersey

Jonathan Dayton (October 16, 1760 – October 9, 1824) was born in Elizabethtown, New Jersey. He was the son of Elias Dayton, a merchant who had served as a militia officer in the French and Indian War, and his wife the former Hannah Rolfe. He graduated from the local academy, where he was classmates with Alexander Hamilton. He attended College of New Jersey (Princeton). He left college in 1775 to fight in the Revolutionary War and received an honorary degree in 1776.

Dayton was 15 at the outbreak of the war in 1775 and served under his father in the 3rd New Jersey Regiment as an ensign. Detached along the frontier constructing Fort Schuyler and Fort Dayton, became Regimental Paymaster 26 Aug 1776. Fought at the Battles of Brandywine and Germantown. On January 1, 1777, he was commissioned a lieutenant and served as paymaster. Marched off to support the army invading Canada, but the unit was diverted to the Mohawk Valley and upstate New York. Detached along the frontier constructing Fort Schuyler and Fort Dayton. He saw service under General George Washington, fighting in the battles of Brandywine Creek and Germantown. He remained with Washington at Valley Forge and helped push the British from their position in New Jersey into the safety of New York City.[2] In October 1780, Dayton and an uncle were captured by Loyalists, who held them captive for the winter before releasing them in the following year. Dayton again served under his father in the New Jersey Brigade. On March 30, 1780, at age 19, he was promoted to the rank of captain and transferred to the 2nd New Jersey Regiment, where he took part in the Battle of Yorktown.

Aide de Camp to General Sullivan 1 May 1779 and during his expedition against the Indians. Captain in the 3rd Regiment NJ Line 30 Mar 1780. Taken prisoner at the Battle of Elizabethtown 5 Oct 1780 and after a winter imprisonment in New York was exchanged. Transferred to the 2nd Regiment NJ Line 1 Jan 1781. Fought in many battles, including being in command of a unit at the Battle of Yorktown and serving under Lafayette. Led his unit in a crucial nighttime bayonet attack on Redoubt 10, under the command of his old classmate Alexander Hamilton, and their teacher Francis Barber. He was retained in and last served in Cumming's New Jersey Continental Battalion from Apr 1783. He served to 3 Nov 1783.

The Revolutionary War records indicate he served as aide-de-camp to General John Sullivan against the Indians from May 1 to November 30, 1779.

At the close of the Revolutionary War, Dayton was admitted as an original member of The Society of the Cincinnati in New Jersey. On July 19, 1799, Dayton was offered a commission as major general in the United States Army, but he declined.

After the war, Dayton studied law and opened a practice, dividing his time between land speculation, law, and politics. After serving as a New Jersey delegate to the Continental Congress and Constitutional Convention (of which he was the youngest member, at age 26), he became a prominent Federalist legislator.

He served as speaker for the Fourth and Fifth Congresses. Like most Federalists, he supported the fiscal policies of Alexander Hamilton, and he helped organize the suppression of the Whiskey Rebellion. He supported the Louisiana Purchase and opposed repeal of the Judiciary Act of 1801.

Dayton married Susan Williamson in 1779 and had two daughters. He died on October 9, 1824. Shortly before Dayton's death, Lafayette visited him.

THOMAS MIFFLIN of Pennsylvania

Thomas Mifflin (January 10, 1744 – January 20, 1800) was born January 10, 1744, in Philadelphia. He was the son of John Mifflin and Elizabeth Bagnall. In 1760, Mifflin graduated from the College of Philadelphia (now University of Pennsylvania) and joined the mercantile business of William Biddle. He married Sarah Morris, March 4, 1767. Their daughter Emily married Joseph Hopkinson, son of Francis Hopkinson. After Sarah's death, Emily was hostess.

Early in the Revolution, Mifflin left Congress to serve in the Continental Army. He was commissioned a major, then became *aide-de-camp* of George Washington.

On August 14, 1775, Washington appointed him to become the army's first quartermaster general, under order of Congress Although it has been said that he was good at the job despite preferring to be on the front lines, questions were raised regarding his failure to properly supply the troops at Valley Forge. When Washington confronted him about this, Mifflin asked to be relieved as quartermaster general but was persuaded to resume those duties.

Mifflin's leadership in the Battle of Trenton and Battle of Princeton led to a promotion to major general. This battle would become classroom to classroom combat in hallways of Princeton. As a result of this debate the Congressional Board of War was created, on which Mifflin served from 1777 to 1778.

Prior to American independence, Mifflin was a member of the Pennsylvania Provincial Assembly (1772–1776). He served two terms in the Continental Congress (1774–1775 and 1782–1784), including seven months (November 1783 to June 1784) as presiding officer.

Mifflin's most important duty as president was to accept on behalf of Congress the resignation of General George Washington on December 23, 1783. After the war, the importance of Congress declined so precipitously that Mifflin found it difficult to convince the states to send enough delegates to Congress to ratify the Treaty of Paris, which finally took place on January 14, 1784, at the Maryland State House in Annapolis. He also appointed Thomas Jefferson as a minister to France on May 7, 1784, and he appointed his former aide, Colonel Josiah Harmar, to be the commander of the First American Regiment.

He was a signatory to the Continental Association and the Constitution. He served in the house of Pennsylvania General Assembly (1785–1788). He was a member of the Supreme Executive Council of the Commonwealth of Pennsylvania, and on November 5, 1788, elected president of the Council, replacing Franklin.

The Whiskey Rebellion and the 1793 Philadelphia yellow fever epidemic happened during his term in office. Fries Rebellion also started during his term. He returned to the state legislature and served until his death the following month.

Mifflin became a member of the American Philosophical Society in 1768 and served for two years as its secretary. Mifflin died in Lancaster, Pennsylvania, on January 23, 1800. He is interred at Holy Trinity Lutheran Church in Lancaster.

THOMAS FITZSIMONS of Pennsylvania

Thomas Fitzsimons (October 1741 – August 26, 1811) was an Irish-born American Founding Father, merchant, banker, and politician. Fitzsimons represented Pennsylvania in the Continental Congress, was a delegate to Constitutional Convention, and served in U.S. Congress. He was a signatory of the Constitution of the United States. He was born in Ireland in 1741. In 1760 his family immigrated to Philadelphia.

They were soon hit by new revenue measures created to help support the finances of Great Britain, including the much-reviled Stamp Act of 1765. Concerned, Fitzsimons became active in the Irish merchant community in Philadelphia. He was a founding member of the Friendly Sons of St. Patrick, and a steering committee organized to protest Coercive Acts.

When Pennsylvania began mobilizing and organizing a militia to fight the British, Fitzsimons became involved. Initially, his company served as part of the soldiers who manned posts along the New Jersey coast. His unit later served in reserve at the 1776 Battle of Trenton.

During the summer of 1776, these citizen-soldiers faced their first crisis. A large British army, supported by the Royal Navy, attacked New York City, and Congress asked the nearby states to reinforce Washington's outnumbered Continental Army regulars. Pennsylvania sent the Associators to the Flying Camp, a mobile reserve stationed in northern New Jersey to prevent any sudden diversion of Redcoats toward Philadelphia. Fitzsimons' company served in outposts under Colonel John Dickinson and guarded the New Jersey shoreline. A month of active duty passed without incident, the assignment provided Fitzsimons valuable time to train his men.

In November, with New York secured, the British invaded New Jersey.

Pennsylvania authorities asked him to serve on an eleven-member board to oversee the Pennsylvania navy, which formed the primary defense of Delaware Bay and the river approaches to Philadelphia. In this role Fitzsimons not only helped plan the capital's defenses, but organized logistics, coordinated defense with neighboring states, and negotiated with a reluctant Continental Congress over strategy. Finding Pennsylvania's river defenses too formidable, the enemy sailed up Chesapeake Bay, marching through poorly defended sections of Maryland and Delaware. Fitzsimons defenses held out for several months.

Fitzsimons' experiences both in uniform and on the states Navy Board convinced him that stronger central authority did not pose a threat to liberty and was in fact the only solution to the new crisis. At this time, he also became associated with Robert Morris, helping to organize the banking facilities that Morris used to support the Continental Army and Navy. He served as a director of the Bank of North America from its founding in 1781 until 1803.

Pennsylvania sent Fitzsimons to the Continental Congress in 1782. There he concentrated on financial and commercial matters, working with Morris and the nationalist faction led by Hamilton and Madison developing a centralized economy.

Thomas Fitzsimons entered politics as a delegate to the Continental Congress in 1782 and 1783. He was a member of the Pennsylvania House of Representatives from 1786 until 1795. He was also a delegate to the U.S. Constitutional Convention in 1787. He supported a strong national government, the United States Congress's powers to impose a tariff on imports and exports, the granting of the House of Representatives power equal to the US Senate. He was one of two Catholic signers of the Constitution, with Daniel Carroll of Maryland.

After the Constitution was established, he served in the first three sessions of the House of Representatives as a Federalist, where he favored protective tariffs and a strong navy, co-drafting the 1794 law authorizing the original six frigates of the United States Navy. Fitzsimons failed to win re-election, defeated by John Swanwick, due to fallout over the Whiskey Rebellion.

In 1796, FitzSimons, was appointed by President John Adams to serve on the five-man debt commission charged under Article VI of the Jay Treaty with examining the claims of British subjects unable to collect debts incurred by Americans prior to the American Revolution. The claims were disposed of by a lump-sum payment and approved by President Jefferson.

Fitzsimons died on August 26, 1811, in Philadelphia, where he was buried in the cemetery of St. Mary's Catholic Church.

JARED INGERSOLL of Pennsylvania

Jared Ingersoll (October 24, 1749 – October 31, 1822) was born in New Haven, Connecticut. In 1778, committed to the cause of independence, Ingersoll returned to Philadelphia and won election to the Continental Congress. Ingersoll became convinced of the need for a stronger national government than was provided by the Articles of Confederation, and he was a delegate to the 1787 Philadelphia Convention.

Born in New Haven, Connecticut, Ingersoll was the son of Jared Ingersoll Sr., a prominent British official whose strong Loyalist sentiment would lead to his being tarred and feathered by radical Patriots. The Ingersoll family was of English descent. In 1765, the year the Stamp Act was imposed on the colonies in America, the British Crown appointed the elder Jared Ingersoll as Stamp Master. The Sons of Liberty hung his effigy in various parts of the colony.

The younger Ingersoll completed Hopkins Grammar School in New Haven in 1762, graduated from Yale College in 1766, studied law in Philadelphia, and was admitted to the Pennsylvania bar in 1773. By training and inclination, a Patriot, the young Ingersoll shied away from the cause at the outset because of loyalty to his distinguished father. His father advised Law, and he studied law at Middle Temple. He spent more than eighteen months in Paris, where he met Benjamin Franklin.

In 1778 he arrived in Philadelphia as a confirmed Patriot. With the help of friends, he established a flourishing law practice, and shortly thereafter he entered the fray as a delegate to the Continental Congress (1780-81).

Shortly after the colonies declared independence, Ingersoll made his personal commitment to the cause of independence and returned home. In 1778 he arrived in Philadelphia as a confirmed Patriot. With the help of friends, he quickly established a flourishing law practice, and shortly after, he entered the fray as a delegate to the Continental Congress (1780–81). In 1781 Ingersoll married Elizabeth Pettit and that same year was elected to the American Philosophical Society.

At the convention, Ingersoll favored revision of the existing Articles of Confederation and supported a plan for a new federal government.

A Legal Scholar, he helped define many of the principles enunciated at Philadelphia. In one definitive case he represented Georgia in *Chisholm v. Georgia* (1793), a landmark case in states' rights. Here the court decided against him, ruling that a state may be sued in federal court by a citizen of another state. (later rescinded by the Eleventh Amendment). In representing Hylton in *Hylton v. US* (1796), Ingersoll was also involved in the first legal challenge to constitutionality of an act of Congress. In this case, the Supreme Court upheld the government's right to impose a tax on carriages.

Jared Ingersoll died in Philadelphia at age 73; interment was in the Old Pine Street Church Cemetery, Fourth and Pine Streets.

Author Biography:

George McCarley's Executive career began with degrees in Management, Business Administration, Economics, Military Science and Engineering, becoming the G.O.A.T. of Corporate Turnaround leaders, with 48 wins and 0 losses, including Fortune 500 and Harvard MBA owned corporations in the Industrial, Mining, Metals, Retail, Automotive, Hardware/Software and Corporate Services sectors. The turnaround background included leadership of Mergers and Acquisitions of 22 "deals." This career activity is often referred to as "Masters of the Universe."

While the turnaround/M&A effort was ongoing, he led Congressional Campaigns and was a force on Presidential Campaigns. Drawn to Religion, he began Preaching in Jails and rehab/Homeless ministry and has Preached to over 20,000 men. He has Docketed a legal case at Supreme Court of the United States, his personal work product.

The Army Veteran has been in four war zones since military exit, including Albania/Kosovo as a Missionary during the terrible Kosovo war, along with two wars you never heard about.

The lifetime reading interest indicated served as a perfect buffer to maintain some normalcy during this overly packed career. The McCarley background and career closely reproduces the lifetime of activity of America's Founding Fathers, thus the perfect and rare background required to coauthor this epic book that links the Brilliance and Heroic act of America's Founding Fathers to the US Constitution.

McCarley recently Authored and published DEMOKRATIA TO DEMOCRACY, THE REQUIEM, which recounts the 7000 year development of Democracy and is available at 40,000 bookstore websites headlined by Barnes & Noble, to include several languages. Simply Google the title and you will be taken to page after page of sources.

Other publications are:

DEMOKRATIA TO DEMOCRACY, THE REQUIEM

MOSES WISDOM, BIBLE 613 SHAPE US CONSTITUTION

"THE FRANCHISE" RESTORE CLEAN ELECTIONS AND GOD'S COUNTRY

INDEX

Most productive Founding Fathers in Revolution and Constitution Era. In order of the importance of each, along with their key contributions to America.

Samuel Adams	Devoted his entire adult life to US Freedom
Benjamin Franklin	Genius = to Edison and Tesla
Robert Morris	Financier of Revolution
John Hancock	Chased by British Assassination Squads
George Washington	Father of our Country
Alexander Hamilton	Washingtons right-hand-man
Thomas Jefferson	President, Constitution Framer
John Adams	President
James Madison	President, Constitution Developer
Roger Sherman	Only Signer of Four Precious Documents
John Dickinson	Signer of Three Documents
John Jay	Judicial Branch Developer
Carrol Family Maryland	War, Constitution, 1st Catholic Bishop
George Mason	Father of Bill of Rights
Benjamin Rush	Medical, Constitution, Founded Univ&Hospitals
Pinckney Family, S. Carolina	Made Charleston Famous, 75% of US Export
Paul Revere	Gunpowder, Cannon, Iron, Copper, US 1st Industrialist
Elbridge Gerry	Vice President
James Wilson	Taught Constitutional Law to Presidents Cabinet
George Wythe	Mentor to Presidents
Gouverneur Morris	Wrote Preamble to US Constitution
Stephen Hopkins	Plymouth Rock roots, Brown U., Cannon Production

John Langdon	74-gun ship, paid troops, Gunships builder
Nathaniel Gorham	President of Convention, 2nd to Washington
Francis Hopkinson	Designer of US Flag
George Taylor	Produced munitions, cannon
Rutledge Brothers	First Supreme Court Justices
James McHenry	Fort McHenry
National Anthem	At Ft. McHenry
Carter Braxton	Finance, Ship Builder
Lee Brothers, Virginia	Fought Taxes, Famous Family Roots
Benjamin Harrison	1 son, 1 grandson became President

Signers of 3 Key Document-10

Josiah Bartlett	Quinine developer, medical treatments
William Ellery	Sons of Liberty, Wrote Charter for Brown U.
George Clymer	Tea, Stamp Act Demonstrations Leader, Financier
Samuel Huntington	President of Congress struck by Smallpox
Francis Lewis	Sons of Liberty, Threw all his Wealth into War.
Thomas McKean	President of Congress, Warfighter North Theater
John Penn	Documents + served Virginia & N. Carolina
George Read	Led Argument for States Rights of Small States
John Witherspoon	James Madison Professor, Recognized Philosopher
Oliver Wolcott	Major General, Cont. Congress, Iroquois Negotiator